HISTORY
OF
BIBLICAL
INTERPRETATION
A READER

HISTORY
OF
BIBLICAL
INTERPRETATION
A READER

WILLIAM YARCHIN

HENDRICKSON
PUBLISHERS

History of Biblical Interpretation
© 2004 by William Yarchin

Hendrickson Publishers, Inc.
P. O. Box 3473
Peabody, Massachusetts 01961-3473

ISBN-13: 978-1-56563-720-7
ISBN-10: 1-56563-720-8

Printed in the United States of America

Second Printing — June 2006

Cover art: Olga Poloukhine. "Witnesses." Egg tempera and photo emulsion on gessoed board. This artwork has been used with the artist's permission. Photo credit: William Haussler.

Library of Congress Cataloging-in-Publication Data

Yarchin, William.
    History of biblical interpretation : a reader / William Yarchin.
       p. cm.
    Includes bibliographical references and index.
    ISBN-13: 978-1-56563-720-7 (hardcover : alk. paper)
    ISBN-10: 1-56563-720-8 (hardcover : alk. paper)
    1. Bible—Criticism, interpretation, etc.—History. I. Title.
    BS500.Y37 2004
    220.6'09—dc22
                         2003027731

TABLE OF CONTENTS

PREFACE

Interest in the history of biblical interpretation is rising among students of the Bible, church history, and theology. Insights from scholars of premodern and ancient generations are increasingly valued in dialogue with contemporary explorations into the meaning of the Bible. Evidence of this growing interest shows in the sheer volume of recent monographs and reference works on biblical interpretation and its history.

Despite this expanding body of valuable resources, no single-volume reader covers the entire span of the Bible's history, presenting examples of how people have thought about interpreting Scripture. This anthology is intended to fill the gap. The selections in this collection include reflections on biblical interpretation as well as examples of actual interpretations. The readings proceed chronologically from the second century B.C.E. to the end of the twentieth century in both the Christian and the Jewish exegetical traditions. Contemporary students of theology and the Bible do not fully equip themselves when their education fails to recognize the contributions made by great thinkers of other generations and other religious traditions. In particular, by including contributions from ancient, medieval, and contemporary Jews, this volume aims to expand the mental horizon within which students of my own faith (Christianity) reflect upon Scripture.

For as long as people have read the Bible, they have interpreted it at many different levels of sophistication and toward many different purposes of understanding and application. A truly comprehensive survey of the history of biblical interpretation might include examples of simple devotional reflections on the text, sermons, political speeches, and many other examples of appropriation from the Bible into social and religious life. This anthology does not cast its net so wide as to reflect the full range of biblical interpretation through the ages. Given the depth and breadth of the Bible's presence in world culture, such a collection would fill many volumes. Instead I have selected only readings representative of the best thinking on the subject from epoch to epoch as well as examples of the most influential exegetical treatments of biblical texts. Consequently, this collection focuses somewhat narrowly on scholarly biblical interpretation. To provide maximum benefit to students of the Bible, I have sought clarity of expression in selecting each piece. In some cases this has meant passing over a more famous work by a given author in favor of a selection more accessible to nonspecialists.

Even with this restriction, many more examples could have been included. Needless to say, the documents of the New Testament present a rich field of insight into interpretation of the Jewish Scriptures at the beginning of the Christian era. But as they constitute a portion of the Christian Bible, they are readily available to students. Readers interested in learning more on exegesis in the New Testament may consult Richard N. Longenecker, *Biblical Exegesis in the Apostolic Period* (2d ed.; Grand Rapids: Eerdmans, 1999). I have also not attempted to introduce the reader to the esoteric, philosophically symbolic world of Jewish kabbalistic interpretation. Interested readers would benefit from the work of Moshe Idel, *Kabbalah: New Perspectives* (New Haven: Yale University Press, 1988) and from the kabbalistic commentary on the Torah called *Zohar: The Book of Enlightenment* (Classics of Western Spirituality; New York: Paulist, 1988). It is my hope, however, that the selections of the present anthology will give students of biblical interpretation a sufficient idea of the interests of learned biblical interpreters over the last twenty-two hundred years.

Dividing history into discrete periods is a subjective enterprise. I have chosen to treat the history of biblical interpretation in five parts. First, however, an Introduction surveys the major trends in twenty-two centuries of learned biblical interpretation. *The selections will be better understood if the introduction has been read.* Part 1 (150 B.C.E.–70 C.E.) features biblical interpretation as it was practiced before Christianity and rabbinic Judaism became firmly established religions. Part 2 (150–1500 C.E.) covers key writers reflecting the classical period of Christian interpretation by the church fathers and their exegetical heirs. Part 3, on rabbinic Judaism, covers key Jewish writers in the same general time span. Part 4 (1500–present) shows some of the ways in which historical concerns came to dominate scholarly interest in the Bible as attention was drawn to questions of philology and ultimately to questions of history and faith. Part 5 (1970–present) brings the reader to the present generation of interpreters, for whom historical questions share the spotlight with concerns about unavoidable subjectivity and ideological motivation in interpretation.

Unique to this collection are selections never before available in English. Three of them are compendia of comments on Psalm 23. During the thirteenth and fourteenth centuries, a number of commentary-anthologies were compiled in Europe for use among Christian churches and Jewish synagogues. Traditional rabbinic comments on Psalm 23 as compiled in the *Yalqut Shim'oni* are rendered from Hebrew and Aramaic into English. English readers can also access the time-honored patristic observations on the psalm as accreted in the Latin text of the *Glossa ordinaria*. Comments by leading humanist scholars of the Renaissance are translated from the sixteenth-century Latin text of the *Critici sacri*. A comparison of these three commentary traditions on the same biblical text makes for an interesting study in itself. Additionally, excerpts from the biblical scholarship of the eighteenth-century Jewish philosopher Moses Mendelssohn are also published here in English for the first time.

To bring readers an accurate sense of how different generations have thought about interpreting Scripture, this collection includes a rather wide range of genres. It thereby runs the risk that some selections will be more challenging than others, particularly where linguistic nuances are difficult to bring across in translation. For this reason, I supply more explanatory footnotes for the pre-1600 C.E. entries than for those from the last four hundred years. All footnotes, unless otherwise marked, are mine. The name of an author or translator at the end identifies a footnote that comes from the edition of the reading's source. Biblical references appear in square brackets when they have been added.

In the writing of this book I have been supported and assisted by more people than I can name here. I am particularly grateful to Azusa Pacific University from whom I received several grants, allowing me time and resources to include the original translations that appear in these pages. The translation of the selection from the *Glossa ordinaria* was produced by James T. Dennison, and the English from the *Critici sacri* section was rendered by J. Derek Halvorson. To these capable scholars I am indebted for their distinctive contributions. This book has been shaped with the help of thoughtful suggestions from many friends and colleagues, including John Hartley, Carole Lambert, Gerald Wilson, Aya Levy, and Yair Barkai. My thanks also go to James Ernest who got the editorial process under way, and to Shirley Decker-Lucke along with her indefatigable associate Sara Scott at Hendrickson for their help in bringing the process to its fruitful end. I will be grateful to readers for suggestions they might share that would improve any future edition of this book. Finally, my deepest gratitude goes to my family—Ann, Molly, and Mitchell—for their love that kept this project in its proper perspective.

This volume leaves untouched many aspects and episodes in the history of biblical interpretation. Readers interested in further exploration into the subject would benefit from consulting any of the following works.

Blowers, Paul M., ed. *The Bible in Greek Christian Antiquity.* The Bible through the Ages 1. Notre Dame, Ind.: University of Notre Dame Press, 1997.

Bray, Gerald Lewis. *Biblical Interpretation: Past and Present.* Downers Grove, Ill.: Inter-Varsity, 1996.

Coggins, R. J., and J. L. Houlden, eds. *A Dictionary of Biblical Interpretation.* London: SCM Press, 1990.

Fowl, Stephen, ed. *The Theological Interpretation of Scripture: Classic and Contemporary Readings.* Oxford: Blackwell, 1997.

Grant, Robert M., with David Tracy. *A Short History of the Interpretation of the Bible.* 2d ed., rev. and enlarged. Philadelphia: Fortress, 1984.

Hagen, Kenneth, ed. *The Bible in the Churches: How Different Christians Interpret the Scriptures.* 2d ed. Milwaukee: Marquette University Press, 1994

Hayes, John H., ed. *Dictionary of Biblical Interpretation.* Nashville: Abingdon, 1999.

Jeffrey, David Lyle, ed. *A Dictionary of Biblical Tradition in English Literature.* Grand Rapids: Eerdmans, 1993.

Kugel, James L., and Rowan A. Greer. *Early Biblical Interpretation.* Philadelphia: Westminster, 1986.

McKim, Donald K., ed. *A Guide to Contemporary Hermeneutics: Major Trends in Biblical Interpretation.* Grand Rapids: Eerdmans, 1986.

McKim, Donald K. *Historical Handbook of Major Biblical Interpreters.* Downers Grove, Ill.: InterVarsity, 1998.

Mulder, Martin Jan, ed. *Mikra: Text, Translation, Reading, and Interpretation of the Hebrew Bible in Ancient Judaism and Early Christianity.* Philadelphia: Fortress, 1988.

Norton, David. *A History of the English Bible as Literature.* Cambridge: Cambridge University Press, 2000.

Old, Hughes Oliphant. *The Reading and Preaching of the Scriptures in the Worship of the Christian Church.* 4 vols. Grand Rapids: Eerdmans, 1998–2002.

Powell, Mark Allan. *The Bible and Modern Literary Criticism: A Critical Assessment and Annotated Bibliography.* New York: Greenwood, 1992.

Smalley, Beryl. *The Study of the Bible in the Middle Ages.* 3rd ed., rev. Oxford: Blackwell, 1983.

Stokes, Mack B. *The Bible in the Wesleyan Heritage.* Nashville: Abingdon, 1981.

Trebolle Barrera, Julio C. *The Jewish Bible and the Christian Bible: An Introduction to the History of the Bible.* Translated by Wilfred G. E. Watson. Grand Rapids: Eerdmans, 1998.

Watson, Duane Frederick, *Rhetorical Criticism of the Bible: A Comprehensive Bibliography with Notes on History and Method.* Leiden: Brill, 1994.

INTRODUCTION: THE HISTORY
OF BIBLICAL INTERPRETATION

Contemporary interpreters approach the Bible from many directions and produce different results. Side by side on a single library shelf today one can find historical studies, sermonic reflections, theological treatises, cultural analyses, and devotional guides—none saying the same things but all presented as reliable interpretations of the Bible. How did such plurality of interpretation happen? Were there always so many different interpretive voices speaking on behalf of Scripture? The purpose of the present anthology, covering the history of biblical interpretation, is to help the reader formulate answers to such questions by becoming more familiar with the many ways in which the Bible has been read for over two thousand years.

The time span during which Scripture has been interpreted is quite broad. So is the range of forms that reflect biblical interpretation. Thousands of years ago scribes and priests were interpreting sacred Hebrew writings even before these became part of the canonical collection we call the Bible. Jews and Christians have been teaching and preaching from canonical biblical texts now for two millennia. Millions of people worldwide continue to make major life decisions on the basis of their understanding of the meaning of Scripture. Beyond the walls of church and synagogue, the influence of the Bible can be seen in a great variety of cultural forms, such as legal codes, scientific treatises, social customs, education systems, linguistic expressions, plays, novels, and films. Extending across such a long period of time and such a broad field of expression, the history of biblical interpretation will obviously include radically different ways in which the Bible has been read. Fully considered, the presence and impact of the interpreted Bible in the West is a subject greater than what any single book can adequately cover.

The aims of this book are more modest. For the sake of practicality in dealing with such a large subject, our survey of the history of biblical interpretation has drawn more or less arbitrary boundaries for itself. As a result, many writings and interpreters from the Jewish and Christian traditions will not appear in this anthology. The focus throughout will remain on selected documents and writers that most clearly and best represent the most important ways interpretation of the Bible has been understood and practiced from the third century B.C.E. to the present.[1] This introduction will offer a tour through these centuries, serving as a general backdrop to the specific readings that constitute the rest of the book.

---

[1] The third century B.C.E. is the earliest point for which we have evidence of scriptural interpretation reflected in documents that did not themselves become part of the biblical canon. On the beginnings of exegetical activity by biblical writers themselves before the Hellenistic age, see

As we shall see, much of the history of biblical interpretation concerns the question of referentiality in the Bible: to what extent are the texts of Scripture to be read for what they *plainly* state, and to what extent *as figures* of something other than their plain reference? Moreover, what constitutes a plain statement in Scripture as distinguished from a figural reference? To understand adequately the nature of these questions, we must first take note of the way readers understood important traditional writings during the age when the Bible began to be interpreted.

Ancient Reading of Traditional Texts: Insights into Mystery
(150 B.C.E.–100 C.E.)

During antiquity, people, for the most part, read sacred texts figuratively. Before there was a Bible, the classical Greek literary canon included many mythological narratives that, as early as the fifth century B.C.E., were being explained allegorically. As the educated classes of the Greco-Roman world grew more philosophically sophisticated, the stories of the gods and heroes preserved in the classical literature became targets for ridicule, or at least produced confusion about how they might be taken other than at face value. According to one of the traditional myths about Hercules, for example, the hero eased the burden of the heavens from the shoulders of Atlas. But Herodorus of Heracleia (fifth century B.C.E.) explained that the tale was an allegory relating how Hercules (Heracles) acquired skill as a priest and scholar in understanding heavenly phenomena. Centuries later Heraclitus (first century C.E.) devoted an entire treatise to showing how Homer had written his poetry as allegories of profound truths about reality.

We would be mistaken to conclude that ancient interpreters had no regard for authorial intent simply because they allegorized. Rather, the meaning derived from allegorical readings of ancient stories was typically taken as the meaning intended by the ancient poet. If the poet were regarded as having been divinely inspired, then the allegorized meaning was the originally inspired meaning. The basic interpretive presupposition was this: due to the inherent limitations of human understanding, there will always be something in the sacred text that remains undisclosed to unglossed reading. *Mystery, then, was characteristic of sacred texts.* God is the speaker, but humans are the writers, and multiplicity of meaning (plain and obscure) is to be expected in the discursive space between what the words humanly say and what they divinely teach. For the ancients, it was not a matter of exposing what is hidden in the text but rather a hope to be guided through figurative reading into a sharing of the divine mind. In this way the truth about divine and mundane reality would be accessible, but only to those who would—through sustained philosophical reflection—put themselves in a position or frame of mind to perceive it. Unlike modern exegesis, in the ancient world the text was not an object for examination vis-à-vis the inquiring subject, testing for truth. Reading and interpreting religious texts in the ancient world was rather a process of participation in the mysteries that they hold. Depending on the setting, the text was sung, memorized, recited, philosophically allegorized—all activities that wove the divine truth of the text into the fabric of the interpreters' social and spiritual existence.

Michael Fishbane, *Biblical Interpretation in Ancient Israel* (Oxford: Clarendon, 1985); and Isaac Rabinowitz, *A Witness Forever: Ancient Israel's Perception of Literature and the Resultant Hebrew Bible* (Bethesda, Md.: CDL Press, 1988).

Some of the earliest biblical interpretation during the Hellenistic and Roman periods reflected this attitude. The Jewish Torah contains stories about warring brothers and wandering patriarchs as well as obscure laws about foods and clothing. But sophisticated readers of the first-century Mediterranean world had come to understand sacred texts largely in terms of moral philosophy. How were such texts in the Torah to be understood? Philo of Alexandria (and also Pseudo-Aristeas) responded to this question by showing how the Jewish Scriptures—figuratively interpreted—could speak to the concerns that framed the Greco-Roman cultural horizon. The words of the Torah constituted a message of divine instruction for the education and edification of the soul, instruction that was delivered through the vehicle of stories about the patriarchs and of laws about kosher foods. By adopting the appropriate point of view through figurative reading, educated people in the Greco-Roman world could understand the Torah for its relevance to the contemplative life: the ancient text could make sense according to the prevailing notions of what cohered as appropriate for divine teaching. Philo's interpretation, though, did not do away entirely with the ordinary reference of the Torah's words. Although the Mosaic laws of purity may, in a way hidden to plain reading, teach a moral philosophy, it was nonetheless expected of Jews to obey the laws of Moses according to their plain sense.

Not all Scripture interpretation at the beginning of the present era was philosophical allegory. The Hebrew Scriptures contained hidden truths of another kind according to readings by the group of Jews (probably the ancient sect called the Essenes) who had established themselves in a settlement near the Dead Sea. The scrolls discovered there in 1947 preserve many examples of a certain way of reading Hebrew Scriptures historically: the ancient documents were taken to speak predictively of historical events that had unfolded only during the time of the Dead Sea community itself. Indeed, the scroll writers at the Dead Sea regarded their own community as the historical fulfillment of the very specific predictions expressed figuratively in lines from certain biblical narratives, psalms, and prophetic scrolls. It seems that, in the light of certain events that transpired among the priestly elite in Jerusalem in the last 150 years B.C.E., the Essenes discerned that these Scriptures were speaking in a mysterious prophetic way about them and their movement's founder, whom they sometimes called the Teacher of Righteousness. By way of illustration, note these lines from one of the scrolls, known as the *Damascus Covenant* (6:2–11):

> But [after the judgment of exile] God remembered the covenant of the forefathers. And he raised from Aaron men of knowledge and from Israel wise men, and made them listen. And they dug the well: 'A well which the princes dug, which the nobles of the people delved with the staff' (Num 21:18).[2] The 'well' is the law. And those who 'dug' it are the converts of Israel, who left the land of Judah and lived in the land of Damascus, all of whom God called 'princes,' for they sought him. . . . And the 'staff' is the interpreter of the law, of whom Isaiah said: 'He produces a tool for his labor' (Isa 54:16). And the 'nobles of the people' are those who came, throughout the whole age of wickedness, to 'dig the well' with the prescriptions that the Law-giver had prescribed for them to walk in. Without these they would never attain until there would arise the true teacher at the end of days.[3]

---

[2] In the book of Numbers, this verse is part of a song with which the Israelites celebrated God's provision of water during the wilderness journey.

[3] Adapted from the translation in Florentino García Martínez and Eibert J. C. Tigchelaar, trans., *The Dead Sea Scrolls Study Edition* (New York: Brill, 1997), 559.

Here again, although the specific form of interpretation is not allegory, the basic pre-supposition of figuration underlying the Dead Sea historical interpretation was the same as for Alexandrian *allegoria:* there can be learned from the inspired text a teaching that speaks to the cultural or historical situation of the interpreter—who himself can share in that same inspiration and so become privy to what otherwise cannot be discerned in the text.

Early Christian and Rabbinic Biblical Interpretation
(100–600 C.E.)

A manner of interpretation roughly analogous to the historical interpretations from the Dead Sea Scrolls is evident in the first century C.E. among the followers of Jesus. As the Jesus followers sought to make sense of what had happened in the teaching career of Jesus and his death and resurrection, it was Scripture that gave insight and voice to their emerging understanding. Certain texts from various parts of the Jewish Scriptures already, in the generations preceding Jesus, had been taken as messianically referential; the earliest Christians found in these texts, and many others, predictions (or at least typological adumbrations) that they believed had found their fulfillment in Jesus—whom they thereby recognized as Christ, the Messiah.[4] (By the second century, a number of Christian writings themselves had come to rank with the traditional Jewish collection as sacred Scripture among the churches, and so the "Old" and the "New" Testaments came to constitute the Christian Bible.) Following this apostolic lead, Christian interpretation of Scripture in subsequent generations developed a more extensive apologetic catalogue of Old Testament texts showing expectations that were properly understood as having been fulfilled in the events surrounding Jesus Christ and his church.

This sort of Christian "expectation-fulfillment" reading is usually known as *typological* interpretation. As interpreters trained in the schools of rhetoric and grammar during late antiquity, the church fathers generally read the narratives of the Old Testament with a sensitivity for their Christian teaching as discerned in their narrative logic. It was from the narrative coherence of the ancient Jewish stories—what the stories were about—that a representation or prefiguration of what had come later could be discerned. Typology, then, would refer not so much to an exegetical technique as it would to a way of approaching the ancient texts whereby they "are invested with meaning by correspondence with other [scriptural] texts of a 'mimetic' or representational kind."[5] The discernment of such correspondences between texts and events, a correspondence that generates meaning otherwise not visible from the text, is probably best understood as a variety of figurative interpretation.[6] Like allegory, typology is a condition of understanding within

---

[4] See Paul M. van Buren, *According to the Scriptures: The Origins of the Gospel and of the Church's Old Testament* (Grand Rapids: Eerdmans, 1998).

[5] Frances Young, "Typology," in *Crossing the Boundaries: Essays in Biblical Interpretation in Honour of Michael D. Goulder* (ed. Stanley E. Porter, Paul Joyce, and David E. Orton; New York: E. J. Brill, 1994), 39.

[6] Young, "Typology." For a broader treatment of the subject, see Erich Auerbach, *Mimesis: The Representation of Reality in Western Literature* (Princeton: Princeton University Press, 1953), esp. 72–76.

which the older text represents more than simply its subject. From this condition is discerned the foreshadowing dimension of the earlier text. Again, like allegory, typological interpretation is more hermeneutical than exegetical because it is less concerned with learning what the ancient texts *say* than with understanding *how they are to be taken* in the light of later texts (the New Testament documents) that the Fathers recognized to be works of interpretation as well as scriptural texts in their own right.

To illustrate, let us note how the following homiletic recitation, attributed to the late-second-century writer Melito of Sardis, alludes to the sense of worshipers' participation in the old Exodus Passover story as it was told—for typological effect—during the Christian eucharistic ritual:

> What is said and done [in the ritual] is nothing, beloved,
> without a comparison and preliminary sketch.
> Whatever is said and done finds its comparison—
> what is said, a comparison,
> what is done, a prefiguration—
> in order that, just as what is done is demonstrated through the prefiguration,
> so also what is spoken may be elucidated though the comparison.
> This is just what happens in the case of a preliminary structure:
> it does not arise as a finished work,
> but because of what is going to be visible through its image acting as a model.
> For this reason a preliminary sketch is made of the future thing. . . .
> As then with the perishable examples,
> so also with the imperishable things;
> as with the earthly things,
> so also with the heavenly.
> For the very salvation and reality of the Lord were prefigured in the people
> [of the Exodus story],
> And the decrees of the gospel were proclaimed in advance by the law.
> The people then was a model [*typos*] by way of preliminary sketch,
> and the law was the writing of a parable;
> The gospel is the recounting and fulfilment of the law,
> and the church is the repository of the reality.[7]

Turning to Jewish exegesis in late antiquity and on into the eighth century (the end of the talmudic period), we see a similar proclivity to interpret one scriptural passage in the light of another, albeit not necessarily by means of a typological correspondence. Solomon, for example, as (traditionally) the author of Proverbs, Ecclesiastes, and the Song of Songs, appears in rabbinic discussion as not only a writer of Scripture but also an inspired authority who in his biblical writings interprets the Torah. We find the matter expressed in the midrash to the Song of Songs:

---

[7] Melito of Sardis, *On Pascha* (ed. and trans. S. G. Hall; Oxford Early Christian Texts; Oxford: Clarendon, 1979), 17–21.

He [Solomon] pondered the words of the Torah and investigated [the meaning of] the words of the Torah. He made handles to the Torah . . . R. Jose said: Imagine a big basket full of produce without any handle, so that it could not be lifted, till one clever man came and made handles to it, and then it began to be carried by the handles. So till Solomon arose no one could properly understand the words of the Torah, but when Solomon arose, all began to comprehend the Torah.[8]

The psalms of David, and indeed the texts from all the scriptural authors, were similarly regarded by the rabbis, so that the whole of the biblical canon presented itself as a self-interpreting text through intertextual illumination. Midrash—the Hebrew term for a notoriously hard-to-define rabbinic mode of interpretation—almost always involved the establishing of connections between biblical texts by any of a number of linkages: philological, paronomastic, thematic, numeric, historical—almost any basis could be employed to shed light from one biblical text upon another. As the supremely abiding gift from God to Israel, the midrashically interpreted Torah was so fully infused with teaching potential that combinations of its elements could endlessly yield insight and understanding.

"Torah" in the rabbinic context, however, does not refer strictly to the books of Moses or even just to the official canon we call the Hebrew Bible. The tradition of the two Torahs—the Written (the books of Moses and, by extension, the whole biblical corpus) and the Oral (the traditional biblical interpretations and legal rulings of the Jewish sages)—holds that both were revealed at Sinai. So, the interpretive tradition does not exist separately from the body of texts it interprets but shares in its authority as both Written and Oral Torahs are spoken in the name of a chain of interpreters going back to Moses and through him to God. Biblical interpretation in this context is a thoroughly social and dialogical phenomenon. Virtually the whole of the vast rabbinic corpus is presented to the reader as though it were a series of conversations across the generations: sometimes page after page of this rabbi offering an interpretation, that rabbi offering an alternative interpretation, and so on. Indeed, within the Jewish tradition of Torah study, it is unthinkable to proceed in isolation: "Why are the words of Torah compared to fire, as it is written, 'Is not my word like fire? Says the Lord' [Jer 23:9]. This is to teach you: What fire is there that can ignite itself? So also the words of Torah do not endure with [one who studies] in solitude."[9] Here again we find biblical interpretation practiced not so much as a method but as a highly participatory form of life, a life of dialogue with the Torah—which is the mind of God.

The innately communal, dialogical nature of rabbinic interpretation presents a challenge to students consulting traditional Jewish biblical interpretations for the first time. Modern readers often puzzle over the lack of finality in biblical interpretation as it is found in the midrashic collections and the Talmuds: multiple interpretations of the same biblical passage and open-ended interpretations constitute the norm rather than the exception.[10] Modern desires for a debate-ending discovery of the final, uncontestable determinate

---

[8] *Song of Songs Rabbah* 1.1.8.

[9] Babylonian Talmud *Ta'anit* 7a. See also *Berakhot* 63a.

[10] The rabbinic notion of a single biblical passage yielding multiple meanings but without redundancy is reflected in this tradition preserved in the Babylonian Talmud (*Sanhedrin* 34a, following the Soncino translation): "One Biblical verse may convey several teachings, but a single teaching cannot be deduced from different Scriptural verses. In R. Ishmael's School it was taught: 'And like a hammer that breaketh the rock in pieces' (Jer 23:29); i.e., just as [the rock] is split into many splinters, so also may one Biblical verse convey many teachings."

meaning in a biblical text, resulting from a methodically impeccable analysis performed upon the text by a transcendent self—such desires are frustrated in the world of rabbinic exegesis, where it seems that no one finally concludes anything. It is a world where students and teachers come together at the *beit midrash* (house of study) with questions driven by the presuppositions that 1) the biblical text has been given by God to illuminate human existence and 2) illumination shines forth only in the *maḥloqet*, the give-and-take of open dialectic around the text. Illumination in the *beit midrash* does not necessarily entail arriving at an interpretive destination. Classical Jewish interpretation repudiates the notion that understanding is coterminous with final graspability and synthesis. Rather, understanding the Bible more authentically resides, perhaps strangely, in the uncertainty of its interpretation, never fully finished. "The words of the wise [rabbinic interpreters] are not added to the text; they are the text as well, linking its words to form not an integrated, hierarchical system but an ongoing tradition, a structure of mutual belonging. The Torah emerges as what it is and comes into its own only in the dialogue it generates; and only by entering into the dialogue can one enter into the Torah. To belong to the dialogue is to belong to Judaism."[11]

On the Christian side, during the first five centuries C.E., differences in biblical interpretation could often become downright contentious. Jews did not generally agree with the way Christians interpreted the Hebrew Scriptures, and among Christian factions there were severe disputes regarding the nature of the Godhead and other issues. Virtually all the disputants agreed that the truth of matters lay in Scripture; the differences frequently boiled down to how the Scriptures (for Jews, the sacred Hebrew scrolls; for the Christian groups, the Old and New Testaments) were to be interpreted. The line of interpretation that eventually prevailed as orthodox among the Christians would require alignment with apostolic teachings as they had gelled in Christian liturgy and worship. The second-century writer Irenaeus of Lyon summarized the orthodox Christian position in his Rule of Faith:

> And this is the drawing-up of our faith, the foundation of the building, and the consolidation of a way of life. God, the Father, uncreated, beyond grasp, invisible, one God the maker of all; this is the first and foremost article of our faith. But the second article is the Word of God, the Son of God, Christ Jesus our Lord, who was shown forth by the prophets according to the design of their prophecy and according to the manner in which the father disposed; and through Him were made all things whatsoever. He also, in the end of times, for the recapitulation of all things, is become a man among men, visible and tangible, in order to abolish death and bring to light life, and bring about the communion of God and man. And the third article is the Holy Spirit, through whom the prophets prophesied and the patriarchs were taught about God and the just were led in the path of justice, and who in the end of times has been poured forth in a new manner upon humanity over all the earth renewing man to God.[12]

---

[11] Gerald Bruns, *Hermeneutics Ancient and Modern* (New Haven: Yale University Press, 1992), 116.

[12] Irenaeus, *Proof of the Apostolic Preaching* (trans. J. P. Smith; Ancient Christian Writers 16; New York: Paulist, 1952), ch. 2, p. 51.

How were the prophets' and patriarchs' texts known to properly yield orthodox teachings? In another polemical document, Irenaeus alluded specifically to the figurative (allegorical/typological) way of reading Scripture, which would reliably uncover what others cannot see:

> If any one, therefore, reads the Scriptures with attention, he will find in them an account of Christ, and a foreshadowing of the new calling. For Christ is the treasure which was hid in the field [Matt 13:44], that is, in this world (for 'the field is the world' [Matt 13:38]); but the treasure hid in the Scriptures is Christ, since He was pointed out by means of types and parables. Hence His human nature could not be understood, prior to the consummation of those things which had been predicted, that is, the advent of Christ. . . . For every prophecy, before its fulfillment, is to men [full of] enigmas and ambiguities. But when the time has arrived, and the prediction has come to pass, then the prophecies have a clear and certain exposition.[13]

With words like these, the early Christians acknowledged that their claim to the Christian meaning of the Jewish Scriptures was less a matter of what these documents said than how they were read. Although here and there patristic discourse regarding the Bible focused on exegetical issues such as philology and literary context, by and large the questions of biblical interpretation were hermeneutical. For passages obviously commensurate with the Rule of Faith, the reading would be literal (with allowance for genre distinctions and figurative expressions) whereas, for passages that required a second reading to agree with apostolic teaching, that second reading would be figurative.[14]

In the fifth century, Augustine refined Christian hermeneutics to a question of reading the Bible in such a way that greater love of God and love of neighbor come of it.[15] Augustine also emphasized what had been affirmed by Origen and all the Fathers as the *sine qua non* for reading the Bible in this way, namely, the perspective that Jesus himself granted the church on the biblical text.[16] Ancient biblical hermeneutics was never simply the application of

---

[13] Irenaeus, *Against Heresies* 4.26, in *The Apostolic Fathers, Justin Martyr, and Irenaeus* (vol. 1 of *The Ante-Nicene Fathers;* ed. and trans. Alexander Roberts and James Donaldson; Grand Rapids: Eerdmans, 1992), 496.

[14] Thus orthodox interpretation was never simply a matter of (allegorical) technique, for opponents of orthodoxy such as the gnostics were themselves accomplished allegorizers.

[15] Augustine, *De doctrina christiana* 1.40, in *Teaching Christianity* (trans. Edmund Hill, O.P.; The Works of Saint Augustine: A Translation for the 21st Century; I/11]. Hyde Park, N.Y.: New City Press, 1996), 124.

[16] One of the key biblical passages on which the early church based this affirmation is the story, near the end of Luke's gospel, in which the resurrected Jesus read himself into the Jewish Scriptures, showing his disciples—probably through some sorts of figuration—how he was the consummate meaning of the Scripture tradition: "And he said to them, 'O foolish men, and slow of heart to believe all that the prophets have spoken! Was it not necessary that the Christ should suffer these things and enter into his glory?' And beginning with Moses and all the prophets, he interpreted to them in all the scriptures the things concerning himself" (24:25–27). Shortly thereafter: "They said to each other, 'Did not our hearts burn within us while he talked to us on the road, while he opened to us the scriptures?'" (24:32). And finally, a little later that same day, addressing a larger group of followers: "Then he said to them, 'These are my words which I spoke to you, while I was still with you, that everything written about me in the law of Moses and the prophets and the psalms must be fulfilled.' Then he opened their minds to understand the scriptures, and said to them, 'Thus it is written, that the Christ should suffer and on the third day rise from the dead'" (24:44–46). Note how this gospel text refers to an opened mind as the necessary condition for perceiving in the Scripture tradition that which was otherwise indiscernable.

method to the text but entailed a living relationship with it; only secondarily was the text transformed in Christian interpretation. Before the biblical text could be converted to Christian reading, there first had to be a conversion of the reader to the interpretive perspective in Christ. Only from this vantage point were such readings possible.

Medieval Christian Interpretation (600–1500 C.E.)

In the minds of the church fathers, figurative interpretation of Scripture became a key part of a larger hermeneutical perspective strongly influenced by neoplatonic philosophical categories of metaphysics. That is, beyond the drafting of ordinary words into the service of expressing extraordinary truth, Christian allegorical interpretation manifested a way of reading not just Scripture but the world itself: visible, tangible things were taken to speak of invisible, spiritual things. As Scripture communicates its divine message, it uses words that signify actual objects or actions in the world (lion, mountain, bread, walking, wrestling, sleeping), which themselves are symbols of intangible, spiritual truths (divine sovereignty, nourishment of the soul, the struggle between godly and ungodly human natures). In this hermeneutical framework, then, it is not only the words of Scripture that God has set forth to communicate divine truth but also the physical world: as the words of Scripture refer to them, things in the tangible world speak symbolically of spiritual realities because God has ordered both—the world and Scripture—to be read together so that humans can be instructed about divinity and morality.[17]

The modern reader sometimes balks at the liberties that ancient and medieval Christian interpreters seem to have taken with biblical texts, as though the literal meaning that words carry were simply disregarded. We note, for example, this comment by the eighth-century British monk Bede on Exod 25:23, where the Israelites are given the specific dimensions for constructing a table to be used in the tabernacle:

> The table made from acacia wood is the Holy Scripture composed out of the bold words and deeds of the holy fathers. . . . This [table] has length, because it suggests to us perseverance in religious undertakings; width, because it suggests the amplitude of charity; height, because it suggests the hope of everlasting reward.[18]

Despite the attention devoted to a figurative sense of Scripture, it was, in the Christian tradition of interpretation, the literal sense that served as the foundation upon which the entire framework of figurative meanings could be built. The grammatical and rhetorical schools of the Greco-Roman world had for generations recognized the establishment of the lexicographical meaning of an author's words as a basic step for interpreting literature.[19]

---

[17] For further information on the neoplatonic philosophical tradition in Christian thought, see the collection of essays in Dominic J. O'Meara, ed., *Neoplatonism and Christian Thought* (Albany: State University of New York Press, 1981).

[18] Bede, *On the Tabernacle* (trans. Arthur G. Holder; Translated Texts for Historians 18; Liverpool: Liverpool University Press, 1994), 21.

[19] E.g., during the late second century, Origen had compiled unparalleled notes on the textual readings of various biblical manuscript traditions. One of the motivations for his scrupulous lexicographical attention to the biblical text was to help establish an accurate semiological basis for allegorical interpretation. A corrupted text would obscure the doctrine that God's Spirit had intended to teach by the selection of only the words that the authentic textual readings preserved.

This discipline continued to influence the Church's figurative exegesis into the Middle Ages, as the standard or literal meaning of a word was important to know in order to identify the correct symbol by which various figurative meanings could be understood: doctrinal (allegorical), moral (tropological), or prophetic (anagogical). An example for this fourfold plurality of meaning is this medieval scriptural allegory attributed to Dante:

> "When Israel went out of Egypt, the house of Jacob from a people of a strange language; Judah was his sanctuary, and Israel his dominion" [Ps 114:1–2]. For if we consider the letter alone, the thing signified to us is the going out of the children of Israel from Egypt in the time of Moses; if the allegory, our redemption through Christ is signified; if the moral sense, the conversion of the soul from the sorrow and misery of sin to a state of grace is signified; if the anagogical, the passing of the sanctified soul from the bondage of the corruption of this world to the liberty of everlasting glory is signified.[20]

However much the spiritual meanings of this passage might edify medieval Christians, the plain meaning—the reference to Israel's flight from Egypt—could not be abandoned. The plain or historical sense always remained the fundament for interpretation. In the twelfth century, French scholastic theologian Peter of Poitiers wrote, "Unless the foundation of history [the literal meaning] is laid beneath, upon which the walls of allegory ought to be erected, and the roof of tropology ought to be placed, the whole edifice of the spiritual understanding will collapse."[21] After stating a similar admonition about the primacy of attending to the literal meaning, Peter's Parisian contemporary Hugh of St. Victor advised his students,

> You have in history the means through which to admire God's deeds, in allegory the means through which to believe his mysteries, in morality the means through which to imitate his perfection. Read therefore [the literal, historical sense]. . . . After the reading of history, it remains for you to investigate the mysteries of allegories, in which I do not think there is any need of exhortation from me since this matter itself appears worthy enough in its own right.[22]

As Hugh's words imply, even with necessary care given to ascertain the biblical text's literal sense, figurative meanings were usually more valued than the literal.

Attention to the plain sense of the Bible was complicated by the fact that the Christian Scriptures for centuries were studied only in translated versions. Since the fifth century, the Latin Bible, known as the Vulgate, had become the standard translation of the Christian Scriptures—indeed, virtually the only Bible—for the Western church. When the Latin text was found to present a strange expression or an odd grammatical construction, the stakes involved in providing a satisfactory explanation were high. After all, the text—even in translation—had recorded the very words of God, the Author of Scripture, whose voice was to be heard in every single word. By the end of the first Christian millennium,

---

[20] Dante Alighieri, *Epistolae: The Letters of Dante* (ed. and trans. Paget Toynbee; 2d ed.; Oxford: Clarendon, 1966), 199.

[21] Peter of Poitiers, *Allegoriae super tabernaculum Moysi* (ed. Philip S. Moore and James A. Corbett; Publications in Mediaeval Studies 3; Notre Dame: University of Notre Dame Press, 1938), 2. The English is taken from G. R. Evans, *The Language and Logic of the Bible: The Earlier Middle Ages* (Cambridge: Cambridge University Press, 1984), 122.

[22] *The Didascalicon of Hugh of St. Victor: A Medieval Guide to the Arts* (trans. Jerome Taylor; New York: Columbia University Press, 1971), 138–39.

however, Latin had ceased to be spoken in Europe as a vernacular. Biblical interpretation thus came to require much greater attention to grammar and syntax than had previously been the case. Such study entailed questions of linguistic signification, particularly the need to explain more clearly how words from a human language (such as Latin) could be taken to communicate suprahuman or divine truth. With refined questions of grammatical functions filling the air and with advanced cultivation of the liberal arts increasing in the twelfth century, understanding how the biblical text could be taken to authentically possess multiple meanings became a more pressing problem. The Aristotelian metaphysical tradition provided heuristic categories for scholars of this age. For instance, God could be understood as the efficient cause of what is expressed whereas the human writers were the operating cause.[23] Along similar philosophical lines, the thirteenth-century theologian Thomas Aquinas articulated how multiple senses can be legitimately derived from the biblical text and employed for the construction of theological subtleties. But the medieval Aristotelian insistence that the hidden essence of things could be humanly discerned only from their manifestation to the senses began to make some of the more exaggerated forms of allegorical interpretation less attractive than the plain sense of Scripture. The literal, historical sense of Scripture was beginning to emerge from centuries of relative neglect.

The intensified study of classical Latin, accompanied by a dynamic complex of commercial, cultural, and political factors, burgeoned into the European Renaissance of the fifteenth century. Scholars took up the study of ancient Greek and applied themselves to proving the authenticity of classical texts, editing them, and translating them from the original. As greater numbers of ancient texts were recovered and manuscripts were compared, it became apparent that texts have a history. So also do words and expressions. Biblical interpretation would now proceed on the recognition that languages and words have a history of meaning. The humanist impulse was to recover, as much as possible, the original meanings of ancient expressions in their social dimensions as they were addressed to their original audiences. In order to support greater historical understanding of the Bible, scholars began to produce voluminous fact-filled compendia, such as dictionaries, encyclopedias, polyglot Bibles, concordances, and philologically oriented commentaries replete with fresh translations for biblical words.[24] Learned interpretation of the Bible was now a journey back into the distant biblical world, and these tools equipped the exegetical traveler for the trek.

Biblical interpretation in the sixteenth century proceeded within a tension between two tendencies. On the one hand, there was the antiquarian motive that fueled the philological and historical inquiries into the long-dead culture of the biblical world. But at the same time, on the other hand, there was the desire to hear in the words of the text the voice of God's Spirit speaking to the individual worshipper. Indeed, among Protestants the sacrament of the proclamation of the word was effectively replacing the Eucharist as the primary mode of Christian participation in divine mystery. Many Protestants were also zealous to build a Christian society on the basis of what Scripture indicates; here the quest to understand the ancient social structures was aimed at living in them again or at least

---

[23] See A. J. Minnis and A. B. Scott, eds., *Medieval Literary Theory and Criticism, c. 1100–c. 1375: The Commentary-Tradition* (rev. ed.; Oxford: Clarendon, 1988), 3.

[24] For insights into the collegial world of Renaissance scholarship as it affected biblical interpretation, see Debora K. Shuger, *The Renaissance Bible: Scholarship, Sacrifice, and Subjectivity* (Berkeley: University of California Press, 1994).

adapting them to the civics of Geneva or Zurich. This tension reflects the Janus face of the Reformation age: the Reformers as servants of the biblical text shared with the medieval world an existential stance regarding the vitality and relevance of Scripture, but as heirs of the Renaissance,their historical objectivism vis-à-vis the antiquity of the biblical world made the distance between sixteenth-century Europe and biblical Palestine ever more evident. The always-present tension between the Bible's ancient signification and its contemporary meaning would increase thanks to the refined historical tools developed at the birth of the modern era.

Post-Talmudic Jewish Interpretation (600–1500 C.E.)

Among the various Jewish communities in southwestern Asia, North Africa, and Europe, midrash had been generally the prevalent form of biblical interpretation during the first eight centuries of the present era. Although exegetical debate among the rabbis had generated the maxim "a biblical passage cannot depart from its plain *[peshat]* meaning,"[25] it was the derived meaning *(derash,* from the same root as for *midrash)* that largely occupied Jewish interpreters, particularly in the haggadic or homiletic traditions but also in halakic or legal exegesis as well. The bases for Jewish interpretation had been firmly established in the corpus of rabbinic traditions.

By the tenth century, however, influence from philosophically sophisticated Arabic intellectual culture could be seen in the increasing attention given to grammatical, scientific, and rhetorical elements in the study of Scripture.[26] Jewish scholars such as Sa'adia ben Joseph (tenth century) in the East and the great scientist and commentator Ibn Ezra (eleventh century) in the West began producing commentaries based much more centrally on the details of Hebrew grammar and philology than had been the case in previous generations. In accord with this approach, there emerged a greater historical awareness and a considerably more consistent focus on the *peshat* and less reliance on midrashic interpretations of biblical passages. Ibn Ezra, for example, insisted on grammatical and contextual factors as primary guides for interpretation, and he sharply criticized the haggadic tradition of midrash when the *derash* seemed to have replaced the *peshat* without warrant. Expressing his dissatisfaction with this characteristic of traditional midrashic interpretation, Ibn Ezra created a play on Eccl 12:12–13: "The end of the matter is—to midrashic interpretation there is no end."[27]

The eleventh-century master commentator R. Shlomo Yitzḥaqi (Rashi) almost always provided explanatory comments along the lines of *peshat.* But he was not averse to including (and sometimes adjusting) the traditional midrashic interpretations where he sensed they contributed to a better understanding of what the text had to teach. His grand-

---

[25] Babylonian Talmud *Yevamot* 11b, 24a, 63a.

[26] At least two aspects of Arabic culture left an imprint on the Jewish commentary tradition. One was the elaboration of Aristotelian thought derived from Arabic translations or commentaries of Greek classics, produced as early as the ninth and tenth centuries. The second was the adaptation of Arabic grammatical concepts in the understanding of Hebrew by Jewish grammarians in the tenth and eleventh centuries.

[27] Taken from Ibn Ezra's introduction to his commentary on the Pentateuch as printed in *Chamishah Chumshei Torah* (Jerusalem: Mossad Harav Kook, 1986),10.

son R. Shmuel ben Meir (Rashbam; twelfth century) was even more insistent on the primacy of the plain meaning when interpreting Scripture. We find almost no midrashic interpretations at all in Rashbam's commentaries but instead explanations of the Torah "in a manner that conforms to the [natural] way of the world."[28] In part, the shift, noted above, among Christian interpreters away from figurative interpretations developed from the influence of the cultivated Jewish knowledge of grammatical details and preference for the *peshat*. Respected Christian scholars such as Nicholas of Lyra (thirteenth century) and Johannes Reuchlin (fifteenth century) consulted Jewish sources and were influenced by them. Overall, there was a parallel trend among Jewish and Christian exegetes during the late Middle Ages: respect for traditional, derived scriptural interpretations continued while there developed a grammatically and philosophically informed insistence that traditional homiletic interpretations could not be maintained at the expense of the Bible's plain sense.

Modern Biblical Interpretation (1500–Present)

As we have seen, by the fifteenth century, an unprecedented historical consciousness was beginning to emerge among European scholars. With a greater concern to establish more clearly what the ancient authors had written, there came also an increased appreciation of the original meaning of an ancient text. Interpreters were less interested in the allegorized meanings that had accumulated from the Fathers and subsequent commentators. In the fifteenth and sixteenth centuries, biblical interpretation became less directed toward aligning a biblical passage with a known Christian teaching through allegory and more directed toward discerning what the biblical author had intended to communicate. We might call this a quest for a certain *determinacy of meaning:* a text is more and more understood to possess a single ("plain," "literal," "historical") meaning—the authorially intended meaning—rather than a multiplicity of moral, theological, and ecclesiological meanings derivative from the things to which the author's words pointed. This is not simply a change of attitude regarding the text of the Bible; the way the world itself was viewed also underwent a transformation. The physical, historical world and all the things in it were seen less and less as symbolic of metaphysical truths or as bearers of spiritual meaning. Instead of providing objects of moral or theological interpretation, the physical world became an object of study in its own right. The task of making the physical universe intelligible (the construction of worldview) was becoming less a theological and more a scientific enterprise.

For biblical scholarship, the significance of this gradual shift in perspective was profound. During the seventeenth and eighteenth centuries, scientific inquiry overwhelmingly proved itself superior to prescientific efforts in accounting for the causation and properties of physical phenomena. Inevitably the modern, scientific frame of mind would be applied to the study of Scripture. Fifteenth-century scholarship had already recognized that there was a history to the biblical manuscript tradition and to biblical linguistic

---

[28] See Lockshin's reference for Rashbam's intriguing Hebrew phrase in *Rashbam's Commentary on Exodus* (ed. and trans. Martin I. Lockshin; Atlanta: Scholars Press, 1997), 225, from which this quote is taken.

conventions. The ability to detect semantic shifts in the ancient languages made it possible to distinguish historical strata in the texts on the basis of the types of words and expressions found in the text. A single text was no longer assumed to come from a single author at a single point in time. Beyond the signs (the words), it was eventually recognized that what the words referred to—the persons, the events, the places mentioned in the Bible—were also historical and therefore best understood when studied in a historical, scientific manner. Scholars applied themselves to the enormous amounts of linguistic and historical information available in newly rediscovered ancient sources such as Josephus, Philo, the Targumim, and rabbinic literature as well as in early Semitic texts discovered at archaeological sites in the Near East. The meaning of Scripture was no longer to be found in a network of doctrinal symbols connoted by the words of Scripture, that is, in a symbolic universe, but rather in the physical and historical universe. The criterion for truth in Scripture no longer resided in that symbolic network but in the correspondence between what is written on the pages of the Bible and what is shown to be true in the historical world of human observation and experience. Modern reading of the Bible highlights the question of what in Scripture can be accepted as literally true in a historical, scientific sense.

Historical criticism is the term frequently used to identify this modern scientific approach to biblical interpretation. The phrase denotes the discernment ("criticism") of historical factors that account for the features of the text: the time when it was written, the real (as distinguished from the attributed) author, and the social, political, and religious circumstances of the author. Through rationally defensible modes of analysis, the reader as investigator seeks to reconstruct the meaning of the text objectively within the time of its origins. Fewer scholars accepted the meaning of the text as it had been determined by (ecclesiastical) authorities that the modern mind now considered external to the world of the text and therefore less binding than the authority of reason and historical evidence. Access to the Bible's meaning was no longer assumed to exist within the reader's world of relations as created and maintained by the teaching authority of the church. This authority had for centuries valorized spiritual and moral figurative readings, and as a result believers had felt a great existential proximity between themselves as reading subjects and Scripture as the textual object.[29] Rather, the starting point of the historical-critical approach was an assumption of separation and distance between subject (reader) and object (text) by virtue of the recognition that the text originated in an ancient world and was written to speak to that world. Understanding the biblical text—now recognized to be an ancient artifact—became a matter of explaining the historical and cultural elements of its world.

Traditional authorities, such as the church fathers and the legacy of medieval scholarship, became less reliable sources for pursuing modern questions about the Bible. Learned biblical interpretation in the modern era required more information about the world of the ancient texts and about the historical development of the biblical documents themselves. The scholarly genre of "biblical introduction" emerged to supply such data. Early examples include the critical histories of the Old and New Testaments published in the late seventeenth century by the erudite French scholar Richard Simon. With particular focus on the textual and philological history of the Bible and through detailed attention to stylistic nuances in the ancient languages, Simon demonstrated, for example, that in the

---

[29] See Hans W. Frei, *The Eclipse of Biblical Narrative: A Study in Eighteenth and Nineteenth Century Hermeneutics* (New Haven: Yale University Press, 1974).

growth of the biblical tradition, Moses could not have authored all of the texts that had long been attributed to him. Simon's purpose was to show that "those who do not sufficiently examine the style of the holy Scriptures are subject to fall into great errors concerning the chronology [of biblical events and texts]."[30] By such charges the Catholic Simon intended to convince Protestants that the historical facts of the Bible demonstrated the need for the church's interpretive authority. But the sharp traditionalist reaction that Simon's work triggered was a harbinger of the sort of conflict that modern biblical study would continue to generate between historical investigation and traditional theological doctrine through subsequent centuries—even to the present day.

During the eighteenth and especially the nineteenth centuries, researchers continued to investigate the nature of the correspondence between the actual history of events mentioned in the Bible and the biblical narration of those events. The results of such study showed that events often differed from how the Bible presents things. For example, the contents of the Pentateuch were seen to derive from several sources that postdated Moses and that were edited together at the end of the Israelite monarchy or later. Scholars identified and reconstructed four main pentateuchal sources: J (for the Yahwist or Jahwist writer, from the early Israelite monarchic period); E (for the Elohist writer, somewhat later in the monarchic period; D (for the Deuteronomic writer, from the late monarchic or exilic period); and P (for the Priestly writer, from the postexilic period). Such reconstructions had larger ramifications for historical understanding of the Hebrew Bible.

For example, the judgments against Israel, announced by the prophets of the monarchic era, could not have been prompted by Israel's violation of the laws that God had established through Moses at Mt. Sinai, as traditionally believed. Instead the judgments were announced *before* the inclusion of these laws in the biblical record. Moreover, historical research indicated that the prophets themselves in some cases were not the originators of everything that appears in the biblical books bearing their names. (It had long been argued that the Hebrew prophecies did not foretell the coming of Jesus so much as they referred to realities on the historical horizon of the Israelites themselves.) The latter portion of the book of Isaiah, for example, was seen as so distinct in style and substance from what is found in the first half, and so relevant to the situation facing the exiled Jews in sixth-century B.C.E. Babylon, that it was concluded that the eighth-century B.C.E. Isaiah of Jerusalem could not have written it. Modern scholars dubbed the anonymous Babylonian prophet Deutero-Isaiah.

Analogously, close attention to the Greek style found in the New Testament epistles to Timothy and Titus—traditionally accepted as having been written by the Apostle Paul—produced the conclusion that they are in fact non-Pauline; similar negative conclusions were reached concerning the authorship of the epistles bearing the names of the Apostle John and the Apostle Peter. Historical examination of the New Testament Gospels generated theories regarding sources used in the writing of the Gospels. Seeking to more directly access the genius of Jesus' teachings, scholars labored to distinguish his genuine words and deeds from later addenda and to reconstruct a more historical account of his life.

Archaeological discoveries in the Near East and intense historical research brought more accurate understanding of ancient cultures and religions as they pertained to biblical

---

[30] Richard Simon, *A Critical History of the Old Testament* (London: Walter Davis, 1682), book 1, p. 42.

studies. As a result, Hebrew and Christian religious beliefs and rituals reflected in the biblical documents were beginning to be understood within the general context of the history of religions. By the first decade of the twentieth century, scholarly study of the Bible in the West was dominated by a concern to interpret the Bible historically as a document of antiquity for the sharpest focus upon the highest religious ideals expressed in its noblest passages.[31]

Greater access to ancient Near Eastern and Mediterranean texts helped twentieth-century biblical interpreters realize that the sources lying behind the present biblical documents were not literary creations in the sense that a modern author would write but rather collections of ancient traditions. The quest to identify the earliest (and so, it was thought, the purest) expressions of biblical thought led scholars to investigate the preliterary traditions that could be discerned behind the written deposits. Such oral traditions had served certain social, cultural, and religious functions in the life of the ancient communities before these traditions had been adapted to the purposes of a written record. So, the practice of source criticism in the nineteenth century was supplemented by form criticism in the twentieth. The narrative and legal traditions currently found in the early part of the book of Exodus could be seen as having originated in the ancient Israelite Passover observances, orally recited. The shape of Jesus' own teachings as recorded in the Synoptic Gospels was seen to have been influenced by Christian proclamation and teaching in the early church. As form-critical studies drew greater attention to the social settings from which the earliest biblical traditions had emerged, biblical scholars began to turn to the social sciences, such as sociology, social and cultural anthropology, and economics, to better understand the social realities of the ancient biblical world.[32]

In short, modern scholars realized that historical understanding of what is written in biblical texts entails far more than linguistics. The necessity of reading specific Bible verses in the light of their larger literary context had been recognized for centuries; the modern insight was that context reaches far beyond the range of a biblical verse's literary neighborhood. The meaning that any given biblical word or expression had for its ancient speakers is contingent upon a wide range of factors constituting the frame of reference that would have been operative at the time of utterance. Much modern biblical scholarship has been devoted to identifying and explicating these factors in an effort to realize the modern ideal for interpreting ancient texts: hearing the text as the ancients would have heard it. Such hearing, many modern biblical interpreters maintain, is what gives access to the meaning of the text.

Late Modern Biblical Interpretation (1970–Present)

The phrase just used—"the meaning of the text"—captures the quintessential stance of the modern interpreter vis-à-vis the text as an object to be interpreted. From that stance, the text is to be examined for the determinate meaning that awaits discovery in its political or historical or religious or psychological or authorial world. This meaning can be

---

[31] For a spirited account of the rise of modern biblical historical criticism, see Howard M. Teeple, *The Historical Approach to the Bible* (Evanston, Ill.: Religion and Ethics Institute, 1982).

[32] See Bruce Malina, "The Social Sciences and Biblical Interpretation," *Interpretation* 37 (1983): 229–42.

recovered for contemporary reflection. Such a manner of interpretation "is principally intent upon circumscribing the text within a specific historical horizon."[33] What is assumed in this stance is that a text's meaning exists in utter distinction from any hermeneutical framework that might be brought to bear upon it from the interpreter's world. Indeed, most of the modern interpretive enterprise has aimed to eliminate any contemporary historical or cultural factor that might insert itself between the reader and the ancient text. Heir to the humanistically charged Reformation and European Enlightenment, with their characteristic aversion to authorized interpretive structures such as church doctrine, the modern mind is uncomfortable with the notion that understanding the biblical text (or any literature) cannot occur without interpretation. The nineteenth-century Oxford don Benjamin Jowett even said as much: "The true use of interpretation is to get rid of interpretation, and to leave us alone with the author."[34]

It is the hallmark of late modern biblical interpretation to acknowledge that Jowett's ideal is not only impossible but also not even desirable. In recent decades scholars have begun to repudiate the notion that the contemporary reader approaches the text as a transcendentally neutral observer. They point out that just as the biblical text was created within a historical and cultural situation that affects the way it was written, so also they themselves as readers are situated within a cultural situation that cannot but affect the way they read. Both biblical text and biblical interpreter are contingent. Any reading of the biblical text, then, will be according to a hermeneutic of some sort (whether or not that fact is acknowledged), and thus the question prompting *interpretatio* is not, "What does this text mean?" but, "How do we interpret this text? How is it to be taken?"[35] The two are very different questions. Instead of pursuing an unencumbered encounter with the pristine text (or the authorial mind behind the text), interpretation in the late modern period entails a more self-conscious recognition of the unavoidability of a hermeneutical system or of presuppositions according to which sense will be made of the text.

The recent emergence of canon-based interpretation may be understood as one way in which biblical scholars attempt to do just that. The framework for interpretation in this case is the biblical canon, the literary assemblage within which the individual biblical compositions have had their home for as long as they have been regarded as Scripture. A canonical approach is a self-consciously theological way of reading biblical texts. Just as, according to structural linguistics, the meaning of a word is not determined by its etymology so much as by its place within a system of signs, so the theological significance of biblical compositions is determined not so much by their earliest versions or settings as by their role within the biblical text-system.[36] Any meaning an ancient composition—such as the Song of Songs—may have had when it was first written became subject to alteration or

---

[33] Michael Fishbane, "Hermeneutics," in *Contemporary Jewish Religious Thought: Original Essays on Critical Concepts, Movements, and Beliefs* (ed. Arthur A. Cohen and Paul Mendes-Flohr; New York: Scribner, 1987), 353–61. Fishbane's term for this approach is *explicatio,* as opposed to *interpretatio.*

[34] David Steinmetz, "The Superiority of Pre-critical Exegesis," *Theology Today* 37 (1980): 27, quoting Benjamin Jowett, "On the Interpretation of Scripture," in *Essays and Reviews* (7th ed.; London: Longman, Green, Longmen & Roberts, 1861) 384.

[35] See Gerald L. Bruns, *Hermeneutics Ancient and Modern* (New Haven: Yale University Press, 1992).

[36] See Gerald T. Sheppard, "Canonical Criticism," in vol. 1 of *Anchor Bible Dictionary* (ed. D. N. Freeman; 6 vols.; New York: Doubleday, 1992), 862.

even obliteration by that text's inclusion in the biblical canon.[37] The function or voice of a biblical composition within the canon, however, is not a given but an intertextual potential the specific contours of which come to light as the faith community (which has received the biblical collection as its textual authority, as its canon) reads the text for relevance to its own historical contingencies. Modern biblical scholarship has identified ways in which some of the biblical compositions were shaped by intertextual resonances with other (earlier) biblical texts during the beginnings of the canonical process.[38] Such shaping was, in part, the outcome of the way the faith community was interpreting its traditional texts. Canonical hermeneutics essentially extends the tradition history of the sacred collection through the ages to the current generation. It is the church and the synagogue—the communities that read the biblical writings as components of their authoritative canon, served by their respective hermeneutical institutions—that will locate among these writings the intracanonical resonances by which the Bible makes sense to them.[39]

We have been speaking of textual meaning as something that readers make or that is made as readers engage with the text. A focus on the text itself as a literary field of potential meaning—instead of a search for the intentions of the author or for the influences of the author's world—is another characteristic of late modern biblical interpretation. Instead of taking biblical writings as a window through which to view the author's meaning (or even divine doctrine), reading the Bible as literature opens the interpreter to meaning evident in the literary artistry of the text itself. By way of a brief example, the Catholic biblical scholar Sean McEvenue writes concerning the poetic line sung by the angels in Luke 2:14,

> Glory to God in the highest,
> and on earth, peace to men and women of good will.

> The meaning . . . does not come from a mimetic reading of the words, but only from a literary reading, noting a trope which is familiar in semitic poetics, the form of parallel stichs. Thus heaven parallels earth, glory parallels peace, and God parallels people: the heavens "in excelsis" are made parallel to the earth and hence the earth to the heavens; the glory of the angels' song is made parallel to the peace which men and women are to experience, and hence our peace is lifted up by angels' singing; and God who receives this song of glory is made parallel to people of good will who receive this angelic peace. . . . To "get" the significance of this little line, one must experience an exhilaration leveraged out of the paralleling of human experience and supernal joy. And if one assents to this feeling, one might be led to change the way one lived.[40]

---

[37] See Moshe Halbertal, *People of the Book: Canon, Meaning, and Authority* (Cambridge: Harvard University Press, 1997), 26.

[38] An entire commentary series currently in production and devoted to explicating this dimension of biblical documents is the Mellen Biblical Commentary (Intertextual) from the Edwin Mellen Press.

[39] One can detect in the canonical approach to interpretation a resemblance to premodern biblical interpretation, when portions of Scripture were almost automatically read in the light of other portions of the canon. Not surprisingly, one of the areas of current scholarly debate is the relationship between canonical interpretation and historical criticism inasmuch as the latter tends to regard biblical compositions in isolation from others not of the same historical context. See Mark Brett, *Biblical Criticism in Crisis? The Impact of the Canonical Approach on Old Testament Studies* (New York: Cambridge University Press, 1991).

[40] Sean McEvenue, "Exegesis as Knowledge of Things Unseen" (paper presented at the annual meeting of the Catholic Biblical Association, San Diego, August 1994).

The phenomenon of interpretation here resembles the aesthetic experience of art. Literary interpretation of Scripture is artistic in that the text is understood to be its own meaning, but not without the necessary engagement by a reader.

Reader-oriented (as distinguished from author-oriented or even text-oriented) interpretation is emerging as another characteristically late modern or postmodern way of understanding the Bible. According to this perspective, all human cultural expression—including linguistic, textual expression—is shaped through institutions, behavioral conventions, practices, and norms that are socially constructed rather than inherent realities of physical being. Interpretation of texts is therefore a dynamic process, attentive not just to what language says but to what language does—and this is never through a single speaking voice but through a dialogical process of interaction.[41] Thus the interaction of voices (a social dynamic)—not the single, individual voice—is the generative matrix of meaning. Meaning in a text certainly qualifies as a socially generated construct, and so, like all social constructs, meanings (i.e., what readers find meaningful) will vary relative to the ideologies or value structures that they support. Such variation inevitably means that the construction of meanings for texts is an unavoidably indeterminate process: there are no fixed, determinate meanings encoded within the texts; texts are made to make sense in terms of indeterminate meanings constructed by readers. There is therefore no such thing as the single, correct meaning of a text, and the role of the reader (or the reading community, sometimes called the interpretive community) is recognized to have a much more prominent place in the construction of meaning.

Truth in biblical texts, then, at the turn of the second millennium is pursued less exclusively according to philosophically based epistemology. Scholars are drawing greater attention to the rhetorical basis of truth as it is constructed both through the way language is used in the texts and through the way it is used by the interpreter. The biblical writers and their interpreters are by definition always situated in one or another web of social interests. So, the presence of a truth-constructing, rhetorical element in biblical interpretation raises the further question of the ideological interests that the rhetoric may be seen to serve—again, both in the world of the text's creators and in the world of the text's interpreters. Biblical interpreters are more and more examining biblical writings for the extent to which they were written or have been taken up by church and synagogue in order to claim divine sanction in favor of, for example, certain class interests, gender prejudices, and power hierarchies in social, ecclesiastical, and political institutions. The "results" of biblical interpretation are no longer restricted to understanding the world that created the Bible. The quest now extends more broadly to include the world that the Bible has created.

In the postmodern world, no single approach to biblical interpretation can claim exclusive validity or relevance. Since the Bible is studied in many different settings—church, university, seminary, home—the questions that are put to it will vary, as will the assumptions regarding the nature of the text. Even in the heyday of historical criticism, figurative reading never died (at least in some circles), and although historical questions now share the stage with reader-oriented queries, they have by no means made a complete exit.

---

[41] Mikhail Bakhtin, *The Dialogic Imagination: Four Essays* (ed. Michael Holquist; trans. C. Emerson and M. Holquist; Austin: University of Texas Press, 1981).

In short, biblical interpretation currently includes a spectrum of methods that reflect elements from every era of its history. Carefully considered, any question or concern brought to the Bible has legitimacy for the Bible-reading audience that presents the question. If all allow for this legitimacy, it may be that interpretive communities can gain insightful perspectives on the Scriptures that otherwise would have remained hidden to them.[42] The world of biblical interpretation has ever been rich and manifold, and so it continues into the twenty-first century.

---

[42] For a sensitive reflection on such prospects, see Daniel Patte, *Ethics of Biblical Interpretation: A Reevaluation* (Louisville: Westminster John Knox, 1995).

Part One

⎯⎯⎯⎯⎯⎯⎯⎯⎯⎯⎯

Prerabbinic Jewish Interpretation
(150 B.C.E.–70 C.E.)

CHAPTER 1

Ancient Greek Translation of Hebrew Scriptures: The Aristeas Legend (late second century B.C.E.)

Before the exile in Babylon (sixth century B.C.E.), ancient Israelite religious texts had been generated and passed down almost exclusively in Hebrew. During subsequent centuries, as more and more Jews took up residence in regions beyond Jerusalem and Judea, eventually Hebrew was supplemented in Jewish communities of the Diaspora with other languages of commerce, law, and diplomacy. Through centuries of Hellenistic rule over much of southwestern Asia and Egypt from the early third century B.C.E., in those regions the Greek language became prominent, especially for literary and philosophical expression. By the turn of the millennium, certain Jewish communities were rendering their religious texts into Greek for liturgical and study purposes. The earliest known manuscripts of Jewish Scriptures in Greek translation are among the scroll fragments from the Dead Sea region and date from the first century B.C.E. Greek translations of Hebrew Scriptures were produced in the second century C.E. and associated with the names Aquila, Symmachus, and Theodotian.

The most enduring Greek translation has come to be known as the Septuagint, a word derived from the Greek term for seventy.[1] The date of the Septuagint translation and the history of its development are difficult to establish with certainty; indeed, scholars are not agreed that there ever was in antiquity an actual single body of Hebrew Scriptures in Greek translation that can be identified as "the Septuagint." But there did circulate an ancient legend accounting for the origin of the Septuagint, written in the form of a letter from a certain Aristeas to his brother Philocrates. Portions of the letter are included here for two reasons.

The first reason is the importance of the Septuagint for the history of Christian interpretation of the Jewish Scriptures. The earliest Christian writings, beginning with the New Testament documents, consistently cited from the Greek Scriptures rather than from the Hebrew. Although Jews would generally cease to regularly use Greek translations of

---

[1] It was early Christian writers who first referred to the Greek Jewish Scriptures as the work of the Seventy, even though the legend counts out seventy-two translators; from this convention is derived the term "Septuagint." The shorthand siglum commonly used to designate the Septuagint is LXX.

Hebrew Scriptures by the fourth century C.E., Christian churches continued with the Septuagint until the Latin Vulgate began its enduring prominence in the Western church in the fifth century. (The Eastern Greek-speaking church has continued to read from the Greek Old Testament to the present time.) At times the Greek rendering of a key scriptural passage has significantly influenced Christian interpretation of the passage. A conspicuous example is Isa 7:14, where, for the Hebrew term meaning "young maiden," the Greek term means "virgin." From this rendering, Christian interpreters argued scriptural support for the doctrine of the virgin birth of Christ. Whereas the Aristeas legend reports only the Torah (the first five books of the Hebrew Scriptures) as having been translated by the seventy-two appointed scholars, among early Christian theologians the legend was embellished to include the whole of Jewish Scriptures—the entire Christian Old Testament—in the work of the seventy translators. Indeed, by the fourth century, many Christian authorities considered the Greek translators (the Seventy) to have been inspired by God's Spirit as a part of the divine plan of salvation.[2]

Second, the Aristeas legend includes some of the earliest examples of prerabbinic Jewish allegorical interpretation of Scripture. Allegory would continue in subsequent centuries as a major mode of biblical interpretation, especially among Christian interpreters. Some prerabbinic exegetes, such as Aristobulus (second century B.C.E.) and Philo of Alexandria (first century C.E.), allegorized Scripture. But except for the Song of Songs, the Jewish Bible was not usually read allegorically in the rabbinic exegetical tradition.[3] Reading the Aristeas allegory of Jewish law can illuminate the early allegorical mind-set regarding Scripture that helped set the tone for centuries of biblical interpretation.

The Aristeas of this legend is presented as presumably a resident of the Jewish community in Alexandria, Egypt. In his letter to Philocrates, Aristeas offers a first-person description of the cooperative diplomatic project, between the Ptolemaic court in Alexandria and the Jewish high-priestly court in Jerusalem, that produced the Greek translation of the Mosaic law. The events depicted would have taken place in the mid-third century B.C.E., but most scholars believe the letter was written in the late second century B.C.E. under a pseudonym.

For further information on the Aristeas legend and the Septuagint:

Collins, Nina L. *The Library in Alexandria and the Bible in Greek.* Supplements to Vetus Testamentum 82. Leiden: Brill, 2000.
Jobes, Karen H., and Moises Silva. *Invitation to the Septuagint.* Grand Rapids: Baker, 2000.
Marcos, Natalio Fernando. *The Septuagint in Context: Introduction to the Greek Version of the Bible.* Leiden: Brill, 2001.

---

[2] See, e.g., Irenaeus, *Against Heresies* 21.1–4; Clement of Alexandria, *Stromata* 1.22.148–149; Cyril of Jerusalem, *Catecheses* 4.34.

[3] A helpful survey of the history of Jewish and Christian interpretation of the Song of Songs is found in R. E. Murphy, *The Song of Songs* (Hermeneia; Minneapolis: Augsburg-Fortress, 1990), 11–41.

The *Letter of Aristeas*[4]

Ptolemy II Philadelphus of the Greek-speaking Ptolemaic dynasty in Egypt was widely respected for his patronage of the arts and scholarship. Aristeas narrates the circumstances and events in Ptolemy's court that led to the decision to produce a Greek translation of the Jewish law books for deposition in the Greek king's royal library. Once the Jewish high priest Eleazar in Jerusalem agrees to assemble a team of scholars for the translation project, Aristeas is dispatched by Ptolemy's chief librarian to convey them to Egypt for the task. Addressing Aristeas and his party while they are in Jerusalem, Eleazar elaborates on the distinctions of the laws of Moses.

"Now our Lawgiver being a wise man and specially endowed by God to understand all things, took a comprehensive view of each particular detail, and fenced us round with impregnable ramparts and walls of iron, that we might not mingle at all with any of the other nations, but remain pure in body and soul, free from all vain imaginations, worshiping the one Almighty God above the whole creation. Hence the leading Egyptian priests having looked carefully into many matters, and being cognizant with (our) affairs, call us 'men of God.' This is a title which does not belong to the rest of mankind but only to those who worship the true God. The rest are men *not of God* but of meats and drinks and clothing. For their whole disposition leads them to find solace in these things. Among our people such things are reckoned of no account, but throughout their whole life their main consideration is the sovereignty of God. Therefore lest we should be corrupted by any abomination, or our lives be perverted by evil communications, he hedged us round on all sides by rules of purity, affecting alike what we eat, or drink, or touch, or hear, or see. For though, speaking generally, all things are alike in their natural constitution, since they are all governed by one and the same power, yet there is a deep reason in each individual case why we abstain from the use of certain things and enjoy the common use of others. For the sake of illustration I will run over one or two points and explain them to you. For you must not fall into the degrading idea that it was out of regard to mice and weasels and other such things that Moses drew up his laws with such exceeding care. All these ordinances were made for the sake of righteousness to aid the quest for virtue and the perfecting of character. For all the birds that we use are tame and distinguished by their cleanliness, feeding on various kinds of grain and pulse, such as for instance pigeons, turtle-doves, locusts, partridges, geese also, and all other birds of this class. But the birds which are forbidden [see Lev 11:13–19] you will find to be wild and carnivorous, tyrannizing over the others by the strength which they possess, and cruelly obtaining food by preying on the tame birds enumerated above. And not only so, but they seize lambs and kids, and injure human beings too, whether dead or alive, and so by naming them unclean, he gave a sign by means of them that those, for whom the legislation was ordained, must practice righteousness in their hearts and not tyrannize over any one in reliance upon their own strength nor rob them of anything, but steer their course of life in accordance with justice,

---

[4] These excerpts from the *Letter of Aristeas* are taken from R. H. Charles, *The Apocrypha and Pseudepigrapha of the Old Testament in English* (Oxford: Clarendon, 1913), vol. 2.

just as the tame birds, already mentioned, consume the different kinds of pulse that grow upon the earth and do not tyrannize to the destruction of their own kindred. Our legislator taught us therefore that it is by such methods as these that indications are given to the wise, that they must be just and effect nothing by violence, and refrain from tyrannizing over others in reliance upon their own strength. For since it is *considered* unseemly even to touch such *unclean* animals, as have been mentioned, on account of their particular habits, ought we not to take every precaution lest our own characters should be destroyed to the same extent?

Wherefore all the rules which he has laid down with regard to what is permitted in the case of these *birds* and other animals, he has enacted with the object of teaching us a moral lesson. For the division of the hoof and the separation of the claws [see Lev 11:1–8] are intended to teach us that we must discriminate between our individual actions with a view to the practice of virtue. For the strength of our whole body and its activity depend upon our shoulders and limbs. Therefore he compels us to recognize that we must perform all our actions with discrimination according to the standard of righteousness—more especially because we have been distinctly separated from the rest of mankind. For most other men defile themselves by promiscuous intercourse, thereby working great iniquity, and whole countries and cities pride themselves upon such vices. For they not only have intercourse with men but they defile their own mothers and even their daughters. But we have been kept separate from such sins. And the people who have been separated in the aforementioned way are also characterized *by the Lawgiver* as possessing the *gift* of memory. For all animals 'which are cloven-footed and chew the cud' [see Lev 11:3] represent to the initiated the *symbol* of memory. For the act of chewing the cud is nothing else than the reminiscence of life and existence. For life is wont to be sustained by means of food wherefore he exhorts us in the Scripture also in these words: 'Thou shalt surely remember the Lord that wrought in thee those great and wonderful things' (Deut 7:18–19 and 10:21). For when they are properly conceived, they are manifestly great and glorious; first the construction of the body and the disposition of the food and the separation of each individual limb and, far more, the organization of the senses, the operation and invisible movement of the mind, the rapidity of its particular actions and its discovery of the arts, display an infinite *resourcefulness*. Wherefore he exhorts us to remember that the aforesaid parts are kept together by the divine power with consummate skill. For he has marked out every time and place that we may continually remember the God who rules and preserves (us). For in the matter of meats and drinks he bids us first of all offer part as a sacrifice and then forthwith enjoy *our meal*. Moreover, upon our garments he has given us a symbol of remembrance (Num 15:38), and in like manner he has ordered us to put the *divine* oracles upon our gates and doors as a remembrance of God (Deut 6:7–9). And upon our hands, too, he expressly orders the symbol to be fastened, clearly showing that we ought to perform every act in righteousness, remembering (our own creation), and above all the fear of God. He bids men also, when lying down to sleep and rising up again, to meditate upon the works of God, not only in word, but by observing distinctly the change and impression produced upon them, when they are going to sleep, and also their waking, how divine and incomprehensible the change from one of these states to the other is. The excellency of the analogy in regard to discrimination and memory has now been pointed out to you, according to our interpretation of 'the cloven hoof and the chewing of the cud.'

For our laws have not been drawn up at random or in accordance with the first *casual* thought that occurred to the mind, but with a view to truth and the indication of right reason. For by means of the directions which he gives with regard to meats and drinks and particular cases of touching, he bids us neither to do nor listen to any-thing thoughtlessly nor to resort to injustice by the abuse of the power of reason. In the case of the wild animals, too, the same principle may be discovered. For the character of the weasel and of mice and such animals as these, which are expressly mentioned, is destructive [see Lev 11:29]. Mice defile and damage everything, not only for their own food but even to the extent of rendering absolutely useless to man whatever it falls in their way to damage. The weasel class, too, is peculiar: for besides what has been said, it has a characteristic which is defiling: It conceives through the ears and brings forth through the mouth. And it is for this reason that a like practice is declared unclean in men. For by embodying in speech all that they receive through the ears, they involve others in evils and work no ordinary impurity, being themselves altogether defiled by the pollution of impiety. And your king, as we are informed, does quite right in destroying such men."

Then I said, "I suppose you mean the informers, for he constantly exposes them to tortures and to painful forms of death."

"Yes," he replied, "these are the men I mean, for to watch for men's destruc-tion is an unholy thing. And our law forbids us to injure any one either by word or deed. My brief account of these matters ought to have convinced you, that all our regulations have been drawn up with a view to righteousness, and that nothing has been enacted in the Scripture thoughtlessly or without due reason, but its purpose is to enable us throughout our whole life and in all our actions to practice righteous-ness before all men, being mindful of Almighty God. And so concerning meats and things unclean, creeping things, and wild beasts, the whole system aims at righteous-ness and righteous relationships between man and man."

He seemed to me to have made a good defense on all the points; for in refer-ence also to the calves and rams and goats which are offered, he said that it was nec-essary to take them from the herds and flocks, and sacrifice tame animals and offer nothing wild, that the offerers of the sacrifices might understand the symbolic mean-ing of the lawgiver and not be under the influence of an arrogant self-consciousness. For he, who offers a sacrifice, makes an offering also of his own soul in all its moods. I think that these particulars with regard to our discussion are worth narrating, and on account of the sanctity and natural meaning of the law, I have been induced to ex-plain them to you clearly, Philocrates, because of your own devotion to learning.

The text goes on to narrate the reception of the Jewish translation team at the Ptolemaic court and a royal banquet scene in which the wisdom of the Jewish scholars is dem-onstrated. A few days later they are set up on the island of Pharos at Alexandria, where they set to work.

As I have already said, they met together daily in the place which was delightful for its quiet and its brightness and applied themselves to their task. And it so chanced that the work of translation was completed in seventy-two days, just as if this had been arranged of set purpose.

When the work was completed, Demetrius collected together the Jewish population in the place where the translation had been made, and read it over to all, in the presence of the translators, who met with a great reception also from the people, because of the great benefits which they had conferred upon them. They bestowed warm praise upon Demetrius, too, and urged him to have the whole law transcribed and present a copy to their leaders. After the books had been read, the priests and the elders of the translators and the Jewish community and the leaders of the people stood up and said, that since so excellent and sacred and accurate a translation had been made, it was only right that it should remain as it was and no alteration should be made in it. And when the whole company expressed their approval, they bade them pronounce a curse in accordance with their custom upon any one who should make any alteration either by adding anything or changing in any way whatever any of the words which had been written or making any omission. This was a very wise precaution to ensure that the book might be preserved for all the future time unchanged. When the matter was reported to the king, he rejoiced greatly, for he felt that the design which he had formed had been safely carried out.

CHAPTER 2

Biblical Commentary in the Dead Sea Scrolls (first centuries B.C.E. and C.E.)

For nineteen centuries caves in the western cliffs of the Dead Sea region have protected numerous manuscripts that were created and copied by Jews who hid them there. How these writings were discovered and studied in modern times is a well-known and fascinating story, which interested readers can review in some detail by consulting F. García Martínez, *The Dead Sea Scrolls Translated: The Qumran Texts in English* (trans. W. G. E. Watson; 2d ed.; Leiden: E. J. Brill, 1996). The translations featured in this chapter come from this work. The biblical passages that are indicated in the text should be read along with the scroll translations.

The hundreds of Dead Sea documents, which date from about 150 B.C.E. to 68 C.E., reflect an intense concern with the scriptures that would later be known as the Hebrew Bible or the Old Testament. Virtually every scroll and fragment—whether a copy of a biblical writing, a commentary on biblical texts, or a sectarian document of liturgy or of community ordinances—is the product of an ancient Jewish group profoundly preoccupied with correct interpretation of the Hebrew Scriptures. One important text from this group suggests that they had geographically and socially separated from the Jerusalem priestly establishment primarily for the sake of correct interpretation and obedience to the halakic requirements of that interpretation:

> These are some of our regulations [concerning the law of G]od, . . . we think that the temple [is the place of the tent of meeting, and Je]rusalem is the camp; and outside the camp is [outside Jerusalem;] it is the camp of their cities . . . [And you know that] we have segregated ourselves from the rest of the peop[le and (that) we avoid] mingling in these affairs and associating with them in these things. And you k[now that there is not] to be found in our actions deceit or betrayal or evil, for concerning [these things w]e give [. . . and further] to you we have wr[itten] that you must understand the book of Moses [and the words of the pro]phets and of David [and the annals] [of eac]h generation . . . [And it is written in the book of] Moses and in [the words of the prop]hets that [blessings and curses] will come upon you which [. . .] [the bl]essings which c[ame upon] him in the days of Solomon the son of David and also the curses which came upon him from the [days of Je]roboam son of Nebat right up to the exile of Jerusalem and of Zedekiah, king of Judah [that] he should bring them in [. . .]. And we are aware that part of the blessings and curses have occurred that are written in the b[ook of Mo]ses. And this is the end of days, when they will return in Israel to the L[aw . . .](4QMMT composite text, lines 3–4, 32–33, 92–96, 103–108).

These lines reflect the self-understanding of a Jewish community that discerns in its own existence and circumstances the fulfillment of expectations expressed in their Scripture. Other texts hint at this same self-perception:

> At the moment of wrath, three hundred and ninety years after having delivered them up into the hand of Nebuchadnezzar, king of Babylon, he visited them and caused to sprout from Israel and from Aaron a shoot of the planting . . . And God appraised their deeds, because they sought him with a perfect heart, and raised up for them a Teacher of Righteousness, in order to direct them in the path of his heart . . . with those who remained steadfast in God's precepts, with those who were left from among them, God established his covenant with Israel for ever, revealing to them hidden matters in which all Israel had gone astray (*Damascus Document* A, I.5–7, 10–11; III.13–14).

> And when these exist/ as a community/ in Israel/ in compliance with these arrangements/ they are to be segregated from within the dwelling of the men of sin to walk to the desert in order to open there His path. As it is written "In the desert, prepare the way of ****, straighten in the steppe a roadway for our God" [Isa 40:3].[1] This is the study of the law which he commanded through the hand of Moses, in order to act in compliance with all that has been revealed from age to age, and according to what the prophets have revealed through his holy spirit (1QS VIII.12–16).

Study of Scripture seems to have served as a *raison d'être* for the community that produced the Scrolls. In the context of a life of study together, correct interpretation of Scripture would be revealed to the community's leadership, and all were expected to follow in obedience to it:

> Whoever enters the council of the Community enters the covenant of God . . . he shall swear with a binding oath to revert to the Law of Moses, with all that it decrees, with whole heart and whole soul, in compliance with all that has been revealed concerning it to the sons of Zadok, the priests who keep the covenant and interpret his will and to the multitude of the men of their covenant who freely volunteer together for this truth and to walk according to his will (1QS V.8–10).

The Dead Sea Scrolls provide insight into the crucial role played by biblical interpretation in the definition of sectarian religious identity at the beginning of the first millennium. The Scrolls are the literary legacy of a Jewish group that, by virtue of interpretations of Scripture that they received as revealed from God, distinguished itself from other Jewish readers of these same texts. Although parallels must be drawn with care, this is not unlike what was later to take place as the followers of Jesus distinguished their movement on the basis of their claim to divinely revealed interpretation of Scripture. In this sense, the emergence of various forms of Judaism and Christianity was largely a matter of biblical interpretation.

Our short selections from the Dead Sea manuscripts cannot cover the extensive range of forms in which Scripture interpretation is attested among the Scrolls. Some of the interpretive writings preserved in the caves, such as *Jubilees, 1 Enoch,* and Tobit, are not exclusive to the Dead Sea provenance. Many documents from the caves, however, preserve early examples of biblical interpretation found virtually nowhere else, and we will attempt

---

[1] The quote from Isa 40:3 includes a scribal convention found occasionally in the Dead Sea Scrolls: the substitution of four dots (****) in the place of the sacred name of God. Where the divine name is written in the Scrolls it is rendered YHWH by Martínez.

to represent these. One category of interpretation distinctive to the Dead Sea Scrolls is known as the pesher method, so called from a Hebrew word that means "interpretation." In the following pages, selections from prominent examples of the pesher manner of biblical interpretation are featured.

The *Pesher Habakkuk* scroll proceeds sequentially through the text of Habakkuk; it explicitly cites a phrase and provides an interpretation for the phrase, using the word *pesher,* which in this usage translates, "the interpretation [of the verse or word just cited] is . . ." In almost every case, the content of Habakkuk, from Babylonian times, is interpreted prophetically to refer, even if in a veiled fashion, to the specific circumstances of the community that produced the pesher scroll in Roman times. The claim to authority for such exclusive interpretations is expressed in column VII, where the community's leader (the Teacher of Righteousness) is said to have received special divine insights on the meaning of prophetic writings. Indeed, the scroll claims that Habakkuk's own words reveal more than he himself understood but that the Teacher would understand the mysteries (VI.12–VII.8).

The document scholars call 4QFlorilegium[2] consists of a selection of cited texts from various books of the Hebrew Scriptures thematically linked to the messianic announcement of 2 Sam 7:5–16. Here the pesher format functions with a midrashic style of textual linkage or juxtaposition, so that seemingly unconnected passages from different parts of Scripture are seen to speak of the same thing. The Hebrew term *midrash* appears in line 14 parallel to *pesher,* as "interpretation," and indeed many scholars consider pesher to be a certain type of midrashic interpretation.[3]

Our last example of biblical commentary from the Dead Sea documents is 4QGenesis Pesher[a] (4Q252), the preserved fragments of which provide commentary on selected passages from Genesis. Some of the commentary in 4Q252 resembles the sort of interpretation seen in contemporary Jewish writings, such as the "rewritten Bible" style found in *Jubilees* and *Liber antiquitatum biblicarum* (Pseudo-Philo) (see 4Q252 on Gen 6:3), and another variation of the pesher technique (see 4Q252 on Gen 49:3–4). But 4Q252 also includes some of the earliest known examples of an exegetical approach that seeks simply to comment on explicit or implicit problems found in certain passages. Thus 4Q252 does not comment on the whole text of Genesis but proceeds through the book focusing on selected lines from Genesis. The comment on Gen 9:24–25, for example, seeks to explain why Noah cursed Ham's son Canaan when it was Ham himself who had transgressed.[4]

For further information on the Dead Sea Scrolls:

Campbell, Jonathan. *Dead Sea Scrolls: The Complete Story.* Berkeley: Ulysses, 1998.
Fitzmyer, Joseph A. *Responses to 101 Questions on the Dead Sea Scrolls.* New York: Paulist, 1992.
VanderKam, James C. *The Dead Sea Scrolls Today.* Grand Rapids: Eerdmans, 1994.

---

[2] The number 4 signifies the cave in which the document was found; the Q signifies the Qumran area of the Dead Sea region; *Florilegium* literally means "gathering of flowers," but as a literary term it signifies a collection or anthology of texts.

[3] For more detailed information on the pesher type of interpretation, see Geza Vermes, "The Qumran Interpretation of Scripture in Its Historical Setting," in *Post-biblical Jewish Studies* (Studies in Judaism in Late Antiquity 8; Leiden: E. J. Brill, 1975), 37–49.

[4] For a more complete discussion of 4Q252, see M. J. Bernstein, "4Q252: From Re-written Bible to Biblical Commentary," *Journal of Jewish Studies* 45 (1994): 1–27; and G. J. Brooke, "4Q252 as Early Jewish Commentary," *Revue de Qumran* 17, nos. 65–68 (1996): 385–401.

1QHabakkuk Pesher (1QpHab)[5]

Column I

10 [. . .] *Hab 1:4a* For the Law falls into abeyance. *11* [The interpretation . . .] that they have rejected the Law of God. *12* [*Hab 1:4bc* And justice does not emerge as the winner, for the evildoer acc]osts the upright man. *blank 13* [Its interpretation: the evildoer is the Wicked Priest[6] and the upright man] is the Teacher of Righteousness[7] *14* [who . . . *Hab 1:4d* This] is why justice emerges *15* [distorted. The interpretation . . .] and not [. . .]

Column II

1 Hab 1:5 you reported it. *blank* [The interpretation of the word concerns] the traitors with the Man of *2* Lies, since they do not [believe in the words of the] Teacher of Righteousness from the mouth of *3* God; (and it concerns) the traito[rs of the] new [covenant] since they did not *4* believe in the covenant of God [and dishonored] his holy name. *5* Likewise: *blank* The interpretation of the word [concerns the trai]tors in the *6* last days. They shall be violators of [the coven]ant who will not believe *7* when they hear all that is going [to happen to] the final generation, from the mouth of the *8* Priest whom God has placed wi[thin the Community,] to foretell the fulfillment of all *9* the words of his servants, the prophets, [by] means of whom God has declared *10* all that is going to happen to his people [Israel]. *Hab 1:6* For see, I will mobilize *11* the Chaldeans, a cru[el and determined] people. *blank 12* Its interpretation concerns the Kittim,[8] who are swift and powerful *13* in battle, to slay many [with the edge of the sword] in the kingdom of *14* the Kittim; they will vanquish [many countries] and will not believe *15* in the precepts of [God . . .] *16* and [. . .]

Column VI

12 Hab 2:1–2 I will stand firm in my sentry-post, *13* I will position myself in my fortress to see what he says to me, *14* what he answers to my allegation. YHWH answered me *15* and said: Write the vision; inscribe it on tablets so that *16* [he who reads it] takes it on the run. *Hab 2:1–2* [. . .]

Column VII

1 And God told Habakkuk to write what was going to happen *2* to the last generation, but he did not let him know the end of the age. *3 blank* And as for what he says: *Hab 2:2* "So that the one who reads it /may run/." *4* Its interpretation concerns the Teacher of Righteousness, to whom God has disclosed *5* all the mysteries of the

---

[5] F. García Martínez, *The Dead Sea Scrolls Translated: The Qumran Texts in English* (trans. W. G. E. Watson; 2d ed.; Leiden: E. J. Brill, 1996). Used with permission.

[6] This figure seems to have been a powerful opponent of the Dead Sea community; most scholars identify him with Jonathan Maccabeus, who became the Jewish high priest at Jerusalem in 152 B.C.E.

[7] This individual apparently helped found and lead the Dead Sea community that produced most of the Scrolls.

[8] A characteristic reference in the Dead Sea Scrolls to the imperial Romans is the term "Kittim."

words of his servants, the prophets. *Hab 2:3a* For the vision has an appointed *6* time, it will have an end and not fail. *blank 7* Its interpretation: the final age will be extended and go beyond all that *8* the prophets say, because the mysteries of God are wonderful. *9 Hab 2:3b* Though it might delay, wait for it; it definitely has to come and will not *10* delay. *blank* Its interpretation concerns the men of truth, *11* those who observe the Law, whose hands will not desert the service *12* of truth when the final age is extended beyond them, because *13* all the ages of God will come at the right time, as he established *14* for them in the mysteries of his prudence. *Hab 2:4* See, *15* [his soul within him] is conceited and does not give way. *blank* Its interpretation: they will double *16* [persecution] upon them [and find no mercy] at being judged. *blank*

Column VIII

1 Its interpretation concerns all observing the Law in the House of Judah, whom *2* God will free from punishment on account of their deeds and of their loyalty *3* to the Teacher of Righteousness. *Hab 2:5–6* Surely wealth will corrupt the boaster *4* and one who distends his jaws like the abyss and is as greedy as death will not be restrained. *5* All the nations ally against him, all the peoples collaborate against him. *6* Are they not all, perhaps, going to chant verses against him, explaining riddles at his expense? *7* They shall say: Ah, one who masses the wealth of others! How long will he load himself *8* with debts? *blank* Its interpretation concerns the Wicked Priest, who *9* is called by the name of loyalty at the start of his office. However, when he ruled *10* over Israel his heart became conceited, he deserted God and betrayed the laws for the sake of *11* riches. And he stole and hoarded wealth from the brutal men who had rebelled against God. *12* And he seized public money, incurring additional serious sin. *13* And he performed repulsive acts of every type of filthy licentiousness. *Hab 2:7–8* Will *14* your creditors not suddenly get up, and those who shake you wake up? you will be their prey. *15* Since you pillaged many countries the rest of the peoples will pillage you. *16 blank* The interpretation of the word concerns the Priest who rebelled *17* [. . .] the precepts of [God . . .]

Column IX

1 being distressed by the punishments of sin; the horrors of *2* terrifying maladies acted upon him, as well as vengeful acts on his fleshly body. And what *3* it says: *Hab 2:8a* "Since you pillaged many countries the *4* rest of the peoples will pillage you." *blank* Its interpretation concerns the last priests of Jerusalem, *5* who will accumulate riches and loot from plundering the peoples. *6* However, in the last days their riches and their loot will fall into the hands *7* of the army of the Kittim. *blank* For they are *Hab 2:8a* "the greatest of the peoples." *8 Hab 2:8b* For the human blood [spilt] and the violence done to the country, the city and all its /occupants/. *blank 9* Its interpretation concerns the Wicked Priest, since for the wickedness against the Teacher of *10* Righteousness and the members of his council God delivered him into the hands of his enemies to disgrace him *11* with a punishment, to destroy him with bitterness of soul for having acted wickedly *12* against his elect. *Hab 2:9–11* Woe to anyone putting ill-gotten gains in his house, placing *13* his nest high up escape the power of evil! You have planned the insult *14* to your house, exterminating many countries and sinning against your soul. For *15* the stones will shout from the walls, and the wooden beams will answer. *16* [The interpretation of the quo]te concerns the [priest] who [. . .]

Column XI

1 deceit. Afterwards, knowledge will be revealed to them, as plentiful as the water *2* in the sea. *Hab 2:15* Woe to anyone making his companion drunk, spilling out *3* his anger! He even makes him drunk to look at their festivals! *4 blank* Its interpretation concerns the Wicked Priest who *5* pursued the Teacher of Righteousness to consume him with the ferocity *6* of his anger in the place of his banishment, in festival time, during the rest *7* of the day of Atonement. He paraded in from of them, to consume them *8* and make them fall on the day of fasting, the sabbath of their rest. *Hab 2:16* You are more glutted *9* with insults than with awards. Drink up also and stagger! *10* The cup of YHWH's right hand will turn against you and disgrace come *11* upon your glory. *blank 12* Its interpretation concerns the Priest whose shame has exceeded his glory *13* because he did not circumcise the foreskin of his heart and has walked on paths of *14* drunkenness to slake his thirst; but the cup of *15* God's anger will engulf him, heaping up [shame upon him.] And the pain

Column XII

1 Hab 2:17 will appal you owing to the human blood and the violence (against) the country, the city, and all its occupants. *2* The interpretation of the word concerns the Wicked Priest, to pay him the *3* reward for what he did to the poor. Because Lebanon is *4* the Council of the Community and the Animals are the simple folk of Judah, those who observe *5* the Law. God will sentence him to destruction, *blank 6* exactly as he intended to destroy the poor. And as for what he says: *Hab 2:17* "Owing to the blood *7* of the city and the violence (against) the country." Its interpretation: the city is Jerusalem *8* since in it the /Wicked/ Priest performed repulsive acts and defiled *9* the Sanctuary of God. The violence against the country are the cities of Judah which *10* he plundered of the possessions of the poor. *Hab 2:18* What use is the sculpture which the craftsman carves, *11* (or) the cast effigy and sham oracle, in whom their craftsman trusts, *12* to make dumb idols? The interpretation of the word concerns all the *13* idols of the nations which they made, to serve them and bow down *14* in front of them. But they will not save them in the day of Judgment. *Hab 2:19* Woe *15* to anyone [saying to wo]od: Wake up! and to silent stone: [Get up!]

4QFlorilegium (4Q174)
(Fragments 1–3)

Column I
[see Deut 23:3]

2 Sam 7:10 1 ["And] an enemy [will trouble him no mo]re, [nor will] the son of iniquity [afflict him again] as at the beginning. From the day on which *2* [I established judges] over my people, Israel." This (refers to) the house which [they will establish] for [him] in the last days, as is written in the book of *3* [Moses: *Exod 15:17–18* "A temple of the Lord] will you establish with your hands. YHWH shall reign for ever and ever." This (refers to) the house into which shall never enter *4* [. . .] either the Ammonite, or the Moabite, or the bastard, or the foreigner, or the proselyte, never, because there [he will reveal] to the holy ones;[9] *5* eternal [glory] will appear over it for ever; foreigners shall not again lay it waste as they laid waste, at the beginning, *6* the tem[ple of Is]rael for its sins. And he commanded to build for himself a temple of man, to offer him in it, *7* before him, the works of thanksgiving. And as for what he said to David: *2 Sam 7:11* "I shall obtain for you rest from all your enemies," (it refers to this:) that he will obtain for them rest from all *8* the sons of Belial, those who make them fall, to destr[oy them for their s]ins, when they come with the plans of Belial to make the s[ons of] *9* light fall, and to plot against them wicked plans so that they are trapped by Belial in their guilty error. *blank 10* And *2 Sam 7:12–14* "YHWH de[clares] to you that he will build you a house. I will raise up your seed after you and establish the throne of his kingdom *11* [for ev]er. I will be a father to him and he will be a son to me." This (refers to the) "branch of David" who will arise with the Interpreter of the law who *12* [will rise up] in Zi[on in] the last days, as it is written: *Amos 9:11* "I will raise up the hut of David which has fallen." This (refers to) "the hut of *13* David which has fallen," who will arise to save Israel. *blank 14* Midrash of "Blessed the man who does not walk in the counsel of the wicked."[10] The interpretation of this sa[ying: they are those who turn] aside from the path [of the wicked], *15* as it is written in the book of Isaiah, the prophet, for the last days: *Isa 8:11* "And it happened that with a strong [hand he turned me aside from walking on the path of] *16* this people." And this (refers to) those about whom it is written in the book of Ezekiel, the prophet, that *Ez 44:10* "[they should] not [defile themselves any more with all] *17* their filth." This refers to the sons of Zadok and to the men of his council, those who seek jus[tice] eagerly, who will come after them to the council of the community. *18 Ps 2:1–2* ["Why do] the nations [become agitated] and the peoples plo[t] nonsense? [The kings of the earth [ag]ree [and the ru]lers conspire together against YHWH and against *19* [his anointed one."[11] Inter]pretation of the saying: [the kings of the na]tions [become agitated and conspire against] the elect of Israel in the last days.

---

[9] The language of Deut 23:3 is clearly here.
[10] Cf. Ps 1:1.
[11] Cf. Ps 2:2.

4QGenesis Pesher^a (4Q252)

This Qumran document is noteworthy as one of the earliest examples of plain-sense commentary on Scripture. In most of the excerpts that follow, the ancient commentator seeks to provide clarification of the biblical text without a tendentious application of the text to the contemporary concerns of the Qumran sect.

Here the commentator seeks to make clear what the Genesis text (Gen 6:3) leaves ambiguous, that is, the meaning of the one hundred twenty-year span of human life.

> Column I
> 1 [In the y]ear four hundred and eighty of Noah's life, Noah reached the end of them. And God 2 [sa]id: "My spirit will not reside in man for ever. Their days shall be fixed at one hundred and twenty years 3 [y]ears until the end of the waters of the flood." . . .

Since the biblical text of the flood narrative presents potentially conflicting chronological references, in these lines the commentator emphasizes that the time spent by Noah and his family in the ark was exactly the span of a solar year (Gen 8:13–19).

> Column II
> 1 On the seventeenth day of the second month 2 the land dried up, on the first (day) of the week. On that day, Noah went out of the ark, at the end of a complete 3 year of three hundred and sixty-four days, on the first (day) of the week. On the seventh 4 *blank* one and six *blank* Noah (went out?) from the ark, at the appointed time of a complete 5 year.

In the biblical narrative (Gen 9:24–25, 27), Noah's son Ham is the one who has committed a violation, but it is Ham's son whom Noah curses. Here the commentator explains why, referring the reader to Gen 9:1.

> *blank* And Noah awoke from his wine and knew what 6 his youngest son had done. And he said: "Cursed be Canaan; he will be, for his br[others], the last of the slaves!" [But he did not] 7 curse Ham, but only his son, for God had blessed the sons of Noah. And they dwelt in the tents of Shem. . . .

> Column IV

With the mention of the name Amaleq in a Genesis genealogical list (Gen 36:12), the Qumran commentator adds the observation that the Amalekite people suffered destruction generations later at the hands of the Israelite king Saul (see Exod 17:14).

> 1 Timnah was the concubine of Eliphaz, Esau's son, and she bore him Amaleq. It was he whom Saul sl[ew], 2 *blank* as he said *blank* through Moses in respect of the last days: Dt 25:19 "I will erase the memory of Amaleq 3 from under the heavens." *blank*

When pronouncing his deathbed blessing upon his eldest son, Reuben, Jacob makes an ob-scure reference to a violation by Reuben that will ultimately compromise the stature of his lineage. The commentator refers the reader back to Gen 35:22 for clarification on Reuben's transgression.

Blessings of Jacob: *Gen 49:3–4* "Reuben, you are my first-born 4 and the first-fruits of my manhood, pre-eminent in stature and pre-eminent in strength; you seethe like water; you shall not enjoy supremacy. You mounted 5 your father's bed; then you defiled it, for he had lain in it." *blank* Its interpretation: That he reproved him, because 6 he lay with Bilhah, his concubine. And as for what he said: "You are my first-born" [. . .] Reuben 7 was the first of his order [. . .]

CHAPTER 3

Philosophical Allegory: Philo of Alexandria (20 B.C.E.–50 C.E.)

The writings of Philo Judaeus reflect the meeting of two important cultural traditions in the Mediterranean world at the beginning of the first millennium C.E. Philo's education as a member of a wealthy Jewish family of cosmopolitan Alexandria in Egypt endowed him with substantial knowledge of Greco-Roman culture as well as a deep respect for Jewish Scriptures. Almost all of his writings—about forty works extant—are concerned in some way with the Torah of Moses, providing exposition of passages, exegetical commentary, or application of Torah to contemporary philosophical and historical issues.

Philo believed that the Jewish Scriptures, as divine communication, revealed divine wisdom. They were written by men such as Moses in a state of inspiration that gave them profound insight into the true nature of the soul, the world, and the divine. But although Moses himself possessed completely accurate knowledge of the divine, the inadequacy of human language for communicating eternal, universal truth required him to adjust language away from its ordinary usage. Philo considered Moses to have utilized standard available words to express what could not be directly articulated in human language. The result is truth written in allegory: "We say that nearly all, or that at all events, the greater part of the history of the giving of the law is full of allegories" (*On the Life of Joseph* 28). For Philo, the allegorical meaning of the Torah exists underneath, or side by side with, the literal meaning. Typically, the allegorical meaning of a scriptural word or passage in Philo's interpretation concerns the essence of God or the development of the human soul in virtue. Allegorical interpretation, then, brings the reader into immediate apprehension of the divine truth Moses seeks to communicate. It also steers the reader away from gross, literal interpretations that would imply anything unworthy of God's perfection, such as contradictions, anthropomorphisms, and mythologies. Ultimately, however, allegory is necessary because of the unspeakable difference between the Creator and creatures. In Philo's intellectual world, the divine word is a *logos* in the rich Hellenistic philosophical sense of the term: the rationality of the order of all things.

When Greek-speaking Jews throughout the ancient Mediterranean world of the first century read Scripture, they typically read in Greek translation. The translation of the Torah of Moses into Greek was for Philo a major event in God's revelation, as now the Greek-speaking world could come to know the revealed truth of the world's Creator and live in harmony with divine law, which corresponded to cosmic law (*On the Life of Moses* 2.43–44). Philo was therefore an assiduous student of the Septuagint, placing the highest confidence in its capacity to carry over into Greek the divine mysteries Moses had inscribed in Hebrew. The *Letter of Aristeas* had stated that when the seventy-two commissioned Jewish scholars produced their independent Greek translations of the Torah, they reached harmony in their work by mutual comparisons. But Philo goes further, claiming divine intervention that guaranteed accuracy:

> They [the translators], like men inspired, prophesied, not one saying one thing and another, but every one of them employed the self-same nouns and verbs, as if some unseen prompter had suggested all their language to them. . . . These translators [were] not mere interpreters but hierophants and prophets to whom it had been granted their honest and guileless minds to go along with the most pure spirit of Moses. (*On the Life of Moses* 2.37, 40)[1]

As an allegorical interpreter of the Torah, Philo alludes to a similar divine inspiration that allows insight into the deeper meaning of scriptural texts. So, for Philo, the ability to allegorize into the philosophical meaning of Scripture is gained through sensitivity to the same divine Spirit that revealed the truth to the inspired writer in the first place. Referring to himself, he writes,

> Sometimes when I have come to my work empty I have suddenly become full, ideas being, in an invisible manner, showered upon me, and implanted in me from on high; so that, through the influence of divine inspiration, I have become greatly excited, and have known neither the place in which I was nor those who were present, nor myself, nor what I was saying, nor what I was writing; for then I have been conscious of a richness of interpretation, an enjoyment of light, a most penetrating sight, a most manifest energy in all that was to be done, having such an effect on my mind as the clearest ocular demonstration would have on the eyes. (*On the Migration of Abraham* 35)[2]

The extant exegetical writings of Philo include running allegorical commentaries on the first half of the book of Genesis, paraphrastic reflection on the meaning of the laws of Moses, and responses to questions about the passages from Genesis and Exodus in canonical sequence. It is not clear whether Philo produced his writings out of his participation in schools or synagogues or in some other specific social setting. In any event, the influence of his approach to biblical interpretation was profound, if not on the development of rabbinic Judaism, then certainly (and indirectly) on Christian theology. For, by reading Scripture with an eye for the divine rationality that can enlighten Jew and Gentile alike, Philo's allegorical method and interpretations helped "scripturize" Hellenistic philosophical concepts that would eventually become key to Christian theology. A prominent example was represented in the *logos:* the divine pattern of creation, the mind of God that models human reason, the mediator between Creator and creature, the sustenance for the soul—a rich theologoumenon that Christian writers would go on to explore extensively. Although not deserving the label "father of Christian theology," Philo showed a way of rendering biblical narratives into theological principles that many Christian theologians would find fruitful in the intellectual milieu of late antiquity.

---

[1] *The Works of Philo* (trans. C. D. Yonge; new updated ed.; Peabody, Mass.: Hendrickson, 1993).

[2] Ibid.

For further information on Philo:

Borgen, Peder. "Philo of Alexandria." Pages 333–42 in vol. 5 of *Anchor Bible Dictionary.* Edited by David Noel Freedman. 6 vols. New York: Doubleday, 1992.
———. *Philo of Alexandria: An Exegete for His Time.* Leiden: Brill, 1997.
Dawson, David. *Allegorical Readers and Cultural Revision in Ancient Alexandria.* Berkeley: University of California Press, 1992.

Selections from Philo[3]

In his work known as Allegorical Interpretation, *Philo argues for the advantage of dealing with difficulties in the text through the discernment of figurative meanings. Here he seeks to clarify the Greek expression* βρώσει φάγη, *"eat freely," as it appears in the Septuagint translation of Gen 2:16.*

XXXI. (97) And the recommendations that he [God] addresses to him [Adam] are as follows: "Of every tree that is in the Paradise thou mayest freely eat" (Gen 3:23). He exhorts the soul of man to derive advantage not from one tree alone nor from one single virtue, but from all the virtues; for eating is a symbol of the nourishment of the soul, and the soul is nourished by the reception of good things, and by the doing of praiseworthy actions.

(98) And Moses not only says, "thou mayest eat," but he adds "freely," also; that is to say, having ground and prepared your food, not like an ordinary individual, but like a wrestler, you shall thus acquire strength and vigour. For the trainers recommend the wrestlers not to cut up their food by biting large pieces off, but to masticate it slowly, in order that it may contribute to their strength; for I and an athlete are fed in different manners. For I feed merely for the purpose of living, but the wrestler feeds for the purpose of acquiring flesh and deriving strength from it; on which account one of his rules of training and exercise is to masticate his food. This is the meaning of the expression, "Thou mayest freely eat."

Elsewhere in Allegorical Interpretation, *Philo seeks to account for an apparent contradiction in Gen 2:17 by demonstrating that the literal meaning of the text cannot be reasonably accepted.*

XXXIII. (105) Accordingly God says, "In the day in which ye eat of it ye shall die the death." And yet, though they have eaten of it, they not only do not die, but they even beget children, and are the causes of life to other beings besides themselves. What, then, are we to say? Surely that death is of two kinds; the one being the death of the man, the other the peculiar death of the soul—now the death of the man is the separation of his soul from his body, but the death of the soul is the destruction of virtue and the admission of vice; (106) and consequently God calls that not merely "to die," but to "die the death;" showing that he is speaking not of common death, but of that peculiar and especial death which is the death of the soul, buried in its passions and in all kinds of evil.[4] And we may almost say that one kind of death is opposed to the other kind. For the one is separation of what was previously existing

---

[3] The following selections are taken from *The Works of Philo* (trans. C. D. Yonge; new updated ed.; Peabody, Mass.: Hendrickson, 1993). Used with permission.

[4] The Hebrew in Gen 2:17 features a grammatical construction designed to bring emphasis and finality to a judicial pronouncement: "you shall certainly die." But because the Hebrew expression is constructed by repeating the verb, it is sometimes awkwardly rendered in translation.

in combination, namely, of body and soul. But this other death, on the contrary, is a combination of them both, the inferior one, the body, having the predominance, and the superior one, the soul, being made subject to it. (107) When, therefore, God says, "to die the death," you must remark that he is speaking of that death which is inflicted as punishment, and not of that which exists by the original ordinance of nature. The natural death is that one by which the soul is separated from the body. But the one which is inflicted as a punishment, is when the soul dies according to the life of virtue, and lives only according to the life of vice.

(108) Well, therefore, did Heraclitus say this, following the doctrine of Moses; for he says, "We are living according to the death of those men; and we have died according to their life."[5] As if he had said, Now, when we are alive, we are so though our soul is dead and buried in our body, as if in a tomb. But if it were to die, then our soul would live according to its proper life, being released from the evil and dead body to which it is bound.

In his Questions and Answers on Genesis, *Philo offers brief responses to questions prompted by details in the text that pose logical or theological difficulties. The following selections from* Questions and Answers on Genesis 1.93–95 *relate to the story of the flood in Gen 6.*

(93) What is the meaning of the expression: "God considered anxiously, because he had made man upon the earth; and he resolved the matter in his mind"? (Gen 6:6).

Some persons imagine that it is intimated by these words that the Deity repented; but they are very wrong to entertain such an idea, since the Deity is unchangeable. Nor are the facts of his caring and thinking about the matter, and of his agitating it in his mind, any proofs that he is repenting, but only indications of a kind and determinate counsel, according to which the displays care, revolving in his mind the cause why he had made man upon the earth.

But since this earth is a place of misery, even that heavenly being, man, who is a mixture compounded of soul and body, from the very hour of his birth to that of his death, is nothing else but the slave of the body. That the Deity therefore should meditate and deliberate on these matters is nothing surprising; since most men take to themselves wickedness rather than virtue, being influenced by the twofold impulse mentioned above; namely, that of a body by its nature corruptible, and placed in the terrible situation of earth, which is the lowest of all places.

(94) Why God, after having threatened to destroy mankind, says that he will also destroy all the beasts likewise; using the expression, "from man to beast, and

---

[5] This quote from Heraclitus is today known as fragment 62. For the text and translation options, see Heraclitus, *Fragments: A Text and Translation with a Commentary* (ed. and trans. T. M. Robinson; Toronto: University of Toronto Press, 1987), 42–43.

from creeping things to flying creatures;" for how could irrational animals have committed sin? (Gen 6:7).

This is the literal statement of the holy scripture, and it informs us that animals were not necessarily and in their primary cause created for their own sake, but for the sake of mankind and to act as the servants of men; and when the men were destroyed, it followed necessarily and naturally that they also should be destroyed with them, as soon as the men, for whose sake they had been made, had ceased to exist.

But as to the hidden meaning conveyed by the statement, since man is a symbol for the intellect which exists in us, and animals for the outward sense, when the chief creature has first been depraved and corrupted by wickedness, all the outward sense also perishes with him, because he had no relics whatever of virtue, which is the cause of salvation.

(95) Why God says, "I am indignant[6] that I made them" (Gen 6:7)? In the first place, Moses is here again relating what took place, as if he were speaking of some illustrious action of man, but, properly speaking, God does not feel anger, but is exempt from, and superior to, all such perturbations of spirit. Therefore Moses wishes here to point out, by an extravagant form of expression, that the iniquities of man had grown to such a height, that they stirred up and provoked to anger even that very Being who by his nature was incapable of anger.

In the second place he warns us, by a figure, that foolish actions are liable to punishment, but that those which proceed from wise and deliberate counsel are praiseworthy.

The well-known biblical passage that posits human existence as directly dependent upon the divine word (Greek logos) *offers Philo an occasion to elaborate on the mediatorial possibilities of the word that comes from God* (Allegorical Interpretation 3.174–178).

LXI. (174) He says also in Deuteronomy, "And he has humbled thee, and suffered thee to hunger, and fed thee with manna, which thou knowest not, neither did thy fathers know, that he might make thee know that man shall not live by bread alone, but by every word which proceedeth out of the mouth of the Lord doth man live" (Deut 8:3). Now this ill-treating and humbling of them is a sign of his being propitiated by them, for he is propitiated as to the souls of us who are wicked on the tenth day. For when he strips us of all our pleasant things, we appear to ourselves to be ill-treated, that is in truth to have God propitious to us.

(175) And God also causes us hunger, not that which proceeds from virtue, but that which is engendered by passion and vice. And the proof of this is, that he nourishes us with his own word, which is the most universal of all things, for manna being

---

[6] Although the Hebrew text of this verse is usually translated, "I regret that I have made them," the Septuagint renders a verb indicating anger rather than sorrow.

interpreted, means "what?" and "what" is the most universal of all things; for the word of God is over all the world, and is the most ancient, and the most universal of all the things that are created. This word our fathers knew not; I speak not of those who are so in truth, but of those who are grey with age, who say, "Let us give them a guide, and let us turn back" (Num 14:1) unto passion, that is to say, to Egypt. (176) Therefore, let God enjoin the soul, saying to it that, "Man shall not live by bread alone," speaking in a figure, "but by every word that proceedeth out of the mouth of God," that is to say, he shall be nourished by the whole word of God, and by every portion of it. For the mouth is the symbol of the language, and a word is a portion of it. Accordingly the soul of the more perfect man is nourished by the whole word; but we must be contented if we are nourished by a portion of it.

LXII. (177) But these men pray to be nourished by the word of God: but Jacob, raising his head above the word, says that he is nourished by God himself, and his words are as follows; "The God in whom my father Abraham and Isaac were well-pleased; the God who has nourished me from my youth upwards to this day; the angel who has delivered me from all my evils, bless these children" (Gen 48:15). This now being a symbol of a perfect disposition, thinks God himself his nourisher, and not the word: and he speaks of the angel, which is the word, as the physician of his evils, in this speaking most naturally. For the good things which he has previously mentioned are pleasing to him inasmuch as the living and true God has given them to him face to face, but the secondary good things have been given to him by the angels and by the word of God. (178) On this account I think it is that God gives men pure good health, which is not preceded by any disease in the body, by himself alone, but that health which is an escape from disease he gives through the medium of skill and medical science, attributing it to science, and to him who can apply it skillfully, though in truth, it is God himself who heals both by these means, and without these means. And the same is the case with regard to the soul, the good things, namely food, he gives to men by his power alone; but those which contain in them a deliverance from evil, he gives by means of his angels and his word.

God's revelation to Abram in Gen 15 includes textual details that could confuse those who read the text literally. An ancient Semitic idiom refers to a proper death as "departing unto one's ancestors," and in verse 15 God applies this idiom to Abram. God also refers to Abram's life, seen in its totality, as a "peaceful" one. In this excerpt from Who Is the Heir of Divine Things? *Philo points out the absurdity of taking such references literally, offering more figurative interpretations as a better way.*

LVI. (275) Having said this much on these subjects [of God's revelation to Abram that his descendants will be enslaved and oppressed in an alien land for four hundred years], the historian proceeds: "And thou shalt depart to thy fathers, having lived in peace, in a good old age" (Gen 15:15). Therefore we, who are imperfect, are made war upon, and we become slaves, and only with difficulty do we find any relief from the dangers which impend over us. But the perfect race, exempt from slavery and free from the perils of war, is bred up in peace and the firmest freedom. (276) And there is a particular lesson to be learnt from his representing the good man not as dying but departing, in order to show that the race of the soul, which is completely purified, cannot be extinguished and cannot die, but only departs in the way of migration from this earth to heaven, not undergoing that dissolution and destruction which death appears to bring with it. (277) And after the words, "Thou shalt depart," he adds, "to thy fathers." It is here worth while to consider what kind of fathers is meant; for God can never mean those who have passed their lives in the country of the Chaldeans, among whom alone he had lived as being his relations, because he had been commanded by a sacred oracle to depart from those who were his kinsmen by blood.

For, says the historian [Moses], "The Lord said unto Abraham, Depart from out of thy land, and from thy kindred, and from thy father's house, to a land which I will show thee; and I will make thee into a great nation" (Gen 12:1). (278) For how can it be reasonable for him who was once been removed from his abode by the interference of Divine Providence, to return and dwell again in the same place? And how could it be reasonable for one who was about to be the leader of a new nation and or another race to be again assigned to his ancient one? For God would never have given to him a new character, and a new nation and family, if he had not wholly and entirely separated himself from his ancient one. (279) For that man is truly a chief of a nation and ruler of a family, from whom, as from a root, sprang that branch so fond of investigating and contemplating the affairs of our nature, by name Israel, since an express command has been given "to remove the old things from before the face of those which are new" (Lev 26:10). For where is any longer the use of investigations into antiquity, and ancient, and long-established customs, to those in whom on a sudden, when they have no such expectation, God rains all kinds of new blessings in a mass?

LVII. (280) Therefore, when he says "fathers," he means not those whose souls have departed from them, and who are buried in the tombs of the land of Chaldea; but, as some say, the sun, and the moon, and the other stars; for some affirm that it is owing to these bodies that the nature of all the things in the world has its existence. But as some other persons think he means the archetypal ideas, those models of these thing which are perceptible by the outward senses and visible; which models, however, are only perceptible by the intellect and invisible; and that it is to these that the mind of the wise man emigrates. (281) Some, again, have fancied that by "fathers," are here meant the four principles and powers of which the world is composed—the earth, the water, the air, and the fire; for they say, that all created things are very properly dissolved into these elements. (282) For as nouns, and verbs, and all the other parts of speech, consist of the elements of grammar, and again are resolvable into these ultimate principles, so, in the same manner, each individual among us, being compounded of the four elements, and borrowing small portions from each essence, does, at certain fixed periods, repay what he has borrowed, giving what he has dry to the earth, what moisture he has to the water, what heat he has to the fire, and what cold he has to the air.

(283) These then are the things of the body; but the intellectual and heavenly race of the soul will ascend to the purest ether as to its father. For the fifth essence, as the account of the ancients tells us, may be a certain one, which brings things round

in a cycle, differing from the other four as being superior to them, from which the stars and the whole heavens appear to be generated, and of which, as a natural consequence, one must lay it down that the human soul is a fragment.

LVIII. (284) And the expression, "After having lived in peace," is used with much propriety; because nearly all or the greater portion of the human race lives rather in war and among all the evils of war. And of wars, one kind proceeds from external enemies, and is brought on by want of reputation, and by lowness of origin, and by other things of that kind. But another kind arises from one's domestic enemies; some about the body, such as weaknesses, stains, all kinds of mutilations, and a whole body of other unspeakable evils; and others affecting the soul, such as passions, diseases, infirmities, terrible and most grievous inflictions, and incurable calamities arising from folly and injustice, and other similar evils.

(285) Therefore he speaks of him who has lived in peace, who has enjoyed a serene and tranquil life, as a man truly happy and blessed. When then shall this happen? When all external things prosper with me, in such a way as to tend to my abundance and to my glory. When the things relating to the body are in a favorable state, so as to give me good health and strength; and when the things relating to my soul are in a similar state, so as to enable it to enjoy the virtues. (286) For each of these requires its own appropriate bodyguards. Now the body is attended in that capacity by glory, and abundance, and a sufficient provision of wealth; and the soul by wholeness, and soundness, and thoroughly healthy state of the body; and the mind by those speculations which are concerned about the sciences.

Since it is plain to all those who are versed in the holy scriptures, that when peace is here mentioned, it is not that peace which cities enjoy. For Abraham bore a part in many terrible wars, out of which he appears to have come triumphantly. (287) And indeed the being forced to depart from his native country, and to leave his home, and his inability to dwell in his native city, and his being driven hither and thither, and wandering about by desolate and unfrequented roads, would have been a terrible war for one who had not put his trust in certain divine oracles and promises.

There would also be a third calamity, of a formidable nature, also to be borne by him, a famine, worse than the departure from his home, or than all the evils of war. (288) What peace then did he enjoy? For I imagine to be driven from his former home, and to have no settled abode, and to be unable to make an effectual resistance to very powerful monarchs, and to be oppressed with hunger, seem like indications, not of one war, but of many wars of various kinds. (289) But, according to those interpretations which are figurative, every one of these events is an instance and proof of unalloyed peace. For an absence of the passions, and a complete scarcity of them, and the destruction of inimical acts of iniquity, and a departure from the opinions of the Chaldeans to the doctrine which loves God, that is to say, from the created being, perceptible by the outward senses, to the great Cause and Creator of all things, who is appreciable only by the intellect, are things which supply a good system of laws and stability.

(290) And God promises the man who enjoys such a peace as this a glorious old age, not indeed one which shall last an exceeding time, but he promises him a life with wisdom. For tranquility and happiness are better than length of years, in proportion as a short period of light is better than everlasting darkness. For well did one of the prophets say: "He had rather live one day in the company of virtue, than ten thousand years in the shadow of death" (Ps 84:10), under this figurative expression of shadow, intimating the life of the wicked. (291) And Moses says the very same thing, intimating it by his actions rather than by his words. For the man who he says shall enjoy a glorious old age, he has at the same time represented as more short-lived than almost any one of those who preceded him. Speaking in a philosophical manner, and teaching us who it is who does truly enjoy a happy old age, that we may not conceive pride respecting old age from anything that affects the visible body; as such pride is full of shame and many disgraceful circumstances. But, that keeping our eyes fixed on wisdom of counsel, and steadiness of soul, we may ascribe to such men and testify in their favor that they have a glorious old age (Gk *gēras*), akin to, and bearing nearly the same name as honor (Gk *geras*). (292) Listen, therefore, in such a spirit as to think his words a good lesson, to this statement of the lawgiver [Moses], that the good man alone has a happy old age, and that he is the most long-lived of men; but that the wicked man is the most short-lived of men, living only to die, or rather having already died as to the life of virtue.

In his work On the Migration of Abraham, *Philo comments at length on Gen 12:1–3. A key theological focus for Philo in this text is the manifold blessing that God commits to bestow upon Abram, a subject that Philo submits to extensive allegorical interpretation. But Philo does not allegorize to the point of rejecting altogether a literal reading of scriptural texts; indeed, in the following excerpt Philo warns against such allegorical excesses.*

XVI. (89) For there are some men, who, looking upon written laws as symbols of things appreciable by the intellect, have studied some things with superfluous accuracy, and have treated others with neglectful indifference; whom I should blame for their levity; for they ought to attend to both classes of things, applying themselves both to an accurate investigation of invisible things, and also to an irreproachable observance of those laws which are notorious. (90) But now men living solitarily by themselves as if they were in a desert, or else as if they were mere souls unconnected with the body, and as if they had no knowledge of any city, or village, or house, or in short of any company of men whatever, overlook what appears to the many to be true, and seek for plain naked truth by itself, whom the sacred scripture teaches not to neglect a good reputation, and not to break through any established customs which divine men of greater wisdom than any in our time have enacted or established. (91) For although the seventh day is a lesson to teach us the power which exists in the uncreated God, and also that the creature is entitled to rest from his labors, it does not follow that on that account we may abrogate the laws which are established respecting it, so as to light a fire, or till land, or carry burdens, or bring accusations, or conduct suits at law, or demand a restoration of a deposit, or exact the repayment of a debt, or do any other of the things which are usually permitted at times which are not days of festival. (92) Nor does it follow, because the feast is the symbol of the joy of the soul and of its gratitude towards God, that we are to repudiate the assemblies ordained at the periodical seasons of the year; nor because the rite of circumcision is an emblem of the excision of pleasures and of all the passions, and of the destruction of that impious opinion, according to which the mind has imagined itself to be by itself competent to produce offspring, does it follow that we are to annul the law which has been enacted about circumcision. Since we shall neglect the laws about the due observance of the ceremonies in the temple, and numbers of others too, if we exclude all figurative interpretation and attend only to those things which are expressly ordained in plain words.

(93) But it is right to think that this class of things resembles the body, and the other class the soul; therefore, just as we take care of the body because it is the abode of the soul, so also must we take care of the laws that are enacted in plain terms; for while they are regarded, those other things also will be more clearly understood, of which these laws are the symbols, and in the same way one will escape blame and accusation from men in general. (94) Do you not see that Abraham also says, that both small and great blessings fell to the share of the wise man, and he calls the great things, "all that he had," and his possessions, which it is allowed to the legitimate son alone to receive as his inheritance; but the small things he calls gifts, of which the illegitimate children and those born of concubines, are also accounted worthy [see Gen 25:5–6]. The one, therefore, resembles those laws which are natural, and the other those which derive their origin from human enactment.

Part Two

---◇◇◇---

Patristic Interpretation and Its Legacy
(150–1500 C.E.)

CHAPTER 4

Christian Fulfillment of Prophecy: Justin Martyr (100–165 C.E.)

After a wide-ranging philosophical education, Justin, who had been born to pagan parents in Roman Syria, converted to Christianity. He had become impressed by the constancy in truth that he perceived in this new religion and also by its moral distinctions, particularly as manifest in the courage of its martyrs. He lived his adult life in a variety of places, eventually founding a school in Rome, where he taught and where he himself was eventually martyred. Justin's extant writings—the *First Apology,* the *Second Apology,* and the *Dialogue with Trypho,* all produced in his role as a Christian apologist—are designed to argue for the truth of Christian claims, to the Roman leadership in the case of the *First* and the *Second Apology* and to the Jews in the case of the *Dialogue.* His work in biblical interpretation reflects a concern to define the distinctions of Christian beliefs relative to existing philosophies and religious traditions of the Greco-Roman world.

The *First Apology* was probably written about 150 C.E.; there Justin aims to draw attention to the moral excellence of Christians and to the great antiquity of their philosophy in the ancient word that was spoken prophetically about Christ. Justin's standard exegetical method is a prophetic one, bringing his reader to the ancient Jewish Scriptures and arguing that passage after passage was written as a prediction of Jesus Christ and the Christian movement. The reader will recognize this method from the writings of the New Testament, and indeed a number of the Old Testament passages understood christologically by Justin were already so interpreted earlier by Christian writers of the New Testament. In the interpretive tradition that Justin represents, Jesus was not simply the figure who fulfilled ancient Jewish prophecy. He was also the inaugural Scripture interpreter who, after his own resurrection, made clear to the disciples meanings from the ancient Scriptures that had hitherto remained hidden. So when Justin points out predictive allegories and analogies from Scripture, he understands himself to be handing down from the apostles the same exegesis they had in their turn learned from Jesus himself. Justin informs his reader to this effect in chapter 100 of the *Dialogue with Trypho:*

> Accordingly He [Christ] revealed to us all that we have perceived by His grace out of the Scriptures, so that we know Him to be the first-begotten of God, and to be before all creatures; likewise to be the Son of the patriarchs, since He assumed flesh by the Virgin of their family, and submitted to become a man without comeliness, dishonoured, and subject to suffering. Hence, also, among His words He said, when He was discoursing about His future sufferings: "The Son of man must suffer many things, and be rejected by the Pharisees and Scribes, and be crucified, and on the third day rise again" [Matt 16:21].

Justin often quotes the text of Jewish Scripture in a form adapted from the Septuagint to fit Christian polemics that he probably received from Christian theologians who had preceded him. The divine authority and accuracy of the Greek translation was important to Justin. Through detailed reference to the Aristeas legend, he commended to his readers a Greek version of the ancient writings that reliably preserves the prophetic meaning shown to be true by its fulfillment in Jesus and the church. The divine Logos had inspired writers such as Moses, David, and Isaiah to record oracles predictive of Jesus; this same Logos became a human called Jesus Christ (*First Apology* 5) and made clear the prophetic meanings of Scripture faithfully available in the Septuagint. Justin thus argues for the Christian faith on the basis of divinely guaranteed truth as found in the Greek Scriptures, which by the second century had become the Bible for Christian churches.

During the first two centuries C.E., Christian writers labored to further define Christianity vis-à-vis established religious traditions, in particular in distinction from Judaism. In their efforts Justin and other Christians of his time read Jewish Scriptures largely as proof texts attesting to the truth of their claims about Jesus as the divine Savior and about themselves as the true inheritors of divine promise and purpose. Rarely did Justin take the words of Scripture in their own historical context to mean what they said more plainly within that context. His characteristic technique is to cite a scriptural passage he takes as prophetic (without connection to the text's historical or literary context) and then to refer to an historical event that he claims to have fulfilled this prophecy. Non-Christian readers of the ancient Scriptures, naturally, did not tend to see in these writings what Christians saw, and in Justin's *Dialogue with Trypho* we find an indication of the sort of debate between Christian and Jewish readers that must have occurred in these early centuries of distinction and separation.

What follows are excerpts from the *First Apology* that amply showcase this early Christian prophetic approach in exegesis.

For further information on Justin Martyr:

Barnard, Leslie W. *Justin Martyr: His Life and Thought.* London: Cambridge University Press, 1967.

Shotwell, Willis A. *The Biblical Exegesis of Justin Martyr.* London: SPCK, 1965.

Skarsaune, Oskar. *Proof from Prophecy: A Study in Justin Martyr's Proof-Text Tradition: Text-Type, Provenance, Theological Profile.* Leiden: Brill, 1987.

The *First Apology of Justin*[1]

Chapter 31

Of the Hebrew Prophets

There were, then, among the Jews certain men who were prophets of God, through whom the prophetic Spirit published beforehand things that were to come to pass, ere ever they happened. And their prophecies, as they were spoken and when they were uttered, the kings who happened to be reigning among the Jews at the several times carefully preserved in their possession, when they had been arranged in books by the prophets themselves in their own Hebrew language. And when Ptolemy king of Egypt formed a library, and endeavoured to collect the writings of all men, he heard also of these prophets, and sent to Herod, who was at that time[2] king of the Jews, requesting that the books of the prophets be sent to him. And Herod the king did indeed send them, written, as they were, in the foresaid Hebrew language. And when their contents were found to be unintelligible to the Egyptians, he again sent and requested that men be commissioned to translate them into the Greek language. And when this was done, the books remained with the Egyptians, where they are until now. They are also in the possession of all Jews throughout the world; but they, though they read, do not understand what is said, but count us foes and enemies; and, like yourselves, they kill and punish us whenever they have the power, as you can well believe. For in the Jewish war[3] which lately raged, Barchochebas, the leader of the revolt of the Jews, gave orders that Christians alone should be led to cruel punishments, unless they would deny Jesus Christ and utter blasphemy. In these books, then, of the prophets we found Jesus our Christ foretold as coming, born of a virgin, growing up to man's estate, and healing every disease and every sickness, and raising the dead, and being hated, and unrecognized, and crucified, and dying, and rising again, and ascending into heaven, and being, and being called, the Son of God. We find it also predicted that certain persons should be sent by Him into every nation to publish these things, and that rather among the Gentiles [than among the Jews] men should believe on Him. And He was predicted before He appeared, first 5000 years before, and again 3000, then 2000, then 1000, and yet again 800; for in the succession of generations prophets after prophets arose.

---

[1] These excerpts are taken from Justin's *First Apology*, in *The Apostolic Fathers, Justin Martyr, and Irenaeus* (vol. 1 of *The Ante-Nicene Fathers*; ed. Alexander Roberts and James Donaldson; Grand Rapids: Eerdmans, 1977). Used with permission.

[2] Justin appears to be chronologically mistaken inasmuch as the Ptolemy who is said to have sponsored the Greek translation project preceded Herod by several generations. It is remotely possible, however, that Justin here reflects a tradition that understood Herod to be the name of Ptolemy's representative in Judea.

[3] Justin here refers to the second Jewish revolt (132–135 C.E.), led by Simeon bar Kokhba against imperial Roman rule in Jerusalem and Judea.

Chapter 32

Christ Predicted by Moses

Moses then, who was the first of the prophets, spoke in these very words: "The sceptre shall not depart from Judah, nor a lawgiver from between his feet, until He come for whom it is reserved; and He shall be the desire of the nations, binding His foal to the vine, washing His robe in the blood of the grape" (Gen 49:10 LXX). It is yours to make accurate inquiry, and ascertain up to whose time the Jews had a lawgiver and king of their own. Up to the time of Jesus Christ, who taught us, and interpreted the prophecies which were not yet understood, (they had a lawgiver) as was foretold by the holy and divine Spirit of prophecy through Moses, "that a ruler would not fail the Jews until He should come for whom the kingdom was reserved" (for Judah was the forefather of the Jews, from whom also they have their name of Jews); and after He (i.e., Christ) appeared, you began to rule the Jews, and gained possession of all their territory. And the prophecy, "He shall be the expectation of the nations," signified that there would be some of all nations who should look for Him to come again. And this indeed you can see for yourselves, and be convinced of by fact. For of all races of men there are some who look for Him who was crucified in Judaea, and after whose crucifixion the land was straightway surrendered to you as spoil of war. And the prophecy, "binding His foal to the vine, and washing His robe in the blood of the grape," was a significant symbol of the things that were to happen to Christ, and of what He was to do. For the foal of an ass stood bound to a vine at the entrance of a village, and He ordered His acquaintances to bring it to Him then; and when it was brought, He mounted and sat upon it, and entered Jerusalem [see Matt 21:1–11], where was the vast temple of the Jews which was afterwards destroyed by you. And after this He was crucified, that the rest of the prophecy might be fulfilled. For this "washing His robe in the blood of the grape" was predictive of the passion He was to endure, cleansing by His blood those who believe on Him. For what is called by the Divine Spirit through the prophet "His robe," are those men who believe in Him in whom abideth the seed of God, the Word. And what is spoken of as "the blood of the grape," signifies that He who should appear would have blood, though not of the seed of man, but of the power of God. And the first power after God the Father and Lord of all is the Word, who is also the Son; and of Him we will, in what follows, relate how He took flesh and became man. For as man did not make the blood of the vine, but God, so it was hereby intimated that the blood should not be of human seed, but of divine power, as we have said above. And Isaiah, another prophet, foretelling the same things in other words, spoke thus: "A star shall rise out of Jacob, and a flower shall spring from the root of Jesse; and His arm shall the nations trust" (Isa 11:1). And a star of light has arisen, and a flower has sprung from the root of Jesse—this Christ. For by the power of God He was conceived by a virgin of the seed of Jacob, who was the father of Judah, who, as we have shown, was the father of the Jews; and Jesse was His forefather according to the oracle, and He was the son of Jacob and Judah according to lineal descent.

Chapter 33

Manner of Christ's Birth Predicted

And hear again how Isaiah in express words foretold that He should be born of a virgin; for he spoke thus: "Behold, a virgin shall conceive, and bring forth a son, and they shall say for His name, 'God with us'" (Isa 7:14 LXX). For things which were incredible and seemed impossible with men, these God predicted by the Spirit of prophecy as about to come to pass, in order that, when they came to pass, there might be no unbelief, but faith, because of their prediction. But lest some, not understanding the prophecy now cited, should charge us with the very things we have been laying to the charge of the poets who say that Jupiter went in to women through lust, let us try to explain the words. This, then, "Behold, a virgin shall conceive," signifies that a virgin should conceive without intercourse. For if she had had intercourse with any one whatever, she was no longer a virgin; but the power of God having come upon the virgin, overshadowed her, and caused her while yet a virgin to conceive. And the angel of God who was sent to the same virgin at that time brought her good news, saying, "Behold, thou shalt conceive of the Holy Ghost, and shalt bear a Son, and He shall be called the Son of the Highest, and thou shalt call His name Jesus; for He shall save His people from their sins" (Matt 1:20–21; Luke 1:35)[4]—as they who have recorded all that concerns our Saviour Jesus Christ have taught, whom we believed, since by Isaiah also, whom we have now adduced, the Spirit of prophecy declared that He should be born as we intimated before. It is wrong, therefore, to understand the Spirit and the power of God as anything else than the Word, who is also the first-born of God, as the foresaid prophet Moses declared; and it was this which, when it came upon the virgin and overshadowed her, caused her to conceive, not by intercourse, but by power. And the name Jesus in the Hebrew language means Σωτήρ (Savior) in the Greek tongue. Wherefore, too, the angel said to the virgin, "Thou shalt call His name Jesus, for He shall save His people from their sins." And that the prophets are inspired by no other than the Divine Word, even you, as I fancy, will grant.

Chapter 34

Place of Christ's Birth Foretold

And hear what part of earth He was to be born in, as another prophet, Micah, foretold. He spoke thus: "And thou, Bethlehem, the land of Judah, art not the least among the princes of Judah; for out of thee shall come forth a Governor, who shall feed My people" (Mic 5:2). Now there is a village in the land of the Jews, thirty-five stadia from Jerusalem, in which Jesus Christ was born, as you can ascertain also from the registers of the taxing made under Cyrenius, your first procurator in Judaea.

---

[4] In Luke's text the angel addresses Mary, but the words Justin cites are from Matthew, where the angel addresses Joseph.

Chapter 35

Other Fulfilled Prophecies

And how Christ after He was born was to escape the notice of other men until
He grew to man's estate, which also came to pass, hear what was foretold regarding
this. There are the following predictions: "Unto us a child is born, and unto us a
young man is given, and the government shall be upon His shoulders" (Isa 9:6);
which is significant of the power of the cross, for to it, when He was crucified, He applied His shoulders, as shall be more clearly made out in the ensuing discourse. And
again the same prophet Isaiah, being inspired by the prophetic Spirit, said, "I have
spread out my hands to a disobedient and gainsaying people, to those who walk in a
way that is not good. They now ask of me judgment, and dare to draw near to God"
(Isa 65:2; 58:2). And again in other words, through another prophet, He says, "They
pierced My hands and My feet, and for My vesture they cast lots" (Ps 22:16). And indeed David, the king and prophet, who uttered these things, suffered none of them;
but Jesus Christ stretched forth His hands, being crucified by the Jews speaking
against Him, and denying that He was the Christ. And as the prophet spoke, they tor-
mented Him, and set Him on the judgment-seat, and said, Judge us. And the expression, "They pierced my hands and my feet," was used in reference to the nails of the
cross which were fixed in His hands and feet. And after He was crucified they cast
lots upon His vesture, and they that crucified Him parted it among them. And that
these things did happen, you can ascertain from the Acts of Pontius Pilate.[5] And we
will cite the prophetic utterances of another prophet, Zephaniah, to the effect that
He was foretold expressly as to sit upon the foal of an ass and to enter Jerusalem. The
words are these: "Rejoice greatly, O daughter of Zion; shout, O daughter of Jerusalem: behold, thy King cometh unto thee; lowly, and riding upon an ass, and upon a
colt the foal of an ass" (Zech 9:9).[6]

Chapter 36

Different Modes of Prophecy

But when you hear the utterances of the prophets spoken as it were personally,
you must not suppose that they are spoken by the inspired [ones] themselves, but by
the Divine Word who moves them. For sometimes He declares things that are to
come to pass, in the manner of one who foretells the future; sometimes He speaks as
from the person of God the Lord and Father of all; sometimes as from the person of
Christ; sometimes as from the person of the people answering the Lord or His Father,
just as you can see even in your own writers, one man being the writer of the whole,
but introducing the persons who converse. And this the Jews who possessed the
books of the prophets did not understand, and therefore did not recognize Christ

---

[5] See J. K. Elliott, *The Apocryphal New Testament: A Collection of Apocryphal Christian Literature in an English Translation* (Oxford: Clarendon, 1993), 169–85.

[6] Here Justin attributes these words, actually found in the book of Zechariah, to the book of
Zephaniah.

even when He came, but even hate us who say that He has come, and who prove that, as was predicted, He was crucified by them.

. . .

Chapter 39

Direct Predictions by the Spirit

And when the Spirit of prophecy speaks as predicting things that are to come to pass, He speaks in this way: "For out of Zion shall go forth the law, and the word of the Lord from Jerusalem. And He shall judge among the nations, and shall rebuke many people; and they shall beat their swords into ploughshares, and their spears into pruning-hooks: nation shall not lift up sword against nation, neither shall they learn war any more" (Isa 2:3). And that it did so come to pass, we can convince you. For from Jerusalem there went out into the world, men, twelve in number, and these illiterate, of no ability in speaking: but by the power of God they proclaimed to every race of men that they were sent by Christ to teach to all the word of God; and we who formerly used to murder one another do not only now refrain from making war upon our enemies, but also, that we may not lie nor deceive our examiners, willingly die confessing Christ. For that saying, "The tongue has sworn, but the mind is un-sworn," might be imitated by us in this matter.[7] But if the soldiers enrolled by you, and who have taken the military oath, prefer their allegiance to their own life, and parents, and country, and all kindred, though you can offer them nothing incorrupt-ible, it were verily ridiculous if we, who earnestly long for incorruption, should not endure all things, in order to obtain what we desire from Him who is able to grant it.

Justin goes on to argue from Ps 19, Pss 1 and 2, and Ps 110 that these songs also foretold as-pects of Christ's death and resurrection.

Chapter 48

Christ's Work and Death Foretold

And that it was predicted that our Christ should heal all diseases and raise the dead, hear what was said. There are these words: "At His coming the lame shall leap as an hart, and the tongue of the stammerer shall be clear speaking: the blind shall see, and the lepers shall be cleansed; and the dead shall rise, and walk about" (Isa 35:6). And that He did those things, you can learn from the Acts of Pontius Pilate. And how it was predicted by the Spirit of prophecy that He and those who hoped in Him should be slain, hear what was said by Isaiah. These are the words: "Behold now the righteous perisheth, and no man layeth it to heart; and just men are taken away, and no man considereth. From the presence of wickedness is the righteous man taken, and his burial shall be in peace: he is taken from our midst" (Isa 57:1).

---

[7] See Euripides, *Hippolytus* 612, in *Euripides* (vol. 3 of *The Complete Greek Tragedies*; ed. David Grene and Richmond Lattimore; Chicago: Univerity of Chicago Press, 1959).

Chapter 49

His Rejection by the Jews Foretold

And again, how it was said by the same Isaiah, that the Gentile nations who were not looking for Him should worship Him, but the Jews who always expected Him should not recognize Him when He came. And the words are spoken as from the person of Christ; and they are these: "I was manifest to them that asked not for Me; I was found of them that sought Me not: I said, Behold Me, to a nation that called not on My name. I spread out My hands to a disobedient and gainsaying people, to those who walked in a way that is not good, but follow after their own sins; a people that provoketh Me to anger to My face" (65:1–3). For the Jews having the prophecies, and being always in expectation of the Christ to come, did not recognize Him; and not only so, but even treated Him shamefully. But the Gentiles, who had never heard anything about Christ, until the apostles set out from Jerusalem and preached concerning Him, and gave them the prophecies, were filled with joy and faith, and cast away their idols, and dedicated themselves to the Unbegotten God through Christ. And that it was foreknown that these infamous things should be uttered against those who confessed Christ, and that those who slandered Him, and said that it was well to preserve the ancient customs, should be miserable, hear what was briefly said by Isaiah; it is this: "Woe unto them that call sweet bitter, and bitter sweet" (Isa 5:20).

Chapter 50

His Humiliation Predicted

But that, having become man for our sakes, He endured to suffer and to be dishonoured, and that He shall come again with glory, hear the prophecies which relate to this; they are these: [Here Justin quotes Isaiah 52:13–53:8]. Accordingly, after He was crucified, even all His acquaintances forsook Him, having denied Him; and afterwards, when He had risen from the dead and appeared to them, and had taught them to read the prophecies in which all these things were foretold as coming to pass, and when they had seen Him ascending into heaven, and had believed, and had received power sent thence by Him upon them, and went to every race of men, they taught these things, and were called apostles.

Chapter 51

The Majesty of Christ

And that the Spirit of prophecy might signify to us that He who suffers these things has an ineffable origin, and rules His enemies, He spake thus: "His generation who shall declare? because His life is cut off from the earth: for their transgressions He comes to death. And I will give the wicked for His burial, and the rich for His death; because He did no violence, neither was any deceit in His mouth. And the Lord is pleased to cleanse Him from the stripe. If He be given for sin, your soul shall see His seed prolonged in days. And the Lord is pleased to deliver His soul from grief, to show Him light, and to form Him with knowledge, to justify the righteous who richly serveth many. And He shall bear our iniquities, Therefore He shall inherit many, and He shall divide the spoil of the strong, because His soul was delivered to death: and He was numbered with the transgressors; and He bare the sins of many, and He was delivered up for their transgressions" (Isa 53:8–12). Hear, too, how He was to ascend into heaven according to prophecy. It was thus spoken: "Lift up the gates of heaven; be ye opened, that the King of glory may come in. Who is this King of glory? The Lord, strong and mighty" (Ps 24:7). And how also He should come again out of heaven with glory, hear what was spoken in reference to this by the prophet Jeremiah.[8] His words are: "Behold, as the Son of man He cometh in the clouds of heaven, and His angels with Him" (Dan 7:13).

Chapter 52

Certain Fulfillment of Prophecy

Since, then, we prove that all things which have already happened had been predicted by the prophets before they came to pass, we must necessarily believe also that those things which are in like manner predicted, but are yet to come to pass, shall certainly happen. For as the things which have already taken place came to pass when foretold, and even though unknown, so shall the things that remain, even though they be unknown and disbelieved, yet come to pass. For the prophets have proclaimed two advents of His: the one, that which is already past, when He came as a dishonoured and suffering Man; but the second, when, according to prophecy, He shall come from heaven with glory, accompanied by His angelic host, when also He shall raise the bodies of all men who have lived, and shall clothe those of the worthy with immortality, and shall send those of the wicked, endued with eternal sensibility, into everlasting fire with the wicked devils. And that these things also have been foretold as yet to be, we will prove. By Ezekiel the prophet it was said: "Joint shall be joined to joint, and bone to bone, and flesh shall grow again; and every knee shall bow to the Lord, and every tongue shall confess Him" (Ezek 37:7–8; Isa 45:24). And in what kind of sensation and punishment the wicked are to be, hear from what was said in like manner with reference to this; it is as follows: "Their worm shall not rest, and their fire shall not be quenched" (Isa 66:24); and then shall they repent, when it profits them not. And what the people of the Jews shall say and do, when they see Him coming in glory, has been thus predicted by Zechariah the prophet: "I will command the four winds to gather the scattered children; I will command the north wind to bring them, and the south wind, that it keep not back. And then in Jerusalem there shall be great lamentation, not the lamentation of mouths or of lips, but the lamentation of the heart; and they shall rend not their garments, but their hearts. Tribe by tribe they shall mourn, and then they shall look on Him whom they have pierced; and they shall say, Why, O Lord, hast Thou made us to err from Thy way? The glory which our fathers blessed, has for us been turned into shame" [Zech 12:10; Isa 63:17; 64:11].

---

[8] Although Justin refers to Jeremiah, the text he cites is from the book of Daniel.

Chapter 53

Summary of the Prophecies

Though we could bring forward many other prophecies, we forbear, judging these sufficient for the persuasion of those who have ears to hear and understand; and considering also that those persons are able to see that we do not make mere assertions without being able to produce proof, like those fables that are told of the so-called sons of Jupiter. For with what reason should we believe of a crucified man that He is the first-born of the unbegotten God, and Himself will pass judgment on the whole human race, unless we had found testimonies concerning Him published before He came and was born as man, and unless we saw that things had happened accordingly—the devastation of the land of the Jews, and men of every race persuaded by His teaching through the apostles, and rejecting their old habits, in which, being deceived, they had had their conversation; yea, seeing ourselves too, and knowing that the Christians from among the Gentiles are both more numerous and more true than those from among the Jews and Samaritans? For all the other human races are called Gentiles by the Spirit of prophecy; but the Jewish and Samaritan races are called the tribe of Israel, and the house of Jacob. And the prophecy in which it was predicted that there should be more believers from the Gentiles than from the Jews and Samaritans, we will produce: it ran thus: "Rejoice, O barren, thou that dost not bear; break forth and shout, thou that dost not travail, because many more are the children of the desolate than of her that hath an husband" (Isa 54:1). For all the Gentiles were "desolate" of the true God, serving the works of their hands; but the Jews and Samaritans, having the word of God delivered to them by the prophets, and always expecting the Christ, did not recognize Him when He came, except some few, of whom the Spirit of prophecy by Isaiah had predicted that they should be saved. He spoke as from their person: "Except the Lord had left us a seed, we should have been as Sodom and Gomorrah" (Isa 1:9). For Sodom and Gomorrah are related by Moses to have been cities of ungodly men, which God burned with fire and brimstone, and overthrew, no one of their inhabitants being saved except a certain stranger, a Chaldaean by birth, whose name was Lot; with whom also his daughters were rescued. And those who care may yet see their whole country desolate and burned, and remaining barren. And to show how those from among the Gentiles were foretold as more true and more believing, we will cite what was said by Isaiah the prophet,[9] for he spoke as follows: "Israel is uncircumcised in heart, but the Gentiles are uncircumcised in the flesh" (Jer 9:26). So many things therefore, as these, when they are seen with the eye, are enough to produce conviction and belief in those who embrace the truth, and are not bigoted in their opinions, nor are governed by their passions.

---

[9] Justin's scriptural source is Jeremiah, not Isaiah.

CHAPTER 5

Penetrating the Inner Meaning of Scripture: Origen (185–254 C.E.)

O rigen was far and away the most influential Christian writer of his time. Born in Alexandria, Egypt, to Christian parents who suffered persecution, Origen developed, through an excellent education, into a highly respected thinker and leader of the Eastern Christian church. He later moved to Caesarea, where he established a school and continued his preaching and writing. In 250 he suffered torture and imprisonment during the persecutions of Christians under Emperor Decius.

Over the course of his adult life, Origen's literary output was enormous, including a vast quantity of homiletical, theological, and exegetical works for the Greek-reading church. (Only a fraction of these works have survived in Greek and also in Latin translation.) His commitment to teaching and preaching the Christian faith is particularly evident in the voluminous commentaries he produced; of the extant manuscripts, eight books are devoted to Matthew's Gospel, nine to John's Gospel, and several more on Paul's Epistle to the Romans. Origen's pastoral duties generated hundreds of homilies on almost every corner of Christian Scripture. He also contributed to the ancient church's academic repository through extensive philological and historical notes on Scripture, although modern knowledge of such scholia is derived not from manuscripts but from indirect testimony of other writers and their sometimes extensive quotes of Origen. The focus of his philological and textual scholarship was primarily on the various Greek translations of the Jewish Scriptures available at the time, but he did not neglect the Hebrew Scriptures, endeavoring to make them accessible to Greek readers though transliteration.

The fundamental, determinative fact of Christian Scripture for Origen was its divine authorship. The collection of various canonical books constituted a single whole, every part of which reflected the fullness of its Author, whose wisdom—verbally expressed in Scripture—nurtured the soul to greater and greater perfection. This was, in fact, for Origen, the purpose of Scripture. The divine wisdom in Scripture was largely accessible by perceiving it through allegorical interpretation, particularly when a literal interpretation would yield a meaning unworthy of God. Origin needed this approach in his opposition to heretics who concluded from the inelegance of Scripture that the biblical deity could not be the true God. Similarly, he sought to prevent strictly literal interpretations from leading simplistic readers to theological conclusions inconsistent with the core of the Christian faith. For the majority of readers, the literal meaning is most accessible, and so no one is necessarily excluded from the written source of God's wisdom. But for the more sophisticated, the hidden treasures of insight are available through allegory. Origen uses the analogy of the text's "body" to refer to the literal, grammatical sense of a passage, and the text's "soul" is the figurative, spiritual meaning intended by God for earnest seekers of divine wisdom. The Bible's rough literary seams are there to invite further investigation and reflection, which lead to knowledge of God not immediately apparent in the text's literal meaning. In this way God can, through Scripture, cultivate the soul's development irrespective of the level from which the text is approached. Origen thus turns what might have been a weakness into a hermeneutical strength: the Christian Bible is divine and effective for salvation not despite its humble appearance but because of it.

In the selection below, Origen offers a reasoned defense of the sort of allegorical interpretation that appears widely in his own work and in that of many of his contemporaries. His argument marks a first in the history of Christian biblical interpretation. Like his predecessors, Origen claims that Christian *meaning* of the Old Testament was delivered to the church through a tradition traceable back to Jesus and his apostles. But he goes further by asserting that the *method* by which the church discerns Christian meaning in Scripture (allegory) is itself also traceable back to the apostles. For Origen, when Paul, for example, uses an allegorical interpretation to make a point in his epistles, Paul is also himself (with apostolic authority) teaching allegory as a method of interpretation. Origen moves beyond other early church exegetes in his claim that God had hidden allegorical meanings not only in Old Testament texts but also in the New Testament writings, and in his assertion that some biblical passages were written not for any literal meaning but only for spiritual significance accessed through allegory.

What brought Origen to raise method in biblical interpretation to the level of systematic reflection and articulation? It was incumbent upon him in view of the larger intellectual program propounded by this church leader. The range of his oeuvre, considered altogether, constitutes an attempt—the first ever—to build the foundations of a complete Christian culture as a viable alternative to the major pagan philosophies and heretical schools on the cultural horizon of the third-century church. Construction of a Christian philosophy or worldview from Scripture would require an explanation of the interpretive method by which this worldview would be hermeneutically derived. The exegetical pattern advocated by Origen follows the same ontological pattern by which all existence is structured, according to his essentially Platonic worldview: every object and event is actually an externality to a deeper spiritual reality. Origen himself, as he comments on the hidden presence of the Christian gospel within the Jewish law, puts it this way:

> The truth of the faith holds that there is one and the same God of the Law and the Gospels, Creator "of the visible and the invisible" (2 Cor 4:18). For the visible holds the highest relationship with the invisible, as the Apostle says, "The invisible is perceived from the creation of the world through the things that were made" (Rom 1:20). Therefore, just as "the visible and invisible," earth and heaven, soul and flesh, body and spirit have mutually this kinship and this world is a result of their union, so also we must believe that Holy Scripture results from the visible and the invisible.[1]

---

[1] Origen, *Homilies on Leviticus* 5.1, in Origen, *Homilies on Leviticus 1–16* (trans. G. W. Barkley; Fathers of the Church 83; Washington, D.C.: Catholic University of America Press, 1990), 89.

Thus the exegetical pattern advocated by Origen derives from the way Scripture, like every visible thing, is constituted when fully considered: there is also the invisible dimension to be taken into account. Indeed, it is that inner, hidden dimension of Scripture that is of most value for spiritual growth. Origen's arguments to this effect constitute part of the rational basis for a Christian school of thought systematically presented in his work *On First Principles.*

For further information on Origen and the Alexandrian interpretation of the Bible:

Dorival, Gilles, and Alain Le Boulluec. *Origeniana Sexta, Origen and the Bible: Actes du Colloquium Origenianum Sextum.* Leuven: Leuven University Press, Peeters, 1995.
Trigg, Joseph W. *Origen.* The Early Church Fathers. New York: Routledge, 1998.
———. *Origen: Bible and Philosophy in the Third-Century Church.* Atlanta: John Knox, 1983.

On First Principles [2]

1. Now that we have dealt, therefore, with this point, that the divine scriptures were inspired by the Holy Spirit, it appears necessary also to explain how some men have involved themselves in numerous errors through not reading or understanding them aright, because the method by which we should approach the interpretation of the divine writings is unknown to the multitude. For the Jews, owing to their hardness of heart and their desire to appear wise in their own sight, have refused to believe in our Lord and Savior because they suppose that the prophecies that relate to him must be understood literally, that is, that he ought actually and visibly to have "proclaimed release to captives" (Isa 61:1), and that he ought to have at once built a city such as they think the "city of God" (Ps 46:4) really is, and at the same time to have "cut off the chariots from Ephraim and the horse from Jerusalem" (Zech 9:10), and also to have eaten "butter and honey" and "chosen the good before he knew how to prefer the evil" (Isa 7:15).

Further, they think that it is the wolf, the four-footed animal, of which it is prophesied that at the coming of Christ it must "feed with lambs, and the leopard lie down with the kids, and the calf and the bull feed with lions and be led to their pastures by a little child, and the ox and the bear lie down together in the green fields and their young ones be brought up side by side, and lions to stand at stalls with oxen and feed on straw" (Isa 11:6–7). Seeing, then, that there was no fulfillment in history of all these things which were prophesied of him and in which they believed that the signs of the advent of Christ were specially to be observed, they refused to acknowledge the presence of our Lord Jesus Christ; nay, contrary to all right and justice, that is, contrary to the faith of prophecy, they nailed him to the cross for assuming for himself the name of Christ.

Then again the heretics, reading in the law, "A fire has been kindled in my anger" (Deut 32:22); and "I am a jealous God, visiting the sins of the fathers upon the children to the third and fourth generation" (Exod 20:5); and "It repenteth me that I have anointed Saul to be king" (1 Sam 15:11); and "I am God, that maketh peace and createth evil" (Isa 45:7); and again "There is no evil in a city, which the Lord hath not done" (Amos 3:6); and "Evils came down from the Lord upon the gates of Jerusalem" (Mic 1:12); and "An evil spirit from God troubled Saul" (1 Sam 18:10), and many other passages of scripture like these, have not dared to say that they are not the writings of God, but have supposed them to belong to that Creator God whom the Jews worshipped, and who they think should be believed to be merely just, and not good as well. For they think that the Savior came here to proclaim to us a more perfect God, who they say is not the Creator of the world, and about whom they entertain diverse opinions; since having once fallen away from their faith in God the Creator, who is the God of all, they have given themselves up to

---

[2] These excerpts are taken from *Origen on First Principles, Being Koetschau's Text of the De principiis Translated into English, Together with an Introduction and Notes* (trans. G. W. Butterworth; London: SPCK, 1936), 4.2, following the Latin text. Used with permission.

various fictions and fables, inventing false opinions and saying that there are certain visible things made by one power and certain invisible things created by another power, just as they are led by the fancy and vanity of their own minds.

Moreover some of the simpler of those who appear to remain within the faith of the Church, while holding that there is none greater than the Creator God, in which they maintain a right and sound opinion, yet believe such things about him as would not be believed even of the most unjust and savage of men.

2. Now the reason why those we have mentioned above have a false apprehension of all these matters is nothing else but this, that the holy scripture is not understood by them in its spiritual sense, but according to the sound of the letter. On this account we shall try to demonstrate, so far as our moderate ability will permit, to those who believe that the holy Scriptures were not composed by means of merely human words but were written under the inspiration of the Holy Spirit and were also handed down and entrusted to us by the will of God the Father through his only-begotten Son Jesus Christ, what is the method of interpretation that appears right to us, who keep to that rule and discipline delivered by Jesus Christ to the apostles and handed down by them in succession to their posterity, the teachers of the heavenly Church.

That there are certain mystical revelations made known through the holy scriptures is admitted, I think, by all, even by the simpler kind of believers; but what these revelations are, or of what nature they are, any man who is fair-minded and not possessed by the vice of boasting will reverently confess that he does not know. If, for instance, we are asked about the daughters of Lot and their apparent unlawful intercourse with their father [Gen 19:30–38], or about the two wives of Abraham, (Gen 16), or the two sisters who were married to Jacob [Gen 29:21–30:24], or the two handmaids who increased the number of his sons (Gen 30:1–13), what else can we reply than that these are sacraments and figures of spiritual things, but that we are ignorant of their precise nature?

When, moreover, we read of the equipment of the tabernacle [see Exod 25–31:11; 35:10–39:43], we hold it as certain that the things described therein are figures of some hidden realities, but to attach them to their appropriate meanings and to bring to light and discuss each separate detail is, I think, a very difficult, not to say impossible task. However, as I said, it does not escape even the common intellect that that description is full of mysteries. And all those narratives which appear to be composed about marriages or the begetting of children or different kinds of battles or any other stories whatever, what else can we believe them to be but the forms and figures of hidden and sacred things? But either because men pay too little attention to the training of their mind, or because they think they already know before they learn, the consequence is that they never begin to know; otherwise if neither earnestness is lacking, nor a master, and if these questions are studied as befits divine, and not merely human matters, that is, in a reverent and pious spirit, and as questions that we hope will in most cases be made clear by the revelation of God, since to human sense they are exceedingly difficult and obscure, then, perhaps, he who thus seeks will at last find all that it is lawful for us to find.

3. But it may possibly be supposed that this difficulty belongs only to the prophetic writings, seeing it is certain to all of us that the prophetic style is everywhere sprinkled with figures and riddles. What, then, when we come to the gospels? Is there not also hidden in them an inner meaning which is the Lord's meaning, and which is only revealed through the grace that was given to him who said, "We have the mind of Christ, that we may know the things that were freely given to us by God. Which things also we speak, not in words which man's wisdom teacheth, but which the Spirit teacheth" [see 1 Cor 2:12, 16]. And who indeed, on reading the revelations made to John, could fail to be amazed at the deep obscurity of the unspeakable mysteries contained therein? For even those who cannot understand what is concealed in these writings yet understand clearly that something is concealed there. And as for the apostolic epistles, which to some appear to be simpler, are they not filled with deep meanings, so that men who can understand the inner meaning of divine wisdom seem through them, as if through some narrow opening, to be flooded with the brightness of immeasurable light?

Seeing, therefore, that these things are so, and that there are many who in this life make mistakes, I do not think that anyone can without danger declare that he knows or understands those things for the opening of which the "key of knowledge" is necessary, which key the Savior said was with those "learned in the law." And at this point, though by a slight digression, I think we should ask those who tell us that before the coming of the Savior the truth did not rest with those who were trained in the law, how it is that our Lord Jesus Christ says that the "keys of knowledge" were with those who had in their hands the books of the law and the prophets. For the Lord spoke as follows "Woe to you, doctors of the law, for ye have taken away the key of knowledge. Ye entered not in yourselves, and them that wished to enter in ye hindered" (Luke 11:52).

4. But, as we had begun say, the right way, as it appears to us, of understanding the scriptures and investigating their meaning, is the following; for indeed we are taught out of scripture itself how we ought to think of it. We find some such rule as this laid down in the Proverbs of Solomon concerning the examination of divine scripture. "Do thou," it says, "portray these things to thyself threefold in counsel and knowledge, so that thou mayest answer words of truth to those who question thee" (Prov 22:20–21, LXX).

Each one must therefore portray the meaning of the divine writings in a three-fold way upon his own soul; that is, so that the simple may be edified by what we may call the body of the scriptures (for such is the name we may give to the common and literal interpretation); while those who have begun to make a little progress and are able to perceive something more than that may be edified by the soul of scripture; and those who are perfect and like the men of whom the apostle says: "We speak wisdom among the perfect; yet a wisdom not of this world, nor of the rulers of this world, which are coming to nought; but we speak God's wisdom hidden in a mystery, the wisdom which God foreordained before the worlds unto our glory" (1 Cor 2:6–7)—such as these may be edified by that spiritual law which has "a shadow of the good things to come" (Heb 10:1), as if by the Spirit. Just as man, therefore, is said to consist of body, soul and spirit, so also does the holy scripture, which has been bestowed by the divine bounty for man's salvation. . . .

5. But we must certainly not forget that there are some passages of scripture in which this that we call the body, that is, the logical and literal meaning, is not found, as we shall show in what follows; and there are places where those meanings which we have called the soul and the spirit are alone to be looked for. I believe that this fact is indicated in the gospels, when six waterpots are said "to be set there for the purifying of the Jews, containing two or three firkins apiece" (John 2:6). Here, as I said, the language of the gospel seems to allude to those who are said by the apostle to be Jews "inwardly" (Rom 2:29), and to mean that these are purified through the word of scripture, by receiving in some cases "two firkins," that is, by accepting the soul meaning and the spiritual meaning in accordance with what we said above, and in other cases three firkins, when the reading also retains for the edification of the hearers a bodily meaning, namely the literal one. And six waterpots are approximately mentioned in allusion to those who are being purified while living in the world. For we read that this world and all that is in it were finished in six days, which is a perfect number.

6. How much value there is in this first meaning, which we have called the literal one, is witnessed by the entire multitude of those believers who accept the faith quite trustfully and simply; and this needs no long argument because it is obvious to all. But of the kind of explanation which we have spoken of above as the soul, as it were, of Scripture, many illustrations are given us by the apostle Paul, as, for example, first of all in his epistle to the Corinthians. "For," he says, "it is written; thou shalt not muzzle the ox that treadeth out the corn."[3] Then in explaining how this precept ought to be understood, he adds: "Is it for the oxen that God careth? Or saith he it altogether for our sake? Yea, for our sake it was written, because he that ploweth ought to plow in hope, and he that thresheth, to thresh in hope of partaking" (1 Cor 9:9–10). Moreover, many other similar passages which are interpreted in this manner out of the law, impart the utmost instruction to those who hear them.

But a spiritual explanation is like this, when one is able to show of what "heavenly things" those who are Jews "after the flesh" serve a copy and a shadow (Heb 8:5; Rom 8:5; Heb 10:1), and of what "good things to come" the law has a "shadow," and any other matters of this kind which may be found in the holy scriptures; or when we inquire what is that "wisdom hidden in a mystery, which God foreordained before the worlds unto our glory, which none of the rulers of this world knew" (1 Cor 2:7–8), or ask the meaning of the same apostle's statement, when he makes use of certain illustrations from Exodus and Numbers and says that "these things happened unto them figuratively, and they were written for our sake, upon whom the ends of the ages are come" (1 Cor 10:11), and when he affords us an opportunity of understanding how we can learn of what those events that happened to them were figures, by saying, "For they drank of that spiritual rock that followed them, and that rock was Christ" (1 Cor 10:4).

---

[3] In the New Testament text, Paul is citing Deut 25:4.

Moreover in another epistle he mentions that command about the tabernacle which was enjoined upon Moses: "Thou shalt make all things according to the figure that was shown thee in the mount" (Heb 8:5).[4] And when writing to the Galatians and reproaching some who believe they are reading the law and yet do not understand it, because they are unaware that there are allegories in these writings, he addresses them in a tone of rebuke: "Tell me, ye that desire to be under the law, do ye not hear the law? For it is written that Abraham had two sons, one by the handmaid and one by the free woman. Howbeit he who was born of the handmaid was born according to the flesh, but he of the free woman was born according to promise. Which things contain an allegory. For these are the two covenants" (Gal 4:21–24), and what follows. Here we must also observe this point, how carefully the apostle says, "Ye that desire to be under the law" (and not, "ye that are under the law") "do ye not hear the law?" Do ye not hear? that is, do ye not understand and know?

Moreover in the epistle to the Colossians he briefly sums up and condenses the meaning of the entire law and says: "Let no man therefore judge you in meat or in drink or in respect of solemn days or a new moon or a sabbath, which are a shadow of the things to come" (Col 2:16–17). Also when writing to the Hebrews and discoursing about those who are of the circumcision he says: "They who serve that which is a copy and shadow of the heavenly things" (Heb 8:5). But probably through the above examples those who accept the apostle's writings as divinely inspired will feel no doubt in regard to the five books of Moses. In regard to the rest of the history, however, they will ask whether the events related therein may also be said to have "happened figuratively" to those about whom they are written. We notice that this point has been spoken of in the epistle to the Romans, where the apostle takes an illustration from the third book of the Kings, which says: "I have left for myself seven thousand men, who have not bowed the knee to Baal" (Rom 11:4).[5] This Paul takes as spoken figuratively of those who are called Israelites "according to election," in order to show that the coming of Christ was beneficial not only to the gentiles but also to very many of the race of Israel who have been called to salvation.

7. This being so, we shall now outline the manner in which divine scripture should be understood on these several points, using such illustrations and examples as may occur to us. And in the first place we must call to mind and point out that the Holy Spirit, who by the providence and will of God through the power of his only-begotten Word who was "in the beginning with God" [John 1:1], enlightened the servants of the truth, that is, the prophets and apostles (wished above all to lend them) to the knowledge of the mysteries connected with those affairs and causes which concern the lives and relationships of men. By men I mean at the present moment souls that are located in bodies. These mysteries which were made known and revealed to them by the Spirit, the prophets portrayed figuratively through the narration of what seemed to be human deeds and the handing down of certain legal ordinances and precepts. The aim was that not everyone who wished should have these

---

[4] In the New Testament text, Exod 25:40 is being cited here.
[5] Paul cites 1 Kgs 19:18 (LXX 3 Kgs 19:18); LXX 3 Kings is 1 Kings in the Hebrew Bible and in most modern versions.

mysteries laid before his feet to trample upon (Matt 7:6), but that they should be for the man who had devoted himself to studies of this kind with the utmost purity and sobriety and through nights of watching, by which means perchance he might be able to trace out the deeply hidden meaning of the Spirit of God, concealed under the language of an ordinary narrative which points in a different direction, and that so be might become a sharer of the Spirit's knowledge and a partaker of his divine counsel.

For in no other way can the soul reach the perfection of knowledge except by being inspired with the truth of the divine wisdom. Therefore it is chiefly the doctrine about God, that is, about the Father, Son and Holy Spirit, which is indicated by those men who were filled with the divine Spirit. Then, too, the mysteries relating to the Son of God, how the Word became flesh, and for what reason he went to the length of "taking upon him the form of a servant" (Phil 2:7), have also been made known by those who were filled, as we have said, with the divine Spirit. After that it followed of necessity that they should instruct the race of mortal men by divine teaching concerning rational creatures, both heavenly and earthly, the more blessed and the lower ones alike, and also concerning the differences between souls and how these differences arose; and then the question what this world is and why it was made, and further, how it comes about that evil is so widespread and so terrible on earth, and whether it is found only on earth or in some other places as well—all this it was necessary that we should learn from the divine teaching.

8. But while it was the intention of the Holy Spirit to enlighten holy souls, who had devoted themselves to the service of the truth, on these and similar subjects, there was in the second place another aim in view, namely, that for the sake of such as either could not or would not give themselves up to this labor and industry in order to prove themselves worthy of being taught and of coming to know matters of such value and importance, the Spirit should wrap up and conceal within ordinary language under cover of some historical record or account of visible things certain secret mysteries. There is introduced therefore an account of the visible creation and of the formation and fashioning of the first man, and then of the descendants that follow in succession from him. There are also recorded certain acts performed by righteous men and occasionally, too, mention is made of the sins these same men committed, seeing they were but human; and then also a considerable number of the licentious and wicked deeds of impious men are related.

In a wonderful manner, too, an account of wars is presented, and the different fortunes now of the conquerors, now of the conquered are described, and by this means, to those who know how to examine writings of this kind, certain unspeakable mysteries are revealed. Further, by a marvelous example of wisdom, in the writings of the law the law of truth is implanted and prophetically indicated; and all these are by the divine skill and wisdom woven together to form a kind of outer covering and veil for spiritual meanings, which is what we meant by the body of holy scripture; with the result that even through this that we have called the outer covering of the letter, woven by the art of wisdom, very many readers may be edified and make progress, who otherwise could not do so.

9. But if in every detail of this outer covering, that is, the actual history, the sequence of the law had been preserved and its order maintained, we should have understood the scriptures in an unbroken course and should certainly not have believed that there was anything else buried within them beyond what was indicated at a first glance. Consequently the divine wisdom has arranged for certain stumbling-blocks and interruptions of the historical sense to be found therein, by inserting in the midst a number of impossibilities and incongruities, in order that the very interruption of the narrative might as it were present a barrier to the reader and lead him to refuse to proceed along the pathway of the ordinary meaning: and so, by shutting us out and debarring us from that, might recall us to the beginning of another way, and might thereby bring us, through the entrance of a narrow footpath, to a higher and loftier road and lay open the immense breadth of the divine wisdom.

And we must also know this, that because the aim of the Holy Spirit was chiefly to preserve the connexion of the spiritual meaning, both in the things that are yet to be done and in those which have already been accomplished, whenever he found that things which had been done in history could be harmonised with the spiritual meaning, he composed in a single narrative a texture comprising both kinds of meaning, always, however, concealing the secret sense more deeply. But wherever the record of deeds that had been done could not be made to correspond with the sequence of the spiritual truths, he inserted occasionally some deeds of a less probable character or which could not have happened at all, and occasionally some which might have happened but in fact did not. Sometimes he does this by a few words, which in their bodily sense do not appear capable of containing truth, and at other times by inserting a large number.

This is found to happen particularly in the law, where there are many things which as literal precepts are clearly useful, but also a considerable number in which no principle of utility whatever is disclosed, while sometimes even impossibilities are detected. All this, as we have said, the Holy Spirit supervised, in order that in cases where that which appeared at the first glance could neither be true nor useful we should be led on to search for a truth deeper down and needing more careful examination, and should try to discover in the scriptures which we believe to be inspired by God a meaning worthy of God.

And not only did the Holy Spirit supervise the writings which were previous to the coming of Christ, but because he is one and the same Spirit and proceeds from the one God he has acted similarly in regard to the gospels and the writings of the apostles. For even the narratives which he inspired through them were not woven together without the spell of that wisdom of his, the nature of which we explained above. And so it happens that even in them the Spirit has mingled not a few things by which the historical order of the narrative is interrupted and broken, with the object of turning and calling the attention of the reader, by the impossibility of the literal sense, to an examination of the inner meaning.

CHAPTER 6

Principles for Typological Interpretation: Tyconius (late fourth century C.E.)

W e must introduce our next ancient interpreter, Tyconius, by noting the historical situation of Donatism, which conditioned his work. Triggered by the aftermath of the Diocletian persecution of the church, Donatists emerged as a prominent Christian group in fourth-century Christian North Africa. The fundamental question behind their emergence was whether morally impure individuals could reside and hold office within the church, the body of Christ. Convinced that the Catholic church was hopelessly compromised on this issue in its consecration of suspect bishops, a certain Donatus led a schismatic departure from the Catholic church. By the early fifth century, the Catholic church had condemned Donatism as a heresy, and by the end of the sixth century, the Donatist church had effectively disappeared.

Although Tyconius himself eventually was excommunicated from the Donatist fold, his only surviving work *(Liber regularum [Book of Rules])* sought, by teaching a particular way of interpreting the Bible, to account for the presence of evil and moral impurity in the church—a question central to the Donatist-Catholic controversy. In the *Rules,* Tyconius assumes a fundamentally oracular conception of Scripture: in any portion of the Bible, God spoke prophetically, by way of types, concerning the composition and nature of the fourth-century North African church. (About 75 percent of the biblical texts Tyconius cites are from the prophets.) But the church cannot discern the oracle apart from knowledge of the logic by which Scripture speaks typologically. The rules that Tyconius laid out were to help the Christian reader discern Scripture's own oracular system, apart from which the reader could only remain oblivious—and therefore in error—as to Scripture's typological depiction of the contemporary church.

For earlier generations, typology had served to help move toward a combination of the Old and New Testaments into a Christian Bible (see 1 Corinthians and Mileto). In the *Book of Rules,* typology functions on a broader horizon, establishing connections between the Bible and the contemporary world of the church. Tyconius maintained that it is by virtue of this typo-logic that Scripture reveals the truth about the contemporary world, namely, that the church contains not only the members of Christ's body but also members of Satan's body at the same time (particularly in Rule 7). The word of God in Scripture speaks comfort and encouragement to the former, and a call for repentance to the latter, as Tyconius argues from Isa 44:21–22:

"I formed you as my servant, you are mine, Israel; do not forget me. For behold, I have swept away your crimes like a cloud and your sins like a mist. Turn to me and I will redeem you." Is the one whose sins he has swept away, to whom he says, "you are mine," and whom he reminds not to forget him, the same one to whom he says, "turn to me"? Are anyone's sins swept away before he is turned? (*Book of Rules* 2.11)

But either way, God's message is accessible only for those who understand the typo-logic by which insight regarding the two bodies is revealed. This logic—woven throughout the biblical text—is taught through the *Rules.*

Thus under Rule 1 Tyconius instructs how to distinguish between prophetic references to Christ himself, on the one hand, and those to Christ's body, the church, on the other. Rule 2 follows accordingly, treating the mystery of the union between Christ and the body of believers who have been baptized into Christ. The church, as the body of Christ, is a bipartite body, consisting of saints and sinners alike. So, prophetic statements of blessing and curse for God's people are not really contradictory, as they refer to different sides of Christ's body, with different natures and different destinies. So also, according to Rule 3, it is the sinning members of the church who are subject to the conditional aspects of God's covenant, whereas the ancient assurance of eternal life applies without mitigation to the other, saintly side of Christ's body. Tyconius's own manner of typological interpretation receives elaboration in Rule 4, where he distinguishes between the "particular" *(specie)* prophecies and the "general" *(genere)* prophecies: the former refer to certain historical events or persons and their typological fulfillment in the life of the church, and the latter present a more immediate figure *(figura)* of the church. Here much of Tyconius's efforts are directed at the complex interweaving of particular and general prophecies in the same passage of Scripture. Turning to a somewhat different aspect of prophecy, Rule 5 addresses the significance of numbers and numerical patterns in biblical chronology. This rule includes apparent temporal inconsistencies in the biblical record as well as numerical symbols, particularly in their allusion to temporal periods in the destiny of the church. Rule 6 carries further the theme of destiny, as it treats the discernment of signs leading to the eventual separation of the good and the evil—within the body of Christ—at the final judgment. Rule 7 concludes the treatise with instruction on interpretation of biblical texts that speak of the opposing antichrist power within the bipartite church body.

Tyconius's treatise on biblical hermeneutics was the first effort of its kind in the Latin church, and its influence is evident, for example, in Augustine's famous *On Christian Doctrine (De doctrina christiana),* which includes a revisionary summary of Tyconius's *Rules.* (The Augustinian revision of Tyconius was enduring; we will note it again in the fourteenth-century work of Nicholas of Lyra.)

For further information on Tyconius:

Bright, Pamela. *The Book of Rules of Tyconius: Its Purpose and Inner Logic.* Notre Dame, Ind.: University of Notre Dame Press, 1988.
Tilley, Maureen. *The Bible in Christian North Africa: The Donatist World.* Minneapolis: Fortress, 1997.

Tyconius's *Book of Rules*[1]

Above everything else that came to mind, I considered it necessary to write a book of rules and so to fashion keys and lamps, as it were, to the secrets of the law. For there are certain mystic rules which obtain in the inner recesses of the entire law and keep the rich treasures of the truth hidden from some people. But if the sense of these rules is accepted without ill will, as we impart it, whatever is closed will be opened and whatever is dark will be illumined; and anyone who walks the vast forest of prophecy guided by these rules, as by pathways of light, will be kept from straying into error.

These are the rules:

I. The Lord and His Body
II. The Lord's Bipartite Body
III. The Promises and the Law
IV. The Particular and the General
V. Times
VI. Recapitulation
VII. The Devil and His Body

I. The Lord and His Body

Whether scripture is speaking about the Lord or about his body, i.e., the church, reason alone discerns, persuading or, such is the force of truth, compelling us to recognize what pertains to each.

In some cases, the subject is a single person; and yet the different functions of the two teach us that the one person is actually twofold. Thus in Isaiah, it says: "he bears our sins and knows sorrow on our behalf; he was wounded for our iniquities and God delivered him up for our sins," and so forth—a passage which the voice of the church universally ascribes to the Lord (Isa 53:4–6). But it goes on to say, still speaking of the same person: "and God wishes to free him from affliction, and God wishes to take away his sorrow, to show him the light and to form him with prudence" [see Isa 53:10]. Does God "wish to show the light" to the same one whom "he delivered up for our sins" or wish "to form him with prudence," especially when that one is himself the very light and wisdom of God? Do not these phrases apply rather to his body? From this it is clear that only reason can tell when there is a transition from the head to the body.

Daniel, too, calls the Lord "a stone cut from the mountain" and says that he "struck" the body of the kingdoms of the world and "ground it into dust," but that his own body "became a mountain and filled the whole earth" (Dan 2:34–35). For it is

---

[1] These selections are taken from *Tyconius: The Book of Rules* (ed. and trans. William S. Babcock; Atlanta: Scholars Press, 1989). Used with permission.

not that the Lord filled the whole earth with his power rather than with the fullness of his body. Some make this claim—which I do not report without sorrow—to the dishonor of God's kingdom and of Christ's unvanquished inheritance. They maintain that the world is filled by the mountain because a Christian may now rightly offer in every place what before was rightly offered only in Zion. But if this is so, there was no need to say that the mountain grew from the stone and took possession of the world by degrees. For Christ our Lord "had this glory before the foundation of the world" (John 17:5, 24); and when the son of God became man in him, he did not receive all power in heaven and on earth little by little like the stone, but all at once. The stone, in contrast, "became a great mountain" by degrees and covered the whole earth by its increase. Furthermore, if he had filled the whole earth not with his body but with his power, he would not be compared to a stone. Power is intangible; but a stone is a tangible body.

Nor is reason alone in showing that the body grows, not the head. This point is also confirmed by apostolic authority: "we are growing in every way into him who is the head, Christ, from whom the whole body, fitted and joined together through every operation supplied according to the measure of each part, makes bodily increase towards building itself up" (Eph 4:15–16). And again: "not holding fast to the head, from whom the whole body, fitted and furnished in its joints and operations, grows into God's increase" (Col 2:19). The head, therefore, does not grow; it is the same from the beginning. Rather the body takes its growth from the head.

Let us return to our thesis. Of the Lord and his body—and reason must discern what pertains to each—it is written: "he charged his angels to guard you in all your ways, to take you in their hands lest you should strike your foot against a stone. You will tread on the asp and the basilisk, and will trample the lion and the serpent under foot. Because he put his hope in me, I will rescue him; I will protect him because he knows my name. He will call upon me and I will heed him; I am with him in tribulation; I will rescue and honor him. I will lengthen his days and show him my salvation" (Ps 91:11–16). Does God "show his salvation" to the same one whose care he has "charged" to "his angels"—or rather to his body?

Again: "he has put a wreath on my head like a bridegroom and has adorned me with jewels like a bride" (Isa 61:10). He speaks of one body of both sexes, bridegroom and bride; but by reason we know what pertains to the Lord, what to the church. And in the Apocalypse the same Lord says: "I am the bridegroom and the bride."[2] And again: "they went to meet the bridegroom and the bride."[3]

And again it is made clear in Isaiah that reason must discern what has to do with the head, what with the body: "thus says the Lord to Christ my Lord, whose right hand I have taken that the nations might heed him"—and it goes on to say what can only pertain to the body—"and I will give you hidden treasures, things unseen I

---

[2] Here Tyconius seems to refer to the marriage motif in Rev 19:6–9 and 22:16–17, but no verse in Revelation corresponds to his quote.

[3] If Tyconius is citing Matt 25:1, the gospel text lacks any mention of the bride.

will disclose to you, that you may know that I am the Lord, the God of Israel, who calls your name, for the sake of Jacob my servant and Israel my chosen one."[4] For the sake of the covenants which he established with the fathers so that they should know him, God discloses to the body of Christ unseen treasures, "what eye has not seen, nor ear heard, nor the heart of man conceived"—but this is the hardened man who does not belong to the body of Christ; to the church, however, "God has revealed" it "through his Spirit" [1 Cor 2:9–10]. Such things, although this too is God's grace, are sometimes seen more easily when set forth by reason.

There are other cases in which reasoning of this kind is less clear, since what is said applies appropriately whether referred to the Lord or to his body. Consequently they can be understood only with the greater grace of God. Thus in the gospel he says: "from this moment you will see the son of man sitting at the right hand of power and coming on the clouds of heaven" (Matt 26:64). In another passage, however, he says that they will not see him coming on the clouds of heaven until the last day: "all the tribes of earth will mourn, and then they will see the son of man coming on the clouds of heaven" (Matt 24:30). Both comings must take place; but first there is the advent of the body, i.e., the church, which comes continuously in the same invisible glory, then the advent of the head, i.e., the Lord, in manifest glory. If he had said, "now you will see him coming," the advent of the body alone would have to be understood; if "you will see," the advent of the head. But in fact he says, "from this moment you will see him coming," since he comes continuously in his body through its birth and through its glory in sufferings like his own. For if those who are reborn become members of Christ and the members make up the body, then it is Christ who comes, since birth is a form of advent, as it is written: "he enlightens every man who comes into this world" (John 1:9). And again: "a generation goes and a generation comes" (Eccl 1:4). And again: "as you have heard that antichrist is coming" (1 John 2:18). Again, with reference to the same body: "for if the one who comes preaches another Jesus" (2 Cor 11:4). Thus, when the Lord was asked about the sign of his coming, he began to talk about that advent of his which the enemy body can imitate with signs and wonders. "Be on guard," he said, "lest anyone lead you astray; for many will come in my name" (Matt 24:4–5), i.e., in the name of my body. In contrast—whatever some may think—no one will speak falsely at the Lord's final advent, i.e., at the consummation and manifestation of his full advent. But we leave a fuller discussion of such matters to its proper place.

. . .

II. The Lord's Bipartite Body

Far more necessary is the rule concerning the bipartite character of the Lord's body; and so we must examine it all the more carefully, keeping it before our eyes

---

[4] Isa 45:1, 3–4. The Isaiah text uses the Hebrew word *meshiach* ("anointed one, messiah") and identifies with it the sixth-century B.C.E. Persian king Cyrus. The Septuagint translates *meshiach* as *christos* ("anointed one").

through all the scriptures. For just as the transition from head to body and back again, as indicated above, is only seen by reason, so also reason alone sees the transition and return from one part of the body to the other, from the right-hand part to the left or from the left to the right, as was clear in the previous section.

For when he tells the one body, "unseen treasures I will disclose to you, that you may know that I am the Lord, and I will take you to myself," he adds, "but you do not know me, that I am God and there is no other God besides me, and you were ignorant of me" (Isa 45:3–5). He is speaking to the one body; but do both phrases—"unseen treasures I will open to you, that you may know that I am God, for the sake of Jacob my servant," and, "but you do not know me"—refer to a single mind? Did Jacob, with one and the same mind, both receive and not receive God's promise? Or again, do both, "but you do not know me" and "you were ignorant of me," apply to the same mind? "You were ignorant" is an expression used only in speaking to someone who now knows; but "you do not know" is addressed to the person who "draws near to God with his lips, yet is far from him in his heart" (Isa 29:13), even though he was called precisely to know and, visibly speaking, belongs to exactly the same body. It is to this person that he says, "but you do not know me."

Again: "I will lead the blind in a way they do not know; and they will tread paths they do not know; and I will turn the darkness into light for them and make the crooked straight. I will do what I say, and I will not forsake them. But they have been turned back" (Isa 42:16–17). Are those who have been turned back the same ones of whom he said "I will not forsake them"—and not rather a part of them?

Again the Lord says to Jacob: "do not be afraid, for I am with you. I will bring your offspring from the east, and from the west I will gather you. I will say to the north, bring them up, and to the south, do not forbid them. Bring back my sons from far away and my daughters from the end of the earth, all among whom my name is invoked. For I fashioned him in my glory, and I formed and made him, and I have brought forth a blind people, and their eyes too are blind, and they have deaf ears" (Isa 43:5–8). Are the blind and the deaf the same ones whom he fashioned in his glory?

Again: "At the first your fathers and their princes committed a crime against me, and your princes defiled my sanctuary, and I gave Jacob to destruction and Israel to the curse. Now listen to me, Jacob my servant, and Israel whom I have chosen" (Isa 43:27–44:1). He shows us that the Jacob he gave to destruction, the Israel who was cursed, was the Jacob he had not chosen.

Again: "I formed you as my servant, you are mine, Israel; do not forget me. For, behold, I have swept away your crimes like a cloud and your sins like a mist. Turn to me and I will redeem you" (Isa 44:21–22). Is the one whose sins he has swept away, to whom he says, "you are mine," and whom he reminds not to forget him, the same one to whom he says, "turn to me"? Are anyone's sins swept away before he is turned?

Again: "I know that as one rejected you will be rejected. For my name's sake I will show you my greatness and will draw my excellence over you" (Isa 48:8–9). Does he show his greatness to the rejected or wrap him in his excellence?

Again: "It was not an elder nor an angel, but he himself who saved them, because he loved them and pitied them; he himself redeemed them and lifted them up and exalted them all the days of their life. But they were rebellious, and they grieved the Holy Spirit" (Isa 63:9–10). If he exalted them all the days of their life, when were they rebellious or when did they grieve the Holy Spirit?

Again, God plainly promises to the one body both that it will be kept safe and that it will be destroyed when he says, "Jerusalem, a rich city, whose tents will not be moved, nor will the pegs of your tent ever be disturbed or its ropes broken," and then adds, "your lines have been broken because the mast of your ship failed, your sails hung slack, and it will not raise its pennon until it is given over to destruction" (Isa 33:20, 23).

. . .

Accordingly it is by this mystery that we must interpret, throughout the scriptures, any passage where God says that Israel will perish as it deserves or that his own inheritance is accursed. For the apostle often argues, especially in Romans, that whatever is said of the whole body must be interpreted as applying to the part. "With respect to Israel, what does he say? All day I reached out my hands to a rebellious people." And to show that this refers to the part, he says, "I ask, has God rejected his inheritance? Not at all. For I am myself an Israelite, descended from Abraham by the tribe of Benjamin. God has not rejected his people whom he foreknew" (Rom 10:21–11:2). And after he has taught us how we are to understand this form of expression, he uses the same kind of expression to show that the one body is both good and evil when he says, "as regards the gospel they are enemies for your sake, but as regards election they are loved for their fathers' sake" (Rom 11:28). Are the enemies the same as the ones who are loved? Can both descriptions apply to Caiaphas? Thus, in all the scriptures, the Lord gives testimony that the one body of Abraham's line, in every case, both grows and flourishes and goes to ruin.

IV. The Particular and the General

I am not referring to the particular and the general as they are used in the rhetorical art devised by human wisdom. Although better able than anyone, Paul did not use that art—for fear that he would have made "the cross of Christ empty" (1 Cor 1:17) if, like falsehood, it needed the aid and ornament of eloquence. Rather I am speaking with reference to the mysteries of heavenly wisdom in relation to the teaching of the Holy Spirit. Making faith the price of truth, the Spirit produced an account marked by mysteries, concealing the general in the particular: for instance, the whole city, now spread throughout the world, in the old Jerusalem or the whole body in a single member such as Solomon. But this was hidden, as were the other things which are hidden not only by abridgment in the particular but also by the multiform character of the narrative. On this account, having asked the help of God's grace, we must spell out the "entries" (Sir 1:7) into reading and the "subtle" discourse of the "manifold Spirit" (Wis 7:22) so that, when he inserts the general into the particular or the particular into the general as an obstacle to understanding, we can easily see whether we are dealing with the particular or the general. For, while relating the particular, he passes over into the general in such a way that the transition is not immediately clear. Rather, in making the transition, he uses words that are appropriate to both until, little by little, he exceeds the mode of the particular, and the transition becomes plain to see. What had begun with the particular now fits only the general. And when he returns to the particular, he moves away from the general in the same manner.

Sometimes, however, he passes from the particular to the general not in the manner just described, but quite obviously, and then returns in the described fashion. Sometimes he makes the transition as described and returns quite obviously. With a similar variety of pattern, he may conclude in the general an account that began with the particular or conclude in the particular one that began with the general. Sometimes he does not altogether turn from the one to the other, and the whole narrative neither exceeds the particular nor omits the general but pertains to both. This variety of transition and order is what exacts the faith that seeks God's grace.

. . .

What shall we say of Solomon? Is he with God, or was he rejected after his idolatry? If we say he is with God, we will be promising impunity to people who worship idols. For scripture does not say that Solomon did penance or that he regained wisdom. But if we say he was rejected, we are stopped by God's voice saying that, for David's sake, he will not even take away Solomon's earthly kingdom, as it is written in Kings: "tearing, I will tear your kingdom from your hand and will give it to your servant. Yet, for the sake of your father David, I will not do this in your day. I will take it from your son's hand. Nor will I take the whole kingdom. For the sake of David my servant and for the sake of Jerusalem, my chosen city, I will give one scepter to your son" (1 Kgs 11:11–13). What good is it to David if, for his sake, his son gains the earthly kingdom only to lose the heavenly? It is clear, then, that Solomon is with God; for David's sake, not even his earthly kingdom was taken away, since he had also said: "I will chastise his sins with the rod of man, but I will not take my compassion from him" (2 Sam 7:14–15). But if it is neither true that he was rejected nor true that idol-worshipers possess the kingdom of God, then it is manifest that Solomon was a figure of the bipartite church: his "vast heart" and his "wisdom" were "like the sand of the sea" (1 Kgs 4:29), and his idolatry terrible.

"Tearing," he says, "I will tear your kingdom from your hand; yet I will not do this in your day. I will take it from your son's hand." "I will tear," would be enough. Why does he say, "tearing, I will tear"? And how is it "from Solomon's hand," if he says, "I will not do this in your day," but "will take it from your son's hand"? "Tearing, I will tear," indicates continuous action, like "blessing, I will bless, and, multiplying, I will multiply your descendants" (Gen 22:17).[5] For he is showing us that Solomon will always be present in his son, i.e., in his posterity. Under the promises made to the fathers, God does not take away the kingdom of this Solomon in later times, but corrects it for ever—and yet, with respect to the idolatry of the Solomon who perseveres in his sin, he constantly takes it away. How else does he either, tearing, tear or not tear the kingdom from Solomon's hand, if Solomon is not now good or evil as present in his sons? In saying, "nor do I take the whole kingdom," however, he returns to the particular and begins a new figure in Solomon's son and servant.

. . .

The foreign city of Nineveh is a figure of the bipartite church. But because it would take too long to go through the reading and explain it point by point, it will be enough to point out what cannot pertain to the particular. "Nineveh," it says, "was a great city with God" (Jonah 3:3), even though, as the chief city of the Assyrians, it was opposed to God since it destroyed Samaria and constantly oppressed all Judea. But, in a figure of the church, the whole city was completely delivered at the preaching of Jonah, i.e., of Christ. In a subsequent prophecy, the same Nineveh is described as destined to perish completely; in preaching to it, the Lord is "the sign of Jonah in the belly of the whale" (Matt 12:39–40). And to make sure that the prophet himself also shows that the city is not to be understood on the level of the particular, he introduces some things which exceed the mode of the particular. "There was no end to its peoples," he says, although it was actually a city of one ethnic stock. And again: "you have multiplied your tradings beyond the stars of heaven," i.e., beyond the church. And again: "upon whom has your malice not fallen all the time" (Nah 3:3, 16, 19)? Could the malice of one city have reached everyone or have done so all the time—unless it was the city that Cain founded in his brother's blood and gave "the name of his son" (Gen 4:17), i.e., his posterity?

The prophet teaches still more clearly that Nineveh is the church. "And," he says, "he will stretch out his hand against the north"—i.e., a people alien to the sun and set in opposition to the south—"and will destroy Assyria and make Nineveh a waste, without water, in the desert; and flocks will feed in the midst of her, all the beasts of the earth. And lizards and hedgehogs will sleep in her fancy ceilings, and beasts will give voice in her trenches and ravens in her gates, because she is as lofty as the cedar. A city of disdain, who dwells in hope, who says in her heart: here I am, and there is none after me! How she has gone to ruin, a pasture for the beasts! All who pass through her will hiss and shake their fists. O illustrious and redeemed city, a dove, who did not listen to the call, who did not accept instruction. She did not trust in the Lord and did not draw near to her God. Her rulers were like raging lions; her judges, like Arabian wolves, did not leave in the morning. Her prophets are puffed-up and disdainful men; her priests profane the holy and disgrace the law. But the Lord is just; he will not do injustice in her midst" (Zeph 2:13–3:5).

. . .

---

[5] Here Tyconius misinterprets, on the basis of the Greek or Latin translation available to him, what is actually a Hebrew grammatical contruction that brings emphasis or resolution to the action denoted by the verb: "I will surely tear"; "I will surely bless."

[The Phoenician city of] Tyre is bipartite, as in Isaiah who, after saying many things that relate to the particular and to the general, also goes on to say: "after the seventy years Tyre will be like the whore in the song: take your lyre, walk about, forgotten whore, forgotten city. Play your best, sing many songs, to make them remember you. And after the seventy years, God will look again to Tyre; and she will be restored to her former state and will have commerce with all the kingdoms of the earth" (Isa 23:15–17). Are we to believe that all the kingdoms of earth will come to Tyre to do business? And if they do come, what is gained by having foretold that Tyre would have "commercial dealings with all the kingdoms of the earth"—unless Tyre is the church, where the world's business is eternal life? For he goes on to show what her business is when he says, "and her business and her profit will be holy to the Lord. For the profit is not taken for themselves, but for those who dwell in the Lord's sight. All her business is to eat and to drink and to be filled as a sign and a memorial in the Lord's sight" (Isa 23:18). If therefore her business is holy to the Lord, how can it deal with all the kingdoms unless this Tyre is everywhere?

For he goes on to show openly what Tyre is, when he says, "behold, the Lord will lay waste the world and make it a desert and scrape its surface bare. He will scatter its inhabitants, priest as well as people"—those belonging to the world whose business is holy to the Lord?—"master as well as slave, mistress as well as maid, seller as well as buyer, creditor as well as debtor, lender as well as borrower. For the earth will be totally laid waste and will be made totally a desert, for the Lord's mouth has declared these things. The earth mourned, the world was laid waste, the depths of the earth mourned. The earth became guilty of crime on account of its inhabitants, because they transgressed the law and altered the precepts, the eternal covenant. Therefore a curse consumes the earth, because its inhabitants sinned. On this account the earth's inhabitants will be in want"—can those be in want whose "business" in "all the kingdoms of the earth" is "to eat and to drink and to be filled," not just for a time, but "as a sign and a memorial in the Lord's sight"?—"and few men will survive. The vine will lament, the wine will lament, all who are glad will sigh. The tambourines' mirth has ended; the shamelessness and the riches of the ungodly have ended." Will the sound of the saints' lyre come to an end? "They have been thrown into confusion; they have not drunk the wine; strong drink has turned bitter to those who drink it. Every city is deserted; they will shut up their houses to keep people out. Wail everywhere about the wine; all merriness has ended on earth; and the deserted cities will remain, and the derelict houses will perish. The earth will suffer all this in the midst of the nations" (Isa 24:1–13). If "every city is deserted," what are the nations in whose midst these things take place?

Even if some of this seems to be happening now in plain sight, it is still true that these are all spiritual matters. He says that every city is deserted inasmuch as it is spiritually dead; but he means the cities of Tyre the whore, not of the Tyre whose business is holy in all the world.

CHAPTER 7

Figurative, Literal, and Christian Meanings from Scripture: Augustine (354–430 C.E.)

B y most accounts Augustine was the greatest Christian leader of late antiquity, and probably the church's most influential figure apart from the apostle Paul. He was educated as a Latin rhetorician, thoroughly Roman in his language and intellect. Augustine's conversion to orthodox Christianity in 386 led him to a monastic way of life, to priesthood, and eventually to become the bishop of Hippo (in what is now called Algeria) in 397.

Among his voluminous works that treat philosophy, theology, and ecclesiology, it is Augustine's many writings in biblical interpretation that concern us here. When he, a highly educated Latin Christian, turned to the scriptures Augustine found himself disheartened by the obscurity of style overall and the sometimes unedifying morals featured in the lives of prominent biblical figures. But when he heard Ambrose of Milan present allegorical interpretations from scripture, Augustine realized that allegory provided a way to acceptably interpret the Bible and to refute the outright rejection of the Old Testament advocated by heretical groups such as the Manicheans (whom he had followed for nine years).[1] Through allegorical interpretation Augustine opened up scripture for pursuit of the Christian ideal of holy living within the philosophical framework of Neoplatonism: the observable world of things and events is actually an exterior manifestation of the true, intelligible world. Signals of the true world beyond visible phenomena can be detected in the phenomena by anyone with understanding who will penetrate the visible to perceive the invisible. Among those visible phenomena are words, which Augustine took to be signs of the doctrines that God was teaching through Scripture. Thus for Augustine what the Christian reader seeks to understand in Scripture is primarily the doctrines underlying the words of the text. The goal of such understanding, Augustine pointed out, is the increase of the Christian virtues: faith in God, hope in God, and love of God.[2]

In *On Christian Doctrine* Augustine was concerned to provide guidance for use of the Christian Scriptures to teachers of the Christian faith. Book One lays out the basic semiotic theory according to which language (as a sign system) and things that make up

---

[1] Manicheanism was a dualistic religion founded in the third century C.E. by the Persian teacher Mani. Manichean doctrine synthesized Christian, Buddhist and Zoroastian elements into a theism that taught the existence of a good deity and an evil deity.

[2] *On Christian Doctrine* 1:39–43.

reality (including the reality of the Christian faith) are to be taken as reliably related to each other. The things that make up reality have their place in an all-embracing heuristical hierarchy with God at its pinnacle; things have meaning for us according to the use to which we put them, but God has meaning apart from use—God is simply to be enjoyed, or loved. Proper use, or love, of all things (including other people) requires a correct understanding of their relative value in the context of God's order.

> But living a just and holy life requires one to be capable of an objective and impartial evaluation of things; to love things, that is to say, in the right order, so that you do not love what is not to be loved, or fail to love what is to be loved, or have a greater love for what should be loved less, or an equal love for things that should be loved less or more, or a lesser or greater love for things that should be loved equally. No sinner, precisely as sinner, is to be loved; and every human being, precisely as human, is to be loved on God's account, God though on his own. (1.28)[3]

Applied to the study of Scripture, this means that interpretation begins and ends with the love of God and love of neighbor. "So if it seems to you that you have understood the divine scriptures, or any part of them, in such a way that by this understanding you do not build up this twin love of God and neighbor, then you have not yet understood them" (1.40). Within the interpretive framework established by the authority of the church, every bit of Scripture properly understood will yield nothing else but the cultivation of this double love or the condemnation of that which is opposed to it. Thus there is to be found everywhere in Scripture, alongside the human author's intended meaning, a deeper meaning pointing the reader to this double love. The purpose of Scripture from the divine perspective is to yield this deeper meaning, and the purpose of exegesis is to uncover it among the signs that constitute the biblical text.

Book Two, then, has to do with exegetical challenges posed by signs the meaning of which is obscure (largely matters of history, grammar, text criticism, and translation[4]). Even if, however, the reader can be sure of the textual reading, or punctuation, or lexicographical details of a given passage, there can still remain interpretive difficulties that arise from signs the meaning of which is ambiguous (largely matters of figurative and literal expressions).

Augustine turned to this set of problems in Book Three, wherein he guided his reader in allegorical interpretation. In keeping with most early Christian hermeneutical practice, Augustine reflected the belief that Scripture bears an allegorical meaning regardless of whether or not the historical author intended any allegorical meaning. Yet the search for allegorical meaning was not to go so far as to obliterate the literal historical meaning. What was key in interpretation for Augustine was the *effect* of the interpretation:

---

[3] Augustine, *De doctrina christiana,* in *Teaching Christianity* (trans. Edmund Hill, O.P.; The Works of Saint Augustine: A Translation for the 21st Century; I/11]. Hyde Park, N.Y.: New City Press, 1996).

[4] The language in which Augustine worked as an interpreter of the Bible was Latin, for his command of Greek was mediocre and his knowledge of Hebrew practically nonexistent. In his exegesis of New Testament texts, Augustine made use of the Latin version once it had been produced by Jerome. But the Latin Old Testament translations Augustine favored were based on the Greek Septuagint, whose translators he believed had enjoyed special divine guidance. Nonetheless Augustine recognized the value for the interpreter to be familiar with both Greek and Hebrew (*On Christian Doctrine* 2.16).

within the horizon of the church's basic teaching (see Book One), if love *(caritas)* of God and neighbor is built up, or if selfish desire *(cupiditas)* is impugned, then the interpretation is a good one, regardless of the means—allegorical or literal—by which one arrives at it.[5]

For more information on Augustine:

Bright, Pamela, ed. *Augustine and the Bible.* Notre Dame: University of Notre Dame Press, 1999.

Fitzgerald, Allan et al., eds. *Augustine Through the Ages: An Encyclopedia.* Grand Rapids: Eerdmans, 1999.

Scott, T. Kermit. *Augustine: His Thought in Context.* New York: Paulist Press, 1995.

---

[5] Book Four is devoted to an adaptation of Tyconius's seven rules of interpretation commensurate with Augustine's Books I–III, and to reflection on the role of rhetoric in teaching and preaching unto salvation.

De doctrina christiana[6]

From the Prologue

1. There are some rules for dealing with the scriptures, which I consider can be not inappropriately passed on to students, enabling them to make progress not only by reading others who have opened up the hidden secrets of the divine literature, but also by themselves opening them up to yet others again. I have undertaken to pass these rules on to those who are both willing and well qualified to learn. . . .

9. . . . [J]ust as the person who knows how to read does not require another reader, when he gets hold of a volume, to tell him what is written in it, in the same way, those who have grasped the rules we are endeavoring to pass on will retain a knowledge of these rules, like letters, when they come across anything obscure in the holy books, and will not require another person who understands to uncover for them what is shrouded in obscurity. Instead, by following up certain clues, they will be able themselves to get the hidden meaning of a passage without any error—or at the very least to avoid falling into any absurdly wrongheaded opinion.

From Book One

39. So what all that has been said amounts to, while we have been dealing with things, is that *the fulfillment and the end of the law* and of all the divine scriptures *is love* (Rom 13:8; 1 Tim 1:5); love of the thing which is to be enjoyed, and of the thing which is able to enjoy that thing together with us, because there is no need for a commandment that we should love ourselves. So in order that we might know how to do this and be able to, the whole ordering of time was arranged by divine providence for our salvation. This we should be making use of with a certain love and delight that is not, so to say, permanently settled in, but transitory, rather, and casual, like love and delight in a road, or in vehicles, or any other tools and gadgets you like, or if you can think of any better way of putting it, so that we love the means by which we are carried along, on account of the goal to which we are being carried.

40. So if it seems to you that you have understood the divine scriptures, or any part of them, in such a way that by this understanding you do not build up this twin love of God and neighbor, then you have not yet understood them. If on the other hand you have made judgments about them that are helpful for building up this love, but for all that have not said what the author you have been reading actually meant in that place, then your mistake is not pernicious, and you certainly cannot be accused of lying. Being a liar, of course, means having the intention of saying what is

---

[6] These excerpts are taken from Augustine, *De doctrina christiana*, in *Teaching Christianity* (trans. Edmund Hill, O.P.; The Works of Saint Augustine: A Translation for the 21st Century; I/11. Hyde Park, N.Y.: New City Press, 1996), using the numbering system found therein. Used with permission.

false; and that is why we find many people intending to lie, but intending to be mistaken, none.

So since a person does the one thing knowingly, experiences the other thing unwittingly, it is abundantly obvious that over one and the same thing the person who is mistaken or deceived is better than the person who tells a lie. Everyone who tells a lie, after all, is committing iniquity; and if it seems to anyone that a lie may sometimes be useful, then it can also seem to him that iniquity is sometimes useful. No liar, after all, in the very act of telling a lie is keeping faith; but what he wants, of course, is that the person he tells it to should have faith in him, faith which by lying he is for all that failing to keep. But every violation of faith, or trust, is iniquitous. Either, therefore, iniquity is sometimes useful, which cannot be, or lying is never useful.

41. But any who understand a passage in the scriptures to mean something which the writer did not mean are mistaken, though the scriptures are not deceiving them. But all the same, as I had started to say, if they are mistaken in a judgment which is intended to build up charity, which is *the end of the law* (1 Tim 1:5), they are mistaken in the same sort of way as people who go astray off the road, but still proceed by rough paths to the same place as the road was taking them to. Still, they must be put right, and shown how much more useful it is not to leave the road, in case they get into the habit of deviating from it, and are eventually driven to take the wrong direction altogether.

But by rashly asserting something that the writer they are reading did not mean, people frequently hit upon other opinions which it is impossible to square with the author's meaning, such that if they are convinced these opinions are true and certain, what the writer meant cannot be true. Then it can happen with them, how I cannot tell, that they start being angrier with scripture than with themselves—a bad attitude which will be totally destructive if they allow it to spread. *For we walk by faith, not by sight* (2 Cor 5:7); but faith will start tottering if the authority of scripture is undermined; then with faith tottering, charity itself also begins to sicken. Because if you fall from faith, you are bound also to fall from charity; it is impossible, after all, to love what you do not believe exists. On the other hand, if you both believe and love, then by doing good and complying with the requirements of good morals, you ensure that you also hope to come eventually to what you love. And so we have these three things, for whose sake all knowledge and all prophecy are pressed into service, faith, hope, charity.

42. But faith gives way to sight, which we shall see, and hope gives way to bliss itself, which we are going to arrive at, while charity will actually grow when these other two fade out. After all, if we love by believing what we cannot yet see, how much more will we do so when we have begun to see it? And if we love, by hoping for it, what we have not yet attained to, how much more when we have attained to it? This, indeed, is the difference between temporal and eternal things, that something temporal is loved more before it is possessed, but loses its appeal when it comes along; this is because it cannot satisfy the soul, whose true and certain abode

is eternity. But anything eternal is loved more fervently when acquired than when just desired. This is because while you are desiring it, you cannot possibly think better of it than it really is, so that it disappoints you when you find it does not come up to your expectations; on the contrary, however great your estimate of it while you are on the way to it, you will find it exceeded when you eventually attain to it.

43. And so people supported by faith, hope and charity, and retaining a firm grip on them, have no need of the scriptures except for instructing others. And so there are many who live by these three even in the desert without books. This leads me to think that the text has already been fulfilled in them, *As for prophecies, they shall be done away with, as for tongues, they shall cease, as for knowledge, it shall be done away with* (1 Cor 13:8). But with them as a kind of scaffolding, such an impressive structure of faith and hope and charity has arisen, that these people, holding on to something perfect, do not seek that which is in part—perfect, of course, insofar as that is possible in this life; because compared with the future life not even the lives of holy and just people here below are perfect. That is why *there abide* he says, *faith, hope, charity; but the greatest of these is charity* (1 Cor 13:13), because when anyone attains to the things of eternity, while the first two fade away, charity will abide, more vigorous and certain than ever.

44. For that reason, when you come to realize *that the end of the law is love, from a pure heart, and a good conscience, and faith without pretense* (1 Tim 1:5), you will relate all the understanding of the divine scriptures to these three, and so be able to approach the study of those books without the least anxiety. When he said *love,* you see, he added *from a pure heart,* meaning that nothing else is loved except what should be loved. He brought in *a good conscience,* though, because of hope; it is those, after all, whose bad consciences trouble them like grit in their shoes, who despair of attaining to what they believe and love. Thirdly, *and faith,* he says, *without pretense.* If our faith lacks any falsity, then we do not love what ought not to be loved, and by living upright lives we hope for what we do love in such a way that our hope cannot possibly be disappointed.

From Book Two

12. . . . [T]he really accomplished investigators of the divine scriptures will be those who have begun by reading them all and becoming familiar with them at least by reading, if not yet by understanding them all—just those, that is, which are called canonical; because the others are best left to be read by people who are well instructed in the truths of faith, or else they may so enthrall the feebler spirits that they delude them with dangerous falsehoods and fancies to the prejudice of sound understanding. But for the canonical scriptures, they should follow the authority of the majority of the Catholic Churches, among which, of course, are those that have the privilege of being apostolic sees and having received letters from the apostles.

They will hold, therefore, to this standard with the canonical scriptures, that they will put those accepted by all the Catholic Churches before those which some do not accept; among these which are not accepted by all they will prefer those accepted by most of them, and by the greater ones among them, to those which fewer Churches and ones of lesser authority regard as canonical. Should they, however, discover that different ones are held to be canonical by the majority of Churches from those so regarded by the greater Churches—though this would be very unlikely—I consider that both should be regarded as having equal authority.

Augustine goes on to review the number, titles, and sequence of the canonical books recognized in the Western Christian churches. The books of the Old Testament, New Testament, and the Apocrypha make up this list.

14. What those who fear God and have a docile piety are looking for in all these books is the will of God. The first step in this laborious search, as I have said, is to know these books, and even if not yet so as to understand them, all the same by reading them to commit them to memory, or at least not to be totally unfamiliar with them. Next, those things that are put clearly in them, whether precepts about how to live or rules about what to believe, are to be studied with the utmost care and diligence; the greater your intellectual capacity, the more of these you will find. The fact is, after all, that in the passages that are put plainly in scripture is to be found everything that touches upon faith, and good morals, that is to say hope and charity, which we dealt with in the previous book.

Only then, however, after acquiring some familiarity with the actual style of the divine scriptures, should one proceed to try to open up and unravel their obscurities, in such a way that instances from the plainer passages are used to cast light on the more obscure utterances, and the testimony of some undoubted judgments is used to remove uncertainties from those that are more doubtful. In this matter what is of the greatest value is a good memory; if this is wanting, these instructions cannot be of any great assistance.

15. Now there are two reasons why texts are not understood: if they are veiled in signs that are either unknown or ambiguous. Signs, for their part, can be either proper or metaphorical. They are said to be proper when they are introduced to signify the things they were originally intended for, as when we say "ox" to signify the animal which everyone who shares the [Latin] language with us calls by this name. They are metaphorical when the very things which we signify with their proper words are made use of to signify something else, as when we say "ox," and by this syllable understand the animal which is usually so called, but again by that animal understand the evangelist, whom scripture itself signified, according to the apostle's interpretation of *You shall not muzzle the ox that threshes the corn* (1 Cor 9:9; Deut 25:4) [see also 1 Tim 5:18].

16. The best remedy for ignorance of proper signs is the knowledge of languages; and in addition to the . . . Latin language, the people whom I have now undertaken to advise have need of the two other languages of the divine scriptures, namely Hebrew and Greek, so that they can have recourse to the earlier versions whenever doubt about the meaning of a text is raised by the infinite variety of Latin . . . translations.

. . .

17. In fact, this state of affairs [i.e., several different available Latin translations from Greek and Hebrew] has been more of a help than a hindrance to the understanding of the scriptures, provided only that readers are not casual and careless. The examination of several versions has often been able to throw light on obscurer passages, as with that text of the prophet Isaiah (58:7 [LXX]), where one translation has, *And do not despise the household of your seed,* and another has, *And do not despise your own flesh.* Each corroborates the other; that is, each can be explained by the other, because on the one hand flesh could be taken in the proper sense, so that the reader could suppose he was being warned not to despise his own body; while on the other the household of one's seed could be understood metaphorically as Christians, born spiritually from the same seed of the word as ourselves.

But now, putting the minds of the translators together, we hit upon the more probable meaning that we are being commanded, according to the literal sense, not to despise our blood relations, because when you connect the household of your seed with your flesh, it is your blood relations that immediately occur to you. I am sure that that is what the apostle meant when he said, *If I may by any means provoke my own flesh to jealousy, in order to save some of them* (Rom 11:14); that is, that by being jealous of those who had believed, they themselves might come to believe as well. By his flesh, clearly, he meant the Jews, because of their blood relationship.

Again, there is that text of the same prophet Isaiah, *Unless you believe, you shall not understand,* which another translator rendered, *Unless you believe, you shall not endure* (Isa 7:9 [LXX]). Which of these two, though, followed the original words one cannot tell, unless one reads copies of the original language. But all the same, for those who are shrewd readers, something important is being suggested by each version. It is difficult, after all, for translators to differ so much from each other, that they do not come close to some extent. So then, understanding refers to everlasting sight, while faith in temporal things as in a kind of cradle is, so to say, nourishing little ones on milk; now, however, *we are walking by faith and not by sight* (2 Cor 5:7), but unless we walk by faith, we shall never be able to reach the sight which does not pass away but endures, when with our understanding purified we cleave to Truth. And that is why one translator says, *Unless you believe, you shall not endure,* while the other has, *Unless you believe, you shall not understand.*

Augustine goes on to give further examples of ambiguities generated by translators.

From Book Three

2. [W]hen ambiguities arise in scripture about the meaning of words used in their proper sense, the first thing we must do is see whether we have phrased or pronounced them wrongly.[7] So when, on paying closer attention, you still see that it is

---

[7] Ancient Greek and Latin manuscripts were usually inscribed in *scriptio continua*, without any space inserted between words or sentences. Reading from such manuscripts—almost always out

uncertain how something is to be phrased, or how to be pronounced, you should refer it to the rule of faith, which you have received from the plainer passages of scripture and from the authority of the Church, about which we dealt sufficiently when we were talking in the first book about *things*. But if both possibilities, or all of them, if it is a multiple ambiguity, are consonant with the faith, it remains to refer to the whole context, to the sections that precede and that follow the ambiguous passage, holding it in the middle between them, so that we may see which of the several meanings that present themselves the context will vote for and allow to fit in with itself.

3. Straightaway now, consider some examples. There is that heretical phrasing: *In principio erat Verbum et Verbum erat apud Deum et Deus erat* [John 1:1–2],[8] adopted in order to give another meaning to the next phrase: *Verbum hoc erat in principio apud Deum;* [9] this is a refusal to confess that the Word is God. But this is to be refuted by the rule of faith, which prescribes for us the equality of the three divine persons, so that we have to say, *et Deus erat Verbum;* and then add, *Hoc erat in principio apud Deum.*[10]

Augustine goes on to offer more examples of ambiguities created by incorrect phrasing during the reading of Scripture.

6. Now everything we have said about ambiguous phrasing is to be observed with ambiguities over pronunciation. These too, except where they arise from the carelessness of the reader, are to be settled either by the standard of faith, or by the context of what precedes and what follows; or if neither serves to resolve the doubt, then whichever way the reader pronounces the word, he will not be at fault.

For example, unless we were held back by the faith by which we believe that God is not going to accuse his chosen ones, and Christ is not going to condemn his chosen ones, we could pronounce the passage, *Who will bring an accusation against God's chosen ones?* as though the reply to this question followed immediately, *God, who justifies them;* and then again when the question is asked, *Who is it that will condemn them?* as though the answer came, *Christ Jesus who died* (Rom 8:33–34). But because it would be the last word in lunacy to believe that, it will be pronounced in such a way that first we have a challenging inquiry, and then this is followed by an interrogatory question. The difference between an inquiry and an interrogatory

---

loud and in the company of others—required great skill and familiarity with the rhetorical cadences of good literature. Incorrectly anticipating the proper breaks between words and phrases would result in misreading; when the text was Christian Scripture, misreading could result in misinterpretations with weighty doctrinal implications. For an excellent introduction to the subject, see M. B. Parkes, *Pause and Effect: An Introduction to the History of Punctuation in the West* (Berkeley: University of California Press, 1993).

8 "In the beginning was the word, and the Word was with God, and God was."
9 "This Word was in the beginning with God."
10 "the Word was with God, and the Word was God; this was in the beginning with God."

question, according to the ancient authors, is that to an inquiry many answers can be given, while to an interrogatory question only a "no" or a "yes." So then it will be pronounced in such a way that after our inquiry, saying *Who will bring an accusation against God's chosen ones?* what follows is spoken in an interrogatory tone, *God, who justifies them?* so that the tacit reply to this is, "No." And again we inquire *Who is it that will condemn them?* and once more ask the interrogatory question, *Christ Jesus who died, or rather who rose again, who is at God's right hand, who is also interceding for us?* so that all the time the tacit answer is "No."

On the other hand, in the passage where it says, *So then, what are we to say? That the nations who were not in pursuit of justice laid hold of justice* (Rom 9:30), unless to the inquiry, *So then, what are we to say?* the affirmative reply comes, *That the nations who were not in pursuit of justice laid hold of justice,* it would not be coherent with the following context. But in whatever tone you pronounce what Nathanael said, *A Nazareth potest aliquid boni esse*[11] (John 1:46); whether as though he were making an affirmation, so that the only interrogatory part would be *A Nazareth?* or as though the whole sentence expressed the questioner's doubt, I cannot see how it should be decided, the sense given in each case presenting no obstacle to faith.

. . .

9. But ambiguities arising from metaphorical language, about which we have to talk from now on, call for no ordinary care and attention. For in the first place, you have to beware of taking a figurative expression literally. And this is where the apostle's words are relevant, *The letter kills, but the spirit gives life* (2 Cor 3:6). When something that is said figuratively, you see, is taken as though it were meant in its proper literal sense, we are being carnal in our way of thinking. Nor can anything more suitably be called the death of the soul than when that in it too, which surpasses the brute beasts, that is to say its intelligence, subjects itself to the flesh by following the letter.

When you follow the letter, you see, you take in their proper literal sense words that are being used metaphorically, and fail to refer what is signified in this proper sense to the signification of something else; but if, for example, you hear the word "sabbath," and all you understand by it is this one of the seven days which recurs week by week; and when you hear the word "sacrifice," your thoughts do not go beyond what is usually done with victims from the flock and the fruits of the earth. This, precisely, is the wretched slavery of the spirit, treating signs as things, and thus being unable to lift up the eyes of the mind above bodily creatures, to drink in the eternal light.

. . .

---

[11] "Can anything good come from Nazareth?"

14. To this warning against treating figurative expressions, that is metaphorical ones, as though they were meant in the literal, proper sense, we also have to add this one, to beware of wanting to treat literal, proper statements as though they were figurative. So first of all we must point out the method for discovering if an expression is proper or figurative. And here, quite simply, is the one and only method: anything in the divine writings that cannot be referred either to good, honest morals or to the truth of the faith, you must know is said figuratively. Good honest morals belong to loving God and one's neighbor, the truth of the faith to knowing God and one's neighbor. As for hope, that lies in everybody's own conscience, to the extent that you perceive yourself to be making progress in the love of God and neighbor, and in the knowledge of them. All this formed the subject of the first book.

15. The human race, however, is inclined to judge sins, not according to the gravity of the evil desire involved, but rather with reference to the importance attached to their own customs. So people frequently reckon that only those acts are to be blamed which in their own part of the world and their own time have been customarily treated as vicious and condemned, and only those acts to be approved of and praised which are acceptable to those among whom they live. Thus it can happen that if scripture either commands something which does not accord with the customs of the hearers, or censures something which does fit in with them, they assume they are dealing with a figurative mode of speech—if, that is, their minds are bound by the authority of God's word. Scripture, though, commands nothing but charity, or love, and censures nothing but cupidity, or greed, and that is the way it gives shape and form to human morals.

Again, if people's minds are already in thrall to some erroneous opinion, whatever scripture may assert that differs from it will be reckoned by them to be said in a figurative way. The only thing, though, it ever asserts is Catholic faith, with reference to things in the past and in the future and in the present. It tells the story of things past, foretells things future, points out things present; but all these things are of value for nourishing and fortifying charity or love, and overcoming and extinguishing cupidity or greed.

16. What I mean by charity or love is any urge of the spirit to find joy in God for his own sake, and in oneself and one's neighbor for God's sake; by cupidity or greed any impulse of the spirit to find joy in oneself and one's neighbor, and in any kind of bodily thing at all, not for God's sake. Now what unrestrained greed does by way of corrupting the human spirit and its body can be called infamous, while whatever it does to harm someone else can be called criminal. And all sins fall into these two categories, but infamous deeds come first. When these have drained the spirit dry and reduced it to a kind of want, it bursts out into criminal acts in order to eliminate obstacles to its infamous behavior, or to secure assistance in it.

Again, what charity does, or love, to profit self is usefulness, while whatever it does to profit the neighbor is called kindness. And here usefulness comes first, because one cannot profit one's neighbor with what one does not have oneself. For the more the kingdom of greed is whittled away, so much the more is that of love increased.

17. So then anything we read of in the scriptures as coming from the person of God or his saints that sounds harsh and almost savage in deed and word is of value for whittling away the kingdom of greed. And if its meaning is crystal-clear, it is not to be referred to something else, as though it were said figuratively like this from the apostle: *He is storing up for himself wrath on the day of wrath and of the revelation of the just judgment of God, who will pay back each and all according to their works; to those indeed who by patient endurance in doing good are seeking glory and honor and imperishability, eternal life; to those however who are given to quarrels and who distrust the truth while they trust iniquity, wrath and indignation. Tribulation and distress upon every human soul that works evil, Jew first and also Greek* (Rom 2:5–9). But this is being addressed to those who are being overthrown together with their greed, because they have been unwilling to overcome it.

But when the kingdom of greed is being undermined in those people it used to dominate, we have this plain statement: *But those who are Jesus Christ's, have crucified their flesh, with its passions and lusts* (Gal 5:24), except that in these instances too some words are to be treated as metaphorical, such as "the wrath of God" and "have crucified"; but they are not so many, or so placed, as to obscure the plain sense and make it all into an allegory or a riddle, which is what I properly call a figurative expression. But coming to what Jeremiah was told, *Behold, I have set you today over nations and kingdoms, to pull down and to destroy, and to scatter and to rout* (Jer 1:10), it is undoubtedly all a figurative utterance, to be referred to that end which we have mentioned.

18. Those things, however, that strike the ignorant as infamous, whether they are only said, or also done, whether attributed to God or to men whose holiness is being commended to us, they are all to be taken as figurative, and their secret meanings have to be winkled out for the nourishment of charity. Anyone, though, who makes use of passing things more sparingly than is customary with those among whom he lives, is either temperate or superstitious, while anyone who makes use of them in a way that exceeds the bounds that are acceptable to the good people among whom he spends his time is either signifying something, or is behaving infamously. In all such cases it is not the use of things, but the caprice of the user that is at fault.

Nor will any in their right mind even begin to believe that the Lord's feet were anointed by the woman with precious ointment (Matt 26:7–12) in the same sort of way as wantonly extravagant and worthless people are familiar with, in those orgies of theirs which we abominate. The good odor, after all, stands for the good reputation which those of good life will have from their works, while they follow in Christ's footsteps, and as it were shed over his feet the most precious fragrance. Thus what is generally infamous in other persons is, in the person of God or a prophet, the sign of some important reality. Certainly, association with a harlot is one thing in men of abandoned morals, another in the prophetic activity of Hosea [see Hos 1:2–3]; nor, if it is infamous conduct to strip off your clothes in drunken and licentious parties, does that mean that it is equally infamous to be naked in the baths.

19. So we have to pay careful attention to what befits places and times and persons, in order not to judge behavior rashly as infamous. It can happen, after all, that a wise person will make use of the most expensive food without a hint of the vice of self-indulgence or greediness, while a fool will be disgustingly on fire with gluttony for the cheapest stuff imaginable. And sane people would much rather eat fish as the Lord did [see Luke 24:42] than lentils in the way Esau, Abraham's grandson, did (Gen 25:34), or oats the way horses do. Just because most wild animals, after all, live on less refined kinds of food than we do, this does not mean that they are more self-restrained than we are. For in all matters of this kind it is not the nature of the things we make use of, but our reason for making use of them and the manner in which we set about getting them, that decides whether what we do deserves approval or disapproval.

20. The just men of old in the earthly kingdom pictured the heavenly kingdom to themselves, and foretold it. Provision of offspring was the reason for the blameless custom of one man having several wives at once; and that is why it was not also decent for one woman to have many husbands, because that does not make her any the more fruitful. To seek either gain or children by sleeping around is simply the disgraceful style of the prostitute. In this sphere of morals scripture does not find fault with whatever the holy men of those times did without lustfulness, although they did what today can only be done out of lust or lechery. And all such stories as are told there are not only to be interpreted literally as historical accounts, but also to be taken figuratively as prophetic in some way, pointing to that end of the love of God or of neighbor, or of both.

Thus it was a matter of infamy among the ancient Romans to wear ankle-long, long-sleeved tunics, whereas now it is infamous for those born to high station not to wear them, even when they are informally dressed. In the same sort of way we have to observe that such lustful inclinations should be banished from every other kind of use we make of things; for not only do they vilely abuse the very customs of the people among whom one is living, but they will even exceed all bounds and erupt, very often, in the most infamous display of their ugliness, which was previously lurking concealed behind the enclosure walls of conventional morals.

21. But anything that fits in with the customs of those among whom this life has to be spent, and is either imposed on one by necessity or undertaken out of duty, is to be seen as directed by good and important people to the end of usefulness and of kindness, either literally, which is how we too should do it, or even figuratively, as befits the prophets.

22. When unlearned people who have other customs come across such deeds in their reading, they think, unless checked by authority, that they are acts of infamy, and they are quite unable to appreciate that the whole of their own way of life, in their marriages, or their parties, or their clothing, and in all other aspects of human

life and culture, would seem infamous to other nations and other times. Some people, moved by the variety of innumerable customs, and half asleep, if I may so put it, being neither sunk in the deep slumber of folly, nor able to wake up fully to the light of wisdom, have supposed that there is no such thing as justice in itself, but that each nation takes it for granted that its own customs are just; as these differ from nation to nation, while justice ought to remain immutable, it becomes obvious, they conclude, that there is no justice anywhere.

They have not understood, to mention just one point, that *What you do not wish done to you, do not do to another* (Tob 4:15) can suffer no variation through any diversity of national customs. When this maxim is referred to love of God, all infamous conduct dies; when to love of neighbor, all crimes. We none of us, after all, like our dwellings ruined; so we ought not to ruin God's dwelling, namely ourselves. And we none of us wish to be harmed by anyone else; therefore let us not harm anyone else ourselves.

23. The tyranny of cupidity or greed being thus overthrown, charity or love reigns supreme with its just laws of loving God for God's sake, and oneself and one's neighbor for God's sake. So this rule will be observed in dealing with figurative expressions, that you should take pains to turn over and over in your mind what you read, until your interpretation of it is led right through to the kingdom of charity. But if this is already happening with the literal meaning, do not suppose the expression is in any way a figurative one.

24. If it is an expression of command, either forbidding infamy or crime, or ordering usefulness or kindness, it is not figurative. But if it seems to command infamy or crime, or to forbid usefulness or kindness, then it is figurative. *Unless you eat,* he says, *the flesh of the Son of man and drink his blood, you shall not have life in you* (John 6:53). He seems to be commanding a crime or an act of infamy; so it is said figuratively, instructing us that we must share in the Lord's passion, and store away in our minds the sweet and useful memory that his flesh was crucified and wounded for our sakes.

Scripture says, *If your enemy is hungry, feed him; if he is thirsty, give him a drink.* Here there can be no doubt that it is enjoining a kindness upon us. But with what follows: *For in doing this you will be heaping coals of fire upon his head* (Rom 12:20; Prov 25:21–22), you might suppose a spiteful crime is being commanded. So you must have no doubt that it is said figuratively; and while it can be interpreted in two ways, in one for doing harm, in the other for giving support, let charity rather call you back to kindness, and to understanding by coals of fire the red hot pangs of repentance, which heal the pride of the man, who is grieved at having been the enemy of the person he is being helped by in his plight.

Again, when the Lord says, *Whoever loves his life, let him throw it away* (John 12:25), he must not be supposed to be forbidding those useful acts by which we all ought to preserve our lives. But "let him throw away his life" is said figuratively; that is, let him do away with and lose that use he now makes of it, namely a perverse and topsy-turvy use, so taken up with temporal things that he gives no thought to eternity.

It is written, *Give to the kindhearted person, and do not support the sinner* (Sir 12:4). The second part of this maxim seems to be forbidding a kindness, in saying *do not support the sinner.* So you should understand that "sinner" is put figuratively for sin, and thus it means you must not support him in his sin.

CHAPTER 8

Anchoring the Text in History

Early Syrian Biblical Interpretation: Theodore of Mopsuestia (350–428 C.E.) and Theodoret of Cyrus (393–457 C.E.)

I n the region of northern Mesopotamia—today found within the borders of Syria, south-western Turkey, and northern Iraq—the Christian church had been established since apostolic times. For the first several centuries, exegesis and liturgy were expressed primarily in Greek and based on the Septuagint, as they were elsewhere in the eastern half of the Roman Empire. By the mid-fifth century, however, Syriac (a dialect of Aramaic) was so widely used in the regional churches as to bring about the emergence of the Syriac Bible, known as the Peshitta. This linguistic shift is indicative of the dual cultural influences upon Syrian religious thought, coming from the Semitic world of the Middle East and the Greco-Roman world of the Mediterranean West. Other results of this cultural blend included a distinctive exegetical orientation, one less enthusiastic for figurative interpretation than what we find in the rest of the church during the first half of the first millennium.

For centuries the city of Antioch was the ecclesiastical hub for this region of the world, and often the more historically oriented interpretive tradition of the early Syriac church is referred to as the Antiochene school (usually contrasted with the more figuratively oriented Alexandrian school of interpretation). Among early Antiochene exegetes, the grounds for theologically understanding narrative texts in the Old and New Testaments were the events to which the words of Scripture referred and not so much the isolated words found in the narratives themselves. At the hands of Alexandrian interpreters such as Origen, allegorical exegesis, so centrally focused on the spiritual significance of the words that make up Scripture, sometimes paid minimal regard to the larger compositional integrity of biblical texts. Antiochene interpreters generally adopted a less atomistic approach to the biblical text and brought a greater emphasis on the literal (or, as they would put it, historical) sense of biblical narratives.

We would be mistaken, however, to suppose that the exegetical relationship between Antioch and Alexandria was one of absolute opposition. Ancient Oriental Christian interpreters shared broad agreement on traditional exegesis while bringing special emphasis on distinct points of view. The nature of this distinction between Antioch and Alexandria may be best understood as the difference in the ancient world between two widely practiced approaches to interpreting literature. In the various philosophical schools, interpretation served to discern abstract metaphysical and moral teachings, and verbal figuration or allegory provided a way for the reader to participate in the truth of such teachings. Among Christians, this can be observed in Origen and other leading allegorists. In the rhetorical schools of antiquity, however, interpretation of texts, supported by the technical details of proper grammatical exegesis, aimed to identify concrete examples of morality and doctrine in the text's narrative presentation. The Antiochene biblical scholars were generally more influenced by Greco-Roman rhetorical schools of thought than by formal philosophical training. Thus Antiochene readings of Scripture offered up models of literary and moral excellence for imitation, exegeted from the way the whole of the biblical book or passage was narratively or discursively constructed. Biblical interpretation that tended to disintegrate literary coherence, as philosophical allegory seemed to do, was considered by Antiochene exegetes methodologically illegitimate and suspect for the theological results it could produce. True to the ideals of ancient rhetorical hermeneutics, the concern for "history" among the Antiochenes had more to do with respecting narrative integrity and rightly understanding the biblical author's intent than with historicity in the strict modern sense (allowing for the possible exception of Theodore of Mopsuestia).

Regarding Old Testament interpretation, the Antiochene approach sometimes produced results at odds with major Christian writers in other parts of the church. As we have seen in earlier selections, many Christian interpreters understood Old Testament texts as characteristically referring prophetically to events of the New Testament or of the early Christian church. Among the Antiochenes, the narrative horizon of the Old Testament historical books served to control and restrict the meaning of other Old Testament texts. For example, David was indeed understood to have prophesied in the Psalms, but his prophecies were largely fulfilled in the era of Hezekiah, Zerubbabel, or the Maccabees, as we find in the Psalms commentary by Theodoret of Cyrus. More extremely, often by virtue of careful attention to verbal tenses in the Septuagint text, Theodore of Mopsuestia denied the presence of any direct messianic prophecies in the Psalms (with the exception of Pss 2, 7, 14, and 110). This tendency remains true throughout Theodore's Old Testament interpretations, most conspicuously in the case of the prophetic books. Only christological types and predictions clearly identified in the Jewish Scriptures by the inspired New Testament writers were accepted by Theodore; he repudiated most others offered by Christian apologists and exegetes. Antiochene exegetes tended to consider carefully the genre of an Old Testament book and the occasion and circumstances for its composition as well as the question of authorship. Theodore regarded these factors so important that in their light he evaluated the degree of inspiration for individual biblical writings. For example, because he concluded that Song of Songs was composed for performance at Solomon's wedding to an Egyptian princess (cf. 1 Kgs 11:1), Theodore denied it was an allegory of God's love for his people, contrary to ubiquitous Jewish and Christian interpretive traditions. Because Theodore took the Psalms' superscriptions to be later additions to the text dating from the Maccabean period, they held almost no importance for him in his exegesis. Compared with Theodore, Theodoret of Cyrus is somewhat more representative of the Antiochene tradition, and of Christian scholarship in general at the time, in that he accepted the Psalms' superscriptions as accurate indicators of their compositional situations.

The textual legacy of these two writers helps indicate the place that Syrian biblical exegesis established in the history of biblical interpretation. During his lifetime Theodore of Mopsuestia was accepted by the church as an orthodox teacher in relation to the heretical movements that proliferated in the fourth and fifth centuries. In subsequent generations, however, his writings fell under severe suspicion when heretics used them amid the elagian and Nestorian controversies. As a result, most of his voluminous oeuvre was condemned and destroyed—including his commentaries on almost every book in the Christian Bible, and an entire treatise refuting allegorical biblical interpretation.[1] Theodore's rigidly historicist views did not widely prevail despite his influence on eastern Syrian biblical hermeneutics when, in the sixth century, his methods were further integrated with Aristotelian principles of interpretation. The situation is different with Theodoret of Cyrus. His extant commentaries (covering most of the Old Testament and the Pauline Epistles) are well attested and were widely utilized in the writings of later Christian writers. This may be owing to Theodoret's brevity of style compared with most ancient Christian commentators as well as to his more nuanced, moderate position on typological and figurative interpretation compared with his Mopsuestian elder. Another consideration must surely be the fact that Theodoret's orthodoxy was never questioned.

The following selection from Theodore's commentary on the Epistle to the Galatians exhibits something of his distinctive hermeneutical position on the topic of literal and allegorical interpretation. The commentary on Psalm 30 by Theodoret of Cyrus represents the more usual way the Old Testament was interpreted in the Syrian Christian tradition.

For further information on Early Syrian Biblical Interpretation:

Genuinot, Jean-Noël. "Theodoret of Cyrus: Bishop and Exegete." Pages 163–93 in *The Bible in Greek Christian Antiquity.* Edited and translated by P. M . Blowers. Notre Dame, Ind.: University of Notre Dame Press, 1997.

Nassif, Bradley. "Spiritual Exegesis in the School of Antioch." Pages 343–77 in *New Perspectives on Historical Theology: Essays in Memory of John Meyendorff.* Edited by Bradley Nassif. Grand Rapids: Eerdmans, 1996.

Wallace-Hadrill, D. S. *Christian Antioch: A Study of Early Christian Thought in the East.* New York: Cambridge University Press, 1982.

Young, Frances. "The Rhetorical Schools and Their Influence on Patristic Exegesis." Pages 182–99 in *The Making of Orthodoxy: Essays in Honour of Henry Chadwick.* Edited by R. Williams. Cambridge: Cambridge University Press, 1989.

Zaharopoulos, Dimitri Z. *Theodore of Mopsuestia on the Bible: A Study of His Old Testament Exegesis.* New York: Paulist, 1989.

---

[1] Theodore of Mopsuestia, *On Allegory and the Historical Sense.* Aside from fragments of his commentaries, only Theodore's work in the Psalms, the Minor Prophets, the Gospel of John (in Syriac translation), and the Pauline Epistles (in Latin translation) remain.

Theodore of Mopsuestia (350–428 C.E.)

Commentary on Galatians [2]

As Theodore makes clear the meaning of Gal 4:22–23 in the context of Paul's larger argument in the epistle, he uses the occasion to point out the illegitimacy and danger of allegorizing as a method of interpretation.

For it is written that "Abraham had two sons, one by a slave and one by a free woman." But the son of the slave was born according to the flesh, the son of the free woman from promise (Gal 4:22–23).

Paul makes plain, above, that the law can have nothing in common with the promises; the Law requires fulfillment of its demands while the promise reveals the giver's generosity. By all of this, Paul wanted to confirm the principle of grace; in the same way, he reminds us of faith and promises along with those other things which we hope to obtain. Over all these things he set the Law—the end of which is righteousness which it promises to those who are, first, obedient to the Law. In fact, it misleads many and, I tell you the truth, probably everyone, because those who try to satisfy the demands of the Law find it impossible to do so.

Paul, therefore, makes it of utmost importance that righteousness is by grace and that such righteousness is better than the righteousness resulting from the fulfillment of the requirements of the Law; God, in his generosity, bestows righteousness, and no one—because of his natural human weakness—is left out. Furthermore, Paul makes that same point over again, the point he illustrated above, with the story of Abraham—that Abraham had two sons, one a natural son from a mere sexual liaison, the other a legitimate son and heir as a divine gift: "For it is written that 'Abraham had two sons, one by a slave and one by a free woman.' But the son of the slave was born according to the flesh"—that is, he was born of a natural physical union. The phrase "according to the flesh" means that birth is an act of the natural, physical body, so Ishmael was born out of a natural physical act of Abraham and Hagar. On the other hand, "the son of the free woman was born through a promise," that is, as a consequence of divine favor. Indeed, all promises are made only by divine favor or grace. So, if one takes the order of nature seriously, one cannot say that Isaac had an ordinary human birth. Sarah could not have had a child for two reasons: she was barren, and, by that time, she was past the age of childbearing in any event. At the same time, Abraham himself was too old to beget a child. Nevertheless, Isaac was born contrary to all expectation and to the laws of nature, solely through the excellence and generosity of him who gave the promise. Now, after reminding us of the story of

[2] Theodore of Mopsuestia's commentary on the Epistle to the Galatians (trans. Paige Lindsey and F. Lewis Shaw; based on H. B. Swete, *Theodori episcopi mopsuesteni in epistolas b. Pauli Commentarii* [2 vols.; Cambridge: Cambridge University Press, 1880–1882], 1:72–81), in Joseph W. Trigg, *Biblical Interpretation* (Message of the Fathers of the Church 9; Wilmington, Del.: Michael Glazier, 1988), 172–77. Used with permission.

Abraham as we read it in the Bible, Paul goes on to add—because he is eager to explain why he has drawn on this story—"Now this is an allegory" (Gal 4:24a).

Countless students of scripture have played tricks with the plain sense of the Bible
and want to rob it of any meaning it contains. In fact, they make up inept fables and call
their inanities "allegories." They so abuse the Apostle's paradigm as to make the holy
texts incomprehensible and meaningless. They go to much trouble to say just what the
Apostle says, "This is by way of an allegory," but they have no idea how far they stray
from what Paul is saying here. That is because he neither dismisses the historical narrative nor is he adding new things to an old story. Instead, Paul is talking about events as
they happened, then submits the story of those events to his present understanding.

For example, he says in one place, "She corresponds to the present Jerusalem"
(Gal. 4:25) and in another, "But as at that time he who was born according to the
flesh persecuted him who was born according to the Spirit" (Gal. 4:29). Above all
else, Paul acknowledges the historicity of the account. Otherwise he could not say
that Hagar "corresponds to the present Jerusalem," thus acknowledging that Jerusalem does exist in the here and now. Neither would he say "just as" had he referred to
a non-existent person. By saying "just as" he demonstrates an analogy, but an analogy cannot be demonstrated if the things compared do not exist. In addition he says
"at that time," indicating the particular time as uncertain or indefinite, but he would
not have had to distinguish the particular time if nothing at all had really happened.
This is the Apostle's manner of speaking.

Those allegorizers, though, turn it all inside out, as if the accounts in the Bible
were no different from dreams in the night. They do their exegesis of scripture "spiritually"—they like to call this silliness "spiritual interpretation." Adam is not Adam,
paradise is not paradise, and the serpent is not a serpent. I want to tell those interpreters this: if they play tricks with history, in the end they will have no history. But, if
they insist on such explanations, let them answer these questions: Who was the first
man made? How was he disobedient? How was the sentence of death introduced? If
they have any answers from the Bible, then what they call "allegory" is exposed as
foolishness, because, throughout, it is proven to be over and above what is necessary. If, however, their "allegory" is true, if the Bible does not retain one account of
actual events but truly points to something else altogether, something so profound as
to require special understanding, something "spiritual," as they wish to call it, which
they have uncovered because they themselves are so spiritual, then where does their
understanding come from? Whatever they call this type of interpretation, has the
Bible itself taught them to read it like this?

I shall not even talk about—if they are right in this—the fact that not even the
reason for the events in Christ's life will be plain. As the Apostle says, Christ canceled
out Adam's disobedience and revoked his death sentence (cf. Rom 5:18ff.). What
are these past events he refers to and where did they happen? According to the
allegorizer, if the scriptural account does not describe actual events, then it means
something altogether different. What are we to make of the Apostle's words, "But I
fear lest, as the serpent seduced Eve" (2 Cor 11:3), if there was no serpent, no Eve,

nor a seduction? So, in many places the Apostle explicitly takes the historical account of ancient writers as unquestionably factual. In this passage he is trying to make his case from real, historical events which the Jews testify to as being true. Indeed, that was what he intended from the beginning—but to what purpose? He desires to demonstrate that the things Christ accomplished are greater than those recounted in the Law and that the righteousness we can have is manifestly more honorable than the righteousness in the Law.

This is why Paul says that there are two covenants, one coming through Moses and the other through Christ. Furthermore, he calls the covenant in Christ the resurrection promised to all of us, Christ himself being the first to rise from the dead. This we explained in detail in our exposition of the Epistle to the Hebrews.

That which was given through Moses was given with the express intention that those given the Law would live under it and, consequently, receive the righteousness which comes from the Law. This was why those who received the Law left Egypt and were settled in a far-off place, so that, separated from every other nation, they would be able to heed with due prudence the law given to them.

So it was the intention and the fulfillment of the work of Christ to cancel out death and, in fact, to raise from death all people, even while they still lived, to an immortal nature. They are no longer, by any means, able to fall into sin, since the Spirit of grace lives in them. Because of this, we will be kept safe from every sin. This is the true and perfect righteousness. For just cause, therefore, Paul calls both of these like things "covenants," since the Law pointed to the very same end as the work of grace, namely, that God and neighbor are to be loved above all else.

The Law, of course, demanded obedience to all its regulations, keeping the people separated from others and so teaching them that no one ought ever to sin. The work of grace, by contrast, fulfills these demands by the resurrection and through immortality which will be ours through the Spirit, so that, governed by the Spirit, we shall not be able to commit any sin.

In any case, righteousness is both within the Law and in Christ, but under the Law one has to earn righteousness by much effort and hard work. This is very difficult; it is, let me assure you, almost impossible to observe scrupulously every requirement of the Law. Sinlessness is not possible in human life; in truth, it can only be obtained by grace. Just so, in the end, we shall sin no more only when we obtain the righteousness which comes from Christ, apart from anything we might be able to do.

For that reason, Paul reminds us of Sarah and Hagar. One bore a child in the course of nature while the other, actually unable to bear a child, bore Isaac through grace, and, of these two sons, the one born because of grace found great esteem and honor. By means of the comparison of Sarah and Hagar the Apostle demonstrates that the righteousness coming through Christ is, even now, far better, far more efficacious, than the righteousness to be found in the Law, because it is a righteousness bestowed by divine grace.

Paul rightly points to the woman who bore a son in the ordinary course of nature as the righteousness of the Law, but to the woman who bore a son against all expectation as the righteousness that comes from grace. Conduct regulated by the Law is well for those who live in the present age, but, in truth, those who are raised up and who are therefore made incorruptible do not need to be circumcised, to offer any sacrifice and vows, nor to observe holy days.

There is, of course, a natural order, the short span given to those born in this life, in which conduct regulated by the law seems to have a place. Nevertheless there is truly a new birth by the grace of God; this is how all those resurrected into the life to come are given new birth. In that birth the righteousness of Christ is to the greatest extent fulfilled. So Paul described the woman who bore a natural son as representing the righteousness of the Law, because, if the Law has any place at all, it governs those born into this life, that is, born according to the natural process of reproduction. However, concerning the woman who bore a child as a result of grace, Paul says that she represented the righteousness of Christ, since righteousness is most truly fulfilled in those who are seen to be raised up from the dead once and for all, and look forward to their second birth through God's grace against all expectation and hope. Therefore, in this place, Paul declares "This is an allegory," terming the comparison by which he compares the past things to things present an "allegory." Then he adds: "These women are the two covenants. One is from Mount Sinai, bearing children to slavery; she is Hagar" (Gal 4:24b).

So, in fact, they are. At this point Paul repeats what he has already said: "This is said by way of allegory." Here he actually desires to tell us that by means of allegory one can illustrate the difference between the covenants by comparing these two women, Hagar and Sarah, and that Hagar represents the order of regulation by law, for the Law was given on Mount Sinai. Therefore, the children she bears are born into slavery because those who live under the Law embrace the Law and its precepts. They are truly punished without means of excuse if they fall into sin, and, equally, they earn praise if they wish to observe the Law in every detail. Now this is a very difficult thing to do, and requires immense effort. It is fitting for slaves, but not for those who are free born, to live this way under the Law's demands. And Paul demonstrates that the comparison he has made to Hagar is not foreign to the Old Testament, adding, "Now Hagar is Mount Sinai in Arabia; she corresponds to the present Jerusalem, for she is in slavery with her children" (Gal 4:25).

"Arabia" was, in earlier times, not only that region now called Arabia, but included all the desert area and all the inhabited regions around the desert, not excluding parts of Egypt, and the place the Israelites inhabited while they were in Egypt was within that part of Arabia. That the name of their land is called Arabia we read in the Bible: "They inhabited the land of Goshen in Arabia" (Gen 45:10; 46:34; 47:1). Since Hagar was from Goshen, Paul wanted to make the point that Mount Sinai belonged to Arabia. Thus Hagar is an apt metaphor for the old covenant which was given in that place, a place associated with Hagar's own people.

Theodoret of Cyrus (393–457 C.E.)

Commentary on Psalm 30[3]

Starting with the psalm's superscription, Theodoret posits two historical narratives as simultaneously proper referential frameworks for understanding Ps 30: the metanarrative of humanity's fall into mortality and Christ's redemption, and a particular episode in the life of the Judahite king Hezekiah according to 2 Chr 32 and 2 Kgs 20. So, although the psalm literally speaks from a historical event, it typologically speaks to realities beyond its immediate historical horizon. By this approach Theodoret secured the text from flights of allegory yet rendered it meaningful to Christian readers of the fifth-century Syrian church.

A psalm for singing at the re-consecration of the house. To the end. Of David.
Blessed David did not build the divine Temple, nor do the verses of the psalm fit the builder. So by *re-consecration of the house* he refers to the restoration of human nature which Christ the Lord accomplished by accepting death on behalf of us, destroying death and giving us hope of resurrection. This psalm as well, however, refers to blessed Hezekiah: after destruction of the Assyrians and cure of his illness, he celebrated a great feast, as was appropriate, giving thanks to God for both granting them salvation and liberating his holy Temple from the fire of the enemy. Consequently, since the celebrations resembled a festival of re-consecration, it was understandable that it also got this title. It should be realized, however, that it is applicable to Hezekiah as a type, but to all human nature in reality: just as he gave admission to lofty thoughts (as the story of the Chronicles taught), received the sentence of death but by divine grace secured his life, so Adam, the first parent, who had built up pretensions to becoming God and formed lofty ambitions against his maker, was consigned to death but by divine loving-kindness attained resurrection.

(2) *I shall extol you, Lord, because you have supported me, and have not let my foes rejoice over me* (v. 1). By taking up our first-fruits, the Lord thus endowed all of nature with salvation, and did not allow the hostile and inimical demons to be gleeful.

O Lord my God, I cried to you, and you healed me. Lord, you brought my soul up from Hades, you saved me from the ranks of those going down into the pit (vv. 2–3). We hear this from the viewpoint of human nature. I mean, the verse *I cried to you and you healed me* is applicable to Hezekiah as far as the obvious sense goes, but not to human nature in this sense: human nature did not beseech God and look for reprieve from destruction; rather, it constantly fell to wailing and weeping, with death in view and no expectation of resurrection. Accordingly, the psalmist made mention of the tears and laments that occur with the sick and dying to show

---

[3] This translation is taken from *Theodoret of Cyrus: Commentary on the Psalms, Psalms 1–72.* (Translated by Robert C. Hill. Vol. 101, *Fathers of the Church.* Washington, D.C.: Catholic University of America Press, 2000), 187–91. Used with permission.

the ineffable loving-kindness of God in return for prayer in that, without being invoked, and seeing only the wailing, he took pity on what was happening and gave a
reprieve from death, death being called *pit* here, too.

(3) *Sing to the Lord, you his holy ones, confess to the memory of his holiness.
Because there is wrath in his anger, and life in his will* (vv. 4–5). He was right to assign the hymn and the confession of favor to the holy ones: since he gave the gift of
resurrection to all human beings, and not all were worthy of the favor, appropriately he consecrated the worthy ones for hymn singing. Now, the other distinction
he made was just right as well, attributing *wrath* to *anger*, giving the name *wrath* to
instruction, and attributing *life* to *will*; he wishes the former, to be sure, not the latter, which is something we bring on ourselves, after all: "God did not make death,"
Scripture says, "and finds no satisfaction in the destruction of the living; he created
everything for existence, in fact, and the generations of the world are wholesome"
[Wis 1:13–14]. And we also hear him saying through the prophet Ezekiel, "Surely
I do not wish the death of the sinner as much as his being converted to me and
living?" [Ezek 18:23]. *Weeping will last till evening, and joy till morning.* Now, things
turned out like this both in the case of Hezekiah and in the case of the salvation of
everyone: after the Assyrians applied those awful threats and moved the city to
weeping, they sustained the blow at night, and in the morning they filled with good
cheer those whom they had forced to weep. The divine Isaiah brought Hezekiah
the sentence of death in the evening, and towards morning brought him in turn the
good news of life. And it happened likewise in the case of the salvation of everyone: the sacred apostles and the believers along with them lamented the Passion of
the Lord, but towards morning the women came and brought the joy of the
Resurrection.

(4) *Now, I said in my prosperity, I shall not be moved forever* (v. 6). Adam had
hopes for this, too, while living in paradise before the deception, as did Hezekiah
after conquering the Assyrian: the book of Chronicles teaches us this clearly when it
says the heart of King Hezekiah was lifted up.

*Lord, by your will you provided my power in beauty, but you turned your face
away, and I was disturbed* (v. 7). This too is applicable both to Hezekiah and all of
human nature. He enjoyed the divine providence on account of virtue and prevailed
over the Assyrians, and in turn when bereft of the divine favor he fell victim to disease and was affected by fear of dying. Adam, too, in the garden was adorned with
the beauty of virtue, and was proof against destruction; but when deprived of the divine providence through the Fall, he experienced the turmoil that comes from living.
Now, Symmachus[4] put it very clearly, "Lord, in your good pleasure you fixed power
in my forefather," so that it would be clear that human nature in person is saying this
to Christ the Lord, who awarded it the great gift of life.

---

[4] During the second century C.E., several Greek translations of the Hebrew Scriptures were
produced as alternatives to the Septuagint. They are known as the translations of Aquila, Theodotian, and Symmachus.

(5) *I shall cry to you, O Lord, and make my petition to my God. What good is there in my blood, in my going down to destruction? Surely dust will not confess to you or proclaim your truth?* (vv. 8–9). Blessed Hezekiah also employed these words, as the fourth book of Kings[5] and the inspired composition of the divine Isaiah teach. Human nature also cried out to God, of course, although not in every case, nevertheless through the holy ones, using words like this, "It is right to sing hymns to you as creator, and to give thanks in words for your favors. This belongs to the living: how could those who have dissolved into dust and ashes and lost their bodily function manage to sing of your kindnesses?"

(6) *The Lord heard and had mercy on me, the Lord became my helper. You turned my lamentation into joy for me. You rent my sackcloth and clad me in joy so that my glory might sing to you and I might feel no compunction* (vv. 10–12). Clad in sackcloth, Hezekiah offered prayer to God against the Assyrians, and human nature put on the guise of grieving. Even today some foolish people in their bewailing the dead are wrong to sit about in sackcloth and have no wish to give ear to the inspired words that cry out unmistakably, *You rent my sackcloth and clad me in joy, and turned my lamentation into joy for me.* I mean, just as Hezekiah was filled with great joy on receiving the promise of the fifteen years, so it is right for us on receiving the hope of resurrection not to mourn the dead but to await joyfully that wonderful outcome. Now, the verse, *so that my glory might sing to you and I might feel no compunction,* Symmachus rendered thus: "so that glory might praise you and not keep silence," that is, "In response to this beneficence it behooves us to sing your praises constantly and celebrate those who have attained such glory, at no time keeping silence." Compunction encourages silence; accordingly, the Septuagint put *compunction* in place of silence. Now, Hezekiah attained glory once such a countless number sustained a divine blow on his account and the sun turned back; we, on the other hand, have a basis of high repute in the evidence given by the God of all of his great affection for us: "God so loved the world," Scripture says, "that he has given his only-begotten Son so that all who believe in him may not perish but have eternal life" (John 3:16). *O Lord my God, I shall confess to you forever:* not only in the present life but also after the resurrection I shall offer hymns to you, constantly recounting your extraordinary and ineffable gifts.

---

[5] LXX 4 Kings is 2 Kings in English versions.

CHAPTER 9

Spiritual Application of the Bible: Gregory the Great (540–604 C.E.)

G regory I, the last of the Latin Fathers of the Western church, was born in Rome to a prominent patrician family and received an outstanding education that prepared him for a high-level political career. In his early thirties Gregory was appointed to one of Rome's most powerful offices, but before a year had passed, he opted for the monastic cloth and resigned his office. His father had by this time died, leaving to Gregory the family's vast Sicilian estates. These holdings afforded Gregory the means and land with which to establish six monasteries, and in Rome he converted his own home into a monastery (dedicated to St. Andrew), where he resided as a monk for three years. His spiritual and administrative reputation brought him an appointment to one of the deaconates of Rome and then to a papal mission to Constantinople that lasted six years. During his residential ambassadorship there, Gregory wrote his famous work, *Moralia in Job.*

Upon returning to Rome, Gregory served as abbott of St. Andrew's Monastery for five years. The death of Pope Pelagius II in 590 occasioned the appointment of Gregory to the church's highest office by popular and ecclesiastical acclaim; he was the first monk to become pope. Gregory served in the papal office for the next fourteen years, skillfully guiding the city of Rome and the Roman church through severely tumultuous times. The governing center of the ancient empire had long since fully transferred to Constantinople, leaving Rome relatively vulnerable to the emerging barbaric kingdoms of Europe. As Rome's leading figure of authority—almost by default—Gregory took control of the city and through skillful diplomacy secured the safety of the city. These accomplishments were to lead in subsequent generations to the increasing power and independence of the papacy among the Western world's political powers. As the leader of the Roman church, he so reorganized the church's holdings throughout Italy that the Christian mission to the poor and indigent advanced significantly.

Gregory's writings—which include hundreds of letters, an authoritative compendium of pastoral rules, reflections on the lives of the saints, and biblical commentary—had an enormous influence on the spiritual life of Western Christians and on the episcopal life of church administrators for centuries after his death. His best-known works in biblical interpretation are commentaries, one on the book of Ezekiel and one on the book of Job. He was drawn to these more obscure books of the Old Testament because they were among the biblical writings least accessible to the Christian readers of the day. Here we see the fruit of hermeneutical efforts from earlier centuries, when figurative method in biblical interpretation was key in the theological and philosophical debates of that earlier formative era in the life of the church. By the sixth century, the figurative modes of biblical interpretation that had been worked out in more ecclesiastically contentious times were available for consistent application to the struggles of the Christian soul against moral temptation and spiritual hunger. Gregory sought to nurture his readers by first attending to the outward, literal sense of the biblical text and from there working inward to the spiritual sense through allegory, to which in turn he would give the moral meaning—thus bringing his readers back out to their own world, where they could live out what they had inwardly discovered in the text with him. His procedure is evident in his *Moralia in Job,* where he first treats the literal meaning (his phrase is "the history" or "the historical sense") of a passage, reviewing the passage again for the allegorical meaning and then returning once more for the tropological or moral significance hidden within the allegory.

Gregory is included in our anthology in order to display the fruits of the formative Western patristic period of biblical interpretation as exhibited in a single commentary on a single biblical book. The following is excerpted from *Moralia in Job,* where Gregory presents a preface to his entire commentary and treats the first five verses of Job 1. The selection contains his historical, allegorical, and tropological comments on only the second verse of Job 1, where it is recorded that Job sired seven sons and three daughters.

For further information on Gregory I:

Evans, G. R. *The Thought of Gregory the Great.* New York: Cambridge University Press, 1986.

Markus, Robert A. *Gregory the Great and His World.* New York: Cambridge University Press, 1997.

Zinn, Grover A. "Exegesis and Spirituality in the Writings of Gregory the Great." Pages 168–80 in *Gregory the Great: A Symposium.* Edited by J. C. Cavadini. Notre Dame, Ind.: University of Notre Dame Press, 1995.

Moralia in Job [1]

From Section One:

They [who requested that Gregory write his commentary] were pleased . . . to drive me by their constant requests to comment on the book of blessed Job and, as far as truth should give me strength, to reveal the book's mysteries in all their profundity for my brothers. To the burden of their request, they added as well the requirement that I should not only shake loose from the words of the historical narrative their allegorical meaning, but should also direct the allegorical interpretation towards moral edification; and that I should also (still another weighty burden) support my interpretations with other scriptural texts and should even interject expositions of those passages if they seemed complicated enough to require unraveling.

. . .

From Section Two:

The reader must realize that some things are expounded here as simple historical narrative, some things examined for their allegorical signification, and some things discussed only for their moral import—but that of course some things are explored carefully in all three ways. First we lay the foundations of historical fact; then we lift up the mind to the citadel of faith through allegory; finally through the exposition of the moral sense we dress the edifice in its colored raiment. The utterances of Truth are nothing but nourishment to refresh the soul. Expounding the text in various ways we offer dishes for the palate of different kinds, so that we may banish the reader's boredom as we might that of a jaded guest at a banquet, who selects what he considers most attractive from the many things set out for him. Sometimes we neglect to expound the overt historical sense lest we be retarded getting to deeper matters. Sometimes passages cannot be expounded literally because when they are taken in that superficial way they offer no instruction to the reader but only generate error.

. . .

Sometimes indeed the very words of the text warn us against taking a text literally. For example, Job says, "Perish the day on which I was born and the night in which it was said, 'A man is conceived'" [see Job 3:3]. And a little later he adds: "May fog cover it, and may it be shrouded in bitterness" [see Job 3:5]. And he goes on cursing that same night: "Let that night be solitary" [see Job 3:7]. But the day of his birth, swept along in the course of time, could not stand still for a minute: how

---

[1] This translation and annotation of the Latin text of Gregory the Great's *Moralia in Job* was done by James J. O'Donnell (online: http://ccat.sas.upenn.edu/jod/gregory.html). Used with permission.

could he ask that it be covered with fog? It had slipped away and existed no longer, and even if it still continued to exist in the natural world could never be aware of bitterness. It is clear that he cannot be speaking of insensate days when he hopes they be smitten with a sense of bitterness. And if the night of his conception had passed away with all the other nights, how could he pray for it to be solitary? Nothing can keep it fixed in the passage of time, so nothing can separate it from the procession of other nights. At another place he says, "How long will it be before you spare me and leave me alone to gulp down my own saliva" [see Job 7:19]? A little before he had said, "Things my soul disdained to touch are now my food in my need" [see Job 6:7]. But everyone knows it is easier to swallow saliva than food, so it is incredible that someone who says he has been eating food should claim he cannot even swallow his saliva. In another place he says: "I have sinned: what shall I do for you, O guardian of mankind" [see Job 7:20]? Or again: "Do you wish to devour me for the sins of my adolescence" [see Job 13:26]? And in another answer he adds: "My heart has never reproached me in my whole life" [see Job 27:6]. How can he confess publicly that he has sinned and yet claim that he has heard no reproach from his heart in his whole life? Sinful deeds and a clear conscience do not ordinarily go together. But undoubtedly the words of the literal text, when they do not agree with each other, show that something else is to be sought in them. It is as if they said to us, "When you see us apparently embarrassed and contradictory, look within us for that which is coherent and consistent."

From Section Four:

Sometimes, of course, the reader who neglects to take the words of the text literally hides the light he had been offered, and while he struggles mightily to find something hidden inside, he loses the thing he could have found on the outside without difficulty. The holy man says: "Did I deny the poor the alms they craved, keep the widow waiting for her pittance, devour my mouthful alone with never an orphan boy to share it? Did I spurn the naked who were ready to perish of cold, too poor to find clothing? Did I never earn thanks from the back that went bare until fleece of my flock warmed it" [see Job 31:16–20]? If we twist these words violently to an allegorical sense, we render all the deeds of his mercy insignificant. This is how divine speech sometimes stirs up the clever with mysteries, but more often provides consolation for the simple with the obvious. It has out in the open food for children but keeps hidden away the things that fill the minds of the eminent with awe. Scripture is like a river again, broad and deep, shallow enough here for the lamb to go wading, but deep enough there for the elephant to swim. As each separate passage provides the opportunity, so the order of this commentary will change its direction designedly to find the sense of the divine words more truly by adapting itself as circumstances demand.

. . .

We have prolonged the preface so that our discourse might, so to speak, sketch and outline the whole of the work. But because we have come to the beginning of our commentary, even after going on this long, we should first plant the root of history so that we might later sate our souls on the fruit of allegory.

Literal

IV.5. *Seven sons were born to him, and three daughters* (1:2).

A large family often stirs the heart of a parent to greed. The more heirs he is blessed with, the more he is stirred to try to build a great estate. To show the holiness of mind of blessed Job, he is proclaimed and shown to have been a just man and shown again to have been the father of a large family. At the very outset of the book he is said to have been devout in offering sacrifice, and later he is reported, in his own words, to have been generous with gifts. We should recognize the great strength he was endowed with when we think how not even love for his many children could make him cling to his property.

Allegorical

XIV.18. *Seven sons were born to him, and three daughters* (1:2).

What does the number seven stand for if not the whole of perfection? We should pass over the arguments of human reason for the perfection of this number (they say it is perfect because it is made up of the first even number [4] and the first uneven one [3], from the first which can be divided and the first which cannot be divided). We certainly know that holy scripture is in the habit of using the number seven as a symbol of perfection. Thus it asserts that the Lord rested from his labors on the seventh day; thus the seventh day is given to men for their rest, that is, for the sabbath. This is why the jubilee year, in which the fulness of repose is signified, is completed by seven sevens with the addition of the number one (sign of our unity).[2]

19. *Seven sons were born to him* (1:2).

These are the apostles going forth manfully to preach. When they accomplish the commands of perfection they symbolize the sturdy life of the higher sex. This is why there were twelve of them chosen to be filled with the seven-fold grace of the spirit, for the number seven is closely related to the number twelve. The parts of the number seven (4+3) multiplied together come to twelve. Whether you take four three times or three four times, seven turns into twelve. Thus the holy apostles, who were sent to preach the three persons of God to the four corners of the world, were chosen twelve in number, so that even by their number they should symbolize the perfection they preached by their words and deeds.

---

[2] [7x7] + 1 = 50; the jubilee was celebrated every fifty years—O'Donnell. See Lev 25:8–55.

20. *And three daughters were born to him* (1:2).

What shall we take the daughters for, if not the flock of less-gifted faithful? Even if they do not stay the course for the perfection of good works by strength and virtue, they cling tenaciously to the faith they know in the trinity. In the seven sons we see the rank of preachers, but in the three daughters the multitude of hearers.

The three daughters can also stand for the three classes of the faithful. After the sons the daughters are named because after the courage displayed by the apostles there came three classes of the faithful in the church's life: pastors, the continent,[3] and the married. This is why the prophet Ezekiel says that he heard three men were set free: Noah, Daniel, and Job [see Ezek 14:14–20]. Noah, who guided the ark through the waves, stands for the order of leaders who, while they preside over the people to set a pattern for living, govern the holy church in the midst of the breakers of temptation. Daniel, who is praised for his wonderful continence, represents the life of the ascetic who, abandoning all the things of this world, despises Babylon and lords over it in the citadel of his spirit. Job then stands for the life of the virtuous lay people in married life, who do good works with the things they possess of this world, following the path of this world to the heavenly fatherland. Since the three orders of the faithful come after the holy apostles, so it is appropriate that after the seven sons the three daughters should be mentioned.

Tropological

XXVII.38. *Seven sons were born to him and three daughters* (1:2).

Seven sons are born for us when the seven virtues of the Holy Spirit quicken to life in us through the conception of right thinking. The prophet counts up this inner progeny that comes from the fertility of the Spirit, saying: "The Spirit of the Lord shall rest upon him, a spirit of wisdom and understanding, a spirit of counsel and strength, a spirit of knowledge and devotion; and the spirit of the fear of the Lord shall fill him" [see Isa 11:2–3]. When wisdom, understanding, counsel, strength, knowledge, devotion and fear of the Lord spring to life for us through the coming of the Spirit, it is like the generation of a long-lived progeny in the mind, which keeps alive our noble lineage from heaven by giving us to share the love of eternity. These seven sons have three sisters in our hearts, because whatever these virtues generate is joined to the three theological virtues of hope, faith and charity. The seven sons cannot achieve the perfection of the number ten unless everything they do is done in hope, faith and charity. Because the thought of good works soon accompanies this abundance of virtues that go on before, it is rightly added:

---

[3] The "continent" are those vowed to a religious life marked by a restraint of bodily appetites, particularly the sexual. —O'Donnell

XXVIII.39. *His wealth included seven thousand sheep and three thousand camels* (1:3).

We can recognize here the accuracy of the historical narrative, while still imitating in the spirit what comes to our hearing through ears of the flesh. We possess seven thousand sheep when in perfect purity of heart we feed our innocent thoughts within on the long-sought food of Truth.

40. We will possess three thousand camels, if we can subdue everything lofty and twisted that is within us to the authority of faith and bow down willingly in humble longing that comes from knowledge of the trinity. We possess camels if we humbly lay down all our lofty thoughts. We surely possess camels when we turn our thoughts to compassion for our brother's weakness so that, bearing one another's burdens, we might know how to come to the aid of another's troubles [see Gal 6:2].

CHAPTER 10

How Can a Text Bear Multiple Meanings?
Thomas Aquinas (1225–1274 C.E.)

From a young age, Thomas Aquinas demonstrated remarkable intellectual strength. Because of his obvious mental abilities, he was soon appointed to the Dominican studium at Paris, where before long his teaching attracted the attention of professors and students. His duties principally consisted in explaining the *Sentences* of Peter Lombard; his comments on this standard compendium of theological knowledge furnished the materials and, in great part, the plan for Thomas's chief work, the *Summa theologiae.* After he received the degree of doctor in theology in 1257, Thomas embarked on his phenomenal career as one of the most illuminating and celebrated constructors of Christian theology.

Among the topics in Thomas's many works is his teaching on the interpretation of Scripture. Beyond his New Testament sermons, Thomas's oeuvre includes commentaries on the books of Job, Isaiah, Jeremiah, the Psalms, two of the Gospels (Matthew and John), and the Pauline Epistles. In most of these works Thomas's approach follows mostly that of his contemporaries and predecessors such as Peter Lombard (1105–1164) and Hugh of St. Victor (1096–1141): a cursory outline of the biblical text's contents is followed by numerous citations from other portions of Scripture and from the Western and Eastern church fathers. His comments on Job, Romans, and John stand out for their depth of philosophical and theological discussion. But probably the most concise expression of his own views on biblical interpretation is found in the pages of the *Summa theologiae,* a complete, systematically arranged exposition of theology and summary of Christian philosophy that draws heavily upon the Aristotelian philosophical heritage. In this magnum opus every subject treated is introduced as a question and divided into articles also expressed as questions. Objections against the proposed thesis are then articulated, followed by Thomas's response, and the discussion concludes with answers to the objections in the order they were initially presented.

As Gregory the Great's sixth-century Job commentary demonstrates, the practice of identifying a multiple spiritual sense of Scripture (allegorical, anagogical, and tropological) had long established itself among Christian interpreters by Thomas's time. But eventually the division of spiritual meanings relative to the literal sense of the text came to pose some problems. Distinctions between the literal sense and the spiritual sense were not always clear when, for example, the biblical text itself presented a trope such as a metaphor. Since tropes are not to be taken literally, what would constitute the literal sense of a metaphor, as distinguished from a spiritual sense that could be derived from it? Another issue for interpretation centered on the value of the literal sense, which medieval Christian exegetes had come characteristically to neglect in their preoccupation with the spiritual senses. Influenced partly by exegesis from European Jews, Christian scholars of the twelfth and thirteenth centuries were developing greater sensitivity to the literal meaning of biblical texts. There grew a need for theoretical arguments supporting the legitimacy of distinguishing literal meaning from spiritual and the value of the literal sense within a Christian philosophical framework. Thomas supplied that need as, in this portion of the *Summa*, he presented a basis for deriving theology from Scripture.

Thomas argued for a union in Scripture of spiritual and tangible dimensions similar to that which he teaches concerning human beings. Thus, whereas God (spiritual) is the Author of Scripture (in Aristotelian terms, the primary cause), human beings (tangible) are the composers of Scripture (the instrumental cause), and both aspects of Scripture factor into interpretation. So, although he defended the legitimacy of discerning multiple meanings in a passage of Scripture, Thomas did not allow for abandonment of the literal sense. Indeed, the basis for theology is the literal sense, and derivative from the literal are the allegorical and moral senses, which God uses to signify deeper dimensions of divine truth.[1] This argument from his *Summa* helped undergird the exegetical practice found in Thomas's own commentaries and widespread in Christian preaching of his era, namely, the citing of other scriptural passages to confirm the meaning of a text under discussion. The single divine Author guarantees that distant biblical passages can illuminate meaning in the present context, and the use of the same words (albeit in Latin) by many different prophets and apostles made available a range of different texts for this exegetical practice. Where the literal sense of a text is expressed metaphorically, Thomas argued that "those things that are taught metaphorically in one part of Scripture, in other parts are taught more openly" (*Summa theologiae* 1.1.9). Moreover, as he states in our selection below, "nothing necessary for faith is contained under the spiritual sense that is not openly conveyed through the literal sense elsewhere." Along these lines, then, Thomas brought support to the long practiced use of Scripture to establish claims on the meaning of Scripture.

For further information on Thomas Aquinas and related subjects in medieval biblical interpretation:

Lampe, G. W. K., ed. *Cambridge History of the Bible.* Vol. 2. Cambridge: Cambridge University Press, 1969.
Smalley, Beryl. *The Study of the Bible in the Middle Ages.* 3d ed. Oxford: Blackwell, 1983.
Torrell, Jean-Pierre. *The Person and His Work.* Vol. 1 of *Saint Thomas Aquinas.* Translated by Robert Royal. Washington, D.C.: Catholic University of America Press, 1996.

---

[1]Elsewhere in this anthology we observe Nicholas of Lyra applying to the text of Ps 23 Thomas's systematic explanation of literal and mystical senses.

Summa theologiae[2]

Whether in Holy Scripture a Word May Have Several Senses?

Objection 1. It seems that in Holy Writ a word cannot have several senses, historical or literal, allegorical, tropological or moral, and anagogical. For many different senses in one text produce confusion and deception and destroy all force of argument. Hence no argument, but only fallacies, can be deduced from a multiplicity of propositions. But Holy Writ ought to be able to state the truth without any fallacy. Therefore in it there cannot be several senses to a word.

Objection 2. Further, Augustine says that "the Old Testament has a fourfold division as to history, etiology, analogy and allegory."[3] Now these four seem altogether different from the four divisions mentioned in the first objection. Therefore it does not seem fitting to explain the same word of Holy Writ according to the four different senses mentioned above.

Objection 3. Further, besides these senses, there is the parabolical, which is not one of these four.

On the contrary, Gregory says: "Holy Writ by the manner of its speech transcends every science, because in one and the same sentence, while it describes a fact, it reveals a mystery."[4]

I answer that, The author of Holy Writ is God, in whose power it is to signify His meaning, not by words only (as man also can do), but also by things themselves. So, whereas in every other science things are signified by words, this science has the property, that the things signified by the words have themselves also a signification. Therefore that first signification whereby words signify things belongs to the first sense, the historical or literal. That signification whereby things signified by words have themselves also a signification is called the spiritual sense, which is based on the literal, and presupposes it. Now this spiritual sense has a threefold division. For as the Apostle says (Heb 10:1) the Old Law is a figure of the New Law, and Dionysius says "the New Law itself is a figure of future glory."[5] Again, in the New Law, whatever

---

[2] This excerpt from the *Summa* is taken from part 1, question 1, article 10 in *The "Summa Theologica" of St. Thomas Aquinas* (trans. Fathers of the English Dominican Province; 22 vols.; 2d rev. ed.; London: Burns, Oates & Washbourne, 1920; online: www.newadvent.org/summa/100110.htm). Used with permission.

[3] Augustine, *De utilitate credendi* 5 ("On the Profit of Believing," in *A Select Library of the Nicene and Post-Nicene Fathers of the Christian Church* [ed. P. Schaff; 14 vols.; Grand Rapids: Eerdmans, 1956], 3:349).

[4] Gregory the Great, *Moralia in Job* 20.1, in Gregory the Great, *Moralia in Job* (ed. M. Adriaen; Corpus Christianorum: Series latina 143A; Turnhout: Brepols, 1979), 1003.

[5] Pseudo-Dionysius, *De caelesti hierarchia* 1, in Pseudo-Dionysius, *The Complete Works* (trans. Colm Luibheid; Classics of Western Spirituality; New York: Paulist, 1987), 147.

our Head has done is a type of what we ought to do. Therefore, so far as the things of the Old Law signify the things of the New Law, there is the allegorical sense; so far as the things done in Christ, or so far as the things which signify Christ, are types of what we ought to do, there is the moral sense. But so far as they signify what relates to eternal glory, there is the anagogical sense. Since the literal sense is that which the author intends, and since the author of Holy Writ is God, Who by one act comprehends all things by His intellect, it is not unfitting, as Augustine says, if, even according to the literal sense, one word in Holy Writ should have several senses.[6]

Reply to Objection 1. The multiplicity of these senses does not produce equivocation or any other kind of multiplicity, seeing that these senses are not multiplied because one word signifies several things, but because the things signified by the words can be themselves types of other things. Thus in Holy Writ no confusion results, for all the senses are founded on one—the literal—from which alone can any argument be drawn, and not from those intended in allegory, as Augustine says. Nevertheless, nothing of Holy Scripture perishes on account of this, since nothing necessary to faith is contained under the spiritual sense which is not elsewhere put forward by the Scripture in its literal sense.

Reply to Objection 2. These three—history, etiology, analogy—are grouped under the literal sense. For it is called history, as Augustine expounds, whenever anything is simply related; it is called etiology when its cause is assigned, as when Our Lord gave the reason why Moses allowed the putting away of wives—namely, on account of the hardness of men's hearts [Mt 19:3–9]; it is called analogy whenever the truth of one text of Scripture is shown not to contradict the truth of another. Of these four, allegory alone stands for the three spiritual senses. Thus Hugh of St. Victor includes the anagogical under the allegorical sense, laying down three senses only—the historical, the allegorical, and the tropological.[7]

Reply to Objection 3. The parabolical sense is contained in the literal, for by words things are signified properly and figuratively. Nor is the figure itself, but that which is figured, the literal sense. When Scripture speaks of God's arm, the literal sense is not that God has such a member, but only what is signified by this member, namely operative power. Hence it is plain that nothing false can ever underlie the literal sense of Holy Writ.

---

[6] Augustine, *Confessions* 12.31.
[7] See book 6 of Hugh of St. Victor, *The Didascalicon: A Medieval Guide to the Arts* (trans. Jerome Taylor; New York: Columbia University Press, 1991).

CHAPTER 11

Medieval Recognition of the Literal Sense: Nicholas of Lyra and the *Glossa ordinaria* on Psalm 23 (1270–1349 C.E.)

The name Nicholas of Lyra is associated with the most famous Bible of the late Middle Ages—*Biblia sacra cum glossa ordinaria* (Holy [or sacred] Bible with the ordinary [or standard] gloss). Nicholas was born about 1270 in the town of Lyre in Normandy (France). His education under the Jewish scholars of Everaux gave him a life-long interest in the Hebrew language, something that distinguished Nicholas from the European tradition of Christian biblical scholarship that had preceded him for hundreds of years. He taught at the Sorbonne from 1309 to 1319 and again from 1333 until his death. After serving as minister provincial for Paris and Burgundy, he became founder of the College of Burgundy at the request of the queen of France. The *Postilla litteralis in Vetus et Novum Testamentum* (Literal postils on the Old and New Testament) was completed in 1331, and his *Postilla moralis in Vetus et Novum Testamentum* (Moral postils on the Old and New Testament) was finished in 1339. His status as a biblical scholar and leader in the Franciscan order was unmatched in the fourteenth century. The endurance of his legacy derived in part from his contribution to the *Glossa ordinaria*.

The glossed Bible[1] harkened back to the early Middle Ages, when explanatory notes were inserted between lines of Jerome's Latin Bible (Vulgate). Postils were also a medieval custom, in which interpretations or expositions of the biblical text were added to the glossed edition.[2] Hugh of St. Cher (ca. 1195–1263) directed the compilation of an authoritative set of postils that became marginal commentary in the glossed Bible, with remarks of the church fathers flanking the Latin biblical text and glosses. The addition of Nicholas's postils crowned the medieval exegetical process: the Latin Bible (Jerome's Vulgate) with glosses,[3] framed by extracts from the church fathers, followed by literal postils beneath and concluded with moral postils underneath these.

As the Ps 23 glosses show, traditional Christian readings of the Old Testament had for centuries remained true to the pattern observed in Gregory the Great's commentary on

---

[1] A gloss is an explanation on a word or phrase in Scripture. Early glosses were taken from the patristic corpus. Hence a "glossed" Bible served as a rudimentary commentary.

[2] *Postilla* may be derived from the phrase *post illa verba* ("after these words").

[3] The glosses in the Psalter have been attributed to Anselm of Laon, who flourished ca. 1080–1117 at the cathedral school of Laon.

Job. The sense of words and phrases in their ancient cultural context tended to be displaced by a central concern for nurturing the soul through spiritual senses claimed for the text. By Nicholas's time, however, knowledge of the Hebrew text and of the historical sense of the text was beginning to increase among Christian scholars. Nicholas understood that soul-nurturing and doctrine-supporting allegorical interpretations of the Old Testament could not stand at the expense of a text's literal meaning. Though not dismissing the mystical sense of the Scriptures, in his postils Nicholas took care to consider the text's expressions within the historical horizon of the life of ancient Israel in general and (in the case of the Psalms) of the life of David. In this respect Nicholas had been influenced by the eleventh-century Jewish commentator Rashi (R. Shlomo Yitzḥaqi), to whom he referred frequently in his literal postils. On the occasions where a psalm was to be christologically (and therefore figuratively) interpreted as prompted by New Testament writers, Nicholas departed from Rashi's historical literalism in favor of allegory. Otherwise, Nicholas's insights into the literal sense as illuminated by Jewish scholars helped cultivate in Christian biblical scholarship a respect for the tradition of Hebrew exegesis of the text. Philosophically, Nicholas was also indebted to Thomas Aquinas for making the case to preserve Scripture's literal sense, apart from which no spiritual sense may be constructed.

Nicholas's voluminous exegetical interest in the literal sense of Scripture helped pave the way for a new emphasis on literal interpretation together with more historically oriented exegesis. Traces of his influence can be detected in the Protestant Reformers' general aversion to allegory two hundred years later. (A similar interest in the ancient historical horizon of biblical texts is evident in our Ps 23 selection from the *Critici sacri*.) Although the ditty *Si Lyra non lyrasset, Lutherus non saltasset* ("If Lyra had not lyred, Luther would not have danced")[4] may claim too much, Lyra's notes with the *Glossa ordinaria* remained a widely used commentary on the Bible well into the sixteenth century.

The following selections are from Nicholas's "Second Prologue," a further prologue, and Commentary on Psalm 23. Some explanatory footnotes have been added for clarification. Also, every attempt has been made to identify the source of patristic citations and allusions—although success is not always possible inasmuch as, in the long history of the glossed Bible, compilers were sometimes rather free in their condensing, transposing, and even paraphrasing of patristic comments. In the translation that follows, the glosses to each line of Ps 23 are printed below the text with alphabetical tags connecting them to the specific biblical expression that is being "glossed."

For further information on Nicholas of Lyra, the *Glossa ordinaria,* and medieval biblical interpretation:

Krey, Philip D. W., and Lesley Smith, eds. *Nicholas of Lyra: The Senses of Scripture.* Studies in the History of Christian Thought 90. Leiden: Brill, 2000.

Lubac, Henri de. *The Four Senses of Scripture.* Vol. 1 of *Medieval Exegesis.* Translated by Mark Sebanc. Grand Rapids: Eerdmans, 1998.

Patton, C. L. "Nicholas of Lyra." Pages 116–22 in *Historical Handbook of Major Biblical Interpreters.* Edited by Donald McKim. Downers Grove, Ill.: InterVarsity, 1998.

---

[4]The pun has been rhymed by Karlfried Froehlich: "Had Lyra not the lyre played, Luther his dance would not have made."

Second Prologue, Concerning the Intention of the Writer and the Mode of Proceeding[5]

"I saw in the right hand of Him that sat upon the throne a book written on the inside and on the outside" (Rev 5[:1]). As was said in the preceding prologue, this book is Holy Scripture, which is said to be written on the outside in terms of the literal sense of the text, and on the inside in terms of the mystical and spiritual sense. It [i.e. the mystical and spiritual sense] is, generally speaking, divided into three categories, as I have already said. Yet in each of these, the number of mystical meanings in any particular place can be multiplied. But all presume the literal sense as a kind of foundation. So, just as a building which begins to part company with its foundations is inclined to collapse, so a mystical exposition which deviates from the literal sense must be considered unseemly and inappropriate, or at any rate less seemly and less appropriate, than other interpretations. So, those who wish to make headway in the study of Holy Scripture must begin by understanding the literal sense, particularly since any argument that is used to prove or explain a doubtful point can only be based on the literal sense, and not on the mystical sense, as Augustine says in his letter against Vincent the Donatist.[6]

One should, moreover, bear in mind that the literal sense, which should be our starting-point, as I have said, seems to be greatly obscured in these modern times. This is partly through the fault of scribes who, misled by similarities between letters, have in many places written something which differs from the true reading of the text *(veritas textus)*. Partly it is the fault of lack of skill on the part of correctors, who in several places have punctuated where they should not, and have begun and ended verses where they should not begin or end, and for this reason the meaning of the text *(sententia literae)* is inconstant, as will be apparent, for this is something which I will have to discuss in the appropriate places, God willing.[7] Partly it is due to the manner of our translation. For often the translation has something quite different from the meaning of the Hebrew text, as Jerome explains in his book *On Questions concerning the Hebrew Text* and in several other places.[8] Other commentators on Holy Scripture say the same in their sermons or writings. Yet, according to Jerome in

---

[5] The translation of Nicholas's "Second Prologue" is from *Medieval Literary Theory and Criticism, c. 1100–1375: The Commentary-Tradition* (ed. A. J. Minnis and A. B. Scott, with David Wallace; rev. ed.; Oxford: Oxford University Press, 1988). Pages 268–70. By permission of Oxford University Press.

[6] Augustine's letter (Letter 93 in *Saint Augustine: Letters*, vol. 2 [trans. Wilfrid Parsons; *The Fathers of the Church*, vol. 18; ed. R. J. Deferrari; New York: Fathers of the Church, 1953], 56–106) reviews the Donatist controversy and contains the following line, which may be what Nicholas is referring to: "Would anyone be so lacking in modesty as to apply to himself something expressed by an allegory, unless he had some clear indication to throw light on its obscure language?"

[7] We have previously noted (ch. 7, n. 7) that during antiquity Latin and Greek manuscripts were usually written without punctuation marking the beginning or ending of sentences. As punctuation marks came to be added in the medieval era, careless scribal work introduced a new potential for misinterpretation into the exegetical process.

[8] See Jerome, *Hebrew Questions on Genesis* (trans. C. T. R. Hayward; Oxford: Clarendon, 1995).

his second prologue on Genesis[9] and in many other places, in order to obtain the true text in the Old Testament one must have recourse to the Hebrew manuscripts. But in so doing one should be very wary of those passages of Old Testament Scripture which speak of the divinity of Christ and the consequences which follow from that. For the Jews have corrupted some of these to defend their own erroneous doctrine. I have, in part, explained this in a question on the divinity of Christ, and will explain it more fully, with God's help, when such passages crop up. In those passages where it is unlikely that they have altered something, since they have had no specific reason for so doing, there appears to be no danger. As Jerome says, in such cases it is safer to have recourse to the Hebrew text, as being the original, in order to make it clear which is the true text.

One should also understand that the literal sense of the text has been much obscured because of the manner of expounding the text commonly handed down by others. Although they have said much that is good, yet they have been inadequate in their treatment of the literal sense, and have so multiplied the number of mystical senses that the literal sense is in some part cut off and suffocated among so many mystical senses. Moreover, they have chopped up the text into so many small parts, and brought forth so many concordant passages to suit their own purpose, that to some degree they confuse both the mind and memory of the reader and distract it from understanding the literal meaning of the text. As I wish to avoid these and similar faults, with God's help I intend to concentrate on the literal sense, and to interpose a very few brief mystical explanations on occasion, but not very often. Likewise, my intention is to cite the statements not only of Catholic but also of Jewish teachers, and especially Rabbi Solomon,[10] who among all the Jewish exegetes has put forward the most reasonable arguments, in order to illuminate the literal meaning of the text.

Nicholas concludes this prologue with a review of seven rules for the exposition of Scripture; they are mostly the same rules as those put forth by Tyconius.

Prologue of the Same Nicholas of Lyra on the Mystical Interpretation of the Bible[11]

"I saw on the right hand sitting upon the throne, a book written within and without" [Rev 5:1]. Sitting upon the throne of glory is the glorious God, who is also

---

[9] Jerome, *Praefatio in Pentateuchum, ad Desiderium* (PL 28:177–84).

[10] R. Shlomo Yitzḥaqi (Rashi).

[11] The translation of the further prologue and Psalm 23 commentary is by James T. Dennison and is based upon *Biblia Sacra cum glossa ordinaria primum quidem a Strabo Fuldensi monacho benedictino: nunc vero novis patrum, cum graecorum, tum latinorum explicationibus locupletata, et postilla Nicolai Lyrani franciscani, nec non additionibus Pauli Burgensis episcopi, et Matthiae Thoringi replicis, opera et studio theologor* (ed. Leander de Sancto Martino and Jean Gallemart; Douai and Antwerp: B. Bellerus and J. Keerbergius, 1617). This edition has been compared with the editio princeps (1480/1481), reprinted in anastatic facsimile with an introduction by K. Froehlich and M. T. Gibson (Turnhout: Brepols, 1992).

the sublime One, ruling the universe, in whose right hand is the divinely given sacred Scripture, according to what is said in Deuteronomy, "In his right hand the fiery law" [Deut 33:2]. For the law of the Old and New Testament is well called fiery because it has been inspired by the revelation of the Holy Spirit (who is divine fire). And this Scripture is well called a book written within and without: without with regard to the literal sense, but within with regard to the mystical sense, concealed beneath the letter. For God who is the author of this Scripture, not only employed words to signify certain things, but also things by words of signification.[12] And so deeds of the Old Testament signified that which is done in the New Testament, just as the apostle says in 1 Corinthians, "All these things happened in a figure" [1 Cor 10:11]. Therefore the sense which is signified by the words is properly called literal: but that which is signified by the things is called mystical. The latter is threefold because if something belonging to matters of faith was signified by such a manner, it is called allegorical; but if it pertains to practical matters, it is called moral; but if it pertains to hope in future blessedness, it is called anagogical, leading us to the highest thing. Hence the verse:

> Litera gesta docet,
> quid credas allegoria.
> Moralis quid agas,
> quotendas anagogia.[13]

> (The letter teaches the act,
> what you should believe, allegory.
> The moral what you should do,
> where you should be heading, anagogy.)

An example of this is the name Jerusalem, which according to the literal sense signifies a certain city situated in the land of Judah; and because this city was chosen by God for divine worship (as is held in 3 Kgs 8)[14] is honored in the mind of the righteous man, both in the church militant and also in the church triumphant. Therefore Jerusalem according to the moral sense in sacred Scripture signifies the faithful soul, according to the allegorical sense the church militant, and according to the anagogical sense the church triumphant.

Moreover knowing that although sacred Scripture has the fourfold sense previously mentioned, yet each does not occur in each of its parts . . . Some places have only a literal sense, as Deut 6, "Hear, O Israel, the Lord your God is one Lord. And you shall love the Lord your God with all your heart" [Deut 6:4, 5], for in these and similar places, the mystical sense is not required. But some places do not have the literal sense properly speaking: for example, Judg 9, "The trees went forth in order to

---

[12] Lyra is describing literal meaning *(vocibus ad aliquid significandum)* as well as figurative meaning *(rebus per voces significatis).*

[13] Augustine of Dacia (died 1282), *Rotulus pugillaris* (ed. Angelus Walz), in *Classica et medievalia* 16 (1955): 139.

[14] Or 1 Kings 8 in English versions.

anoint a king over them" [Judg 9:8]. And Matthew, "If your hand offends you, cut it off and cast it from you" [Matt 5:30]. For the literal sense is properly that which is signified by the words, as has been said, and no such sense is found here: nor in other places like them: for it follows that the literal sense of sacred Scripture would be false, because trees never have done this, nor are they able to do it. Likewise the Savior has not suggested that a man cut off his own hand literally; rather in these things there is a mystical sense, which is understood through the things signified. For by the trees is understood the inhabitants of the city of Shechem, who made Abimelech king over them, as is explained in the same text; and by cutting off the hand, is understood a friend, a neighbor, who becomes an occasion for ruin, and from such familiarity a man ought to cut himself off. Moreover because some teachers say the metaphorical sense is the literal sense, this must be understood in general, because where there is no sense signified by the words, the metaphorical sense is the primary sense and thus loosely speaking it is called the literal sense because the literal sense exists when no other is there; and to signify this they say the metaphorical is included under the literal sense. In this manner of speaking, I have also called the metaphorical sense literal in many places in my writing upon the books of sacred Scripture. But some places of sacred Scripture have both the literal and the mystical sense; as in Genesis it is said that Abraham had two sons, namely Isaac and Ishmael: and this is true according to the literal sense, and likewise according to the mystical sense. For by these two, the two testaments were allegorically signified, as the apostle says in Gal 4:22–24. And in the same way, two spiritual sons of a prelate may be signified morally, one of whom acts positively and the other acts negatively; also anagogically signified are the angels who stood and those who fell. Again, as has been said, the mystical sense is that signified by the things indicated by the words, and subjectively speaking there are many real properties of one thing which sometimes are very different. Thus one thing, speaking subjectively, sometimes signifies many different things mystically. As the lion signifies Christ by the property of steadfastness, "Behold the lion from the tribe of Judah has conquered" [Rev 5:5]; and by its voracity it signifies the devil, "Your adversary, the devil, as it were goes about like a roaring lion seeking whom he may devour" [1 Pet 5:8].

Moreover as soon as I have expounded sacred Scripture with the help of God according to the literal sense and God grants me a measure of life: confident of the help of God, I propose then to expound according to the mystical sense, where it must be mystically expounded, as the Lord will grant it to me; yet I do not intend to write down all the mystical senses, nor to discuss everything on individual words, but to handle some briefly, to which readers of the Bible and preachers of the Word of God may return, as and when it will seem expedient to them. Do not be surprised, if I shall omit many mystical things in my exposition. I will do this for the sake of brevity and because previous expositors have done so, and also because of the one who expounds the parable of the sower—that which is said at the end: "They brought forth fruit, some one hundred fold, some sixty fold, some thirty fold" [Matt 13:8; Mark 4:8]. He left this unexpounded. And in other expositions of parables, Christ does the same thing. . . .

A Psalm of David 22[15]

Text and Ordinary Gloss

The ªLord ᵇrules me, and nothing will he
ªIn whom I am secure.

ᵇElsewhere [sometimes the Latin texts reads], shepherds.

ªwithhold from ᵇme. In the ᶜplace of pasture, he ᵈplaced ᵉme. ᶠBeside
ªIn the future.

ᵇBecause he believes the spiritual substance needed to be granted to him by God (Cassiodorus).[16]

ᶜIn prayerful reading of Scripture.

ᵈNot I myself.

ᵉFeeding.

ᶠHe, so to speak, first instructs me in faith and afterwards leads me forth.

the ªwater of refreshing, he ᵇleads me; he ᶜconverts my ᵈsoul.
ªBaptism, by which is restored what men lost, and the soul, barren from the sterile effects of sin, is nourished (Cassiodorus).[17]

ᵇLittle by little as children.

ᶜBut first he teaches my soul, etc. And afterwards that it may be holy and just.

ᵈAlienated in Adam.

He ªleads me upon the ᵇpaths of ᶜrighteousness on ᵈaccount of his name.
ªFrom that place. As a shepherd leads the sheep. He makes me persevere in the precepts of love; or he leads me forth to this knowledge so that I may teach his precepts.

ᵇIn which few walk.

ᶜHis.

ᵈNot on account of my merit, and if this appears to be so, not on account of others (Augustine).[18]

---

[15] Ps 23 in the Hebrew Bible (MT); Ps 22 according to the Septuagint and Vulgate. The reason for this is that the Septuagint, followed by the Vulgate, combines MT Pss 9 and 10 into one (i.e., Ps 9). From this point on in the Psalter, every number of the psalms in the Septuagint and Vulgate is one less than the number in the Hebrew Bible until Ps 147. At that point, the Septuagint and Vulgate make two psalms (Pss 146 and 147) out of one (MT Ps 147) in order to preserve the 150 psalms.

[16] Cassiodorus, *Explanation of the Psalms* (trans. P. G. Walsh; 3 vols.; New York: Paulist, 1990), 1:235.

[17] Cassiodorus, *Psalms*, 1:236.

[18] Augustine, *On the Psalms* (trans. D. S. Hebgin and D. F. Corrigan; Ancient Christian Writers 29; Westminster, Md.: Newman, 1960), 229; cf. Augustine, *Enarrationes in psalmos* (Corpus Christianorum: Series latina 38–40; Turnhout: Brepols, 1956), 1:134.

And ^aeven if I ^bwalk in the midst of the shadow of ^cdeath, I will not fear

^aHe leads me, because even if.

^bSo that I may be converted from those ignorant of God.

^cOf this life which is the shadow of death (Augustine).[19] Or heretics are the shadow of death because they bear the form of destruction (Cassiodorus).[20]

evil because you are with me. Your ^arod and your staff

^aI will not fear for. . . . Chastisement (which is for the flock; the rod for growing children) by which the life of the flesh advances to the spiritual life (Augustine).[21]

have ^acomforted me. You have ^bprepared a ^ctable in my ^dpresence

^aBy chastening, they are not discouraged (Augustine).[22]

^bBy which they have been comforted.

^cThe communion of the body of Christ (Augustine).

^dSo that now I have been strengthened against them not by sucking the milk of infancy, but by solid food (Augustine).[23]

^aagainst those who oppress me. You have ^banointed my ^chead

^aBecause the good have been laid hold of by the unworthy, they are hurt by evils (Augustine).

^bYou have gladdened my mind with spiritual joy.

^cThe mind.

in ^aoil, and my ^bcup running over, how ^cmagnificent it is!

^aWith spiritual grace.

^bGiving over to oblivion various delights (Augustine). Or, your cup.

^cFor he gives the splendor of eternal life.

Your mercy also follows me ^aall the days

^aAfter everything. As long as I live here (Cassiodorus).

of ^amy life so ^bthat I may dwell in the ^chouse of the Lord ^dforever.

^aNot your.

^bIt will follow me; moreover not merely here, but also that I may dwell. And to observe precedence, so that I may dwell.

^cNot made with hands.

^dEternally.

---

[19] Augustine, *On the Psalms*, 229.

[20] Cassiodorus, *Explanation of the Psalms* 1:237.

[21] Augustine, *On the Psalms*, 229.

[22] Augustine, *On the Psalms*, 229.

[23] Augustine, *On the Psalms*, 229.

Nicholas of Lyra Postilla

Psalm 22

The Lord rules me. To this Psalm, the following title is prefaced in Hebrew—A Psalm of David; and in Jerome's translation[24] along with the Hebrew—A Song of David. The meaning is the same because "song" and "psalm" signify the same thing. This explanation is also clear from what has been said before, except that Rashi says here that sometimes the Holy Spirit was touching the mind of David earlier.[25] Afterwards he sang a psalm and then put ahead of it in the title of the following psalm, a song by his own name, David. But on the contrary, David sometimes began to sing with an instrument to stir up his devotion; as it is said concerning Elisha, "And when the musician sang, the Spirit of the Lord came into him" (2 Kgs 3:15).[26] Then David felt the touch of the Holy Spirit. In this manner, the name David was actually set in front in the title of the psalm and prefaced to the song.

1. The Lord rules me. Some say that David composed this psalm in the Spirit foreseeing the return from the Babylonian captivity. In this character he says, "The Lord rules me" because he came back into the land of Israel by means of divine direction. "And nothing will he withhold from me" because he had no notable deficiency on the way. "In the place of pasture, he placed me," i.e., in the land of Israel which is fertile. But that does not agree well with Neh 5:5, where it is said that the people who had returned from captivity were in such poverty that some were arranging to sell their daughters into bondage and others were arranging to sell their possessions in order to have food to eat. For that reason, Rashi explains it in a different way, namely of the person of David himself, who, in fear of Saul, fled with his men to the king of Moab, as it is put in 1 Sam 22:1–5.[27] But because the fugitive men and those with debts of obligation were with David and also were pursuing idolatry and other evil inclinations, the prophet Gad spoke to David himself concerning the commandment of the Lord, that he was not to remain there, but go into the land of Judah, which he did.

Hence also it is added, "And David set out and came into the forest of Hereth" (1 Sam 22:5), confident of the divine provision. And Rashi[28] says here that by the divine power that place was abounding in fruits and animals and fountains of water so that David and his men were able to be sustained there and had no opportunity of worshipping the idols remaining in the land of Moab (which had been given over to idolatry). It can also be said, apart from such a miracle, that that forest was fertile and

---

[24] Jerome's translation is the Vulgate.

[25] Cf. R. Shlomo Yitzḥaqi (Rashi), *Commentary on Psalms 1–89* (trans. M. I. Gruber; Atlanta: Scholar's Press, 1998), 132–33.

[26] Nicholas follows the Septuagint/Vulgate enumeration, where MT 2 Kings is 4 Kings. The two books of Samuel are counted 1 and 2 Kings in the Septuagint/Vulgate.

[27] Nicholas's text reads 1 Kings 22; cf. the preceding note.

[28] Yitzḥaqi (Rashi), *Commentary on Psalms 1–89*, 132.

abounding in food and that it was that forest about which it was said, "And all the people of the land came into the forest in which there was honey upon the face of the ground" (1 Sam 14:25), namely flowing from the trees in which bees were making honey in great abundance. And Ps 10[11], mentioned above, is about the same thing. Nevertheless, it differs in this, that the former is a thanksgiving for protection against the attack of Saul. But this one is about the provision of God in food. In accordance with this sense, David says, "The Lord rules me." Also he was saying this about his men who were afraid to return to the land of Judah before they needed to because of debts of obligation, as is held by 1 Sam 22. The sense is, "The Lord rules me" by calling me back to the land of Judah through his prophet.

1. "And nothing will he withhold from me." For he recalled me from that to the promised land for his worship. I am holding firmly that he will make preparation for me and my comrades concerning food.

2. "In the place of pasture," i.e., of good sufficiency or well sufficient for living.

3. "He placed me." Because the forest of Hereth was a place sufficient for living, as has been said, from which his meaning is clear because it is added

4. "Beside the water of refreshing." Because at first I wanted to remain in the land of the Gentiles from fear of Saul; now I want the contrary.

5. "He leads me upon the paths of righteousness," i.e., he has brought me back to the place of his worship, which is perfect righteousness.

6. "On account of his name," i.e., neither I nor my men would do anything against the honor of his name, as has been said.

7. "And even if I walk in the midst of the shadow of death, I will not fear evil," i.e., in danger of death from the persecution of Saul inside his kingdom.

8. "I will not fear evil," having been chosen by him.

9. "Because you are with me," as it were a strong defender. Also in this remark David directs his expression to God himself.

10. "Your rod and your staff," i.e., your protections which also are designated by the names rod and staff.

11. "You have prepared a table in my presence," i.e., sufficient food.

12. "Against those," namely, Saul and his confederates.

13. "You have anointed in oil," as if he says, not only have you provided me food, but also suitable spices, which is designated by the name oil.

14. "And my cup," i.e., not only have you provided me food, but also suitable water.

15. "Your mercy also follows me." By providing for me sufficiently in the succeeding time.

16. "So that I may dwell in the house of the Lord," i.e., in the land where the worship of God flourishes.

17. "Forever." The psalm can be explained allegorically of the devout man fleeing from the world as from a dangerous place, and entering the place of devotion, chiefly of the mendicants, confident of the divine provision and defense against adversaries not only of the body, but also of the soul.

Allegorically

1. **The Lord rules me.** Just as Ps 10[29] is about David's confidence on returning to the land of Israel, confident also that in that very place he was protected from his enemies by divine help, so this psalm speaks about his confidence because in that very place he was nourished in the wilderness. Therefore he says, "The Lord rules me and nothing will he withhold from me." Moreover, it can be explained allegorically about passing through any place whatever to the wilderness of religion, and most of all of the mendicant confident that the necessities of life will be sufficiently provided to him there by divine help. And so he says, "The Lord rules me" by calling me to himself.

2. "And nothing will he withhold from me," concerning the necessities of life. "Seek first the kingdom of God and his righteousness and those things will be added to you" (Matt 6:33).

3. "Beside the water of refreshing," i.e., of saving wisdom.

4. "He leads me." Not only bodily, but also spiritually.

5. "He converts my soul." To himself from the vanity of the world.

6. "He leads me upon the paths of righteousness." By the observance of his counsels which are indeed short paths with respect to the life of his public commandments.

7. "For even if I walk in the midst of the shadow of death," i.e., heavy temptation.

8. "I will not fear evil." The act and the assent.

---

[29] MT Psalm 11; cf. n. 14 above.

9. "Because you are with me." As it were a strong defender; therefore it is added.

10. " Your rod and your staff," i.e., the strength of your passion (which is the rod wounding the devil) and your staff sustains me.

11. "Have comforted me." In adversities and temptations; therefore it is added.

12. "You have prepared a table in my presence," i.e., refreshing consolation.

13. "Against those who oppress me," i.e., against the devil, his temptations and evil men oppressing me with injustices.

14. "You have anointed in oil." Your mercies.

15. "My head," i.e., my mind, which is the most valuable part of men.

16. "And my cup running over," i.e., the sacrament of the altar overflowing with fervent love. "Imbibe, O lovers" (Song 5:1).

17. "How magnificent it is." Effectively because it leads to the glory of heaven.

18. "And your mercy also follows me all the days of my life." Through an increase of grace.

19. "So that I may dwell in the house of the Lord." Namely, heaven without end.

Part Three

―⊗⊗⊗―

Rabbinic Interpretation and Its Legacy (150–1500 C.E.)

CHAPTER 12

An Overview of the Classical Jewish Interpretive Tradition (fourth through thirteenth centuries C.E.)

T wo thousand years ago, different Jewish groups were studying the Hebrew Scriptures in somewhat different ways. Elsewhere in this anthology we have observed the products of some of these approaches, such as that represented by Philo and that found in the Dead Sea Scrolls. Additionally, many New Testament documents are themselves the results of exegetical efforts by other Jews of the late Second Temple period. From other schools of thought in this early Jewish world, such as the Sadducees, however, almost nothing of scriptural interpretation has survived. After the Roman destruction of the Jerusalem temple in 70 C.E. and the Roman victory over the Bar Kokhba rebellion in 135, no forms of Judaism survived that depended primarily on Jewish political institutions. Only the rabbinic form of Judaism lived on, and it is to the exegetical efforts of the ancient rabbis and the enduring interpretive tradition they engendered that we now turn.

In the era when Julius and Augustus ruled from Rome, the religious and social order of Jewish life centered on the temple in Jerusalem and its attendant religio-political institutions. The aftermath of the temple's destruction included the need to raise up a new structure of authority around which Jewish communal life could be oriented. To this end, in about 90 C.E. Rabban Johanan ben Zakkai established a council at Yavneh composed of sages (teaching masters) from the various Jewish districts of Palestine. There the formal ordination process was established for the passing of teaching authority to students of subsequent generations. This development helped distinguish the sages—tradition would come to call them rabbis—as a recognized authority-laden social class among Jews worldwide. From this point on, the collective opinions of the rabbis would determine the contours of religious and social life in the Jewish world—and all of it was built upon interpretation of Scripture.[1]

The question of the earliest appearance of rabbinic interpretation is a subject of scholarly debate. Certain portions of the Dead Sea documents seem to reflect a rabbinic or

---

[1] The chief exception to this statement was the Karaite Jews, who distinguished themselves from rabbinic Judaism by rejecting the rabbinate as a social, legal, and hermeneutical authority. Karaite interpretation of Scripture was known for its literalness and autonomy: each individual was expected to interpret Scripture without recourse to the rabbinic tradition and according to the literal sense of the text. Karaism first emerged in Mesopotamia during the late eighth century, expanding into the Levant and Egypt in the tenth century. In later centuries Karaite communities were to survive in greater numbers in the Crimea and in Russia.

"protorabbinic" interpretative stance, as do selected passages of the New Testament; such cases point to first-century C.E. origins. The earliest collections of rabbinic interpretive thought were compiled in the fourth century, and regardless of the question of earlier antecedents, we can safely say that rabbinic interpretation of Scripture had become a well-established *written* tradition by that time.

The ancient rabbis themselves, however, understood the origins of Jewish biblical interpretation differently. They would consider it mistaken to think that there existed, on the one hand, the Scriptures that God had revealed at Sinai (and, by implication, to the prophets and other inspired writers) and, on the other hand, the later rabbinic commentary applied to these Scriptures. Rather, the Oral Torah, the body of rabbinic Scripture interpretation, had been revealed to Moses at Sinai just as had the biblical laws, or Written Torah. Whereas the Written Torah was transmitted over the generations in manuscript form, the Oral Torah remained an unwritten tradition.

Rabbinic documents express this idea in a variety of ways. For example, the Mishnah tractate *Avot* (Fathers) begins with the words "Moses received the Torah from Sinai and passed it on to Joshua, and Joshua to the elders, and the elders to the prophets, and the prophets passed it on to the men of the Great Synagogue." There follows an annotated list of scholars down to the first century C.E., each having received and passed on the Oral Torah that originated from Sinai. In the Palestinian Talmud we find this teaching: "Everything which any advanced disciple may teach in the presence of his master at any time in the future, was already told to Moses on Mount Sinai" (*Pe'ah* 2.6). A somewhat different expression of the idea that the same divine source lies behind both the biblical law and its body of interpretation appears in *Midrash Rabbah Numbers* (Chukkat 19:6): "Matters that had not been disclosed to Moses were disclosed to R. Akiva and his colleagues."[2] Thus, from the perspective of the classical Jewish interpretive tradition, the notion of Torah—a text-based, authoritative divine revelation—is not strictly a matter of an original meaning that is at first expressed textually and subsequently made clearer through interpretation consistently distinguished from that original meaning. "Torah" in its full sense refers to the ongoing human reception of revelation as well as its divine granting.

The Oral Torah has long been understood to consist of two types of teaching, halakah and haggadah. Halakah is a legal ruling that determines correct observance of a biblical law. The chief repositories of these rulings are the Mishnah (compiled in the third century C.E.) and the Talmuds—the Palestinian (also called Yerushalmi; compiled ca. 550 C.E.) and the Babylonian (also called Bavli; compiled ca. 650 C.E.). These voluminous compendia do not constitute biblical commentaries per se. Instead of being organized according to the sequence of biblical texts, they proceed through a series of general conceptual themes, such as prayer, purity, and observance of religious holy days. Although the Mishnah is devoted to the legal application of Scripture to Jewish life, it in fact cites Scripture with relative infrequency. Not so with the Talmuds. For the purposes of the present survey, we may understand the Talmuds as the accumulated results of efforts over many generations to identify specific scriptural bases for halakic rulings found in the Mishnah. For this task, the Talmuds draw heavily upon, and often expand considerably upon, older sources of Scripture commentary known as midrash (see below).

---

[2] For more about R. Akiva, see below.

Haggadah (or aggadah) is an ethical or theological interpretation of Scripture, usually derived from a narrative portion of text rather than from a legal passage.[3] Often the occasion for an haggadic comment lies in the unspoken narrative background to a biblical episode, in an odd or rare Hebrew expression or grammatical form, or in the potential for intertextual connection between one biblical text and another, such as the actions and legacies of two biblical characters, each from a different story. A wide range of theological and moral themes appears in the haggadah. Often the emphasis lands on the unique relationship between God and Israel as evident in the events of biblical history and especially in the giving and the study of the Torah.

Both halakic and haggadic interpretations of Scripture characteristically address the biblical text in a fashion that is often called midrash. Defining this term has prompted considerable debate among scholars, but the following allows for the range of significance inherent in the word:

> The term *Midrash* (plural, *Midrashim*) is used . . . [traditionally] to refer either to (1) a rabbinic interpretation, virtually always of a scriptural word, phrase, or verse, which searches, or ferrets out, a meaning which is not immediately obvious upon first encounter with the text; (2) a compilation of such interpretations; (3) the totality of all rabbinic compilations of such interpretations; and (4) the act of interpreting Scripture in the manner described above.[4]

Here we are primarily concerned with the first and second meanings in this definition.

Usually a single midrashic interpretation will develop from a very small unit of Scripture—a phrase, a verse, a word, even a letter. Frequently, however, the outcome or insight generated by a *darshan* (one who teaches a midrash) implicitly speaks of much larger theological and moral themes reflected throughout the whole of Scripture. The trigger for a midrashic interpretation is usually something in the biblical text that is unusual, anomalous, or otherwise unexpected—apparent contradictions, repetitions, obscure words, unusual spelling or grammar, implied moral or theological questions—ranging in scale from the conspicuous to the exceedingly minute. Indeed, many midrash-triggering "bumps" in the text are so subtle that they cannot be detected apart from a close scrutiny of the Hebrew biblical text. (This characteristic of midrash makes it difficult for non-Jewish students of the Bible to grasp the significance of many midrashim and turns into a formidable challenge the task of economically translating rabbinic documents.) Underlying most midrashic attempts to address problems in the text is the presupposition that, as God's revelation, Scripture cannot contain anything that is without meaning—not even letters within words (or, in the extreme, the very shape of the letters). Thus, there can be no superfluity or imperfection such as might be implied by the presence of a repetition or any other element in the text.[5] Over the generations the rabbinic houses of study would

---

[3] The haggadah also includes legends about the ancient rabbinic sages, but here we are restricting ourselves to the *haggadot* that more directly concern biblical interpretation.

[4] Richard Kalmin, "Patterns and Development in Rabbinic Midrash of Late Antiquity," in *Hebrew Bible/Old Testament: The History of Its Interpretation* (ed. Magne Sæbø; Göttingen: Vandenhoeck & Ruprecht, 1996), 287.

[5] To help provide guidelines for the development of explanations for these features of the text, and even more for providing scriptural bases for halakic rulings, certain rules for scriptural exegesis *(middot)* became part of the rabbinic tradition. These *middot*, originally seven in number, were traditionally attributed to the great first-century authority Hillel; an expanded list of thirteen exegetical principles was passed down in the name of the early-second-century sage Ishmael ben

naturally come up with more than one solution to a perceived textual problem. It is common, then, to find in the rabbinic documents multiple responses to a question once it has been introduced from the biblical text. Rarely is there an effort evident in the midrashic documents themselves to adjudicate definitively among these various interpretations; they are allowed each to take their place before the reader, often in the same midrashic volume, even on the same page. This characteristic of midrashim in the aggregate points to the conspicuously social dimension of rabbinic interpretation.

Rabbinic exegesis came by social engagement in the house of study *(beit midrash)* and in any other setting where scholars dialogued. It was not the cultural practice for ancient rabbis to teach through the composition of texts but through the training of disciple-scholars. Not one of the rabbinic interpretations of Scripture, as they have been committed to writing, is in the form of a book or essay from the pen of an identifiable author, such as we find in the Christian interpretive tradition. (This is true despite the frequent attributions of specific teachings to individual authorities by name.) Rabbinic documents are the products not of the sages themselves but of anonymous editors who selected from the various rabbinic teaching traditions and arranged them into collections that subsequently became traditions in their own right and were passed down through the ages.[6] Moreover,

---

Elisha, and a further expanded list of thiry-two rules is said to have been taught by the mid-second-century rabbi Eliezer ben Yose. The sevenfold Hillel list is as follows (adapted from D. I. Brewer, *Techniques and Assumptions in Jewish Exegesis before 70 C.E.* [Tübingen: J. C. B. Mohr (Paul Siebeck), 1992], 226):

1. *Qal wa-ḥomer* ("light and heaviness"): inference from a minor application to a larger application of the same theological or behavioral principle, and vice versa;

2. *Gezerah shavah* ("equal decree"): inference by verbal similarity;

3. *Binyan av mekatuv eḥad* ("building a family from one text"): homogenization through the creation of a conceptual category on the basis of one biblical passage and applying that category to similar texts;

4. *Binyan av meshnei ketuvim* ("building a family from two texts"): homogenization through the creation of a conceptual category on the basis of two biblical passages and applying that category to similar texts;

5. *Kelal u-pherat u-pherat ukelal* ("general and particular, and particular and general"): a general term is qualified by a subsequent particular term, and a particular term is qualified by a subsequent general term;

6. *Keyitzeh bo' bemaqom aḥer* ("as is similar with it in another place"): exposition of one passage by means of a similar passage;

7. *Davar hilamed me'inyano* ("meaning is learned from its context"): the meaning may be deduced from nearby texts.

Although at times the *darshanim* made use of some of these principles (even by name), midrashic interpretations, by and large, do not necessarily work by virtue of following any one *middah*. Regardless, it is interesting to note that the mid-fifth-century *Mekilta of R. Simeon ben Joḥai* on Exodus (at 21:1) refers to R. Ishmael's teaching of the thirteen *middot* "by which the Torah is interpreted, and which were passed on [from God] to Moses at Sinai."

[6] The rabbinic corpus of midrash is vast and includes such documents as *Genesis Rabbah, Leviticus Rabbah, Lamentations Rabbah, Pesiqta of Rab Kahana, Song of Songs Rabbah,* and *Ruth Rabbah,* to mention but a few. For a concise introduction to the general subject of midrash and midrashic documents, see M. D. Herr, "Midrash," in *Encyclopaedia Judaica* (16 vols.; Jerusalem: Keter, 1971), 11:1507–14.

these rabbinic compilation documents typically share a distinctive characteristic: they are presented as though they were the recording of a conversation between rabbinic authorities. It is possible that this format preserves faint traces of the exegetical debates that took place in the ancient rabbinic schools of Palestine and Babylonia. Be that as it may, the dialogical nature of rabbinic interpretive discourse manifests an engagement with the biblical text as an eminently social phenomenon. The rabbis "knew themselves in dialogue with each other and with generations of wise men extending both backward to Koheleth and Solomon (and beyond to Moses and to God himself, who is frequently pictured as studying his own texts) and forward to the endless openings of the Scriptures upon new questions that are put to them. Thus the midrashic collections that have come down to us are structured as conversations rather than as systematic expositions."[7] The twelfth-century Spanish philosopher and poet Judah ha-Levi expressed the rabbinic dialogical ideal with a succinct play on words: *Meppo sopherim velo' meppo sepharim* "(Learn) from scholars and not (just) from books."[8]

The scholars active from 90 to 220 C.E., when the codification of the Mishnah was definitively accomplished by Judah ha-Nasi, were known as the Tannaim (from a word that means "repeaters" [of what they had been taught]). With the promulgation of the Tannaitic traditions in the Mishnah, the next generations of rabbis, known as Amoraim (from a word meaning "speakers" [of teachings]), followed until about 500 C.E. The Amoraim typically deferred to the authority of what their Tannaitic predecessors had taught.

The vast corpus of rabbinic literature mentions by name thousands of rabbinic authorities from the Tannaitic and Amoraitic eras (although it is not uncommon for names to appear in variant or corrupted forms). It is not always possible to distinguish in the sources between two or more rabbis who had the same name. The following summations of individuals mentioned in our selections are restricted to information relevant to biblical interpretation. These rabbinic authorities are reviewed here in the general order of their historical sequence.

Tannaim

Rabbi Ishmael ben Elisha (early second century)

Rabbi Ishmael ben Elisha was a contemporary of another important Tannaitic figure, R. Akiva, and the midrashim often feature differences between the two in interpretation and interpretive method. R. Ishmael characteristically allowed for figures of speech and repetitions in the biblical text as functions of the natural expressiveness in human language. As a result, he did not consider it necessary, as did R. Akiva, to assume that every linguistic twist or repetition was a bearer of meaning that required its own interpretation: *Dibberah torah ke-lashon beney adam* ("The Torah speaks according to human expression") (*Sifre* to Num 15:31). R. Ishmael tended to favor more literal interpretations. Several important halakic compilations are attributed to the school of Ishmael: the *Mekilta* (on

---

[7] Gerald Bruns, "Midrash and Allegory," in *The Literary Guide to the Bible* (ed. Robert Alter and Frank Kermode; Cambridge, Mass.: Belknap, 1987), 630.

[8] Judah ha-Levi, *Kitab al Khazari (Book of Kuzari)* (trans. Hartwig Hirschfeld; Brooklyn: P. Shalom, 1969), pt. 2, sec. 72.

Exodus), the *Sifre* (on Numbers), and 1–54 of *Sifra Deuteronomy*. To R. Ishmael also are attributed the thirteen principles for exegetical reasoning, an expansion of the seven principles attributed to the first-century master Hillel.

Rabbi Akiva (early second century)

Although in his younger years he had despised scholarship, during his adult life Akiva went on to become a profoundly influential Tanna and the very picture of devotion to Torah study. The school he founded grew to be among the most respected of its time. Akiva taught that since the Torah came from God, there could be in it nothing superfluous, no meaningless redundancies, no spelling or grammatical variations without a purpose or significance. At Akiva's encouragement, one of his students, Aquila, produced a slavishly literal Greek translation of the Torah that reflected many of the halakic readings from the Akiva school. Onkelos, who produced the most enduring Aramaic translation (Targum) of the Torah, was similarly influenced by Akiva. The midrashic works *Sifre* and *Sifra* (on Leviticus) characteristically reflect the halakic views taught by Akiva. In one of his most far-reaching accomplishments, Akiva brought order to the burgeoning body of halakic traditions of the pre–Bar Kokhba period; the order he established would eventually be refined by R. Judah ha-Nasi and known as the Mishnah.

Rabbi Neḥunia (late first century)

R. Neḥunia was R. Ishmael's teacher; the latter handed down to his own students his master's teaching on the hermeneutical principle of *kelal u-pherat*. According to this view, halakic principles derived from Scripture are to be systematized by categories of general positions related to particular refinements. This differs from the *ribbui u-mi'ut* approach taught by the Akiva school, according to which halakic principles are applied by extension or limitation.

Rabbi Eleazar ben Azariah (early second century)

Born to a wealthy priestly family, R. Eleazar was selected to serve at age eighteen as *nasi* (civic governor of the Palestinian Jewish community) and later shared this office with its previous holder, Gameliel II. As an interpreter, R. Eleazar tended to favor the more literal readings associated with the school of R. Ishmael. Although greatly respected for his halakic rulings, most of R. Eleazar's surviving interpretations are haggadic. In his exegetical arguments, he made copious use of the *qal wa-ḥomer* principle.

Rabbi Jose the Galilean (early second century)

A student of R. Akiva, R. Jose earned a level of respect unusual in a master-pupil relationship. But despite this distinction and his participation at the Yavneh council, no disciples of R. Jose's are known as such. His biblical interpretations usually follow the more elaborate tradition of Akiva.

Rabbi Simon ben Menasiah (late second–early third century)

A contemporary of Judah ha-Nasi, this Tanna was known for his strict discipline in abstinence and in Levitical purity. In the Babylonian Talmud at *Yoma* 85b appears a tradition by the authority of R. Simon that is also included in our *Mekilta* selection but attributed to R. Nathan.

Rabbi Nathan (mid-second century)

R. Nathan is also referred to as Nathan ha-Bavli, as he had immigrated from Babylon to Israel in order to study under R. Ishmael and R. Jose. During the Hadrianic persecution, he returned to Babylon. Tradition attributes to R. Nathan a commentary on an early form of the the haggadic Mishnah tractate *Avot* and an articulation of forty-nine *middot,* or exegetical principles.

Rabbi Eleazar of Modim (late first–early second century)

R. Eleazar was well known as a haggadist, with only one halakic opinion attributed to him. Other interpreters sometimes found his homiletic interpretations excessive in figural reach from the literal meaning of the text.

Rabbi Ḥanina (first century)

A man of very meager means, R. Ḥanina was widely respected for his piety and the efficacy of his prayers (which were sometimes said to be associated with miracles). His teachings, to the extent that they are preserved, are largely haggadic.

Rabbi Isaac (second century)

Among the first of the Babylonian Tannaim, R. Isaac eventually immigrated to Palestine. He was known for his skill as both a haggadist and a halakist.

Rabbi Aḥai ben Josiah (late second century)

R. Aḥai earned renown as a halakic authority in the tradition of R. Ishmael's exegetical school. He established a yeshiva in Babylon.

Rabbi Judah ben Bathyra (second century)

After spending his youth in Rome, Judah moved to Palestine, where he studied with R. Akiva, and settled in Babylon, where he founded a yeshiva. In Babylon his authority grew to compare with that of R. Akiva in Palestine.

Rabbi Dostai (late second century)

This Palestinian Tanna was known for his humor and practical wisdom.

Rabbi Eliezer (late first–early second century)

Having participated in the council at Yavneh, R. Eliezer went on to establish an influential academy whose students included Akiva and Aquila. In his halakic rulings R. Eliezer was severely conservative, resisting most attempts to adjust halakah to the realities of the Jewish world after the temple had been destroyed. His contentions with the majority of rabbis over such issues brought upon him excommunication (a decision by the majority to disregard his authority and his rulings). The story of his excommunication (Baba Meṣiʻa 59b in the Babylonian Talmud) illustrates the principle that the majority opinion prevailed over the authority of even such a prominent scholar as R. Eliezer. Later, following his death, his rulings were reinstated for official study.

Rabbi Eleazar ben Perata (early second century)

This Tanna, who adhered to his practice of teaching and observing Torah even to the point of imprisonment under Hadrian's edict, was well known for his homiletic interpretations.

Rabbi Eliezer ben Jacob (early second century)

R. Eliezer was a Palestinian Tanna who studied under R. Akiva. Much of the Mishnah tractate *Middot* is attributed to him.

Rabbi Judah ha-Nasi (late second–early third century)

Among the last of the Tannaim, R. Judah was born into a lineage of political leadership tracing back to Hillel in the first century. His family's wealth, his authority as a scholar, and the profound respect accorded him by the Jewish community brought him recognition by the Roman authorities as the ruler of the Jews in Palestine—reflected in the epithet "Judah the Prince." R. Judah used his civic and religious authority to firmly establish the communal cohesion of the Jewish people in their religious and judicial institutions within the imperial Roman context. Perhaps the most enduring of his achievements was the definitive codification of Tannaitic halakic rulings called the Mishnah. In our selection he is referred to as Rabbi.

Amoraim

Rabbi Simeon ben Laqish (third century)

During a difficult period for Jews in Palestine, this Amora was very active as a community leader and scholar in Tiberias, where he had studied at the academy. R. Simeon worked energetically to promote the study of Torah not only through his teaching efforts but through his generosity. The Babylonian Talmud often refers to him as Resh Laqish.

Rabbi Hoshaiah (late third–early fourth century)

Although the Talmud cites him, this Babylonian Amora was never formally recognized as a halakic authority. He was therefore known as an "associate of the rabbis."

Rabbi Ḥuna (fourth century)

R. Ḥuna grew up and studied in Babylon and later immigrated to Palestine, where he took an active role in the academic and civic life of the Jewish community. His teachings, which appear frequently in the Palestinian Talmud, often refer to the authority of Babylonian scholars. R. Ḥuna was known for his homiletic interpretations.

Rabbi Ḥiyya (late second century)

After spending his youth in Babylon, Ḥiyya moved to Palestine in order to study under R. Judah ha-Nasi, becoming one of his most noteworthy students. R. Ḥiyya went on to establish his own *beit midrash,* there preserving and teaching the *baraitoth* (rulings) that R. Judah did not include in his codification of the Mishnah. In addition to his expertise in halakah, R. Ḥiyya was known for his dedication in supplying poorer communities with Torah scrolls.

Rabbi Zeirah (early fourth century)

Although he grew up in Babylon, R. Zeirah became convinced of the superior halakic training available in the Palestinian academies and so immigrated there. Widely cited in the Talmuds, R. Zeirah was distinguished by his extraordinary precision in learning and teaching halakoth.

Rabbi Yudan (fourth century)

R. Yudan was a Palestinian Amora whose views are recorded only in the Palestinian Talmud and midrashim. He was known for his encouragement to the Jewish people as they endured oppressive government policies under Christian emperors.

Rabbi Abbahu (early fourth century)

A member of a wealthy family residing in Caesarea, R. Abbahu had opportunities to travel and to acquire an education in mathematics, Greek, and classical rhetorical training. His civic prominence and enthusiasm for learning of all sorts won him respect from the Roman authorities. By the fourth century, Caesarea had become a center of Christian learning; R. Abbahu seems to have been an Amora who engaged in disputes about Christian interpretations of Scripture.

Rabbi Yoḥanan (late second–early third century)

Widely cited in the Palestinian Talmud for his halakic opinions, R. Yoḥanan was also known for his transmission of traditions about the destruction of the Jewish temple at Jerusalem in 70 C.E.

Rabbi Hamma ben Ḥanina (third century)

This Palestinian Amora used part of his family's wealth to underwrite construction of a synagogue in Sepphoris. R. Hamma earned a reputation as a great homelist, bringing to his preaching a treasury of haggadoth.

Rabbi Samuel (early third century)

Although he was a Babylonian Amora, tradition says that R. Samuel was a student of Judah ha-Nasi. His family's wealth afforded him a fine education; his erudition included knowledge of medicine and astronomy. R. Samuel became a major authority in civil law and was appointed to lead a *beit din* (law court) that left a long-lasting legacy of justice. His education and prominent place in society brought him into constructive engagement with non-Jewish leaders and scholars.

Rabbi Issi ben Akiva (late third–early fourth century)

Born in Babylon to a priestly family, R. Issi moved to Palestine, where he eventually was named to teach at the Tiberian academy. His haggadic and halakic teachings are frequently cited in both Talmuds.

Rabbi Abbaye (late third–early fourth century)

R. Abbaye was a Babylonian Amora with a priestly heritage who was appointed to lead the academy at Pumbeditha. The halakic disputes between R. Abbaye and another Amora named Rava are so prominent in the Babylonian Talmud that their names together sometimes constitute a shorthand reference to the distinctive talmudic mode of dialectical argumentation. R. Abbaye assimilated *haggadoth* from Palestine for teaching in Babylon.

For further information on midrash and the classical Jewish interpretive tradition:

Fishbane, Michael, ed. *The Exegetical Imagination: On Jewish Thought and Theology.* Cambridge: Harvard University Press, 1998.

Halivni, David Weiss. *Peshat and Derash—Plain and Applied Meaning in Rabbinic Exegesis.* Oxford: Oxford University Press, 1991.

Neusner, Jacob. *Introduction to Rabbinic Literature.* New York: Doubleday, 1994.

———. *What Is Midrash?* Philadelphia: Fortress, 1987.

Porton, Gary G. *Understanding Rabbinic Midrash: Text and Commentary.* Hoboken, N.J.: KTAV.

Stern, David. "Midrash." Pages 613–20 in *Contemporary Jewish Thought.* Edited by A. A. Cohen and P. Mendes-Flohr. New York: Scribner, 1987.

CHAPTER 13

Halakic Interpretation of the Scriptures

Sabbath Law in Exodus 31:12–17;
The *Mekilta of Rabbi Ishmael;*
The Palestinian Talmud, Tractate *Yoma* 8.3–5;
Rabbi Shlomo Yitzḥaqi (Rashi);
Rabbi Moses ben Naḥman (Ramban, Naḥmanides)
(fourth through thirteenth centuries C.E.)

P resented here are samples of halakic interpretation from a sequence of rabbinic and later sources centered on the theme of Sabbath law and focused on Exod 31:12–17. They briefly represent the transgenerational interpretive dialogue so characteristic of the classical Jewish exegetical tradition. The commentary sequence—spanning almost a millennium—includes comments from the *Mekilta of Rabbi Ishmael,* the Palestinian Talmud, Rashi, and Ramban and notes how each subsequent interpreter builds on, and responds to, the inherited halakic tradition.

Sabbath Law in Exodus 31:12–17

In the biblical presentation of these verses, Exod 31:12–17 shows the very beginnings of halakic interpretation, as the verses elaborate on the basic Sabbath commandment that appears initially in Exod 20:8–11. Originally the Israelites are commanded to cease from work in the seventh day of the week, but no penalty for Sabbath violation is mentioned. Here in Exod 31 the law is repeated, with special attention to the consequences of any violation, to the jurisdiction of this commandment over everyone in the Israelite community, and to the enduring irrevocability of the Sabbath requirement.[1] One might say that as far as the classical Jewish interpretive tradition regarding Sabbath law is concerned, it is God who begins the halakic process:

---

[1] In Exod 35:2–3 a further refinement is added to the Sabbath law, specifying the kindling of fire as an action that would violate the Sabbath law if done on that day.

Exodus 31:12–17

And the Lord said to Moses, "And you, speak to the people of Israel, 'But [*ach*] my Sabbaths you shall observe, for this is a sign between me and you throughout your generations, in order to know that I am the Lord who sanctifies you. And you shall observe the Sabbath for it is holy unto you. Anyone who profanes it shall surely be put to death, for whoever does any work during it, that soul shall be cut off from among his people. For six days work may be done, but the seventh day is a Sabbath of complete rest, holy unto the Lord; whoever does work on the Sabbath day shall surely be put to death. The Israelites shall observe the Sabbath, to make the Sabbath an eternal covenant for their generations. Between me and the Israelites it is a sign forever that in six days the Lord made the heavens and the earth, but on the seventh day he rested and relaxed.' "

The *Mekilta of Rabbi Ishmael* (fourth century C.E.)

The *Mekilta of Rabbi Ishmael* is primarily a halakic commentary on Exodus, concentrating on the legal sections, from Exod 12 to 35. This midrashic collection was redacted into its final form about the third or fourth century C.E.; its contents indicate that its sources are some of the oldest midrashim, dating back perhaps to the time of R. Akiva.

The following selection features teachings that, for the most part, explore nuances of the Sabbath law left untouched by the Exod 31 text: What exactly constitutes work that would violate the Sabbath? Would the work involved in lifesaving activity violate the Sabbath? By what reasoning do we justify a decision on this question? Are the nighttime hours included in the commandment to rest? These and other questions prompt from the rabbis responses typical of early halakic exegesis.[2]

Mekilta of Rabbi Ishmael [3]

And the Lord said to Moses.
Directly and not through the medium of an angel or a messenger.

But my Sabbaths you shall observe.
Why is this said? Because it says: "You shall not do any manner of work" (Exod 20:10), from which I know only about activities that can be regarded as labor. But how about activities that can be regarded as merely detracting from the restfulness of the Sabbath? Scripture says here: "Verily [*ach*] ye shall keep My Sabbaths," thus prohibiting even such activities as only detract from the restfulness of the day.[4]

Once R. Ishmael, R. Eleazar b. Azariah and R. Akiba were walking along the road followed by Levi the netmaker and Ishmael the son of R. Eleazar b. Azariah. And the following question was discussed by them: Whence do we know that the duty of saving life supercedes the Sabbath laws? R. Ishmael, answering the question,

---

[2] Other halakic midrashim include the following:

> *Sifra:* A commentary that works through all of Leviticus verse by verse. The core of this text developed in the mid-third century as a critique and commentary of the Mishnah, although subsequent additions and editing went on for some time afterward.

> *Sifre Numbers:* Largely halakic, this midrash on the book of Numbers includes a long haggadic piece. References in the Talmud indicate that the original core of *Sifre* was centered on Numbers, Exodus, and Deuteronomy; but because of vicissitudes in the textual transmission by the Middle Ages, only the commentary on Numbers and Deuteronomy remained. The core material was redacted about the middle of the fourth century.

> *Sifre Deuteronomy:* An exegetical and halakic midrash on Deuteronomy, redacted in the late third century.

[3] This translation is reprinted from *Mekilta de-Rabbi Ishmael,* © 1961, vol. 3, The Jewish Publication Society with the permission of the publisher, The Jewish Publication Society. Edited and translated by Jacob Z. Lauterbach.

[4] Verse 13 begins—somewhat oddly—with the Hebrew particle *ach;* at this point in the *Mekilta,* it is taken as an expression of emphasis or extension. See n. 9 below.

said: Behold it says: "If a thief be found breaking in," etc. (Exod 22:1).[5] Now of what case does the law speak? Of a case when there is a doubt whether the burglar came merely to steal or even to kill. Now, by using the method of *kal vaḥomer* [inference from a minor application to a larger application of the same theological or behavioral principle], it is to be reasoned: Even shedding of blood, which defiles the land and causes the Shekinah [divine presence] to remove, is to supercede the laws of the Sabbath if it is to be done in protection of one's life.[6] How much more should the duty of saving life supercede the Sabbath laws! R. Eleazar b. Azariah, answering the question, said: If in performing the ceremony of circumcision, which affects only one member of the body, one is to disregard the Sabbath laws, how much more should one do so for the whole body when it is in danger! The sages however said to him: From the instance cited by you it would also follow that just as there the Sabbath is to be disregarded only in the case of certainty,[7] so also here the Sabbath is to be disregarded only in a case of certainty.[8]

R. Akiba says: If punishment for murder sets aside even the Temple service, which in turn supercedes the Sabbath, how much more should the duty of saving life supercede the Sabbath laws!

R. Jose the Galilean says: When it says: "But my Sabbath ye shall keep," the word "but" *(ach)* implies a distinction. There are Sabbaths on which you must rest and there are Sabbaths on which you should not rest.[9]

R. Simon b. Menasiah says: Behold it says: "And you shall keep the Sabbath for it is holy unto you" (31:14). This means: The Sabbath is given to you but you are not surrendered to the Sabbath.

R. Nathan says: Behold it says: "Wherefore the children of Israel shall keep the Sabbath to observe the Sabbath throughout their generations" (31:16). This implies that we should disregard one Sabbath for the sake of saving the life of a person so that that person may be able to observe many Sabbaths.

For it is a sign between me and you
But not between Me and the nations of the world.

---

[5] In their discussions the rabbinical sages characteristically referred to passages of Scripture by quoting only the first few words of the cited passage. This does not necessarily mean that only the quoted words are pertinent to the point at issue. The whole of Exod 22:1 reads, "If a man steals an ox or a sheep, and kills it or sells it, he shall pay five oxen for an ox, and four sheep for a sheep. He shall make restitution; if he has nothing, then he shall be sold for his theft."

[6] The law in Exod 22:1 does not make any distinction as to whether the burglar breaks in on a Sabbath or on a week-day. —Lauterbach

[7] If the child is born at twilight of Friday evening or of Saturday evening, in which case it is not certain that the following Sabbath is the eighth day after birth, the circumcision may not be performed on that Sabbath day (see Mishnah *Shabbat* 19.5 and *Shabbat* 134b–135a [in the Babylonian Talmud]). —Lauterbach

[8] I.e., that life will be saved by work done on the Sabbath. —Lauterbach

[9] Here the Hebrew particle *ach* in Exod 31:13 is understood to limit, rather than extend, the principle of Sabbath rest. See n. 4 above.

Throughout their generations

This law should obtain throughout the generations.

That ye may know [in order to know]

Why is this said? Because it says: "Wherefore the children of Israel shall keep the Sabbath" (ibid.), from which I might understand that the deaf and dumb, the insane and the minor are also included in this commandment. Therefore it says here: "That ye may know." So I must interpret it as speaking only of such persons as have understanding.

That I am the Lord Who sanctifies you

In the future world, which is characterized by the kind of holiness possessed by the Sabbath of this world. We thus learn that the Sabbath possesses a holiness like that of the future world. And thus it says: "A Psalm: A song of the Sabbath day" (Ps 92:1), referring to the world in which there is Sabbath all the time.

And ye shall observe the Sabbath for it is holy unto you

This is the verse that R. Simon b. Menasiah interpreted as saying: The Sabbath is given to you but you are not surrendered to the Sabbath.

For it is holy unto you

This tells that the Sabbath adds holiness to Israel. Why is the shop of so-and-so closed? Because he keeps the Sabbath. Why does so-and-so abstain from work? Because he keeps the Sabbath. He thus bears witness to Him by whose word the world came into being that He created His world in six days and rested on the seventh. And thus it says: "Therefore ye are my witnesses, saith the Lord, and I am God" (Isa 43:12).

Everyone that profanes it shall surely be put to death

Why is this said? Because it says: "Whoever does any work on the Sabbath day, he shall surely be put to death" (31:15). We have thus heard the penalty. But we have not heard the warning.[10] Therefore it says: "But the seventh day is a Sabbath unto the Lord thy God, in it you shall not do any sort of work" (Exod 20:10). I thus know only the penalty for and the warning against work on the Sabbath during the daytime. How do I know that there is also a penalty for and a warning against work during the nighttime of the Sabbath? It says here: "Everyone who profanes it shall surely be put to death." From this however we only learn about the penalty. But we have not heard any warning.[11] Scripture says: "But the seventh day is a Sabbath unto the Lord thy God." Now there would be no purpose in saying "a sabbath" except to include the nighttime in the warning—these are the words of R. Ahai the son of Josiah.

---

[10] The assumption here is that for every warning or admonition there must be a penalty for transgressing the warning. The discussion in the rabbinic commentary collection called *Sifra* (Qedoshim 10–12), concerning sexual relations, includes extended arguments for the warning-penalty connection.

[11] I.e., against work during the nighttime of the Sabbath. —Lauterbach

R. Judah b. Bathyra says: Suppose the Gentiles surrounded Israelitish cities and the Israelites in self-defense had to profane the Sabbath. The Israelites should not in such a case say: Since we had to profane part of the Sabbath, we might as well continue to profane the rest of the day. For it says: "Everyone that profanes it shall surely be put to death," meaning: Everyone that profanes it even for one moment shall be put to death.[12]

For whoever does work during it

Provided that he does a complete act of work. But suppose he writes one letter [of a word] on Sabbath morning and the other letter in the afternoon, or he spins one thread in the morning and another thread late in the afternoon, I might understand that he should also be guilty. But it says: "For whoever does any work therein"—that is, provided he does a complete act of work at one time.

That soul shall be cut off from among his people

Why is this said? Since it says: "Everyone that profanes it shall surely be put to death," I know only that one who does it presumptuously, despite the warning of witnesses, incurs the penalty. But how about one who acts presumptuously but privately? Scripture says here: "Shall be cut off"—to include even one who profanes the Sabbath presumptuously even though only privately.[13]

Shall be cut off

To be cut off merely means to cease to exist.

That soul

This means the soul acting presumptuously.—These are the words of R. Akiba.

From among his people

And his people is left in peace.

Six days shall work be done

One passage says: "Six days shall work be done," and another passage says: "Six days shall you labor and do all your work" (Exod 20:9).[14] How can both these passages be maintained? When the Israelites do the will of God, then: "Six days shall work be done." Their work is done for them by others. And thus it says: "And strangers shall stand and feed your flocks, and aliens shall be your plowmen and your vinedressers" (Isa 61:5). But when the Israelites do not do the will of God, then: "Six

---

[12] The problem of Sabbath observance during wartime was already broached during Hellenistic times, according to 1 Maccabees, which narrates the slaughter that Jews suffered as a result of refusal to fight on the Sabbath. The story reflects the decision to fight on the Sabbath (2:29–41). Here in the *Mekilta*, the recognition of this practical necessity is qualified by the insistence that temporary suspension of Sabbath observance must not continue for even "a blinking of the eye" (R. Judah b. Bathyra's actual phrase) longer than necessary.

[13] Verse 14 mentions two penalties for Sabbath violation: execution and extirpation from the community. Here the penalties are applied to public and private Sabbath violations respectively.

[14] The Hebrew formulation cited from Exod 20 renders the verb "do" in the active voice whereas the formulation in Exod 31 uses the passive voice.

days shall you labor and do your work." They themselves must do their work. And not only this but even the work of others is done by them, as it is said: "You shall serve your enemy," etc (Deut 28:48).[15]

But the seventh day is a Sabbath of complete rest holy unto the Lord

Why is this said? Because it says: "These are the appointed seasons of the Lord, even holy convocations, which ye shall proclaim in their appointed season" (Lev 23:4). One might think that just as the holiness of the festival depends on the *bet din*[16] that fixes their dates, so also shall the holiness of the Sabbath depend on the proclamation of the *bet din*. Therefore it says: "But the seventh day is a Sabbath of complete rest holy unto the Lord," meaning that the Sabbath is in the charge of God who definitely fixed the day, and it does not depend on the *bet din*. And thus it says: "Ye shall keep the Sabbath," etc.

Wherefore the children of Israel shall keep the Sabbath to observe the Sabbath

This is the verse that R. Nathan interpreted as implying that we should profane one Sabbath for the sake of saving the life of a person in order that he may be able to observe many Sabbaths.

R. Eliezer says:

To observe the Sabbath throughout their generations for a perpetual covenant—to do on the Sabbath that for which a covenant has been made. And what is this? It is circumcision.[17]

R. Eleazar b. Perata says: How can you prove that if one keeps the Sabbath it is accounted to him as if he had made the Sabbath? It says: "Wherefore the children of Israel shall keep the Sabbath to make the Sabbath."[18]

Rabbi says: How can you prove that if one keeps but one Sabbath properly, it is accounted to him as if he had observed all the Sabbaths from the day that God created his world to the time of the resurrection of the dead? It is said: "Wherefore the children of Israel shall keep the Sabbath to observe the Sabbath throughout their generations."

---

[15] "Therefore you shall serve your enemies whom the Lord will send against you, in hunger and thirst, in nakedness, and in want of all things; and he will put a yoke of iron upon your neck, until he has destroyed you."

[16] I.e., the tribunal which proclaims the new moon and thus determines on which day the festival should fall. —Lauterbach

[17] Here R. Eliezer expresses the halakic tradition that the circumcision ritual, established in Gen 17 as a "perpetual covenant" using terminology virtually identical to that found in this Exod 31 passage, takes precedence over the Sabbath law.

[18] Following the masoretic phrasing of the biblical text in Exod 31:12–17, at verse 16 in our translation we have connected the verb "to make" to the phrase "eternal covenant" as its object: "to make the Sabbath an eternal covenant for their generations." But in this case the *darshan* is reading the final words of verse 16 as a separate clause: "[It is] for your generations a perpetual covenant," leaving the preceding words in this verse as the *darshan* has quoted them.

Between me and the Israelites

But not between me and the nations of the world.

It is a sign forever

This tells that the Sabbath will never be abolished in Israel. And so you find that anything to which the Israelites were devoted with their whole souls has been preserved among them. But anything to which the Israelites were not devoted with their whole souls has not been retained by them. Thus the Sabbath, circumcision, the study of the Torah, and the ritual of immersion,[19] for which the Israelites laid down their lives, have been retained by them. But such institutions as the Temple, civil courts, the sabbatical and jubilee years, to which the Israelites were not whole-heartedly devoted, have not been preserved among them.

For in six days . . . and on the seventh day he ceased from work and rested

He ceased from the thought of work. Perhaps also from administering justice? It says: "and rested." This tells that his administration of justice never stops. And thus it says: "Righteousness and justice are the foundations of your throne" (Ps 89:15). "Clouds and darkness are round about him, righteousness and justice," etc. (Ps 97:2),[20] "The Rock, his work is perfect, for all his ways are justice," etc. (Deut 32:4).[21]

---

[19] I.e., the ritual bath which the Jewish woman takes after the completion of each period of menstruation. —Lauterbach

[20] "Clouds and darkness are round about him; righteousness and justice are the foundation of his throne."

[21] "The Rock, his work is perfect; for all his ways are justice. A God of faithfulness and without iniquity, just and right is he."

The Palestinian Talmud, Tractate *Yoma* 8.3–5 (sixth century C.E.)

The enormous compendium of commentary on the Mishnah is known as the Talmud; it has been handed down since the seventh century in two different versions: the Babylonian Talmud (Bavli) and the Palestinian Talmud (Yerushalmi; also referred to as the Jerusalem Talmud and Talmud Eretz Yisrael [Talmud of the Land of Israel]). The Yerushalmi was redacted in the mid-sixth century C.E., probably in the Galilee region of Palestine. The Bavli has long been the more widely used Talmud, as it is far more complete in its treatment of tractates from the Mishnah. Where there are contradictions between the two, it is Bavli that is followed in Jewish jurisprudence. Much halakic discussion preserved in the Palestinian Talmud, however, is not found in the Babylonian. Such is the case in the following selection from the tractate *Yoma* (meaning, in this application, the ordering of time).

Often the halakic discussions regarding one biblical text have relevance for halakah derived from a different biblical text. In the *Yoma* tractate of the Palestinian Talmud, a discussion (centered on Leviticus 23) that explores the extent of work cessation observances for Yom Kippur (Day of Atonement) leads to the expression of an exegetical principle pertinent to our Exodus 31 text. The *Yoma* selection also displays the sorts of exegetical reasoning not uncommon in the Talmuds as rabbis developed elaborate chains of logic from the biblical text into a network of halakic consistency. The footnotes should help in guiding the reader through the arguments. One begins to understand why proficiency in Talmud requires years of serious study in order to participate in this multigenerational dialogue that proceeds according to its own rules of discourse, often found obscure by outsiders.

Yoma[22]

8.3

An admonition concerning not working on the Day [of Atonement]: "You shall do no work on this same day" (Lev 23:28).

The penalty: "And whoever does any work on this same day—that person I will destroy from among his people" (Lev 23:30).

An admonition as to afflicting the soul on that day: "For whoever is not afflicted on this same day shall be cut off from his people" (Lev 23:29).

The penalty: " . . . shall be cut off from his people" (Lev 23:29).

There is no admonition against work by night, nor is there a statement governing the penalty; there is no admonition governing afflicting the soul by night, nor is there a penalty.[23]

[As to the view that there is no explicit reference to penalty for doing so by night,] said R. Simeon b. Laqish, "What should the Scripture have said, 'You should not afflict [your soul]'?!"

. . .

Said R. Hoshaiah, "[What Scripture could have said is] 'Take heed, lest you not afflict . . .' *which would have yielded three admonitions."*

Said R. Hunah, " 'Take heed' serves as it does in that statement that I have made to you: 'Take heed, in an attack of leprosy, to be very careful to do according to all that the Levitical priests shall direct you; as I commanded them, so you shall be careful to do' " (Deut 24:8).

R. Hiyya taught, "Scripture need not have made reference [at Lev 23:30] to the penalty with respect to performing prohibited acts of labor. Why not? I could have derived the fact of the penalty from the law governing affliction of the soul [see Lev 23:29]. Now if in the case of afflicting the soul, which is a lesser matter, if one does not do so, he is liable to extirpation, in the case of performing a prohibited act of

---

[22] The translation is taken from *The Talmud of the Land of Israel: A Preliminary Translation and Explanation* (trans. Jacob Neusner; 35 vols.; Chicago Studies in the History of Judaism; Chicago: University of Chicago Press, 1982–1994), vol. 14. Used with permission.

[23] The question here in the rabbinic discussion centers on whether the daytime prohibition and penalty regarding work on Yom Kippur extend to the nighttime. Essentially the same question, regarding work on the Sabbath, was treated in the *Mekilta* section above.

labor, which is a serious matter, is it not a matter of logic that one should be liable to extirpation on that account?

"Accordingly, the purpose of stating the penalty inhering in performing a prohibited act of labor is solely to serve to provide an admonition to that which lies before it, with the following consequence: Just as the penalty stated with regard to performing a prohibited act of labor serves as an admonition for the preceding item, so the penalty stated with regard to afflicting the soul serves as an admonition for the act."[24]

Said R. Zeirah, "Is that to say that they derive the law by means of analogical reasoning *[gezera shavah], even in the case of a verse left without exegesis as to one aspect of said verse?"*[25]

Said R. Yudan, "But does this mode of exegetical reasoning not follow the method of R. Aqiba? For R. Aqiba said, 'They do indeed derive a law by analogical exegesis, even in a case in which there is no aspect of the verse left open for that purpose.' "

R. Eliezer b. Jacob says, "With respect to an act of labor, it is said, 'For whoever does any work on this same day . . . ,'" (Lev 23:30), and with respect to afflicting the soul, it is said, 'For whoever is not afflicted on this same day . . .' (Lev 23:39).

"Just as in the case of the reference to 'this same day,' in regard to a prohibited act of labor, there is no distinction between day and night, whether as to penalty or as to admonition, so when we read 'on this same day,' with regard to afflicting the soul, we should not make any distinction whatsoever between day and night, between penalty and admonition."

Up to this point we have followed the problem through the exegetical reasoning of R. Aqiba.[26] *How shall we approach it in line with the thinking of R. Ishmael?*[27]

---

[24] Lev 23:28–30 states a warning and a penalty regarding work on the Day of Atonement and a warning and a penalty for failing to self-afflict on the Day of Atonement. But since the statements applied to self-affliction would automatically—through *qal va-ḥomer*—apply also to the greater violation of performing work, this would render the warning-penalty statement about work superfluous. But actually it is not superfluous, for its purpose—understood through *gezarah shavah*—is to express a warning-penalty for *nighttime* violations of both the work and the self-affliction stipulations.

[25] The *gezerah shavah* that R. Ḥiyya just stated makes a connection of similarity between two verses (one about prohibiting work, the other about failing to self-afflict on the Day of Atonement), but in fact the similarity is imported from the verse regarding work prohibition into the verse regarding self-affliction, a one-sided connection of similarity.

[26] The authority of R. Akiba is lent to such uses of *gezerah shavah* interpretation.

[27] The Palestinian Talmud characteristically presents traditional rabbinic teachings as having originated in either the school of R. Akiba, whose teachings tended to expand the range of exegetical techniques, or that of R. Ishmael, whose use of the same techniques was less expansive.

R. Ishmael taught: " 'And it shall be a statute for you for ever that in the seventh month, on the tenth day of the month, you shall afflict yourselves and shall do no work' (Lev 16:29). The matters of afflicting oneself and working are thus joined together.

"Just as the forms of labor that I have prohibited for you are those on account of which one is liable to extirpation, so the forms of afflicting the soul that I have placed on you are those on account of which one is liable to extirpation."

The text continues with further refinements of what constitutes acceptable fasting for the Day of Atonement and what constitutes acceptable methods of resuscitation of those who faint from hunger. This raises the general principle of taking lifesaving actions on a holy day without violating the strictures of that day.

8.4

R. Abbahu in the name of R. Yohanan: "This is dealt with as a case of doubt concerning life and death, and in any case concerning life and death the needs of the sick person override the prohibitions of the Sabbath [and hence, also, of the Day of Atonement]."

. . .

8.5

How do we know that a matter of doubt concerning life or death overrides the prohibitions of the Sabbath?

R. Abbahu in the name of R. Yohanan: " '[Say to the people of Israel,] But *(ach)* you shall keep my Sabbaths, [for this is a sign between me and you throughout your generations, that you may know that I, the Lord, sanctify you]' (Exod 31:13). The word 'but' serves as an exclusionary clause [indicating that there are circumstances in which one does not keep the Sabbath]."

There is he who proposes to say, "Profane the Sabbath [one time] on a person's account, so that he may sit and observe many Sabbaths."

Rabbi Shlomo Yitzḥaqi (Rashi) (1040–1105 C.E.)

Rashi stands out as one of the most important scholars of the Hebrew Bible and the Talmud. Born in France and educated in the Jewish academies of Mainz and Worms, Rashi established in his hometown of Troyes a school that would eventually become almost synonymous with European academic Jewish culture. Even today, nine hundred years after his death, every edition of the Babylonian Talmud features his halakic commentary, and most Jewish study editions of the Hebrew Bible give his comments pride of place.

Rashi's biblical commentary, which covers the entire Hebrew Bible, is one of the outstanding representatives of the postclassical era in biblical interpretation.[28] In the hands of Rashi and other scholars, the Bible was studied with much greater attention to the details of Hebrew grammar and with a more consistent intention to make clear the *peshat,* or plain sense of the text. (*Peshat* is often contrasted with the *derash,* or derived, midrashic sense of the text.) He informed his reader of this intention with his well-known comment on Gen 3:8:[29] "There are many aggadic midrashim and our rabbinic predecessors have already compiled them in Genesis Rabbah and other midrashic collections. As for myself, my purpose has only to do with the plain sense of scripture and with any aggadah that explain the words of scripture fittingly." By no means did Rashi abandon the midrashic tradition, but his use of the midrashim in his biblical commentary is judicious. Indeed, Rashi sometimes quotes a traditional midrash in order to show that, along with the plainer meaning, the text has a richness that rewards pious reflection as well as careful study. Rashi's commentary tended to mediate the *peshat* and the *derash* as two types of interpretation that synergistically face one another, with a resulting interplay that helped maintain the ancient Eastern midrashic way of exegetical thinking amid the growing Western rationality of Rashi's world.

Before turning to his comments on the Sabbath law in Exod 31, we can briefly observe this dynamic in Rashi's biblical commentary on the story of Moses' murder of an Egyptian (Exod 2:12–13). The Egyptian had beaten an unfortunate Hebrew man, identified by rabbinic tradition as the husband of Shelomith, the daughter of Dibri (Lev 24:11). The Egyptian taskmaster had contrived to seduce Shelomith. When, the next day, the Egyptian noticed that the husband was aware of this, he beat him all day long. Moses' "turning this way and that" refers to his taking note of what the Egyptian had done to the Hebrew within the privacy of the house ("this way") and in the field ("and that"). So, when "Moses saw that there was no man," the midrash takes this to mean that Moses saw no possible merit in this individual. The plain sense informs that Moses killed the Egyptian for beating an Israelite, even though the killing cannot be justified. But according to the midrash, the Egyptian was beyond any hope of redemption, nor would any of his descendants embrace true faith or a righteous life. Rashi endorses this traditional view and amplifies it with reference to Lev 24:10. Yet he also notes that the *peshat* follows the ordinary sense. So,

---

[28] Other prominent scholars who began to move the Jewish interpretive tradition beyond midrashic exegesis include the famous leader of the Jewish Babylonian community Sa'adia ben Joseph (Gaon) (892–942) and Rashi's younger contemporary, the Spanish philosopher-physician Abraham Ibn Ezra (1089–1164).

[29] The Genesis text reads, "and they [Adam and Eve] heard the voice of the Lord in the garden."

in taking punitive action, Moses first makes sure that it is safe to do so *(peshat)* while, from the point of view of morality, he is justified in this respect *(derash)*.[30]

Rashi's remarks on the Exod 31 Sabbath pericope serve to paraphrase a particular biblical sentence for a more accurate understanding or to make explicit what is implied in the biblical text. We can observe his engagement with the midrashic and talmudic tradition at several points. For example, at Exod 31:13, where (in the *Mekilta*) R. Jose the Galilean takes the word *ach* ("but") as a qualification of the Sabbath requirement subordinating it to the requirement to build the sanctuary, Rashi disagrees, calling upon an exegetical rule expressed in the Palestinian Talmud: occurrences of the word *ach* in the Bible serve to restrict or exclude. So, for Rashi, the Sabbath is excluded from (has priority over) the imperative to build the sanctuary. But at 31:14, "that soul shall be cut off from among his people," Rashi approvingly brings in the traditional comment concerning witnesses found in the *Mekilta*. Finally, regarding the phrase in 31:17, "but on the seventh day he rested and relaxed," both the *Mekilta* and Rashi respond to the same potential misunderstanding, but not in the same way. The ancient rabbis argued, by citing passages from the Psalms, that the notion of God's cessation from work does not entail a cessation from the universal administration of justice. Rashi, on the other hand, first determines the precise meaning of the biblical word "rest" through comparative philology and then interprets the biblical expression as a linguistic accommodation for human understanding and therefore not as something to be taken literally.

For further information on Rashi:

Pearl, Chaim. *Rashi.* New York: Grove, 1988.
Shereshevsky, Esra. *Rashi: The Man and His World.* New York: Sepher-Hermon, 1982.

---

[30] For a more detailed examination of this and many other instances of Rashi's mediation of immediate and applied exegesis, see Benjamin J. Gelles, *Peshat and Derash in the Exegesis of Rashi* (Leiden: Brill, 1981).

Rashi's Commentary[31]

And you, speak to the Israelites.

And you

[a grammatically repetitive element in this sentence, as the verb "speak" already contains the "you" element—ed.], although I have commissioned you to command them regarding the work of the sanctuary, do not consider it a casual thing to neglect the Sabbath for the sake of that very work.

But [ach] my Sabbaths you shall observe

Even though you will be eager to rush enthusiastically in the work [on the sanctuary], the Sabbath is not to be pushed aside on account of it.

[In the Torah] every occurrence [of the words] ach and raq stipulates a limiting exclusion [of the legal principle in question]. Here [ach] serves to exclude the Sabbath from the work of the sanctuary.

For it is a sign between me and you

It is a great sign between us [signifying] that I chose you through my bestowing unto you my day of rest for your rest.

to know

[So that] the nations [know] by it "that I am the Lord who sanctifies you."

shall be put to death

If there are witnesses and a warning.

[that soul] shall be cut off

In the case of [a Sabbath violation] without warning.

The one who profanes it

The one who behaves during it as though it were profane, despite its sanctity.

A Sabbath of cessation

An intentionally relaxing rest, and not a merely opportune rest.

Holy unto the Lord

Observance of [the Sabbath's sanctity] is for my sake and by my command.

---

[31] The following selection is translated by William Yarchin from *Mikra'ot gedolot; hamishah humshei Torah 'im shishim perushim ve-hosafot* (New York: Shulsinger Bros. 1950).

and he rested [vayyinafesh]

As the Onqelos [Aramaic version] translates this: "and he rested." All forms of *nofesh* are connotations of the word *nefesh* ["soul"]; so one restores one's soul and breath by relaxing from the toil of work. Now, the One of Whom it is written, "He neither tires nor grows weary" [Isa 40:28], and whose every work is accomplished through utterance, had the notion of rest written about Himself in order to explain to the ear that which it is able to hear.

Rabbi Moses ben Naḥman (Ramban, Naḥmanides) (1194–1270 C.E.)

R. Moses ben Naḥman (RaMBaN, or Ramban) grew up in Gerona, Spain, in a prominent rabbinical family. After receiving the finest rabbinical education available in Europe at the time, Ramban eventually gained recognition as the acknowledged authority among Spanish Jews in questions of religious jurisprudence. He had also studied medicine and during his lifetime practiced as a physician, but he spent most of his adult years in Gerona teaching Torah. Among his many writings, he is probably best known for his commentary on the Torah and for his commentary on the Talmud. Ramban's biblical commentary is philologically informed and responds (sometimes at length) to Rashi and Ibn Ezra, often in disagreement with them. He has obviously learned to respect the *peshat,* but at the same time he seeks to allow for the deeper meanings of the text as suggested by the traditional midrashim. Ramban also had a high regard for the teachings of the Kabbalah, and his commentary was one of the first to include kabbalistic teachings. This theosophical system, a product of Jewish mysticism of the tenth and eleventh centuries, perceived in the words of the biblical text the symbolic reality of divine presence and had been hitherto taught for generations as a secret doctrine. Ramban's references to kabbalistic teachings in his commentary are found in idiosyncratic expressions that are difficult to understand unless one is already initiated into the system of kabbalistic symbolism.

In 1263 Ramban was brought, by the royal orders of King James of Aragon, to participate in a religious disputation with Pablo Christiani, a Christian convert from Judaism. The debate concluded in Ramban's favor, but in reply to subsequent controversies over the proceedings, he published an account of the arguments. His account was eventually regarded as sufficiently blasphemous against Christian teachings to exile him from Spain. The aging exile settled in Israel, where he wrote the bulk of his commentaries and provided much-needed leadership to the Jewish communities.

A distinctive feature of our selection from Ramban's commentary on the Torah is his rigorous examination of the manner of reasoning by which a halakic interpretation is reached. Ramban brings focused attention to the precise nuance of the key word *ach* in Exod 31:13. If this Hebrew particle can serve in the Torah to indicate a limitation of the Sabbath rest requirement, is this force of the particle relevant to this particular biblical passage? Rashi said yes, but Ramban alludes to the ancient sages' halakic precedent on the question as well as to biblical literary context as he both differs and agrees with Rashi. Our final reading in halakic exegesis, then, displays a key characteristic of classical Jewish biblical interpretation: exegesis is not only a response to the features of the biblical text but also a transgenerational conversation.

For further information on Ramban:

Ramban: Writings and Discourses. Translated by Charles Chavel. New York: Shilo, 1978.

Ramban's Commentary[32]

But [ach] my Sabbaths you shall observe

Even though you will be eager to rush enthusiastically in the work [on the sanctuary], the Sabbath is not to be pushed aside on account of it.

[In the Torah] every occurrence [of the words] *ach* and *raq* stipulates a limiting exclusion [of the legal principle in question]. Here [*ach* serves] to exclude the Sabbath from the work of sanctuary construction. This is what Rashi says.

But this [Rashi's reasoning] is incorrect as I see it, because according to the midrashic interpretive method of our rabbis [during the Tannaitic and Talmudic periods], the words *ach* and *raq* would indicate a diminution of the Sabbath rest requirement [thus allowing for Sabbath-day work on the sanctuary]. For in every place we find it the diminution pertains to the specific practice being commanded [in this case, the Sabbath]. If one were to interpret the diminution [indicated by *ach*] with the question of the building the sanctuary in mind, it would indeed be permitted to perform that work on the Sabbath.

However, the [Sabbath] diminution we are talking about here more properly applies to [the work entailed in] circumcision or to the saving of someone's life and to related scenarios in which the Sabbath rest requirement is set aside. And thus they said in *Yoma:* "On what basis is the rest requirement for Sabbath set aside [for the sake of saving a life], even when it is not certain that life is in danger? R. Abohu said in the name of R. Yochanan: '*ach* my Sabbaths you shall observe'— has an effect of diminution [of Sabbath requirements]."[33]

Now the work [entailed in constructing] the sanctuary does not set aside the rest requirement for Sabbath, but that is because [Moses] gave warning about it *here* [at this point in the story, just before the Israelites were to begin constructing the sanctuary].[34]

---

[32] The following selection is translated from *Perush ha-Ramban 'al ha-Torah (Commentary to the Pentateuch by Moshe ben Nachman)* (Jerusalem: Makor Publishing, 1962), from the 1470 edition produced in Rome, corrected by the edition printed in *Mikra'ot gedolot; ḥamishah ḥumshei Torah 'im shishim perushim ve-hosafot* (New York: Shulsinger Bros., 1950).

[33] As is often the case in halakic interpretation, the point in question is a highly refined one. Although the ancient rabbis cited Exod 31:13 for its attestation of Sabbath requirement limitation, Ramban observes that they did not apply this limitation to sanctuary construction but to other cases. His concern at this juncture is the way one argues about the force of *ach* in this context.

[34] Ramban agrees with Rashi that the Sabbath takes priority over the sanctuary work, but disagrees regarding the exegetical reasoning as to why that is true. For Rashi, it is a matter of correctly understanding *ach*. For Ramban, it has not so much to do with ach as with understanding the literary context. By explaining Exod 31:13 from its narrative context at the conclusion of the section of sanctuary-building instructions (chapters 25–31), Ramban reads the text in a strict chronological order. But Rashi's comment at 31:18—where he repeats the midrashic tradition that the materials in the Torah are not necessarily presented in chronological order—suggests that the narrative context was not the dominant factor for his interpretation of the Sabbath law in 31:12–17.

One would interpret according to the plain sense *[peshat]*, then, in this way: "You are to perform the work of [constructing] the Tent of Meeting, but [nonetheless] my Sabbaths you shall always observe."

As we read in the Torat Kohanim:[35] "I might conclude that the building of the sanctuary takes precedence over the Sabbath. But Scripture says, 'My Sabbaths you shall observe, and my sanctuary you shall respect; I am the LORD' [Lev 19:30]."

---

[35] *Sifra Qedoshim* 3, 7:7.

CHAPTER 14

Haggadic Interpretation of the Scriptures: Psalm 23 in *Yalqut Shim'oni* (thirteenth century C.E.)

Y*alqut* means "compilation," an apt description of this rambling compendium of ten thousand haggadic interpretations on biblical passages. The collected interpretation segments are drawn from a wide range of older midrashic sources that the compiler usually identifies and that span the range of haggadic literature, including Tannaitic, Amoraic, geonic, and even midrashic sources as late as the twelfth century.[1] A few of these sources are today accessible only by virtue of their inclusion in the *Yalqut*.

We are not certain who accomplished this compilation. A sixteenth-century edition features the name of a certain R. Simeon of Frankfurt on the title page, concerning whom virtually nothing is known. An alternative opinion that attributed the work to an eleventh-century R. Simeon is unlikely because of the presence in the *Yalqut* of some midrashim from a later date. It may be that this compilation does not owe its existence to any one author, given the variations of textual readings found in source citations throughout the work. At any rate, the Simeon tradition of authorship accounts for the title *Yalqut Shim'oni*. It is probable that the *Yalqut* was compiled in the early thirteenth century, for we do not find any of the twelfth-century Jewish masters, such as Rashi, using or even referring to this work. By the fifteenth century, this collection had become quite popular among Jewish preachers and scholars across Europe, and it has gone through about eleven editions. (A similar, more limited compilation, of uncertain date, attributed to Machir b. Abba Mari is known as *Yalqut Hamakhiri*.)

Haggadic collections traditionally had arranged their materials according to the sequence of subjects covered in the talmudic tractates. The *Yalqut* broke from this convention by arranging the collected interpretations according to the sequence of the portions

---

[1] These terms refer to specific periods of Jewish leadership during the formative rabbinic era, from the first to the early sixth century C.E. The period of the Tannaim (literally, the "repeaters" of tradition from their masters) extended from the mid-first century C.E. to 220 C.E., primarily in the land of Israel; the period of the Amoraim (literally, the "sayers") extended from the early third century to the end of the fifth century C.E. in both the land of Israel and Babylonia. By the end of the seventh century, both Talmuds had been compiled. From that point to the beginning of the eleventh century, the geonim in Babylonia provided leadership for most of the Jewish world in talmudic interpretation.

of the Jewish Bible upon which they comment. A certain influence from the Christian exegetical tradition is possible, since for centuries Christian scholars had produced similar collections of patristic commentary (known as *catenae,* or "chains") arranged in this fashion. *Catenae* on the book of Psalms were especially popular. The interpretation segments in the *Yalqut* can be lengthy or quite abbreviated; in the latter cases, the citations from ancient sources are often abridged or are only partially quoted, the remainder being more fully quoted elsewhere in the collection. It is not unusual therefore to find only the beginning of an interpretation given.

Prompted by the opening phrase of Ps 23, the homiletic comments begin with scriptural reflections on theological metaphors, celebrating some of the ways Scripture speaks metaphorically about God. There follows a section on the theme of divine presence and provision, illustrated at length with midrashic references not to David but to the wilderness travels of the Israelites. With the words "my cup overflows" in verse 5b, the focus returns to David and references to the coming messianic age.

For further information on *Yalqut Shim'oni:*

Elbaum, Jacob. "Yalqut Shim'oni." Pages 707a–708b in vol. 16 of *Encyclopaedia Judaica.* 16 vols. Jerusalem: Keter, 1971.
———. "*Yalqut Shim'oni* and the Medieval Midrashic Anthology." *Prooftexts* 17 (1997): 133–51.

23 [2]

Mizmor of David

The Lord is my shepherd, I shall not lack.

David was the shepherd of Israel ("You will shepherd my people Israel" [2 Sam 5:2]), but who was David's shepherd? The Holy One, Blessed be He, as it is written "The Lord is my shepherd, I shall not lack."

Abraham was the one who blessed everyone, as it is written "and in you all the families of the earth shall be blessed" (Gen 12:3), but who was the one who blessed Abraham? The Holy One, Blessed be He, as it is written "And the Lord had blessed Abraham in all things" (Gen 24:1).

Moses was the banner [*nes*] of Israel, as it is written "by all the signs and wonders that Moses did" (Deut 34:11), but who was Moses' banner? The Holy One, Blessed be He, as it is written "And he called it 'The Lord is my banner [*nisso*]' " (Exod 17:15).[3]

Jerusalem is the light for the world, as it is written "And the nations shall walk by your light" (Isa 60:3), but who is the light of Jerusalem? The Holy One, Blessed be He, as it is written "the Lord will be unto you an everlasting light" (Isa 60:19).

So also it is said, "My beloved is mine and I am his" (Song 2:16); He is for me God, "I am the Lord your God," (Exod 20:2) and I am for him a nation, "Listen to me, O my nation" (Isa 51:4). He is to me as a brother, "Would that you were as a brother to me" (Song 8:1), and I am to him a sister, "Open to me, O my sister, my betrothed" (Song 5:2). I am to him a sheep, "O you my flock" (Ezek 34:17), "the sheep of my pasture" (Ezek 34:31), and he is to me a shepherd, "The Lord is my shepherd."

Said R. Hamma b. Ḥanina: "You will find no trade more vile than that of a shepherd, who spends his entire day walking with his rod and satchel, yet David calls The Holy One, Blessed be He, a shepherd?!" But David has said: "I have learned from the elders (Ps 119:100): Jacob called him shepherd, as it is written 'the God who has shepherded me' (Gen 48:15), so also I call him shepherd, 'The Lord is my shepherd, I shall not lack.' "

---

[2] The following selection is translated from the 1898 Wilna edition.

[3] As is frequently the case in midrash, the rhetorical point is made through a play on Hebrew words. The Hebrew word *nes* means both "flag" and "miracle." Here Moses' reputation for miraculous "signs and wonders" introduces the theme of miracle *(nes)*, which linguistically allows for a midrashic application of the term to Moses himself as Israel's "banner," even as the biblical text had already done for God at Exod 17:15. (Reading according to the *Yalqut*'s source, *Genesis Rabbah* 59:5.)

<u>Another interpretation</u>: "For the Lord your God has blessed you" (Deut 2:7). Is it possible [that you are blessed] sitting idly? No, for we are taught, "[the Lord has blessed you] in all the works of your hands" (Deut 2:7); thus if a man works, he is blessed, but if he does not work, he is not blessed. What does this mean, "He intimately knows your path/ways/doings/footsteps" (Deut 2:7)? [It means that the Lord is familiar with] the steps you must take, the soiling hardships you endure while earning a living.[4]

<u>R. Yehudah in the name of R. Eleazar said</u>, "Three things happen during a journey: garments wear out, the body withers, and funds deplete, but with The Holy One, Blessed be He, this is not so; "Your garment did not wear out from upon you, etc" (Deut 8:4), "and you did not lack anything" (Deut 2:7). This refers to the fact that you did not have to spend anything of your own account: "These forty years the Lord your God has been with you" (Deut 2:7).

<u>Said R. Yudan</u>: On the merit that you said, "**This** is my God and I will praise him" (Exod 15), I gave you **this** [God's sustaining presence] these forty years.[5]

<u>R. Yehudah said</u>, "[This compares to] when a king resides in his country, the country does not lack anything; so 'the Lord has been with you—you did not lack anything'" (Deut 2:7).

Customarily, when someone receives a guest, on the first day [of the visit] he slaughters [and prepares] a calf for him, and on the second day a lamb, on the third day chickens, the fourth day beans, the fifth day still less, and so on. The first day is nothing like the last day [of the visit]. We could have thought the same [would occur in the wilderness], but we are taught 'These forty years the Lord your God has been with you' the first day as the last day."

<u>R. Nehunia said</u>, "What is the meaning of 'You did not lack a **thing**" (Deut 2:7)? If you were to lack nothing, [you had] only to say a word and it was performed: such as, 'let the manna taste like veal,' and it was done; 'Let it taste like a hen,' and it was done; 'Let it taste like a turkey,' and it was done." What do you seek? Flour? "And the people gathered" etc. (Num 11:8)[6]: Spice? "They crushed it in a mortar" (Num 11:8). Cakes? "They made it into cakes" (Num 11:8), and thus it is written

---

[4] Starting with the Hebrew expression in Deut 2:7, the midrash here continues with a series of words that resound both phonetically and semantically: "he knows your *lekhtkha halokhkha likhlukhkha*"; the combination of these words richly connotes the notion of walking and working on a gritty path through life.

[5] R. Yudan's midrash turns playfully on the repetition of the Hebrew word *zeh* ("this") in Deut 2:7; cf. *Yalqut Shim'oni* at Deut 2:7.

[6] The full verse in Numbers reads, on the subject of manna, "The people went around and gathered it, ground it in mills or beat it in mortars, then boiled it in pots and made cakes of it; and the taste of it was like the taste of cakes baked with oil."

"You did not lack [but] a **word**"[7] —rather, that which you would **speak** [as your desire] was there in your mouth: "I desire manna."— "I rain it upon you" (Exod 16:4). "It's water I want."— "Behold, he smote the rock, and the waters gushed out" (Ps 78:20). "I desire quail,"— "And the quails came up" (Exod 16:13).

They said, "We desire meat." When Moses heard that he went to The Holy One, Blessed be He. He [Moses] said to him, "Your children ask for meat." The Holy One, Blessed be He, answered, "Give it to them." Moses said to him, "Whence do I have meat (Num 11:13), sheep and cattle to slaughter for them" (Num 11:22)? The Holy One, Blessed be He, said, "Didn't you have frogs in Egypt? You were then so rich, but now you have nothing?" He said before him, "Master of the Universe, [back there] whatever was yours was mine." He said to him "So, in Egypt 'I have,' but now [in the wilderness] 'I don't have'?" "Is the hand of the Lord shortened" (Num 11:23)?

He has me lie down in green pastures
R. Eleazar asked R. Simeon, "When Israel went out from Egypt, did they bring with them weaving looms?"[8] He replied, "No." "Then by what means did they clothe themselves all the forty years?" He answered, "The ministering angels clothed them, as it is written 'I clothed you also with embroidered cloth'" (Ezek 16:10). And what is meant by embroidered cloth? R. Dostai said, "A royal cloak." He said to him, "Didn't they wear out?" He answered him, "Haven't you read, 'And your garment did not wear out from upon you'" (Deut 8:4)? He said to him, "But did not the children grow up [and out of their smaller clothing]?" He replied, "Go out and learn from the snail, that as it grows its shell grows with it." And he said, "Wouldn't they [the garments] become stained?" He replied, "The cloud of fire[9] laundered them; go out and learn [from] amiant[10] which is not cleansed but by fire." He said to him, "But wouldn't they be ruined from vermin?" He replied, "When they were dead, mildew would not touch them, how much more when they were alive." He said to him, "But wouldn't there develop a stench from the sweat, seeing they would never change their clothes?" He replied, "The well would bring up for them all sorts of green herbs and [thus] all sorts of scents, and in these they would roll themselves,[11] as it is written 'He has me lie down in green pastures.' And the fragrance dispersed from one end of the earth to the other, bringing Solomon to remark [concerning Israel], 'the scent of your garments is like the scent of Lebanon'" (Song 4:11).

And he [Solomon] added, "Nard and saffron, calamus and cinnamon" (Song 4:14)—whence all these? [From] "a garden fountain, a well of living water" (Song 4:15). When Israel saw how The Holy One, Blessed be He, pampered them in the

---

[7] The midrash here turns on the semantic flexibility of the Hebrew root *dbr:* it can mean "thing" (and so the Israelites lacked no*thing* in the wilderness) and "word" and "speak." Here R. Neḥunia seems to be linking all three meanings, indicated in the text with bold print.

[8] Reading *qoriyot* with most other versions of this midrash; the *Yalqut Shim'oni* text reads *qoriyas,* "leather garments."

[9] See Exod 40:38.

[10] Amiant is an asbestos-like material.

[11] Reading the root *g'g'* with most versions of this midrash; the *Yalqut Shim'oni* text reads the root *n'n',* "shake."

wilderness, they began praising him and saying, "You are the one who is a good shepherd; you never withhold your goodness."

The Lord is my shepherd, I shall not lack, etc.

He leads me beside still waters
R. Samuel said, "You have waters that are suitable for drinking but not for bathing, and also waters suitable for bathing but not for drinking; but the waters of this well are suitable for both."

He restores my soul by means of Torah; "The Torah of the Lord is perfect, reviving the soul" (Ps 19:8 [7 English versions]).

He leads me in the paths of righteousness: [this refers to] manna and the well and quail meat and clouds of glory, not because of any merit in us[12] but rather **for his name's sake.**
Another comment: **He leads me beside steady waters** means that as the water passed from tent to tent [during the wilderness journey] it maintained its volume and none of them had to draw water from any other source.

Though I walk through the valley of the shadow of death [refers to] the fiercest part of the wilderness.

I will fear no evil as it is written "And the Lord went before them by day" (Exod 13:21).

Your rod these are afflictions;
and your staff this is Torah.[13]

They comfort me Is it possible without affliction? The scripture says, "Only [= it's not possible without affliction] [goodness and mercy . . .]" Does it mean [such blessing without affliction] is possible in this world? The scripture says, "Only [after affliction] will goodness and mercy follow me" [= only in the world to come is it possible without affliction].
R. Eleazar of Modim said, "At a time yet to come the tutelary angels of all the nations of the world will come and make accusations before the Master of the Universe: 'These are idolators, and those are idolators, and these had illicit sexual relations, and those had illicit sexual relations, and these shed [innocent] blood, and

---

[12] Reading *lanû* with *Yalqut Hamakhir;* the *Shim'oni* text reads *lô,* "him."

[13] Suffering and Torah are not infrequently found as twin themes in rabbinic literature, often in comments that cite Ps 94:12: "How honored is the one whom you discipline, O Lord, and whom you teach out of your law." An interesting contrast is found between the Babylonian Talmud (*Berakhot* 5a), "Afflictions stay far from the one who engages in Torah" (with the related discussion there), and the Mishnah (*Avot* 6:4), "Such is the way of Torah: You eat bread with salt, 'and water you drink by rationed measure' [Ezek 4:11], and on the ground you sleep, and you live a life of trouble as you toil in Torah."

those shed [innocent] blood, and these [the nations] are going to Gehenna, but these are not going down?' He said to them, 'If so, each nation that goes down [into punishment] will be accompanied by its deity, as it is written 'For all the peoples walk each in the name of its own god'" (Mic 4:5).

R. Ḥanina in the name of R. Reuven said, "Were it not written in scripture, it would be impossible to say! It does not say 'For by fire the Lord is executing justice' (Isa 66:16), but rather 'For by fire the Lord is being judged' and so David says *Though I walk through the valley of the shadow of death* [here under judgment], *I will fear no evil for you [too] are with me*.

Another interpretation:

Indeed, though I walk through the valley of <u>the shadow of death</u>

R. Isaac said, "This is a reference to one who sleeps in the shade of a single palm tree or in the shade of the moon." But this [statement about] the shade of a single palm tree was not spoken [about any instance] except when the shadow of its fellow[-palm tree] does not fall upon it; it applies to an instance in a field, but [also] in a courtyard even though the shadow of its fellow[-palm tree] does fall upon it; [the instance involving] the shade of the moon was not spoken [as applicable] except when [the shade] is in the west, but [when it is] in the east there is nothing to be concerned about.[14]

You prepare a table before me

This is the manna.

Issi b. Akiva said, "The [piled] height of the manna [in the wilderness] was fifty cubits, and the one who does not believe it will not witness this same abundance, as it is written, 'He will not look upon the rivers, the streams flowing with honey and curds'"(Job 20:17).

In the presence of my enemies

The manna that came down for them, the Israelites, grew and piled up until all the kings of the east and of the west could see it.

My cup overflows

Said R. Abbaye, "From here we learn that the cup of David in the times to come [Messianic age] will hold 221 logs [133 liters]."

Overflows, in gematria[15] means 221.

---

[14] This obscure comment is found in the Babylonian Talmud (*Pesahim* 111a). It may pertain to vulnerability to certain demons who try to hide in shadows.

[15] In Hebrew, each letter possesses a numerical value. Gematria is the calculation of the numerical equivalent of letters, words, or phrases. Here the Hebrew word for "overflows" is *rwyh. r =* 200; *w* = 6; *y* = 10; *h* = 5. The sum of these values is 221, and thus the means for realizing the volume capacity of David's cup is revealed.

Another interpretation:

He has me lie down in green pastures

It speaks of David when he was fleeing from Saul, as it is written "And David departed, and went into the forest of Heret" [1 Sam 22:5]. Why is the forest called "Heret," which means arid? The Holy One, Blessed be He, watered it with the goodness of the world, as it is written, "My soul is feasted as with marrow and fat" [Ps 63:5].

He restores my soul

This [refers to David's] kingdom, not due to my worthiness but rather **for his name's sake.**

Indeed, though I walk through the valley of the shadow of death

This speaks of the desert Ziph. Why? **For you are with me.**[16]

Your rod

This [refers to] affliction.

And your staff

This [refers to] Torah, **They comfort me.**

You prepare a table before me

This [refers to David's] kingdom.

In the presence of my enemies

This [refers to] Doeg and Ahitophel.[17]

You anoint my head with oil

Is it possible without affliction? The scripture says "Only." Can it be ever in this world? Teaching us: "Only [then, in the world to come] **will goodness and mercy follow me.**"

And I will dwell in the house of the Lord for ever

This [refers to] the Temple.

Our teachers interpreted as if all that is said here were about Israel [and not only about David].

---

[16] Probably a reference to 1 Sam 23:14, "And David remained in the strongholds in the wilderness, in the hill country of the Wilderness of Ziph. And Saul sought him every day, but God did not give him into his hand."

[17] In the biblical narrative of David's life, both Doeg and Ahitophel brought support to David's enemies (for Doeg, see 1 Sam 21 and 22; for Ahitophel, see 2 Sam 15–17:23).

He has me lie down in green pastures [refers to] Israel, as it is written, "I myself will be the shepherd of my sheep, and I will make them lie down" [Ezek 34:15].

He leads me beside still waters
    "And on the river there will grow, on its banks (all types of trees)" [Ezek 47:12].[18]

He restores my soul
    This [refers to] the goodness of the world to come.

---

[18] The entire Ezekiel verse reads, "And by the river at its banks, this side and that side, there will grow every tree for food, whose leaf will not wither, and whose fruit will not fail; it will bring forth new fruit every month, because these waters will flow out of the Temple; and the fruit will be for food, and the leaves for healing."

CHAPTER 15

Systematically Philosophical Jewish Exegesis: Sa'adia ben Joseph (892–942 C.E.)

Because he was born and raised in the Fayyum district of Upper Egypt, Sa'adia was known to the Jewish world during his lifetime as Sa'adia ben Joseph al-Fayyumi. Little has passed down to us concerning his youth, but given that by his twentieth year he had completed a Hebrew lexicon—the first ever—it is obvious that he possessed intellectual abilities that he applied with industry and creativity early on. His education led him to study in Palestine, Syria, and finally Baghdad. There, in the context of a controversy over the Jewish calendar (and its critical implications for festival observances), Sa'adia established himself as a leading halakic authority and was invited to serve as gaon (chief scholar-in-residence) over the great Babylonian academy. In later generations he became known as Sa'adia Gaon, the most highly regarded authority of the geonic period.[1]

Sa'adia's literary productivity was as formidible as his learning, and as pioneering as his early lexicographical work. He was the first to write a grammar of the Hebrew language and an introduction to the Talmud. His translation of the Jewish Bible into Arabic was the first made from the Masoretic Text and produced in Arabic characters rather than Hebrew. (It remains in use among Arabic-speaking Jews to this day.) Much of his halakic writing has not survived in manuscript form, but the deference shown to him by subsequent generations testifies to the imprint of his thinking upon Jewish law. Sa'adia's biblical commentaries include works on the Torah, the Minor Prophets, Isaiah, the Psalms, Proverbs, and Job. He was very effective in opposing the Karaite movement.[2] Perhaps his greatest legacy

---

[1] The geonim led the ancient talmudic academies from ca. 660 to 1000 C.E. Eventually the Babylonian geonim eclipsed the older Palestinian centers of Judaism and were acknowledged as the leading spiritual authorities by the majority of the world's Jews. They established the Babylonian Talmud as the foremost canonical work of rabbinic literature and the primary guide to religious practice. As a rcsult, a predominantly Babylonian version of Judaism was brought to newer centers of Judaism in North Africa and Europe.

[2] With the codification of the Palestinian and Babylonian Talmuds, the Jewish religion had committed itself to engaging with Scripture according to the rabbinic interpretive tradition. During the eighth century, there began in Babylon a movement of Karaites (from a Hebrew word meaning "Scripture"), who opposed rabbinic authority in determining the structures of Judaism. Parallel with literalistic trends in Qur'anic scholarship among Muslims at the time, the Karaites called for a strict literalism in biblical interpretation and in halakic observances. Sa'adia's polemics against the Karaites, followed by those of Maimonides two hundred years later, effectively confirmed the rabbinic legacy and character of Judaism for perpetuity. Partly as a consequence of polemical

lies in his unequaled reputation as a systematizer of Jewish religious thought in the context of the flourishing scientific and philosophical thought of medieval Islamic culture.

This cultural background is key to understanding the contribution Sa'adia made to biblical interpretation. In the sixth century C.E., Syrian Christians had translated much of the Greek philosophical works into Syriac; during the eighth and ninth centuries, Islamic scholars brought Greek philosophical thought into the Arabic-speaking world through translation. As had been the case with Christianity's Scriptures, so among Muslims the use of Hellenistic reasoning tools gave rise to distinct Islamic schools of thought impinging on rational beliefs about God vis-à-vis the revelation received in the Qur'an. The Mutazilites in particular were concerned to work out a system of Islamic belief based on reason and the consistent application of logic. Much of the contention centered on the problem of anthropomorphisms attributed to God in the sacred revelation; for progressive Muslims, rational coherence in religious faith required understanding problematic expressions in the sacred text as meaning something other (and more rationally coherent) than what the text literally said. It was argued that rational reflection would arrive at *ta'wil*, the "hidden meaning" of the sacred text. Such proposals prompted highly contentious debates over the limits and legitimacy of interpretation, debates that played a significant role in the cultural and political life of medieval Islam.

Jews of the Islamic world, from Baghdad to North Africa and Spain, confronted essentially the same intellectual challenge of comprehending their traditional revelation-based beliefs in the face of the resurgence of reason-based Greek philosophies. Given the traditional Jewish disagreement with Christian allegorization of Scripture, and the contemporary debates over *ta'wil*, the option of allegory available to Philo of Alexandria would no longer serve to address the issue. Sa'adia sought to produce a systematization of Jewish thought that would support Jewish belief in God at this cultural moment, chiefly through his *Book of Beliefs and Opinions.* There Sa'adia makes the case, according to the philosophical standards of the day and in keeping with the traditions constitutive of rabbinic Judaism, for faithful Jewish adherence to the Scriptures and to belief in the God that they reveal. A representative statement of his is found in treatise 3, chapter 10: "[T]he Bible is not the sole basis of our religion, for in addition to it we have two other bases. One of these is anterior to it; namely, the fountain of reason. The second is posterior to it; namely the source of tradition. Whatever, therefore, we may not find in the Bible, we can find in the other two sources." [3]

Central to the *Book of Beliefs and Opinions* is Sa'adia's concern to preserve—consistent with Hellenistic metaphysical categories—the ineffability and transcendence of God by addressing the key issue of divine anthropomorphisms. Here the rabbinic tradition was not always a help, as the following passage from the Babylonian Talmud attests:

> When the Holy One, Blessed be He, wished to create man, He [first] created a company of ministering angels and said to them: "Is it your desire that we make a man in our image?" They answered: "Sovereign of the Universe, What will be his deeds?" "Such and such will be his deeds," He replied. Thereupon they exclaimed: "Sovereign of the Universe, 'what is man

---

engagement with Karaite scholars, major Jewish interpreters cultivated an enduring sensitivity to the Bible's literal sense along with their respect for traditional rabbinic midrash.

[3] Sa'adia proceeds to provide responses to twelve objections to the Bible as a self-consistent source for knowledge of God.

that thou art mindful of him, and the son of man that thou dost care for him?'" (Ps 8:4). Thereupon He stretched out His little finger among them and consumed them with fire. . . .

The first man reached from one end of the world to the other. . . . But when he sinned, the Holy One, Blessed be He, laid His hand upon him and diminished him, as it is written "Thou dost beset me behind and before, and layest thy hand upon me" (Ps 139:5).[4]

Sa'adia treats the issue fundamentally as a problem of language. In the Bible, the linguistic manifestation of theological beliefs takes the form of literary expressions, so interpretation (Arabic *ta'wil*) appropriate to the Bible's literary use of language is essential for correct understanding. In *Beliefs and Opinions* Sa'adia introduces *ta'wil* into his interpretive system with safeguards against esoteric or allegorical excess, as he outlines in treatise 7, chapter 2, with reference to understanding biblical statements about the resurrection of the dead literally or figuratively:

[W]e, the congregation of the Israelites, accept in its literal sense and its universally recognized meaning whatever is recorded in the books of God that have been transmitted to us. The only exceptions to this rule are those instances in which the generally recognized and usual rendering would lead to one of the four [following] results: either (a) the contradiction of the observable senses . . . (b) the contravention of reason . . . (c) a conflict with some other Scriptural utterance . . . , or, finally, (d) conflict with what has been transmitted by rabbinic tradition.

Sa'adia's discursive procedure on the question, as we see in the following selection from *Beliefs and Opinions,* is twofold. First he relativizes divine "somatic" expressions by observing how, elsewhere in the Bible, such expressions are applied to humans yet are obviously not to be taken literally. Even the earth is at times referred to anthropomorphically in Scripture without any pretense of literal attribution. Then he reasons *a fortiori* that such expressions cannot be applied to God with a literal meaning. (Sa'adia's readers would doubtless recognize his employment of ontological categories from the Aristotelian philosophical tradition so influential in medieval Christian and Islamic theological reflection.)

Another major issue in the Islamic theological debates that affected contemporary Jewish belief was faith in the absolute justice of the single sovereign God. In his commentary on the book of Job, Sa'adia was concerned that his reader understand the lesson of the book as a whole, which he preferred to call the *Book of Theodicy*. To this end, Sa'adia provided a fresh Arabic translation and commentary along with an introduction that lays out the plan of the book of Job as a coherent theological argument—another scholarly first from Sa'adia's pen. In his opinion, the question of innocent suffering is resolved by what the character Elihu has to say (in Job 32–37), refuting the arguments of Job's previous interlocutors and maintaining that God tests (and thereby strengthens) the loyalty of the righteous. Thereby the stage is set for God to speak to Job and restore his fortunes.

Inasmuch as Sa'adia seeks to bring his readers to a rationally consistent understanding of the text of Job, his translation sometimes transforms into a metaphoric expression what the Hebrew text seems to present as a statement of fact. An example appears in an articulation of Job's suffering that Sa'adia translates, "Were my agony weighed out *as it were,* in a single scale that bore it and its counterpart together, it would now outweigh the sand

[4] The translation is from I. Epstein, *The Babylonian Talmud: Seder Nezikin, Sanhedrin* (London: Soncino, 1935), 242–43.

of the sea, and therefore my speech is choked" (Job 6:2–3, emphasizing Sa'adia's addition), and similarly in Job 9:25, rendered, "My days are more fleet than a runner; they are done, and *it is as though* I have seen no good in them." Common sense, as do the first verses of the book, tell us that Job's days have not been devoid of good. Despite Sa'adia's poetic sensibilities demonstrated in his own liturgical compositions, rhetorical flourishes in the text of Job run the risk of obscuring the intended message of the larger composition, so he feels obliged to preserve the literal sense by making conspicuous the simile.

Given Sa'adia's conviction that exegesis must be guided by reason toward theological results that do not impugn the rationally comprehended truth about God, he translates to avoid any diminution of God's uniqueness and absolute sovereignty, as in Elihu's rebuke of Job: "Thou are not right in this for God's *power* is more than man" (Job 33:12). God is unique in that there can be no comparison with any other being. So also in our selection from Sa'adia's Job commentary: God's power is unique in that it cannot be shared with any other being; hence Sa'adia adds the word "God" to provide an unambiguous subject to the verb "smite" and provides a detailed justification (Job 2:7). Moreover, given his conviction that God rules in direct sovereignty over all, Sa'adia finds it irrational and exegetically unnecessary to regard the *śatan* figure as anything but a human being, and certainly not as an angelic being. Our selection includes Sa'adia's full defense of his position, which he wrote to counter the prevailing traditional view among most Jewish and Christian interpreters.

For further information on medieval philosophical Jewish exegesis:

Brody, Robert. *The Geonim of Babylonia and the Shaping of Medieval Jewish Culture.* New Haven: Yale University Press, 1998.

The Book of Beliefs and Opinions [5]

Part of Sa'adia's tome explicates Jewish theological beliefs in contradistinction to those of Christianity, particularly on the unity of God. After responding to Christian arguments from Scripture for the divine Trinity, Sa'adia observes that many times Christians take scriptural statements such as Ps 33:6 ("By the word of the Lord were the heavens made . . .") as supportive of Trinitarian teaching in Scripture: "I note that this, too, is due to [the Trinitarians'] unfamiliarity with the language of scripture." The gaon then includes in his summation of Jewish beliefs a section on how scriptural descriptions and statements about God are best interpreted. He begins by noting several texts that declare the utter incomparability of God.

Treatise 2, Chapter 9

Thus the Scriptures, taking into account everything that exists, exclude the possibility of its resembling the Creator or the Creator's resembling it. These explicit statements are, then, to be regarded as the basic principles that are to serve as the foundation of belief to which every doubtful expression with a figurative meaning must be referred in order to be brought into agreement with them. Among the Biblical utterances, now, with a figurative meaning is the statement of Scripture: *and God created man in His own image, in the image of God created He him* (Gen 1:27). This [linking of the image with God], I must explain, is merely a way of conferring honor. That is to say just as, even though all lands belong to Him, God honored one of them by saying: "This is My land," and although all mountains are His, He honored one mountain by saying: "This is My mountain," so did He, [although] all forms are His, honor one of them by saying: "This is My form," by way of distinction, not in a material sense.

Another one of these passages with a figurative meaning is the statement of Scripture: *For the Lord thy God is a devouring fire* (Deut 4:24). Now I must explain that what Scripture means hereby is that God is as punishing and destructive to unbelievers and heretics as fire. I find, moreover, that in the language of Scripture comparisons are sometimes expressed without [the use of the Hebrew preposition] *kaf.* Thus we read: *And He brought you forth out of the iron furnace* (Deut 4:20), the meaning of which is [really] *as out of an iron furnace.* [We read] also: *after a dead dog? After a flea?* (1 Sam 24:15), the actual meaning of which is: *as after a dead dog and as after a flea.* Finally [we read] concerning the Gadites that *Their faces were the faces of lions* (1 Chr 12:9), the meaning of which is [of course] *like the faces of lions.* Similarly must the meaning of *He is a devouring fire* be construed as: He is as punishing *as a devouring fire.*

---

[5] This selection was taken from Sa'adia Gaon, *The Book of Beliefs and Opinions* (trans. Samuel Rosenblatt; Yale Judaica Series 1; New Haven: Yale University Press, 1948). © Copyright, 1948, by Yale University Press. Pages 114–27. Used with permission.

[The] next [subject I shall discourse] about [in connection with the nature of God is that of] quantity. I say, then, that the concept of quantity calls for two things neither of which may be applied to the Creator. One of these is the measurement of length, width, and depth. The other is division and combination whereby things are divided from one another or combined with each other. None of these things can be asserted of the Creator, as it is proven by reason, Scripture, and tradition.

As far as the rational proof is concerned, it consists herein, that it was a Creator of these combinations and compositions, as demanded by our reason, that we were looking for and we found that there was nothing left of these [combinations] that would not be included in the concept that He was the author thereof.

As for the proof from Scripture, it is contained in the verse we have mentioned previously, namely: *Lest ye deal corruptly* (Deut 4:16), and the rest of that passage.[6]

As for the proof from tradition, again, we find that whenever our sages, who were considered trustworthy authorities in regard to our religion, encountered any such comparisons of God to physical beings, they did not translate them in an anthropomorphic sense, but rendered them in such a way as to correspond to the previously established principle. Now they were the disciples of the prophets and better acquainted than others with the speech of the prophets. If, therefore, it had seemed to them that these expressions were meant to be taken in their material sense, they would have translated them literally. However, they knew for certain from the prophets, aside from what their reason dictated to them, that by means of these anthropomorphic expressions they meant to designate lofty, exalted ideas. They therefore translated them in accordance with their clear understanding of the underlying thoughts.

One example of this type of translation is:

Behold, the hand of the Lord (Exod 9:3) = *Behold, a plague from before the Lord.*[7]

Another illustration of this sort of rendering is:

And under His feet (Exod 24:10) = *And under the throne of His glory.*

A further instance is:

According to the mouth of the Lord (Exod 17:1) = *According to the word of the Lord.*

A still further sample of this mode of translating on their part is:

---

[6] Sa'adia refers here to the presupposition underlying biblical prohibitions against graven images, that God cannot be truly represented in any tangible form.
[7] All these examples are taken from *Targum Onqelos.*

In the ears of the Lord (Num 11:18) = *Before the Lord.* Thus also did they translate all passages of a similar nature.

Chapter 10

And now that I have made it clear that reason, Scripture, and tradition are in agreement on the exclusion of any comparison from the personality of our Lord, I shall elaborate on these anthropomorphic terms, that are employed by Scripture in speaking of God, and say that there are ten of them, namely:

head, as in its statement: *And a helmet of salvation upon His head* (Isa 59:17);

eye, as in its statement: *The eyes of the Lord thy God are always upon it* (Deut 11:12);

ear, as in its statement: *For ye have wept in the ears of the Lord* (Num 11:18);

mouth, as in its statement: *According to the mouth of the* Lord (Exod 17:1);

lip, as in its statement: *Nor will I alter that which is gone out of My lips* (Ps 89:35);

face, as in its statement: *The Lord make His face to shine upon thee* (Num 6:25);

hand, as in its statement: *Behold, the hand of the Lord* (Exod 9:3);

heart, as in its statement: *And the Lord said in His heart* (Gen 8:21);

entrails, as in its statement: *Therefore My entrails yearn for him* (Jer 31:20);

and *foot,* as in its statement: *And prostrate yourselves at His footstool* (Ps 99:5).

Such statements, now, and others resembling them, are instances of the usage of language and its extension, each of them pointing to some idea [in connection with God]. As for their interpretation, it is such as we find it to be in matters other than those pertaining to the Creator. Thus we know that it is really of the nature and the peculiarity of language thus to extend and transfer meanings and employ figures of speech.

Such an extension of meaning is employed by the language of Scripture when it says

that heaven speaks: *The heavens declare the glory of God* (Ps 19:2);

that the sea talks: *For the sea hath spoken, the stronghold of the sea, saying* (Isa 23:4);

that death utters speech: *Destruction and Death say* (Job 28:22);

that stones can hear: *Behold, this stone shall be a witness against us; for it hath heard* (Josh 24:27);

that the mountains speak: *The mountains and the hills shall break forth before you into singing* (Isa 55:12);

and that the hills put on garments: *And the hills are girded with joy* (Ps 65:13).

There are also other such passages that cannot be enumerated in haste.

Now if someone were to ask, "But what advantage is there in this extension of meaning that is practiced by language and that is calculated only to throw us into doubt? Would it not have done better if it had restricted itself to expressions of unequivocal meaning and thus have enabled us to dispense with this burden of discovering the correct interpretation?" my answer would be that, if language were to restrict itself to just one term, its employment would be very much curtailed and it would be impossible to express by means of it any more than a small portion of what we aim to convey. It therefore preferred rather to extend its use of words so as to transmit every meaning, relying for the correct interpretation upon reason and acquaintance with the texts of Scripture and with history. Were we, in our effort to give an account of God, to make use only of expressions that are literally true, it would be necessary for us to desist from speaking of Him as one that hears and sees and pities and wills to the point where there would be nothing left for us to affirm except the fact of His existence.

And now that I have made this clear, let me go back to the ten terms listed before in order to explain their actual meaning. I say, then, that [when they used the word] *head* [in connection with God], the prophets wished [to convey] the thought of distinction and elevation, as Scripture expresses itself elsewhere in regard to human beings: *My glory, and the lifter up of my head* (Ps 3:4). By *eye*, again, they meant solicitude, as in the statement found in Scripture: *That I may set mine eye upon him* (Gen 44:21). By *face* [as applied to God] they meant either good will or anger. Thus Scripture says in one instance: *In the light of the king's countenance is life* (Prov 16:15); and in another: *And her countenance was no more sad* (1 Sam 1:18). By *ear* they meant the acceptance of a plea, as Scripture says: *Let thy servant, I pray thee, speak a word in my lord's ears* (Gen 44:18). By *mouth* and *lip* they meant explanation and command, as in the statements of Scripture: *At the mouth of Aaron and his sons* (Num 4:27), and *The lips of the righteous feed many; [but the foolish die for want of understanding]* (Prov 10:21). By *hand* they meant power, as in the statement of Scripture: *Therefore their inhabitants were short of hand* (2 Kgs 19:26). *By heart* they meant wisdom, as in the statement of Scripture: *A young man void of* heart (Prov 7:7). By *entrails* they meant tenderness, is in the statement of Scripture: *Yea, Thy Law is in my inmost parts* (Ps 40:9). By *foot*, finally, they meant domination by force, as in the statement of Scripture: *Until I make thine enemies thy footstool* (Ps 110:1).

Since, then, at certain times we find such expressions used of human beings in a nonmaterial sense how much more fittingly should they be construed in this non-material sense when applied to the Creator! Furthermore I say that we find that expressions similar to these are used in speaking of inanimate things which cannot properly be said to possess any of these organs. We find, namely, that in the language of Scripture thirteen such terms are applied to the earth and water.

The first of them is *head*—*Nor the head of the dust of the world* (Prov 8:26).

[Another is] *eye*, as in the statement of Scripture: *And they shall cover the eye of the earth* (Exod 10:5).

[A third is] *ear*, as in the statement of Scripture: *And give ear, Oh earth* (Isa 1:2).

[A fourth is] *face*, as in the statement of Scripture: *Above the face of the earth* (Num 11:31).

[A fifth is] *mouth*, as in the statement of Scripture: *And the earth opened her mouth* (Num 16:32).

[A sixth is] *wing*, as in the statement of Scripture: *From the wing of the earth* (Isa 24:16).

[A seventh is] *hand*, as in the statement of Scripture: *By the hand of the river* (Dan 10:4).

[An eighth is] *lip*, as in the statement of Scripture: *By the river's lip* (Exod 2:3).

[A ninth is] *heart*, as in the statement of Scripture: *The deeps were congealed in the heart of the sea* (Exod 15:8).

[A tenth is] *navel*, as in the statement of Scripture: *That dwell in the navel of the earth* (Ezek 38:12).

[An eleventh is] *belly*, as in the statement of Scripture: *Out of the belly of the netherworld cried I, and Thou heardst my voice* (Jonah 2:3).

[A twelfth is] *womb*, as in the statement of Scripture: *Or who shut up the sea with doors, when it broke forth, and issued out of the womb* (Job 38:8).

[A thirteenth is] *thigh,* as in the statement of Scripture: *And I shall gather them from the thighs of the earth* (Jer 31:8).

Thus we find that the language of Scripture employs these expressions in speaking of things, which, according to the testimony of our senses, possess none of these organs, on which account they must all be construed as merely figures of speech. It must, therefore, do the same for whatever our reason testifies possesses none of these organs. In that case, too, these expressions can be only figures of speech. He, therefore, who alleges that the language of Scripture uses words only in their material sense, must find these thirteen organs for us in the earth and the water.

Now just as the above-mentioned terms for the organs of the body [when applied to God] are used only figuratively, so also are all acts connected with these organs. [This would hold true where such words are addressed to God] as *incline Thine ear, open Thine eyes, stretch forth Thy hand,* and the like. The same thing would also apply to the special functions ascribed to these organs, [as when it is asserted of God] that *He hears and sees and speaks and thinks* and the like. Each one of these has an interpretation other than its literal sense. Hence even such a statement as *And the Lord smelled,* the true implication of which is difficult to construe, would have the meaning of "to receive," which [the word "smell" necessarily has] in the statement of Scripture: *Through the smell of water it will bud* (Job 14:9). [Such a construction would be] in keeping with reason and Scripture and tradition.

Peradventure however, someone, attacking our view, will ask: "But how is it possible to put such constructions on these anthropomorphic expressions and on what is related to them, when Scripture itself explicitly mentions a form like that of human beings that was seen by the prophets and spoke to them and to which they imputed God's words, let alone the description by it of God's being seated on a throne, and His being borne by the angels on top of a firmament, as Scripture says: *And above the firmament that was over their heads was the likeness of a throne, as the appearance of a sapphire stone; and upon the likeness of the throne was a likeness as the appearance of a man above it?* (Ezek 1:26). Furthermore, this form is also mentioned as having been seen seated on a throne with angels on its right and its left, as Scripture says: *I saw the Lord setting on His throne, and all the host of heaven standing by Him on His right hand and on His left"* (1 Kgs 22:19).

Our answer to this objection is that this form was something [specially] created. Similarly the throne and the firmament, as well as its bearers, were all of them produced for the first time by the Creator out of fire for the purpose of assuring His prophet that it was *He* that had revealed His word to him, as we shall explain in the third treatise of this book. It is a form nobler even than [that of] the angels, magnificent in character, resplendent with light, which is called *the glory of the Lord.* It is this form, too, that one of the prophets described as follows: *I beheld till thrones were placed, and one that was ancient of days did sit* (Dan 7:9), and that the sages characterized as šᵉ*khinah.* Sometimes, however, this specially created being consists of light without the form of a person. It was, therefore, an honor that God had conferred on

His prophet by allowing him to hear the oracle from the mouth of a majestic form created out of fire that was called *the glory of the Lord,* as we have explained.

What further proves the correctness of our thesis is the statement of the prophet concerning this form: *And He said unto me: "Son of man, stand upon thy feet, and I will speak with thee"* (Ezek 2:1). Now it is inconceivable that this interlocutor was the master of the universe, because the Torah says that the Creator has never spoken to anyone without an intermediary except to *our teacher Moses* alone. That is the import of its statement, *And there hath not arisen a prophet since in Israel like unto Moses, whom the Lord knew face to face* (Deut 34:10) As for the rest of the prophets, however, it was only the angels that addressed them. When, then, we find the text directly mentioning the title *angel,* we have an explicit reference to a created being. if, again, it uses the phrase *glory of the Lord,* that too implies something created. If, however, it mentions the name *Lord* but does not attach to it the word *glory* or *angel* but only such expressions as *vision* or *throne* or some human attribute, there can be no doubt but that there is something suppressed in that utterance, the full form of which should be *glory of the Lord* or *angel of the Lord,* in accordance with the practice of the language of Scripture to leave out words by ellipsis.

Chapter 11

Next I shall discourse upon [the category of] *quality,* that is to say the accidents, [in their relationship to God]. I say, then, that in reality it cannot be asserted at all that accidents could apply to God, in view of the fact that He is the creator of all accidents. When, therefore, we find Him saying that He loves or hates a certain thing, what is meant thereby is that whatever He has commanded us to do is designated by Him as lovable in His sight, since He has made the love of that thing obligatory upon us. Thus, for example, Scripture says: *For the Lord loveth justice* (Ps 37:28), and *For the Lord is righteous, He loveth righteousness* (Ps 11:7), and the like. It also makes this assertion about the virtues in general, saying: *For in these things I delight, saith the Lord* (Jer 9:23). Whatever, again, He has forbidden us to do is designated by Him as hateful in His sight, since He has made the hating of that thing obligatory upon us. Thus Scripture says: *There are six things which the Lord hateth* (Prov 6:16), and *I hate robbery with iniquity* (Isa 61:8). It also makes this assertion about vices in general, saying concerning them: *For all these are things that I hate, saith the Lord* (Zech 8:17).

Furthermore, whenever we note that, [according to Scripture], God says that He is pleased or angry, what is meant thereby is that whenever happiness and reward are decreed for some of God's creatures, that is characterized as God's pleasure. This is illustrated in such statements of Scripture as *The Lord taketh pleasure in them that fear Him* (Ps 147:11), and *Lord, Thou hast taken pleasure in Thy land* (Ps 85:2). Again, when some of them are deserving of hardship and punishment, that is characterized as God's anger. This is illustrated in such statements of Scripture as *The anger of the Lord is against them that do evil* (Ps 34:17), and *But His power and His wrath is against all them that forsake Him* (Ezra 8:22). As for physical anger and pleasure or physical love and hate, they can be possessed only by beings that desire and fear. It is out of the question, however, that the Creator of all things should entertain a desire for aught that He has created or be in fear of it. The same exegesis is to be given to all other apparently anthropomorphic descriptions of God occurring in Scripture that fall under the category of quality.

With respect to [the category of] *relation* I say that it would be improper to connect anything with the Creator in an anthropomorphic manner or to relate it to Him, because He has existed since eternity, [that is a time] when none of the things created were connected with Him or related to Him. Now, that they have been created by Him, it would be necessary to make the inadmissible assumption that a change has taken place in His essence, permitting them to become related to and connected with Him in an anthropomorphic fashion, subsequent to the existence of a contrary situation.

When, therefore, we note that the Scriptures call God *king* and present human beings as His slaves and the angels as ministering to Him, as is done in the statements of Scripture: *The Lord is king forever and ever* (Ps 10:16), and *Praise, O ye servants of the Lord* (Ps 113:1), and *The flaming fire His ministers* (Ps 104:4), all that is merely a means of expressing reverence and esteem. For the human beings most highly esteemed by us are the kings. God is also called "king" in the sense that He can do whatever He wishes and that His command is always carried out, as Scripture says: *Forasmuch as the king's word has power; and who may say unto Him: "What doest thou?"* (Eccl 8:4).

Again, when we find that the Scriptures ascribe to God friends and enemies, as is done in such statements of Scripture as *O ye that love the Lord, hate evil* (Ps 97:10), and *The haters of the Lord should dwindle away before Him* (Ps 81:16), that is merely a metaphorical usage of these terms on their part for the purpose of expressing esteem or disapproval. Esteem is shown of those men that obey God by applying to them the designation of *lovers* of God, whilst disapproval of the disobedient is expressed by the application to them of the designation of *haters*. In the same vein must everything else that falls under this category be interpreted.

Apropos of [the category of] *place,* I say that it is inconceivable for several reasons that the Creator should have need for occupying any place whatsoever. First of all He is Himself the Creator of all space. Also He originally existed alone, [that is, at a time] when there was [as yet] no [such thing as] place. It is unthinkable, therefore, that as a result of His act of creation He should have been transported into space. Furthermore, space is required only by a material object which occupies the place of the object that it meets and comes in contact with, so that each one of the two contiguous objects forms the place of the other. This is, however, out of the question so far as the Creator is concerned.

As for the assertion of the prophets that God dwells in heaven, that was merely a way of indicating God's greatness and His elevation, since heaven is for us the highest thing we know of. This is borne out by such explanations offered by the Scriptures as *For God is in heaven, and thou upon earth* (Eccl 5:1); as well as *Behold, heaven and the heaven of heavens cannot contain Thee* (1 Kgs 8:27). The same applies to statements to the effect that God dwells in the Temple, such as, *And I will dwell among the children of Israel* (Exod 29:45), and *And the Lord dwelleth in Zion* (Joel 4:21). The purpose of all this was to confer honor upon the place and the people in question. Besides that it is to be remembered that God had also revealed in that place His specially-created light, of which we have made mention previously, that was called *šᵉkhinah* and *glory*.

As regards [the category of] *time,* it is inconceivable that the concept of time could be applied to the Creator because of the fact that He is Himself the Creator of all time. Furthermore, He existed originally alone when there was as yet no such thing as time. It is, therefore, unthinkable that time should have effected any locomotion or change in Him. Moreover, time is nothing else than the measurement of the duration of corporeal beings. He, however, who has no body, is far removed from such concepts as time and duration. If, nevertheless, we do describe God as being enduring and permanent, that is done only by way of approximation, as has been stated by us previously.

Again, when we find the Scriptures making such statements as *Even from everlasting to everlasting, Thou art God* (Ps 90:2), as well as *Yea, since the day was I am He* (Isa 43:13), and again, *Before Me there was no God formed, neither shall any be after Me* (Isa 43:10), all the points of time referred to therein revert solely to God's acts. Those, therefore, who say *Even from everlasting to everlasting, Thou art God,* mean thereby: "From the beginning of time Thou hast always helped Thy servants." Thus Scripture expresses it elsewhere: *God is unto us a God of deliverances* (Ps 68:21).

As for His statement, blessed be He, *Before Me there was no God formed,* that was meant to convey the thought: "Before I sent My messenger and after I sent Him there was no God outside of Myself." For immediately prior to this remark He says: *My servant whom I have chosen.* In the popular idiom, in fact, it is quite proper for a person to say "before me" when he means "before I act." This was done by Joab when he said: *I may not tarry thus before thee* (2 Sam 18:14). Also one may say "after me" when one means "after I have acted," as Nathan did when he said: *I also will come in after thee, and confirm thy words* (1 Kgs 1:14).

Similarly is there, in the statement *Yea, since the day was I am He,* an allusion to some distinguished day, either the day of the revelation at *Sinai* or another such day. What God says, in effect, in this statement is: "From that time on have I been the one commanding you to do such and such a thing and forbidding you to do that, and saving you from this," because He concludes the statement with the remark: *I will work, and who can reverse it?*

As regards [the matter of] *possession,* inasmuch as all creatures are God's creation and handiwork, it is not seemly for us to say that He possesses one thing to the exclusion of another, nor that He possesses the one to a greater and the other to a lesser degree. If we, nevertheless, see the Scriptures assert that a certain people is His peculiar property and His possession and His portion and *inheritance,* [as they do in the statement]: *For the portion of the Lord is His people, Jacob the lot of His inheritance* (Deut 32:9), that is done merely as a means of conferring honor and distinction. For, as it appears to us, every man's portion and lot are precious to him. Nay the Scriptures even go so far as to declare God, too, figuratively to be the lot of the pious and their portion, as they do in their statement: *O Lord, the portion of mine inheritance and of my cup* (Ps 16:5). This is, therefore, also an expression of special devotion and esteem.

It is also in this sense that one must construe the designation of God as the Master of the prophets and of [all] believers, as He is called in such expressions used by Scripture as *The God of Abraham,* [*the God of Isaac and the God of Jacob*] (Exod 3:6), and *The God of the Hebrews* (Exod 3:18). Such a designation is entirely in order, since God is the Master of all. This [special attachment of God's name] to the pious is, then, merely an expression of His esteem and high regard for them.

As for [the category of] *position* [in relation to God], inasmuch as the Creator, blessed and exalted be He, is not a physical being, it is unseemly [to speak] of Him as having any such position as sitting or standing or the like. Nay, it is impossible because He is not a physical being, and because originally there existed nothing outside of Himself. Also by position is meant the extension of one body over another. Finally the various positions assumed necessarily produce some change or alteration in him that assumes them.

If, nevertheless, the Scriptures make such assertions as *Yea, the Lord sitteth as king forever* (Ps 29:10), their object therein is solely to indicate the permanence of God's existence. Such statements on the part of the Scriptures, again, as *Rise up, O Lord, and let Thine enemies be scattered* (Num 10:35) mean nothing else than readiness for help and punishment. In such utterances, moreover, as *And He stood with him there* (Exod 34:5), the subject referred to is the divine light called *šᵉkhinah.* Finally, by such Scriptural remarks as *And the Lord went His way, as soon as He had finished* (Gen. 18:33) is meant the removal of that light. The same sort of exegesis must be given to any Scriptural statements resembling these.

Commentary on Job[8]

When it was the day that God's beloved came and presented themselves before Him, Job's adversary was present along with them. [Job 1:6]

I rendered *the children of God* as "God's beloved" in accordance with the widespread usage of the nation, as in *Children are ye to the Lord your God* (Deut 14:1), *My first-born child Israel* (Exod 4:22), *Is corruption His? No, His children's is the fault* (Deut 32:5), and the like. These beloved would gather in a special place on appointed days to worship God and do His bidding. For it says, *When it was the day that the children of God,* etc. The gathering was for worship of Him, as shown by the words to *present themselves before Him* (see Exod 23:17, 34:23, Deut 16:16).

I translated *to present themselves* as "and presented themselves" because I took the sense of the verb to be in the perfect tense—as in *If a man hath transgressed against his fellow to slay him* (Exod 21:14), where the meaning is "and hath slain him." Likewise in *The daughter of a man who is a priest, if she hath profaned herself to fornicate* (Lev 21:9), the meaning is "and hath fornicated." So here *to present themselves* means "and presented themselves."

As for the *adversary (śaṭan),* he was in fact an ordinary human being, like the one mentioned when Scripture says, *The Lord raised an adversary (śaṭan) to Solomon,* Hadad the Edomite (1Kgs 11:14). It also says, *And God raised up against him an adversary (śaṭan), Rezon, son of Eliada* (1 Kgs 11:23). Both of these were mortal men. Similarly, the Bible says of Joshua son of Jehozadak, *And the adversary (śaṭan) standing to his right, to accuse him (le-śiṭno)* (Zech 3:1). That too was a human adversary, specifically, *Rehum the chancellor and Shimshai the scribe* (Ezra 4:8), whose opposition to Joshua is mentioned explicitly by the Bible when it says, *And in the reign of Ahasuerus, at the outset of his reign, they wrote an accusation (śiṭnah) against the inhabitants of Judah and Jerusalem* (Ezra 4:6). And in like fashion is the entire passage in Zechariah (3:2) to be treated in which occur the words *The Lord rebuke thee, O adversary (haś-śaṭan).*

So commonly is this word *(śaṭan)* applied to people who oppose one another that it occurs in many passages of Scripture which I shall not enumerate. Examples: *They are my adversaries where I pursue good* (Ps 38:21), *In place of my love they oppose me* (Ps 109:4), *This be the recompense of my adversaries from God* (Ps 109:20), and again, in the story of Isaac, *And they strove over that also, and he called it Śiṭnah* (Gen 26:21). On the basis of this and other parallels, the adversary here would be a human being. It is farfetched in the extreme to infer that he would be an angel. For all monotheists agree that the Creator made His angels, who minister to Him, in the knowledge that they would not disobey Him, just as He chose the prophets, who

---

[8]This selection comes from *The Book of Theodicy: Translation and Commentary on the Book of Job* (ed. and trans. L. E. Goodman; Yale Judaica Series 25; New Haven: Yale University Press, 1988). Pages 153–59, 174–75. Copyright © by Yale University. Used with permission.

bear His messages, in the knowledge that they would not disobey Him. But opposing God's righteous beloved is among the most egregious acts of rebellion. So one who claims that this adversary to Job was an angel has made angels rebels and contravened the principle upon which we agree.

As you know, the soul has three faculties: thought, irascibility, and appetite. Thought is the power by which a person discriminates right from wrong and true from false. Irascibility is that by which animals show aggressiveness and mettle, to pursue their interests and to react and retaliate against attack. And appetite is the faculty by which animals crave nourishment, procreation, and satisfaction of other needs. You know also that the mark of justice in a rational being is subordination of the powers of irascibility and appetite to thought. If either of these dominates, that is injustice or wrong. Thus one who allows that angels might act out of envy, which is one species of irascibility, implies that appetitive actions are assignable to them as well, such as eating, drinking, sexual intercourse, and other vile and squalid functions, from which God preserved His angels.

Besides, God foreknew that the angels would never disobey Him, and it is not possible for what contravenes His foreknowledge to take place. For if things were to take place contrary to what we have supposed, God would have foreknown that instead.

I understand that one sectary was so carried away with this view that Job's adversary was an angel that he even claimed that envy, jealousy, and lust may actually occur in angels, as the story of Job and this adversary's envy of him seemed to him to suggest. Seeing that this position of his could not be maintained without allowing eating and drinking to be predicable of angels, he stopped up this hole in his position by declaring even such characterizations of the angels permissible. He realized that this in turn implied that angels might be described as cohabiting and mating, so he allowed this as well, finding in the verse *The children of God saw [the daughters of men that they were fair . . .*] (Gen 6:2ff.) a reference to the angels seeking forbidden mates upon falling from heaven and becoming like human beings. And he read an allusion to this into the verse *I had said ye are gods, all children of the most High, yet like men shall ye die and like any officer shall ye fall* (Ps 82:6–7). Thus nothing remained too foul or obscene to ascribe to the angels. Yet all this was simply the consequence of his original thesis. He concocted these monstrous absurdities because he had so little discernment in interpreting discourse linguistically. With God's help I shall now explain where he went wrong in everything that he posits.

You should know that the miscue which led this thoughtless tamperer and others to hold that the śatan is an angel lay in the words of God to the śatan, *Lo, all that he hath is in thy hand; only against him do not loose thy hand* (1:12), and again, Only *preserve his soul* (2:6), and in the verse *And he smote Job with pestilent boils* (2:7)— which seems to attribute this action to the adversary.

I shall elucidate these three verses so as to remove the misunderstanding conclusively. To begin with, I point out that design and intent are called "hand" in the language of the Israelites. For David said to the woman who petitioned him, *Is the hand of Joab with thee in all this?* (2 Sam 14:19), meaning Joab's design and intent. Likewise, Joab's saying that Sheba the son of Bichri had *raised his hand against the king, against David* (2 Sam 20:21), when Sheba had not actually laid hands upon the king but had only the purpose and intent. And similarly, *Also in Judah the hand of God was to give them one heart* (2 Chr 30:12), meaning God's intent. There are many parallels. Accordingly, the words *Lo, all that he hath is in thy hand* would mean "is subject to your design, purpose, or intent." I shall explain the other two problem verses along similar lines in their proper places in this book, and the fantasies of this dreamer will be dispelled.

Having dissolved this first problem, I must say that this interpreter went wrong in his exegesis of *The children of God saw . . .* (Gen 6:2) even more shamefully than in his misreading of the story of Job. The reason: he had no understanding whatever of the usage of Israelites as to the general and the special. For it is their custom to say, "the exceptional do thus, and the masses thus," when these elite are humans, mentioned separately only as a mark of distinction. Thus, after treating of special cases, "the doings of human beings" refers simply to the generality, as in the verse of Jeremiah, *That hast set signs and wonders on the land of Egypt to this day, both on Israel and on men* (Jer 32:20)—Israel are men too, and Jeremiah singled them out only to indicate that they are special. Similarly in Zechariah, *When upon the Lord shall be the eye of man and of all the Tribes of Israel* (Zech 9:1)—the Tribes of Israel are likewise human beings, and he singles them out only as a mark of their distinction. On this basis, the words *The children of God saw . . .* (Gen 6:2) refer also to human beings, singled out from the generality only as a mark of distinction.

This is a credible explanation that clears God's ministrants of all reproach. It is reinforced and supported by the words that follow, *And God saw that many were the evils of man* (Gen 6:5), where the angels are not included in the censure, and by God's words about the punishment, *I will blot out man that I have created* (Gen 6:7), where He does not visit punishment upon the angels as well. What can you possibly say about someone who would succumb to such a delusion?

His error regarding the passage *Yet like men shall ye die* (Ps 82:7) is still more grave, yet more readily cleared up, since it shows that he did not even look at the beginning of the passage. For the beginning is a remonstrance against judges charged with the conduct of justice who have shown partiality and injustice. God rebukes them accordingly, saying, *How long will ye render iniquitous judgment and favor the wicked? Selah* (Ps 82:2). He then commands them to treat the orphan fairly, *Judge the helpless and the orphan, vindicate the poor and the lowly, rescue the helpless and downtrodden,* etc. (Ps 82:3–4). He blames them for not heeding what He is telling them, as though they did not comprehend Him, saying, *They do not know; they do not understand* (Ps 82:5). Then He reveals to them what He had held in store for them had they been fair, *I had said, "ye are gods"* (Ps 82:6), meaning, "I had intended to elevate and ennoble you." And now He informs them how low and lacking they will become: *But like men shall ye die* (Ps 82:7), meaning like ordinary men, *and like any officer shall ye fall*—like some chief stricken from his rank. This is like His saying to Nebuchadnezzar, *How art thou fallen from heaven, O shining one, son of the dawn?* (Isa 14:12). Nebuchadnezzar was not in the heavens. This is mere verbal hyperbole and sarcasm.

The entire passage, then, deals with judges and magistrates, and we find nothing about angels appointed by God as judges or magistrates. For there are two forms of judgment: (1) the reckoning with men and their retribution, which is reserved exclusively to the Sovereign of the two worlds and which it is unthinkable that He would delegate to another, as it says, *I shall draw nigh to you for judgment, and I shall be a ready witness* (Mal 3:5); and (2) the legal disputes of human beings, but these we must settle with one another. No report comes down to us, nor even the slightest indication, that in any age these were entrusted to an angel. This being so, the claims of this man are refuted fully and drop out of view.

One who states that this adversary is sinfulness itself is closer to interpreting the expression soundly than was the preceding interpreter. For sinfulness does act as an adversary to man, pleading against him so as to triumph over him, as our fathers said, *Our iniquities answer against us,* etc. (Jer 14:7), and again, *Our sins testify against us* (Isa 59:12). Indeed God might even place one in this adversary's hand, in the sense of *Thou hast undone us by our sins* (Isa 64:6).

This idea of the adversary would fit rather well, were it not for the Book's testifying that Job was without sin—as when it says unequivocally that Job was *blameless and upright, God-fearing and shunning evil* (1:1, 8)—and the displeasure with his companions for speaking nonsense about him, when God says, *For ye have not spoken unto Me that which is right* (42:8), as I shall explain with God's help.

Since the belief that the adversary is an angel does not stand up to scrutiny, inasmuch as angels are elevated beings and inasmuch as God knows that they will choose not to sin, and since the adversary is not sinfulness, as the book bears witness that Job was free of sinfulness, no third alternative remains for us but to take the term as referring to a human being like Hadad the Edomite, Rezon, Rehum, Shimshai, the shepherds of Gerar, and their like.

We say, then, that with all Job's probity and plenty, there were folk in that land who envied him on both accounts, who said of him that he served God only out of solicitude for His blessings, and that if some disaster befell him or if he were deprived of some of those blessings, he would falter in his faithfulness and turn apostate. Therefore God willed to reveal to His prophet [Moses by the Rabbinic account] the falsity and groundlessness of these charges against Job and permitted those misfortunes to befall him; and when Job bore them steadfastly, God rewarded and recompensed him and confuted the charges of his adversaries.

Most likely this man who opposed Job had many followers, and the book singled him out solely because he was preeminent among them. The intent in God's addressing him would be like that of His addressing Abimelech in the interest of Abraham (Gen 20:3), Laban in the interest of Jacob (Gen 31:24), and Balaam in the interest of Israel (Num 22). These received God's words not so as to edify those addressed but so as to elevate the faithful. And the same would be the reason for God's addressing the adversary here—to ennoble His righteous servant and remove from him all taint of the outrageous charge which his envious accuser had leveled against him.

Summing up, I would say that for any prophet or upright servant of God defamed by slanderers as Job was, it would be fitting for God to try him so as to clear him of their outrageous charges. But I also say that God may or may not please to do so. He might simply hold the detractors in contempt and disregard their libels. In Job's case, however, He was pleased to vindicate his servant and so to test him by way of sufferings.

So when the adversary went out from before God, God smote Job with sore abcesses from heel to crown. [Job 2:7]

The dissolution of the third difficulty is plain. For the Book says, [*the adversary went out from before God,*] *and he smote Job with sore abcesses.* The verb cannot pertain to the *śaṭan;* the only possible subject is God, since God's name is mentioned just prior, where it says, *from before God.* The clause *and he smote Job* is conjoined to it, giving the meaning, "and God smote Job." That is why I have supplied the noun "God" and clarified the syntax as I have [rendering the first clause of the verse as a subordinate rather than an independent clause].

But truth to tell and certain as the foregoing, even if the word "God" had been further from *smote* than was *śaṭan* in the word order, and the word *śaṭan* had been closer, we could still ascribe the action to God, on the model of the words *They cry out and the Lord heareth* (Ps 34:18), which refer back to *the righteous,* who are further removed, in the verse *The eyes of the Lord are upon the righteous* (v. 16), while the wicked are closer, in the verse *The face of the Lord is against the wicked* (v. 17). There are many examples of this pattern of skipping over the adjacent and referring to the remote. All the more evident is it when God's name is nearer and that of the adversary is further that the proper subject of the verb is He.

So now all the confusions about the *śaṭan* are dissolved, and the context confirms that he was a man. If the unreclaimed had the least inkling of this they would not have enmeshed themselves in the dreadful stories that we have been obliged to hear.

Part Four

Modern Interpretation (1500–Present)

CHAPTER 16

Renaissance Scholarship: Psalm 23 in
Critici sacri (1660)

The European Renaissance was the new cultural life that began to flower in fourteenth-century Italy and continued to develop in France, Holland, Germany, and England into the sixteenth century. The term has come to refer to the period when, responding to a complex array of political, technological, and commercial circumstances, rapid departures from the previously dominant cultural traditions became evident in various parts of Europe. Scholars do not agree on when the Renaissance began and ended and to what extent it was discontinuous with medieval life before and modern life afterward. We will attempt no reduction of such a broad and diverse movement to a simple definition. For our purposes, what is of interest in this period is the birth of a more historical mind-set in biblical scholarship.

The general humanist enterprise during the Renaissance would obviously include the attempt to understand classical sources better. To serve this end, scholars endeavored to correct corrupted texts, update the critical methods of the medievals, and acquire a more authentic sense of classical pagan ideas by removing centuries of accreted Christian assumptions. All this had a profound effect on how the Bible was studied. Refined examination of the texts of the Vulgate clearly revealed the need for extensive revision of its Latin in order to establish a more accurate text and a superior translation. Broadened access to printed texts fueled the desire among scholars to make available not only better Latin translations of the Bible but more accurate editions of the Greek New Testament and the Hebrew Old Testament. As scholars sought to understand biblical idioms better, they turned to ancient translations such as the Septuagint, Targumim, and other ancient versions. Soon improved editions of these literatures were also produced and printed.

In the sixteenth and seventeenth centuries, ecclesiastical patrons commissioned massive polyglot-Bible printing projects. One of the most widely used was the London Polyglot, supervised by the churchman Brian Walton and completed in 1657. This six-volume Bible included in side-by-side columns the Hebrew Old Testament with Latin interlinear translation, the Samaritan Pentateuch, the Septuagint with variant readings, the corrected Vulgate, the Syriac Peshitta, an Arabic translation, the Aramaic Targumim, the Ethiopic Psalms (all with Latin translations), and the New Testament in Greek with textual variants.

In 1660 the English churchman John Pearson and a team of fellow divines completed an enormous compendium of biblical commentary authored by a selection of Renaissance scholars. Conceived as an addition to Walton's polyglot, the nine volumes of the

Critici sacri totaled 9,679 double-columned, folio-sized pages. Beyond the biblical commentaries themselves, this compendium included hundreds of scholarly excurses on a wide variety of philological, historical, and cultural topics—for example, the mandrakes mentioned in Gen 30; the land where Job lived; the style of New Testament Greek; and the Ephesian cult mentioned in Acts 19. In later editions the number and length of the excurses grew, constituting of themselves a four-volume thesaurus appended to the original volumes of the collection.

For comparison with the other commentary compendia in our anthology (the *Yalqut Shim'oni* and the *Glossa ordinaria*), our selection from the *Critici sacri* is Ps 23. The contributors here do not include the full range of exegetes who appear elsewhere in the *Critici sacri,* but they fairly represent the state of biblical scholarship from the sixteenth century. At that time, the focus of humanist biblical scholarship in the Old Testament was primarily philological. Much energy was expended in the writing of Hebrew grammars and related lexicographical resources in close consultation with rabbinic commentaries and contemporary Jewish experts such as Elijah Levita. Biblical commentaries employed this newly available material in pursuit of two different purposes. One was to press Christian Hebrew scholarship into the service of defending aspects of Christian theology so that the text could speak to the contemporary church. The other interpretive purpose followed the humanist respect for the true antiquity of the world that produced the biblical writings. The entries throughout the *Critici sacri* are, for the most part, of the latter sort, offering detailed explanation of ancient social customs, clothing, instruments, and, above all, words and phrases. (In this respect, what we find here is typical of the information that many commentaries of the modern period feature.) In our Ps 23 selection, the focus is overwhelmingly on philology, although the intensity of this focus varies from commentator to commentator. The contributors are reviewed here in the order in which they appear in the *Critici sacri* at Ps 23.

Sebastian Münster (1489–1552)

Münster had been a Franciscan but turned Protestant in 1524. In 1528 he began teaching at the university in Basel, where he remained until his death. An enormously influential Christian Hebraist, Münster was for his time the best Christian source for Hebrew grammar (much of which was generated by his translation of the work of Elijah Levita). His extensive oeuvre included authoritative Semitic dictionaries and his own copiously annotated Latin-Hebrew polyglot, which reflected rabbinic learning in his translation. Over one hundred thousand volumes of his work were in circulation by the end of the sixteenth century. He dedicated his Latin Old Testament to Henry VIII with words that expressed clearly the spirit of Renaissance biblical scholarship:

> In our era we are assisted by the multitude of books, which we know were unavailable in earlier ages. For St. Jerome himself had no help interpreting the Old Testament except a naked Bible and an uneducated (and untrustworthy) teacher; no Aramaic translation or Targum, no commentaries, not even a Hebrew grammar—without which many places of Scripture cannot possibly be accurately explained, no matter what some people say.[1]

[1] Taken from D. K. Shuger, *The Renaissance Bible: Scholarship, Sacrifice, and Subjectivity* (Berkeley: University of California Press, 1994), 33.

Interestingly, Münster's comments on Ps 23 are entirely allegorical, in this respect setting them apart from all the other *Critici sacri* contributions on this psalm.

François Vatable (died 1547)

A Catholic scholar who taught in Paris at the Collège de France, Vatable was a highly erudite and excellent teacher whose students included even Jews. His lectures included ample references to medieval Jewish exegetes such as David Kimchi. He himself published nothing during his lifetime. To his students are owed his comments on Ps 23, which consist of explanations of certain Hebrew idioms and suggestions for the most accurate Latin translation.

Isidore Clarius

A Roman Catholic (Italian Benedictine) who produced his own Latin version.

Johannes Drusius (1550–1616)

Although he began his studies of Semitics at Louvain, Drusius fled intra-Protestant persecution in the Netherlands to London, where he continued his study of Semitic languages at Cambridge. After teaching Syriac, Aramaic, and Hebrew at Oxford, he returned to the Netherlands and settled in 1584 at the new university in Franeker. His work there helped to establish the university as the foremost center of its time for the philological study of the Hebrew Bible. Drusius was an avid student of rabbinic literature yet, unlike some of his Christian contemporaries, was free from any motivation to engage in Christian apologetics. His usual manner of exegesis is to offer strictly grammatical or lexical notes, as we see in his comments on Ps 23.

Sixtinus Amama (1593–1629)

In 1616 Amama was appointed professor of Oriental languages at the University of Franeker as the successor to Drusius, who died in his arms. Over the next ten years, Amama published his teacher's massive commentaries and essays in ten volumes. Amama appears to have had a good measure of rabbinic learning. His comments on Ps 23 are the most lengthy of the group, and they include tangents into Gen 4:7 and the biblical terminology for Gehenna.

Hugo Grotius (1583–1645)

Grotius was one of the Netherlands' most celebrated intellects. By age eight, he had produced elaborate Latin compositions, and by age fifteen, he had received his doctorate from the University of Leiden. Grotius went on to become a recognized international law theorist, political philosopher, poet, and biblical scholar. In the latter vein he wrote complete works on the Scriptures: *Annotata ad Vetus Testamentum* (1644); *Annotata ad Evangelia* (1641); *Annotata ad Novum Testamentum* (1644)—all works that were written and revised over a long period of time. The exegetical work of Grotius was not inclined to dogmatics or directly concerned with any sense of the text other than the philological, as his brief comments on Ps 23 attest.

Our review of the *Critici sacri* and its intellectual milieu points to the technical nature of its contents, so some explanation of the layout in our selection is in order. Lemmata from Ps 23, as given in the *Critici sacri* text, are set off by bold print. The commentators sometimes quote the Septuagint Psalter, which is indicated by the abbreviation LXX in square brackets [LXX]. At other times, commentators quote the Hebrew Psalter as translated by Jerome, indicated by the abbreviation Heb. in square brackets [Heb.]. In the cases in which the Latin translation of the Septuagint Psalter and the Latin translation of the Hebrew Psalter agree with one another and are quoted by one of the commentators, both are indicated in square brackets [LXX & Heb.]. Contributors to the *Critici sacri* often provided their own Latin translation of the Hebrew or Greek original—that is, they offered a translation variant from the accepted Latin Vulgate editions of their day and commented on this, or they provided variant readings in the body of their comment. In such cases we have set off the translated passage or variant reading in small capital letters, and neither the Septuagint nor the Hebrew Psalter is indicated. For the sake of rendering an accurate translation of the Latin Vulgate in the idiom of the seventeenth century, all translations of the Vulgate are taken from the Douay-Rheims version of the Bible.[2] To represent something of the page appearance that readers of this compendium had before them (relative to earlier sources), most of the Hebrew and Greek fonts are preserved in our selection. At certain points, the seventeenth-century printer has confused Hebrew characters, which are here printed correctly.

For further information on the *Critici sacri* and Renaissance biblical scholarship:

Bentley, Jerry H. *Humanists and Holy Writ: New Testament Scholarship in the Renaissance.* Princeton: Princeton University Press, 1983.

Evans, Gillian. R. *The Language and Logic of the Bible: The Road to Reformation.* Cambridge: Cambridge University Press, 1985.

Friedman, Jerome. *The Most Ancient Testimony: Sixteenth-Century Christian Hebraica in the Age of Renaissance Nostalgia.* Athens, Ohio: Ohio University Press, 1983.

McKane, William. *Selected Christian Hebraists.* New York: Cambridge University Press, 1989.

Shulvass, Moses A. *The Jews in the World of the Renaissance.* Leiden: Brill, 1973.

---

[2] The translation of the Old Testament in this version was first published at the English College at Douay in 1609, and the translation of the New Testament was first published at the English College at Rheims in 1582. It is currently available as *The Holy Bible, Translated from the Latin Vulgate: Douay-Rheims Version* (Rockford, Ill.: Tan, 1971).

Psalm xxiii[3]

MUNSTERUS.

1. **MY SHEPHERD** This allegory is used frequently in Scripture, where the Lord is called SHEPHERD and pious men are called "sheep." What TO LEAD A SHEEP TO THE PASTURE means he [the Psalmist] shows next with these words: HE WILL LEAD AND ESCORT MY SOUL ALONG PATHS OF JUSTICE, etc. Furthermore, the "staff" by which rational sheep are led is the Word of God; the "table" is the promises by which man is strengthened against the enemy; the "oil" is the benificence of God; and the "chalice which inebriateth"[4] is the grace of consolation.

VATABLUS.

1. **He shepherds me** [Heb.] רעי MY SHEPHERD; SHEPHERDING ME.

I WILL LACK אחסר I WILL WANT FOR NOTHING: that is to say, I will not be able to lack anything.

2. **IN ABODES MADE OF SHOOTS** בנאות דשא IN FIELDS OF GRASS, IN GRASSY PASTURES.

TO STILL WATERS על מי מנוחות TO QUIET WATERS; or, GENTLE: that is, placid and gently flowing waters, which are free from all danger.

He transforms [LXX] ישובב HE REVIVES; or HE CAUSES TO REVIVE, subject to IN THE GOOD WAY. In other [Latin readings] HE MAKES TO REST; HE RESTORES PEACEFULNESS; HE REESTABLISHES."

Of righteousness [LXX & Heb.] צדק This particular term describes STRAIGHT AND CLEAR PATHS, or LEVEL paths, that are not mountainous, on which a sheep does not become exhausted.

4. **I will have walked** [LXX & Heb.] אלך To me this means WERE I WALKING; or WERE I CONSTANTLY PRESENT IN: that is, even were I constantly in deadly darkness and the greatest danger.

---

[3] The translation by J. Derek Halvorson is of *Critici sacri; sive, Annotata doctissimorum virorum in Vetus ac Novum Testamentum, quibus accedunt tractatus varii theologico-philologici: Editio nova in novem tomos distributa, multis anecdotis commentariis, ac indice ad totum opus locupletissimo, aucta* (Sacred criticisms; or, Annotations of the most learned men on the Old and New Testaments, to which they add various theological-philological treatises: A new edition, distributed in nine volumes, with many unpublished commentaries and a complete index to the entire collection added) (ed. John Pearson; 8 vols. in 9; Amsterdam: Boom, 1698), vol. 3, col. 133, line 17–col. 136, line 56.

[4] "Cup that runneth over" is the translation adopted in the *King James Version* and in many subsequent English versions.

And thy staff [LXX & Heb.] ומשענתך AND THY SHEPHERD'S CROOK. With these he [the Psalmist] signifies the care and zeal of the shepherd.

5. **YOU PREPARE** תערך YOU WILL FURNISH. Hebrew future tense for the present tense. With these he [the Psalmist] signifies a bounty of all things, or those that will be necessary or pleasant.

Thou hast anointed my head with oil [LXX] דשנת בשמן ראשי YOU POUR PER-FUME OVER MY HEAD. Or, YOU ADMINISTER ANOINTING TO MY HEAD WITH PERFUME. Hebrew past tense for the present.

6. **BUT NEVERTHELESS GOOD** אך טוב SURELY GOODNESS: or, HAPPINESS.

Unto length of days [LXX & Heb.] לארך ימים This is a Hebraism for FOR MANY DAYS.

CLARIUS.

1. **The Lord ruleth[5] me** [LXX]) Or, HE SHEPHERDS ME. In this Psalm he [the Psalmist] preaches the wonder and security and happiness of trust in God. This allegory—in which pious men are called "sheep" and God is called "shepherd"—is found frequently in Scripture.[6] It is nothing other than a beast of the field that depends on the works of the shepherd, [that is] not able to look out for itself at all (whence the proverb was born, "the behavior of little sheep"), and that nevertheless is equally capable of being useful for man. Thus man will surely die, unless God leads and refreshes him with his Spirit; and if he is abandoned by that Spirit, then none of those things by which he gains salvation is able to remain or to be found [in him].

2. **In a place of pasture** [LXX] Or, IN A PLEASANT AND FERTILE PLACE. Those who shepherd flocks best have stables not far from the pasture, especially in Judea, where the shade of the woods is rare. For in the middle of the day, when the heat is fierce, they [the sheep] should be led into the shade, which the Poet [Virgil] advises:

> But at day's hottest seek a shadowy vale,
> Where some vast ancient-timbered oak of Jove
> Spreads his huge branches, or where huddling black
> Ilex on ilex cowers in awful shade.[7]

The Psalmist adds that he [the shepherd] leads TO THE WATERS OF REFRESH-MENT, or COOLING and GENTLY FLOWING waters, which he is in the habit of doing twice a day. Actually he drives [them] to the waters, because experienced [shep-

---

[5] Some manuscripts read *reget* ("will rule").

[6] See Munsterus on verse 1, above.

[7] Virgil, *Georgica*, 3.331–334; Latin text and English translation in Virgil, *Bucolics, Aeneid, and Georgics* (ed. J. B. Greenough; Boston: Ginn, 1900).

herds] typically provide for the well-being of [their] flocks of sheep by means of drinking troughs, which the sheep returning from pasture lap at, and by the taste of which they sate [their] desire for drinking and grazing.

3. **He hath converted my soul** [LXX] Or, HE HAS RESTORED TO ME, or HE LEADS AND ESCORTS ALONG THE PATHS OF JUSTICE. That which he [the Psalmist] has said through allegory in the preceding verse he declares here. The Hebrews, however, consider that term "he hath converted" as if [it meant] "he has led gently," because with this word the Psalmist was considering the indulgent care of the Father. For this they taught, that the vigilant and circumspect one who follows the flock should re-strain it with great clemency, and in rounding up and retrieving the sheep [should be-have] more like a leader than a lord, driving [them] with shouting and a staff and never by hurling [his] spear.

4. **Thy rod** [LXX & Heb.] Nothing other is to be understood by the SHEPHERD'S STAFF AND CROOK than pastoral care and earnestness. It is a synecdoche, of course, so you understand the deed through the instrument. Therefore, the "staff", by which rational sheep are led, is the word of God; the "table" is the promises, by which man is strengthened against his enemies; the "oil" is the benificence of God; and the "chalice which inebriateth" is the grace of consolation.[8]

5. **Thou hast prepared a table before me** [LXX] He [the Psalmist] indicates with a different allegory that he overflows with an abundance of all things through the shepherding of God.

Thou has anointed my head with oil [LXX] Especially in Palestine the anointed are later admitted to lavish banquets.

6. **And that I may dwell** [LXX] We see here the end result of his [the Psalmist's] devotion, that having been rescued from throngs of enemies, he is naturally made more peaceful with God.

DRUSIUS.

2. בִּנְאוֹת דֶּשֶׁא יַרְבִּיצֵנִי Aquila and Symmachus [translate as], ἐν ὡραιότητι πόας κατεσχήνωσέν με, HE HAS PLACED ME IN THE BEAUTY OF THE FIELD.

3. יְשׁוֹבֵב Symmachus [translates as], ἀνεκτήσατό με.

בְּמַעְגְּלֵי Symmachus [translates as], δι' ἀτραπῶν, THROUGH PATHS [Heb.].

5. כּוֹסִי Theodotion [translates as], Ποτήριόν μου. Symmachus [translates it as] ποτήριον. Quinta's edition [provides], καὶ ποτήριόν μου. Sexta [translates it as] τὸ ποτήριόν μου.

---

[8] See Munsterus on verse 1, above.

רְוָיָה וְאַךְ טוֹב Symmachus [translates as] μεθύσκον πλὴν ἀγαθόν and Quinta [does so] in the same manner. You should render it in Latin as MY CUP THAT RUNNETH OVER, IN TRUTH IS GOOD (calix inebrians, verum bonus). Sexta's edition [renders it as] μεκύσκων ὡς κράτισον RUNNING OVER SO AS TO BE SPLENDID.

6. שַׁבְתִּי Symmachus [translates as] ἡ κατόικησίς μου, MY HABITATION.

Amama.[9]

23. The Psalmist is a teacher who explains his faith in the benificence of God. He is a comforter who consoles himself against fear of poverty. And he seeks justification (for his faith) in the originating cause, namely the paternal care of God for David. Deod.[10] He declares his own faithfully blessed state, both in body and in spirit. [The Psalm was] written, as is seen, while he was in exile, fleeing from Saul. He proceeds allegorically, comparing God to the Shepherd and himself to the sheep. He proposes the allegory in verse one.

רָעָה, רֹעִי to SHEPHERD. The term embraces in its transitive signification all the duties of the good shepherd that pertain to the pasture. Here we have a metaphor for "to rule." TO RULE and TO HAVE DOMINION explain in turn TO SHEPHERD. Micah 5[:2], FROM YOU ONE WILL GO FORTH FOR ME IN ORDER THAT HE MIGHT BE RULER OVER ISRAEL (Ex te exibit mihi לִהְיוֹת מֹשֵׁל ut sit Dominator in Israel). Matthew 2:1: ὅς τις ποιμανεῖ τὸν λαὸν; hence in Hom. ποίμην λαῶν.[11]

אֶחְסָר From חָסַר with the force of כָּל I SHALL NOT WANT ANY THING, that is, anything. Thus, it will not be justifiable [that he should lack anything] in view of your care for all people. Rabbi Solomon[12] [supplies] כְּלוּם "anywhere" (quopiam), or דבר. חָסַר, or חֵסֶר, "to be absent from," "to be far away from." חָסֵר "to cheat." Hence חֶסֶר חֶסְרוֹן & חֹסֶר.

Here חֶסֶר, which is opposed to מָלֵא in the Masoretic Text. The propositions in verse one cohere syllogistically.

2. He explains the allegory in verses two and three by enumerating the aspects pertaining to the office of the good pastor. The exposition of the argument is by aspects. Then he continues with bucolic and pastoral phrases and recounts the good gifts of God, such as a bountiful supply of sustenance.

---

[9] This commentary by Sixtinus Amama is not included in the first edition of the *Critici sacri* (1660) or in the Frankfurt edition of 1695.

[10] This is a shorthand reference to Giovanni Diodati, *Pious and Learned Annotations upon the Holy Bible* (London: James Flesher, 1651).

[11] This Greek phrase, translated "shepherd of the people," is a stock phrase in Homer's *Iliad* and *Odyssey*.

[12] On the use of R. Shlomo Yitzḥaqi (Rashi) (1028–1105) outside Jewish circles in the Middle Ages and later, see Herman Hilperin, *Rashi and the Christian Scholars* (Pittsburgh: University of Pittsburgh Press, 1963).

בְּנָאוֹת IN FIELDS, IN ABODES. נָוָה TO DWELL IN, here נָוֶה DWELLING PLACE, HUT, COTTAGE. Plural נָוִים & נָוֹת. According to normal [Hebrew grammar] נָוֹת & נְאוֹת are exchanged with ease using an "Ehevi" letter.[13] This he desires: not to give me so much rich food, but to give me quiet and comfort in due proportion.

דֶּשֶׁא TENDER GRASS. עֵשֶׂב MORE MATURE GRASS, LONGER-LASTING GRASS. Where [it appears] in the Hiphil[14] הִדְשִׁיא "to grow, sprout." תַּדְשֵׁא הָאָרֶץ דֶּשֶׁא.[15]

יַרְבִּיצֵנִי From רָבַע TO LIE DOWN, TO LIE DOWN NEARBY. [This term is] specific to quadrupeds, as שָׁכַב [is] to humans. It is also said of birds, sheep, and chicks that lie down, as in Deuteronomy 22:6, where the mother רוֹבֶצֶת lies down with her chicks. Hiphil הִרְבִּיץ TO MAKE TO LIE DOWN NEARBY.

תַּרְבִּיצֵנִי Jun.[16] HE MAKES ME TO LIE DOWN. Gen.[17] HE STABLES ME. Varro, *De Re Rustica* [*On Agriculture*], Book I, "... the best practice is, [after selling the forage,] for him to feed and fold the flocks of a neighbor in his pasture."[18] Nevertheless, "I stable" and "I am stabled" are customarily neutral [i.e., they can both be used actively or passively]. Properly speaking, this is said with regard to quadrupeds and birds. Genesis 4:7: IF IN TRUTH YOU DO NOT DO WELL, SIN LIES WAITING AT THE DOORWAY. חַטָּאת רוֹבֵץ ["sin is crouching"] like a dog, ἐπὶ θυραῖς, "in front of the doors", as in Mt 24:33: YOU KNOW THAT HE IS NEAR AND BEFORE THE DOORS. The anomaly is reconciled either by supplying the synonym חֵטְא ["sin'] or through metonomy, as it is for עֹנֶשׁ הַחַטָּאת ["penalty of sin"]. Thus Deut 29:20 [MT v. 19], AND EVERY CURSE THAT IS WRITTEN IN THE BOOK OF THE LAW WILL REST [וְרָבְצָה] ON HIM. Nevertheless, I find in the manuscripts of D.D. Sculteti, which he committed to me in good faith, a peculiar sentence (given) by the illustrious Baro of Dhona to Melvinus, LYING DOWN, YOU ARE AT THE DOORWAY OF SIN *(ad ostium peccati recubans es)*, that is, you lie down. Thus it is shown to be an anomaly. And "the greatest security" will signify "in the greatest rest," as is said of the flock lying down in the shade to escape the summer heat. [Cf.] Song of Songs 1:7. [It is] as if to say, you lie down safely and you sleep soundly with

---

[13] "Ehevi" is shorthand for the Hebrew letters—aleph, he, waw, and yod—that are sometimes present and other times dropped from words without affecting the meaning of the word.

[14] Hiphil is a conjugation that usually connotes a causative force to the verb.

[15] Here Amama quotes the Hebrew phrase from Gen 1:11 to show the noun and Hiphil verbal forms of the same root for "grass" or "vegetation," awkwardly (but literally) translated, "let the earth vegetate vegetation."

[16] This is a shorthand reference to Franciscus Junius (1545–1602), who was a pupil of the converted Jew Immanuel Tremellius and worked with him on a widely used Latin translation of the Bible. Their translation is usually very sparse and literal, reading almost like an interlinear translation.

[17] This is a shorthand reference to Gilbertus Genebrardus, a sixteenth-century Benedictine who wrote a commentary on the Psalms.

[18] Varro, *De re rustica* 1.21.1, in Cato and Varro, *On Agriculture* (trans. W. D. Hooper and H. B. Ash; Loeb Classical Library; Cambridge: Harvard University Press, 1941), 236–37. Amama's version of Varro's text differs from that provided in the Loeb edition: Amama leaves out "having sold the forage" *(pabulo vendito)* and gives "in his pasture" *(in suo pascuo)* instead of "in his field/farm" *(in suo fundo)*.

the greatest danger threatening you. Two things remain: 1. Analysis and Scope, which [shows that it] is a warning, not a reproach; 2. לְפֶתַח ;ל includes the article.

peaceful [waters] נֹחַ It is quiet. Aquila, PEACEFUL, that is, hardly moving, peaceful [waters], flowing mildly, which lack danger. See Genesis 24:20, 29:2, and 30:38.

יְנַהֲלֵנִי HE DRIVES ME. To drive is to lead the flock. Festus, "leading the horses of Agasonis," that is, driving well. It is close to shepherding. Germanicus Caesar,

—"driving with a staff" *(baculoque minatur).*

It [the term "to drive"] is used in the Vulgate at Exodus 3:1, "and he drove the flock to the inner parts of the desert." Thus James 3:4 [states], in a popular idiom in use in France, Spain, and Italy, "Behold also ships, whereas they are great, and are driven by strong winds."

3. בַב From שׁוֹב שׁוּב HE RESTORES, HE MAKES PEACEFUL, or HE LEADS MY SOUL BACK INTO THE GOOD WAY, that is, my languishing [soul]. Or, HE MAKES TO RETURN: for when the afflicted man is lifted up by consolation, his soul seems in a way to return [to the right way].

נָחָה ["he leads"] In Hiphil, הנחה "to lead," "to lead away" gently, as a shepherd would [his] sheep or as one would a child.

בְמַעְגְּלֵי ["in paths"] From עֶגֶל, here עָגֹל "rolling smooth," עֲגָלָה "wagon." And thus מַעֲגָל and מַעֲגָלָה [indicate] the routine path that a wagon impresses [in the ground]. מַעֲגָל even signifies the place of an encampment, which seems to have been fortified by the ancients at one time with wagons. [Hence, the] Belgian Wagenburg, [or] "city of wagons."

צֶדֶק OF RIGHTEOUSNESS, that is, [a path that is] level, flat, minimally uneven, [and] leveled, on which the sheep is not wearied.

4. בְּגֵיא ["through the valley"] גַּיְא and גֵּיא or גַּיְא likewise גַּי and גֵּי VALLEY. He explicates the allegory through the hypothesis whence גֵּי גֶן־הִנֹּם and thrice גֵּי הִנֹּם Valley of Hinnom. [This is] the place outside of Jerusalem, named after its owner, in which the Jews sacrificed their children to Moloch. After this it was profaned. The pious King Josiah saw to it that sordid things, carrion, and every type of filth were carried off to that place, and since the air there was infected, he saw to it that there was a אֵשׁ תָּמִיד "perpetual fire" there by which these things were consumed. Whence in subsequent ages it was called the place of the damned, גֵּי הִנָּם, or γεέννα in the New Testament and throughout Rabbinical literature. In the Old Testament that place תֹּפֶת was called by תֹּפִים *Tympanis,* because while the infant was being sacrificed and consumed by fire the sacrificial priests beats drums, so that the parents standing nearby would not be moved to pity by the wailing and crying of the innocent infants. Indeed, it was a horrible spectacle. And here also burning is called smoky with [the ad-

dition of] הּ. Note תָּפְתֶּה in Isa 30[:33], BUT FOR A LONG TIME תפתה HAS BEEN READY (*iam ab heri parata est* תפתה). Similarly, the place of the blessed is denoted by the garden of pleasure, paradise.

Moloch Two huge pyres were constructed, and the boy, having been handed over, was thrown in by his feet by the priests on both sides. Whence [we get], "to make children to pass through fire by Moloch."

Shadow of death is said first of all about present danger, as in this case. Secondly, [it is said] about the grave, [as in] Job 10:21, INTO THE LAND OF DARKNESS AND OF THE SHADOW OF DEATH. Thirdly, [it is said] regarding the darkness of errors, [as in] Isa 9:1 [MT 9:2], Mt 4:16, and Lk 1:71 [actually, 1:79], IN ORDER TO APPEAR TO THOSE WHO SIT IN DARKNESS AND THE SHADOW OF DEATH. The image of death [is] a composite of צֵל and מָוֶת which is from מָוֶת and צֶלֶם, so that it signifies such an image as is seen by the eyes of the dying. [This is] the most sorrowful image of death.

Shadow of death From צֵל "shadow," and מָוֶת. From צלל "to overshadow with a covering, to be concealed, to be covered," whence [we get] צֵל "by means of shadow" for "by means of defense." [Hence,] "in the shadow of your allies" (*in umbra alarum tuarum*). [Consider also] Ps 121:5, THE LORD YOUR SHADOW, [and the Septuagint] LXX, "your protection." Others suggest צֶלֶם but then it should have been צַלְמוּת. However, it signifies the gloomiest place, which is able to cast upon us the image of death by the dread of darkness, or which knocks the wind out of us by our dread. Certainly, [it is] a deadly and most dangerous place.

thy rod Ἡ ῥάβδος σου, שֵׁבֶט is the πολύσημος [polysemous] voice, signifies: 1. TRIBE, 2. SCEPTER, 3. ROD or STAFF, THE ROD OF CORRECTION. Here it signifies the staff, which is made from a tree or from the root of a tree. It is mentioned otherwise at Gen 49[:10], THE SCEPTER WILL NOT BE REMOVED FROM JUDAH, NOR THE RULER'S STAFF FROM HIS FEET (*Non removebitur* שבט *de Juda, nec Legislator de pedibus ejus*), that is, lordship, power [will not be removed from it]. And because this passage was corrupted by the Jews, which the Aramaic translates with שֻׁלְטָן LORDSHIP, POWER, RULE, and this supports that which follows מְחֹקֵק. שֵׁבֶט does not signify a "thin and flexible rod," "a switch" (*een Roede*),[19] but a THICK AND FIRM ONE. [Consider] II Sam 18:14, JOAB TOOK THREE SPEARS AND THRUST THEM INTO THE HEART OF ABSOLOM (*Joab accepit tria* שְׁבָטִים *hastilia, et infixit in cor Absolomi*). [Consider also] Lev 27:32, WHATEVER PASSES UNDER THE STAFF, A TENTH IS HOLY TO THE LORD. II. SCEPTER, STAFF OF THE KING. Achilles, in Book I of the *Iliad*, swears thus: Ναὶ μὰ τὸ δεσκ. τὸ μὲν οὔποτε φύλλα καὶ ὅσους φύσει ἐπειδὴ πρῶτα τομὴν ἐν ὀρέσσι λέλοιπεν.[20] "Nor shall it become green again, [for] the iron has stripped its leaves and bark on all sides."

מִשְׁעָן ["staff"] From שָׁעַן in Niphal. נִשְׁעַן HE RESTED ON, HE LAY DOWN, HE RECLINED, and figuratively TO BE CONFIDENT. Hence, מִשְׁעָן, STAFF: a shepherd's crook,

---

[19] Amama gives the Dutch here for "rod, wand, switch."

[20] Homer, *Iliad* 1.234–235, in Homer, *Opera* (ed. David B. Monro and Thomas W. Allen; 5 vols.; Oxford: Oxford University Press, 1920).

which was placed at his feet, by which the shepherd was supported while he stood by shepherding his flock. And מִשְׁעֶנֶת [means] the SUPPORT, POST, FOOT by which we are supported, in either body or spirit, whence . . .

נחם in Niphal נִחַם TO BE CONSOLED, passive, GRIEVE, Piel "to be consoled," נֹחַם "consolation," תַּנְחוּמִים and תַּנְחוּמוֹת "consolations," whence the Book of Tanchuma.[21]

5. Now he applies the allegory to his own person, and [he does so] in a dual manner: I. by enumerating [his] present blessings in verse 5; II. [by enumerating] future blessings, both in this life and in the future.

עָרַךְ TO ARRANGE, TO DISPENSE, TO GATHER BY HIS ORDER. Hiphil, TO APPRAISE, TO FURNISH.

שֻׁלְחָן ["table"] From שלח "I place," because dishes are placed before him, which from this are called place-settings.

צוררי ["my enemies"] From צָרַר "to tie up," "to handle with limitations."

With oil With perfume, with ointment. You render my head anointed. He is saying that he abounds in all things, both necessities and related luxuries. שֶׁמֶן [is] the general name for all fatness, both natural and fabricated. And thus that which is gluey and fatty is called aromatic ointment and liniment. The ancients applied it for the purpose of propriety and cheerfulness, whence Mt 6:17. Later Christ reproaches the Pharisees because whenever they fasted they darkened their faces and acted as if dead and made known to men that they were fasting. He [Christ] says, WHEN YOU FAST, ANOINT YOUR HEAD (Σὺ δὲ νεσεύων ἄλειψαί σου τὴν κεφαλὴν), that is, show by this external sign that you are cheerful, so they will not know that you are fasting. Based on this, the mourning abstain from [being anointed with] oil. II Sam 14:3 [14:2–3], JOAB SENT TO TEKOA, AND BROUGHT FROM THERE A WISE WOMAN, AND SAID TO HER, 'TAKE UP MOURNING, PUT ON MOURNING CLOTHES, AND DO NOT ANOINT YOURSELF WITH OIL, AND GO TO THE KING.'

רְוָיָה RUNNING OVER, from רוה "to inundate," "to saturate." רָוֶה "soaked," רָוָה and ה with yod רַוָּיָה.

6. אַךְ ["surely"] NOTHING IF NOT, Jun. ACTUALLY, PARTICULARLY.

They will follow [Used] both in a good and in a bad [sense]. [In] bad, [see, for example,] Ps 141[143:3], "The enemy hath persecuted my soul" [LXX]. And throughout [the Scriptures], רָדַף "to be pursued intensely," הַרְדִּיף "to cause to be pursued."

וְשַׁבְתִּי ["and I will dwell"] "and I will rest." שׁוּב also [means] "he was peaceful," from the nominative שׁוּבָה. Isa 30:15, בְּשׁוּבָה וּבְנַחַת "you will be saved in quiet and in rest."

---

[21] *Tanchuma* is the title of a midrashic collection on the Torah.

חֶסֶד MERCY, KIND-HEARTEDNESS. חָסִיד "kind-hearted," "pious," "merciful," "holy"; hence חֲסִידִים Hasidim. And the Aramaic חַסִי ὅσιος קְדֹשׁ חָסִיד ὅσιος, ἅγιος, "holy." Hence חֲסִידָה "stork," due to its natural inclination to mercy towards offspring. Πέλαργος.

לְאֹרֶךְ יָמִים ["forever"] AFTER A LENGTH OF DAYS, FOR A LONG TIME. Ald. Belg. A PROLONGED TIME *(een langdurige tijd).*[22] Jun. "As long as the days are long."

GROTIUS.

1. **The Lord ruleth me** [LXX] The Aramaic considers [this psalm as a] song to have been made referring to the Israelites who were in the desert. For poetry often is a depiction of things that once might have been said, such as is [the case with] the prophecy of Nereus in Horace.[23]

5. **Thou has prepared a table before me** [LXX] Not a wooden [table], or a stone [table], but one that is easy to pick up quickly from the ground.

Thou hast anointed my head with oil [LXX] It is proper for you to insert "with fat" *(pinguibus)* for "with oil" *(oleo)*, as the Aramaic [does] here. For thus שמן is employed in Proverbs 21:20, Psalm 109:24, and Isaiah 5:1. But understand here, with the Aramaic, those very fat birds with which the Israelites were fed in the desert, whether those were ὀρτυγομῆτραι, "mothers of quail" or something else.

---

[22] Amama here gives a translation in Old Belgian.
[23] Horace, *Odes* 1.15, in Horace, *Odes and Epodes* (trans. C. E. Bennett; Loeb Classical Library; Cambridge: Harvard University Press, 1927), 44–47.

CHAPTER 17

Allegory, Authorial Intent, and Christian Doctrine: John Calvin (1509–1564)

Destined to become one of the most influential figures in the history of the Christian church, John Calvin was born to upper-middle-class parents in France and in his youth trained for the priesthood and later for a career in law. His earliest scholarly works were thoroughly in the humanist vein, dedicated to explicating classical writers such as Seneca. In his mid-twenties Calvin departed from the Roman Catholic faith to become a Protestant, and his conversion led him to devote his scholarly energies to the service of what he called "true religion."[1]

The legacy of his exegetical output is prodigious, including about forty-five volumes of biblical commentary produced over a twenty-eight-year career of ecclesiastical and civic leadership at Geneva. Most of these commentaries were developed in lectures Calvin delivered at the Geneva Academy, where he taught many students who would go on to become important Protestant theologians in their own right. Students and secretaries transcribed his lectures into notes that he edited for publication.

Calvin's approach to the biblical text reflected his classical humanist training, paying close attention to grammatical and rhetorical features of the text in its original languages and in its historical context. Reading the text first from the Hebrew or Greek, Calvin would then translate into Latin, frequently explaining why he had chosen certain Latin formulations. His concern for the best manuscript readings brought him to rely on Erasmus's Greek edition of the New Testament.

The humanist quest for the best manuscript readings and the attentiveness to the grammar and style of the original language expressions were fueled by the desire to discern the genuine meaning of the ancient text, that is, the meaning that was in the mind of the author. Writing to the prominent Greek scholar Simon Grynaeus in a letter that came to serve as the preface to his own commentary on the book of Romans, Calvin opined that "since about the only business he [the commentator] has is to lay open the mind of the writer he has set out to explain, the more he leads the reader away from it, the more he deviates from his own purpose and is sure to wander out of bounds." This may be characterized as a literalist approach to the text, as opposed to a figurative approach. Indeed, Calvin rather regularly expressed disagreement with patristic tendencies toward allegorization.

---

[1] See the prefatory dedication of John Calvin, *A Commentary on the Psalms* (London: James Clarke, 1965).

His commentaries sometimes reflect the exegetical polemics of his era, for he would some-times express his disdain for the figurative exegesis of a given biblical passage as advanced by his theological opponents and other contemporary writers. The basis for Calvin's disre-gard for allegory was his belief that such interpretation did not represent what the biblical author intended. For Calvin, any exegesis that departed from the obvious historical mean-ing was only an attempt to find something in the text that simply was not there—the antithesis of the humanist mind-set.

Given the quantity of his output and the extent of his influence, clearly there is much more to be said about Calvin as an interpreter of Scripture. The selections below are cho-sen simply to highlight Calvin's attitude toward figurative exegesis (and his low regard for apocryphal books such as Sirach), and to clearly represent the more historically minded exegetical direction taken by prominent Protestant interpreters of the Reformation era.

For further information on John Calvin and humanist biblical scholarship:

Oberman, Heiko A. *The Reformation: Roots and Ramifications.* Grand Rapids: Eerdmans, 1994.

Parker, Thomas Henry L. *Calvin's New Testament Commentaries.* 2d ed. Edinburgh: T&T Clark, 1993.

Puckett, David Lee. *John Calvin's Exegesis of the Old Testament.* Louisville: Westmin-ster/John Knox, 1995.

Rabil, Albert, Jr., ed. *Renaissance Humanism: Foundations, Forms, and Legacy.* Philadelphia: University of Pennsylvania Press, 1988.

Selections from Calvin

Institutes of the Christian Religion[2]

In this passage from his Institutes of the Christian Religion *(2.5.17, 19) the subject is the role of human free will relative to divine sovereignty in salvation; Calvin is opposing those who argue that the exercise of free will is necessary to respond to divine grace.*

17. They [Calvin's opponents] appeal, moreover, to the testimony of the Apostle Paul, because he says, "It is not of him that willeth, nor of him that runneth, but of God that showeth mercy" (Rom 9:15). From this they infer, that there is something in will and endeavor, which, though weak in themselves, still, being mercifully aided by God, are not without some measure of success. But if they would attend in sober earnest to the subject there handled by Paul, they would not so rashly pervert his meaning. I am aware they can quote Origen[3] and Jerome[4] in support of this exposition. To these I might, in my turn, oppose Augustine. But it is of no consequence what they thought, if it is clear what Paul meant. He teaches that salvation is prepared for those only on whom the Lord is pleased to bestow his mercy—that ruin and death await all whom he has not chosen. He had proved the condition of the reprobate by the example of Pharaoh, and confirmed the certainty of gratuitous election by the passage in Moses, "I will have mercy on whom I will have mercy" [see Exod 33:19; Rom 9:6–18]. Thereafter he concludes, that it is not of him that willeth, nor of him that runneth, but of God that showeth mercy. If these words are understood to mean that the will or endeavor are not sufficient, because unequal to such a task, the apostle has not used them very appropriately. We must therefore abandon this absurd mode of arguing, "It is not of him that willeth, nor of him that runneth;"—therefore, there is some will, some running. Paul's meaning is more simple—there is no will nor running by which we can prepare the way for our salvation—it is wholly of the divine mercy. He indeed says nothing more than he says to Titus, when he writes, "After that the kindness and love of God our Saviour toward man appeared, not by works of righteousness which we have done, but according to his mercy he saved us" (Titus 3:4, 5). Those who argue that Paul insinuated there was some will and some running when he said, "It is not of him that willeth, nor of him that runneth," would not allow me to argue after the same fashion, that we have done some righteous works, because Paul says that we have attained the divine favour, "not by works of righteousness which we have done." But if they see a flaw in this mode of arguing, let them open their eyes, and they will see that their own mode is not free from a similar fallacy. The argument which Augustine uses is well founded, "If it is said, 'It is not of him that willeth, nor of him that runneth,' because neither will nor running are sufficient; it may, on the other hand, be retorted, it is not

---

[2] This translation of Calvin's *Institutes of the Christian Religion* is from *Institutes of the Christian Religion* (trans. Henry Beveridge; Grand Rapids: Eerdmans, 1953), vol. 1. Used with permission.

[3] Origen, *Commentarii in Romanos* 7.16 (PG 14:1145).

[4] Jerome, *Adversus Pelagianos dialogi III* 1.5 (PL 23:500f.).

'of God that showeth mercy,' because mercy does not act alone." This second proposition being absurd, Augustine justly concludes the meaning of the words to be, that there is no good will in man until it is prepared by the Lord; not that we ought not to will and run, but that both are produced in us by God.[5] Some, with equal unskillfulness, wrest the saying of Paul, "We are laborers together with God" (1 Cor 3:9). There cannot be a doubt that these words apply to ministers only, who are called "labourers with God," not from bringing anything of their own, but because God makes use of their instrumentality after he has rendered them fit, and provided them with the necessary endowments.

18. They appeal also to Ecclesiasticus,[6] who is well known to be a writer of doubtful authority. But, though we might justly decline his testimony, let us see what he says in support of free will. His words are, "He himself made man from the beginning, and left him in the hand of his counsel; If thou wilt, to keep the commandments, and perform acceptable faithfulness. He hath set fire and water before thee: stretch forth thy hand unto whether thou wilt. Before man is life and death; and whether him liketh shall be given him" (Sir 15:14–17). Grant that man received at his creation a power of acquiring life or death; what, then, if we, on the other hand, can reply that he has lost it? Assuredly I have no intention to contradict Solomon, who asserts that "God has made man upright;" that "they have sought out many inventions" (Eccl 7:29). But since man, by degenerating, has made shipwreck of himself and all his blessings, it certainly does not follow, that everything attributed to his nature, as originally constituted, applies to it now when vitiated and degenerate. Therefore, not only to my opponents, but to the author of Ecclesiasticus himself (whoever he may have been), this is my answer: If you mean to tell man that in himself there is a power of acquiring salvation, your authority with us is not so great as, in the least degree, to prejudice the undoubted word of God; but if only wishing to curb the malignity of the flesh, which, by transferring the blame of its own wickedness to God, is wont to catch at a vain defence, you say that rectitude was given to man, in order to make it apparent he was the cause of his own destruction, I willingly assent. Only agree with me in this, that it is by his own fault he is stript of the ornaments in which the Lord at first attired him, and then let us unite in acknowledging that what he now wants is a physician, and not a defender.

19. There is nothing more frequent in their mouths than the parable of the traveller who fell among thieves, and was left half dead (Luke 10:32). I am aware that it is a common idea with almost all writers, that under the figure of the traveller is represented the calamity of the human race. Hence our opponents argue that man was not so mutilated by the robbery of sin and the devil as not to preserve some remains of his former endowments; because it is said he was left half dead. For where

---

[5] Augustine, *Enchiridion* 9.32, in Augustine, *Confessions and Enchiridion* (trans. Albert C. Outler; Library of Christian Classics 7; Philadelphia: Westminster, 1955), 358.

[6] Ecclesiasticus (also called Sirach) is the name of a book included in the Apocrypha, a collection of ancient Jewish books traditionally regarded by most of the Christian churches throughout history as part of the biblical canon. One of the distinctions of the Reformation Protestants was their low regard for the doctrinal authority of apocryphal books.

is the half living, unless some portion of right will and reason remain? First, were I to deny that there is any room for their allegory, what could they say? There can be no doubt that the Fathers invented it contrary to the genuine sense of the parable. Allegories ought to be carried no further than Scripture expressly sanctions: so far are they from forming a sufficient basis to found doctrines upon. And were I so disposed I might easily find the means of tearing up this fiction by the roots. The Word of God leaves no half life to man, but teaches that, in regard to life and happiness, he has utterly perished. Paul, when he speaks of our redemption, says not that the half dead are cured (Eph 2:5, 30; 5:14) but that those who were dead are raised up. He does not call upon the half dead to receive the illumination of Christ, but upon those who are asleep and buried. In the same way our Lord himself says, "The hour is coming, and now is, when the dead shall hear the voice of the Son of God" (John 5:25). How can they presume to set up a flimsy allegory in opposition to so many clear statements? But be it that this allegory is good evidence, what can they extort out of it? Man is half dead; therefore there is some soundness in him. True! he has a mind capable of understanding, though incapable of attaining to heavenly and spiritual wisdom; he has some discernment of what is honorable; he has some sense of the Divinity, though he cannot reach the true knowledge of God. But to what do these amount? They certainly do not refute the doctrine of Augustine—a doctrine confirmed by the common suffrages even of the Schoolmen,[7] that after the fall, the free gifts on which salvation depends were withdrawn, and natural gifts corrupted and defiled. Let it stand, therefore, as an indubitable truth, which no engines can shake, that the mind of man is so entirely alienated from the righteousness of God that he cannot conceive, desire, or design anything but what is wicked, distorted, foul, impure, and iniquitous; that his heart is so thoroughly envenomed by sin, that it can breathe out nothing but corruption and rottenness; that if some men occasionally make a show of goodness, their mind is ever interwoven with hypocrisy and deceit, their soul inwardly bound with the fetters of wickedness.

Commentary on Galatians[8]

In this selection from Calvin's Commentary on Galatians *(at 4:21–26), Calvin follows the humanist commentary pattern: phrase-by-phrase commentary, with reference to the Apostle Paul's grammar and rhetoric where this would help bring out the intended sense. This New Testament passage in context treats the question of the place of the Jewish law in salvation by faith in divine grace. The biblical text reads,*

> Tell me, you who desire to be subject to the law, will you not listen to the law? For it is written that Abraham had two sons, one by a slave woman and the other by a free woman. One, the child of the slave, was born according

---

[7] Calvin here refers to the tradition of Roman Catholic scholastic authorities, whose interpretations of Scripture opposed Calvin's emphasis on the inefficacy of the human will for salvation.

[8] The commentary selections are taken from Calvin's *Commentaries on the Epistles of Paul to the Galatians and Ephesians* (trans. J. W. Pringle; Grand Rapids: Eerdmans, 1948). Used with permission.

to the flesh; the other, the child of the free woman, was born through the promise. Now this is an allegory: these women are two covenants. One woman, in fact, is Hagar, from Mount Sinai, bearing children for slavery. Now Hagar is Mount Sinai in Arabia and answers, on the other hand, to the present Jerusalem, for she is in slavery with her children. But the other woman corresponds to the Jerusalem above; she is free, and she is our mother.

21. **"Tell me."** Having given exhortations adapted to touch the feelings, he [Paul] follows up his former doctrine by an illustration of great beauty. Viewed simply as an argument, it would not be very powerful; but, as a confirmation added to a most satisfactory chain of reasoning, it is not unworthy of attention.

"To be under the law," signifies here, to come under the yoke of the law, on the condition that God will act toward you according to the covenant of the law, and that you, in return, bind yourself to keep the law. In any other sense than this, all believers are under the law; but the apostle treats, as we have already said, of the law with its appendages.

22. **"For it is written."** No man who has a choice given him will be so mad as to despise freedom, and prefer slavery. But here the apostle teaches us, that they who are under the law are slaves. Unhappy men! who willingly choose this condition, when God desires to make them free. He gives a representation of this in the two sons of Abraham, one of whom, the son of a slave, held by his mother's condition; while the other, the son of a free woman, obtained the inheritance. He afterwards applies the whole history to his purpose, and illustrates it in an elegant manner.

In the first place, as the other party armed themselves with the authority of the law, the apostle quotes the law on the other side. *The law* was the name usually given to the Five Books of Moses. Again, as the history which he quotes appeared to have no bearing on the question, he gives to it an allegorical interpretation. But as the apostle declares that these things are *allegorized* (ἀλληγορουμενα), Origen, and many others along with him, have seized the occasion of torturing Scripture, in every possible manner, away from the true sense. They concluded that the literal sense is too mean and poor, and that, under the outer bark of the letter, there lurk deeper mysteries, which cannot be extracted but by beating out allegories. And this they had no difficulty in accomplishing; for speculations which appear to be ingenious have always been preferred, and always will be preferred, by the world to solid doctrine.

With such approbation the licentious system gradually attained such a height, that he who handled Scripture for his own amusement not only was suffered to pass unpunished, but even obtained the highest applause. For many centuries no man was considered to be ingenious, who had not the skill and daring necessary for changing into a variety of curious shapes the sacred word of God. This was undoubtedly a contrivance of Satan to undermine the authority of Scripture, and to take away from the reading of it the true advantage. God visited this profanation by a just

judgment, when he suffered the pure meaning of the Scripture to be buried under
false interpretations.

Scripture, they say, is fertile, and thus produces a variety of meanings. I acknowledge that Scripture is a most rich and inexhaustible fountain of all wisdom; but
I deny that its fertility consists in the various meanings which any man, at his pleasure, may assign. Let us know, then, that the true meaning of Scripture is the natural
and obvious meaning; and let us embrace and abide by it resolutely. Let us not only
neglect as doubtful, but boldly set aside as deadly corruptions, those pretended expositions, which lead us away from the natural meaning.

But what reply shall we make to Paul's assertion, that these things *are allegorical?* Paul certainly does not mean that Moses wrote the history for the purpose of
being turned into an allegory, but points out in what way the history may be made to
answer the present subject. This is done by observing a figurative representation of
the Church there delineated. And a mystical interpretation of this sort (ἀναγωγή) was
not inconsistent with the true and literal meaning, when a comparison was drawn
between the Church and the family of Abraham. As the house of Abraham was then
a true Church, so it is beyond all doubt that the principal and most memorable
events which happened in it are so many types to us. As in circumcision, in sacrifices,
in the whole Levitical priesthood, there was an allegory, as there is an allegory at the
present day in our sacraments,—so was there likewise in the house of Abraham; but
this does not involve a departure from the literal meaning. In a word, Paul adduces
the history, as containing a figurative representation of the two covenants in the two
wives of Abraham, and of the two nations in his two sons. And Chrysostom, indeed,
acknowledges that the word *allegory* points out the present application to be different (κατάχρησις) from the natural meaning; which is perfectly true.

23. **"But he who was of the bond woman."** Both were sons of Abraham according to the flesh; but in Isaac there was this peculiarity, that he had the promise of
grace. In Ishmael there was nothing besides nature; in Isaac there was the election of
God, signified in part by the manner of his birth, which was not in the ordinary course,
but miraculous. Yet there is an indirect reference to the calling of the Gentiles, and the
rejection of the Jews: for the latter boast of their ancestry, while the former, without
any human interference, are become the spiritual offspring of Abraham.

24. **"These are the two covenants."** I have thought it better to adopt this
translation, in order not to lose sight of the beauty of the comparison; for Paul compares the two διαθῆκαι [the Greek word Paul uses for "covenants"], to two mothers,
and to employ *testamentum* (a testament), which is a neuter noun, for denoting a
mother, would be harsh. The word *pactio* (a covenant) appears to be, on that account, more appropriate; and indeed the desire of obtaining perspicuity, as well as
elegance, has led me to make this choice.

The comparison is now formally introduced. As in the house of Abraham there
were two mothers, so are there also in the Church of God. Doctrine is the mother of
whom we are born, and is twofold, Legal and Evangelical. The legal mother, whom

Hagar resembles, gendereth to bondage. Sarah, again, represents the second, which gendereth to freedom; though Paul begins higher, and makes our first mother Sinai, and our second, Jerusalem. The two covenants, then, are the mothers, of whom children unlike one another are born; for the legal covenant makes slaves, and the evangelical covenant makes freemen.

But all this may, at first sight, appear absurd; for there are none of God's children who are not born to freedom, and therefore the comparison does not apply. I answer, what Paul says is true in two respects; for the law formerly brought forth its disciples, (among whom were included the holy prophets, and other believers,) to slavery, though not to permanent slavery, but because God placed them for a time under the law as "a schoolmaster" (Gal 3:25). Under the vail of ceremonies, and of the whole economy by which they were governed, their freedom was concealed: to the outward eye nothing but slavery appeared. "Ye have not," says Paul to the Romans, "received the spirit of bondage again to fear" (Rom 8:15). Those holy fathers, though inwardly they were free in the sight of God, yet in outward appearance differed nothing from slaves, and thus resembled their mother's condition. But the doctrine of the gospel bestows upon its children perfect freedom as soon as they are born, and brings them up in a liberal manner.

Paul does not, I acknowledge, speak of that kind of children, as the context will show. By the children of Sinai, it will afterwards be explained, are meant hypocrites, who are at length expelled from the Church of God, and deprived of the inheritance. What, then, is the *gendering to bondage,* which forms the subject of the present dispute? It denotes those who make a wicked abuse of the law, by finding in it nothing but what tends to slavery. Not so the pious fathers, who lived under the Old Testament; for their slavish birth by the law did not hinder them from having Jerusalem for their mother in spirit. But those who adhere to the bare law, and do not acknowledge it to be "a schoolmaster to bring them to Christ" (Gal 3:24), but rather make it a hinderance to prevent their coming to him, are the Ishmaelites born to slavery.

It will again be objected, why does the apostle say that such persons are born of God's covenant, and are considered to belong to the Church? I answer, strictly speaking, they are not God's children, but are degenerate and spurious, and are disclaimed by God, whom they falsely call their Father. They receive this name in the Church, not because they are members of it in reality, but because for a time they presume to occupy that place, and impose on men by the disguise which they wear. The apostle here views the Church, as it appears in this world: but on this subject we shall afterwards speak.

25. **"For Hagar is mount Sinai."** I shall not waste time in refuting the expositions of other writers; for Jerome's conjecture, that Mount Sinai had two names, is trifling; and the disquisitions of Chrysostom about the agreement of the names are equally unworthy of notice. Sinai is called Hagar, because it is a type or figure, as the Passover was Christ. The situation of the mountain is mentioned by way of contempt. It lies in Arabia, beyond the limits of the holy land, by which the eternal inheritance was prefigured. The wonder is, that in so familiar a matter they erred so egregiously.

"And answers, on the other hand." The Vulgate translates it, "is joined" *(conjunctus est)* to Jerusalem; and Erasmus makes it, "borders on" *(confinis)* Jerusalem; but I have adopted the phrase, "on the other hand," *(ex adverso,)* in order to avoid obscurity. For the apostle certainly does not refer to nearness, or relative position, but to resemblance, as respects the present comparison. The word, σύστοιχει, which is translated "corresponding to," denotes those things which are so arranged as to have a mutual relation to each other, and a similar word, συστοιχία, when applied to trees and other objects, conveys the idea of their following in regular order. Mount Sinai is said (συστοιχεῖν) *to correspond to* that which is now Jerusalem, in the same sense as Aristotle says that Rhetoric is ἀντίστοφος, the *counterpart* to Logic, by a metaphor borrowed from lyric compositions, which were usually arranged in two parts, so adapted as to be sung in harmony. In short, the word, συστοιχεῖ, *corresponds,* means nothing more than that it belongs to the same class.

But why does Paul compare the present Jerusalem with Mount Sinai? Though I was once of a different opinion, yet I agree with Chrysostom and Ambrose, who explain it as referring to the earthly Jerusalem, and who interpret the words, *which now is,* τῇ νῦν Ἰερουσαλὴμ, as marking the slavish doctrine and worship into which it had degenerated. It ought to have been a lively image of the new Jerusalem, and a representation of its character. But such as it now is, it is rather related to Mount Sinai. Though the two places may be widely distant from each other, they are perfectly alike in all their most important features. This is a heavy reproach against the Jews, whose real mother was not Sarah but the spurious Jerusalem, twin sister of Hagar; who were therefore slaves born of a slave, though they haughtily boasted that they were the sons of Abraham.

26. **"But Jerusalem, which is above."** The Jerusalem which he calls *above,* or heavenly, is not contained in heaven; nor are we to seek for it out of this world; for the Church is spread over the whole world, and is a "stranger and pilgrim on the earth" (Heb 11:13). Why then is it said to be from heaven? Because it originates in heavenly grace; for the sons of God are "born, not of blood, nor of the will of the flesh, nor of the will of man," (John 1:13) but by the power of the Holy Spirit. The heavenly Jerusalem, which derives its origin from heaven, and dwells above by faith, is the mother of believers. To the Church, under God, we owe it that we are "born again, not of corruptible seed, but of incorruptible," (1 Pet 1:23) and from her we obtain the milk and the food by which we are afterwards nourished.

Such are the reasons why the Church is called the mother of believers. And certainly he who refuses to be a son of the Church in vain desires to have God as his Father; for it is only through the instrumentality of the Church that we are "born of God" (1 John 3:9), and brought up through the various stages of childhood and youth, till we arrive at manhood. This designation, "the mother of us all," reflects the highest credit and the highest honor on the Church. But the Papists are fools and twice children, who expect to give us uneasiness by producing these words; for their mother is an adulteress, who brings forth to death the children of the devil; and how foolish is the demand, that the children of God should surrender themselves to her to be cruelly slain! Might not the synagogue of Jerusalem at that time have assumed such haughty pretensions, with far higher plausibility than Rome at the present day? And yet we see how Paul strips her of every honorable distinction, and consigns her to the lot of Hagar.

Commentary on Corinthians[9]

In 2 Cor 3:6, as Paul is distinguishing between the nature of the new covenant in Christ relative to the nature of the older Sinai covenant, he uses the phrase "for the letter kills, but the Spirit gives life." Calvin takes the occasion in his commentary on this text to polemicize against allegorical interpretation of Scripture. The verse reads,

[God,] who has made us competent to be ministers of a new covenant, not of letter but of spirit; for the letter kills, but the Spirit gives life.

"Not of the letter but of the spirit." He [Paul] now follows out the comparison between the law and the gospel, which he had previously touched upon. It is uncertain, however, whether he was led into this discussion, from seeing, that there were at Corinth certain perverse devotees of the law, or whether he took occasion from something else to enter upon it. For my part, as I see no evidence, that the false apostles had there confounded the law and the gospel, I am rather of opinion, that, as he had to do with lifeless declaimers, who endeavored to obtain applause through mere prating, and as he saw, that the ears of the Corinthians were captivated with such glitter, he was desirous to show them what was the chief excellence of the gospel, and what was the chief praise of its ministers. Now this he makes to consist in the efficacy of the Spirit. A comparison between the law and the gospel was fitted in no ordinary degree to show this. This appears to me to be the reason why he came to enter upon it.

There is, however, no doubt, that by the term *letter,* he means the Old Testament, as by the term *spirit* he means the gospel; for, after having called himself *a minister of the New Testament,* he immediately adds, by way of exposition, that he is a *minister of the spirit,* and contrasts the *letter* with the *spirit.* We must now inquire into the reason of this designation. The exposition contrived by Origen has got into general circulation—that by the *letter* we ought to understand the grammatical and genuine meaning of Scripture, or the *literal* sense (as they call it), and that by the *spirit* is meant the allegorical meaning, which is commonly reckoned to be the *spiritual* meaning. Accordingly, during several centuries, nothing was more commonly said, or more generally received, than this—that Paul here furnishes us with a key for expounding Scripture by allegories, while nothing is farther from his intention. For by the term *letter* he means outward preaching, of such a kind as does not reach the heart; and, on the other hand, by *spirit* he means living doctrine, of such a nature as *worketh effectually* (1 Thess 2:13) on the minds of men, through the grace of the

---

[9] The commentary selections are taken from Calvin's *Commentaries on the Epistles of Paul to the Corinthians* (trans. J. W. Pringle; Grand Rapids: Eerdmans, 1948), vol. 2. Used with permission.

Spirit. By the term *letter,* therefore, is meant *literal* preaching—that is, *dead* and *ineffectual,* perceived only by the ear. By the term *spirit,* on the other hand, is meant *spiritual* doctrine, that is, what is not merely uttered with the mouth, but effectually makes its way to the souls of men with a lively feeling. For Paul had an eye to the passage in Jeremiah, that I quoted a little ago (Jer 31:31), where the Lord says, that his law had been proclaimed merely with the mouth, and that it had, therefore, been of short duration, because the people did not embrace it in their heart, and he promises the Spirit of regeneration under the reign of Christ, to write his gospel, that is, the new covenant, upon their hearts. Paul now makes it his boast, that the accomplishment of that prophecy is to be seen in his preaching, that the Corinthians may perceive, how worthless is the loquacity of those vain boasters, who make incessant noise while devoid of the efficacy of the Spirit.

. . .

"**For the letter killeth**." This passage was mistakenly perverted, first by Origen, and afterwards by others, to a spurious signification. From this arose a very pernicious error—that of imagining that the perusal of Scripture would be not merely useless, but even injurious, unless it were drawn out into allegories. This error was the source of many evils. For there was not merely a liberty allowed of adulterating the genuine meaning of Scripture, but the more of audacity any one had in this manner of acting, so much the more eminent an interpreter of Scripture was he accounted. Thus many of the ancients recklessly played with the sacred word of God, as if it had been a ball to be tossed to and fro. In consequence of this, too, heretics had it more in their power to trouble the Church; for as it had become general practice to make any passage whatever mean anything that one might choose, there was no frenzy so absurd or monstrous, as not to admit of being brought forward under some pretext of allegory. Even good men themselves were carried headlong, so as to contrive very many mistaken opinions, led astray through a fondness for allegory.

The meaning of this passage, however, is as follows—that, if the word of God is simply uttered with the mouth, it is an occasion of death, and that it is *lifegiving,* only when it is received with the heart. The terms *letter* and *spirit,* therefore, do not refer to the exposition of the word, but to its influence and fruit.

CHAPTER 18

Enlightenment Rationality for Understanding Scripture: Baruch Spinoza (1632–1677)

Baruch Spinoza was born and raised in the Jewish community of Amsterdam, the son of Portugese Jews who had fled the threat of the Inquisition. As he progressed brilliantly though his education—which included Talmud, Hebrew Bible, and Kabbala in addition to training in the lens-polishing craft—Spinoza found little to bridge the distance he perceived between the traditional beliefs of his faith and the rapidly expanding world of seventeenth-century scientific and philosophical learning. At the age of twenty-four, upon his expulsion from the Amsterdam synagogue for his departure from traditional Jewish beliefs, Spinoza took up residence elsewhere in Holland, supporting himself as an optical-lens grinder. His livelihood afforded him the opportunity to continue his philosophical studies, and before long Spinoza had gained a reputation for his mastery of the sort of rationalism characteristic of the philosophy of René Descartes.

The seventeenth century was, for European learning, a remarkable time of ever increasing departures from traditional dogma in the study of the physical world, mathematics, and philosophy. In these and other areas, long-standing traditions of scholarly method—hitherto dominated by appeal to authority (usually ancient)—were increasingly challenged by appeal to observable experience and consistency with reason. In short, the scientific worldview was emerging. Spinoza reveled in this new world of rationalism, and over a fourteen-year period, his publications included a systematic presentation of Descartes's philosophy, a five-volume system of his own philosophical ethics, an essay on rational method, and a discursive essay on the civic implications of reasonable religion.

It is this last mentioned work that interests us, the *Tractatus theologico-politicus,* published in 1670. In this work Spinoza intended to provide sophisticated and philosophically inclined readers with a method for interpreting the Bible that comports above all with rational consistency. Drawing upon the legacy of the Protestant Reformers' axiom *sola scriptura* (Scripture itself—instead of ecclesiastical traditions and authorities—provides the basis for determining the meaning of Scripture), Spinoza repudiated any interpretive method that served primarily to align texts with ecclesiastical dogma. Inasmuch as the Bible formed a basis for religious teachings that, for better or for worse, affected the lives and societies of Europeans, Spinoza wrote,

> I determined to examine the Bible afresh in a careful, impartial, and unfettered spirit, making no assumptions concerning it, and attributing to it no doctrines, which I do not find clearly therein set down. With these precautions I constructed a method of Scriptural interpretation, and thus equipped proceeded to inquire . . . [as a result] I was easily able to conclude, that the authority of the prophets has weight only in matters of morality, and that their speculative doctrines affect us little." [preface][1]

The reason Spinoza could find value in the Bible's moral law was its rational basis. The same could not be said for the Bible's other contents, such as its theology, cosmology, or anthropology, for these were validated not by timeless reason but by virtue of the culture-specific circumstances of their historical expression.

The basis for Spinoza's conclusion about the biblical writers was the recognition that much of what is found in the Scriptures derives not from the timelessness of divine revelation but from the customs and practices of the particular culture in which the writers found themselves. He was able to adduce well-established results of biblical research demonstrating that the Bible itself had a history and bore the marks of ancient literary and theological assumptions not shared by enlightened seventeenth-century Europeans. Consequently the Bible was to be studied and understood inductively according to the same methods that demystify the natural world and make it understandable. In short, Spinoza advocated a thoroughly historical approach for biblical interpretation. This represents Spinoza's breakthrough in the history of biblical interpetation: he placed the Bible entirely within the natural realm, where, like any other manifestation of natural processes, it could be subject to critical examination *in toto*. By this approach Spinoza could argue that it was the long discarded worldview of ancient (including biblical) authors that gave their words particular historical meaning. Failure to take seriously their ancient conceptual system of meaning would be to misinterpret their words.

His work on biblical interpretation did not receive immediate widespread acceptance, partly because it was redolent of his nonsupernatural metaphysics. Philosophically Spinoza had moved well beyond his exegetical predecessors, such as Sa'adia ben Joseph, Ibn Ezra, and especially Maimonides among the Jews and John Calvin, Louis Cappel, and Ludwig Meyer among the Christians. These had all wrestled with the problem of the Bible's literary forms, and out of a quasi-apologetic motivation had argued that the Bible's crude or unscientific statements were to be interpreted according to external standards of rationality or coherence and thereby rescued for religious relevance and contemplation. (Actually, this had been the motivation underlying the great systems of figurative interpretation for over eighteen hundred years.) But Spinoza insisted that biblical statements were to be judged historically on the Bible's own terms, without requiring them to align with the interpreter's sense of logical or religious correctness. This is why he found so little of the Bible's content to have genuine theological value.

His emphasis on the value of historical methodology for biblical study eventually prevailed and would go on to preoccupy learned biblical interpretation well into the twentieth century. In this sense, Spinoza's contribution firmly places us in the modern period of

---

[1] It is important to note that in seventeenth-century Europe the policies of state regimes were shaped in part by theological and ecclesiological teachings of the church, whether Catholic or Protestant. The larger purpose of Spinoza's treatise is to delineate clearly the areas of theology and politics that belong to the private sphere of the individual relative to those areas where the regime has the right to prevail.

biblical interpretation. Henceforth the task would be less a matter of mining the texts for timeless theological doctrines (the quest for what is true) and more a matter of determining historically contextualized meanings (the quest for what was meant), following by necessity the same interpretive procedures as are applied to nonscriptural texts.

For further information on Spinoza and his times:

Nadler, Steven M. *Spinoza: A Life*. Cambridge: Cambridge University Press, 1999.

Popkin, Richard. "Spinoza and Bible Scholarship." Pages 383–407 in *The Cambridge Companion to Spinoza*. Edited by D. Garrett. Cambridge: Cambridge University Press, 1996.

Preus, J. Samuel. *Spinoza and the Irrelevance of Biblical Authority*. Cambridge: Cambridge University Press, 2001.

Tractatus theologico-politicus[2]

Chapter 7

Of the Interpretation of Scripture

On every side we hear men saying that the Bible is the Word of God, teaching mankind true blessedness, or the path to salvation. But the facts are quite at variance with their words, for people in general seem to make no attempt whatsoever to live according to the Bible's teachings. We see that nearly all men parade their own ideas as God's Word, their chief aim being to compel others to think as they do, while using religion as a pretext. We see, I say, that the chief concern of theologians on the whole has been to extort from Holy Scripture their own arbitrarily invented ideas, for which they claim divine authority. In no other field do they display less scruple and greater temerity than in the interpretation of Scripture, the mind of the Holy Spirit, and if while so doing they feel any misgivings, their fear is not that they may be mistaken in their understanding of the Holy Spirit and may stray from the path of salvation, but that others may convict them of error, thus annihilating their personal prestige and bringing them into contempt.

Now if men were really sincere in what they profess with regard to Holy Scripture, they would conduct themselves quite differently; they would not be racked by so much quarrelling and such bitter feuding, and they would not be gripped by this blind and passionate desire to interpret Scripture and to introduce innovations in religion. On the contrary, they would never venture to accept as Scriptural doctrine what was not most clearly taught by Scripture itself. And finally, those sacrilegious persons who have had the hardihood to alter Scripture in several places would have been horrified at the enormity of the crime and would have stayed their impious hands. But ambition and iniquity have reached such a pitch that religion takes the form not so much of obedience to the teachings of the Holy Spirit as of defending what men have invented. Indeed, religion is manifested not in charity but in spreading contention among men and in fostering the bitterest hatred, under the false guise of zeal in God's cause and a burning enthusiasm. To these evils is added superstition, which teaches men to despise reason and Nature, and to admire and venerate only that which is opposed to both. It is therefore not surprising that, to make Scripture appear more wonderful and awe-inspiring, they endeavor to explicate it in such a way that it seems diametrically opposed both to reason and to Nature. So they imagine that the most profound mysteries lie hidden in the Bible, and they exhaust themselves in unravelling these absurdities while ignoring other things of value. They ascribe to the Holy Spirit whatever their wild fancies have invented, and devote their utmost strength and enthusiasm to defending it. For human nature is so constituted that what men conceive by pure intellect, they defend only by intellect and reason, whereas the beliefs that spring from the emotions are emotionally defended.

---

[2] The selection is taken from *Tractatus theologico-politicus* (trans. Samuel Shirley, with introduction by Brad S. Gregory; New York: E. J. Brill, 1989) (Gebhardt ed., 1925). Used with permission.

In order to escape from this scene of confusion, to free our minds from the prejudices of theologians and to avoid the hasty acceptance of human fabrications as divine teachings, we must discuss the true method of Scriptural interpretation and examine it in depth; for unless we understand this we cannot know with any certainty what the Bible or the Holy Spirit intends to teach. Now to put it briefly, I hold that the method of interpreting Scripture is no different from the method of interpreting Nature, and is in fact in complete accord with it. For the method of interpreting Nature consists essentially in composing a detailed study of Nature from which, as being the source of our assured data, we can deduce the definitions of the things of Nature. Now in exactly the same way the task of Scriptural interpretation requires us to make a straightforward study of Scripture, and from this, as the source of our fixed data and principles, to deduce by logical inference the meaning of the authors of Scripture. In this way—that is, by allowing no other principles or data for the interpretation of Scripture and study of its contents except those that can be gathered only from Scripture itself and from a historical study of Scripture—steady progress can be made without any danger of error, and one can deal with matters that surpass our understanding with no less confidence than those matters which are known to us by the natural light of reason.

But to establish clearly that this is not merely a sure way, but the only way open to us, and that it accords with the method of interpreting Nature, it should be observed that Scripture frequently treats of matters that cannot be deduced from principles known by the natural light; for it is chiefly made up of historical narratives and revelation. Now an important feature of the historical narratives is the appearance of miracles; that is, as we showed in the previous chapter, stories of unusual occurrences in Nature, adapted to the beliefs and judgment of the historians who recorded them.[3] The revelations, too, were adapted to the beliefs of the prophets, as we showed in chapter 2; and these do, indeed, surpass human understanding.[4] Therefore knowledge of all these things—that is, of almost all the contents of Scripture—must be sought from Scripture alone, just as knowledge of Nature must be sought from Nature itself.

As for the moral doctrines that are also contained in the Bible, although these themselves can be demonstrated from accepted axioms, it cannot be proved from such axioms that Scripture teaches these doctrines: this can be established only from

---

[3] In chapter 6 Spinoza had argued from certain details in Scripture that "everything related in Scripture as having truly happened came to pass according to the laws of Nature, as everything does." Still, "Scripture does not explain things through their proximate causes; in its narratives it merely employs such order and such language as is most effective in moving men—and particularly the common people—to devotion . . . its aim being not to convince on rational grounds but to appeal to and engage men's fantasy and imagination."

[4] From chapter 2: "God adapted his revelations to the understanding and beliefs of the prophets, who may well have been ignorant of matters that have no bearing on charity and moral conduct but concern philosophical speculation, and were in fact ignorant of them, holding conflicting beliefs. Therefore knowledge of science and of matters spiritual should by no means be expected of them. So we conclude that we must believe the prophets only with regard to the purpose and substance of the revelation; in all else one is free to believe as one will."

Scripture itself. Indeed, if we want to testify, without any prejudgment, to the divinity of Scripture, it must be made evident to us from Scripture alone that it teaches true moral doctrine; for it is on this basis alone that its divinity can be proved. We have shown that the chief characteristic which established the certainty of the prophets was that their minds were directed to what was right and good; hence this must be made evident to us, too, before we can have faith in them. We have already shown that miracles can never give proof of God's divinity, apart from the fact that they could be wrought even by a false prophet. Therefore the divinity of Scripture must be established solely from the fact that it teaches true virtue. Now this can be established only from Scripture. If this could not be done, our acceptance of Scripture and our witness to its divinity would argue great prejudice on our part. Therefore all knowledge of Scripture must be sought from Scripture alone.

Finally, Scripture does not provide us with definitions of the things of which it speaks, any more than Nature does. Therefore, just as definitions of the things of Nature must be inferred from the various operations of Nature, in the same way definitions must be elicited from the various Biblical narratives as they touch on a particular subject. This, then, is the universal rule for the interpretation of Scripture, to ascribe no teaching to Scripture that is not clearly established from studying it closely. What kind of study this should be, and what are the chief topics it should include, must now be explained.

1. It should inform us of the nature and properties of the language in which the Bible was written and which its authors were accustomed to speak. Thus we should be able to investigate, from established linguistic usage, all the possible meanings of any passage. And since all the writers of both the Old and the New Testament were Hebrews, a study of the Hebrew language must undoubtedly be a prime requisite not only for an understanding of the books of the Old Testament, which were written in that language, but also for the New Testament. For although the latter books were published in other languages, their idiom is Hebraic.

2. The pronouncements made in each book should be assembled and listed under headings, so that we can thus have to hand all the texts that treat of the same subject. Next, we should note all those that are ambiguous or obscure, or that appear to contradict one another. Now here I term a passage obscure or clear according to the degree of difficulty with which the meaning can be elicited from the context, and not according to the degree of difficulty with which its truth can be perceived by reason. For the point at issue is merely the meaning of the texts, not their truth. I would go further: in seeking the meaning of Scripture we should take every precaution against the undue influence, not only of our own prejudices, but of our faculty of reason in so far as that is based on the principles of natural cognition. In order to avoid confusion between true meaning and truth of fact, the former must be sought simply from linguistic usage, or from a process of reasoning that looks to no other basis than Scripture.

For further clarification, I shall give an example to illustrate all that I have here said. The sayings of Moses, "God is fire," and "God is jealous," [see Deut 4:24] are perfectly clear as long as we attend only to the meanings of the words; and so, in spite of their obscurity from the perspective of truth and reason, I classify these sayings as clear. Indeed, even though their literal meaning is opposed to the natural light of reason, this literal meaning must nevertheless be retained unless it is in clear opposition to the basic principles derived from the study of Scripture. On the other hand, if these statements in their literal interpretation were found to be in contradiction with the basic principles derived from Scripture, they would have to be interpreted differently (that is, metaphorically) even if they were in complete agreement with reason. Therefore the question as to whether Moses did or did not believe that God is fire must in no wise be decided by the rationality or irrationality of the belief, but solely from other pronouncements of Moses. In this particular case, since there are several other instances where Moses clearly tells us that God has no resemblance to visible things in heaven or on the earth or in the water, we must hence conclude that either this statement or all those others must be explained metaphorically. Now since one should depart as little as possible from the literal meaning, we should first inquire whether this single pronouncement, "God is fire," admits of any other than a literal meaning; that is, whether the word "fire" can mean anything other than ordinary natural fire. If the word "fire" is not found from linguistic usage to have any other meaning, then neither should this statement be interpreted in any other way, however much it is opposed to reason, and all other passages should be made to conform with it, however much they accord with reason. If this, too, should prove impossible on the basis of linguistic usage, then these passages would have to be regarded as irreconcilable, and we should therefore suspend judgment regarding them. However, since the word "fire" is also used in the sense of anger or jealousy (Job 31:12), Moses' pronouncements are easily reconciled, and we can properly conclude that these two statements, "God is fire" and "God is jealous" are one and the same statement.

Again, as Moses clearly teaches that God is jealous and nowhere tells us that God is without passions or emotions, we must evidently conclude that Moses believed this, or at least that he intended to teach this, however strongly we may be convinced that this opinion is contrary to reason. For, as we have shown, it is not permissible for us to manipulate Scripture's meaning to accord with our reason's dictates and our preconceived opinions; all knowledge of the Bible is to be sought from the Bible alone.

3. Finally, our historical study should set forth the circumstances relevant to all the extant books of the prophets, giving the life, character and pursuits of the author of every book, detailing who he was, on what occasion and at what time and for whom and in what language he wrote. Again, it should relate what happened to each book, how it was first received, into whose hands it fell, how many variant versions there were, by whose decision it was received into the canon, and, finally, how all the books, now universally regarded as sacred, were united into a single whole. All these details, I repeat, should be available from an historical study of Scripture; for in order to know which pronouncements were set forth as laws and which as moral teaching, it is important to be acquainted with the life, character and interests of the author. Furthermore, as we have a better understanding of a person's

character and temperament, so we can more easily explain his words. Again, to avoid confusing teachings of eternal significance with those which are of only temporary significance or directed only to the benefit of a few, it is also important to know on what occasion, at what period, and for what nation or age all these teachings were written down. Finally, it is important to know the other details we have listed so that, in addition to the authenticity of each book, we may also discover whether or not it may have been contaminated by spurious insertions, whether errors have crept in, and whether these have been corrected by experienced and trustworthy scholars. All this information is needed by us so that we may accept only what is certain and incontrovertible, and not be led by blind impetuosity to take for granted whatever is set before us.

Now when we possess this historical account of Scripture and are firmly resolved not to assert as the indubitable doctrine of the prophets anything that does not follow from this study or cannot be most clearly inferred from it, it will then be time to embark on the task of investigating the meaning of the prophets and the Holy Spirit. But for this task, too, we need a method and order similar to that which we employ in interpreting Nature from the facts presented before us. Now in examining natural phenomena we first of all try to discover those features that are most universal and common to the whole of Nature, to wit, motion-and-rest and the rules and laws governing them which Nature always observes and through which she constantly acts; and then we advance gradually from these to other less universal features. In just the same way we must first seek from our study of Scripture that which is most universal and forms the basis and foundation of all Scripture; in short, that which is commended in Scripture by all the prophets as doctrine eternal and most profitable for all mankind. For example, that God exists, one alone and omnipotent, who alone should be worshipped, who cares for all, who loves above all others those who worship him and love their neighbors as themselves. These and similar doctrines, I repeat, are taught everywhere in Scripture so clearly and explicitly that no one has ever been in any doubt as to its meaning on these points. But what God is, in what way he sees and provides for all things and similar matters, Scripture does not teach formally, and as eternal doctrine. On the contrary, we have clearly shown that the prophets themselves were not in agreement on these matters, and therefore on topics of this kind we should make no assertion that claims to be the doctrine of the Holy Spirit, even though the natural light of reason may be quite decisive on that point.

Having acquired a proper understanding of this universal doctrine of Scripture, we must then proceed to other matters which are of less universal import but affect our ordinary daily life, and which flow from the universal doctrine like rivulets from their source. Such are all the specific external actions of true virtue which need a particular occasion for their exercise. If there be found in Scripture anything ambiguous or obscure regarding such matters, it must be explained and decided on the basis of the universal doctrine of Scripture. If any passages are found to be in contradiction with one another, we should consider on what occasion, at what time, and for whom they were written. For example, when Christ says, "Blessed are they that mourn, for they shall be comforted" [see Matt 5:4], we do not know from this text what kind of mourners are meant. But as Christ thereafter teaches that we should take thought for nothing save only the kingdom of God and his righteousness, which he commends as the highest good (Matt 6:33), it follows that by mourners he means only those who mourn for man's disregard of the kingdom of God and His righteousness; for only this can be the cause of mourning for those who love nothing but the kingdom of God, or justice, and utterly despise whatever else fortune has to offer.

So, too, when Christ says, "But if a man strike you on the right cheek, turn to him the left also" [see Matt 5:39] and the words that follow, if he were laying this command on judges in the role of lawgiver, this precept would have violated the law of Moses. But he expressly warns against this (Matt 5:17). Therefore we should consider who said this, to whom, and at what time. This was said by Christ, who was not ordaining laws as a lawgiver, but was expounding his teachings as a teacher, because (as we have already shown) he was intent on improving men's minds rather than their external actions. Further, he spoke these words to men suffering under oppression, living in a corrupt commonwealth where justice was utterly disregarded, a commonwealth whose ruin he saw to be imminent. Now we see that this very same teaching, which Christ here expounds when the ruin of the city was imminent, was also given by Jeremiah in similar circumstances at the first destruction of the city (Lam 3:30). Thus it was only at the time of oppression that the prophets taught this doctrine which was nowhere set forth as law; whereas Moses (who did not write at a time of oppression, but—please note—was concerned to found a good commonwealth), although he likewise condemned revenge and hatred against one's neighbor, yet demanded an eye for an eye. Therefore it clearly follows simply on Scriptural grounds that this teaching of Christ and Jeremiah concerning the toleration of injury and total submission to the wicked applies only in situations where justice is disregarded and at times of oppression, but not in a good commonwealth. Indeed, in a good commonwealth where justice is upheld, everyone who wants to be accounted as just has the duty to go before a judge and demand justice for wrongdoing (Lev 5:1), not out of revenge (Lev 19:17, 18), but with the purpose of upholding justice and the laws of his country, and to prevent the wicked from rejoicing in their wickedness. All this is plainly in accord with natural reason. I could produce many more similar examples, but I think this is sufficient to explain my meaning and the usefulness of this method, which is my only object at present.

Now up to this point we have confined our investigation to those Scriptural pronouncements which are concerned with moral conduct, and which can be the more easily elucidated because on such subjects there has never been any real difference of opinion among the writers of the Bible. But other Biblical passages which belong only to the field of philosophical speculation do not yield so easily to investigation. The approach is more difficult, for the prophets differed among themselves in matters of philosophical speculation (as we have already shown) and their narratives conform especially to the prejudices of their particular age. So we are debarred from deducing and explaining the meaning of one prophet from some clearer passage in another, unless it is most plainly established that they were of one and the same mind. I shall therefore briefly explain how in such cases we should elicit the meaning of the prophets from the study of Scripture. Here, again, we must begin from considerations of a most general kind, first of all seeking to establish from the clearest Scriptural pronouncements what is prophecy or revelation and what is its essential nature; then what is a miracle, and so on with other subjects of a most general nature. Thereafter we must move on to the beliefs of individual prophets, and from there finally to the meaning of each particular revelation or prophecy, narrative, and miracle. We have already pointed out with many apposite examples what great caution we should exercise in these matters to avoid confusing the minds of the prophets and historians with the mind of the Holy Spirit and with factual truth, and so I do not think it necessary to say any more on this subject. But with regard to the meaning of revelation, it should be observed that this method only teaches us how to discover what the prophets really saw or heard, and not what they intended to signify or represent by the symbols in question. The latter we can only guess at, not infer with certainty from the basis of Scripture.

The text continues by dismissing as unreliable the authority of the major interpretive traditions of rabbinic Judaism and the Roman Catholic magisterium, leaving only Spinoza's method as the reliable means for understanding Scripture.

At this point I have to discuss any difficulties and shortcomings in our method which may stand in the way of our acquiring a complete and assured knowledge of the Holy Bible. The first important difficulty in our method is this, that it demands a thorough knowledge of the Hebrew language. Where is this now to be obtained? The men of old who used the Hebrew language have left to posterity no information concerning the basic principles and study of this language. At any rate, we possess nothing at all from them, neither dictionary nor grammar nor text-book on rhetoric. The Hebrew nation has lost all its arts and embellishments (little wonder, in view of the disasters and persecutions it has suffered) and has retained only a few remnants of its language and of its books, few in number. Nearly all the words for fruits, birds, fishes have perished with the passage of time, together with numerous other words. Then again, the meanings of many nouns and verbs occurring in the Bible are either completely unknown or subject to dispute. We are deprived not only of these, but more especially of the knowledge of Hebrew phraseology. The idiom and modes of speech peculiar to the Hebrew nation have almost all been consigned to oblivion by the ravages of time. So we cannot always discover to our satisfaction all the possible meanings which a particular passage can yield from linguistic usage; and there are many passages where the sense is very obscure and quite incomprehensible although the component words have a clearly established meaning.

Besides our inability to present a complete account of the Hebrew language, there is the further problem presented by the composition and nature of that language. This gives rise to so many ambiguities as to render it impossible to devise a method[5] that can teach us with certainty how to discover the true meaning of all Scriptural passages; for apart from the sources of ambiguity that are common to all

---

[5] That is, impossible for us who are not used to this language and lack a systematic account of its phraseology. —Spinoza

languages, there are others peculiar to Hebrew which give rise to many ambiguities. These I think it worth listing here.

The text continues with examples of the difficulties certain obscurities in the Hebrew language and in the Hebrew biblical-manuscript tradition can pose for interpretation.

To return to our theme, such being the structure and nature of the Hebrew language, it is quite understandable that such a number of ambiguities must arise that no method can be devised for deciding them all. For we have no grounds for expecting that this can be completely achieved from a comparison of different passages, which we have shown to be the only way to elicit the true meaning from the many senses which a particular passage can yield with linguistic justification. It is only by chance that a comparison of passages can throw light on any particular passage, since no prophets wrote with the deliberate purpose of explaining another's words, or his own. And furthermore, we can draw no conclusion as to the meaning of one prophet or apostle from the meaning of another except in matters of moral conduct, as we have already convincingly demonstrated; no such conclusions can be drawn when they are dealing with philosophical questions, or are narrating miracles or history. I could bring further examples to prove this point, that there are many inexplicable passages in Scripture; but I prefer to leave this subject for the present, and I shall proceed to a consideration of the points that still remain: the further difficulties we encounter in this true method of Scriptural interpretation, or in what way it falls short.

One further difficulty consequent upon this method is this, that it requires an account of the history of all the Biblical books, and this for the most part we cannot provide. As I shall make clear at some length at a later stage, we either have no knowledge at all or but doubtful knowledge of the authors—or if you prefer the expression, the writers—of many of the books. Again, we do not even know on what occasion or at what time these books of unknown authorship were written. Furthermore, we do not know into whose hands all these books fell, or in whose copies so many different readings were found, nor yet again whether there were not many other versions in other hands. When I touched on this topic I did make a brief reference to the importance of knowing all these details, but there I deliberately passed over certain considerations which must now be taken up.

If we read a book relating events which are incredible or incomprehensible, or which is written in a very obscure style, and if we do not know the author or the time or the occasion of its composition, it will be vain for us to try to achieve a greater understanding of its true meaning. Deprived of all these facts we cannot possibly know what was, or could have been, the author's intention. But if we are fully informed of these facts, we are in a position to form an opinion free from all danger of mistaken assumptions; that is to say, we ascribe to the author, or to him for whom he wrote, no more and no less than his just meaning, concentrating our attention on what the author could have had in mind, or what the time and the occasion demanded. I imagine that everyone is agreed on this; for it often happens that we read in different books stories that are much alike, and form very different judgments of them according to our opinions of the writers. I remember once having read a book about a man named Orlando Furioso who used to ride a winged monster in the sky, fly over any regions he chose and single-handed slay huge numbers of men and giants, together with other similar fantastic happenings which are quite incomprehensible in respect to our intellect. Now I had read a similar story in Ovid about Perseus, and another story in the books of Judges and Kings about Samson, who single-handed and unarmed slew thousands of men, and of Elijah, who flew through the air and finally went to heaven in a chariot and horses of fire. These stories, I repeat, are obviously similar, yet we form a very different judgment of each. The first writer was concerned only to amuse, the second had a political motive, the third a religious motive, and it is nothing else but our opinion of the writers that brings us to make these judgments. It is therefore evident that in the case of obscure or incomprehensible writings, it is essential for us to have some knowledge of the authors if we seek to interpret their writings. And for the same reasons, to choose the correct reading out of the various readings of unclear narratives, we have to know in whose manuscript these different readings are found, and whether there were ever some other versions supported by men of greater authority.

. . .

Thus we can conclude that, with the help of such an historical study of Scripture as is available to us, we can readily grasp the meaning of its moral doctrines and be certain of their true sense. For the teachings of true piety are expressed in quite ordinary language, and being directed to the generality of people they are therefore straightforward and easy to understand. And since true salvation and blessedness consist in true contentment of mind and we find our true peace only in what we clearly understand, it most evidently follows that we can understand the meaning of Scripture with confidence in matters relating to salvation and necessary to blessedness. Therefore we have no reason to be unduly anxious concerning the other contents of Scripture; for since for the most part they are beyond the grasp of reason and intellect, they belong to the sphere of the curious rather than the profitable.

I consider that I have now displayed the true method of Scriptural interpretation and have sufficiently set forth my opinion on this matter. Furthermore, I have no doubt that it is now obvious to all that this method demands no other light than the natural light of reason. For the nature and virtue of that light consists essentially in this, that by a process of logical deduction that which is hidden is inferred and concluded from what is known, or given as known. This is exactly what our method requires.

The text continues with responses to certain objections to Spinoza's method. To the objection that supernatural light is necessary for interpretation of Scripture, Spinoza notes that the original audiences who received the words of the prophets and apostles needed no such thing. This proves that the religious value of Scripture is accessible to all even though the rational justification for religious truth often requires more extensive philosophical effort.

Therefore, as the sovereign right to free opinion belongs to every man even in matters of religion, and it is inconceivable that any man can surrender this right, there also belongs to every man the sovereign right and supreme authority to judge freely with regard to religion, and consequently to explain it and interpret it for himself. The supreme authority to interpret laws and the supreme judgment on affairs of state is vested in magistrates for this reason only, that these belong to the sphere of public right. Thus for the same reason the supreme authority to explain religion and to make judgment concerning it is vested in each individual, because it belongs to the sphere of individual right.

It is, then, far from true that the authority of the Hebrew High Priest in interpreting his country's laws enables us to infer the Pope's authority to interpret religion; on the contrary, a more obvious inference is that the interpretation of religion is vested above all in each individual. And this again affords further proof that our method of Scriptural interpretation is the best. For since the supreme authority for the interpretation of Scripture is vested in each individual, the rule that governs interpretation must be nothing other than the natural light that is common to all, and not any supernatural right, nor any external authority. Nor must this rule be so difficult as not to be available to any but skilled philosophers; it must be suited to the natural and universal ability and capacity of mankind. We have shown that our rule answers to this description; for we have seen that such difficulties as are now to be found in it have arisen from the negligence of men, and are not inherent in our method.

CHAPTER 19

Renewing the Jewish Past to Engage with the Present: Moses Mendelssohn (1729–1786)

T he cultural and intellectual movement known as the Enlightenment did not sweep through Europe in a single generation. Different regions encountered this new worldview at different times; the earliest developments took place in England, France, and the Netherlands during the seventeenth century. In central Europe, the Age of Reason began to flower in the eighteenth century with the work of philosophers such as Christian Wolff and Gotthold Ephraim Lessing. Berlin was emerging as the core of the German Enlightenment *(Aufklärung),* attracting Jewish intellectuals eager to stimulate their minds in a way that was not possible, for the most part, in their own Jewish communities. At the time among Jews in the German-speaking world, education did not stress learning vernacular languages or biblical Hebrew (traditionalist Jews often knew only Yiddish and Hebrew). Talmud study was preeminent. Knowledge of the Bible was secondary, deriving mostly from talmudic and classical midrashic interpretations that dominated Jewish education. The natural sciences were rarely taught. As German Jews began to encounter the boader cultural world of central Europe through newly expanded educational and commercial opportunities, they often experienced the pull of two different responses to the religious changes of the day: total assimilation into non-Jewish culture or retreat from engagement with the larger European cultural world. The lack of a middle way was due, in part, to a lack of intellectual coherence that traditional Judaism offered vis-à-vis the emerging scientifically rational worldview. As was true for their contemporary Protestant counterparts, the faith of German Jews faced serious challenges in the Enlightenment.[1]

Among the Jewish intellectuals attracted to Berlin was Moses Mendelssohn, a self-taught philosopher whose writings in metaphysical rationalism and moral philosophy made him a leading figure in the German Enlightenment (and in the Jewish Enlightenment, known as the Haskalah). An observant Jew, Mendelssohn was concerned to bridge the distance between the new secular learning and traditional Jewish education, for he saw nothing in Judaism that was antithetical to a scientific worldview or to human reason. In-

---

[1] Most European Jews found the work of Baruch Spinoza too extreme in its metaphysical implications and too antagonistic against the Jewish exegetical tradition to be of much help for authentic Jewish engagement with the emerging modern European world.

deed, he was convinced that the Jewish Torah and way of life rested on "eternal truths of reason" and, when properly taught, functioned to facilitate rational enlightenment in Jews.

From his own experience in training his children in Torah, Mendelssohn saw the value in making available an edition of the Torah that would help German Jews become better acquainted with the Hebrew of their Scriptures and with excellent German at the same time. Previously published Yiddish translations of Jewish Scripture were not true to the biblical Hebrew, and the existing German translations were Christian projects that tended to read the New Testament into the Jewish Bible. In collaboration with the accomplished Masoretic grammarian Solomon Dubno and other contributors, Mendelssohn added commentary to explain the reasoning behind his translation text-by-text. The resulting publication included an introduction to the Hebrew biblical text for Jewish readers. Published as *Sepher Netivot Shalom* ("The Book of the Paths of Peace"), Mendelssohn's Torah project was completed in 1783. For religious Jews, it would assist entrance into German culture, and for Jews closer to assimilation, it offered a way back to study of Torah.[2] - Mendelssohn hoped that his efforts would help European Jewish communities experience a cultural rebirth through a greater awareness of the moral and aesthetic values of the Jewish Bible.

In his introduction ("Light for the Path"), Mendelssohn addresses the question of pentateuchal authorship. Contemporary Christian historical investigation had begun to conclude that Moses could not have written the entire Pentateuch (passages such as Deut 34:5–12 figured prominently in the debate). In Mendelssohn's argument supporting full Mosaic authorship, his citation of Jewish authorities demonstrates that for centuries Jewish scholars had been aware of the historical implications such passages posed. Much of Mendelssohn's introduction makes a case for the accuracy of the Masoretic Hebrew text of the Torah, including the vowels and accents, which he claims were delivered to Moses from God. (For some time Jewish and Christian scholars alike had been questioning the antiquity of the Masoretic vowel-and-accent system in the Hebrew Bible.) Mendelssohn also introduces his readers to the ancient and more recent translations of the Torah, the weaknesses of which call for the fresh translation and commentary that he offers. Beyond the issues of the text, Mendelssohn's Introduction also argues at length for the originary antiquity of the Hebrew language, claiming that it is the primordial tongue (which God used in speaking the universe into existence) and as such it is a vital medium effective for all ranges of discourse and artistic expression.

Mendelssohn's commentary[3] was not revolutionary. He referred frequently to classical sources, including talmudic and midrashic authorities, for the *derash* (homiletic, nonliteral) sense of the text. But he draws most liberally upon the great *pashtanim* (authorities in literal interpretation) Rashi, Rashbam, Ibn Ezra, and Ramban, whose exegesis usually rested on detailed attention to Hebrew grammar and literary context. In this

---

[2] For hundreds of years, Ashkenazic Jews had been accustomed to reading Yiddish in Hebrew characters. Mendelssohn had his German translation printed in Hebrew characters in order to make knowledge of the Bible and of the German language more immediately accessible to Yiddish speakers.

[3] Mendelssohn himself produced commentary on Gen 1:1–6:8; the rest of Genesis was annotated by Mendelssohn's associate Solomon Dubno. Exodus commentary came from Mendelssohn's pen whereas commentaries on the books of Leviticus, Numbers, and Deuteronomy were the work of various others under Mendelssohn's editorial guidance.

regard, Mendelssohn helped reintroduce into modern Jewish study the less midrashic exegetical tradition that reached back to Sa'adia ben Joseph. But Mendelssohn himself was not averse to the *derash* as opposed to the *peshat* (literal):

> If it is impossible for him [the translator] to combine the two meanings well in his transla-
> tion, and to hide the second [homiletic] meaning in the shade of the first [literal] meaning, as
> it is in the language which is before us, he can only choose the first and simple meaning, and
> should not deviate from it to the left or to the right, and he should leave the *derash* to the ex-
> pert in the translated book. But, however, if, in the way that appears to us, the *peshat* of the
> Scripture is hidden from us and opposed to the accepted way of the *derash,* which was copied
> for us by our sages (may their memory be blessed) so that it is impossible for both of them to
> be correct, as the contradiction prevents it, then it is obligatory for us to go the way of the
> *derash,* and to translate the Scripture according to it, for we have only the tradition of our
> sages, may their memory be blessed, and in their light may we see light. (introduction)

In the face of Enlightenment criticism of the *derash*, Mendelssohn sometimes defended traditional Jewish exegesis, pointing out the multivalence of language: in the natural course of human speech, words and expressions can bear a primarily intended meaning and a secondarily intended meaning simultaneously. Drawing an analogy from physical elements and structures, such as air and the body's limbs, that can be shown to serve more than one purpose, he argued that words can and do transmit more than one intention. This argument, as it reasons from what is observable in nature, appealed to a core Enlightenment logic on behalf of a traditional Jewish interpretive stance.

The *Sepher Netivot Shalom* was intended to provide educated Jews with a reference to the Hebrew Bible's language, to the literalist tradition of Jewish exegesis, and to rabbinic tradition. Neither wholly modern nor wholly medieval, it represented not so much an effort to reject previous Jewish exegetical tradition as an attempt to renew it. Despite initial negative reactions to its publication by some conservative Jewish leaders, Mendelssohn's translation was widely accepted by German-speaking Jews, who made use of it for generations to come. (Some later editions printed the translation in Roman characters and dropped the commentary.) The impact of Mendelssohn's translation on European Jewry was enormous, prompting a far more pronounced presence of Bible study in Jewish education and a deeper engagement of Jews in European culture.

For further information on Mendelssohn and the Haskalah:

Altmann, Alexander. *Moses Mendelssohn: A Biographical Study.* Tuscaloosa: University of
     Alabama Press, 1973.
Harris, Jay M. *How Do We Know This? Midrash and the Fragmentation of Modern Judaism.*
     Albany: State University of New York Press, 1995.
Sorkin, David. *The Berlin Haskalah and German Religious Thought.* Portland, Oreg.:
     Vallentine Mitchell, 2000.
———. *Moses Mendelssohn and the Religious Enlightenment.* Los Angeles: University of
     California Press, 1996.

The Book of the Paths of Peace[4]

Responding to doubts about Moses' authorship of the Pentateuch that had become increasingly endorsed in critical introductions to the Old Testament produced mostly by Christian scholars, Mendelssohn makes a case for Mosaic authorship from traditional Jewish scholarship.

Behold, Moses our Teacher, peace be upon him, wrote the entire Torah from "In the beginning" (Gen 1:1) to "in the sight of all Israel" (Deut 34:12). He even included the last verses from "And Moses died" (Deut 34:5) to the end of the Torah.

Mendelssohn goes on to review several remarks from venerable Jewish authorities regarding the dictation of the Torah by God to Moses; in these remarks the episode of Jeremiah's dictation to the scribe Baruch (see Jer 36) is adduced as a model of immediate scribal accuracy in the writing of divinely inspired words.

But it appears to me that they brought proof from Baruch for good reason, since it could be possible to question whether the Holy One, praised be He, spoke and Moses wrote the entire Torah. How could he say all the things that were written about them in the third person, and not as they would speak among themselves? For example, in each place where it says, "And God spoke to Moses . . ." it would have been even better if it had said, "I, the Lord, spoke to Moses . . . ," or, "And God spoke to me." Is this from the point of view of the speaker who speaks for himself, or is it from the point of view of the writer who speaks for himself? For what reason did they change the way of the language, speaking in the third person by a third person?

This is a well-known matter, for others have already found it difficult. This difficulty almost caused them to have doubt in the authorship of the Torah. For this reason [one of the Jewish authorities] brings proof from Baruch, who himself testifies that he wrote the scroll from the mouth of Jeremiah. In spite of this, the book always mentions Jeremiah and Baruch as speaking in the third person. Reading the scroll to the people [is found] in this wording, "And Jeremiah ordered Baruch, saying . . ." (Jer 36:5) and it does not say, "I, Jeremiah, commanded Baruch . . ." nor "Jeremiah commanded me . . ." This proves that the prophets wrote from the mouths of their masters in this manner. . . .

But it is clearly the truth that Moses was the one who wrote the entire Torah from the beginning of the book of Genesis to " . . . in the sight of all of Israel" (Deut

---

[4] The following selections are adapted from David Fox Sandmel's unpublished translation of *Sepher Netivot Shalom*, based on the text as printed in *Gesammelte Schriften, Jubiläumsausgabe* (Stuttgart-Bad Cannstatt: F. Frommann, 1971–), vol. 14 (ed. Haim Bar-Dayan;), and vol. 15, part 2 (ed. Werner Weinberg). David Fox Sandmel, "A Translation and Critical Analysis of Sections I and II of Moses Mendelssohn's Introduction to His Commentary ("Bi'ur") on the Pentateuch as well as the Part of the Genesis Commentary Written by Himself"; Rabbinic Thesis, Hebrew Union College (Cincinnati), 1983. Pages 3–8, 141–45, 152–56, 255–58. Used with permission.

34:12) from the mouth of the Almighty. For this reason it is written, "And when Moses had finished writing the words of this law in a book, to the very end" (Deut 31:24). The word "end" proves the definite wholeness of all its parts, that he finished writing the song "Give Ear" (Deut 32) and the blessing [Deut 33:1–29] and that which is said after, until "in the sight of all Israel," (Deut 34:12) as will be explained there [in this multivolume commentary], with God's help.

This is the proof that R. Shimon offers: "Is it conceivable that the Torah is missing even one letter? Is it not written, 'Take this book of the Law' (Deut 31:26)?" For if Moses' book was missing the eight verses [reporting his death: Deut 34:5–12], how could he have given it to the priests and the Levites to place it in the ark, without first having given it to Joshua to finish and to add the story of his death? Thus, [in that sense] it is certain that Moses wrote all of it, and he did not leave the Torah lacking one letter " . . . by the side of the ark of the covenant of the Lord" (Deut 31:26).

Behold, we, the entire congregation of the community of Israel, believe that just as Moses our Teacher (peace be upon him), wrote his Torah, thus is it now in our hands, today. Not one item in it has changed from then until now. Nor did anything happen to it as had happened to secular books, such that the scribes and copiers over the course of time made changes in them with additions or deletions or transpositions, sometimes in error due to laziness, and sometimes with intent, in their desire to change the words of the author, to the point that, after a long time, the proper reading was completely forgotten, and the book was permanently reformulated.

But this is not what the faithful God promised us in His covenant, as is written, "for it shall live unforgotten in the mouths of their descendants" (Deut 31:21). He taught by His holy prophets, when He says, "And as for me, this is my covenant with them, says the Lord: my spirit which is upon you, and my words which I have put in your mouth, shall not depart out of your mouth, or the mouth of your children, or the mouth of your children's children, says the Lord, from this time forth and for evermore" (Isa 59:21).

Therefore he appointed for us scribes and Masoretes,[5] who counted all the letters in the Torah, to guard them from addition and deletion. They supervised the books that were copied to prevent any error in writing, according to the laws passed down from the days of Ezra the scribe and his co-workers.

A perennial theological problem of theodicy entails the biblical statement in Gen 1:31 that everything that God had created was good despite the fact that there is so much evil and suffering in the world. Mendelssohn addresses the problem in his commentary to this verse.

AND GOD SAW ETC.: The enlightened man will understand that on the days which preceded, it only says, "And God saw that it was good," but here, on the sixth day, it says, "everything that He had made, and behold, it was very good." The

---

[5] Scribal scholars known as Masoretes (seventh to tenth centuries C.E.) were the experts in the rules, practices, and data regarding the accurate transmission of the text of the Jewish Bible.

meaning is that the specific objects of reality do not contain complete and definite goodness, but good and evil mixed and contained with one another. Many evils are found in the specific things that were created, and there are those of them that are continued from the point of view that they were created, for it prevented any creation from being complete in relation to the perfect end, and it was necessary that it be composed of existence and absence, and the absence is the source of evil. Some of them continue in the chain of cause and effect, according to the chance of time and its accidents. Some of them continued by choice, and they are the evil qualities and acts, and all of them are evil from one side, and good from the other, evil from the point of view of the specific part, and good from the point of view of the general, all of it, for there is no reality at all to definite evil with an evil purpose, since it is an impossible thing and contains an internal contradiction. For every existing thing, from the point of view of its existence, is good. Were these evil things not good from one aspect, they would be unable to exist in the universe created by the Good One who does good, who loves goodness with a perfect love, and abhors definite evil with complete abhorrence. Know from this that the specific evil is also good and fitting to the intended end of all creation, and must exist, as is the meaning when it says, "For every thing there is a season, and a time for every matter . . ." (Eccl 3:1). I will give you an example: death is bad, from the point of view that it is the loss of life, however, from the general point of view, it is good, since destruction and existence are intertwined, stuck together, and joined, so that every loss is the cause of an existence, and every existence is the cause of a loss. Through both, every creation is changed from one form to another, according to the desired purpose of God, may He be blessed. Likewise, the evils of choice and of acts are evil from the point of view of the one who chooses them; desire and free will, however, are a great good and advantage for the world in general, and existence would not be possible without them, and there is no free will without the possibility of a thing and its opposite. The evil choices, therefore, are also good, from that point of view, and God will also turn them and direct them to goodness through his providence and mercy, since this is the purpose of creation: to correct evil and change it to good.

Therefore, in all the days [of creation] which preceded, it only mentions the specifics of creation, and the complete good is not found among them, but rather, evil and good mixed. However, from the point of view that evil is also necessary for the continuance of good, God (may He be praised) saw that it fit the purpose and desired its continuance, not from the point of view that it is evil, but rather, from the aspect that it is necessary for the good. He desired death, not because it is a loss of a form, but, rather, because it a cause of existence. Thus He desired the evil inclination, not because it leads men away to evil, but because it is necessary for the continuance of the world. This is the meaning of "and God saw that it was good." But now, on the sixth day, when all of the work was completely finished, God saw all that he had made, and behold, there was no evil at all in the world as a whole. For, from the point of view of the general, everything was good and very fitting for the end which God (may He be praised) intended. If it were possible for this end to be achieved in a manner which agreed more closely to the desire of the Creator, there is no doubt that He would have chosen this manner, but since He chose this rule and order, there is no doubt that it agrees with the desire of the Creator (may He be praised). Through this, the intended end by Him will be achieved in the way which is the most good and satisfactory before Him, and that is the meaning of "behold, it was very good." The particulars of creation are called "good," but the general is called "very good."

Understand this, and know and be enlightened by what our rabbis, may their memory be blessed, said in *Genesis Rabbah:* " 'And behold, it was very good,' and 'behold it was very good,' this is death," (9:5) and they also mentioned that it is the evil inclination (9:7), and that it is the punishment of evil (9:8).[6] And in the *Zohar* (47a) to Genesis, " 'And God saw all that he had made, behold, it was very good.' Here the word 'very' makes good the omission of the words 'that it was good' in the account of the second day. On the second day death was created, and according to our colleagues, the expression 'very good' refers to death." In the matter of the generality of creation, and that which is desired in it, I found there a precious section (*Zohar* 47a) "God now also saw all the generations which were to be, and everything which was to happen in the world in each generation before it came into existence. 'Which he had made': these words indicate all the works of the creative period, recounted in the section Bereshit,[7] in which was created the foundation and basis of all that was to be and come to pass in the world subsequently. God foresaw all, and placed all potentiality in the work of creation."[8] According to this, included in this verse is everything which He made, not only things which came forth then into existence, but also everything which would become and be produced afterwards, to the end of all the generations. About the totality of this reality alone, which contains all the worlds and all the times, it is said that it is very good. Understand this!

During the eighteenth century, scholars such as the German Protestant H. B. Witter and the French Roman Catholic Jean Astruc postulated that, instead of originating from the pen of Moses, the text of the Pentateuch was compiled from sources that each tended to use (among other things) a different name for the Deity: for example, Elohim (God) in Gen 1:1–2:4a and YHWH (Lord) in Gen 2:4b–3:34. Various versions of source-documentary theories for the composition of the Pentateuch have prevailed among most biblical scholars to the present day. Mendelssohn's accounting for the change in divine names also endured into the twentieth century, appearing (although not always with attribution) in the works of more conservative Jewish and Christian scholars objecting to source-documentary theories for the composition of the Pentateuch.

THE LORD GOD: In the chapter above [Gen 1], it only mentions the name God (elohim), but here it says the Lord God (YHWH elohim). The Lord is the one whose name is God, who rules and judges all, and this is its interpretation in every

---

[6] *Genesis Rabbah* is a collection of exegetical midrashic comments on the book of Genesis. It was compiled in the sixth century C.E. from the same rabbinic sources as are found in the Jerusalem Talmud. The point Mendelssohn makes here is that rabbinic tradition offered insights into the existence of evil in a world created and governed by a benevolent deity.

[7] *Bereshit* ("In the beginning") is the name of the first reading section in the Jewish liturgical cycle (Gen 1:1–6:8).

[8] The *Zohar* is a mystical commentary on the Torah, purportedly by the second-century Palestinian rabbi Shimon ben Yoḥai.

case, according to its simple meaning, "Lord is He who is God." Our rabbis (may their memory be blessed) interpreted these two names as the attribute of Justice and the attribute of Mercy. It is plausible that the first chapter, from "In the beginning" to "had made" (Gen 1:1–2:3) was received by special individuals from the days of the holy patriarchs, and it is possible that it is from the days of Adam and Seth, transmitted by mouth from the fathers to the sons. These holy ones would teach their sons and their students the secret of the act of creation and the origination of the universe. And from here, this faith was publicized in all the ends of the world to every people and tongue, so that there is no people and tongue found which does not have a little knowledge or an allusion of this subject. However, this tradition was perverted among some of them by the vanity of those affecting wisdom, and the lies of the poets who turned their faces to heaven, and concocted, on their own, things which were not so, to draw away the hearts of the multitude, upon which the light of the Torah of God had not shone. And they mixed truth with falsehood, and nothing remained for them except small allusions, like the light which shines in the darkness of light and deep darkness. Behold, it is well known that the proper name [YHWH], which teaches about the personal providence of God for special men and the devotion of God for those who preserve His words, was only publicized by the signs and portents which He performed for the children of Israel, when He brought them out from Egypt, and separated them for His service, as we will explain, God willing, about the verse, "but by my name the Lord I did not make myself known to them" (Exod 6:3), see there [further in the commentary]. Since, when Moses our teacher, peace be upon him, wrote the Torah from the mouth of God, he set this traditional chapter in the beginning, but only mentioned the word *elohim* in it, to show the complete power and rule over every possible thing, to bring forth to the bounds of existence, and to make it behave according to His will. He added and said, "these are the generations of the heavens and the earth when they were created. In the day that the Lord God made," (Gen 2:4) to show that this essence that has power over all is the revered name, who looks after His servants, and who reveals His secret to His prophets, and who is there for them at the time when they call to Him, He is the Lord God. The [present] German translator has interpreted this revered name as *das ewige Wesen,* and sometimes as *der Ewige,* which contains "was, is, and will be;" see the Book of Exodus, the verse "this is my name forever" (Exod 3:15), for that is its place. Onkelos[9] translates the name of God in the first chapter with the word "Lord" (yy) and the words "the Lord God" he interpreted as "Lord God" (yy elohim) but I do not know his intention.

(5) WHEN [NO] PLANT OF THE FIELD ETC.: The purpose of this chapter is to inform you of the particulars of the formation of Adam and his wife, for in the previous chapter, it only mentioned that God created them, male and female. Now it will inform you how the providence of God, the revered essence, was upon Adam, to regulate everything for his good, and to form a helper for him from his ribs, and gave them a commandment, and set aside for the man knowledge to understand His

---

[9] "Onkelos" *(Onqelos)* refers to the most authoritative Aramaic translation (Targum) of the Pentateuch, named after the second-century Jewish proselyte to whom tradition attributes its production.

creatures etc. I have seen, in the *baraita*[10] of R. Eliezer the son of R. Yosi Hagelili, which Rashi (may his memory be blessed) quotes in this chapter, "concerning the thirty-two hermeneutical rules by which the Torah is interpreted, [that] this is one of them, a general statement, followed by a specific act, the latter is then a particular of the former. 'And He created man' is the general statement, it conceals His creation after that, and it conceals His deeds. Then it repeats and explains, 'And the Lord God formed etc.' (Gen 2:7). He planted for him the garden of Eden, and He placed him in the garden of Eden, and he made a deep sleep fall upon him. He who hears this might think that this is another account altogether [by a different writer], but it is only a particular of the first [account]. And so with the animals it repeats and writes, 'So out of the ground the Lord God formed every beast of the field' (v. 19) in order to explain, 'and brought them to Adam to see what he would call them' *(ibid.)* and to teach about the winged birds that they were created from the mire." Thus far his words. Remember this rule, for it is a great foundation and essence for the understanding of Scripture, and by it many places in the Scripture will be explained for you, which would be impossible to understand without this rule. Sometimes all the commentators are unable, and not one man of valor is able to understand the simple meaning of the text, but if you remember this rule by which the Torah is interpreted, you will find that they are simple things, very easy to understand, as you will see, God willing, in several places in our explanation.[11]

As was often the case in antiquity, the anthropopathic depictions of God's character in biblical stories create problems for intellectually defensible theology also in modern times. Here Mendelssohn explains how the reference to God's regret over creating humankind (Gen 6:6) can be intelligently understood.

AND IT GRIEVED HIM TO HIS HEART: Onkelos translated, "and he said to himself that he would break their strength according to his will." The meaning is that the Omnipresent considered to sadden man. He [Onkelos] strayed from the plain meaning of the Scripture in order to expand on the attribute of sorrow from God (may He be exalted) which is elevated and lofty above every lesser attribute. In the words of our rabbis (may their memory be blessed) in *Genesis Rabbah* (27:4), "A certain skeptic asked R. Joshua b. Qarha, he said to him 'Do you not maintain that the Holy One, praised be He, foresees the future?' He said to him, 'Yes.' He said to him, 'But it is written, and it grieved him to his heart?' He said to him, 'Has a son ever been born to you?' He said to him, 'Yes.' He said to him, 'And what did you do?' He said to him, 'I rejoiced and made all others rejoice.' He said to him, 'Yet did you not know that he would eventually die?' He said to him, 'Gladness at the time of gladness, and mourning at the time of mourning.' He said to him, 'Even so was it with the Holy One (blessed be He),' even though it was revealed before Him that their end would be to sin, and His end would be to destroy them, He did not cease from creating them." The enlightened man will understand that the spiritual attributes which are called passions *(Leidenschaften),* or the emotions of the soul are divided into two

---

[10] The word *baraita* refers to any ancient rabbinic interpretive tradition from the first two centuries C.E. that had not been included in the authoritative compilation of the Mishnah.

[11] See rule 5 on p. 113, n. 5.

kinds, between which there is a great difference. The first kind branches off from the possessions and from the true powers of the soul, and they arouse the power of desire to cling to a thing or be removed from it, according to the good or the evil that is found in it, like love or hate, amusement or anger, satisfaction and joy or sorrow. All of these are complete in essence and first praiseworthy proofs in the mind of the enlightened man. They do not cause sin, except when they come out of the bounds of equilibrium and transgress the set law, for then they trouble the thoughts of man, and confuse his mind, and through them he comes to great foolishness, for the power of desire prevailed over the power of understanding, and this is the source of all rebellion and wickedness, as we wrote above. But, as long as they do not escape their bounds, they are in man for splendor, and, in essence, there is no degradation or destruction in them.

The root of the second kind is lack and negation, and they only have reality in a limited sense. Positing this lack from which they branch off, these are their examples: avarice, remorse, cowardice, despair and the like, for avarice is not conceivable without the many needs of the avaricious person, when he worries that he will not find all his needs. Remorse is not conceivable without the changing of the idea and the counsel, and cowardice is not conceivable without the weak person, nor despair unless hope is lacking. The same with all of them. These ways are deficiencies in essence and at first, but from the point of view of man, they are sometimes praiseworthy, for they can bring him to good deeds, as is known from remorse and the like. Behold, it seems, from the words of our sages (may their memory be blessed) that they did not refrain from relating the first kind to God (may He be exalted). They said about Him that He was angry, joyous, happy, and saddened, since, with Him, these ways are clean of any lack and from all degradation and vanity in the world. He is angry in judgment, and joyous in righteousness. He is happy in the complete good, and saddened by the truly evil, without any confusion of thought and delusion. His name is exalted because of this, an exaltation without end. Therefore, no change or lack comes out from any of His attributes, God forbid. But if they are sometimes lacking in the bosom of man, they will produce in him the lesser attributes. This is only because of the reason which we mentioned, that they transgress their law, and they confuse the mind with a shortness of perception. All of this is from the first kind of emotions which we mentioned. However, they do not mention the second kind of emotions about God (may He be exalted) at all, except metaphorically, and to speak in human language, so that the hearers will understand. Therefore we said about the word "was sorry" *(wayyinnaḥem),* whose meaning is an emotion of the second kind, that the Torah speaks in human language. However, with the word "was grieved" *(wayyit'atsev),* which shows hatred for the truly evil, it is said that in the hour of sadness, He is truly sad, as we have mentioned.

Chapter 20

Historical Criticism Rigorously Applied to the Gospels: David Friedrich Strauss (1808–1874)

Born in the German town of Ludwigsburg to devout Lutheran parents, David Friedrich Strauss excelled as a student from the very beginning of his education. Moving on from the local Protestant theological lyceum, or seminary, where he began a lifelong friendship with F. C. Baur, Strauss took his university education at Tübingen (where Baur moved) and Berlin (where F. D. E. Schleiermacher was teaching). While at Berlin, Strauss began to develop notes for lectures on the New Testament Gospels historically critiqued, notes that eventually became the basis for his widely read *Life of Jesus Critically Examined*—a 1550-page analysis of over ninety events narrated in the Gospels. The first edition was published in 1835, and by its fourth edition in 1840, the work had reached a surprisingly wide audience. Indeed, the breadth of readership helps explain the professional outfall for Strauss from his *Life of Jesus:* he was removed from the teaching position to which he had been appointed at Tübingen primarily because he essentially denied the historical foundation of the gospel accounts—something the Protestant theological authorities were not prepared to accept. Never to teach again in a university, he lived from royalties on several best-selling works and the pension from a teaching appointment in Zurich that he accepted but that was withdrawn from him because of the ongoing controversy.

The basic data treated in Strauss's *Life of Jesus,* of course, were not new. Theologians had for years attempted to reconcile for the modern mind the various miraculous elements and historical contradictions in the New Testament Gospels through rationalizations and harmonizations. Rejecting these approaches as alien to the nature of the New Testament materials themselves, Strauss systematically drew attention to the mythical characteristics of the gospel narratives. By the term "myth" Strauss meant "the representation of an event or of an idea in a form which is historical, but at the same time characterized by the rich pictorial and imaginative mode of thought and expression of the primitive ages."[1] Such representations were based on historical events in the life of the historical Jesus but had undergone considerable mythic embellishment expressive of religious ideas

---

[1] D. F. Strauss, *The Life of Jesus Critically Examined* (trans. George Eliot; 2d ed.; London: Swan Sonnenschein, 1892), p. 53.

conforming to the messianic expectations of those who passed on the stories. In the context of some of Strauss's later publications,[2] it is evident that the critical work found in his *Life* was intended to prepare for a more constructive theological appropriation of the religious and philosophical ideas latent in the New Testament, albeit without illusions about their roots in history. Indeed, the second part of Strauss's *Life of Jesus* looks forward from "that which has been destroyed critically" to that of the Bible's teaching and the church's faith which can be "re-establish[ed] dogmatically."[3]

The work of Strauss is important for the history of biblical interpretation on at least two accounts. First, the publication of his *Life of Jesus Critically Examined* brought to a head a fundamental issue facing modern Christian readers of the New Testament, namely, the differences in worldview that lie between the writers of the ancient documents and the modern readers of those writings. Since the seventeenth century, the scientific study of the natural world—for example, the discovery of the motion of the planets—had begun to cast doubt on the Bible's literal truth. The (to the modern mind) reasonable practice of studying the text and content of the Bible as if it were any other ancient document could not but raise disturbing questions on the nature of its truth. Faced with the sort of material that one would otherwise, outside the pages of Scripture, classify as unhistorical, modern educated Christians by the mid-nineteenth century had been struggling for some time to revere the Bible religiously while comprehending its contents historically. Certain more conspicuously implausible portions of the Bible, such as the Eden story, the flood story, or even the virgin birth narratives and the reports of the ascension of Jesus, had already begun to be taken by many as nonhistorical. What Strauss introduced was a devastating negative historical judgment on virtually the whole of the gospel narratives, and his elegant arguments appealed to the modern mind so well that he helped shape the question of history in the Bible as a dominant issue in biblical studies for generations to come. Strauss did not, of course, work in a vacuum, and the writings of many other scholars can be credited for shaping the issue during the eighteenth and nineteenth centuries.[4] But Strauss's impact was profound, without question.

Second, Strauss anticipated a key theme of biblical scholarship that was to flower in the twentieth century. His approach to the gospel material clearly recognized that the material exhibited the traits of a tradition that itself had a history, a tradition that found expression in genres the characteristics of which themselves had to be taken into account. So, whatever eyewitnesses to the historical Jesus might have actually seen and heard, the reports of what was witnessed were bound to undergo certain changes during the decades of transmission of the Jesus tradition. These changes would bear the imprint of the religious consciousness motivating the community that passed on the tradition. As a result, by the time the Jesus tradition was committed to writing, it had been shaped to speak to the religious needs and expectations of the church that had come to cherish the tradition and sought to live by it. Thus, partly from the influence of Strauss's work, biblical scholarship would go on in the later nineteenth and twentieth centuries to seek to uncover the historical Jesus as he actually was, apart from the accretions of tradition about him. An important exegetical methodology known as gospel form criticism emerged in the twentieth

---

[2] D. F. Strauss, *Critical History of Doctrine* (1840–1841); *Life of Jesus for the German People* (1864); *The Christ of Faith and the Jesus of History* (1865).

[3] Strauss, *Life of Jesus Critically Examined*, p. 757.

[4] The more prominent names include F. C. Baur, H. S. Reimarus, and J. S. Semler.

century as scholars sought to understand better the nature of the Jesus tradition in its development within the life of the early church. Clearly, Strauss helped set the stage for much of what was to come in scholarly biblical interpretation.

For further information on D. F. Strauss and related modern biblical scholarship:

Cromwell, Richard S. *David Friedrich Strauss and His Place in Modern Thought.* Fair Lawn, N.J.: Burdick, 1985.
Pals, Daniel L. *The Victorian "Lives" of Jesus.* San Antonio: Trinity University Press, 1982.

The Life of Jesus Critically Examined[5]

The Possibility of *Mythi* in the New Testament Considered on Internal Grounds

In this chapter of Strauss's book, his thesis is presented in the form of responses to questions or objections, printed within quotation marks.

Seeing from what has already been said that the external testimony respecting the composition of our Gospels, far from forcing upon us the conclusion that they proceeded from eye-witnesses or well-informed contemporaries, leaves the decision to be determined wholly by internal grounds of evidence, that is, by the nature of the Gospel narratives themselves: we might immediately proceed from this introduction to the peculiar object of the present work, which is an examination of those narratives in detail. It may however appear useful, before entering upon this special inquiry, to consider the general question, how far it is consistent with the character of the Christian religion that mythi should be found in it, and how far the general construction of the Gospel narratives authorizes us to treat them as mythi. Although, indeed, if the following critical examination of the details be successful in proving the actual existence of mythi in the New Testament, this preliminary demonstration of their possibility becomes superfluous.

If with this view we compare the acknowledged mythical religions of antiquity with the Hebrew and Christian, it is true that we are struck by many differences between the sacred histories existing in these religious forms and those in the former. Above all, it is commonly alleged that the sacred histories of the Bible are distinguished from the legends of the Indians, Greeks, Romans, etc., by their moral character and excellence.

"In the latter, the stories of the battles of the gods, the loves of Krishna, Jupiter, etc., contain much which was offensive to the moral feeling even of enlightened heathens, and which is revolting to ours: whilst in the former, the whole course of the narration, offers only what is worthy of God, instructive, and ennobling."

To this it may be answered with regard to the heathens, that the appearance of immorality in many of their narratives is merely the consequence of a subsequent misconception of their original meaning: and with regard to the Old Testament, that the perfect moral purity of its history has been contested. Often indeed, it has been contested without good grounds, because a due distinction is not made between that which is ascribed to individual men (who, as they are represented, are by no

---

[5] These excerpts are taken from *The Life of Jesus Critically Examined* (trans. George Eliot; 2d. ed.; London: Swan Sonnenschein, 1892), 75–92, translated from the fourth (1840) German edition. Eliot has left untranslated the Latin term *mythi* (plural of *mythus*), which Strauss used to designate nonhistorical elements of the gospel narratives.

means spotless examples of purity), and that which is ascribed to God: nevertheless it is true that we have commands called divine, which, like that to the Israelites on their departure out of Egypt to purloin vessels of gold, are scarcely less revolting to an enlightened moral feeling, than the thefts of the Grecian Hermes. But even admitting this difference in the morality of the religions to its full extent (and it must be admitted at least with regard to the New Testament), still it furnishes no proof of the historical character of the Bible; for though every story relating to God which is immoral is necessarily fictitious, even the most moral is not necessarily true.

"But that which is incredible and inconceivable forms the staple of the heathen fables; whilst in the biblical history, if we only presuppose the immediate intervention of the Deity, there is nothing of the kind."

Exactly, if this be presupposed. Otherwise, we might very likely find the miracles in the life of Moses, Elijah, or Jesus, the Theophany and Angelophany of the Old and New Testament, just as incredible as the fables of Jupiter, Hercules, or Bacchus: presuppose the divinity or divine descent of these individuals, and their actions and fate become as credible as those of the biblical personages with the like presupposition.

Yet not quite so, it may be returned. Vishnu appearing in his three first avatars as a fish, a tortoise, and a boar; Saturn devouring his children; Jupiter turning himself into a bull, a swan, etc.—these are incredibilities of quite another kind from Jehovah appearing to Abraham in a human form under the terebinth tree [see Gen 18:1–8], or to Moses in the burning bush [see Exodus 3]. This extravagant love of the marvelous is the character of the heathen mythology.

A similar accusation might indeed be brought against many parts of the Bible, such as the tales of Balaam [see Num 22], Joshua [see Josh 1–10], and Samson [see Judg 13–16]; but still it is here less glaring, and does not form as in the Indian religion and in certain parts of the Grecian, the prevailing character. What however does this prove? Only that the biblical history *might* be true, sooner than the Indian or Grecian fables; not in the least that on this account it *must* be true, and can contain nothing fictitious.

"But the subjects of the heathen mythology are for the most part such, as to convince us beforehand that they are mere inventions: those of the Bible such as at once to establish their own reality. A Brahma, an Ormusd, a Jupiter, without doubt never existed; but there still is a God, a Christ, and there have been an Adam, a Noah, an Abraham, a Moses."

Whether an Adam or a Noah, however, were such as they are represented, has already been doubted, and may still be doubted. Just so, on the other side, there may have been something historical about Hercules, Theseus, Achilles, and other heroes of Grecian story. Here, again, we come to the decision that the biblical history *might* be true sooner than the heathen mythology, but is not necessarily so. This decision however, together with the two distinctions already made, brings us to an important observation. How do the Grecian divinities approve themselves immediately to us as non-existing beings, if not because things are ascribed to them which we cannot reconcile with our idea of the divine? whilst the God of the Bible is a reality to us just in so far as he corresponds with the idea we have formed of him in our own minds. Besides the contradiction to our notion of the divine involved in the plurality of heathen gods, and the intimate description of their motives and actions, we are at once revolted to find that the gods themselves have a history; that they are born, grow up, marry, have children, work out their purposes, suffer difficulties and weariness, conquer and are conquered. It is irreconcilable with our idea of the Absolute to suppose it subjected to time and change, to opposition and suffering; and therefore where we meet with a narrative in which these are attributed to a divine being, by this test we recognize it as unhistorical or mythical.

It is in this sense that the Bible, and even the Old Testament, is said to contain no mythi. The story of the creation with its succession of each day's labor ending in a rest after the completion of the task; the expression often recurring in the farther course of the narrative, God repented of having done so and so;—these and similar representations cannot indeed be entirely vindicated from the charge of making finite the nature of the Deity, and this is the ground which has been taken by mythical interpreters of the history of the creation. And in every other instance where God is said to reveal himself exclusively at any definite place or time, by celestial apparition, or by miracle wrought immediately by himself, it is to be presumed that the Deity has become finite and descended to human modes of operation. It may however be said in general, that in the Old Testament the divine nature does not appear to be essentially affected by the temporal character of its operation, but that the temporal shows itself rather as a mere form, an unavoidable appearance, arising out of the necessary limitation of human, and especially of uncultivated powers of representation. It is obvious to every one, that there is something quite different in the Old Testament declarations, that God made an alliance with Noah, and Abraham, led his people out of Egypt, gave them laws, brought them into the promised land, raised up for them judges, kings, and prophets, and punished them at last for their disobedience by exile;—from the tales concerning Jupiter, that he was born of Rhea in Crete, and hidden from his father Saturn in a cave; that afterwards he made war upon his father, freed the Uranides, and with their help and that of the lightning with which they furnished him, overcame the rebellious Titans, and at last divided the world amongst his brothers and children. The essential difference between the two representations is, that in the latter, the Deity himself is the subject of progression, becomes another being at the end of the process from what he was at the beginning, something being effected in himself and for his own sake: whilst in the former, change takes place only on the side of the world; God remains fixed in his own identity as the I AM [see Exod 3:13–14], and the temporal is only a superficial reflection cast back upon his acting energy by that course of mundane events which he both originated and guides. In the heathen mythology the gods have a history: in the Old Testament, God himself has none, but only his people: and if the proper meaning of mythology be the history of gods, then the Hebrew religion has no mythology.

From the Hebrew religion, this recognition of the divine unity and immutability was transmitted to the Christian. The birth, growth, miracles, sufferings, death, and resurrection of Christ, are circumstances belonging to the destiny of the Messiah, above which God remains unaffected in his own changeless identity. The New Testament therefore knows nothing of mythology in the above sense. The state of the question is however somewhat changed from that which it assumed in the Old Testament: for Jesus is called the Son of God, not merely in the same sense as kings under the theocracy were so called, but as actually begotten by the divine spirit, or from the incarnation in his person of the divine λόγος [logos, "word"]. Inasmuch as he is one with the Father, and in him the whole fullness of the godhead dwells bodily, he is more than Moses. The actions and sufferings of such a being are not external to the Deity: though we are not allowed to suppose a *theopaschitic* union with the divine nature, yet still, even in the New Testament, and more in the later doctrine of the Church, it is a divine being that here lives and suffers, and what befalls him has an absolute worth and significance. Thus according to the above accepted notion of the mythus, the New Testament has more of a mythical character than the Old. But to call the history of Jesus mythical in this sense, is as unimportant with regard to the historical question as it is unexceptionable; for the idea of God is in no way opposed to such an intervention in human affairs as does not affect his own immutability; so that as far as regards this point, the gospel history, notwithstanding its mythical designation, might be at the same time throughout historically true.

Admitting that the biblical history does not equally with the heathen mythology offend our idea of Deity, and that consequently it is not in like manner characterized by this mark of the unhistorical, however far it be from bearing any guarantee of being historical,—we are met by the further question whether it be not less accordant with our idea of the world, and whether such discordancy may not furnish a test of its unhistorical nature.

In the ancient world, that is, in the east, the religious tendency was so preponderating, and the knowledge of nature so limited, that the law of connection between earthly finite beings was very loosely regarded. At every link there was a disposition to spring into the Infinite, and to see God as the immediate cause of every change in nature or the human mind. In this mental condition the biblical history was written. Not that God is here represented as doing all and every thing himself:—a notion which, from the manifold direct evidence of the fundamental connection between finite things, would be impossible to any reasonable mind:—but there prevails in the biblical writers a ready disposition to derive all things down to the minutest details, as soon as they appear particularly important, immediately from God. He it is who gives the rain and sunshine; he sends the east wind and the storm; he dispenses war, famine, pestilence; he hardens hearts and softens them, suggests thoughts and resolutions. And this is particularly the case with regard to his chosen instruments and beloved people. In the history of the Israelites we find traces of his immediate agency at every step: through Moses, Elijah, Jesus, he performs things which never would have happened in the ordinary course of nature.

Our modern world, on the contrary, after many centuries of tedious research, has attained a conviction, that all things are linked together by a chain of causes and effects, which suffers no interruption. It is true that single facts and groups of facts, with their conditions and processes of change, are not so circumscribed as to be unsusceptible of external influence; for the action of one existence or kingdom in nature intrenches on that of another: human freedom controls natural development, and material laws react on human freedom. Nevertheless the totality of finite things forms a vast circle, which, except that it owes its existence and laws to a superior power, suffers no intrusion from without. This conviction is so much a habit of thought with the modern world, that in actual life, the belief in a supernatural manifestation, an immediate divine agency, is at once attributed to ignorance or imposture. It has been carried to the extreme in that modern explanation, which, in a spirit exactly opposed to that of the Bible, has either totally removed the divine causation, or has so far restricted it that it is immediate in the act of creation alone, but mediate from that point onwards,—i.e., God operates on the world only in so far as he gave to it this fixed direction at the creation. From this point of view, at which nature and history appear as a compact tissue of finite causes and effects, it was impossible to regard the narratives of the Bible, in which this tissue is broken by innumerable instances of divine interference, as historical.

It must be confessed on nearer investigation, that this modern explanation, although it does not exactly deny the existence of God, yet puts aside the idea of him, as the ancient view did the idea of the world. For this is, as it has been often and well remarked, no longer a God and Creator, but a mere finite Artist, who acts immediately upon his work only during its first production, and then leaves it to itself; who becomes excluded with his full energy from one particular sphere of existence. It has therefore been attempted to unite the two views so as to maintain for the world its law of sequence, and for God his unlimited action, and by this means to preserve the truth of the biblical history. According to this view, the world is supposed to move in obedience to the law of consecutive causes and effects bound up with its constitution, and God to act upon it only mediately: but in single instances, where he finds it necessary for particular objects, he is not held to be restricted from entering into the course of human changes immediately. This is the view of modern Supranaturalism; evidently a vain attempt to reconcile two opposite views, since it contains the faults of both, and adds a new one in the contradiction between the two ill-assorted principles. For here the consecutiveness of nature and history is broken through as in the ancient biblical view; and the action of God limited as in the contrary system. The proposition that God works sometimes mediately, sometimes immediately, upon the world, introduces a changeableness, and therefore a temporal element, into the nature of his action, which brings it under the same condemnation as both the other systems; that, namely, of distinguishing the maintaining power, in the one case from individual instances of the divine agency, and in the other from the act of creation.

Since then our idea of God requires an immediate, and our idea of the world a mediate divine operation; and since the idea of combination of the two species of action is inadmissible:—nothing remains for us but to regard them both as so permanently and immoveably united, that the operation of God on the world continues for ever and every where twofold, both immediate and mediate; which comes just to this, that it is neither of the two, or this distinction loses its value. To explain more closely: if we proceed from the idea of God, from which arose the demand for his

immediate operation, then the world is to be regarded in relation to him as a Whole:
on the contrary, if we proceed from the idea of the finite, the world is a congeries of
separate parts, and hence has arisen the demand for a merely mediate agency of
God:—so that we must say—God acts upon the world as a Whole immediately, but
on each part only by means of his action on every other part, that is to say, by the
laws of nature.

This view brings us to the same conclusion with regard to the historical value of
the Bible as the one above considered. The miracles which God wrought for and by
Moses and Jesus, do not proceed from his immediate operation on the Whole, but
presuppose an immediate action in particular cases, which is a contradiction to the
type of the divine agency we have just given. The supranaturalists indeed claim an
exception from this type on behalf of the biblical history; a presupposition which is
inadmissible from our point of view, according to which the same laws, although varied by various circumstances, are supreme in every sphere of being and action, and
therefore every narrative which offends against these laws, is to be recognized as so
far unhistorical.

The result, then, however surprising, of a general examination of the biblical
history, is that the Hebrew and Christian religions, like all others, have their mythi.
And this result is confirmed, if we consider the inherent nature of religion, what essentially belongs to it and therefore must be common to all religions, and what on
the other hand is peculiar and may differ in each. If religion be defined as the perception of truth, not in the form of an idea, which is the philosophic perception, but
invested with imagery; it is easy to see that the mythical element can be wanting only
when religion either falls short of, or goes beyond, its peculiar province, and that in
the proper religious sphere it must necessarily exist. . . . [This would be] a sphere of
divine existences whose relations to one another, actions, and influences, can be
represented only after human analogy, and therefore as temporal and historical.
Even when the mind has raised itself to the conception of the Divine unity, still the
energy and activity of God are considered only under the form of a series of acts: and
on the other hand, natural events and human actions can be raised to a religious significance only by the admission of divine interpositions and miracles. It is only from
the philosophic point of view that the world of imagination is seen again to coincide
with the actual, because the thought of God is comprehended to be his essence, and
in the regular course itself of nature and of history, the revelation of the divine idea is
acknowledged.

. . .

Whatever view may be taken of the heathen mythology, it is easy to show with
regard to the New Testament, that there was the greatest antecedent probability of
this very kind of fiction having arisen respecting Jesus without any fraudulent intention. The expectation of a Messiah had grown up amongst the Israelitish people long
before the time of Jesus, and just then had ripened to full maturity. And from its beginning this expectation was not indefinite, but determined, and characterized by
many important particulars. Moses was said to have promised his people a prophet

like unto himself (Deut 18:15), and this passage was in the time of Jesus applied to the Messiah (Acts 3:22; 7:37). Hence the rabbinical principle: as the first redeemer *(Goël),* so shall be the second; which principle was carried out into many particulars to be expected in the Messiah after his prototype Moses. Again, the Messiah was to come of the race of David, and as a second David take possession of his throne (Matt 22:42; Luke 1:32; Acts 2:30): and therefore in the time of Jesus it was expected that he, like David, should be born in the little village of Bethlehem (John 7:42; Matt 2:5f.). In the above [Deuteronomy] passage Moses describes the supposed Messiah as a prophet; so in his own idea, Jesus was the greatest and last of the prophetic race. But in the old national legends the prophets were made illustrious by the most wonderful actions and destiny. How could less be expected of the Messiah? Was it not necessary beforehand, that his life should be adorned with that which was most glorious and important in the lives of the prophets? Must not the popular expectation give him a share in the bright portion of their history, as subsequently the sufferings of himself and his disciples were attributed by Jesus, when he appeared as the Messiah, to a participation in the dark side of the fate of the prophets (Matt 23:29ff.; Luke 13:33ff.; cf. Matt 5:12)? Believing that Moses and all the prophets had prophesied of the Messiah (John 5:46; Luke 4:21; 24:27), it was as natural for the Jews, with their allegorizing tendency, to consider their actions and destiny as types of the Messiah, as to take their sayings for predictions. In general the whole Messianic era was expected to be full of signs and wonders. The eyes of the blind should be opened, the ears of the deaf should be unclosed, the lame should leap, and the tongue of the dumb praise God (Isa 35:5f.; 42:7; cf. 32:3–4). These merely figurative expressions soon came to be understood literally (Matt 11:5; Luke 7:21f.), and thus the idea of the Messiah was continually filled up with new details, even before the appearance of Jesus. Thus many of the legends respecting him had not to be newly invented; they already existed in the popular hope of the Messiah, having been mostly derived with various modifications from the Old Testament, and had merely to be transferred to Jesus, and accommodated to his character and doctrines. In no case could it be easier for the person who first added any new feature to the description of Jesus, to believe himself its genuineness, since his argument would be: Such and such things must have happened to the Messiah; Jesus was the Messiah; therefore such and such things happened to him.

Truly it may be said that the middle term of this argument, namely, that Jesus was the Messiah, would have failed in proof to his contemporaries all the more on account of the common expectation of miraculous events, if that expectation had not been fulfilled by him. But the following critique [i.e., Strauss's book] on the Life of Jesus does not divest it of all those features to which the character of miraculous has been appropriated: and besides we must take into account the overwhelming impression which was made upon those around him by the personal character and discourse of Jesus, as long as he was living amongst them, which did not permit them deliberately to scrutinize and compare him with their previous standard. The belief in him as the Messiah extended to wider circles only by slow degrees; and even during his lifetime the people may have reported many wonderful stories of him (cf. Matt 14:2). After his death, however, the belief in his resurrection, however that belief may have arisen, afforded a more than sufficient proof of his Messiahship; so that all the other miracles in his history need not be considered as the foundation of the faith in this, but may rather be adduced as the consequence of it.

It is however by no means necessary to attribute this same freedom from all conscious intention of fiction, to the authors of all those narratives in the Old and New Testament which must be considered as unhistorical. In every series of legends, especially if any patriotic or religious party interest is associated with them, as soon as they become the subject of free poetry or any other literary composition, some kind of fiction will be intentionally mixed up with them. The authors of the Homeric songs could not have believed that every particular which they related of their gods and heroes had really happened; and just as little could the writer of the Chronicles have been ignorant that in his deviation from the books of Samuel and of the Kings, he was introducing many events of later occurrence into an earlier period; or the author of the book of Daniel that he was modeling his history upon that of Joseph, and accommodating prophecies to events already past; and exactly as little may this be said of all the unhistorical narratives of the Gospels, as for example, of the first chapter of the third, and many parts of the fourth Gospel. But a fiction, although not undesigned, may still be without evil design. It is true, the case is not the same with the supposed authors of many fictions in the Bible, as with poets properly so called, since the latter write without any expectation that their poems will be received as history: but still it is to be considered that in ancient times, and especially amongst the Hebrews, and yet more when this people was stirred up by religious excitement, the line of distinction between history and fiction, prose and poetry, was not drawn so clearly as with us. It is a fact also deserving attention that amongst the Jews and early Christians, the most reputable authors published their works with the substitution of venerated names, without an idea that they were guilty of any falsehood or deception by so doing.

The only question that can arise here is whether to such fictions, the work of an individual, we can give the name of mythi? If we regard only their own intrinsic nature, the name is not appropriate; but it is so when these fictions, having met with faith, come to be received amongst the legends of a people or religious party, for this is always a proof that they were the fruit, not of any individual conception, but of an accordance with the sentiments of a multitude.

A frequently raised objection remains, for the refutation of which the remarks above made, upon the date of the origin of many of the gospel mythi, are mainly important: the objection, namely, that the space of about thirty years, from the death of Jesus to the destruction of Jerusalem, during which the greater part of the narratives must have been formed; or even the interval extending to the beginning of the second century, the most distant period which can be allowed for the origin of even the latest of these gospel narratives, and for the written composition of our gospels;—is much too short to admit of the rise of so rich a collection of mythi.

But, as we have shown, the greater part of these mythi did not arise during that period, for their first foundation was laid in the legends of the Old Testament, before and after the Babylonian exile; and the transference of these legends with suitable modifications to the expected Messiah, was made in the course of the centuries which elapsed between that exile and the time of Jesus. So that for the period between the formation of the first Christian community and the writing of the Gospels, there remains to be effected only the transference of Messianic legends, almost all ready formed, to Jesus, with some alterations to adapt them to Christian opinions, and to the individual character and circumstances of Jesus: only a very small proportion of mythi having to be formed entirely new.

Definition of the Evangelical *Mythus* and Its Distinctive Characteristics

The precise sense in which we use the expression *mythus,* applied to certain parts of the gospel history, is evident from all that has already been said; at the same time the different kinds and gradations of the mythi which we shall meet with in this history may here by way of anticipation be pointed out.

We distinguish by the name *evangelical mythus* a narrative relating directly or indirectly to Jesus, which may be considered not as the expression of a fact, but as the product of an idea of his earliest followers: such a narrative being mythical in proportion as it exhibits this character. The mythus in this sense of the term meets us, in the Gospel as elsewhere, sometimes in its pure form, constituting the substance of the narrative, and sometimes as an accidental adjunct to the actual history.

The *pure mythus* in the Gospel will be found to have two sources, which in most cases contributed simultaneously, though in different proportions, to form the mythus. The one source is, as already stated, the Messianic ideas and expectations existing according to their several forms in the Jewish mind before Jesus, and independently of him; the other is that particular impression which was left by the personal character, actions, and fate of Jesus, and which served to modify the Messianic idea in the minds of his people. The account of the Transfiguration, for example [see Matt 17:1–8; Mark 9:2–8; Luke 9:28–36], is derived almost exclusively from the former source; the only amplification taken from the latter source being—that they who appeared with Jesus on the Mount spoke of his decease. On the other hand, the narrative of the rending of the veil of the temple at the death of Jesus [see Matt 27:51; Mark 15:38] seems to have had its origin in the hostile position which Jesus, and his church after him, sustained in relation to the Jewish temple worship. Here already we have something historical, though consisting merely of certain general features of character, position, etc.; we are thus at once brought upon the ground of the historical mythus.

The *historical mythus* has for its groundwork a definite individual fact which has been seized upon by religious enthusiasm, and twined around with mythical conceptions culled from the idea of the Christ. This fact is perhaps a saying of Jesus such as that concerning "fishers of men" [see Matt 4:18–22; Mark 1:16–20] or the barren fig-tree [see Matt 21:18–22; Mark 11:12–14], which now appear in the Gospels transmuted into marvelous histories: or, it is perhaps a real transaction or event taken from his life; for instance, the mythical traits in the account of the baptism were built upon such a reality [see Matt 3:13–17; Mark 1:9–11; Luke 3:21–22; John 1:31–34]. Certain of the miraculous histories may likewise have had some foundation in natural occurrences, which the narrative has either exhibited in a supernatural light, or enriched with miraculous incidents.

All the species of imagery here enumerated may justly be designated as mythi, . . . inasmuch as the unhistorical which they embody—whether formed gradually by tradition, or created by an individual author—is in each case the product of an *idea*. But for those parts of the history which are characterized by indefiniteness and want of connection, by misconstruction and transformation, by strange combinations and confusion,—the natural results of a long course of oral transmission; or which, on the contrary, are distinguished by highly colored and pictorial representations, which also seem to point to a traditionary origin;—for these parts the term *legendary* is certainly the more appropriate.

Lastly. It is requisite to distinguish equally from the mythus and the legend, that which, as it serves not to clothe an idea on the one hand, and admits not of being referred to tradition on the other, must be regarded as *the addition of the author,* as purely individual, and designed merely to give clearness, connection, and climax, to the representation.

It is to the various forms of the unhistorical in the Gospels that this enumeration exclusively refers: it does not involve the renunciation of the *historical* which they may likewise contain.

Criteria by which to Distinguish the Unhistorical in the Gospel Narrative

Having shown the possible existence of the mythical and the legendary in the Gospels, both on extrinsic and intrinsic grounds, and defined their distinctive characteristics, it remains in conclusion to inquire how their actual presence may be recognized in individual cases.

The mythus presents two phases: in the first place it is not history; in the second it is fiction, the product of the particular mental tendency of a certain community. These two phases afford the one a negative, the other a positive criterion, by which the mythus is to be recognized.

I. *Negative.* That an account is not historical—that the matter related could not have taken place in the manner described is evident,

First. When the narration is irreconcilable with the known and universal laws which govern the course of events. Now according to these laws, agreeing with all just philosophical conceptions and all credible experience, the absolute cause never disturbs the chain of secondary causes by single arbitrary acts of interposition, but rather manifests itself in the production of the aggregate of finite casualities, and of their reciprocal action. When therefore we meet with an account of certain phenomena or events of which it is either expressly stated or implied that they were produced immediately by God himself (divine apparitions, voices from heaven, and the like), or by human beings possessed of supernatural powers (miracles, prophecies), such an account is *in so far* to be considered as not historical. And inasmuch as, in general, the intermingling of the spiritual world with the human is found only in unauthentic records, and is irreconcilable with all just conceptions; so narratives of angels and of devils, of their appearing in human shape and interfering with human concerns, cannot possibly be received as historical.

Another law which controls the course of events is the law of succession, in accordance with which all occurrences, not excepting the most violent convulsions and the most rapid changes, follow in a certain order of sequence of increase and decrease. If therefore we are told of a celebrated individual that he attracted already at his birth and during his childhood that attention which he excited in his manhood; that his followers at a single glance recognized him as being all that he actually was; if the transition from the deepest despondency to the most ardent enthusiasm after his death is represented as the work of a single hour; we must feel more than doubtful whether it is a real history which lies before us. Lastly, all those psychological laws, which render it improbable that a human being should feel, think, and act in a manner directly opposed to his own habitual mode and that of men in general, must be taken into consideration. As for example, when the Jewish Sanhedrin are represented as believing the declaration of the watch at the grave that Jesus was risen, and instead of accusing them of having suffered the body to be stolen away whilst they were asleep, bribing them to give currency to such a report [see Matt 28:11–15]. By the same rule it is contrary to all the laws belonging to the human faculty of memory, that long discourses, such as those of Jesus given in the fourth Gospel, could have been faithfully recollected and reproduced.

It is however true that effects are often far more rapidly produced, particularly in men of genius and by their agency, than might be expected; and that human beings frequently act inconsequently, and in opposition to their general modes and habits ; the two last mentioned tests of the mythical character must therefore be cautiously applied, and in conjunction only with other tests.

Secondly. An account which shall be regarded as historically valid, must neither be inconsistent with itself, nor in contradiction with other accounts.

The most decided case falling under this rule, amounting to a positive contradiction, is when one account affirms what another denies. Thus, one gospel represents the first appearance of Jesus in Galilee as subsequent to the imprisonment of John the Baptist [see Matt 4:12; Mark 1:14], whilst another Gospel remarks, long after Jesus had preached both in Galilee and in Judea, that "John was not yet cast into prison" [see John 3:24]. When on the contrary, the second account, without absolutely contradicting the first, differs from it, the disagreement may be merely between the incidental particulars of the narrative; such as *time* (the clearing of the

Temple), *place* (the original residence of the parents of Jesus), *number* (the Gad-arenes, the angels at the sepulchre), *names* (Matthew and Levi), or it may concern the essential substance of the history. In the latter case, sometimes the character and circumstances in one account differ altogether from those in another. Thus, accord-ing to one narrator, the Baptist recognizes Jesus as the Messiah destined to suffer [see John 1:29]; according to the other, John takes offense at his suffering condition [see Matt 11:2–6]. Sometimes an occurrence is represented in two or more ways, of which one only can be consistent with the reality; as when in one account Jesus calls his first disciples from their nets whilst fishing on the sea of Galilee [see Matt 4:18–22], and in the other meets them in Judea on his way to Galilee [see John 1:35–42]. We may class under the same head instances where events or discourses are represented as having occurred on two distinct occasions, whilst they are so simi-lar that it is impossible to resist the conclusion that both the narratives refer to the same event or discourse.

It may here be asked: is it to be regarded as a contradiction if one account is wholly silent respecting a circumstance mentioned by another? In itself, apart from all other considerations, the *argumentum ex silentio* is of no weight; but it is certainly to be accounted of moment when, at the same time, it may be shown that had the author known the circumstance he could not have failed to mention it, and also that he must have known it had it actually occurred.

II. *Positive.* The positive characters of legend and fiction are to be recognized sometimes in the form, sometimes in the substance of a narrative.

If the form be poetical, if the actors converse in hymns, and in a more diffuse and elevated strain than might be expected from their training and situations, such discourses, at all events, are not to be regarded as historical. The absence of these marks of the unhistorical do not however prove the historical validity of the narra-tion, since the mythus often wears the most simple and apparently historical form: in which case the proof lies in the substance.

If the contents of a narrative strikingly accords with certain ideas existing and prevailing within the circle from which the narrative proceeded, which ideas them-selves seem to be the product of preconceived opinions rather than of practical ex-perience, it is more or less probable, according to circumstances, that such a narrative is of mythical origin. The knowledge of the fact, that the Jews were fond of representing their great men as the children of parents who had long been childless, cannot but make us doubtful of the historical truth of the statement that this was the case with John the Baptist; knowing also that the Jews saw predictions everywhere in the writings of their prophets and poets, and discovered types of the Messiah in all the lives of holy men recorded in their Scriptures; when we find details in the life of Jesus evidently sketched after the pattern of these prophecies and prototypes, we cannot but suspect that they are rather mythical than historical.

The more simple characteristics of the legend, and of additions by the author, after the observations of the former section, need no further elucidation.

Yet each of these tests, on the one hand, and each narrative on the other, considered apart, will rarely prove more than the possible or probable unhistorical character of the record. The concurrence of several such indications, is necessary to bring about a more definite result. The accounts of the visit of the Magi, and of the murder of the innocents at Bethlehem [see Matt 2], harmonize remarkably with the Jewish Messianic notion, built upon the prophecy of Balaam, respecting the star which should come out of Jacob [see Num 24:15–19]; and with the history of the sanguinary command of Pharaoh [see Exod 1:15–22]. Still this would not alone suffice to stamp the narratives as mythical. But we have also the corroborative facts that the described appearance of the star is contrary to the physical, the alleged conduct of Herod to the psychological laws; that Josephus, who gives in other respects so circumstantial an account of Herod, agrees with all other historical authorities in being silent concerning the Bethlehem massacre; and that the visit of the Magi together with the flight into Egypt related in the one Gospel [see Matt 2:13–15], and the presentation in the temple related in another Gospel [see Luke 2:22–40], mutually exclude one another. Wherever, as in this instance, the several criteria of the mythical character concur, the result is certain, and certain in proportion to the accumulation of such grounds of evidence.

It may be that a narrative, standing alone, would discover but slight indications, or perhaps, might present no one distinct feature of the mythus; but it is connected with others, or proceeds from the author of other narratives which exhibit unquestionable marks of a mythical or legendary character; and consequently suspicion is reflected back from the latter, on the former. Every narrative, however miraculous, contains some details which might in themselves be historical, but which, in consequence of their connection with the other supernatural incidents, necessarily become equally doubtful.

In these last remarks we are, to a certain extent, anticipating the question which is, in conclusion, to be considered: viz., whether the mythical character is restricted to those features of the narrative, upon which such character is actually stamped; and whether a contradiction between two accounts invalidate one account only, or both? That is to say, what is the precise boundary line between the historical and the unhistorical?—the most difficult question in the whole province of criticism.

In the first place, when two narratives mutually exclude one another, one only is thereby proved to be unhistorical. If one be true the other must be false, but though the one be false the other may be true. Thus, in reference to the original residence of the parents of Jesus, we are justified in adopting the account of Luke which places it at Nazareth [see 2:4, 39], to the exclusion of that of Matthew, which plainly supposes it to have been at Bethlehem [see 2:1–6; 19–23]; and, generally speaking, when we have to choose between two irreconcilable accounts, in selecting as historical that which is the least opposed to the laws of nature, and has the least correspondence with certain national or party opinions. But upon a more particular consideration it will appear that, since one account is false, it is possible that the other may be so likewise: the existence of a mythus respecting some certain point, shows that the imagination has been active in reference to that particular subject (we need only refer to the genealogies [see Matt 1:1–17; Luke 3:23–38]); and the historical accuracy of either of two such accounts cannot be relied upon, unless substantiated by its agreement with some other well authenticated testimony.

Concerning the different parts of one and the same narrative: it might be thought for example, that though the appearance of an angel, and his announcement to Mary that she should be the Mother of the Messiah [see Luke 1:26–38], must certainly be regarded as unhistorical, still, that Mary should have indulged this hope before the birth of the child, is not in itself incredible. But what should have excited this hope in Mary's mind? It is at once apparent that that which is credible in itself is nevertheless unhistorical when it is so intimately connected with what is incredible that, if you discard the latter, you at the same time remove the basis on which the former rests. Again, any action of Jesus represented as a miracle, when divested of the marvelous, might be thought to exhibit a perfectly natural occurrence; with respect to some of the miraculous histories, the expulsion of devils for instance, this might with some limitation, be possible. But for this reason alone: in these instances, a cure, so instantaneous, and effected by a few words merely, as it is described in the Gospels, is not psychologically incredible; so that, the essential in these narratives remains untouched. It is different in the case of the healing of a man born blind. A natural cure could not have been effected otherwise than by a gradual process; the narrative states the cure to have been immediate; if therefore the history be understood to record a natural occurrence, the most essential particular is incorrectly represented, and consequently all security for the truth of the otherwise natural remainder is gone, and the real fact cannot be discovered without the aid of arbitrary conjecture.

The following examples will serve to illustrate the mode of deciding in such cases. According to the narrative, as Mary entered the house and saluted her cousin Elizabeth, who was then pregnant, the babe leaped in her womb, she was filled with the Holy Ghost, and she immediately addressed Mary as the mother of the Messiah [see Luke 1:39–45]. This account bears indubitable marks of an unhistorical character. Yet, it is not, in itself, impossible that Mary should have paid a visit to her cousin, during which everything went on quite naturally. The fact is however that there are psychological difficulties connected with this journey of the betrothed; and that the visit, and even the relationship of the two women, seem to have originated entirely in the wish to exhibit a connection between the mother of John the Baptist, and the mother of the Messiah. Or when in the history of the transfiguration it is stated, that the men who appeared with Jesus on the Mount were Moses and Elijah: and that the brilliancy which illuminated Jesus was supernatural; it might seem here also that, after deducting the marvelous, the presence of two men and a bright morning beam might be retained as the historical facts [see Matt 17:1–8; Mark 9:2–8; Luke 9:28–36]. But the legend was predisposed, by virtue of the current idea concerning the relation of the Messiah to these two prophets, not merely to make any two men (whose persons, object and conduct, if they were not what the narrative represents them, remain in the highest degree mysterious) into Moses and Elijah, but to create the whole occurrence; and in like manner not merely to conceive of some certain illumination as a supernatural effulgence (which, if a natural one, is much exaggerated and misrepresented), but to create it at once after the pattern of the brightness which illumined the face of Moses on Mount Sinai [see Exod 34:29–35].

Hence is derived the following rule. Where not merely the particular nature and manner of an occurrence is critically suspicious, its external circumstances represented as miraculous and the like; but where likewise the essential substance and groundwork is either inconceivable in itself, or is in striking harmony with some Messianic idea of the Jews of that age, then not the particular alleged course and mode of the transaction only, but the entire occurrence must be regarded as unhistorical. Where on the contrary, the form only, and not the general contents of the narration, exhibits the characteristics of the unhistorical, it is at least possible to suppose a kernel of historical fact; although we can never confidently decide whether this kernel of fact actually exists, or in what it consists; unless, indeed, it be discoverable from other sources. In legendary narratives, or narratives embellished by the writer, it is less difficult,—by divesting them of all that betrays itself as fictitious imagery, exaggeration, etc.—by endeavoring to abstract from them every extraneous adjunct and to fill up every hiatus—to succeed, proximately at least, in separating the historical groundwork.

The boundary line, however, between the historical and the unhistorical, in records, in which as in our Gospels this latter element is incorporated, will ever remain fluctuating and unsusceptible of precise attainment. Least of all can it be expected that the first comprehensive attempt to treat these records from a critical point of view should be successful in drawing a sharply defined line of demarcation. In the obscurity which criticism has produced, by the extinction of all lights hitherto held historical, the eye must accustom itself by degrees to discriminate objects with precision; and at all events the author of this work, wishes especially to guard himself in those places where he declares he knows not what happened, from the imputation of asserting that he knows that nothing happened.

CHAPTER 21

Recognizing Genres in Scripture:
Hermann Gunkel (1862–1932)

Johannes Heinrich Hermann Gunkel's German university education thoroughly grounded him in the historical study of theology and religion. His earliest scholarly publication on ancient Christian notions of the divine Spirit adumbrated his lifelong interest in the vibrant religious consciousness of ancient peoples who produced religious texts. When a move from Göttingen to an academic appointment at Halle required him to shift into Old Testament studies, Gunkel brought his interests in ancient nonbiblical religions and folklore research to bear on the Bible. He continued his groundbreaking studies in Old Testament later when he taught at Berlin, and afterwards, Giessen, and finally when he returned to Halle. As he continued in Old Testament studies over the course of his career, he cultivated knowledge from experts in a variety of disciplines, such as classics, Egyptology, Germanics, and literature. In an age of rapidly increasing specialization, this was somewhat unusual, and it helped him consistently develop fresh approaches to biblical studies.

Scholarly study of biblical texts in the eighteenth and nineteenth centuries had come to focus on the history of the composition of the texts. Close scrutiny of the laws and narratives of the Pentateuch, for example, led scholars to identify material from different sources that had been edited into a single Torah narrative. Source criticism of this sort was primarily concerned with the history of editing and the sequence of editors who had shaped the material in the late monarchic and exilic periods.

In the hands of Gunkel and other scholars whom he influenced,[1] many laws and narrative pieces that had been thought to come from later periods of Israelite history were recognized to derive from earlier centuries of the Old Testament period. Some of the information that prompted this rethinking came from the modern historical study of religions, which had revealed the intensely social dimension of religious institutions and traditions, particularly in hoary antiquity. During biblical times, religion was, generally speaking, more a matter of communal experience than of individual engagement with the divine. This meant that ancient religious texts, such as the documents of the Bible, were

---

[1] Sigmund Mowinkel, *The Psalms in Israel's Worship* (trans. D. R. Ap-Thomas; Nashville: Abingdon, 1962); Albrecht Alt, *Essays on Old Testament History and Religion* (trans. R. A. Wilson; Garden City, N.Y.: Doubleday, 1967); Hugo Gressmann, *Mose und seine Zeit: Ein Kommentar zu den Mose-Sagen* (Göttingen: Vandenhoeck & Ruprecht, 1913).

more likely the products of what nameless social groups (rather than individual authors) had passed down through the ages. Gunkel sought to study the history of this transmission by examining the history of the literary forms (in German, *Formgeschichte* or *Gattungsgeschichte,* usually rendered in English as "form criticism"). The Old Testament provided a rich trove of traditional material for this kind of analysis. Gunkel applied himself in particular to 1) the poetry of the Psalms as typical expressions of Israel's worship through the ages, 2) the prophetic texts as reflections of regular oracular activity in Israelite court and temple, and 3) the stories in Genesis as expressions of the folk mentality and ultimately the national identity of Israel.

Gunkel pointed out that the individual stories in Genesis feature certain typical elements that allow for reconstruction of the social contexts in which they were used over time. That is, Gunkel sought to locate the stories in their original *Sitz im Leben* (setting in life) and to trace the stages through which they passed as they were incorporated into later literary compositions that ultimately yielded the present Torah narrative. In so doing, Gunkel was not seeking out a record of what actually happened in Israel's history, but rather searched for traces of the religious faith that found expression in these stories. This search led him to conclude that some of the stories were not Israelite in their original forms but had undergone adaptations as they had become "Israelitized." Gunkel's method emphasized the importance of oral tradition in the origination and transmission of ancient religious and ethnic thought. For example, the stories of the ancestors were originally short anecdotes or episodes that, in their oral retelling, became narrated together in longer sequences of episodes long before they were committed to writing. Recovery of the earliest forms of the stories allowed scholars to penetrate into the earliest stages of the history of Hebrew religion, stages that antedated by centuries the documentary editing of these same traditions.

A similar tradition history may be posited for collections of prophetic oracles and stories of the prophets in the Old Testament. Applying form criticism to the prophetic texts, Gunkel argued that the biblical prophets were not writers of books bearing their names but speakers of ecstatic proclamations that had been uttered orally and only later committed to writing. Gunkel was able to show that in their utterances the prophets made use of standard speech and poetic forms taken from existing conventions in ancient life. For example, the ubiquitous prophetic phrase "Thus says the Lord" could be shown to derive from standard formulaic expressions used by messengers dispatched to communicate messages from one party to another as a part of ancient Near Eastern diplomatic and commercial protocol. This may indicate that the prophets understood themselves to act as messengers from God to announce the divine will to Israel. Gunkel and other form critics suggested that much of what appears narratively and poetically in the Old Testament as inherently religious expressions were probably originally nonreligious forms that were taken up into religious use in the Israelite prophetic tradition.

Gunkel's fertile mind applied *Gattungsgeschichte* to the Psalms, with similarly groundbreaking results. From consistent patterns of components found in many of the psalmic compositions, he was able to discern five basic types of psalms (hymns, laments sung by the community, laments sung by individuals, thanksgiving songs by individuals, and psalms sung on behalf of the royal court). Gunkel posited general settings in the life of ancient Israel in which the psalms would have been created and sung. He reasoned that many of the communal psalms were probably created in and for public worship in the ancient Israelite cult. One effect of the research of Gunkel and his students was to demonstrate the probability that many of the psalms derived from preexilic times, contrary to the late (Maccabean) dating asserted by many scholars in the nineteenth century. Another fruitful avenue of form-critical investigation in the Old Testament led to insights into the role that prophets may have played in ancient Israelite cult. Indeed, it has been suggested that some of the famous Old Testament prophets were cultic oracular speakers or otherwise had adapted conventional cultic oracular expressions for announcing their own messages from God.

The investigations into preliterary stages of Israelite writings pioneered by Gunkel left a profound impression on biblical interpretation in the twentieth century. Gunkel helped establish that much of what is found in the Old Testament bears the mark of ancient life as it played out in various settings, such as royal court, village and farm, cultic shrine, and marketplace. He drew attention to the relationship between the actual life of Israel and the emotional tones and verbal expressions found in the texts that would attend to that life. Gunkel's remarkable sensitivity to the sociological and psychological depth dimensions of the texts introduced a welcome corrective to the rather dry cataloguing of ancient editorial hands in the making of the Bible.

It is worth noting at least one other area of biblical studies where Gunkel introduced new thinking. The study of religions in the nineteenth century had revealed much about the mythological elements in ancient Near Eastern religions. In some of his earlier work in biblical creation and apocalyptic texts, Gunkel recognized similar mythological elements and attributed their presence in the biblical writings to influence from Mesopotamian religions. He did not suggest a literary dependency but rather a reception of the Babylonian elements into ancient Israelite worship via oral tradition. Generations of scholars after Gunkel have continued to explore this dimension of biblical traditions with great success.

For further information on Gunkel, his influences, and his legacy:

Frazer, James George. *Folklore in the Old Testament.* 3 vols. London: Macmillan, 1919.
Gaster, Theodor Herzl. *Myth, Legend, and Custom in the Old Testament.* New York: Harper & Row, 1969.
Gunkel, Hermann. *Water for a Thirsty Land: Israelite Literature and Religion.* Edited by K. C. Hanson. Fortress Classics in Biblical Studies. Minneapolis: Fortress, 2001.
Hayes, John H., ed. *Old Testament Form Criticism.* San Antonio: Trinity University Press, 1974.
Westermann, Claus. *Basic Forms of Prophetic Speech.* Philadelphia: Westminster, 1967.

The Types of Stories in Genesis[2]

God and People in the Stories

Two groups of stories stand out clearly among the great mass of material in Genesis. The first group consists of stories about the origin of the world and the primal ancestors of the human race. This includes the stories up to the tower of Babel [see Gen 1–11]. The scene of these narratives is the distant past and their sphere of interest is the whole world. The second group consists of stories about the fathers of Israel—Abraham, Isaac, Jacob and their sons [see Gen 12–50]. Their setting is the land of Canaan and its environs; and interest is centered on one family, with the thought ever hovering with more or less clarity in the background that from it God's people is to come.

There is also a difference in the idea of God. In the primeval stories he is more universal. Yahweh is the creator of heaven and earth (Gen 2:4b; or at least of human beings and animals, Gen 2:5ff.) and is the lord and judge of the human race (in the stories of the garden, the angel marriages, the flood, the building of the tower). But the god who appears in the patriarchal narratives, who visits Abraham and protects Jacob, who intervenes in the minor happenings of the life of the individual, who prospers the journey and provides for hospitality, seems more like a family god. To be sure, however, he is a god with whom the God of the people of Israel and the numen of the localities of Canaan are connected.

There are other differences as well. An aloof and baneful mood prevails in the primeval stories. They tell of fearful divine judgments and presuppose a deep gulf between the human race and the divinity which humans do not overstep with impunity. But in the patriarchal narratives there appears a god whose inviolable grace even watches over children and grandchildren. Furthermore, in the patriarchal stories the divinity is always there in secret, unnoticed, or simply speaking from heaven, or just in a dream. But in the primeval stories the idea of God is more anthropomorphic. God moves intimately among people and no one is surprised at this. The story of the garden presupposes that God came to visit them every morning [see Gen 3:8]. He shut the door of the ark after Noah [see Gen 7:16], and came to him in person, allured by his sacrifice [see Gen 8:20–22]. He even formed people and animals with his own hands, experimenting unsuccessfully [see Gen 2:7; 18–20]. In the flood narrative he repented that he created human beings [see Gen 6:5–7], and then at the end promised never again to inflict so horrible a punishment [see Gen 9:14–15]. In the story of the tower he seems for a moment to be almost afraid of the growing power of the human race [see Gen 11:1–9], and so on.

---

[2]These excerpts are taken from *The Stories of Genesis* (trans. John J. Scullion; Vallejo, Calif.: BIBAL, 1994), translated from the third edition of the introduction to Gunkel's commentary on the book of Genesis. Used with permission.

The actors in the patriarchal stories are always people. If the divinity appears, it is by way of exception. But in the primeval stories it is the divinity who carries the action (in the creation) or is at least the main contributor (the garden, the angel marriages of Gen 6:1ff., the flood, the building of the tower). This difference is merely relative, because the divinity makes its appearance in certain patriarchal stories, such as the Hebron and Sodom narratives (Gen 18–19), as well as in the Penuel episode (Gen 32:25ff.). On the other hand people are the actors or main actors in the Cain and Abel story as well as in the cursing of Canaan. These too are to be numbered among the stories. The predominance of the activity of the divinity in the primeval stories means that these stories have a mythical stamp; they are faded myths.

Myth In Genesis

Myths—let no one be frightened of the word—are stories about the gods, differing from stories proper in which the actors are humans. Now the mythical narratives of Genesis have come to us in relatively faded colors. We perceive this from the narratives themselves because we are in a position, at certain points, to infer an older form than that handed down. For example, the present text of Gen 6:1–4 is but a torso. We also see this when we compare the primeval stories with the mythological references that we encounter in the Old Testament poets and prophets and in the later apocalyptic writers. We come to the same conclusion (and here it is very clear) when we compare the primeval stories with oriental myths, especially the biblical creation and flood stories with the Babylonian versions. The vast contours, the characteristically brilliant colors proper to these myths in their origin, have become blurred in the biblical accounts. These would include the equation of divine figures with natural objects or areas, the struggles between the gods, the begetting of gods, etc.—none of which is present in Genesis. It is here that one can discern what is characteristic of Israelite religion, namely that it was not favorable to myth. From the outset it was directed towards monotheism. But a history of the gods requires at least two divinities.

And so the Israel that we come to know in the Old Testament did not tolerate unadulterated myths, at least not in prose. Concessions to myth were, however, allowed to the poet. Poetry therefore preserves the remnants of a more ancient attitude, preceding the Genesis tradition. This older attitude came to terms with myth without embarrassment. The primeval stories preserved for us in Genesis, however, are dominated throughout by an unspoken reserve in the face of myth. The monotheism of Israel admits only of those myths in which either God acts alone (as in the creation account) or else in which the story takes place between God and humans. The former can not really be considered (hi)story since in (hi)story a third situation results from action and counteraction. As regards the latter, Israel's understanding was that humans are too weak to be worthy opponents of God and thus to enter into conflict with him on a major scale. As soon as God intervenes, all is decided. If one wants in such a case to narrate any (hi)story at all, then the initiative must come from below. This is what is done in the stories of the garden and the tower. The flood story is different since God appears in it at the very beginning. But as a consequence the listener is not drawn into any suspense about the fate of the human race.

One should further note that the stories handed down which have mythical echoes are far fewer in number than the patriarchal stories, where there is no mythical element. Here too one can perceive the effect of an aversion to myth.

Israel Reflects

Genesis has no pure myths of its own. Hence it is not necessary to enter into a detailed discussion here about the origins, type and primal meaning of myth. We can be content with the simple definition of myth as "a story about the gods" and with a few remarks relevant to Genesis.

There is a series of myths in which it is possible to recognize that the narrative of a primeval event has been colored by a similar phenomenon which occurs often (or else regularly) in the real world. The creation of the world, for example, is portrayed as a great springtime, and the frequent appearance of the rainbow after rain was the occasion of a narrative about its origin after the flood.

Many myths answer questions and teach. So it is with the primeval stories of Genesis. The creation story asks: Where do heaven and earth come from? Why is the sabbath holy? The garden narrative asks: Whence the human intellect and the fate of death? Whence the human body and spirit? Whence language? Whence the love between the sexes (Gen 2:24)? How is it that the woman experiences such pain in childbirth and that the man has to till the recalcitrant land or that the snake crawls on its belly? And so on. In these cases the answer to the question constitutes the intrinsic content of the story. It is different with the flood story which appears to reproduce a historical event. However the etiological element (giving the reason) is there at the end: Why doesn't the flood come again (Gen 8:21–22; 9:8ff.)? What does the rainbow mean (Gen 9:12ff.)? The natural conclusion of such a story is "and so." "And so a man leaves his father and his mother and cleaves to his wife" (Gen 2:24). But none of these questions is concerned with matters peculiar to Israel—and here myths differ specifically from stories in that myths are concerned with matters affecting the whole world.

. . .

The Patriarchal Stories

The primeval stories are followed by the patriarchal stories. Their heroes are the tribal fathers or ancestors of the nations, particularly of Israel. Basic to these stories is the notion that each nation, and so Israel, took its origin from the family of one of the ancestors which then continually expanded. This notion found expression in Israel in the formula which in many (though not all) instances described the nation or people as "sons of PN." Such a theory was also current among the Arabs and was known to the Greeks, at least in the more ancient period. However, there is no trace of it in either Egypt or Babylon. A consequence of this concept is that relationships between peoples were explained by means of the family tree. Two peoples, it was said, had brothers as ancestors. This meant that the peoples were closely related and stood as equals. If one happened to be richer, stronger or nobler, this was explained by saying that its tribal ancestor was the firstborn brother, or that he descended from the better mother, and that the other was the younger, or was descended from the concubine. The division of Israel into twelve tribes was explained by conceiving the ancestor, Israel, as having had twelve sons. If some of the tribes were closely linked, then it was because they derived from the same mother. More distant relationships existed between the uncle and the nephew, Abraham and Lot, and between the ancestors of Israel on the one hand, and Moab and Ammon on the other.

There is something sound in this theory, inasmuch as the bond which forms the unity of the family or tribe in the simple relationships of desert peoples is not some sort of political organization but has the sense of blood relationship. Furthermore, many families do in fact descend from the male, or at least claim the one after whom they call themselves as their leader. On the other hand, we know enough about the origin of peoples and tribes to be able to say that they are also formed in quite different ways. For example, foreign groups may be assimilated or there may be a fusion of immigrants with residents. Israel's constantly vaunted purity of blood is a figment of the imagination.

Hence the theory that peoples generally take their origin from the family of a single ancestor proceeds not from observation of facts, but from mythical thinking which tried to comprehend everything—and so peoples—as arising from procreation. In any case, a numerous tribe or a whole people is too far removed in time from the tribal ancestor to whom it lays claim to be able to have any oral information about him. In cases where there is not only a family tree extant, but certain stories are also narrated about the ancestor, the explanation is that the experiences and circumstances of the people itself have been transferred to the primeval figure. This is perfectly obvious in many cases. When a person named Shechem, the ancestor of the city of Shechem, is described as a popular young man who was killed by Simeon and Levi, the ancestors of two tribes, everyone regards this not as history, but as historical experiences clothed in story [see Gen 34]. We are not distorting the stories or story fragments that deal with such tribal figures. On the contrary we only grasp their real meaning and make it accessible when we try to understand the heroes about whom they speak as peoples and tribes, and to explain the stories about them as being primarily the experiences of peoples.

However, one must proceed very cautiously here. We must reckon with the possibility that some of these figures did not originally represent peoples. It may have only been later tradition that subsequently elevated them to ancestor status. Furthermore, after the "ancestral" figures had become established as heroes in narratives, narratives of a different sort which did not have their origin in popular (tribal) history became attached to them. We can be sure that certain figures may be understood as personifications of peoples and tribes, particularly those whose names are known to us as names of peoples, e.g., Cain, Canaan, Ishmael, Ammon, Moab, the twelve tribes and their families. But it is different with figures like Abraham, Isaac, and Jacob, the ancestors of Israel; with Lot, the tribal ancestor of Ammon and Moab; with Esau, the tribal ancestor of Edom; and with Laban "the Aramaean." These figures do not bear the names of the peoples and tribes which they represent. They must have originally had another significance and were only elevated to become representatives of their peoples by the demands of tradition. Hence it follows that certain details narrated about them can go back to the historical development of their people, though all is not to be understood as a systematic account of what happened. One must proceed with even more reserve in the case of such figures as Abel and with the women: Sarah, Hagar, Rebekah, Leah, Rachel, Dinah, and Tamar. It is not at all clear that each of these is meant to represent a tribe. It is to be noted further that Shem, Ham and Japheth were perhaps primal peoples and that Jacob and Esau may have represented two groups of peoples. Many of the narratives which deal with the ancestors (and we speak cautiously here) originally portrayed the experiences of peoples.

We can suppose that in ancient times there were disputes about wells between the inhabitants of Gerar and the roving Bedouin until they finally made a treaty in Beer-sheba. The story describes these events as a dispute and treaty between Abimelech of Gerar and the ancestors Abraham and Isaac (Gen 21:22ff.; 26). Simeon and Levi insidiously murdered the young Shechem, but Jacob dissociated himself from the brothers (Gen 34). The history that gave rise to this would have been as follows. The Canaanite city of Shechem was treacherously overcome by the tribes of Simeon and Levi, but the other tribes of Israel remained neutral. A part of the Tamar story, Gen 38, describes the ancient situation of the tribe of Judah. In the story of Hirah, the Adullamite, and Judah's wife Shua, Judah co-operated with the Canaanites. A number of Judahite-Canaanite groups (Er and Onan) disappeared early and finally two new groups (Perez and Zerah) arose.

. . .

It is the very nature of story that we do not perceive ancient events clearly in them, but rather as through a mist. The story has spun its poetic web over the historical reminiscences and obscured its outlines. The process of popular transmission has added all sorts of things to that which was their own. Thus figures of entirely different origins, as we have just seen, have coalesced to form ancestors; and the historical and the imaginative have been woven into the single, unified web which we now see. The result is that the period in which the event took place cannot for the most part be determined from the story. Often not even the place is certain, and now and again not even the matter at issue. Story has forgotten where Jacob and Esau, Cain, Shem and Japheth actually lived or what Jacob and Esau originally meant. The scholar who would derive historical events from stories needs to be urgently warned not to proceed pedantically, and not to surrender to the belief that it is possible to directly recover historical facts by simple retrojection into the popular history of peoples from the patriarchal stories (see below).

Although these stories might obscure rather than reveal the events of the past, only a barbarian would despise them for that reason. They are often more precious than straightforward prose accounts of what happened. For example, if we were to have an accurate historical account of Ishmael, we would remain more or less indifferent to it because this "wild ass" accomplished scarcely anything for the human race. But because an imaginative hand has painted him, he lives on forever.

. . .

The Period when the Stories Originated

Because these narratives are available to us from two sources (J and E) which come from somewhere in the 9th and 8th centuries, it has been commonly believed that the stories themselves originated in essence in the period of the Israelite monarchy and provide no information about history previous to this (cf. J. Wellhausen, *Prolegomena to the History of Ancient Israel,* Eng. 1957, pp. 318–319). In fact, however, they are much older. The names that occur in them attest to this; they have been almost entirely forgotten even when we can vouch for their historicity. We know nothing from the process of historical transmission in Israel about Shem, Ham, and Japheth, scarcely anything about Reuben, Simeon and Levi; and it is only the oldest (or older) transmission that tells us anything about Ishmael and Cain. These then are names of ancient peoples and tribes older than historical Israel. It is quite obvious that the stories of Jacob and Esau are very ancient. It is true that these figures were subsequently equated with Israel and Edom; however, the double names and a number of traits in the story which do not fit the historical peoples of Edom and Israel demonstrate that the old narrative had a very different situation in view. In the story, Jacob was in craven fear of his brother. Historically, Israel overcame Edom in war. In the story, Esau was stupid. Historically, he was famed for his wisdom.

We can advance another proof for the antiquity of such stories from the history of story in Israel. The stories in the book of Judges in general no longer speak of the ancestors of tribes or peoples (except Judg 1), but of individual tribal leaders. The last historically datable story which is colored by the old style is the story of the attack on Shechem—the Dinah story of Gen 34. As far as we can see, therefore, this type of narrative disappeared in the ancient period of the judges. From that time on such narratives were still transmitted, but not created anew.

Stories and Motifs: Historical, Ethnographic, Etiological, Ethnological, Etymological, Cultic

We call stories historical stories when they reflect historical events and ethnographic stories when they portray predominantly the status of peoples. The stories about the treaty at Beer-sheba, the attack on Shechem, the dying out of the older Judahite tribes are historical. The stories of Cain and of Ishmael are ethnographic.

Together with these motifs the Genesis narratives contain etiological motifs, i.e., motifs whose purpose it is to explain something (a motif in this sense is a basic, self-contained unit of poetic material). There was an abundance of questions which might preoccupy an ancient people. The child looks wide-eyed at the world and asks, "Why?" The answer that it gives and with which it is readily content is perhaps quite childish and so quite wrong. Nevertheless, if it is a well-disposed child, the answer is fascinating and stimulating, even for adults. Ancient people raised such questions and answered them as best they could. These questions were usually the same as those we raise and try to answer in our scientific disciplines. We are dealing here, then, with the beginnings of human science—very modest beginnings to be sure, but beginnings which demand our respect. This is particularly stimulating and attractive for us because these answers articulate ancient Israel's most intimate impressions, clothed in the colorful garment of poetry.

Some questions of this sort are ethnological. What are the reasons for the relationships between peoples? Why is Canaan a slave to its brothers? Why has Japheth so vast a territory (Gen 9:24ff.)? Why do the sons of Lot dwell in the unproductive east? How was it that Reuben lost his right of primogeniture (Gen 49:3–4)? Why must Cain wander about homeless and a fugitive? Why will sevenfold vengeance be taken on the one who slays Cain? Why is Gilead the boundary facing the "sons of the east" (Gen 31:52)? Why does Beer-sheba belong to us and not to the people of Gerar (Gen 21:22ff.; 26:25ff.)? Why does Joseph own Shechem (Gen 48:22)? Why did Ishmael become a desert people with this as its possession and with this God (Genesis 16)? Why is it that the Egyptian peasants have to bear the heavy tax of one fifth of their produce while the fields of the priests are free (Gen 47:13ff.)? The question is very often raised: Why does Israel possess the beautiful land of Canaan? The stories narrate in a number of ways how the fathers acquired this land. God promised it to Abraham because of his obedience (Gen 12:7); when Lot chose the east at the parting at Bethel, the west became Abraham's property (Gen 13); Jacob acquired the blessing of the better land from Isaac by trickery (Gen 27); God promised it to Jacob at Bethel (Gen 28:13), and so on.

In individual cases it is often scarcely possible to distinguish between ethnological stories of this kind, which narrate a fictitious event in order to explain the relationship between peoples, and historical stories, which contain a fragment of a tradition of an event that really happened. Ethnological and ethnographic elements are usually found side by side in the same story. The relationships presupposed are historical, the way in which they are explained is poetic.

The answer given to these questions always follows the same line—explaining the present circumstances from something that the primal fathers have done. It was the primal ancestor who dug the well at Beer-sheba, and so it belongs to us, his heirs (Gen 26:25ff.); the primal ancestors established Gilead as a boundary (Gen 31:52); Cain's tribal ancestor was cursed by God to eternal wandering, and so on. A favorite device is to find an explanation of something in an extraordinary oracle pronounced by God himself or by one of the fathers. The story narrates the original circumstances that led to the oracle (Gen 9:25ff.; 12:2–3; 15:18; 27:28ff.; etc.). These explanations were found to be so satisfactory that they gave rise to a specific literary type, the blessing. However childish they seem to us, however incapable these ancients were of arriving at a correct explanation of things, we must not fail to recognize the profundity that speaks out of these poetic stories. The contemporary relationships between peoples (this is what the narratives presuppose) were not due to chance, but had their causes in events that took place of old. They were in a certain sense predestined. The ethnological stories contain the beginnings of a philosophy of history.

Gunkel goes on to describe folk-etymological motifs in the Genesis text, whereby the origin of the names of certain ancient locations and people are explained, such as the city Zoar (Gen 19:20–22) and the personal name Isaac (Gen 18:12).

. . .

More important than these etymological stories are the cultic motifs whose purpose is to explain prescriptions for worship. Such prescriptions played a major role in the life of the ancients. There is a great number of customs of this sort which, already in the most ancient period accessible to us, were no longer comprehensible, either wholly or in part, to the one who carried them out. Customs are far more tenacious than attitudes, and cult is extraordinarily conservative. The situation is similar with us. Our worship underwent a mighty process of purification during the Reformation and again under rationalism; and now in many cases we do not understand (or we understand but partly) what we see and hear in our churches.

Ancient Israel reflected on the origin of many of its cultic customs. Even though the adults, dulled by constant usage, no longer took notice of the unusual and incomprehensible, they were roused from their torpor by the questions of the children. When children saw their fathers carrying out all sorts of unusual rites at the Feast of Passover, they asked—and this is expressly prescribed (cf. Exod 12:26; 13:14)—"What does this mean?" The story of the passover was then narrated to them. It was the same with the twelve stones at the Jordan (Josh 4:6). The father was to explain them to the children as a commemoration of the crossing of the river. These examples show us vividly how a story of this kind is an answer to a question.

The question is similarly raised about the origin of circumcision and of the sabbath —Why do we not eat the sinew of the hip (Gen 32:33)? For what reason does one anoint the holy stone at Bethel and offer the tithe there (Gen 28:18,22)? Why is it that we do not offer a child at Jeruel, the place where Isaac was offered (Gen 22:1–19), but a ram?

No Israelite could possibly have given the real reason for all these things; the reasons were far too old. But it was from this need that myth or story began. One narrated an event and thereby explained the holy custom—a long time ago something took place which naturally gave rise to what is now done; we carry out this custom in memory and imitation of what happened then. But the event which is meant to explain the present practice was said to have taken place regularly in the early period. Thus the ancient people presented the quite correct impression that the worship customs go back to time immemorial. The trees of Shechem (Gen 12:6) and Hebron (Gen 18:4) are older than Abraham! We practice circumcision because of Moses, whose firstborn was circumcised in place of him, and whose blood God wanted (Exod 4:14ff.). We rest on the seventh day because God rested on the seventh day at the creation of the world (Gen 2:2–3; which is a myth, because it is God himself who is acting). The sinew of the hip is sacred to us because Jacob struck God or, as was said later, God struck Jacob there at Penuel (Gen 32:33). Jacob was the first to anoint the stone at Bethel because he used it as a pillow when the divinity appeared to him (Gen 28:18). At Jeruel God first demanded Abraham's child, but was then satisfied with the ram (Gen 22).

On such occasions we hear continually of particular places, Bethel, Penuel, Shechem, Beer-sheba, Lahai-roi, Jeruel, etc., and of the trees, springs, and memorial stones there. These were the primal sanctuaries of the tribes and generations of Israel. A remote age had perceived immediately something of the very divinity itself in these elements of nature; but a later age, to which this link no longer appeared so patently obvious, raised the question: Why is it that this place and this symbol are so sacred? The stock answer was that it was because the divinity appeared to the ancestor there. We honor God there in memory of this elemental revelation. The cult story, then, had its origin (and this is of the utmost importance for the history of religion) in a time when the religious sense no longer had immediate experience of the sacredness of the place or natural object, and no longer understood the meaning of the sacred custom. The immediate impression of the sacredness of the holy symbol became in the story a unique experience of the primal ancestor, and the internal conviction was objectivized in an external event.

The story then had to establish how God and the tribal ancestor happened to meet at this place. Abraham was sitting under a tree in the midday heat when the men appeared before him; hence the tree is holy (Gen 18:1ff.). The well in the desert, Lahai-roi, became Ishmael's sanctuary because his mother met God there on her flight in the desert and he comforted her (Gen 16:7ff.). Jacob happened to pass the night at a particular place, lay down with a stone under his head, and then saw a ladder reaching to heaven; hence the stone is our sanctuary (Gen 28:10ff.). Moses happened to come to the holy mountain and thornbush with his herds (Exod 3:1ff.). Each of the more important sanctuaries of Israel would have had a story of origin of this kind.

We can well imagine that such sanctuary stories were originally narrated on the occasion of the solemn festival at the particular place; Passover and the exodus story, Purim and the Esther legend, the Babylonian New Year feast and the creation hymn, all belong together. Our own Christmas and Easter would be quite unthinkable without their proper stories.

These cult stories are very useful to us because we learn from them of the sacred places and customs of Israel, and because they transplant us into the living world of ancient religious experience. They are our main sources for the oldest religion of Israel. Genesis is full of them, and there are a few in the later books. Almost everywhere that God appears at a particular place, there is a story of this sort at base. We have in them the beginnings of the history of religion.

. . .

The Mingling of Motifs

There are almost always a number of different motifs united in the stories and mingled together in a variety of ways. The story of Hagar's flight (Gen 16) is ethnographic inasmuch as it portrays Ishmael's way of life. It is ethnological inasmuch as it intends to explain this situation. A part of it is cultic, giving the reason why Lahai-roi is sacred. And it is also etymological because it explains the names Ishmael and Lahai-roi.

. . .

In the older narratives of Genesis the etymological motifs never appear independently, but are only subsidiary. Cases in which they prevail or even fill out the whole narrative are due to later narrative inventiveness. This is the case in the meeting of Jacob and Esau, and is particularly obvious in the account of the birth of the sons of Jacob. . . .

This shows how the stories grew in many cases. Hence it is very clear that, with the majority of etymological motifs, those parts of the stories which explain the names were created precisely for that purpose.

. . .

In many cases we learn from parallels which present history as story that the story contains material that has come from elsewhere. . . . [And] that subsequent Israelite interest has taken over the story and that dimensions of Israelite history have entered into it. Jacob and Esau have been equated with the peoples Israel and Edom, and the treaty between Jacob and Laban has been given an ethnohistorical meaning. But we can also imagine the opposite case where a story arose out of a historical event or in order to answer a question, and has been heavily elaborated by the addition of all sorts of poetic and other motifs. . . . Drawing together all these observations which hold more or less true for every ancient story, we come to the conclusion that *the material treated in the patriarchal stories is on the whole neither historical nor etiological in origin.* Many of the narratives or their raw material must have already existed before they acquired their new meaning in the life of Israel. They must have circulated for a long time as pleasant stories, and in origin were pure products of the creative spirit. Such passages, which do not admit of an explanation, are, for want of a better word, called "story-like" *(novellistisch)* in the commentary; perhaps "fable-like" *(märchenhaft)* would be a better term. [*Translator*—or "fabulous" in the literal and original meaning of the word.]

CHAPTER 22

Searching for the Origins of the Jesus Tradition: Rudolph Bultmann (1884–1976)

Over the span of his forty-five-year career, Rudolf Bultmann played a major role in biblical interpretation during the twentieth century. His stature is evidenced not only by the three hundred books, articles, essays, monographs, and reviews he produced but also in the numerous outstanding students he attracted who went on to make significant scholarly contributions in their own right. Born in northern Germany to Evangelical Lutheran parents, Bultmann's life work as a scholar and Lutheran preacher revolved around the construction of a modern understanding of human existence in the face of the mystery of divine grace as proclaimed in the New Testament gospel—a task he considered merely the carrying out of Luther's (and Paul's) idea of faith to its logical conclusion.

The key word here is "modern." Bultmann's theological training was heavily influenced by the history-of-religions approach dominant during the late nineteenth and early twentieth centuries in many European universities. In this approach the origins of the Christian faith as expressed in the New Testament were to be understood within the religious and cultural milieu of the Greco-Roman world. Bultmann thus recognized that the New Testament expressions of faith and salvation were conditioned by a mythical worldview no longer shared by modernity. He argued that a distinction needs to be made between what ancient myth is as a conceptual mode (of the otherworldly) and what myth intends to communicate, namely, an understanding of human existence in the world. It is to this understanding of human existence that Bultmann felt modern Christian theology and biblical interpretation were to attend, rather than the mythological conceptual framework in which it is found on the pages of the New Testament. Thus, responsible theology in the modern world calls for the translation of mythic cosmological categories—heaven, miracle working, the divine in human form, the spirit, resurrection from the dead—into categories of authentic human existence, which is what these ancient notions were ultimately about. Adapting for theology from the work of his existentialist philosopher colleague Martin Heidegger, Bultmann maintained that authentic human existence was a genuine openness to the future based on nothing from the world itself but solely on faith in the proclaimed Word of God.

Because he sought to speak of God responsibly in the modern world, Bultmann was a theologian. But crafting modern, coherent theological statements from the Bible is challenging, given the Bible's unsystematized range of theological nuance. Bultmann thus recognized the *theological* necessity for critical interpretation of Scripture, both historically and in terms of the sense conveyed by scriptural passages. That is, Bultmann maintained that New Testament writings must be correctly placed in their respective locations in the history of the tradition and they must also be evaluated for their centrality to the biblical author's fundamental intention and to the Christian gospel. The latter task entails a degree of circular reasoning. The interpreter—who automatically brings to the interpretive task a certain preunderstanding of the question at hand—tends to confirm what has been established through that preunderstanding as central by qualifying the elements that seem to fall outside the central intention. Bultmann was aware of this problem and agreed with others that the circle is unavoidable.[1]

The historical task brought Bultmann to focus on the history of the Jesus tradition. He was impressed by Gunkel's insights into the history of ancient Israelite traditions through form-critical analysis. In a similar fashion, Bultmann intended to reach behind the Gospels' literary accretions to uncover the earliest Jesus tradition. But as the following selection shows, Bultmann's form-critical analysis of the synoptic-gospel tradition led him to a negative conclusion regarding the historical accuracy of much that is found in the Gospels.[2] He went further, however, by seriously doubting the viability of attempts to reconstruct the life and personality of the historical Jesus. His research showed that at a very early stage in the process of tradition, the memories of Jesus' words and deeds were recast and embellished with accretions demonstrably not original. What was recoverable was not the historical Jesus but the ways in which the earliest bearers of the gospel tradition interpreted the tradition for the purpose of a faith-catalyzing reception of the divine word. Bultmann concluded that the gospel tradition was shaped more by a concern for theology than for history. Thus the Gospels do not present history but rather theology in story form.

This insight—that the Gospels represent a *narrative* (rather than historical) theological tradition—would eventually lead scholars to pay greater attention to how the shapers of biblical tradition constructed their narratives as literary expressions of their faith. Bultmann's legacy includes the suggestion that the Gospels' very obfuscation of history points to an experience of faith so dominant in the processes of tradition that even Jesus' original message and historical personality were secondary to the imperatives of proclamation. The following essay reflects something of the exegetical research that led Bultmann to his provocative theological conclusions.

For further information on Bultmann and related subjects:

Harrisville, R. A., and W. Sundberg. *The Bible in Modern Culture: Theology and Historical-Critical Method from Spinoza to Käsemann.* Grand Rapids: Eerdmans, 1995.

Johnson, Roger. *Rudolf Bultmann: Interpreting Faith for the Modern Era.* San Francisco: Collins, 1987.

McKnight, Edgar. *What Is Form Criticism?* Philadelphia: Fortress, 1969.

Morgan, Robert. "Rudolf Bultmann." Pages 68–86 in *The Modern Theologians.* Edited by D. Ford. Oxford: Blackwell, 1997.

---

[1] R. Bultmann, "Is Exegesis without Presuppositions Possible?" in *Existence and Faith: Shorter Writings of Rudolph Bultmann* (ed. and trans. Schubert Ogden; London: Hodder & Stoughton, 1960), 289–96.

[2] See also R. Bultmann, *History of the Synoptic Tradition* (rev. ed.; New York: Harper & Row, 1976); and *Primitive Christianity in Its Contemporary Setting* (New York: Thames & Hudson, 1956).

"The New Approach to the Synoptic Problem"[3]

The phrase "the synoptic problem" has usually denoted the question concerning the mutual relationships of the gospels of Matthew, Mark, and Luke. Ever since the end of the eighteenth century critical research has been engaged in examining the various hypotheses that might explain these relationships. By the end of the nineteenth century there was general agreement that the correct solution of the problem had been found. This solution went by the name of "The Two-Document Hypothesis." According to this theory the general content of the synoptic tradition can be traced essentially to two sources. One of these is the Gospel of Mark, which the authors of Matthew and Luke used as a source. The other is a collection of sayings of Jesus, which both Matthew and Luke used and which each combined with the text of Mark in his own way. It is true that Matthew and Luke used some other sources, but nearly all of the material in these gospels can be traced to Mark and to the collection of sayings (often called the *Logia*). In tracing these relationships it should be noted that both Mark and the collection of sayings were subjected to editorial redaction. It is quite possible that Matthew and Luke possessed Mark and the *Logia* in different recensions, and it is quite probable that the form of the Gospel of Mark used by them was earlier than the one with which we are familiar. However, the differences between these forms cannot have been very great. The *Urmarkus* (as this supposed earlier form was called) must have been essentially identical with Mark as it lies before us, minus a few slight later additions.

Two difficult questions, however, remained to be considered. First: How was the relationship between Mark and the *Logia* to be defined? Which was older, Mark or the *Logia*? Did Mark use the *Logia* at all? The second related question concerned the sources that the writer of Mark used in the composition of his gospel. Did he employ oral tradition simply, or did he have written sources as well? These two questions were considered important because of the goal toward which all this critical work was believed to lead, viz., the attainment of the most accurate possible picture of the life and the teaching of the historical Jesus.

Bultmann reviews the assumptions of earlier research into the life of Jesus, particularly the reliance on the content and sequence of events as they appear in Mark as essentially historical. More recent analyses of the Synoptic Gospels by scholars such as Wilhelm Wrede and Julius Wellhausen discussed the problem of the distinction between the oldest traditions about Jesus and the additions or modifications introduced in the eventual redaction of the gospel documents. The quest for the historical Jesus advanced with the recognition that the oldest traditions were preserved in small fragments of the sayings of Jesus that did not disclose or reflect a continuous narrative line of Jesus' career. Bultmann observes that "a literary work or fragment of [the Jesus] tradition is a primary source for the historical situation out of which it arose, and is only a secondary source for the historical details concerning which it gives information."

---

[3] R. Bultmann, "The New Approach to the Synoptic Problem," *Journal of Religion* 6 (1926): 337–62. Used with permission.

If we define the total undertaking as that of distinguishing the different stages of the synoptic tradition from one another in order to identify the oldest, the very first task is to make a critical distinction between tradition and editorial redaction in the Synoptic Gospels. Now it is easy to discover the method of redaction employed in Matthew and Luke, since here we can compare the gospels with Mark and can note the way in which Matthew and Luke combined this gospel with the material of the *Logia*. When the process of gospel-making has been observed in this case, it becomes possible with considerable certainty to distinguish between tradition and redaction in the Gospel of Mark. This undertaking was systematically carried out by K. L. Schmidt, in his book entitled *Der Rahmen der Geschichte Jesu* [The Framework of the Story of Jesus] (1919). By means of such an analysis it becomes clear that the original tradition underlying Mark (with perhaps the exception of the story of the Passion) consisted almost entirely of small isolated fragments; and that virtually all the descriptions of place or time which connect the individual fragments into a larger whole are due to redaction. In the case of Mark, this editorial redaction is still quite primitive; but in Matthew, and especially in Luke, it is already considerably developed. All three Evangelists have typical forms of transition from one incident to another. They ring the changes on a rather limited amount of material in order thus to construct the background of individual scenes and to construct a framework for the entire life of Jesus. They mention such items as the house, the road, the mountain, the seashore; situations such as Jesus in a ship, on a journey, as a guest at a meal, in the synagogue at a religious service. As conventional accompaniments appear the popular crowd, the foes of Jesus, and the ever-present disciples. In my own book, *Die Geschichte der synoptischen Tradition* (1921), I presented in full these conclusions of K. L. Schmidt and carried the study somewhat further.

As a result of this investigation it appears that the outline of the life of Jesus, as it is given by Mark and taken over by Matthew and Luke, is an editorial creation, and that as a consequence our actual knowledge of the course of Jesus' life is restricted to what little can be discovered in the individual scenes constituting the older tradition. This conclusion, however, is not simply a negative one. It has also its positive significance, since critical analysis has brought out portions that can be regarded as original traditions.

Now a new problem arises. In the first place, we must ask whether all the traditional bits are equally original or whether we are not obliged to distinguish here also between earlier and later tradition. In the second place, it must be asked whether these traditions have been preserved intact or whether, through redaction by the Evangelists or in the course of previous transmission, they have not been altered, abridged, or expanded. What means do we possess for answering these questions?

The method of investigation called *Formgeschichte* is believed to furnish such means. This method starts from the observed fact that all literary presentations, particularly in primitive culture and in the ancient world, follow relatively fixed forms. This is true not only of written narratives, but also of oral tradition. It is to be noticed, for example, that folk tales, or proverbs, or folk songs transmitted orally, have their definite styles. Two factors must be noted in a study of form: first, the stylistic pattern which prevails in a particular kind of utterance, such as folk tales or riddles; and secondly, the laws conditioning the transmission of a literary fragment in either oral or written tradition. Certain examples of this will be given later.

. . .

In the New Testament this task of literary analysis is admittedly much more difficult [than its application to the Old Testament], because the material is of much smaller compass and the period of its development is much shorter. Nevertheless, it is possible to distinguish in the material of the synoptic tradition certain specific literary types which have their own laws of style. If, now, the content of the tradition is expressed in the form of such special types, it is possible to place great reliance on this tradition, for these forms always offer definite resistance to any radical alteration. This resistance, of course, is only relative; for it is undeniable that the material actually underwent changes. If, however, we can succeed in identifying a particular literary type and its laws of style, we can then frequently distinguish an original tradition from secondary additions. We thus obtain a test for determining the age of a literary utterance by noting whether it appears in the original pure form belonging to this type of literature or whether it shows marks of further stylistic development. It is easily understood that such investigation is very difficult and must be carried on with great caution. Conclusions, however, are reinforced when we not only note the laws of style belonging to a given type, but also discover the general laws which govern the transmission of material.

This last task, viz., the study of the laws which govern literary transmission, can be approached by observing the manner in which the Marcan material was altered by Matthew and Luke; and also how Matthew and Luke worked over what they took from the *Logia*. Here we observe a certain regular procedure which becomes still more evident when we carry the investigation to a later tradition, particularly to the apocryphal gospels, and see how in these the gospel material received further literary development. When once the laws governing such transmission of tradition are established we may assume that these laws prevailed also in the case of Mark and in the collection of the *Logia*. Then, it is frequently possible to attempt provisionally to reconstruct a literary form older than the one lying before us. The ability to make the necessary distinctions can be developed by studying the general laws which govern popular transmission of stories and traditions in other instances, for example, in the case of folk tales, anecdotes, and folk songs.

The primary task of identifying the specific types of the synoptic material and the laws of style governing each is made simpler through the fact that we are acquainted with similar species in contemporary rabbinical and Hellenistic literature. Just what types can be identified and more accurately described with the help of this material will be made clear in the following discussion.

Bultmann goes on to describe how accretions typically add to the old tradition, such as in the attempt to provide names and identities to persons originally anonymous in the stories. (Additional biblical references have been added in brackets by the editor.)

Let us now ask what literary types the *formgeschichtliche* investigation can identify in the material of the synoptic tradition.

We can easily identify the type of miracle stories. . . . Characteristic miracle stories are those in which the miracle constitutes the main theme and is described with considerable detail, such as the healing of the Gerasene demoniac [see Mark 5:1–20; Matt 8:28–34; Luke 8:26–39], the cure of the woman with the issue of blood [see Mark 5:25–34; Matt 9:20–22; Luke 8:43–48], the raising of the daughter of Jairus from death [see Mark 5:22–24; Matt 9:18–26; Luke 8:40–56], the stories of the stilling of the storm [see Mark 4:35–41; Matt 8:23–27; Luke 8:22–24], of walking on the sea [see Mark 6:45–52; Matt 14:22–33], of the feeding of the five thousand [see Mark 6:30–44; Matt 14:13–21; Luke 9:10–17], and others. These miracle stories, particularly the accounts of miraculous healing, reveal one and the same style with definite characteristics. Since we know a great many miracle stories of Jewish and Hellenistic origin, we can make a careful comparative study of the miracle stories found in the Gospels. We thus discover that the gospel stories have exactly the same style as the Hellenistic miracle stories. Accounts of miraculous healing run as follows: First, the condition of the sick person is depicted in such fashion as to enhance the magnitude of the miracle. In this connection it is frequently said that the sickness had lasted a long time. Occasionally it is stated that many physicians had attempted in vain to cure the sick person. Sometimes the terrible and dangerous character of the sickness is emphasized. All these traits are found in the synoptic narratives, just as they also appear in the stories which are told concerning the pagan miracle-worker Apollonius of Tyana.[4] After this introductory description of the illness comes the account of the healing itself. The Hellenistic miracle stories often tell of unusual manipulations by the miracle-worker; the Gospel accounts, however, seldom mention this trait (Mark 7:33 and 8:23). The Gospels do, however, retain other typical items. They narrate that the Savior came near to the sick person—perhaps close to his bed—that he laid his hand upon the patient or took him by the hand and then uttered a wonder-working word. Following a custom also characteristic of pagan miracle stories, the narratives of healing in the Gospels occasionally reproduce this wonder-working word in a foreign tongue, as, for example, *Talitha Kumi* (Mark 5:41) and *Ephphatha* (Mark 7:34). Another typical trait appears when it is sometimes said that no one was permitted to see the actual working of the miracle (Mark 7:33 and 8:23). The close of the miracle story depicts the consequence of the miracle, frequently describing the astonishment or the terror or the approval of those who witnessed the miraculous event. In other cases the close of the narrative shows the one who is healed demonstrating by some appropriate action that he is entirely cured. Thus, in Mark 2:11ff., the lame man who was healed carried away the bed on which he had been brought. Precisely the same thing is narrated in a Hellenistic miracle story told by Lucian of Samosata.[5] In the Hellenistic stories of the exorcism of demons, the process was often described in drastic fashion by representing the demon on his expulsion as indulging in some destructive action, such as shattering a

---

[4] See *The Life of Apollonius of Tyana: The Epistles of Apollonius and the Treaties of Eusebius* (trans. F. C. Conybeare; Cambridge: Harvard University Press, 1960).

[5] See *Lucian* (trans. A. M. Harmon; 8 vols.; Cambridge: Harvard University Press, 1960–1969).

pillar or overturning a vessel containing water. In similar fashion, in the account in the fifth chapter of Mark, the demon who was expelled entered into a herd of swine and drove them into the sea. Many of the foregoing traits are also found in the rabbinical miracle tales. All of them appear in Hellenistic accounts. On the basis, then, of the similarity between the miracle stories in the Synoptic Gospels and those in Hellenistic literature we are forced to conclude that these miracle stories do not belong to the oldest strata of tradition, but, at least in their present form, were elaborated in Hellenistic Christianity.

It is true that the older Palestinian tradition also narrates miracles of Jesus, but, . . . only [of] those miracles which give occasion for a controversy between Jesus and his opponents. One of the oldest types of the synoptic tradition consists of controversial utterances. This type is common to both the rabbinical and the synoptic tradition, and precisely the same characteristics of style may be observed in both. An act or attitude of someone (in the case of the Christian tradition, Jesus or a disciple of his) gives the occasion for an attack by an opponent. Familiar instances are the violation of the Sabbath requirements or a failure to observe some ritual of purification. The attack is answered by a defense, which appears in a specific form, very frequently an *ad hominem* query, or an illustration, or perhaps both together. To the charge that Jesus was healing on the Sabbath day came the answer in the form of the question, "Is it lawful to do good on the sabbath day or to do evil?" (Mark 3:4). In answer to the inquiry why his disciples did not fast, Jesus replied: "Can the children of the bridegroom fast when the bridegroom is with them?" Another way of replying is to give a Scripture citation.

It is characteristic of the style of these controversial discourses, as may be observed in similar rabbinical material, that the dialogue proceeds in crisp and trenchant form. The question asked or the illustration given in rejoinder contains the complete refutation of the opponent. We therefore conclude that, in the Synoptic Gospels, where the answer receives further elaboration, the elaborating words are a secondary contribution. This is undoubtedly the case in Mark 2:19, 20, where the question cited above is elaborated as follows: "So long as they have the bridegroom with them they cannot fast; but the days will come when the bridegroom shall be taken from them, and then will they fast in that day." The content of these words reinforces this conclusion, for they contain an allegorical prophecy of the death of Jesus and a justification of the later custom of fasting in the Christian community. Careful investigation shows that similar elaborations of an original tradition are found in other places.

The form of these controversial dialogues shows that this part of the tradition originated in the primitive Palestinian community, and the general content, along with many incidental observations, confirms this hypothesis. Accordingly, we must picture the life of this community moving within the limits of Judaism, engaged in disputes with the Jewish schools, and seeking to justify the correctness of its point of view by appeal to words of Jesus and by citations from Scripture. These controversial passages, then, precisely as in the case of rabbinical utterances, were transmitted not as historical narratives, but as polemic and apologetic material. It is therefore incorrect to regard these controversial utterances as accounts of actual historical scenes in the life of Jesus. It is true that the spirit of Jesus breathes in them; for his activity called the community into life and from him the community received the peculiar views with which the controversies are concerned. There is no reason to doubt that many genuine utterances attributed to Jesus in these discourses rest back upon accurate historical recollection; but it must also be admitted that the scenes depicted in them are not to be taken as narratives of actual events.

In confirmation of this conclusion, a further observation may be made. In many of the controversial discourses we find that it is not an objectionable attitude of Jesus, but rather the behavior of his disciples, that furnishes the occasion for opposition. Thus we read that the disciples did not fast, that they plucked the heads of wheat on the Sabbath, that they did not practice ritual purification before eating. Why now were the disciples rebuked? Clearly Jesus could not have maintained a correct attitude in all these matters. The disciples must have learned their independent attitude only from him. When, now, we trace the origin of such a narrative to the apologetic necessities of the Christian community, the whole matter becomes clear. The "disciples" are nothing other than the community. This community, under the influence of Jesus, had broken with the old customs, and was defending its position against its opponents by appealing to an utterance of Jesus. This appeal, following the method of rabbinical literature, expresses itself in terms of a controversial discourse.

Bultmann goes on to analyze the form of the controversy narrative as an example of an apophthegma (apothegm), a recognizable episodic frame that features an important utterance of the key figure, usually a hero or philosopher.

We have seen that the controversial utterances cannot be regarded as actual historical scenes. The same is true of the biographical *apophthegmata*. These are pictorial creations of the Christian community in which is brought to clear expression what the community held to be the character of their Master, what they experienced in relation to him, or how he fared in popular estimation. Thus, for example, the stories of the calling of the first disciples from their occupation as fishermen are not actual historical events. They lack entirely any portrayal of adequate motives or historical verisimilitude. These scenes simply give symbolic expression, such as one might find in a picture, to the general experience of the disciples when, through the wonderful power of Jesus, they were diverted from their previous manner of life. Thus the well-known story of Jesus preaching in Nazareth and his rejection there (Mark 6:1–6) is not a definite historical occurrence, but is a symbolic picture which vividly represents the attitude of the people as a whole to the preaching of Jesus.

When we undertake a critical investigation of the recorded words of Jesus we face a very difficult task. Is it possible here also to distinguish between a more ancient content and a later reworking? The first step in this investigation is to detach the utterances themselves from the setting given to them in the Gospels, for this setting is due to the editorial work of the Evangelists or of earlier collectors of the discourses. It is only when the utterances are thus disentangled from their setting that the real meaning of the words can be obtained; for in the editorial setting an artificial meaning is often given. Take, for example, the statement, "Agree with thine adversary quickly, while thou art with him in the way, etc." In Matt 5:25–26 these words urge a reconciliation. But in Luke 12:57–59 they take the form of a parable of warning, saying in effect: Exactly as in his earthly life a person, up to the very last, tries to settle a dispute out of court by some mutual agreement because it is impossible to be sure what judgment the court will make, so ought one, while it is still possible to do so, to take pains that he shall not appear as a defendant before the court of the heavenly judge. It is probable that in this case Luke has preserved the original meaning of the utterance. Frequently, however, it is no longer possible for us to determine what the original meaning of a statement was.

. . .

We can see with especial clearness in the parables the way in which the content of tradition was influenced by the interpretation given to it by the Evangelists. . . . The Evangelists no longer understand the style of the ancient parables—a style common to both the synoptic and the rabbinical literature—but they regard the parables as allegories which in obscure fashion prophesied the fate of Jesus or of his community. As a matter of fact the parables were originally intended not to conceal ideas, but to make them clear and effective. The Evangelists, however, frequently add secondary utterances to the original parables. These additions can occasionally be identified by a comparative study of the Gospels themselves. In the parable of the royal feast (Matt 22:6–7) some of those who were invited attacked and slew the king's servants who invited them to the feast; the king consequently sent his army against them, slew them, and burned their city. This is a very improbable item in the original parable, and the fact that Luke says nothing about it shows that it is an addition of Matthew's. Matthew intends this incident to refer allegorically to the destruction of Jerusalem as a punishment for the death of the prophets and messengers of God. It is only when we free ourselves completely from the interpretation which the Evangelists have given to the parables and when we free the parables from secondary additions that we can hope to discover their original meaning. It is true that we are compelled to admit that in many cases we cannot determine the original meaning with any certainty. But in the process of analysis we receive much help by a comparison with the rabbinical parables, which reveal clearly the general method arid and style of parabolic utterances.

Moving beyond the parables, Bultmann shows how the same sort of analysis can apply to traditions about other utterances of Jesus, categorized as typically Jewish "wisdom utterances," the behavioral precepts of Jesus, and the prophctic or apocalyptic utterances.

In conclusion we may note briefly the relationship between *formgeschichtliche* [history of literary and oral forms] investigation and the *religionsgeschichtliche* [history of religions] interpretation of primitive Christianity. We showed earlier in this article how the traditional picture of Jesus has been dissolved, principally by the investigations of Wrede and Wellhausen. *Formgeschichtliche* analysis continues further this process of criticism and comes at first to the negative conclusion that the

outline of the Gospels does not enable us to know either the outer course of the life
of Jesus or his inner development. We must frankly confess that the character of Jesus
as a human personality cannot be recovered by us. We can neither write a "life of
Jesus" nor present an accurate picture of his personality. . . .

The outcome of *formgeschichtliche* investigation, however, is not merely negative. When critical analysis has been carried through and the different strata of tradition have been isolated; when, further, we keep in mind the fundamental principle
that the first undertaking is to obtain a clear picture of the primitive community, then
we may inquire concerning the more important matter, viz., the preaching of Jesus.
On the basis of the three typical forms in which utterances of Jesus appear we can
form three pictures of the preaching of Jesus: Jesus as a teacher of wisdom, Jesus as a
lawgiver, and Jesus as a prophet. If we leave out of account the first picture as being
the least probable, the fundamental problem as to the nature of the preaching of
Jesus may be formulated as follows: How are the ethical and the eschatological utterances related to each other? Do they belong to one single picture or, as many investigators think, do they stand in such contrast that we must choose between them
when we seek to know what the historical Jesus taught? Was Jesus a lawgiver, or was
he a prophet? It is my conviction that these questions must be asked seriously; but I
also believe that the answer must be: He was both; the ethical and eschatological utterances belong in a larger unity. I cannot here give the reasons for my conviction. I
can only indicate the complicated nature of the *religionsgeschichtliche* questions by
citing a particular instance. I have several times alluded to the fact that when we
have isolated the various strata of tradition the question arises whether a given narrative originated in the Palestinian community or in the Hellenistic. The importance of
this distinction was made clear by W. Bousset in his *Kyrios Christos* (second edition,
1921). He showed that primitive Palestinian Christianity was very different from Hellenistic Christianity. The former remained within the limits of Judaism and regarded
itself as the true Israel; its piety was eschatological and it awaited Jesus as the coming
Son of Man. Primitive Hellenistic Christianity, on the other hand, was a religion of
cult, in the center of which stood Jesus Christ as the "Lord" who communicated his
heavenly powers in the worship and the sacraments of the community. It goes without saying that the recognition of this difference is of great importance in the analysis
of the synoptic tradition. It means that the elements of cult-religion contained in the
Synoptic Gospels are secondary, coming from Hellenistic sources.

Recent investigations and discoveries, however, have made it questionable
whether primitive Palestinian Christianity can be regarded as a definite unity. It has
been suggested that we must distinguish here two developments or two historical
motives. The researches of the philologist [Richard] Reitzenstein, have led to the
probable conclusion that already in certain circles of Judaism there were stronger influences than had hitherto been supposed of oriental, Iranian-Babylonian redemp-
tionist religion and speculation, such as we find later in Gnosticism.[6] This type of

---

[6] Richard Reitzenstein, *Studien zur antiken Synkretismus aus Iran und Griechenland* (Leipzig:
B. G. Teubner, 1926); *Antike und Christentum: Vier religionsgeschichtliche Aufsätze* (Darmstadt:

religion spread among groups of apocalyptists and in small sects which practiced various rituals, particularly baptism. Such a sect within Judaism seem to have been the Essenes, about whom, unfortunately, we know very little. It is quite probable that John the Baptist and the sects bearing his name should be classed here. On this point new material of a surprising nature has recently come to light, although there is as yet no agreement as to the exact significance of the discovery. The orientalist [Mark] Lidzbarski, who edited and translated the writings of the Gnostic sect of the Mandaeans, has given weighty reasons for the conjecture that these Mandaeans, who were formerly believed to have had their rise in Babylonia, really originated by the Jordan River, and that they were nothing other than the sect of John the Baptist.[7] The sect, of course, later underwent a development in doctrine and practice. Characteristics of this sect were the ritual of baptism and certain remarkable cosmological and eschatological speculations. The Mandaeans also called themselves Nasoreans, meaning probably "Observers." It is to be noted that in Christian tradition Jesus also was frequently described by the title "The Nasorean," a word which cannot be etymologically derived from Nazareth, his actual or alleged home. Probably he was called Nasorean because he originally belonged to the sect of John the Baptist. The evangelical tradition preserves the memory of this in the statement that Jesus permitted himself to be baptized by John. In addition to this the earliest Christian tradition reveals a peculiar relationship to John the Baptist. The followers of Jesus and those of John the Baptist stood together in opposition to orthodox Judaism, but in relation to each other they were rivals. This is especially clear in the Fourth Gospel, but traces of it are retained also in the synoptic tradition. It seems probable, then, that Jesus and his community must be regarded as an offshoot from the community of John the Baptist. If this is true we must reckon with the possibility that the preaching of Jesus and of his first followers was perhaps more strongly influenced by oriental-syncretistic conceptions than would be indicated by the later tradition, and that possibly eschatology played a much greater part in that early preaching than in later tradition. Here, however, most of the details are still quite uncertain. What has here been said is primarily to indicate some of the important problems which lie as yet unsolved before us.

Wissenschaftliche Buchgesellschaft, 1963); *Hellenistic Mystery-Religions: Their Basic Ideas and Significance* (trans. J. E. Stuly; Pittsburgh: Pickwick, 1978).

[7] Mark Lidzbarski, *Ginzä, der Schatz, oder das grosser Buch der Mandäer übersetzt und erklärt* (Göttingen: Vandenhoeck & Ruprecht, 1925).

CHAPTER 23

Archaeology and Biblical Interpretation: William F. Albright (1891–1971)

B y the time he entered the Oriental Seminary at Johns Hopkins University in Baltimore for graduate study under the famed German scholar Paul Haupt, William F. Albright was well equipped for advanced study of the Bible. His childhood in the Chilean mission field had brought him fluency in Spanish, French, and German as well as a serious interest in history and the Bible. During college he had taught himself Hebrew and Akkadian, and he had already published on Semitic philology in a German technical journal. Having long since discovered his destiny as a scholar, at Baltimore Albright launched a lengthy and distinguished career that would fashion him into a true generalist: authoritative historian, master ancient Near Eastern philologist, pioneering field archaeologist—in the words of his biographers, "a twentieth-century genius." Albright's impact on biblical interpretation, particularly in North America, was exceptional not only by virtue of his own research discoveries and voluminous scholarly output (more than eight hundred publications) but also through a cluster of energetic students whom he trained after he had replaced Haupt at Johns Hopkins. These students, many of whom secured high-profile appointments at major American universities and divinity schools, would themselves go on to influence subsequent generations of scholars through their own publications.

During the early twentieth century, the American religious landscape was marked by contention between liberal and conservative theological perspectives. In the light of the great advances in the study of the history of religions and the literary history of the Bible, the liberal (sometimes called modernist) view traced in the Bible a great, millennia-spanning movement in human consciousness from primitive polytheism to more sophisticated monotheism. The Bible's presentation of a monotheistic Israelite faith during the time of Moses was taken to be a retrojection from a much later era of a more fully developed religious faith. Historical literary analyses by scholars such as Julius Wellhausen convinced many students that the biblical narratives could not offer anything like reliable history. On the other hand, the conservative (also called fundamentalist) view affirmed the historical reliability of biblical accounts and the uniqueness of central elements of Israelite faith such as (early) teachings of monotheism.

In a modern cultural context deeply imprinted with the triumph of scientific method—stunningly displayed by scientists and engineers through remarkable accomplishments in chemistry and physics—Albright attempted to demonstrate the basic truth of orthodoxy on the basis of a scientifically unassailable history of Western religion that culminated in Judeo-Christian monotheism. Albright's historical research program sought a full explanation of the Bible in its ancient context according to the scientific examination of empirical philological and archaeological evidence. He thus became the champion and pioneering practitioner of "biblical archaeology," the results of which could command respect by any scientific measure—thus securing a position of relevance and influence over modern biblical interpretation. Some of the results and their significance for understanding the Bible can be learned from our selection, which is taken from "The Bible after Twenty Years of Archeology (1932–1952)."

Through a synthesis of inscriptional, archaeological, textual, and historical evidence, the Albrightean school made a claim to greater confidence in the basic historicity of biblical accounts. For example, season upon season of archaeological excavations in Palestine revealed evidence of city destruction patterns in the thirteenth century B.C.E. consistent with the biblical account of the conquest under Joshua. Additionally, the discoveries of greater quantities of ancient Semitic documents permitted greater refinement in modern knowledge of the history of ancient Hebrew. Thus, evidence became available to help identify certain poems such as Deborah's song in Judg 5 as authentically ancient compositions chronologically proximate to the events they celebrate. In this fashion, many events from Israel's early history were placed on surer historical footing. Such syntheses provided the basis for one of Albright's students, John Bright, to publish a reconstruction of ancient Israelite history that stands out from most other major works of this sort by claiming essential historicity for much of what the Hebrew Bible narrates. (First published in 1959, Bright's *History of Israel* is now in its fourth edition.)

A reciprocal dynamic of interest and influence played between the Albrightean historical program and the biblical-theology movement in North America. If scientific historical research indicated that the biblical writings were centrally concerned with real historical events and their ancient interpretation, then the events of the Bible would have to factor into modern biblical-theological work—contrary to the methodological assumptions of primarily European nineteenth- and early-twentieth-century theologians. Thus, a certain theological motivation prompted Albright and his students to work toward reconstruction of the actual events underlying the biblical narratives about ancient Israel encountering God. Apart from such securely established historical bases, it was felt that ancient Israel's theological witness would not command serious attention from the modern historically conscious mind and so could not constructively contribute to theology. The assumption behind this conception of biblical theology was that study of the Bible in its ancient context, as established by scientific historical methods, would unveil what the biblical writers were actually saying about God. This touchstone—the historical-critically authenticated witness of the biblical writers to God's active presence in the historical process that they experienced—became a key element incorporated into much of the work by biblical theologians in the mid–twentieth century. G. Ernest Wright, another of Albright's students, played an especially prominent role in the biblical-theology movement through works such as *God Who Acts: Biblical Theology as Recital*.

In the selection that follows, the reader will notice Albright's tone of confidence in the objectivity of method and in the certainty of historical results as they pertain to understanding the Bible. Today few biblical scholars would endorse Albright's enthusiasm for such conclusive historical claims. This is so for at least two reasons. First, through further refinement of the very methods that Albright had introduced, archaeological experts have gone on to produce more-refined syntheses of evidence far less supportive of key

Albrightean conclusions. For example, it is no longer certain that the thirteenth-century destruction layers among the ruins of Canaanite cities can be attributed to Israelite conquest. Second, Albright's confidence derived in part from the astounding breadth of his historical and linguistic expertise. The now firmly established trend toward academic specialization—prevalent in all fields from medicine to literature—makes it doubtful whether any longer a single individual could acquire the scope of training and experience sufficient for the authoritatively integrative task to which Albright aspired in such projects as *From the Stone Age to Christianity: Monotheism and the Historical Process* (Baltimore: Johns Hopkins University Press, 1940). Irrespective of this, Albright's legacy for biblical interpretation endures in numerous historical and textual insights as well as in the very methodological advances that have since dated his work.

For further information on William F. Albright and biblical archaeology:

Dever, William G. *Recent Archaeological Discoveries and Biblical Research.* Seattle: University of Washington Press, 1990.

King, Philip J. *American Archaeology in the Mideast: A History of the American Schools of Oriental Research.* Philadelphia: American Schools of Oriental Research, 1983.

Running, Leona G., and David Noel Freedman. *William Foxwell Albright: A Twentieth Century Genius.* New York: Morgan, 1975.

"The Bible after Twenty Years of Archeology (1932–1952)"[1]

Periodical stock-taking is a necessity in all progressive fields. The more recent the development of any scientific or scholarly field of investigation, the more necessary does such stock-taking become. What is a commonplace in nuclear physics or genetics should also be taken for granted in any archeological field. In biblical archeology the past generation has been revolutionary in every sense of the word. In 1951 the present writer contributed to a symposium two chapters on the progress of the archeology of Palestine and surrounding Bible lands in the thirty years from 1920 to 1950.[2] Just twenty years have elapsed since he published his first book intended for the general reader: *The Archaeology of Palestine and the Bible*. The advance made since that book was written is almost incredible; it easily dwarfs the sum of all relevant discoveries during the preceding century in its total impact on our knowledge of the Bible.

I

In surveying the most important discoveries since 1932 which bear on the Bible it is hard not to include all archeological finds in Bible lands, since the greatest achievement of archeology during this period has been to consolidate fragmentary materials into a synthesis of the history of ancient Eastern civilization, in which the Bible appears in its true historical perspective. However, if one must choose, one may suggest the following subjects as particularly important: (1) stabilizing the chronology; (2) the tablets of Mari and Ugarit; (3) new documents bearing on the exilic and postexilic periods, especially the Lachish letters and new Aramaic papyri and ostraca from Egypt; (4) the Dead Sea Scrolls and similar finds in Palestine; (5) the early Gnostic and Manichean codices from Egypt.

Stabilizing ancient chronology may not seem very important, but it is impossible to understand the course of events or the history of civilization unless one can set events and cultures in correct time relation. Twenty years ago the archeological chronology of Palestine was still in a state of chaos, with scholars differing in their dates by centuries in the Iron Age and even by thousands of years before the second millennium. At that time there was no agreement on the correlation of Babylonian, Egyptian, and Syro-Palestinian chronologies before about 1500 B.C. Now we have many cross-checks, both documentary and archeological, on the relation between successive cultural stages in these countries; we also have much more abundant information for the political chronologies of Mesopotamia and Egypt, checked by astronomical data. Above all, radiocarbon dating has developed since 1947, and we

---

[1] This extract comes from "The Bible After Twenty Years of Archeology (1932–1952)" by William F. Albright. *Religion in Life* vol. 21 1952. ©1952 by Pierce and Smith. Used by permission of Abingdon Press.

[2] In *The Old Testament and Modern Study: A Generation of Discovery and Research*, ed. H. H. Rowley. Oxford: Oxford University Press, 1951.—Albright

now have many approximate dates for archeological materials of organic origin, covering the last 8,000 years of Near-Eastern history.

Second (in chronological order) come Mari and Ugarit. The excavation of Mari began in 1933, under the direction of André Parrot. Situated on the Middle Euphrates, Mari was one of the most important centers of the Northwest Semitic life of Patriarchal times. In 1936, M. Parrot unearthed many thousands of cuneiform tablets dating mostly from about 1700 B.C., which are now in course of being studied and published. These tablets throw direct light on the background of the Patriarchal traditions of Genesis.[3]

Four years before the commencement of the Mari excavations, C. F. A. Schaeffer had begun excavations at Ras Shamrah on the coast of northern Syria, finding rich remains from the wealthiest of all Canaanite cities immediately before the Mosaic Age. He started almost at once to find tablets, and by 1933 he had unearthed extensive fragments of a whole temple library. The cuneiform alphabet of Ugarit was deciphered in 1930, and the first recovered tablet of the great Baal Epic was published by Ch. Virolleaud at the end of the following year.[4] In 1931, several scholars took up the study of the new texts, which were not long in yielding most of their secrets. By 1940 it was possible for C. H. Gordon to publish an admirable pioneer grammar of Ugaritic, which was revised and expanded in 1947.[5] The excavation of Ugarit, interrupted in 1939, was resumed by M. Schaeffer in 1948, and we look forward to continuation of this most important undertaking. The remains of three epics, which had been composed previously in Phoenicia, have survived in copies made not long before the great earthquake of c. 1360 B.C.; the light they shed on the earliest poetical literature of the Bible has completely revolutionized our approach to it.

Third in our brief survey we mention the new documents from the sixth and fifth centuries B.C. which have come to light since 1935. In 1935 the late J. L. Starkey discovered the Ostraca of Lachish, consisting chiefly of letters written in ink on potsherds. Together with several additional ostraca found in 1938, they form a unique body of Hebrew prose from the time of Jeremiah. Further light on the time of the Exile comes from the ration lists of Nebuchadnezzar, found by the Germans at Babylon and partly published by E. F. Weidner in 1939. Other new evidence will be discussed below. Somewhat later but of decisive value for our understanding of the history and literature of the Jews in the time of Ezra and Nehemiah are the continuing finds and publications of Aramaic papyri and ostraca from Egypt. Four large groups of this material are being published, and their complete publication will more than double the total bulk of such documents available twenty years ago.

---

[3] These appear in the series Archives royales de Mari and Archives royales de Mari, transcrite et traduite.

[4] Charles Virolleaud, "Un poème phénicien de Ras-Shamra: La lutte de Môt, fils des dieux, et d'Aleïn, fils de Baal," *Syria* 12 (1931): 103–224.

[5] Cyrus H. Gordon, *Ugaritic Handbook: Revised Grammar, Paradigms, Texts in Transliteration, Comprehensive Glossary* (Rome: Pontifical Biblical Institute, 1947).

In 1947 some Bedouin made a discovery south of Jericho which could not have been foreseen by the most optimistic specialist—a cave containing many scrolls of leather covered with Hebrew and Aramaic writing, to say nothing of over 600 fragments. News reached the world in the spring of 1948 and publication began a few months later. In early 1949 the cave was rediscovered and cleared by G. L. Harding and Père R. de Vaux, the most competent archeologists in the Kingdom of Jordan. The first lot of manuscripts went partly to the Syrian Archbishop, Athanasius Yeshue Samuel, and partly to E. L. Sukenik at the Hebrew University. John C. Trever was responsible for recognizing the approximate date and importance of the Syrian collection; Sukenik had previously recognized the age and value of the manuscripts in the Hebrew University, but did not announce his acquisition until later. In early 1952 new caves containing fragments of later scrolls in Hebrew, Aramaic and Greek were discovered, and the announcement of this find was followed by news of the recovery of additional scrolls in still another cave.

The discovery of the original group of these scrolls was followed by a series of fantastic onslaughts on their antiquity and even on their authenticity, over the signatures of some well-known scholars in America and Europe, both Christian and Jewish. Only in Palestine, where the finds were too well known to be suspect, was there virtually unanimous agreement about their general age. It is true that such sensational discoveries are always challenged, but in this case the data are so well substantiated that the attacks must be connected with the fact that the new finds disprove the already published views of the attacking scholars.

Here we have threefold evidence in support of a date for the Dead Sea Scrolls well before A.D. 70. The vases (over forty of which were found) in which the scrolls had been placed, as well as lamps found with them, are Hellenistic and cannot have been manufactured after the time of Herod the Great (37 B.C.–A.D. 4). The linen in which the scrolls were wrapped has been dated by radiocarbon count to the period between c. 175 B.C. and A.D. 225 (in round numbers). The forms of letters used by scores of different scribes over a period of more than a century are intermediate between the known script of the third century B.C. and of the Apostolic period. All competent students of writing conversant with the available materials and with paleographic method date them in the 250 years before A.D. 70,[6] and most are divided between dates for the sealing of the cave between about 50 B.C. and just before A.D. 70; the writer's own preferred date for nearly all the Scrolls remains in the last century B.C. Subsequent finds date partly (when coming from the first cave) from the same period and partly from the second century A.D. (when coming from later caves). These latter fragments are in considerably later script, bridging the gap between the Dead Sea Scrolls and the earliest previously known papyrus and parchment fragments in Hebrew from the third and fourth centuries A.D.

The contents of the new scrolls are partly biblical (two scrolls of Isaiah, one of which is complete, most of the first two chapters of Habakkuk, etc.), and partly

---

[6] There is still disagreement among specialists as to the date of the fragments of Deuteronomy in a script intermediate between old Hebrew cursive and the earliest Samaritan. —Albright

intertestamental. Their historical and philological importance is very great indeed, and they are already revolutionizing our approach to the text of the Old Testament and the background of the New Testament.

Our last category of outstanding discoveries carries us down into the Christian era and may seem too late to be of significance for biblical studies. First comes the discovery in 1930 of seven Manichean codices composed in part by Mani, founder of this Gnostic sect, in the third century A.D.; translated into Coptic soon afterwards and copied for us by fourth-century scribes. The publication, chiefly due to the talent of H. J. Polotsky, began in 1934 and was interrupted in 1940 by the war.[7] Before this our only firsthand knowledge of Manichean literature came from fragments translated into Central-Asiatic languages and discovered in Turkestan by German explorers before the First World War. Now we have a mass of original material, which, among other things, establishes the secondary character of Mandeanism in relation to Manicheism; the former has been regarded by many scholars as in part older than the Gospel of John.

In 1947 a second, even more remarkable, discovery of Gnostic books was made in Egypt, this time a lot of some forty treatises bound together in codices, at Chenoboscium (Chenoboskion) in Upper Egypt. These books are also in Coptic; the extant copies date from the third and fourth centuries and the original Greek works from which they were translated must go back to the second and third centuries. We have here for the first time the original writings of the strange early Gnostic groups called the Barbelo Gnostics, the Ophites, Sethians, and others, as well as several Hermetic treatises. At last we can control and expand the information given us by Hippolytus, Irenaeus, and Epiphanius about these early Gnostics and their beliefs. The new documents will have extraordinary significance in connection with the debate about the alleged Gnostic affinities of the Gospel of John. Fortunately all (or nearly all) of these codices have been acquired by the Egyptian government, and it is to be hoped that they will be published before long. Meanwhile we have very reliable information from the first student of these texts, Jean Doresse.

II

It is just as hard to select biblical books and periods of biblical history for illumination as it is to choose between discoveries. The scope for eventual choice is too wide and there are too many interesting matters on which the finds of the past twenty years have thrown light. We shall take (1) the Patriarchal traditions of Genesis, (2) the early poetry of Israel, (3) the contrast of Israelite faith with Canaanite religion, (4) Exile and Restoration, and (5) the Gospel of John.

In 1932 the writer gave much attention in his book, *The Archeology of Palestine and the Bible,* to the way in which Patriarchal tradition had been confirmed by archeology. That was before the discoveries at Mari, which we have sketched briefly

---

[7] Hans Jakob Polotsky, *Manichäische Homilien* (Stuttgart: W. Kohlhammer, 1934).

above. Now we can speak even more emphatically, and with a wealth of additional detail. For example, the "city of Nahor" which plays a role next to Harran in the Patriarchal stories (Gen 24:10) turns up frequently along with Harran in the Mari documents from about 1700 B.C. The name of a prince of Mari, *Arriyuk*, is evidently the same as the "Arioch" of Gen 14. "Benjamin" often appears as a tribal name at Mari. And so on. Other parallels have come to light with G. Posener's publication of many new Egyptian texts cursing Palestinian chieftains of the late nineteenth century B.C.[8]

It is becoming increasingly clear that the accounts of the Patriarchs go back largely to early narrative poems transmitted orally into Israelite times and then written down in shortened prose paraphrases of the poetic originals. In no case are these Patriarchal stories mere reflections of the life of Israel in the Divided Monarchy, as used to be held by most literary critics; they actually do go back almost a thousand years to the Middle Bronze Age. Of course, in the process of oral transmission there has been a good deal of refraction and rearrangement of materials, with changed emphases and modernizations. These phenomena are characteristic of oral transmission of such materials, and they are more than balanced by the gain to the pedagogical and ethical content of the narratives. Written records of tribal warfare would be of less significance to the historian and of immeasurably less value to our day than the moving stories of Abraham, Jacob, and Joseph.

III

The recovery of the Ugaritic epics, briefly described above, provides us with many thousands of lines of Canaanite verse, antedating the time of Moses and the emergence of Israel as a people. These epics contain innumerable close parallels to the poetry of the Hebrew Bible, especially to the earliest poems but also in less measure to later biblical verse. The parallels are stylistic, grammatical, and verbal; they include whole verses, phrases, and single words. We find that the earliest poetry of the Bible abounds in verse forms which are characteristic of the Canaanite poems of Ugarit, such as the pattern of repetitive parallelism called *abc:abd* by H. L. Ginsberg, who was the first to recognize it. For example, in Ugaritic we have many such three-unit (tricolon) verses as the following, from the Epic of Danel (the Danel of the consonantal text of Ezek 14:14, etc.):

> *Ask for life,* O youth Aqhat,
>> *Ask for life,* and I will give (it) thee,
>>> Eternal life, and I will grant (it) to thee!

Compare this with a similar three-unit verse in the Baal Epic:

> *Behold thine enemies,* O Baal,
>> *Behold thine enemies* shalt thou crush,
>>> Behold thou shalt crush thy foes!

---

[8] Georges Posener, *Princes et pays d'Asie et de Nubie* (Brussels: Fondation égyptologique reine Élisabeth, 1940).

This tricolon has been preserved with only minor changes in wording and a major transformation in theological meaning in Ps 92:10:

> For behold thine enemies, O Yahweh,
>> For behold thine enemies shall perish,
>> All doers of evil shall be scattered!

Among far-reaching parallels in style we have no fewer than forty pairs of parallel synonyms documented from both biblical and Canaanite verse. All eighty words are the same. In view of the limited amount of Canaanite literature yet available to us and of the relatively late date of most biblical poetry which has been preserved, this similarity between the two literatures is very striking. We also have a great many close parallels in grammar. It is remarkable how many apparent anomalies in early Hebrew verse, which have been explained away or emended by scholars, turn out to be accurate reflections of Canaanite grammatical peculiarities which were forgotten long before the time of the Masoretes, who vocalized the consonantal Hebrew text of the Bible in the seventh to ninth centuries A.D. These grammatical peculiarities grow fewer and fewer in later Hebrew verse and are scarcely to be found at all in our latest biblical poetry.

With this new independent criterion for dating it becomes possible to push back the dates generally accepted for many early Hebrew poems. The Song of Deborah (Judg 5) has always been dated early by the great majority of scholars, but most emendations of its text by textual critics must now be discarded. However, the Song of Miriam (or of Moses, Exod 15), which resembles the Song of Deborah so closely in style and meter that they should never have been far separated in time, has usually been dated after the building of the Temple of Solomon, or even after the Exile. The key reason for such a late date has been verse 17, with its reference to "the mountain of thine inheritance, O Yahweh," which has quite naturally been referred to Mount Zion and the Temple. However, we have the very same expression used in the Canaanite Baal Epic, where Baal speaks of "the mountain of mine inheritance," referring to the partly terrestrial, partly celestial mountain where he resides in the far north. Biblical scholars had inferred long before the discovery of the Canaanite literature that ancient phraseology which applied originally to the cosmic mountain in the far north had been utilized in poetic descriptions of Zion. It now becomes absurd to use the verse as an argument for such an improbably late date of the Song of Miriam. This beautiful triumphal hymn, which may rightfully be termed the national anthem of ancient Israel, must now be pushed back to Israelite beginnings, substantially perhaps to the time of Moses in the thirteenth century B.C. The Oracles of Balaam (Num 22–24) also go back to the thirteenth century B.C., or perhaps in part to the following century. Similarly, the Blessings of Jacob (Gen 49) and of Moses (Deut 33) cannot be later than the eleventh century B.C.

In harmony with the earlier date which must be assigned to Pentateuchal poetry, we must date many of the Psalms back to early Israelite times. We find that early Psalms contain so much Canaanite material that they may safely be treated as Israelite adaptations of pre-Israelite hymns to Baal. Psalm 68 turns out to be a catalogue of early Israelite hymns and lyric poems, apparently all composed between the thirteenth and the tenth centuries and swarming with archaic expressions, only recently explained by Canaanite parallels. This Psalm has often been attributed to the Maccabean period (second century B.C.), in spite of the fact that the Jewish scholars who translated it into Greek in the same century did not understand it any better than the Masoretes a thousand years later. This is typical of the utter absurdity of much so-called "critical" work in the biblical field. A rapidly increasing number of scholars today deny any Maccabean Psalms and doubt whether any part of the Psalter is later than the fourth or even fifth century B.C.

IV

Until the Ugaritic tablets were published, it was impossible to make an effective contrast between the early faith of Israel and the religion of ancient Canaan, since we had scarcely any original Canaanite literature on which to base such a contrast. Before the discovery of the Ugaritic epics the present writer had emphasized that the leading Canaanite deities, such as Baal, were "high gods," not merely vegetation spirits or local deities. This was proved conclusively by the Ugaritic texts, where Baal plays a role closely comparable to that of the Homeric Zeus, who was "father of men and of gods" and whose authority was limited only by the boundaries of the world. The first scholar after the publication of the new material to stress the impossibility of the views of Wellhausen on the evolution of Israelite religious culture was, strangely enough, no conservative theologian, but a leading French agnostic and anticlerical, René Dussaud.[9]

The days when Yahweh was thought to have won a victory over Baal because he was chief god of a whole tribe, whereas Baal was merely a term designating a host of local deities, each ruling only in a single town and its vicinity, are over. We now know that the followers of Yahweh and of Baal both considered their own gods as cosmic in power; the main difference between them was that Baal was storm-god, head of a whole pantheon of deities, while Yahweh was sole God of the entire known universe, with no pantheon. The gods of Baal's pantheon included relatives and even foes; neither the gods nor the world were in general his creation. Yahweh, on the other hand, was creator of all that existed. This is not the place to describe the total breakdown of Wellhausenism under the impact of our new knowledge of antiquity; suffice it to say that no arguments have been brought against early Israelite monotheism that would not apply equally well (with appropriate changes in specific evidence) to postexilic Judaism. Nothing can alter the now certain fact that the gulf between the religions of Israel and of Canaan was as great as the resemblance between their material cultures and their poetic literatures.

---

[9] René Dussaud, *Les découvertes de Ras Shamra (Ugarit) et l'Ancien Testament* (Paris: P. Guethner, 1941).

V

The period of Old Testament history beginning with Joiachin in 598 B.C. and ending with Ezra and Nehemiah less than two centuries later, was regarded two generations ago as the cornerstone of Old Testament history. Then in 1895 and 1896 W. H. Kosters and C. C. Torrey began their onslaughts on postexilic history, followed by S. A. Cook and others.[10] Torrey started by denying the authenticity of the Ezra Memoirs and went on to reject that of the Book of Ezekiel and finally that of the Book of Jeremiah. Continuing with remorseless logic (given his totally inacceptable premises), he denied that there had been a thoroughgoing devastation of Judah and Jerusalem by the Chaldeans in the time of Nebuchadnezzar, that there had been any real Exile or Restoration, and that there was an Ezra. The figure of Nehemiah he regarded as obscure and unimportant.

In 1923, G. Hölscher, followed twenty years later by W. A. Irwin, with a train of scholars holding mediating positions, reduced Ezekiel, previously considered as the most solid foundation of the Wellhausen structure, to a tiny nucleus of allegedly authentic verses, all the rest of the book being treated as much later than the sixth century B.C.[11] Torrey, of course, rejected Ezekiel entirely.[12] The theological implications of these views are very extreme. Having eliminated this major series of crises in Old Testament history, the predictions of the Prophets are automatically nullified, with respect both to the coming doom and to the consequent Restoration of Israel. The Old Testament loses most of its majesty, and its meaning for our day is reduced immeasurably.

The views of these scholars have been categorically disproved by the archeological discoveries of the past twenty years. Excavation and surface exploration in Judah have proved that the towns of Judah were not only completely destroyed by the Chaldeans in their two invasions, but were not reoccupied for generations— often never again in history. This is solidly demonstrated by the evidence of pottery (which serves the archeologist as fossils serve the geologist in dating periods), confirmed by a steadily increasing number of inscriptions from the last years of the Kingdom of Judah. Vivid light is shed on these events by the Lachish Ostraca and other recently discovered documents.

For instance, several stamped jar handles bearing the name of "Eliakim, steward of YWKN," have been found in the ruins of the last occupation of two towns of

---

[10] Willem Hendrik Kosters, *Die Wiederherstellung Israels in der persischen Periode* (Heidelberg: J. Hörning, 1895); Charles Cutler Torrey, *The Composition and Historical Value of Ezra-Nehemiah* (Giessen, Germany: J. Ricker, 1896), and *Ezra Studies* (Chicago: University of Chicago Press, 1910); Stanley Arthur Cook, "The Inauguration of Judaism," in *Macedon, 401–301 B.C.* (Cambridge Ancient History 6; Cambridge: Cambridge University Press, 1927).

[11] Gustav Hölscher, *Hesekiel, der Dichter und das Buch* (Giessen, Germany: Töpelmann, 1924); William A. Irwin, *The Problem of Ezekiel* (Chicago: University of Chicago Press, 1943).

[12] Charles Cutler Torrey, *Pseudo-Ezekiel and the Original Prophecy* (New Haven: Yale University Press, 1930).

Judah before the final catastrophe. *YWKN* was at once identified with King Joiachin, in spite of certain apparent difficulties in the form of the name. A few years later (1939) E. F. Weidner published several ration lists of Nebuchadnezzar excavated by the Germans at Babylon, in which one of the recipients appears repeatedly (in the year 592, six years after Joiachin had been exiled to Babylon) as "Yawkin, king of Judah." It would be difficult to find more clear-cut evidence of the time of the destruction and the authenticity of Joiachin's exile in Babylon.[13] Incidentally, Torrey asserted that no Jewish *gardeners* can possibly have been taken as captives to Babylon—but we have in these same ration lists, among other captive Jews, a Jewish *gardener*! The attempt by Torrey and Irwin to show that there was no Jewish dispersion in Babylonia to which Ezekiel can have preached—assuming that he existed at all—has collapsed entirely. That neither language nor content of the Book of Ezekiel fits any period or place outside of the early sixth century B.C. and Babylonia, has been proved in detail by C. G. Howie (1950).[14]

If we turn to the Book of Ezra, recent discoveries have vindicated the authenticity of its official documents in the most striking way. Here again Torrey and others have insisted that the language of the book is late, dating from the third century B.C., after Alexander the Great. The publication of the fifth-century Elephantine Papyri (1904–1911) from a Jewish colony near Assuan in upper Egypt[15] had already made Torrey's position difficult, but subsequent discoveries by Mittwoch, Eilers, and others have dealt it the *coup de grâce*.[16] For example, Torrey insisted that certain words, among them *pithgama*, "matter, affair," were of Greek origin and could not, therefore, have been taken into biblical Aramaic before 330 B.C. In the last twenty years these very same words have turned up in Egyptian Aramaic and Babylonian cuneiform documents from the late fifth century, that is, from the very time of Ezra! The forced Greek etymologies which he proposed are now mere curiosities. The great ancient historian, Eduard Meyer, fifty-five years ago[17] insisted on the substantial authenticity of the Persian decrees and official letters preserved in Ezra; during the past twenty years strong additional evidence for them has been published by H. H. Schaeder and Elias Bickerman.[18] If it were practicable to quote from still

---

[13] Ernest Friedrich Weidner, "Jojachin, König von Juda in babylonischen Keilschrifttexten," in *Mélanges syriens offerts à René Dussaud* (Paris: Geuthner, 1939), 923–35.

[14] Carl Gordon Howie, *The Date and Composition of Ezekiel* (Philadelphia: Society of Biblical Literature, 1950).

[15] Archibald H. Sayce and A. E. Cowley, *Aramaic Papyri Discovered at Assuan* (London: A. Moring, 1906).

[16] Eugen Mittwoch, "Neue aramäische Urkunden aus der Zeit der Achämenidenherrschaft in Ägypten," *Monatschrift für Geschichte der Wissenschaften der Judentums*, Neue Folge 47 (1939): 93–100; Wilhelm Eilers, "Keilinschriften und antike Rechtsgeschichte," *Orientalistische Literaturzeitung* 34 (1931): 922–37, and "Iranische Beamtennamen in der keilschriftlichen Überlieferung, I," *Abhandlungen für die Kunde des Morgenlandes* 25 (1940): 71–201.

[17] Eduard Meyer, *Die Entstehung des Judenthums: Eine historische Untersuchung* (Halle: Max Niemeyer, 1896.)

[18] Hans Heinrich Schaeder, *Esra der Schreiber* (Beiträge zur historischen Theologie 5; Tübingen: J. C. B. Mohr, 1930); Elias Bickerman, "The Edict of Cyrus in Ezra 1," *Journal of Biblical Literature* 65 (1946): 247–75.

unpublished Aramaic documents from fifth-century Egypt, the weight of factual evidence would crush all opposition.

Archeological data have thus demonstrated the substantial originality of the Books of Jeremiah and Ezekiel, Ezra and Nehemiah, beyond doubt; they have confirmed the traditional picture of events, as well as their order. Of course, there are minor modifications; it is probable that Nehemiah preceded Ezra instead of following him, and it is certain that Nehemiah's foes, Sanballat and Tobiah, were not pagans and were regarded by some of their contemporaries as being as good, if not better, Jews than Nehemiah. The picture of more than 40,000 Babylonian Jews leaving soon after the Cyrus decree in order to return to the land of their fathers is quite unjustified by the facts of tradition and it has now become incredible. The Jews actually returned in smaller groups, and the census list in question belongs to the third quarter of the fifth century, a century after the Decree of Cyrus.

VI

Passing from the end of the Old Testament period to the New Testament, we immediately encounter the problem of the Gospel of John. Since the School of Tübingen in the first half of the nineteenth century and the Dutch School in the second half of the century, radical critics have placed John's Gospel about the middle of the second century A.D., or even a little later. There was a reaction over a generation ago against this extreme view, which is now excluded by striking finds of Greek papyrus fragments of the Gospel itself and of a secondary compilation based partly on it (both published in 1935), both of which must date before about A.D. 150. At present, however, it is safe to say that most "liberal" New Testament scholars date the Gospel between A.D. 90 and 130. Many insist with R. Bultmann on its alleged Gnostic background. All these scholars, even including many moderately conservative students, separate the Gospel from the authentic tradition which is believed to underlie the Synoptic Gospels, and treat it as an essentially apocryphal document of interest only to historians of later Christianity and systematic theologians.

There can, of course, be no doubt that the Gospel of John is largely independent of the Synoptic tradition and that early Christian tradition dated it later than it dated them. Nor can there be any doubt that the Gospel of John was a favorite book of many Gnostics, including particularly the Valentinians. Yet this is no more a reason for regarding the Gospel itself as coming from a Gnostic milieu than for treating Plato as a Gnostic because Valentine's metaphysics was strongly influenced by him.

But the recent discoveries of Gnostic books in Egypt have completely changed the picture with respect to Gnosticism. We now know that the Church Fathers did not appreciably exaggerate their accounts of Gnosticism, and that the gap between Christianity and any form of second-century Gnosticism was tremendous. The efforts of recent historians of religion to picture a Gnosticism which resembled the Gospel of John more closely than anything known from Patristic tradition have been nullified by the discoveries at Chenoboscium, briefly described above. And Bultmann's attempt to derive the thought of John's Gospel from the Mesopotamian Gnostics known as Mandeans[19] has been disproved by the demonstration of a late date for Mandeanism (fifth century A.D. and later) by E. Peterson, F. C. Burkitt, and H. Lietzmann.[20] The *coup de grâce* to the Mandean hypothesis came after the publication of three Manichean codices in 1933–1940, as described above. Yet there remains a faint suggestion of Gnostic ways of thinking in our Gospel, which will be discussed below.

A very important step forward in the historical interpretation of the Gospel of John was taken when several Semitic scholars recognized that the Greek of this Gospel reflects an Aramaic background. It is not the vernacular (*Koine*) Greek of the contemporary papyri discovered in Egypt, but a vernacular Greek with very strong Semitic coloring, both in vocabulary and in syntax. Few would go as far as C. C. Torrey, who insists that it is a *translation* from a written Aramaic original. But every scholar with comparable knowledge of both Greek and Aramaic has recognized the Aramaizing quality of the language.[21] Hence Torrey makes the Gospel earlier than the Synoptics, and he was followed in this respect by the late A. T. Olmstead, who maintained in his *Jesus in the Light of History* (1942) that the narratives of the Gospel were written *before* A.D. 40, while the "sermons" were later (though not as late as believed by other New Testament scholars).

In the writer's Pelican *Archeology of Palestine* (1949) he demonstrated with numerous examples that the references to places, persons, and things in John went back to before the First Jewish Revolt in A.D. 66–70, which ended with the destruction of Jerusalem and the exile of the Christians from Western Palestine. It becomes hypercritical to insist on a second-century date for material which goes back so clearly to Aramaic informants in Palestine before A.D. 70.

In 1945, Erwin Goodenough, Yale historian of religion and authority on Philo, the great Jewish contemporary of Paul, pointed out with great emphasis that there is nothing specifically Gnostic in John's Gospel. On the contrary, Goodenough held, it is "a primitive Gospel," going back to the very beginnings of Christianity. He pointed out that the currently accepted critical order, Paul's Epistles, the Synoptic Gospels, and John, does not do elementary justice to the fact that there is much more in common, in some respects, between Paul and John than between either of them and the Synoptics. Goodenough did not touch on the linguistic or archeological aspects of the question, but limited himself to ideas and their development.[22]

---

[19] Rudolph Bultmann, "Die Bedeutung der neuerschlossenen mandäischen und manichäischen Quellen für das Verständnis des Johannesevangeliums," *Zeitschrift für die neutestamentliche Wissenschaft* 24 (1925): 100–146.

[20] Hans Lietzmann, "Ein Beitrag zur Mandäerfrage," *Sitzungsberichte der preussischen Akademie der Wissenschaften: Philosophisch-historische Klasse* (1930): 596–608; Francis Crawford Burkitt, *Church and Gnosis* (Cambridge: Cambridge University Press, 1932).

[21] Charles Cutler Torrey, "The Aramaic Origin of the Fourth Gospel," *Harvard Theological Review* 16 (1923): 305–44.

[22] Erwin Goodenough, "John: A Primitive Gospel," *Journal of Biblical Literature* 64 (1945): 145–82.

There remained, however, a serious weakness in the position of Good-enough—there was no extant literature illustrating the climate of ideas assumed by him as antecedent to John's Gospel. Nor could the present writer's earlier position (*From the Stone Age to Christianity,* 1940) be directly confirmed, that there were proto-Gnostic influences behind John's Gospel, which, without being in any way specifically Gnostic, provided the soil in which Gnosticism could grow in the second half of the first century A.D.

With the publication of the Dead Sea Scrolls since 1948, this is entirely changed, and we now have remarkably close parallels to the conceptual imagery of John in the new Essene documents from the last century and a half before Jesus' ministry. To be sure, parallels had been noted in the earlier sectarian Jewish literature from intertestamental times, such as the Book of Jubilees, the Testaments of the Twelve Patriarchs, and Enoch, probably all dating in the main from the early decades of the second century B.C. But in our new scrolls we have much closer contacts with both John and Paul, especially with the former. Most striking is the simple cosmic dualism common to both: God against Satan; light against darkness; "truth, right," against "falsehood, deception, error"; "good, holy," against "evil, wicked"; "flesh" against "spirit," etc. On the other hand, the Gospel of John does not reflect the use of "mystery" and "knowledge" *(gnosis)* which is common to the Dead Sea Scrolls and to Paul. As A. D. Nock has lately shown, the use of these concepts in the New Testament has little in common with the conceptual world of the mystery religions or Gnosticism; it goes back to intertestamental literature.[23] The new scrolls confirm and illustrate Nock's demonstration.

In other words, the thought content of John's Gospel reflects the Jewish background of John the Baptist and Jesus, not that of later times. Sayings and deeds of Jesus, narratives and sermons are all of one piece and cannot be separated from the person of our Lord. To be sure, the order in which the memories of the Beloved Disciple were transmitted to posterity by a pupil or secretary is no longer historically exact, and the boundaries between happenings in the flesh and events in the spirit have sometimes been dissolved, but the Gospel of John carries us straight back to the heart of Jesus. No valid distinction between a suprahistorical Christ and a historical Jesus can be made on the basis of misleading historical assumptions, and there is no room for existentialist *Entmythologisierung* in the manner of Bultmann. There is no reason to date the Gospel after A.D. 90; it may be earlier.

VII

In conclusion we emphasize the fact that archeological discovery has been largely responsible for the recent revival of interest in biblical theology, because of the wealth of new material illustrating text and background of the Bible. As the

---

[23] Arthur Darby Nock, "The Vocabulary of the New Testament," *Journal of Biblical Literature* 52 (1933): 131–39.

reader will have seen from this article, new archeological material continues to pour in, compelling revision of all past approaches to both Old and New Testament religion. It becomes clearer each day that this rediscovery of the Bible often leads to a new evaluation of biblical faith, which strikingly resembles the orthodoxy of an earlier day. Neither an academic scholasticism nor an irresponsible neoorthodoxy must be allowed to divert our eyes from the living faith of the Bible.

CHAPTER 24

Disconnection between Ancient and Modern Worldviews: Langdon Gilkey (1919–)

Langdon Gilkey grew up in the academic environment of the University of Chicago, where his father served as a minister at a nearby Baptist church and later became the first dean of the University Chapel. For his own college education, Gilkey went to Harvard, where he majored in philosophy. During World War II, he spent almost five years in China, including a period of internment in a prison camp. Upon returning to America in 1945, Gilkey went to Union Theological Seminary in New York, where he studied under Reinhold Niebuhr. After teaching appointments at Vassar and Vanderbilt in the 1950s, Gilkey accepted a position at the University of Chicago in 1963, where he remained until his retirement in 1989.

Gilkey's theological interests have led him to produce influential works in a number of areas, including interfaith dialogue with Buddhism and assessment of Roman Catholicism. Probably his most noteworthy theological writing addresses the confrontation of religious faith with modern scientific thought. In particular, Gilkey has been concerned to explore how talking about God can be meaningful in a secular age. In this context, "secular" connotes a fundamental reliance on empirical criteria for meaning and validity applied to any claims of truth. But traditional religions such as Christianity developed categories of theological discourse in an age permeated by a deeply religious worldview. The problem is not new, of course, but it had generated a new approach from biblical theologians in the mid-twentieth century, and Gilkey addressed this approach as a philosopher of religion. Here a few words on the American biblical-theology movement are in order.

As historical criticism grew to dominate biblical interpretation in the nineteenth and twentieth centuries, the key questions emphasized the reconstruction, from all available sources, of the history and thought of ancient Israel and early Christianity. In this endeavor of historical science, it was established that, by and large, the elements of Israelite and Christian faith are not easily distinguishable from the general history of the ancient world. The notion that we have a uniquely revelatory history in the events of the Bible (the German term is *Heilsgeschichte*) is not demonstrable from the data of the text themselves but derives from the wishes or faith of the interpreter. Consequently, many Christian theologians of the later nineteenth and early twentieth centuries tended to shy away from traditional assertions about the supernatural, especially as it pertains to ideas of divine revelation. This tendency came to be known as theological liberalism.

The biblical-theology movement of the 1950s and 1960s developed as a reaction to the liberal alienation of the biblical text from theological vitality. Primarily an American intellectual phenomenon, this movement embraced historical criticism while seeking to construct a more biblically derived theology. Regarding the question of divine revelation, the approach generally taken in the biblical-theology movement was to contrast the mode of theologizing found in the Bible—centered on events that took place in history—with mythologizing from the phenomena of nature (as in ancient Israel's neighbors) or with philosophical doctrines (as in the pagan Greco-Roman world). The biblical writers testified to the revelation of God that took place in historical events, such as the deliverance of the Israelites from Egypt and the resurrection of Jesus. The very faith of ancient Israel and the early church, then, was understood as a matter of confessing and making known the saving acts of God. Biblical interpretation would require historical-critical effort to reconstruct as accurately as possible the historical events that gave birth to the community of God and sustained it. In the hands of biblical theologians, the results of rapidly advancing archaeological work in the Near East and comparative Semitics were applied to biblical studies in support of the uniqueness and historical basis of biblical faith. From such reconstruction, a basis for modern testimony to God's action in the world could be established.[1]

Like many Christian intellectuals of the mid-twentieth century, Gilkey was attracted by the attempt in biblical theology to bring the voice of the ancient biblical texts to the modern world. But as the selection here, "Cosmology, Ontology, and the Travail of Biblical Language," spells out, he was bothered by inconsistencies evident within the biblical-theology enterprise. These inconsistencies are symptomatic of a major characteristic of modern biblical interpretation: the problem of a modern worldview facing an ancient one. Although Gilkey does not write as a biblical exegete, the essay serves to critique clearly and insightfully a major trend in twentieth-century biblical interpretation in America.

For further information on Langdon Gilkey and the biblical-theology movement:

Childs, Brevard S. *Biblical Theology in Crisis.* Philadelphia: Westminster, 1970.
Gilkey, Langdon B. *The Theology of Langdon B. Gilkey: Systematic and Critical Studies.* Edited by K. A. Pasewark and J. B. Pool. Macon, Ga.: Mercer University Press, 2000.
Smart, James D. *The Past, Present, and Future of Biblical Theology.* Philadelphia: Westminster, 1979.
Wright, George E. *God Who Acts: Biblical Theology as Recital.* London: SCM Press, 1952.

---

[1] There were many more aspects to the twentieth-century biblical-theology movement. This brief review is restricted to the problem of revelation and history, since this is what Gilkey addresses in his essay.

"Cosmology, Ontology, and the Travail of Biblical Language"[2]

This is a paper on the intelligibility of some of the concepts of what we commonly call "biblical theology," or sometimes "the biblical point of view," or "the biblical faith." Although my remarks relate only to the Old Testament and at some points concern only two distinguished American representatives of the "biblical viewpoint," G. E. Wright and B. Anderson, the number of scholars of both testaments whose thoughts are based on the so-called "biblical view," and so who share the difficulties outlined below, is very great indeed. My paper stems not from a repudiation of that theological point of view. Speaking personally, I share it, and each time I theologize I use its main categories; but I find myself confused about it when I ponder it critically, and this paper organizes and states rather than resolves that confusion.

My own confusion results from what I feel to be the basic posture, and problem, of contemporary theology: it is half liberal and modern, on the one hand, and half biblical and orthodox, on the other, i.e., its world view or cosmology is modern, while its theological language is biblical and orthodox. Since this posture in two different worlds is the source of the difficulties and ambiguities which exist in current biblical theology, I had best begin with its elucidation.

Our problem begins with the liberal repudiation of orthodoxy. One facet of this repudiation was the rejection of the category "revelation through the special activity of God," what we now call "special revelation," "Heilsgeschichte," [salvation history] or popularly "the mighty acts of God." Orthodoxy, taking the Bible literally, had seen this special activity in the simple biblical twofold pattern of wondrous events (e.g., unexpected children, marvelous victories in battle, pillars of fire, etc.), on the one hand, and, on the other hand, a divine voice that spoke actual words to Abraham, to Moses, and to their prophetic followers. This orthodox view of the divine self-manifestation through special events and actual voices offended the liberal mind on two distinct grounds: (1) In understanding God's acts and speech literally and univocally, the orthodox belief in special revelation denied the reign of causal law in the phenomenal realm of space and time, or at least denied that that reign of law had obtained in biblical days. To the liberals, therefore, this orthodox view of revelation represented a primitive, prescientific form of religion and should be modernized. (2) Special revelation denied that ultimately significant religious truth is universally available to mankind, or at least in continuity with experiences universally shared by all men. On these two grounds of causal order and universality, liberalism reinterpreted the concept of revelation: God's acts ceased to be special, particular, and concerned with phenomenal reality (for example, the stopping of the sun, a visible pillar of fire, and audible voices). Rather, the divine activity became the

---

[2] Langdon Gilkey, "Cosmology, Ontology, and the Travail of Biblical Language," *Journal of Religion* 41 (1961): 194–205. Copyright 1961 by the University of Chicago. Used with permission.

continual, creative, immanent activity of God, an activity which worked through the natural order and which could therefore be apprehended in universal human experiences of dependence, of harmony, and of value—experiences which in turn issued in developed religious feeling and religious consciousness. The demands both of world order and of universality were thus met by this liberal reconstruction of religion: The immanent divine activity was now consistent throughout experience, and whatever special activity there was in religious knowledge was located subjectively in the uniquely gifted religious leader or culture which possessed deeper insight and so discovered deeper religious truth.

Against this reduction of God's activity to his general influence and of revelation to subjective human insight, neo-orthodoxy, and with it biblical theology, reacted violently. For them, revelation was not a subjective human creation but an objective divine activity; God was not an inference from religious experience but he who acts in special events. And Hebrew religion was not the result of human religious genius or insight into the consistent continuity of God's activity; rather, biblical religion was the response of faith to and the recital of the "mighty acts of God." Both contemporary systematic and contemporary biblical theology are in agreed opposition to liberalism in emphasizing that revelation is not a possibility of universal human experience but comes through the objective, prior, self-revelation of God in special events in response to which faith and witness arise. Whether or not this self-understanding is accurate is a question we shall try to answer.

Contemporary systematic and biblical theology have, however, often failed to note that in repudiating the liberal emphasis on the universal and immanent as against the special and objective activity of God, they have *not* repudiated the liberal insistence on the causal continuum of space-time experience. Thus contemporary theology does not expect, nor does it speak of, wondrous divine events on the surface of natural and historical life. The causal nexus in space and time which Enlightenment science and philosophy introduced into the Western mind and which was assumed by liberalism is also assumed by modern theologians and scholars; since they participate in the modern world of science both intellectually and existentially, they can scarcely do anything else.

Now this assumption of a causal order among phenomenal events, and therefore of the authority of the scientific interpretation of observable events, makes a great difference to the validity one assigns to biblical narratives and so to the way one understands their meaning. Suddenly a vast panoply of divine deeds and events recorded in Scripture are no longer regarded as having actually happened. Not only, for example, do the six days of creation, the historical fall in Eden, and the flood seem to us historically untrue [see Gen 1, 3, 6–9], but even more the majority of divine deeds in the biblical history of the Hebrew people become what we choose to call symbols rather than plain old historical facts. To mention only a few: Abraham's unexpected child [see Gen 21]; the many divine visitations; the words and directions to the patriarchs [see Gen 22]; the plagues visited on the Egyptians [see Exod 7–12]; the pillar of fire [see Exod 13:20–22]; the parting of the seas [see Exod 14:19–31]; the verbal deliverance of covenantal law on Sinai [see Exod 19–24:11]; the strategic and logistic help in the conquest; the audible voice heard by the prophets; and so on—all these "acts" vanish from the plane of historical reality and enter the never-never land of "religious interpretation" by the Hebrew people. Therefore when we read what the Old Testament seems to say God did, or what precritical commentators said God did (see Calvin), and then look at a modern interpretation of what God did in biblical times, we find a tremendous difference: the wonder events and the verbal divine commentaries, commands, and promises are gone. Whatever the Hebrews believed, we believe that the biblical people lived in the same causal continuum of space and time in which we live, and so one in which no divine wonders transpired and no divine voices were heard. Nor do we believe, incidentally, that God could have done or commanded certain "unethical" deeds like destroying Sodom and Gomorrah [see Gen 18–19] or commanding the murder of the Amalekites [see Deut 25:17–19]. The modern assumption of the world order has stripped bare our view of the biblical history of all the divine deeds observable on the surface of history, as our modern humanitarian ethical view has stripped the biblical God of most of his mystery and offensiveness.

Put in the language of contemporary semantic discussion, both the biblical and the orthodox understanding of theological language was univocal. That is, when God was said to have "acted," it was believed that he had performed an observable act in space and time so that he functioned as does any secondary cause; and when he was said to have "spoken," it was believed that an audible voice was heard by the person addressed. In other words, the words "act" and "speak" were used in the same sense of God as of men. We deny this univocal understanding of theological words. To us, theological verbs such as "to act," "to work," "to do," "to speak," "to reveal," etc., have no longer the literal meaning of observable actions in space and time or of voices in the air. The denial of wonders and voices has thus shifted our theological language from the univocal to the analogical. Our problem is, therefore, twofold: (a) We have not realized that this crucial shift has taken place, and so we think we are merely speaking the biblical language because we use the same words. We do use these words, but we use them analogically rather than univocally, and these are vastly different usages. (b) Unless one knows in some sense what the analogy means, how the analogy is being used, and what it points to, an analogy is empty and unintelligible; that is, it becomes equivocal language. This is the crux of our present difficulty; let us now return to biblical theology to try to show just how serious it is.

We have said that there is a vast difference between ourselves and the Bible concerning cosmology and so concerning the concrete character of the divine activity in history and that this difference has changed biblical language from a univocal to an analogical form. If, then, this difference is there, what effect has it had on the way we understand the narratives of Scripture, filled as they undoubtedly are with divine wonders and the divine voice? A perusal of such commentators as Wright and Anderson will reveal that, generally speaking, there has been a radical reinterpretation of these narratives, a reinterpretation that has been threefold. First, the divine activity called the "mighty deeds of God" is now restricted to one crucial event, the Exodus-covenant complex of occurrence. Whatever else God may not have done, we say, here he really acted in the history of the Hebrew people, and so here their faith was born and given its form.

Second, the vast panoply of wonder and voice events that preceded the Exodus-covenant event, in effect the patriarchal narratives, are now taken to be Hebrew interpretations of their own historical past based on the faith gained at the Exodus. For us, then, these narratives represent not so much *histories* of what God actually did and said as *parables* expressive of the faith the post-Exodus Jews had, namely, belief in a God who was active, did deeds, spoke promises and commands, and so on. Third, the biblical accounts of the post-Exodus life—for example, the proclamation and codification of the law, the conquest, and the prophetic movement—are understood as the covenant people's interpretation through their Exodus faith of their continuing life and history. Having known God at the Exodus event, they were able now to understand his relation to them in terms of free covenant and law and to see his hand in the movement of their subsequent history. In sum, therefore, we may say that for modern biblical theology the Bible is no longer so much a book containing a description of God's actual acts and words as it is a book containing Hebrew interpretations, "creative interpretations" as we call them, which, like the parable of Jonah, tell stories of God's deeds and man's response to express the theological beliefs of Hebrew religion. Thus the Bible is a book descriptive not of the acts of God but of Hebrew religion. And though God is the subject of all the verbs of the Bible, Hebrew religious faith and Hebrew minds provide the subjects of all the verbs in modern books on the meaning of the Bible. Incidentally, we avoid admitting these perennial human subjects by putting our verbs in the passive voice: "was seen to be," "was believed to be," etc. For us, then, the Bible is a book of the acts Hebrews believed God might have done and the words he might have said had he done and said them—but of course we recognize he did not. The difference between this view of the Bible as a parable illustrative of Hebrew religious faith and the view of the Bible as a direct narrative of God's actual deeds and words is so vast that it scarcely needs comment. It makes us wonder, despite ourselves, what, in fact, do we moderns think God *did* in the centuries preceding the incarnation; what *were* his mighty acts?

The nub of this problem is the fact that, while the object of biblical recital is God's acts, the object of biblical theological inquiry is biblical faith—that is to say, biblical theology is, like liberalism, a study of Hebrew religion. Thus while the language of biblical theology is God-centered, the whole is included within gigantic parentheses marked "human religion." This means that biblical theology is fundamentally liberal in form and that without translation it provides an impossible vehicle for biblical-theological confession, since it is itself a witness to Hebrew religion and not to the real acts of God. For of course the real action and revelation of God must precede and be outside these great parentheses of Hebrew faith if the content of that faith—as a response to God's acts—be not self-contradictory and illusory, beguiling but untrue, like the poetic religion in Santayana's naturalism.

As we noted, most modern Old Testament commentators reduce the mighty acts of God to one event: the Exodus-covenant event. Let us, therefore, look at our

understanding of this event, for around it center the problems we see in biblical theology. Here, we are told, God acted, and in so doing, he revealed himself to the Hebrew people and established his covenant relation to them. Since current biblical
theology is, like most contemporary theology, passionately opposed to conceptions
of God based on natural theology or on general religious experience, we may assume that before this initial divine deed there was no valid knowledge of God at all:
if knowledge of God is based only on his revelatory acts, then prior to those acts he
must have been quite unknown. Exodus-Sinai, then, is the pivotal point of biblical
religion.

Now this means that the Exodus event has a confessional as well as a historical
interest for us. The question of what God did at Sinai is, in other words, not only a
question for the scholar of Semitic religion and theology, it is even more a question
for the contemporary believer who wishes to make his witness today to the acts of
God in history; and so it poses a question for the systematic theologian who wishes
today to understand God as the Lord who acted there. We are thus not asking
merely the historical question about what the Hebrews believed or said God did—
that is a question for the scholar of the history of religions, Semitic branch. Rather,
we are asking the systematic question, that is, we are seeking to state in faith what *we*
believe God actually did. For, as biblical scholars have reminded us, a religious confession that is biblical is a direct recital of God's acts, not a recital of someone else's
belief, even if it be a recital of a Hebrew recitation. If, therefore, Christian theology is
to be the recitation in faith of God's mighty acts, it must be composed of confessional and systematic statements of the form: "We believe that God did so and so,"
and not composed of statements of biblical theology of the form: "The Hebrews believed that God did so and so."

If we had asked an orthodox theologian like Calvin this confessional and systematic question: "What do you believe God did at the Exodus?" he would have
given us a clear answer. "Look at the book of Exodus," he would have answered,
"and see what it says that God did." And in his commentary he recites that deed of
God just as it appears on the pages of Scripture; that is, his confessional understanding of the event includes the divine call heard by Moses [see Exod 3–4], all the
plagues [see Exod 7–12], the pillar of fire [see Exod 13:20–22], the parting of the seas
[see Exod 14:21–30], the lordly voice booming forth from Sinai, and the divinely
proclaimed promises and legal conditions of the covenant [see Exod 19–24:11]. At
the Reformation, therefore, statements in biblical theology and in systematic theology coalesced because the theologian's understanding of what God did was drawn
with no change from the simple narratives of Scripture, and because the verbs of the
Bible were thus interpreted univocally throughout. Thus in Reformation theology, if
anywhere, the Bible "speaks its own language" or "speaks for itself" with a minimum
of theological mediation.

When, however, one asks Professors Wright or Anderson the systematic or
confessional question: "What did God actually do in the Exodus-Sinai event, what
actually happened there?" the answer is not only vastly different from the scriptural
and orthodox accounts, but, in fact, it is extremely elusive to discover. Strangely

enough, neither one gives the questions "What did God *really* do?" "What *was* his mighty act?" much attention. First of all they deny that there was any miraculous character to the event, since "the Hebrews knew no miracles." They assert, therefore, that outwardly the event was indistinguishable from other events,[3] revelation to the Hebrews always being dependent on faith. And finally they assert that probably there was a perfectly natural explanation of the objective side of the event. As Anderson puts it, the rescue of the Hebrews resulted "probably from an East wind blowing over the Reed Sea" ;[4] and in a single sentence Wright makes one mysterious reference to "certain experiences that took place at the Holy mountain . . . which formed the people into a nation."[5] Considering that each writer clearly feels that the Bible is about the real acts of God, that our religion is founded thereon, and that Christian theology must recite these acts of God, this unconcern with the character of the one act that God is believed actually to have done is surprising.

In any case, this understanding of the event illustrates the uneasy posture in two worlds of current biblical theology and thus its confusion about two types of theological language. When modern biblical writers speak *theologically* of the revelatory event, their attention focuses on the prior and objective event, and they speak in the biblical and orthodox terms of a God who speaks and acts, of divine initiation and human response, and of revelation through mighty, divine deeds in history. When, however, they function as *scientific* historians or archeologists and ask what actually happened, they speak of that same prior event in purely naturalistic terms as "an ordinary though unusual event," or as "an East wind blowing over the Reed Sea." Thus they repudiate all the concrete elements that in the biblical account made the event itself unique and so gave content to their theological concept of a special divine deed. In other words, they continue to use the biblical and orthodox theological language of divine activity and speech, but they have dispensed with the wonders and voices that gave univocal meaning, and thus content, to the theological words "God acts" and "God speaks."

This dual posture in both biblical orthodoxy and modern cosmology, and the consequent rejection of univocal meanings for our theological phrases, raises our first question: "Are the main words and categories in biblical theology meaningful?" If they are no longer used univocally to mean observable deeds and audible voices, do they have any intelligible content? If they are in fact being used as analogies (God acts, but not as men act; God speaks, but not with an audible voice), do we have any idea at all to what sort of deed or communication these analogies refer? Or are they just serious-sounding, biblical-sounding, and theological-sounding words to which we can, if pressed, assign no meaning? Note I am not making the empiricist or positivist demand that we give a naturalistic, empirically verifiable meaning to these theological words, a meaning outside the context of faith and commitment. I am asking for a confessional-theological meaning, that is, a meaning based on thought

---

[3] G. E. Wright, *Books of the Acts of God* (Garden City, N.Y.: Doubleday, 1959), p. 18.—Gilkey
[4] B. Anderson, *Understanding the Old Testament* (Englewood Cliffs, N.J.: Prentice-Hall, 1957), 47–49.—Gilkey
[5] Wright, *Acts of God*, 86.—Gilkey

about our faith concerning what we mean by these affirmations of faith. The two affirmations I especially wish to consider are, first, "God has acted mightily and specially in history for our salvation, and so God is he who acts in history." And second,
"Our knowledge of God is based not on our discovery of him but on God's revelation of himself in historical events." My point is that, when we analyze what we
mean by these theological phrases, we can give no concrete or specifiable content so
that our analogies at present are empty and meaningless. The result is that, when we
push the analysis of these analogical words further, we find that what we actually
mean by them contradicts the intent of these theological phrases.

Let us take the category of "mighty act" first. Perhaps the most important theological affirmation that modern biblical theology draws from the Scripture is that
God is he who acts, meaning by this that God does unique and special actions in history. And yet when we ask: "All right, what has he done?" no answer can apparently
be given. Most of the acts recorded in Scripture turn out to be "interpretations by
Hebrew faith," and we are sure that they, like the miracles of the Buddha, did not really happen at all. And the one remaining objective act, the Exodus, becomes on
analysis "the East wind blowing over the Reed Sea," that is, an event which is objectively or ontologically of the same class as any other event in space and time. Now if
this event is validly to be called a mighty act of God, an event in which he really did
something special—as opposed to our just believing he did, which would be religious subjectivism and metaphysical naturalism—then, ontologically, this must in
some sense be more than an ordinary run-of-the-mill event. It may be
epistemologically indistinguishable from other events to those without faith, but for
those of faith it must be objectively or ontologically different from other events. Otherwise, there is no mighty act, but only our belief in it, and God is the God who in
fact does not act. And then our theological analogies of "act" and "deed" have no
referent, and so no meaning. But in current biblical theology such an ontologically
special character to the event, a special character known perhaps only by faith but
really "out there" nevertheless, is neither specified nor specifiable. For in the Bible itself that special character was understood to be the very wonders and voices which
we have rejected, and nothing has appeared in modern biblical thought to take their
place. Only an ontology of events specifying what God's relation to ordinary events
is like, and thus what his relation to special events might be, could fill the now empty
analogy of mighty acts, void since the denial of the miraculous.

Meanwhile, in contemporary biblical theology, which dares to stray into the
forbidden precincts of cosmology and ontology only far enough to deny miracles, all
that can be said about the event leaves the analogy of the mighty act quite empty.
We deny the miraculous character of the event and say its cause was merely an East
wind, and then we point to the unusual response of Hebrew faith. For, biblical theology, that which remains special about the event, therefore, is only its subjective result, namely, the faith response. But if we then ask what this Hebrew response was
to, what God did, we are offered merely an objectively natural event. But this means
merely that the Hebrews, as a religious people, were unusual; it does not mean that
the event to which they responded was unusual. One can only conclude, therefore,
that the mighty act of God is not his objective activity in history but only his inward

incitement of a religious response to an ordinary event within the space-time continuum. If this is what we mean, then clearly we have left the theological framework of "mighty act with faith response" and returned to Schleiermacher's liberalism, in which God's general activity is consistent throughout the continuum of space-time events and in which special religious feeling apprehends the presence of God in and through ordinary finite events. Thus our theological analogy of the mighty act seems to have no specifiable referent or meaning: like the examples of God's speaking, the only case turns out on analysis to be an example, not of God's activity at all, but of Hebrew insight based on their religious experience.

A similar problem arises when we ask what is meant by "revelation" in a modern mighty acts theology. The correlation of ordinary event and faith response is basic for contemporary theology: no event, we say, becomes revelatory (i.e., is known to be revelatory) unless faith sees in it the work of God. Now this correlation of ordinary event with discerning faith is intelligible enough once the covenant relation between God and his people has been established: then God is already known, faith has already arisen, and so God's work can be seen by faith in the outwardly ordinary events of Hebrew existence. But can the rule that revelatory events are only discerned by faith be equally applied to the event in which faith takes its origin? Can it, in other words, provide a theological understanding of *originating* revelation, that is, of God's original self-manifestation to man, in which man does not discern an already known God but in which God reveals himself to men who know nothing of him? Certainly it is logical to contend that faith cannot be presupposed in the event which purportedly effects the origination of faith.

When we consider the description that biblical theology makes of the origination of faith, moreover, the problems in this view seem vast indeed. Theologically it is asserted that God is not known through general, natural, historical, or inward experience. Thus presumably the Hebrews fled from Egypt uncognizant of God, having in their minds no concepts at all of the transcendent, active, covenant deity of later Hebrew religion. How, then, did they come to know this God? The answer of contemporary theology, of course, is that at this point the East wind over the Red Sea rescued the Hebrew people from the Egyptians, and so, according to Wright, their faith arose as the only assumption that could make sense of this great stroke of good fortune: "They did not have the power themselves (to effect the rescue); there was only one explanation available to them. That was the assumption that a great God had seen their afflictions, had taken pity on them. . . ."[6] Thus Hebrew faith is here presented as a human hypothesis, a religious assumption arising out of intuition and insight into the meaning of an unusual and crucial experience.

One can only wonder at this statement. First of all in what sense can one speak of *revelation* here? Is this not a remarkably clear example of natural religion or natural theology? The origination of Hebrew faith is explained as a religious assumption based on an unusual event but one which was admittedly consistent with, of the

---

[6] Wright, *Acts of God*, 73. —Gilkey

same order as, other events within the nature-history continuum. In what way does this faith come from God and what he has done rather than from man and what he has discovered, or even just poetically imagined? It seems to be only the religious insight and imagination of the Jews that has created and developed this monotheistic assumption out of the twists and turns of their historical experience. And second, why was there "only one explanation available" to them? Why was this response so inevitably tied with this event as to make us feel that the response was revealed in the event? Why could not the Hebrews have come to believe in a god of the East Wind, or a benevolent Fate, or any of the thousands of deities of unusual events that human religion has created? Surely on neo-orthodox principles, the theological concept or religious assumption *least* available to the imagination of men who knew not God was that of the transcendent, covenant God of history—exactly the assumption now called "inevitable" when an East wind had rescued them.

Furthermore, we should recall that for biblical theology the entire meaning of the concept of revelation through divine activity rather than through subjective experience or insight hangs on this one act of divine revelation. Thus the admission at this vital point that Hebrew faith was a daring human hypothesis based on a natural but unusual event is very puzzling. For it indicates that despite our flowery theological language, our actual understanding of Hebrew religion remains inclosed within liberal categories. When we are asked about what actually happened, and how revelation actually occurred, all we can say is that in the continuum of the natural order an unusual event rescued the Hebrews from a sad fate; from this they concluded there must be somewhere a great God who loved them; thus they interpreted their own past in terms of his dealings with them and created all the other familiar characteristics of Hebrew religion: covenant, law, and prophecy. This understanding of Hebrew religion is strictly "liberal": it pictures reality as a consistent world order and religious truth as a human interpretation based on religious experience. And yet at the same time, having castigated the liberals, who at least knew what their fundamental theological principles were, we proclaim that our real categories are orthodox: God acts, God speaks, and God reveals. Furthermore, we dodge all criticism by insisting that, because biblical and Christian ideas of God are "revealed," they are, unlike the assumptions and hypotheses of culture and of other religions, beyond inspection by the philosophical and moral criteria of man's general experience.

What has happened is clear: because of our modern cosmology, we have stripped what we regard as "the biblical point of view" of all its wonders and voices. This in turn has emptied the Bible's theological categories of divine deeds and divine revelations of all their univocal meaning, and we have made no effort to understand what these categories might mean as analogies. Thus, when we have sought to understand Hebrew religion, we have unconsciously fallen back on the liberal assumptions that do make some sense to us. What we desperately need is a theological ontology that will put intelligible and credible meanings into our analogical categories of divine deeds and of divine self-manifestation through events.

Our point can perhaps be summarized by saying that, without such an ontological basis, the language of biblical theology is neither univocal nor analogical but equivocal, and so it remains empty, abstract, and self-contradictory. It is empty and abstract because it can provide us with no concrete cases. We say the biblical God acts, but we can give neither concrete examples nor an analogical description; we say he speaks, and no illustrative dialogues can be specified. What has happened is that, as modern men perusing the Scriptures, we have rejected as invalid all the innumerable cases of God's acting and speaking; but as neo-orthodox men looking for a word from the Bible, we have induced from all these cases the theological generalization that God is he who acts and speaks. This general truth about God we then assert while denying all the particular cases on the basis of which the generalization was first made. Consequently, biblical theology is left with a set of theological abstractions, more abstract than the dogmas of scholasticism, for these are concepts with no known concreteness. Finally, our language is self-contradictory because, while we use the language of orthodoxy, what we really mean is concepts and explanations more appropriate to liberal religion. For if there is any middle ground between the observable deed and the audible dialogue which we reject, and what the liberals used to call religious experience and religious insight, then it has not yet been spelled out.

In the cases both of the mighty act of God and of the speech of God, such a spelling-out is an enterprise in philosophical theology. While certainly this enterprise cannot be unbiblical, it must at least be ontological and philosophical enough to provide theological meaning to our biblical analogies of divine deeds and words, since today we have abandoned the univocal, literal meanings of these words. One example may illustrate. Commenting on the "biblical view," Wright says: "He [God] is to be known by what he has done and said, by what he is now doing and saying; and he is known when we do what he commands us to do."[7] Unless we can give some analogical meaning to these concepts "do," "say," and "command," we are unable to make any confessional sense at all of this sentence, since every actual case of doing, saying, or commanding referred to in the Scripture has for us vanished into subjective Hebrew religious experience and interpretation. One might almost conclude that without a theological ontology, biblical theology is in danger of becoming a version of Santayana's poetic view of religion, in which believing man paints the objective flux of matter in the pretty subjective pictures of religious language and myth.

Two changes in our thinking can, I believe, rescue us from these dilemmas. First of all, biblical theology must take cosmology and ontology more seriously. Despite the undeniable but irrelevant fact that the Hebrews did not think much about cosmology, cosmology does make a difference in hermeneutics. When we say "God acts," we mean something different cosmologically than the writers of JED and P,[8] or even than Calvin, did. Thus the modern discipline of "biblical theology" is more tricky than we perhaps assumed when we thought we could just lift out theological abstractions (God speaks, God acts) from the narratives of Scripture and, calling

---

[7] Wright, *Acts of God*, 32. —Gilkey
[8] These letters are the sigla that scholars, since the middle of the nineteenth century, have used to designate authors or redactors of the varying materials in the Pentateuch.

them "the biblical point of view," act as if they were the only theology we needed. If in doing this we pretend that we are "just letting the Bible speak for itself," we are fooling no one but ourselves. Actually we are translating the biblical view into our own, at least in rejecting its concrete content of wonders and voices and so changing these categories from univocal concepts to empty analogies. But we have done this translating without being aware of the change we have made and thus without thinking out the problems in which this shift in cosmology and the resultant translation of biblical language involve us. Hence the abstractness and self-contradictory character of our categories in present "biblical theology." To speak the biblical word in a contemporary setting is a difficult *theological* task as well as a difficult existential task.

This means in turn that two very different enterprises must be distinguished in Christian theology, for they cannot be confused without fatal results. First there is the job of stating what the biblical writers meant to say, a statement couched in the Bible's own terms, cosmological, historical, and theological. This is "biblical theology," and its goal is to find what the Bible truly says—whether what in specific instances the Bible says seems to us in fact to be true or not. Then there is the other task of stating what that Word might mean for us today, what *we* believe God actually to have done. This is confessional and systematic theology, and its object is what *we* believe the truth about God and about what he has done to be. To use Wright's language, we must distinguish between *Hebrew* recital (biblical theology) and *our* recital (confessional or systematic theology) if our confessions are to make any sense at all. To confuse the two, and to try to make a study of what the biblical writers said also and at the same time an attempt to say what we believe to be true about God, is fatal and leads to the kind of confusions we have outlined.

Second, it is clear that throughout this paper our central problem has been that, in the shift of cosmology from ancient to modern, fundamental theological concepts have so changed their meaning as almost to have lost all reference. The phrases "God acts" and "God speaks," whatever they may ultimately mean to us, do not signify the wonders and voices of ancient days. As we have seen, it is no good repeating the abstract verbs "to act" and "to speak," if we have no intelligible referents with which to replace the vanished wonders and voices; and if we use these categories as analogies without any discussion of what we mean by them, we contradict ourselves over and over. When we use the analogies "mighty act," "unique revelatory event," or "God speaks to his people," therefore, we must also try to understand what we might mean in systematic theology by the general activity of God. Unless we have some conception of how God acts in ordinary events, we can hardly know what our analogical words mean when we say: "He acts uniquely in this event" or "this event is a special divine deed." Thus if we are to give content to the biblical analogy of a mighty act, and so to our theological concepts of special revelation and salvation, we must also have some understanding of the relation of God to general experience, which is the subject of philosophical theology. Put in terms of doctrines, this means that God's special activity is logically connected with his providential activity in general historical experience, and an understanding of the one assumes a concurrent inquiry into the other. For this reason, while the dependence of systematic and philosophical theology on biblical theology has long been recognized and is obvious, the dependence of an intelligible theology that is biblical on the cosmological and ontological inquiries of believing men, while now less universally accepted, is nonetheless real. There is no primary discipline in the life of the church, for all of us—biblical scholars and theologians—live and think in the present and look for the truth in documents from the past. And for all of us, a contemporary understanding of ancient Scriptures depends as much on a careful analysis of our present presuppositions as it does on being learned in the religion and faith of the past.

CHAPTER 25

Salvation History and Modern Historiography: Christian Hartlich (ca. 1952–1978)

S ince the seventeenth century, learned interpretation of the Bible has been dominated by historical concerns, asking the sorts of questions modern scholars pose to any ancient writings: What historical person authored this text? What sources were used? When did the events reported in the text occur relative to their being reported? How reliable is the reporting? Which of the reported events can be established as having actually happened? The results of such historical-critical investigations were often negative, as fewer and fewer of the events attested in the Bible could be accepted as historical fact according to modern standards. Several selections in our anthology represent this historical mind-set as it has been applied to Scripture. We have also noted Langdon Gilkey's (and, long before him, Baruch Spanoza's) dissatisfaction with some attempts to maintain faith in Scripture's historical references. The determination of historical truth in the Bible is a central preoccupation of modern biblical interpretation. How is theological reading or preaching of Scripture possible in the light of the historian's negative conclusions?

One response, advocated by the more conservative wings of Jewish and Christian communities, has been simply to deny the validity of historical-critical methodologies altogether when they are applied to Scripture. These communities have sometimes regarded also other areas of scientific research, such as evolutionary biology or paleogeology, with similar suspicion inasmuch as scientific reconstruction of the very ancient state of the earth is often at odds with a literal historical reading of the Bible. Other responses include attempts by some biblical scholars to demonstrate a basic historical reliability in the Bible without pressing for the accuracy of every detail.

But an answer of a different kind, and very influential, came from neoorthodox Christian theologians. The most famous was the Swiss theologian Karl Barth (1886–1968). Historical-critical investigation of the Bible posed no problem for Barth except when it is elevated to the primary place in biblical interpretation. Accurate historical understanding is necessary but insufficient for what the Scriptures—unique among all other writings—exist to do, for the Scriptures are among us to impart not historical knowledge but faith.[1]

---

[1] See Karl Barth, "The Strange New World within the Bible," in *The Word of God and the Word of Man* (trans. D. Horton; [Boston]: Pilgrim, 1928), 28–50.

For Christian theology and existence, the Bible serves as a sort of gateway into a "strange new world" where the objectivity of *human speech about God* (the object of scientific inquiry) is secondary to the subjectivity of *divine speech addressing humans* (inaccessible to scientific inquiry). Scientifically intelligible historical reconstructions of what actually happened in biblical history cannot take center stage for the theological interpretation of Scripture, as they cannot trigger faith that will accept the grace that God extends for salvation. This is because scientific historiography is rooted in the program of modern epistemology launched in the seventeenth century by René Descartes, which operates according to a methodology of doubt.

An exceptionally clear exposition of this very point, but from a different perspective, was written by Christian Hartlich. Trained in Germany at Tübingen and Leipzig in theology and philosophy, Hartlich is known for his work in the philosophy of history and has written on the origins of modern scientific concepts of myth. In 1978 he published an essay explaining the bases for scientific assessment of historical sources and the implications of such assessment for theological reading of the Bible.[2]

For further information on historical science and faith in the Bible:

Miller, J. Maxwell. *The Old Testament and the Historian.* Philadelphia: Fortress, 1976.

Minear, Paul S. *The Bible and the Historian: Breaking the Silence about God in Biblical Studies.* Nashville: Abingdon, 2002.

Van Harvey, A. *The Historian and the Believer: The Morality of Historical Knowledge and Christian Belief.* Champaign: University of Illinois Press, 1996.

---

[2] Christian Hartlich, "Historisch-kritische Methode in ihrer Anwendung auf Geschehnisaussagen der Hl. Schrift," *Zeitschrift für Theologie und Kirche* 75 (1978): 467–84.

Historical-Critical Method in Its Application to Statements Concerning Events in the Holy Scriptures[3]

In present day theology—in the exegetical disciplines as well as dogmatics—one encounters a profound uncertainty about the validity of the historical-critical method that is connected with its application to statements concerning events in the Holy Scriptures. Alongside the methodologically uncertain and unfinished treatment of all other miracle stories, the interest of research focuses on the question whether and to what extent the historical-critical method is competent to make a judgment with regard to the central miracle of Christianity, the affirmation of the resurrection of Jesus as an event that really took place. Positions have recently been taken on this subject in numerous theological publications—with the prevailing tendency, in spite of the diversity of arguments, to protect the ontic primacy of Jesus affirmed by his resurrection, which elevates him above all other creatures, against historical criticism. The resurrection of Jesus is supposedly a singular fact; and regarding its determination the historical-critical method founders, and, according to its own presuppositions, must founder.

The fundamental theological axiom at work here can be summarized in one sentence: Without an objective, ontic grounding for christology in the resurrection event Christian faith has no basis. At the same time, however, there is also the desire—so far as possible—to proceed in a historical-critical way, in order to make the event of the resurrection of Jesus historically plausible. What results from this combination of a dogmatically established fact, on the one hand, and the undergirding of this factuality by historical substantiation, on the other, is the creation of a historical method for the private use of Christians: namely, a method whose consistent and unlimited application to similar statements about events in other religions is not questioned by Christian theology, but whose extension is nevertheless broken off by the same theology at that point where it enters into conflict with the theological axiom just stated.

. . .

In so far as opinions have been recently set forth regarding the theological relevance of the historical-critical method, they move almost without exception . . . in the direction of granting only limited validity to the human discovery of truth with regard to statements about events in the Holy Scriptures, thus limiting human rationality to merely a *usus instrumentalis* [heuristic practice] in service of a presupposed theologumenon. In view of this situation, it is imperative to develop the basic premises of the historical-critical method with a step-by-step rationale, for only in this

---

[3] This English translation is by D. Doughty, "Historical-Critical Method in Its Application to Statements Concerning Events in the Holy Scriptures," *Journal of Higher Criticism* (Fall 1995): 122–39. Used with permission.

way can their full jurisdiction even over statements about events in Holy Scripture, including the resurrection of Jesus, first become visible. What therefore is historical-critical methodology in its application to statements about events in the Holy Scriptures? How does it justify itself? What consequences does it have for theology?

Thesis 1: Under no conditions can the historian presuppose the truth of statements regarding events in documents from the past; he must ascertain the truth with critical procedures.

Rationale: Being faced with documents which affirm something to be an event, the business of the historian is the determination whether what is affirmed in such documents did in fact take place and took place in such a way as the documents state.

With reference to documents of this kind, therefore, the historian must arrive at a determination whether what they represent as an "event" actually took place, or was merely supposed to be an "event" by the narrator. In other words, the historian must determine whether what is related as an event can be granted a factuality that will stand independently of the individual and subjective representation by the narrator that it took place. If this is the case, then, the historian affirms objectivity for what is related as an event and truth for the account of the event.

The procedure of the historian, therefore, is necessarily critical, in so far as it is an investigation of whether what is related as an event in the document before him was merely conceived to be an event in the mind of the narrator—or whether, beyond this, it must be judged to be an event in fact. The necessity for criticism in the investigation of history as a discipline is established by the possibility for error in every human statement —as diverse as the grounds for error might be in individual cases.

Even where the intention of truthfulness is presupposed, no human opinion that an event has taken place (even when it is forcefully expressed), simply as such and without further consideration, can guarantee the factuality of an event that is merely thought to be a fact. The historian thus requires something more than the mere presence of an opinion that something really took place—namely, a conducted demonstration that the opinion presented concerning an event having taken place actually corresponds with reality. The conduct of this demonstration, through which an opinion concerning an event found in a document from the past is in each case established to be true (verified), mediates truth in the sense of the historical knowledge of events.

As applied to statements regarding events found in the Bible, this means that the historian always addresses these statements—without placing in question the subjective conviction of the biblical writers—only as still having to be verified. This is true even for reports which are found (as far as can be determined) in the oldest strata of tradition, or derive from eyewitnesses.

In contrast, therefore, to an exegesis which, remaining in the horizon of events as conceived by the biblical writers, confines itself to mediating the literal sense, the historian moves beyond the opinion of the writer to an investigation of the truth of the statements regarding events and makes the decision concerning this dependent on the result of his critical procedure. Expressed in the language of eighteenth-century hermeneutics: The interpreter may not—as Ernesti still wanted to do—limit himself to the mediation of the *quid dictum* [that which is taught], but beyond this must inquire concerning the *quid verum* [that which is true], or in what sense a *veritas* can be ascribed to the *dictum*. . . .

This can be illustrated by the phenomenon of "sacred history."

Thesis 2: "Sacred history" is characterized by the fact that beings which are not ascertainable in the context of ordinary experience—beings of divine, demonic, and supernatural origin—are active in an otherwise empirical and natural sequence of events. Statements concerning such "sacred history" are fundamentally unverifiable, and in this sense, from the perspective of that which has in fact taken place, without value for the historian.

Rationale: When the historian, in his intention to determine the truth of statements concerning events, encounters "sacred history" (in the Bible, for example), he is faced with a "history" of a special kind, which is characterized by the fact that—from the perspective of ascertainable truth—events of a fundamentally different kind are linked together in the unity of a narrated inter-connection of events.

What constitutes the fundamental difference in kind of the events linked together in such a "sacred history" is their basic difference with regard to the determination of the truth of what is narrated: With regard to events of one kind there exists for us as human beings the fundamental possibility to determine their truth or falsehood, while for the other kind of events this possibility just as fundamentally does not exist—namely, wherever it is related that supernatural beings as such directly appear and become active in an otherwise empirical and natural sequence of events.

This fundamental difference in the character of events, as they are related, for example, in the sacred history of the Bible, can be clarified by a consideration of Matt 28:2ff. Here it is related that—as the women came to the grave—a great earthquake took place, "for an angel of the Lord descended from heaven and came and rolled back the stone, and sat upon it. His appearance was like lightning, and his raiment white as snow. And for fear of him the guards trembled and became like dead men. But the angel said to the women . . ."

The earthquake referred to here is an event whose factuality we are fundamentally able to verify, perhaps by means of some ascertainable effect. In principle, we therefore have at our disposal the stipulations by means of which the statement that there and then an earthquake took place can be tested with regard to its truth. When in the same narrative, however, the descent of an angel from heaven is given as the cause of the earthquake, this is a statement regarding an event for which every determination of truth or falsehood is fundamentally withdrawn. For the assertion that an angel descended from heaven refers not merely to the descent of a being of a certain appearance, ascertainable by our senses ("his appearance was like lightning, and his raiment white as snow"), this assertion refers also to the descent of a being of supernatural origin and supernatural character, a "heavenly" being, in the sense of a being having been sent from God and acting in his service and with his authority. In all these respects, however, an angel as such is fundamentally removed from every verification.

That means, however, that none of the objective data accessible to human beings —his robe as white as snow and his appearance like lightning—can ever be identified with an "angel" in the sense referred to, in the same way as no person is able to provide the stipulations by means of which a determination might be made regarding the movement, presence, and activity of an "angel" in a certain place and time. Consequently, no human being is in a position to verify, as based on an accessible object, his belief (or that of someone else) that then and there an "angel" was present and active.

From this it follows further that there is no other possibility for statements about events by human subjects in the past to be true for us than to verify their statements according to the same stipulations (and in the same manner) by which we determine the truth of such statements concerning events today. And if we encounter statements in documents from the past concerning events whose verifiability is fundamentally denied to us, in so far as they fall totally outside the sphere of our own stipulations for knowledge of verifiable realities, there is then no way in which the truth of such statements—conceivable in itself—can become really true for us. As statements concerning events, they are and necessarily remain for us without truth, and that which is stated by them without objectivity.

It follows, therefore, that the historian can take account of statements about the direct appearance and activity of supernatural beings, as he finds them in "sacred history," only in the sense of their having been so stated. He can deal with them only as mere opinions of persons in the past concerning events, but not as statements which are true and thus able to serve as sources for knowledge of what in fact took place.

Thesis 3: The mediation of the truth of statements concerning events in documents from the past is only possible by means of the historical-critical method. This is rooted in the way human knowledge is constituted, and the stipulations for the mediation of such knowledge, therefore, are not arbitrarily chosen, but necessary and generally mandatory for all persons who desire historical truth.

Rationale: This thesis indicates the only possible and also necessary presuppositions by which the historian can and must make judgments about statements concerning events of the past. He may and can presuppose nothing else than those means for the determination of historical truth which are necessary according to the human conception of knowledge. All other presuppositions abrogate the objective character of his endeavor.

Against this thesis, it will be objected that, because the historian's means of knowledge are so determined, they are able to grasp only a part of history as it really happened. This objection amounts to a confusion of history which is possible to conceive with history as it really happened. Given the way human knowledge is constituted, there is an unbreakable correlation between knowledge of the reality of events and the actual reality of events. A possible reality of events only becomes an actual reality for human beings through the procedure by which they come to know reality as such. Consequently, any mediation of the reality of events for human beings is only possible by means through which they themselves come to know the reality of such events. An event which is possible to conceive only becomes a real event for human beings if they are able to confirm it by means of their own way of knowing reality.

If an accusation of limitation can be made at all in this matter, the accusation must be addressed not to the human being and his method for knowledge of real events, but to that being who is responsible for establishing the constitution of knowledge for human beings.

To be sure, God might have given us a capability for knowing that would have enabled us to recognize as historical reality that which, with the conditions of knowledge as given, must necessarily remain for human beings only a history that is possible to conceive. And one might feel that this condition for knowledge is unfortunate. But one should see things as they are, and not deceive oneself. No human striving, not even theological striving, can make that become reality which, according to the way knowledge is constituted for us, is merely a possibility.

Thesis 4: There is no other criterion for determining whether an event referred to in a document from the past actually took place than the possibility of locating it in the context of the framework of experience constituted by the discipline in its present state of knowledge. Whether other frameworks of experience were present yesterday, or might be present tomorrow—these conceivable possibilities do not abrogate the validity of this thesis.

Rationale: In documents from the past, the historian is presented first of all with merely individual and subjective opinions concerning what should be regarded as true. The historian's task is to test whether objectivity can be granted to these opinions.

This can be illustrated with an example. The Roman historian Suetonius reports that, following the death of Caesar Augustus, a highly placed official with the rank of praetor swore that at the funeral celebration he observed the figure of Caesar, who had just been cremated, ascend into heaven. The modern historian is presented, therefore, with a report, mediated by a reliable writer of history from the ancient world, of a statement by an eyewitness, an honorable senator, confirmed by an oath.

Why does the historian not immediately accept this statement as truth? Is it perhaps because of his limited conception of reality? Why should it not have been possible for God, or the gods, to take up into heaven the Caesar who had just died? Does the fault lie with the "atheistic" methodology of the historian? Now, no historian doubts that for a being conceived to be endowed with almighty power all things are possible. The question is only whether the sworn statement of an eyewitness suffices to insert the heavenly journey of Caesar Augustus, in itself a conceivable possibility, into the course of history as a fact—in such a way, therefore, that in a historical presentation it must be said: "After his death Augustus was taken up into heaven," with a footnote saying, "The fact is confirmed by an eyewitness; cf. Suetonius, *Vita Divi Augusti,* cap. 100."

[The relevant section of Suetonius reads:

> *Two funeral orations were pronounced in his praise, one before the temple of Julius, by Tiberius; and the other before the rostra, under the old shops, by Drusus, Tiberius's son. The body was then carried upon the shoulders of senators into the Campus Martius, and there burnt. A man of praetorian rank affirmed upon oath that he saw his spirit ascend from the funeral pile to heaven. The most distinguished persons of the equestrian order, bare-footed, and with their tunics loose, gathered up his relics, and deposited them in the mausoleum, which had been built in his sixth consulship between the Flaminian Way and the bank of the Tiber; at which time likewise he gave the groves and walks about it for the use of the people.]*[4]

No historian who is aware of his methodological instrumentation for the confirmation of statements about events would be able to reach such a conclusion. He has no instruments of knowledge at his disposal which places him in a position to validate such assertions concerning journeys into heaven because they fall outside the continuum of ordinary knowledge. With regard to historical events, ordinary knowledge is only possible on the basis of a partial identifiability of what is reported in a fundamentally repeatable continuum of knowledge. An event must cohere in principle with other events, i.e., stand in a verifiable connection. An absolutely incoherent event is not verifiable as an event, but merely a conceivable possibility.

This is also the case with regard to the concept of contingency, so very dear to many theologians. If one understands by a contingent event an event for which every ascertainable connection with other ascertainable events is withdrawn, such an event is indeed possible to conceive, but is not assertable as having really taken place.

Returning to our example of the heavenly journey of Augustus, since the historian therefore can grant no objectivity to the sworn sense-perception, he will now attempt to investigate the individual and subjective conditions which may have led the Praetor to make this statement. Do we have to do here with a vision? Was that which he supposedly saw nothing else than an inner reworking by the heart of conceptions deriving from the Caesar cult in the exceptional situation of grief for his imperial Lord,

---

[4] Suetonius, *The Lives of the Twelve Cæsars* (trans. A. Thomson; rev. and corr. ed.; New York: R. Worthington, 1883).

who already during his lifetime was revered as God and Lord, as *Theos kai Kyrios*? In that time did reports of this kind belong to the repertoire of Caesar legends? What are we to make in general of such widely attested stories of heavenly journeys?

Another historical writer, namely Dio Cassius, relates the same incident. From him we learn the name of the official. Much more important, however, is his information that Livia, Caesar's wife, paid the Praetor 250,000 denar for his oath.

[The relevant section of Dio Cassius reads:

> Now these (aforementioned) rumors began to be current at a later date. At the time they declared Augustus immortal, assigned to him priests and sacred rites, and made Livia, who was already called Julia and Augusta, his priestess; they also permitted her to employ a lictor when she exercised her sacred office. On her part, she bestowed a million sesterces upon a certain Numerius Atticus, a senator and ex–praetor, because he swore that he had seen Augustus ascending to heaven after the manner of which tradition tells concerning Proculus and Romulus.][5]

Even this statement, which to begin with seems very plausible, cannot be simply accepted by the historian without further consideration. He will have to determine whether such an act could be attributed to Livia, and, if so, what motives may have produced it; or whether we have to do with a false accusation by her political opponents. The historian will further have to investigate which sources the report by Dio Cassius concerning the bribery of the Praetor by Livia is based on, and whether his own historical work or the sources he used are characterized by a negative view of the house of Caesar. Even if it is possible, however, to cleanse the statement of the Praetor from every suggestion of dishonesty, there is one thing that the historian may not do under any circumstances: namely, thereby conclude that what the Praetor claimed to have seen—the entrance of Augustus into heaven—can be elevated to the status of an objective event.

To apply what has become clear from this example to statements concerning events in the New Testament, we see that the historian faces the same problem with reference to the ascension of Jesus: whether or not he can grant to the statement concerning the ascension of Jesus the status of an objective event. He is just as unable to do so in this instance as in the case of a corresponding secular report of an ascent into heaven—and indeed for the same reason. From statements concerning events for which no conditions for verification exist he cannot derive facts which can be inserted into the course of history that has actually taken place. The only fact which he sees before him is the fact of the statement, but not the factuality of that which is stated as fact.

The decision that the historian makes here is fully independent from whether the statement in question is found in an earlier or later strata of tradition. For in so far

---

[5] Dio Cassius, *Roman History* (trans. E. Cary and H. B. Foster; 9 vols.; Loeb Classical Library; Cambridge: Harvard University Press, 1961), vol. 7, bk. 66, p. 105.

as we have to do here with a statement that is unverifiable, even the fact that it belongs to the earliest strata of tradition is no basis for the objectivity of the event related. No such indication can be gained from the results of literary critical analysis.

This point must be maintained over against a common false assumption, according to which from the temporal "originality" of a portrayal of an event conclusions are drawn regarding its origin in a given occurrence. From the perspective of theology, for example, the account of the ascension of Jesus into heaven is judged to be a "late legend," in contrast to the original statements concerning the exaltation of Jesus, where there is no mention of a forty-day earthly sojourn of the resurrected one [Phil 2:6–11]; but from the temporal priority of the earlier conception of the event no basis can be derived for its priority with regard to objectivity. Given the fundamental unverifiability of a portrayal of exaltation, an earlier portrayal of the event can claim no higher degree of objectivity than a later.

These observations are wholly valid with regard to the assertion that the event of the resurrection of Jesus is a historically demonstrable reality. When one asserts from a theological perspective, for example, as an historical affirmation, "that only the event of the resurrection of Jesus and the confession to this deed of God fulfilled in Jesus makes the historical development of the primitive Christian mission understandable,"[6] one is reasoning backward from the historically demonstrable consequences of the resurrection faith and its history to the factual reality of the resurrection. No historian, who has thought through the means of his knowledge, would be able to accept such a conclusion. For if the maxim which leads to this conclusion became a general rule for historical investigation, then wherever supernatural accounts accompany or ground the introduction of a religion, a cult, or a belief, it would be required that the reported events be granted historical reality.

No historian would question that belief in the resurrection is historically demonstrable to have been of fundamental significance for the introduction of the Christian faith. What must be rejected as a serious error, however, is the assertion that the resurrection of Jesus itself is therefore the historically demonstrable fact that grounds the Christian faith. Here also it holds true: the factuality of what is believed cannot be derived from the historical demonstrability of the consequences of the resurrection faith.

Consistent application of the historical-critical method leads to a different result: the resurrection of Jesus is not the basis of the Christian faith, but the content. Given the demonstration that statements concerning events of sacred history cannot be granted objectivity, the critical historian questions further, concerning the conditions under which statements of this kind could arise at all. Sacred history as a problem for history as a discipline is the subject of our next thesis.

---

[6] P. Stuhlmacher, *Schriftauslegung auf dem Wege zur biblischen Theologie* (Göttingen: Vandenhoeck und Ruprecht, 1973), 141. —Hartlich

Thesis 5: The writers of "sacred history" have at their disposal no "higher capability of knowledge" that places them in a position to make truthful statements concerning events which lie outside the boundaries drawn by the constitution of knowledge common to all human beings.

Rationale: The wide presence of sacred history in religious documents from the past seems to support the view that the narrators of sacred history should be granted a higher means of knowledge. At first glance, it appears improbable to declare all statements of this kind, en bloc, to be error, deception, illusion, invention, and the like.

Against the view that the narrators of sacred history should be ascribed a special, higher capability of knowledge, different from the structure of knowledge common to all human beings, stands the observation that in all other points of their human constitution these narrators appear to be subject to the same human conditions as the rest of humanity. The supposition of a special capability of knowing belonging only to these narrators, therefore, would signify a constitutional exception at a single point—with constitutional identity at all other points. This identity at all other points, which includes, for example, the demonstrable possibility of error with regard to empirical facts, makes it probable that statements in the form of sacred history result from subjective conditions which are possible on the basis of the constitution of knowledge common to all humankind.

This probability increases to the extent that we can disclose the concrete, purely subjective conditions under which the statements in the form of sacred history could become real. The historian now attempts, therefore, in pursuit of further understanding, to make the statements of sacred history reconstructively understandable in their purely subjective possibility and necessity. In other words, he seeks to answer the question: What conditions must have been present in the subjectivity of the writers of sacred history in order to relate historical happenings as if they had really taken place, even though they never took place in fact? How can it be explained that in their accounts the biblical writers seldom if ever seem disturbed by the very question that nevertheless concerns everyone today who assumes responsibility for the truth in reporting events, namely, the question whether these events in fact took place?

Thesis 6: The concept of factuality *(Tatsächlichkeit)* was unknown to the writers of sacred history. Their way of narrating is naive, insofar as it takes place without thorough critical reflection on the conditions underlying statements about events with claims of truth. In their narrations of events they thus allow heterogeneous elements to flow together which the historian today must fundamentally separate.

Rationale: First of all, it should be noted that the word *Tatsache* ("fact") first surfaced in German writing in the middle of the 18th century.[7] As can be gathered from

---

[7] See R. Staats, "Der theologiegeschichtliche Hintergrund des Begriffs 'Tatsache,'" *Zeitschrift für Theologie und Kirche* 70 (1973), 316–45. —Hartlich

the Grimm Dictionary, it was probably employed for the first time in 1756 by the theologian Johann Joachim Spalding as a translation for *res facti* ("matter of fact"). A statement by Lessing is significant. He expresses his amazement that this newly created word so quickly found entrance into the literature: "I am well able to remember the time when it was not yet in anyone's mouth. However, I do not know from whose mouth or pen it first emerged. Even less do I know how it came to be that, contrary to the usual fate of new words, it has had so great a success in a brief time, nor for what reason it has earned such a great acceptance that in certain writings one cannot turn one page without running into the word *Tatsache*."[8]

One will not go wrong in the supposition that the rapid introduction of the word *Tatsache* was not accidental, but stands in relationship with the scientific movement of that time. In withdrawal from the ambiguous term "reality" *(Wirklichkeit)*, that in the often-changing history of its use had become laden with many equivocations, science created a precise concept for a methodologically verified, confirmed, and demonstrated reality.

The naiveté of the narrators of sacred history, asserted in the thesis, can be explained in terms of a level in the development of reflection on the criticism of knowledge determined by its time. It is, namely, a datum of human historical experience that the formal principles of true objective knowledge were not available from the beginning in a fundamental way, but had to be acquired step by step, as the consequence of prolonged fruitless attempts. The awareness of verification as a necessary condition for truth concerning external objects (regardless of what kind) is a result which could first be obtained at a time when reason, in view of a multitude of conflicting opinions about reality, each one asserted as true, recognized the need for basic reflection concerning the necessary conditions for the truth of such judgments. So long, however, as reflection was not carried out in such a fundamental way, opinions concerning truth in statements about events were not grounded, even subjectively, by any necessary relationship with objective conditions for truth in such judgments. This means: in this area of human possibility for judgment, not yet decisively governed by reason, what was believed to be objective in statements of narrative form could at once be set forth as objective, i.e., as objective truth. This is confirmed by a series of observations, some of which relate to the narrator of sacred history, and some to the community to which the narrator addresses himself.

There are biblical stories that relate occurrences for which, because of the situation portrayed, no human being was a witness, nor could have been, and which even so are simply related by the writers as if they had observed the event themselves (e.g., the report of creation—monologues by Yahweh—the burial of Moses by Yahweh). Such a narrative style excludes the possibility that a viewpoint concerning the objectivity of what is related—in the sense of a suitable distinction between belief about reality, on the one hand, and reality which has been demonstrated or must still be demonstrated, on the other—was present at all in the perspective of the narrator.

---

[8] J. and W. Grimm, *Deutsches Wörterbuch* 10.1.1, 322. —Hartlich

A concern for the objectivity of these narratives was no more crucial for the community which received them than for the writers of sacred history. For the fact that the church accepted narratives into its canon that contradict one another with regard to the course of events shows that the process of canonization took place under a perspective that was indifferent with regard to the contradictions of this kind present in the canonized histories. And it should be especially noted that contradictions of this kind are to be found not only at peripheral points, but also at the center of christological affirmations—in the genealogies of Jesus, for example, and even in the resurrection accounts.[9]

From the canonization of such narratives, which clearly contradict one another with regard to the course of events, it can be concluded that their inclusion in the canon did not take place with a view to determining the actual course of events. For if it had been carried out with this view, it would have been necessary to authoritatively determine, in the case of contradictory narratives, which course of events was factual and which report was true. But this is precisely what the community did not do in the process of canonization. Given the presence of several incongruous narratives, neither was a particular course of events declared to be objective, nor did incongruous accounts become subjects of discussion for the purpose of verification. Rather, through their inclusion in the canon these accounts obtained an equal authority, even though with regard to the objectivity of the related events they could not all be true at the same time. It becomes clear from this that the community derived a unified and authoritative truth from these narratives, whose unity and authority could not be called into question by the incongruity of the courses of events as related.

The attempts to create a harmony of the Gospels, which can be traced through all of church history since Tatian, show, on the one hand, the endeavor to establish a chronologically and historically unified course of events, as expressed, for example, in the title of a thirteenth-century manuscript: *Historia evangelica, conjuncta in unum evangelium ex evangeliis evangelistarum, secundum consequentiam historiae* ["A gospel history, joined in one gospel out of the gospels of the evangelists, in accordance with the succession of history"—ed.]. On the other hand, however, the rejection of such harmonizations by the church shows a correct instinct, namely, the feeling that the narratives are not to be evaluated according to the criteria of historical truth, but that they pursue an entirely different intention.

Thesis 7: The writers of sacred history, like that found in the Bible, make use of history as a form in order by this means—an indirect appeal—to call forth faith. Whoever is misled by a misunderstanding of their form of expression and thus conceives the statements of sacred history to be assertions of facts commits a fundamental hermeneutical error.

---

[9] Matt 1:1–17; Luke 3:23–38; Matt 27:62–28:10; Luke 24:1–12; John 20:1–18.

Rationale: It can be exegetically demonstrated that the historical material which the narrators of sacred history offer represents a plastic substance that can be formed according to the intention of the narrator, one that is not oriented by the concept of facts. In other words, their objectifying statements function in service of a basic intention, which is not directed towards a discerning (historical-critical) acceptance by the hearer, but appeals to the hearer to grasp the possibility of a new life.

Whoever therefore treats the history-like statements of sacred history as assertions of fact removes them from their exegetically demonstrable, functional context and places them under the knife edge of the modern conception of fact, which is the product of recent scientific thinking. Through this hermeneutical misinterpretation, these statements are delivered to the knife of a criticism which must necessarily refute them.

Thesis 8: A disastrous theological error arises as a consequence of this false hermeneutical perspective, namely, when this "sacred history," which wants to serve and be understood as a means of expression, is itself made the primary object of faith. Faith in the forgiveness of God is something essentially different from holding a story about the forgiveness of God to be true.

Rationale: In the New Testament, Christian preaching used the form of history in service of the appeal for existential faith. Christian preaching today may make use of this form in so far as it is assured that preacher and hearer understand sacred history appropriately, i.e., as it intends to be understood. And that means when it is understood not as a rendering of objective events, but as an indirect appeal for authentic faith making use of history as a form.

However, the appropriateness of this form of preaching finds its limits when sacred history, which wants to serve and be understood as a means of expression, is itself made the primary object of faith—so that, first of all, sacred history must be regarded as true, so that one may then advance from this history so regarded to faith in the unconditional grace of God. With such a grounding of faith in the grace of God in a history regarded to be true, faith decays, because the hearer is required to first give attention to something other than the grace of God, namely, to the truth of this history, in order afterward to also have faith in the grace of God. Faith in God's forgiveness, however, is something different from holding the story of God's forgiveness to be true.

It has thus become clear as to when the radical application of the historical-critical method to biblical statements about events becomes a requirement for Christian faith: namely, at that point when the pseudo-historical statements of sacred history themselves become dogmatized and made obligatory for faith.

. . .

Conclusion

From the side of theology, all conceivable grounds are advanced in order to demonstrate the inappropriateness of the method for verifying events used by historical criticism with regard to biblical narratives—and in particular with regard to the resurrection narratives. In essence, all such objections are variations of the assertion that the historical-critical method is based on arbitrary presuppositions.

The preceding discussion had as its purpose the demonstration that this accusation is unjustified. In determining the truth of statements concerning events from the past, the critical historian begins not with arbitrary assumptions ("fact-specific," "ideological," "conditioned by a predetermined concept of history"), nor is he a Cartesian, Kantian, Positivist, Atheist, or any other such label, which so often appear in the place of argumentative refutation. Rather—as a representative of humankind concerned with the truth—he simply applies, in a methodical way, the universally accessible conditions for knowledge of truth to statements about events from the past.

Part Five

---⚬⚬⚬---

Late Modern Interpretation (1970–Present)

CHAPTER 26

Canonical Interpretation: Brevard Childs (1923–)

The academic career of Brevard Childs has been devoted to biblical exegesis and theology. His studies in Switzerland with systematician Karl Barth, biblical theologian Walter Eichrodt, and Old Testament exegete Walter Baumgartner immersed him in the history of ancient Israel's traditions and in Christian theological reflection. Upon returning to America in the mid-1950s, Childs was appointed to a teaching position at Yale Divinity School, where, over the course of three decades, he became one of the most productive and influential Old Testament scholars in North America. His early publications included investigations into the ways older Israelite traditions were transformed from their original meanings as they were taken up into the emerging canon of Jewish Scripture. In particular, Childs sought to describe how the larger collection, the biblical canon itself, came to provide hermeneutical standards by which its constitutive components—the canonical books—were interpreted by the early Jewish and Christian communities. His research began to move away from quests to recover the earliest stages of the biblical traditions or the editorial programs of the final redactors. Instead Childs opened up new questions, exploring how the assembled writings as canon constitute a theological framework of interpretation rather than only an historical one.

Childs's interest in scriptural canon for theological interpretation arose, in part, from important developments in the post-World War II biblical-theology movement. As mentioned earlier, this movement had gained influence, particularly in America, as a reaction against nineteenth-century liberalism, which had emphasized historical interpretation of biblical texts as the only defensible exegetical enterprise—diminishing the legitimacy of theological interpretation of the Bible. Biblical theologians of the 1950s and 1960s argued for taking the Bible seriously by recognizing that what had emerged from Israel's history was genuine theology: God had been revealed in certain historical acts, and Israel's testimony to this revelation resulted eventually in oral and literary traditions that ultimately became Scripture. Biblical research, whether archaeological or textual, served to bring the Bible interpreter as close as possible to the saving event in which God had been revealed.

But rigorous philosophical and exegetical critiques from scholars such as Langdon Gilkey and James Barr had undermined confidence that the historical events of biblical faith could be recovered. Even Childs's own work had raised serious questions whether such a historical enterprise was even faithful to the theological nature of Scripture. Childs's concern was to succeed where the biblical-theology movement had failed: to find a way of

308   HISTORY OF BIBLICAL INTERPRETATION

reading the biblical text theologically and yet with modern historical consciousness at the same time. In the rich tradition of premodern biblical interpretation, Childs discovered indications of an interpretive approach that held promise for his quest. Although modern biblical historical critics excelled at analysis, distinguishing the segments of the biblical traditions in the history of their development, they could not provide a way to understand the Bible, wherein the segments cohere as books and a scriptural collection. The premoderns were better at this because they read the portions within the biblical context of *canon*. It was this canonical context for biblical interpretation that modern scholarship had largely ignored.

Childs's call to postmodern biblical scholarship was for a canonical criticism of the Bible. It is postmodern in that it does not repudiate the analytic insights of historical-critical research yet moves beyond the modern assumption that the historical-critical approach is the only legitimate one. Indeed, Childs welcomes the light that modern criticism shines on unharmonized differences that lie between texts within the boundaries of the canonical collection. But it is through canonical criticism that the interpreter can understand how the intracanonical dialogue between biblical texts yields a theological testimony greater than the sum of the canon's parts. Childs's insight is that a text's embeddedness in the biblical canon is a decisive datum, inasmuch as the reader interprets it as Scripture.

In Childs's exegesis, "canonical criticism" (a term that he does not use) does not denote a new critical methodology alongside redaction criticism or form criticism. Instead Childs's canonical program has more to do with an exegete's evaluative understanding of the nature of the biblical text at the outset. Recognition of the Bible as the sacred canon of the church that receives it as such immediately posits the reader's own embeddedness within the received tradition of a community of faith. That place of reading within the church further entails the acceptance of Scripture as a mode of God's active address to the church in its world. Childs's program is an experiment in reading the Bible critically from this faith stance.

The following selections are taken from *Introduction to the Old Testament as Scripture*, one of Childs's most influential and provocative works. With this publication he challenged the way in which critical biblical scholarship had carried on for over two hundred years, by offering a full-scale example (more than 650 pages) of how it could be done differently. In the first part of the selection, Childs offers a critique of modern approaches to the Old Testament; he then goes on to propose a way of exegesis that is responsive to historical criticism but simultaneously mindful of the canonical dimension of the biblical texts. In order to illustrate the approach that Childs advocates, the second part of the selection features his canonical treatment of a particular historical-critical problem in the book of Jonah.

For further information on Brevard Childs and canonical criticism:

Childs, Brevard S. *The Book of Exodus*. Old Testament Library. Philadelphia: Westminster, 1974.
———. *Isaiah*. Old Testament Library. Louisville: Westminster John Knox, 2000.
Sanders, James A. *Canon and Community: A Guide to Canonical Criticism*. Philadelphia: Fortress, 1984.
———. *From Sacred Story to Sacred Text*. Philadelphia: Fortress, 1987.
Sheppard, Gerald. "Canonical Criticism." Pages 861–66 in vol. 1 of *Anchor Bible Dictionary*. Edited by D. N. Freedman. 6 vols. New York: Doubleday, 1992.

Introduction to the Old Testament as Scripture[1]

Childs begins his own Old Testament introduction with an assessment of the Old Testament introduction as a scholarly discipline. After reviewing the history of the introduction genre, he offers his own critique of such works, particularly as they have been produced since the Enlightenment.

The most common opinion is to view this history [of Old Testament Introductions] in terms of scholarly progress and substantial gain. In a burst of enthusiasm some nineteenth-century scholars portrayed the history as a journey from ignorance and error in which ecclesiastical dogma stifled free research into a era of freedom measured only by critical standards of objective truth. Conversely, some conservative Christians have described this history as a growth in unbelief in which the truth of the Bible has been sacrificed on the altar of human wisdom and pride.

In my judgment, both of these evaluations have missed the mark. On the one hand, it seems to me impossible to deny the enormous gains which have been achieved in many areas of the study of the Old Testament. To compare the church fathers, or the Reformers for that matter, with modern scholarship in terms of philology, textual and literary criticism, or of historical knowledge and exegetical precision should convince any reasonable person of the undeniable achievements of historical critical scholarship in respect to the Old Testament.

On the other hand, there have been serious losses reflected in the victory of the critical Introduction. By this evaluation I do not include the psychological impact of the new knowledge on traditional Jewish and Christian beliefs, which is a subject lying outside the scope of this discussion. Rather in terms of the subject matter, serious reservations can be held regarding the form of the critical Introduction as an adequate approach to the literature it seeks to illuminate.

In the first place, the historical critical Introduction as it has developed since Eichhorn[2] does not have for its goal the analysis of the canonical literature of the synagogue and church, but rather it seeks to describe the history of the development of the Hebrew literature and to trace the earlier and later stages of this history. As a result, there always remains an enormous hiatus between the description of the critically reconstructed literature and the actual canonical text which has been received and used as authoritative Scripture by the community.

Secondly, because of the predominantly historical interest, the critical Introduction usually fails to understand the peculiar dynamics of Israel's religious literature, which has been greatly influenced by the process of establishing the scope of

---

[1] Reprinted from *Introduction to the Old Testament as Scripture* by Brevard S. Childs, copyright © 1979 Brevard S. Childs, admin. Augsburg Fortress (www.fortresspress.org). Used with permission.

[2] Johann Gottfried Eichhorn, *Einleitung ins Alte Testament* (3 vols.; Leipzig: Bey Weidmanns Erben und Reich, 1787).

the literature, forming its particular shape, and structuring its inner relationships. The whole dimension of resonance within the Bible which issues from a collection with fixed parameters and which affects both the language and its imagery is lost by disregarding the peculiar function of canonical literature.

Thirdly, the usual historical critical Introduction has failed to relate the nature of the literature correctly to the community which treasured it as Scripture. It is constitutive of Israel's history that the literature formed the identify of the religious community which in turn shaped the literature. This fundamental dialectic which lies at the heart of the canonical process is lost when the critical Introduction assumes that a historically referential reading of the Old Testament is the key to its interpretation. It assumes the determining force on every biblical text to be political, social, or economic factors which it seeks to establish in disregard of the religious dynamic of the canon. In sum, the issue is not whether or not an Old Testament Introduction should be historical, but the nature of the historical categories being applied.

How does this criticism relate to the history of scholarship leading up to the development of the critical Introduction which we have outlined? It suggests that the friction which characterized the history of the discipline and is still present today between a liberal versus conservative, scientific versus ecclesiastical, objective versus confessional approach to the Old Testament poses a false dichotomy of the problem. Because this issue has been confused throughout its history, the development of critical biblical scholarship has brought both great gains and also serious losses in understanding the Old Testament. In my judgment, the crucial issue which produced the confusion is the problem of the canon, that is to say, how one understands the nature of the Old Testament in relation to its authority for the community of faith and practice which shaped and preserved it.

Childs goes on to discuss modern efforts toward describing the process of canonization. He concludes that while on the one hand, canonization is clearly a relevant historical fact for understanding the Bible as scripture, on the other hand the motives and causes for the biblical books and book-collections taking the shape that they have in the canon elude historical-critical reconstruction. Childs poses what he considers the key question (p. 45): "Is it possible to understand the Old Testament as canonical Scripture and yet to make full and consistent use of the historical critical tools?" In his chapter "Canon and Criticism," Childs sets out to answer this question.

Exegesis in a Canonical Context

. . .

The major task of a canonical analysis of the Hebrew Bible is a descriptive one. It seeks to understand the peculiar shape and special function of these texts which comprise the Hebrew canon. Such an analysis does not assume a particular stance or faith commitment on the part of the reader because the subject of the investigation is the literature of Israel's faith, not that of the reader. However, apart from unintentional bias which is always present to some extent, the religious stance of the modern reader can play a legitimate role after the descriptive task has been accomplished, when the reader chooses whether or not to identify with the perspectives of the canonical texts of Israel which he has studied. Because this literature has had a special history as the religious literature of ancient Israel, its peculiar features must be handled in a way compatible to the material itself. A corpus of religious writings which has been transmitted within a community for over a thousand years cannot properly be compared to inert shreds which have lain in the ground for centuries. This observation is especially in order when one recognizes that Israel's developing religious understanding—the Bible speaks of God's encounter with Israel—left its mark on the literature in a continuing process of reshaping and growth.

Canonical analysis focuses its attention on the final form of the text itself. It seeks neither to use the text merely as a source for other information obtained by means of an oblique reading, nor to reconstruct a history of religious development. Rather, it treats the literature in its own integrity. Its concern is not to establish a history of Hebrew literature in general, but to study the features of this peculiar set of religious texts in relation to their usage within the historical community of ancient Israel. To take the canonical shape of these texts seriously is to seek to do justice to a literature which Israel transmitted as a record of God's revelation to his people along with Israel's response. The canonical approach to the Hebrew Bible does not make any dogmatic claims for the literature apart from the literature itself, as if these texts contained only timeless truths or communicated in a unique idiom, but rather it studies them as historically and theologically conditioned writings which were accorded a normative function in the life of this community. It also acknowledges that the texts served a religious function in closest relationship to the worship and service of God whom Israel confessed to be the source of the sacred word. The witness of the text cannot be separated from the divine reality which Israel testified to have evoked the response.

It is a misunderstanding of the canonical method to characterize it as an attempt to bring extrinsic, dogmatic categories to bear on the biblical text by which to stifle the genuine exegetical endeavor. Rather, the approach seeks to work within that interpretative structure which the biblical text has received from those who formed and used it as sacred Scripture. To understand that canonical shape requires the highest degree of exegetical skill in an intensive wrestling with the text. It is to be expected that interpreters will sometimes disagree on the nature of the canonical shaping, but the disagreement will enhance the enterprise if the various interpreters share a common understanding of the nature of the exegetical task.

The Canonical Approach Contrasted with Others

Several crucial methodological issues are raised when the canonical approach is described as focusing on the final form of the text. Perhaps these issues can be most sharply profiled by contrasting the approach which I am suggesting with other familiar methods of critical biblical scholarship.

The canonical study of the Old Testament shares an interest in common with several of the newer literary critical methods in its concern to do justice to the integrity of the text itself apart from diachronistic reconstruction. One thinks of the so-called "newer criticism" of English studies, of various forms of structural analysis, and of rhetorical criticism. Yet the canonical approach differs from a strictly literary approach by interpreting the biblical text in relation to a community of faith and practice for whom it served a particular theological role as possessing divine authority. For theological reasons the biblical texts were often shaped in such a way that the original poetic forms were lost, or a unified narrative badly shattered. The canonical approach is concerned to understand the nature of the theological shape of the text rather than to recover an original literary or aesthetic unity. Moreover, it does not agree with a form of structuralism which seeks to reach a depth structure of meaning lying below the surface of the canonical text.

Then again, the canonical method which is being outlined differs sharply from the so-called "kerygmatic exegesis" which was popularized by [Gerhard] von Rad and his students in the 50s and 60s. Classic examples of this method can be found in the writings of H. W. Wolff, C. Westermann, W. Brueggemann, among others.[3] For several years beginning in 1966 [the widely-read periodical] *Interpretation* ran a series of articles under the rubric "*Kerygma* of the Bible." This method attempted to discover the central intention of a writer, usually by means of formulas or themes, which intention was then linked to a reconstruction of a historical situation which allegedly evoked that given response. Its major concern was to combine historical critical analysis with a type of theological interpretation. A major criticism of the method is the extremely subjective, reductionist method in which the form-critical method has been extended beyond its original function to derive a theological message. Often the assumption that the theological point must be related to an original intention within a reconstructed historical context runs directly in the face of the literature's explicit statement of its function within the final form of the biblical text. . . .

Again, the canonical study of the Old Testament is to be distinguished from the traditio-critical approach in the way in which it evaluates the history of the text's formation. By assuming the normative status of the final form of the text the canonical approach evokes the strongest opposition from the side of traditio-historical criticism for which the heart of the exegetical task is the recovery of the depth dimension. Form critics raise familiar questions: Why should one stage in the process be accorded a special status? Were not the earlier levels of the text once regarded as canonical as well, and why should they not continue to be so regarded within the exegetical enterprise? Is not the history which one recovers in the growth of a text an important index for studying Israel's development of a self-understanding, and thus the very object of Old Testament theology? Having been trained in the form-critical

---

[3] See G. von Rad, *Genesis: A Commentary* (trans. John H. Marks; Old Testament Library; Philadelphia: Westminster, 1961); H. W. Wolff and W. Brueggemann, *The Vitality of Old Testament Traditions* (Atlanta: John Knox, 1975); C. Westermann, *Essays in Old Testament Hermeneutics* (trans. J. L. Mays; Richmond: John Knox, 1964).

method, I feel the force of these questions and am aware of the value of the approach. Still I feel strongly that these questions miss the mark and have not fully grasped the methodological issues at stake in the canonical proposal.

The Final Form of the Text and its Prehistory

The reason for insisting on the final form of scripture lies in the peculiar relationship between text and people of God which is constitutive of the canon. The shape of the biblical text reflects a history of encounter between God and Israel. The canon serves to describe this peculiar relationship and to define the scope of this history by establishing a beginning and end to the process. It assigns a special quality to this particular segment of human history which became normative for all successive generations of this community of faith. The significance of the final form of the biblical text is that it alone bears witness to the full history of revelation. Within the Old Testament neither the process of the formation of the literature nor the history of its canonization is assigned an independent integrity. This dimension has often been lost or purposely blurred and is therefore dependent on scholarly reconstruction. The fixing of a canon of scripture implies that the witness to Israel's experience with God lies not in recovering such historical processes, but is testified to in the effect on the biblical text itself. Scripture bears witness to God's activity in history on Israel's behalf, but history *per se* is not a medium of revelation which is commensurate with a canon. It is only in the final form of the biblical text in which the normative history has reached an end that the full effect of this revelatory history can be perceived.

It is certainly true that earlier stages in the development of the biblical literature were often regarded as canonical prior to the establishment of the final form. In fact, the final form frequently consists of simply transmitting an earlier, received form of the tradition often unchanged from its original setting. Yet to take the canon seriously is also to take seriously the critical function which it exercises in respect to the earlier stages of the literature's formation. A critical judgment is evidenced in the way in which these earlier stages are handled. At times the material is passed on unchanged; at other times tradents select, rearrange, or expand the received tradition. The purpose of insisting on the authority of the final canonical form is to defend its role of providing this critical norm. To work with the final stage of the text is not to lose the historical dimension, but it is rather to make a critical, theological judgment regarding the process. The depth dimension aids in understanding the interpreted text, and does not function independently of it. To distinguish the Yahwist source from the Priestly in the Pentateuch often allows the interpreter to hear the combined texts with new precision. But it is the full, combined text which has rendered a judgment on the shape of the tradition and which continues to exercise an authority on the community of faith. Of course, it is legitimate and fully necessary for the historian of the ancient Near East to use his written evidence in a different manner, often reading his texts obliquely, but this enterprise is of a different order from the interpretation of sacred scripture which we are seeking to describe.

Then again, the final form of the text performs a crucial hermeneutical function in establishing the peculiar profile of a passage. Its shaping provides an order in highlighting certain elements and subordinating others, in drawing features to the foreground and pushing others into the background. To work from the final form is to resist any method which seeks critically to shift the canonical ordering. Such an exegetical move occurs whenever an overarching category such as *Heilsgeschichte* [salvation history] subordinates the peculiar canonical profile, or a historical critical reconstruction attempts to refocus the picture according to its own standards of aesthetics or historical accuracy. . . .

The Canonical Process and the Shaping of Scripture

The formation of the canon took place over an extended period of time in close relation to the development of the Hebrew literature. But the canonical process was not simply an external validation of successive stages of literary development, but was an integral part of the literary process. Beginning in the pre-exilic period, but increasing in significance in the post-exilic era, a force was unleashed by Israel's religious use of her traditions which exerted an influence on the shaping of the literature as it was selected, collected and ordered. It is clear from the sketch of the process that particular editors, religious groups, and even political parties were involved. At times one can describe these groups historically or sociologically, such as the reforming Deuteronomic party of Jerusalem, or the editors associated with Hezekiah's court (Prov 25:1). But basic to the canonical process is that those responsible for the actual editing of the text did their best to obscure their own identity. Thus the actual process by which the text was reworked lies in almost total obscurity. Its presence is detected by the effect on the text. Moreover, increasingly the original sociological and historical differences within the nation of Israel—Northern and Southern Kingdom, pro- and anti-monarchial parties, apocalyptic versus theocratic circles— were lost, and a religious community emerged which found its identity in terms of sacred scripture. Israel defined itself in terms of a book! The canon formed the decisive *Sitz im Leben* [setting in life] for the Jewish community's life, thus blurring the sociological evidence most sought after by the modern historian. When critical exegesis is made to rest on the recovery of these very sociological distinctions which have been obscured, it runs directly in the face of the canon's intention.

The motivations behind the canonical process were diverse and seldom discussed in the biblical text itself. However, the one concern which is expressly mentioned is that a tradition from the past be transmitted in such a way that its authoritative claims be laid upon all successive generations of Israel. Such expressions of intent are found in the promulgation of the law (Deut 31:9ff.), in the fixing of rituals (Exod 12:14), and in the provisions for transmitting the sacred story (Exod 12:26ff.). A study of the biblical text reveals that this concern to pass on the authoritative tradition did not consist in merely passively channelling material from one generation to another, but reflects an involvement which actively shaped both the oral and written traditions. A major hermeneutical move was effected in the process of forming an original law, prophetic oracles, or ancient narrative into a collection of scripture through which every subsequent generation was to be addressed.

It is not clear to what extent the ordering of the oral and written material into a canonical form always involved an intentional decision. At times there is clear evidence for an intentional blurring of the original historical setting (cf. the discussion of "Second Isaiah"). At other times the canonical shaping depends largely on what appear to be unintentional factors which subsequently were incorporated within a canonical context (e.g., the sequence of the proverbs in Prov 10ff.). But irrespective of intentionality the effect of the canonical process was to render the tradition accessible to the future generation by means of a "canonical intentionality," which is coextensive with the meaning of the biblical text.

. . . T[he modern hermeneutical impasse which has found itself unable successfully to bridge the gap between the past and the present, has arisen in large measure from its disregard of the canonical shaping. The usual critical method of biblical exegesis is, first, to seek to restore an original historical setting by stripping away those very elements which constitute the canonical shape. Little wonder that once the biblical text has been securely anchored in the historical past by "decanonizing" it, the interpreter has difficulty applying it to the modern religious context. (I am indebted to Gerald T. Sheppard for this formulation of the issue.)

Some of his comments on the book of Jonah are presented here to illustrate the approach Childs advocates. Following a review of the book's major historical-critical problems, Childs turns to the prayer in Jonah 2, which most critical scholars explain as a later interpolation into the story.

The Canonical Shape of Jonah

In an effort to describe how the book of Jonah functions in its canonical context, it seems wise to begin with the form-critical problem. What is the form and function of the Jonah story? It has long been noticed that the book reaches a climax in ch. 4 with a didactic point. Indeed once this point has been made, the book comes to an abrupt end. Moreover, the retrospective explanation in 4:2 succeeds in closely tying the preceding scenes to the didactic point of the final chapter. It is crucial to observe how the point is made. It emerges from the dialogue between God and Jonah and is self-contained. It does not need to be explained by the author of the story. The form-critical implication to be drawn from this observation is that the story now functions in a way analogous to that of a parable. In spite of the probability that the elements of the story may have once circulated independently of its present form, the story now functions as a unit in which the audience receives the word in unmediated form from the narrative itself.

However, there are several reasons why we prefer the term "parable-like" rather than making an immediate identification of the Old Testament book with the form of the parable. First, the nature of the genre of parable is itself a highly controversial issue, particularly from the side of New Testament scholarship, and the term introduces into the discussion many extraneous issues. The logic of the book is not affected by making more precise the exact relationship of the Old Testament story to the complexities within the genre. Secondly, there are certain unique features within the book of Jonah which are not part of the parabolic form. The book begins with the stereotypical literary formula of the prophetic books: "the word of Yahweh came to Jonah." Although the book of Jonah is not a collection of prophetic words, but rather a story about the prophet, the author has adapted the prophetic formula to his own didactic purposes. By beginning with this formula, the author has cast his story into the style of the other prophecies. Finally, there is considerable flexibility within the form which must not be sacrificed to an overly rigid formal classification.

The significance of this parable-like form of the book can be elucidated by contrasting its form and function with other suggested genres. The story is different from a prophetic legend whose meaning is supplied by means of a redactor's framework imposed upon the story (e.g., I Kgs 16:29ff.). Again, the story of Jonah is not symbolic action which points to another dimension of reality by means of carefully contrived adumbration. Moreover, the story does not belong to the genre of midrash even though there are elements of midrashic technique involved because the major concern of the narrative does not turn on explaining a difficulty in a biblical text. Finally, the story does not function as an allegory which requires the proper key in order for its hearers to perceive its meaning. However, although this form-critical analysis of how the story functions does rule out certain interpretations, it does not offer in itself a criterion for adjudicating between the two conflicting interpretations which were discussed above. To resolve this problem, we shall have to seek evidence of canonical shaping in the final form of the book.

The majority of critical scholars are convinced that the prayer in ch. 2 is a later interpolation into the original story. Among the various reasons brought forward against the originality of the prayer, two stand out. It is argued that the prayer has not only disturbed the structure of the story, but also has introduced a confusing note into the one clear message of the book. In terms of the original structure, the first and second commissions to Nineveh are clearly parallel (1:1 and 3:1). In each of these two chapters the focus of the story falls on the heathen reaction, the threat of judgment, the prayer for deliverance, and the ensuing rescue. Chapter 4 shifts the perspective to Jonah. His reaction to Nineveh's repentance is described, which in turn evokes the lesson in a divine response.

In this reconstruction of the original story Jonah never changes in voicing his opposition to his mission. He first flees, but is compelled to return by God's direct intervention. He then carries out his commission, but is angry at its success. His explanation (4:2) indicates his consistent resistance from the beginning. He knows in advance that God will not carry through with his threat. The issue turns on the fullfilment of the prophet's word. Jonah resisted because he did not want to be a false prophet. In his response God defends his right as Creator to let his mercy to his creation override the prophetic word. By the removal of ch. 2 the sharp lines of the original story emerge, thus confirming the interpretation which related the purpose of the book to the issue of unfulfilled prophecy.

But what is the effect on the story when in its final form the lengthy prayer of Jonah is introduced in ch. 2? This move appears to have been a crucial one in the canonical shaping. First of all, the structure of the book is substantially altered by the introduction of the prayer of ch. 2. As has been convincingly demonstrated by Landes,[4] ch. 2 now functions as a parallel to ch. 4. The similar introductory formulas as well as the consistent structure serve as literary evidence for an intentional structural paralleling of the chapters. The effect of the parallel is that the meaning of ch. 4 is now strongly influenced by ch. 2.

In ch. 2 Jonah prays to God from the belly of the fish. The prayer is not a cry for help, but is a prayer of thanksgiving for deliverance already experienced. The Hebrew text is unequivocal in its use of verbs of completed action in striking contrast to the Septuagint's attempt to remove this problem. In its present narrative context the threat to Jonah's life lay in his being drowned in the sea. The large fish was the divine means of deliverance! The prayer of Jonah is a veritable catena of traditional phrases from the Psalter. Jonah prays in the stereotypical language of the psalms which every faithful Jew had always used. He first describes the threat to his life in the language of the complaint psalm, which, however, because of the context of the ongoing narrative, works to provide a new and remarkable dimension of historical specificity. Jonah is thankful for his rescue and ascribes praise to his God: "Deliverance belongs to Yahweh!" (v. 10; English versions v. 9).

In ch. 4 Jonah again prays to his God and once again he makes use of traditional language. The formula of v. 2 appears first in Exod 34:6 in the giving of the covenant to Israel at Sinai, but has become an integral part of the liturgical language of the Psalter as well (Pss. 86:15; 103:8; 111:4; 112:4; 116:5; 145:8). This time, however, the appeal to the same divine attribute of mercy evokes a negative response from the prophet. He is angry because God has "repented of the evil" intended for Nineveh.[5] If his anger had once stemmed from concern over the fulfillment of the prophetic word, there has been a noticeable shift in the expanded narrative. The structural parallelism of chs. 2 and 4, which contrasts the two prayers of Jonah, refocuses the narrative. The issue now turns on the scope of divine mercy. Jonah is thankful for his own deliverance, but resentful of Nineveh's inclusion within the mercy which had always been restricted to Israel. This interpretation is further supported by the prayer of the king. His response: "Who knows, God may yet repent and turn from his fierce anger," is a citation from Joel 2:14, and a continuation of the same covenant formula which Jonah uses in 4:2. Clearly the issue is now on the recipient of the divine mercy.

The inclusion of the prayer of Jonah in ch. 2 has had another effect on the interpretation of the story. The prayer affords the reader an avenue into the faith of the prophet. Obviously, Jonah's personality is not the issue, but rather Jonah is portrayed as a typical Jew who shares Israel's traditional faith. In his trouble he renders

---

[4] G. M. Landes, "The Kerygma of the Book of Jonah," *Interpretation* 21 (1967): 3–31.

[5] Cf. J. Jeremias, *Die Reue Gottes* (Biblische Studien 65; Neukirchen-Vluyn: Neukirchener Verlag, 1975), 98ff. —This note is an expansion of Childs's own abbreviated citation.

thanksgiving to God and is confident of divine rescue. In sum, the effect of the prayer from a canonical perspective is to typify Jonah! The lesson which was directed to Jonah now also serves a larger audience. The book addresses those other faithful Jews who have been set apart from the nations by the Mosaic covenant, and who were sustained by the sacred traditions of their Psalter.

There are several other observations which can be made in regard to the effect of the prayer in ch.2 on the interpretation of the book as a whole. The initial characterization of the book as a parable-like story which directly communicates its message to its hearers still holds. Nevertheless, the inclusion of the prayer has had the effect of complicating the simple parabolic form which is an additional reason for characterizing the final form of the story with the less precise terminology. The story has been given a different literary structure and another internal dynamic has been set in motion. Jonah no longer serves simply as the reluctant messenger of God to whom the message of ch. 4 is directed. Rather his role has been expanded by fashioning him into a representative figure and thus establishing a link between Israel and the heathen. Of course, it is the complexity of the form within the final shape of the book which has caused the difficulty of interpretation and has afforded genuine warrants for the various critical analyses.

The crucial question now arises as how one is to relate these two different interpretations found in the book. If the above analysis is at all correct, the final form of the story does seek to address the issue of God's salvation being extended to the nations as well as to Israel. Moreover, this redactional stamp has not obliterated the earlier form of the story, but refocused it. In my judgment, the final reworking of the story simply extended the original point. In the "first edition" the theological point turned on God's right as Creator to override his prophetic word for the sake of his entire creation. The "second edition" merely amplified the point respecting the whole creation in terms of the nations, but it did not alter the basic creation theology by substituting one of election.

Is it possible to make any further observations as to the historical process lying behind the development of the canonical shape of the story? There is no evidence to suggest that the two levels of the story were separated by a long historical development. Not only is the language of one piece, but the midrashic method of handling the tradition is represented just as much by the reconstructed first stage as by the final form. It seems more likely to suggest that the force which effected a shift in the function of the book derived from the canonical process itself. When the book was collected within a corpus of other sacred literature, the need arose to specify the addressee as the covenant community. Thus the original prophetic problem of unfulfilled prophecy against the nations was expanded. Again, the effect of ordering the book within a larger collection can be seen on the new reading of the significance of Nineveh. To be sure the idiom within the biblical text is neutral and lacks any specific reference to Israel's historical relationship to the Assyrians. But this larger historical dimension is now supplied by the role of the larger canon. Thus, the reader brings to the story a common memory respecting the Ninevites to whom Jonah was sent with a message of repentance, and he has in his canon the book of Nahum!

Finally, the canonical setting of the story in the period of Jeroboam II (2 Kgs 14), rather than placing it in the post-exilic period, ensures seeing the issue raised by the book as constitutive to the theological relation between Israel and the nations. The issue is not to be historicized and derived from an allegedly post-exilic narrowness of Hellenistic Judaism, but serves as a critical prophetic judgment on Israel in line with the rest of the prophetic witnesses of the Old Testament.

Theological and Hermeneutical Implications

(a) By determining that the book of Jonah functions in its canonical context as a parable-like story the older impasse regarding the historicity of the story is by-passed as a theological issue. Because the book serves canonically in the role of an analogy, it is as theologically irrelevant to know its historicity as it is with the Parable of the Good Samaritan. In both instances historical features have been incorporated within the narrative, but this determination does not affect the canonical role which the book plays. This is a judgment respecting the canonical function of Jonah and is not to be generalized into a principle that history is unimportant for the Bible.

(b) The canonical shape of the book of Jonah offers an example of an editorial process which retained intact elements of an earlier interpretation. A subsequent editing of the book shifted the focus, but did not eliminate the earlier level. To the extent to which the earlier interpretation has been retained in the final shape of the book, it continues to offer a genuine canonical witness. In the case of the book of Jonah, the final form did subordinate one interpretation to another and offered a clear guideline as to the primary message. Thus, the two interpretations reflect an inner relationship within the canon and are not to be played off against each other.

(c) The form of the book of Jonah is unique in the Book of the Twelve.[6] The book does not contain the oracles of Jonah, nor is the material biographical in the strict sense. Rather, the authority of the book rests on the prophetic function of the book as bearer of a message. All attempts, therefore, to defend the prophet's reputation—he fled out of love of Israel (Rashi), or he resisted the divine decision from concern over God's glory—miss the purpose of the book within the canon. Such apologetics serve to weaken rather than enhance the truth of the book.

(d) The canonical shape of the book of Jonah resists the attempts of both Jew and Christian to politicize the biblical message. On the one hand, the divine attack on Jonah's resistance is not to be derived from post-exilic narrowness, but is theologically grounded in the nature of God as Creator. On the other hand, the case for seeing Jonah's resistance arising because of the inclusion of the nations is not to be dismissed as a later Christian bias, but is a genuine Old Testament witness directed against a misunderstanding of the election of Israel.

---

[6] In the Hebrew Bible, the last twelve books of the Prophets (Hosea to Malachi) are known collectively as the Book of the Twelve.

CHAPTER 27

The Wisdom of the Fathers:
David C. Steinmetz (1936–)

Not long after he earned a doctorate at Harvard Divinity School, David C. Steinmetz won wide recognition for his careful scholarship in church history. Beginning with his earliest published work, Steinmetz has continued to make important contributions to his specialization: Christian history of the later Middle Ages and the Reformation. He has paid particular attention to the interpretation of the Bible in this era. Steinmetz's influence has triggered a rethinking of the conventionally assumed divide between biblical interpretation in the medieval period and that in the Reformation era, bringing the later Middle Ages out from behind the shadow of the Reformation.

The following essay by Steinmetz, "The Superiority of Pre-critical Exegesis," has subsequently appeared in a number of anthologies and so is one of his most widely read pieces. He challenges the hegemony of historical-critical interpretation of the Bible with a boldness similar to Walter Wink's (see chapter 29) but with more detailed attention to the wisdom of premodern scholarship. Like Wink, Steinmetz regards the value of strictly historical-critical interpretation to be somewhat exaggerated and often counterproductive for the life of the church. The biblical author's intended meaning (usually equated with the plain or literal meaning and enshrined as the goal of historical-critical scholarship) should not be pursued as the only legitimate meaning a text can yield. Steinmetz points out that as contemporary literary critics have correctly argued, meanings beyond what a writer may have intended are always generated in the encounter between author and reader. Pre-critical interpreters were superior to their modern historical-critical counterparts because they recognized this productive dynamic and—following the precedents within the pages of the Bible itself—found in it a way for Scripture to speak to the church in all eras.

The reader may recall that, about 720 years earlier, Thomas Aquinas had defended the practice of finding multiple meanings in a single biblical passage. In this essay Steinmetz incorporates elements of Thomas's argument into his own but with an important difference. As a premodern interpreter, Thomas did not hesitate to claim that the nonliteral meanings in Scripture are legitimate because they were intended by the author of Scripture, who is God. When Steinmetz argues for the legitimacy of multiple meanings, he does not require that all legitimate meanings are authorially intended meanings latent in the divine dimension of Scripture. For Steinmetz, biblical texts can generate multiple meanings not because they are divinely authored but because they are texts. When readers interpret texts—any texts—they engage in a dynamic exchange with the author that will come up with meanings not originally intended, because this is what readers do. Although Steinmetz comes to the same conclusion as his medieval predecessors regarding multiple meanings, he does so without appealing to any divine quality inherent in the texts by virtue of their divine authorship. In this sense, precritical interpreters and modern historical critics assume the same locus of legitimate meaning: in the mind of the author, human or divine. Steinmetz allows for meanings—sometimes the more important ones—that are freshly created apart from what might have ever been authorially intended.

For further information on the rediscovery of precritical biblical interpretation:

Fowl, Stephen E. *Engaging Scripture: A Model for Theological Interpretation.* Oxford: Blackwell, 1998.

Frei, Hans W. *The Eclipse of Biblical Narrative: A Study in Eighteenth and Nineteenth Century Hermeneutics.* New Haven: Yale University Press, 1980.

Lindbeck, George. "The Story-Shaped Church: Critical Exegesis and Theological Interpretation." Pages 39–52 in *Scriptural Authority and Narrative Interpretation.* Edited by G. Green. Philadelphia: Fortress, 1987.

Ochs, Peter, ed. *The Return to Scripture in Judaism and Christianity: Essays in Postcritical Scriptural Interpretation.* New York: Paulist, 1993.

The Superiority of Pre-critical Exegesis[1]

In 1859 Benjamin Jowett, then Regius Professor of Greek in the University of Oxford, published a justly famous essay on the interpretation of Scripture.[2] Jowett argued that "Scripture has one meaning—the meaning which it had in the mind of the Prophet or Evangelist who first uttered or wrote, to the hearers or readers who first received it."[3] Scripture should be interpreted like any other book and the later accretions and venerated traditions surrounding its interpretation should, for the most part, either be brushed aside or severely discounted. "The true use of interpretation is to get rid of interpretation, and leave us alone in company with the author."[4]

Jowett did not foresee great difficulties in the way of the recovery of the original meaning of the text. Proper interpretation requires imagination, the ability to put oneself into an alien cultural situation, and knowledge of the language and history of the ancient people whose literature one sets out to interpret. In the case of the Bible, one has also to bear in mind the progressive nature of revelation and the superiority of certain later religious insights to certain earlier ones. But the interpreter, armed with the proper linguistic tools, will find that " . . . universal truth easily breaks through the accidents of time and place"[5] and that such truth still speaks to the condition of the unchanging human heart.

Of course, critical biblical studies have made enormous strides since the time of Jowett. No reputable biblical scholar would agree today with Jowett's reconstruction of the gospels in which Jesus appears as a "teacher . . . speaking to a group of serious, but not highly educated, working men, attempting to inculcate in them a loftier and sweeter morality."[6] Still, the quarrel between modern biblical scholarship and Benjamin Jowett is less a quarrel over his hermeneutical theory than it is a disagreement with him over the application of that theory in his exegetical practice. Biblical scholarship still hopes to recover the original intention of the author of a biblical text and still regards the pre-critical exegetical tradition as an obstacle to the proper understanding of the true meaning of that text. The most primitive meaning of the text is its only valid meaning, and the historical-critical method is the only key which can unlock it.

But is that hermeneutical theory true?

---

[1] David C. Steinmetz, "The Superiority of Pre-critical Exegesis," *Theology Today* 37 (1980): 27–38. Used with permission.

[2] Benjamin Jowett, "On the Interpretation of Scripture," *Essays and Reviews*, 7th ed. (London: Longman, Green, Longman and Roberts, 1861), 330–433. —Steinmetz

[3] Jowett, "Interpretation," 378. —Steinmetz

[4] Jowett, "Interpretation," 384. —Steinmetz

[5] Jowett, "Interpretation," 412. —Steinmetz

[6] Helen Gardner, *The Business of Criticism* (London: Oxford University Press, 1959), p. 33. —Steinmetz

I think it is demonstrably false. In what follows I want to examine the pre-critical exegetical tradition at exactly the point at which Jowett regarded it to be most vulnerable—namely, in its refusal to bind the meaning of any pericope to the intention, whether explicit or merely half-formed, of its human author. Medieval theologians defended the proposition, so alien to modern biblical studies, that the meaning of Scripture in the mind of the prophet who first uttered it is only one of its possible meanings and may not, in certain circumstances, even be its primary or most important meaning. I want to show that this theory (in at least that respect) was superior to the theories which replaced it. When biblical scholarship shifted from the hermeneutical position of Origen to the hermeneutical position of Jowett, it gained something important and valuable. But it lost something as well, and it is the painful duty of critical scholarship to assess its losses as well as its gains.

I

Medieval hermeneutical theory took as its point of departure the words of St. Paul: "The letter kills but the spirit makes alive" (2 Cor 3:6). Augustine suggested that this text could be understood in either one of two ways. On the one hand, the distinction between letter and spirit could be a distinction between law and gospel, between demand and grace. The letter kills because it demands an obedience of the sinner which the sinner is powerless to render. The Spirit makes alive because it infuses the forgiven sinner with new power to meet the rigorous requirements of the law.

But Paul could also have in mind a distinction between what William Tyndale later called the "story-book" or narrative level of the Bible and the deeper theological meaning or spiritual significance implicit within it. This distinction was important for at least three reasons. Origen stated the first reason with unforgettable clarity:

> Now what man of intelligence will believe that the first and the second and the third day, and the evening and the morning existed without the sun and moon and stars? And that the first day, if we may so call it, was even without a heaven? And who is so silly as to believe that God, after the manner of a farmer, "planted a paradise eastward in Eden" and set in it a visible and palpable "tree of life," of such a sort that anyone who tasted its fruit with his bodily teeth would gain life, and again that one could partake of "good and evil" by masticating the fruit taken from the tree of that name? And when God is said to "walk in the paradise in the cool of the day" and Adam to hide himself behind a tree. I do not think anyone will doubt that these are figurative expressions which indicate certain mysteries through a semblance of history and not through actual event.[7]

Simply because a story purports to be a straightforward historical narrative does not mean that it is in fact what it claims to be. What appears to be historical may be metaphor or figure instead and the interpreter who confuses metaphor with

[7] Origen, *On First Principles*, ed. by G. W. Butterworth (New York: Harper and Row, 1966), 288. —Steinmetz

literal fact is an interpreter who is simply incompetent. Every biblical story means something, even if the narrative taken at face value contains absurdities or contradictions. The interpreter must demythologize the text in order to grasp the sacred mystery cloaked in the language of actual events.

The second reason for distinguishing between letter and spirit was the thorny question of the relationship between Israel and the church, between the Greek Testament and the Hebrew Bible. The church regarded itself as both continuous and discontinuous with ancient Israel. Because it claimed to be continuous, it felt an unavoidable obligation to interpret the Torah, the prophets, and the writings. But it was precisely this claim of continuity, absolutely essential to Christian identity, which created fresh hermeneutical problems for the church.

How was a French parish priest in 1150 to understand Psalm 137, which bemoans captivity in Babylon, makes rude remarks about Edomites, expresses an ineradicable longing for a glimpse of Jerusalem, and pronounces a blessing on anyone who avenges the destruction of the temple by dashing Babylonian children against a rock? The priest lives in Concale, not Babylon, has no personal quarrel with Edomites, cherishes no ambitions to visit Jerusalem (though he might fancy a holiday in Paris), and is expressly forbidden by Jesus to avenge himself on his enemies. Unless Psalm 137 has more than one possible meaning, it cannot be used as a prayer by the church and must be rejected as a lament belonging exclusively to the piety of ancient Israel.

A third reason for distinguishing letter from spirit was the conviction, expressed by Augustine, that while all Scripture was given for the edification of the church and the nurture of the three theological virtues of faith, hope, and love, not all the stories in the Bible are edifying as they stand. What is the spiritual point of the story of the drunkenness of Noah,[8] the murder of Sisera,[9] or the oxgoad of Shamgar, son of Anath?[10] If it cannot be found on the level of narrative, then it must be found on the level of allegory, metaphor, and type.

That is not to say that patristic and medieval interpreters approved of arbitrary and undisciplined exegesis, which gave free rein to the imagination of the exegete. Augustine argued, for example, that the more obscure parts of Scripture should be interpreted in the light of its less difficult sections and that no allegorical interpretation could be accepted which was not supported by the "manifest testimonies" of other less ambiguous portions of the Bible. The literal sense of Scripture is basic to the spiritual and limits the range of possible allegorical meanings in those instances in which the literal meaning of a particular passage is absurd, undercuts the living relationship of the church to the Old Testament, or is spiritually barren.

---

[8] Gen 9:20–27.
[9] Judg 4.
[10] Judg 3:31.

II

From the time of John Cassian, the church subscribed to a theory of the four-fold sense of Scripture.[11] The literal sense of Scripture could and usually did nurture the three theological virtues, but when it did not, the exegete could appeal to three additional spiritual senses, each sense corresponding to one of the virtues. The allegorical sense taught about the church and what it should believe, and so it corresponded to the virtue of faith. The tropological sense taught about individuals and what they should do, and so it corresponded to the virtue of love. The anagogical sense pointed to the future and wakened expectation, and so it corresponded to the virtue of hope. In the fourteenth century Nicholas of Lyra summarized this hermeneutical theory in a much quoted little rhyme:

> Littera gesta docet,
> Quid credas allegoria,
> Moralis quid agas,
> Quo tendas anagogia.[12]

This hermeneutical device made it possible for the church to pray directly and without qualification even a troubling Psalm like 137. After all, Jerusalem was not merely a city in the Middle East, it was, according to the allegorical sense, the church; according to the tropological sense, the faithful soul; and according to the anagogical sense, the center of God's new creation. The Psalm became a lament of those who long for the establishment of God's future kingdom and who are tramped in this disordered and troubled world, which with all its delights is still not their home. They seek an abiding city elsewhere. The imprecations against the Edomites and the Babylonians are transmuted into condemnations of the world, the flesh, and the devil. If you grant the fourfold sense of Scripture, David sings like a Christian.

III

Thomas Aquinas wanted to ground the spiritual sense of Scripture even more securely in the literal sense than it had been grounded in patristic thought. Returning to the distinction between "things" and "signs" made by Augustine in *De doctrina christiana* (though Thomas preferred to use the Aristotelian terminology of "things" and "words"). Thomas argued that while words are the signs of things, things designated by words can themselves be the signs of other things. In all merely human sciences, words alone have a sign-character. But in Holy Scripture, the things designated by words can themselves have the character of a sign. The literal sense of Scripture has to

---

[11] For a brief survey of medieval hermeneutical theory which takes into account recent historical research see James S. Preus, *From Shadow to Promise* (Cambridge, Mass.: Harvard University Press, 1969), 9–149; see also the useful bibliography, 287–93.—Steinmetz

[12] The letter teaches the act,
what you should believe, allegory.
The moral what you should do,
where you should be heading, anagogy.

do with the sign-character of words; the spiritual sense of Scripture has to do with the sign-character of things. By arguing this way, Thomas was able to show that the spiritual sense of Scripture is always based on the literal sense and derived from it.

Thomas also redefined the literal sense of Scripture as "the meaning of the text which the author intends." Lest Thomas be confused with Jowett, I should hasten to point out that for Thomas the author was God, not the human prophet or apostle. In the fourteenth century, Nicholas of Lyra, a Franciscan exegete and one of the most impressive biblical scholars produced by the Christian church, built a new hermeneutical argument on the aphorism of Thomas. If the literal sense of Scripture is the meaning which the author intended (presupposing that the author whose intention finally matters is God), then is it possible to argue that Scripture contains a double literal sense? Is there a literal-historical sense (the original meaning of the words as spoken in their first historical setting) which includes and implies a literal-prophetic sense (the larger meaning of the words as perceived in later and changed circumstances)?

Nicholas not only embraced a theory of the double literal sense of Scripture, but he was even willing to argue that in certain contexts the literal-prophetic sense takes precedence over the literal-historical. Commenting on Ps 117, Lyra wrote: "The literal sense in this Psalm concerns Christ; for the literal sense is the sense primarily intended by the author." Of the promise to Solomon in 1 Chr 17:13, Lyra observed: "The aforementioned authority was literally fulfilled in Solomon; however, it was fulfilled less perfectly, because Solomon was a son of God only by grace; but it was fulfilled more perfectly in Christ, who is the Son of God by nature."

For most exegetes, the theory of Nicholas of Lyra bound the interpreter to the dual task of explaining the historical meaning of a text while elucidating its larger and later spiritual significance. The great French humanist, Jacques Lefèvre d'Etaples, however, pushed the theory to absurd limits. He argued that the only possible meaning of a text was its literal-prophetic sense and that the literal-historical sense was a product of human fancy and idle imagination. The literal-historical sense is the "letter which kills." It is advocated as the true meaning of Scripture only by carnal persons who have not been regenerated by the life-giving Spirit of God. The problem of the proper exegesis of Scripture is, when all is said and done, the problem of the regeneration of its interpreters.

IV

In this brief survey of medieval hermeneutical theory, there are certain dominant themes which recur with dogged persistence. Medieval exegetes admit that the words of Scripture had a meaning in the historical situation in which they were first uttered or written, but they deny that the meaning of those words is restricted to what the human author thought he said or what his first audience thought they heard. The stories and sayings of Scripture bear an implicit meaning only understood by a later audience. In some cases that implicit meaning is far more important than the restricted meaning intended by the author in his particular cultural setting.

Yet the text cannot mean anything a later audience wants it to mean. The language of the Bible opens up a field of possible meanings. Any interpretation which falls within that field is valid exegesis of the text, even though that interpretation was not intended by the author. Any interpretation which falls outside the limits of that field of possible meanings is probably eisegesis and should be rejected as unacceptable. Only by confessing the multiple sense of Scripture is it possible for the church to make use of the Hebrew Bible at all or to recapture the various levels of significance in the unfolding story of creation and redemption. The notion that Scripture has only one meaning is a fantastic idea and is certainly not advocated by the biblical writers themselves.

V

Having elucidated medieval hermeneutical theory, I should like to take some time to look at medieval exegetical practice. One could get the impression from Jowett that because medieval exegetes rejected the theory of the single meaning of Scripture so dear to Jowett's heart, they let their exegetical imaginations run amok and exercised no discipline at all in clarifying the field of possible meanings opened by the biblical text. In fact, medieval interpreters, once you grant the presuppositions on which they operate, are as conservative and restrained in their approach to the Bible as any comparable group of modern scholars.

In order to test medieval exegetical practice I have chosen a terribly difficult passage from the Gospel of Matthew, the parable of the Good Employer or, as it is more frequently known, the parable of the Workers in the Vineyard (Matt. 20:1–16). The story is a familiar one. An employer hired day laborers to work in his vineyard at dawn and promised them the standard wage of a denarius. Because he needed more workers, he returned to the market place at nine, noon, three, and five o'clock and hired any laborers he could find. He promised to pay the workers hired at nine, noon, and three what was fair. But the workers hired at the eleventh hour or five o'clock were sent into the vineyard without any particular promise concerning remuneration. The employer instructed his foreman to pay off the workers beginning with the laborers hired at five o'clock. These workers expected only one twelfth of a denarius, but were given the full day's wage instead. Indeed, all the workers who had worked part of the day were given one denarius. The workers who had been in the vineyard since dawn accordingly expected a bonus beyond the denarius, but they were disappointed to receive the same wage which had been given to the other, less deserving workers. When they grumbled, they were told by the employer that they had not been defrauded but had been paid according to an agreed contract. If the employer chose to be generous to the workers who had only worked part of the day, that was, in effect, none of their business. They should collect the denarius that was due them and go home like good fellows.

Jesus said the kingdom of God was like this story. What on earth could he have meant?

VI

The church has puzzled over this parable ever since it was included in Matthew's Gospel. St. Thomas Aquinas in his *Lectura super Evangelium Sancti Matthaei* offered two interpretations of the parable, one going back in its lineage to Irenaeus and the other to Origen. The "day" mentioned in the parable can either refer to the life-span of an individual (the tradition of Origen) in which case the parable is a comment on the various ages at which one may be converted to Christ, or it is a reference to the history of salvation (the tradition of Irenaeus), in which case it is a comment on the relationship of Jew and Gentile.

If the story refers to the life span of a man or woman, then it is intended as an encouragement to people who are converted to Christ late in life. The workers in the story who begin at dawn are people who have served Christ and have devoted themselves to the love of God and neighbor since childhood. The other hours mentioned by Jesus refer to the various stages of human development from youth to old age. Whether one has served Christ for a long time or for a brief moment, one will still receive the gift of eternal life. Thomas qualifies this somewhat in order to allow for proportional rewards and a hierarchy in heaven. But he does not surrender the main point: eternal life is given to late converts with the same generosity it is given to early converts.

On the other hand, the story may refer to the history of salvation. Quite frankly, this is the interpretation which interests Thomas most. The hours mentioned in the parable are not stages in individual human development but epochs in the history of the world from Adam to Noah, from Noah to Abraham, from Abraham to David, and from David to Christ. The owner of the vineyard is the whole Trinity, the foreman is Christ, and the moment of reckoning is the resurrection from the dead. The workers who are hired at the eleventh hour are the Gentiles, whose complaint that no one has offered them work can be interpreted to mean that they had no prophets as the Jews have had. The workers who have borne the heat of the day are the Jews, who grumble about the favoritism shown to latecomers, but who are still given the denarius of eternal life. As a comment on the history of salvation, the parable means that the generosity of God undercuts any advantage which the Jews might have had over the Gentiles with respect to participation in the gifts and graces of God.

Not everyone read the text as a gloss on Jewish-Christian relations or as a discussion of late conversion. In the fourteenth century the anonymous author of the *Pearl*, an elegy on the death of a young girl, applied the parable to infancy rather than to old age. What is important about the parable is not the chronological age at which one enters the vineyard, but the fact that some workers are only in the vineyard for the briefest possible moment. A child who dies at the age of two years is, in a sense, a worker who arrives at the eleventh hour. The parable is intended as a consolation for bereaved parents. A parent who has lost a small child can be comforted by the knowledge that God, who does not despise the service of persons converted in extreme old age, does not withhold his mercy from boys and girls whose eleventh hour came at dawn.

Probably the most original interpretation of the parable was offered by John Pupper of Goch, a Flemish theologian of the fifteenth century, who used the parable to attack the doctrine of proportionality, particularly as that doctrine had been stated and defended by Thomas Aquinas. No one had ever argued that God gives rewards which match in exact quantity the weight of the good works done by a Christian. That is arithmetic equality and is simply not applicable to a relationship in which people perform temporal acts and receive eternal rewards. But most theologians did hold to a doctrine of proportionality: while there is a disproportion between the good works which Christians do and the rewards which they receive, there is a proportion as well. The reward is always much larger than the work which is rewarded, but the greater the work, the greater the reward.

As far as Goch is concerned, that doctrine is sheer nonsense. No one can take the message of the parable of the vineyard seriously and still hold to the doctrine of proportionality. Indeed, the only people in the vineyard who hold to the doctrine of proportionality are the first workers in the vineyard. They argue that twelve times the work should receive twelve times the payment. All they receive for their argument is a rebuke and a curt dismissal.

Martin Luther, in an early sermon preached before the Reformation in 1517, agreed with Goch that God gives equal reward for great and small works. It is not by the herculean size of our exertions but by the goodness of God that we receive any reward at all.

But Luther, unfortunately, spoiled his point by elaborating a thoroughly unconvincing argument in which he tried to show that the last workers in the vineyard were more humble than the first and therefore that one hour of their service was worth twelve hours of the mercenary service of the grumblers.

The parable, however, seems to make exactly the opposite point. The workers who began early were not more slothful or more selfish than the workers who began later in the day. Indeed, they were fairly representative of the kind of worker to be found hanging around the marketplace at any hour. They were angry, not because they had shirked their responsibilities, but because they had discharged them conscientiously.

In 1525 Luther offered a fresh interpretation of the parable, which attacked it from a slightly different angle. The parable has essentially one point: to celebrate the goodness of God which makes nonsense of a religion based on law-keeping and good works. God pays no attention to the proportionately greater efforts of the first workers in the vineyard, but to their consternation, God puts them on exactly the same level as the last and least productive workers. The parable shows that everyone in the vineyard is unworthy, though not always for the same reason. The workers who arrive after nine o'clock are unworthy because they are paid a salary incommensurate with their achievement in picking grapes. The workers who spent the entire day in the vineyard are unworthy because they are dissatisfied with what God has promised, think that their efforts deserve special consideration, and are jealous of their employer's goodness to workers who accomplished less than they did. The parable teaches that salvation is not grounded in human merit and that there is no system of bookkeeping which can keep track of the relationship between God and humanity. Salvation depends utterly and absolutely on the goodness of God.

VII

The four medieval theologians I have mentioned—Thomas Aquinas, the author of the *Pearl,* the Flemish chaplain Goch, and the young Martin Luther—did not exhaust in their writings all the possible interpretations of the parable of the Workers in the Vineyard. But they did see with considerable clarity that the parable is an assertion of God's generosity and mercy to people who do not deserve it. It is only against the background of the generosity of God that one can understand the relationship of Jew and Gentile, the problem of late conversion, the meaning of the death of a young child, the question of proportional rewards, even the very definition of grace itself. Every question is qualified by the severe mercy of God, by the strange generosity of the owner of the vineyard who pays the non-productive latecomer the same wage as his oldest and most productive employees.

If you were to ask me which of these interpretations is valid, I should have to respond that they all are. They all fall within the field of possible meanings created by the story itself. How many of those meanings were in the conscious intention of Jesus or of the author of the Gospel of Matthew, I do not profess to know. I am inclined to agree with C. S. Lewis, who commented on his own book, *Till We Have Faces:* "An author doesn't necessarily understand the meaning of his own story better than anyone else. . . ."[13] The act of creation confers no special privileges on authors when it comes to the distinctly different, if lesser task of interpretation. Wordsworth the critic is not in the same league with Wordsworth the poet, while Samuel Johnson the critic towers over Johnson the creative artist. Authors obviously have something in mind when they write, but a work of historical or theological or aesthetic imagination has a life of its own.

VIII

Which brings us back to Benjamin Jowett. Jowett rejected medieval exegesis and insisted that the Bible should be read like any other book.[14] I agree with Jowett that the Bible should be read like any other book. The question is: how does one read other books?

---

[13] W. H. Lewis, ed., *Letters of C. S. Lewis* (New York: Harcourt, Brace and World, 1966), 273. —Steinmetz

[14] Jowett, "Interpretation," 377. —Steinmetz

Take, for example, my own field of Reformation studies. Almost no historian that I know would answer the question of the meaning of the writings of Martin Luther by focusing solely on Luther's explicit and conscious intention. Marxist interpreters of Luther from Friedrich Engels to Max Steinmetz have been interested in Luther's writings as an expression of class interests, while psychological interpreters from Grisar to Erikson have focused on the theological writings as clues to the inner psychic tensions in the personality of Martin Luther. Even historians who reject Marxist and psychological interpretations of Luther find themselves asking how Luther was understood in the free imperial cities, by the German knights, by the landed aristocracy, by the various subgroups of German peasants, by the Catholic hierarchy, by lawyers, by university faculties—to name only a few of the more obvious groups who responded to Luther and left a written record of their response. Meaning involves a listener as well as a speaker, and when one asks the question of the relationship of Luther to his various audiences in early modern Europe, it becomes clear that there was not one Luther in the sixteenth century, but a battalion of Luthers.

Nor can the question of the meaning of Luther's writings be answered by focusing solely on Luther's contemporaries. Luther's works were read and pondered in a variety of historical and cultural settings from his death in 1546 to the present. Those readings of Luther have had measurable historical effects on succeeding generations, whose particular situation in time and space could scarcely have been anticipated by Luther. Yet the social, political, economic, cultural, and religious history of those people belongs intrinsically and inseparably to the question of the meaning of the theology of Martin Luther. The meaning of historical texts cannot be separated from the complex problem of their reception and the notion that a text means only what its author intends it to mean is historically naive. Even to talk of the original setting in which words were spoken and heard is to talk of meanings rather than meaning. To attempt to understand those original meanings is the first step in the exegetical process, not the last and final step.

Modern literary criticism has challenged the notion that a text means only what its author intends it to mean far more radically than medieval exegetes ever dreamed of doing. Indeed, contemporary debunking of the author and the author's explicit intentions has proceeded at such a pace that it seems at times as if literary criticism has become a jolly game of ripping out an author's shirt-tail and setting fire to it. The reader and the literary work to the exclusion of the author have become the central preoccupation of the literary critic. Literary relativists of a fairly moderate sort insist that every generation has its own Shakespeare and Milton, and extreme relativists loudly proclaim that no reader reads the same work twice. Every change in the reader, however slight, is a change in the meaning of the text. Imagine what Thomas Aquinas or Nicholas of Lyra would have made of the famous statement of Northrop Frye:

> It has been said of Boehme that his books are like a picnic to which the author brings the words and the reader the meaning. The remark may have been

intended as a sneer at Boehme, but it is an exact description of all works of literary art without exception.[15]

Medieval exegetes held to the sober middle way, the position that the text (any literary text, but especially the Bible) contains both letter and spirit. The text is not all letter, as Jowett with others maintained, or all spirit, as the rather more enthusiastic literary critics in our own time are apt to argue. The original text as spoken and heard limits a field of possible meanings. Those possible meanings are not dragged by the hair, willy-nilly, into the text, but belong to the life of the Bible in the encounter between author and reader as they belong to the life of any act of the human imagination. Such a hermeneutical theory is capable of sober and disciplined application and avoids the Scylla of extreme subjectivism, on the one hand, and the Charybdis of historical positivism, on the other. To be sure, medieval exegetes made bad mistakes in the application of their theory, but they also scored notable and brilliant triumphs. Even at their worst they recognized that the intention of the author is only one element—and not always the most important element at that—in the complex phenomenon of the meaning of a text.

IX

The defenders of the single meaning theory usually concede that the medieval approach to the Bible met the religious needs of the Christian community, but that it did so at the unacceptable price of doing violence to the biblical text. The fact that the historical-critical method after two hundred years is still struggling for more than a precarious foothold in that same religious community is generally blamed on the ignorance and conservatism of the Christian laity and the sloth or moral cowardice of its pastors.

I should like to suggest an alternative hypothesis. The medieval theory of levels of meaning in the biblical text, with all its undoubted defects, flourished because it is true, while the modern theory of a single meaning, with all its demonstrable virtues, is false. Until the historical-critical method becomes critical of its own theoretical foundations and develops a hermeneutical theory adequate to the nature of the text which it is interpreting, it will remain restricted—as it deserves to be—to the guild and the academy, where the question of truth can endlessly be deferred.

---

[15] This quotation is cited by E. D Hirsch. Jr., *Validity in Interpretation* (New Haven: Yale University Press, 1967), 1, at the beginning of a chapter which sets out to elaborate an alternative theory.
—Steinmetz

CHAPTER 28

Jews, Christians, and Theological Interpretation of the Bible: Jon Levenson (1949–)

From the impulse provided by Jewish intellects such as Moses Mendelssohn in the eighteenth century there emerged a serious interest among some nineteenth-century Jews to study Judaism scientifically. Scholars such as Leopold Zunz (1794–1886) and Abaham Geiger (1810–1874) sought to use the same modern critical methods of inquiry as were being applied successfully to the study of classical texts and culture, history, and philosophy, in order to describe and understand the origins and development of Jewish traditions. As the *Wissenschaft des Judentums* movement developed, there was generally a more intense focus brought to bear on Jewish texts and beliefs from the postbiblical era than on the biblical text itself. (At the same time, critical research into the composition of the Bible was advancing apace among Protestant scholars.) Generally speaking, Jews who valued historical-critical methods of research did not consider the ancient documents and culture of the Bible relevant for investigation or for application to contemporary cultural issues. Conversely, Jews who valued the biblical past and biblical study were not inclined to employ critical methods of research; rather they preferred to study Torah within the framework of traditional historical assumptions of the Bible's composition and meaning.

Later in the nineteenth century and in the twentieth century, the situation began to change. The Italian scholar S. D. Luzzatto (1800–1865), for example, applied critical research methods to the Hebrew Bible, albeit with more enthusiasm when studying wisdom or prophetic texts than when turning to the Torah. This pattern was generally true for other Jewish scholars before World War II: they might conclude, along with Protestant scholars, that the latter half of the book of Isaiah was a product of exilic writers or that some psalms were composed during the Maccabean age, but the books of the Pentateuch were still accepted as a single literary entity deriving from the era of Moses.

By the mid-twentieth century, critical biblical scholarship practiced by Jews had become a force to be reckoned with, particularly in linguistic and historical disciplines. Figures such as Max Margolis (textual criticism and philology), Julius Morgenstern (history of Israelite religion), Ephraim Speiser (Semitics and ancient Near Eastern cultures), and Cyrus Gordon (ancient Near Eastern languages and history) became leading lights in a tradition of Jewish scholarship that advanced biblical learning by expert application of extrabiblical material to the study of Jewish Scriptures. At the same time, other Jewish scholars were moving beyond the historicist pattern of biblical studies into more focused specializations in issues of biblical interpretation per se. Pioneers in this respect include H. L. Ginsburg (philologically and historically based biblical interpretation) and Harry M. Orlinsky (textual criticism, English translation, and the history of ancient Israel). Jewish scholars continue to distinguish themselves as leaders in linguistic and historical studies of the Bible, but more recently others have integrated a historicist approach (applied now to the whole of the Hebrew Bible, including the Torah) with sensitive literary analysis; the names of Baruch Levine, Jacob Milgrom, and Nahum Sarna, among others, come to mind.

The reader will note, however, that, though excelling in historical disciplines such as philology and textual criticism, modern Jewish biblical scholarship has not emphasized theology—an area that has long preoccupied many Christian scholars. Several factors have contributed to this. Works by the leading modern Jewish intellects, such as Moses Mendelssohn and Martin Buber, were, by and large, produced in German and remained untranslated into English until after World War II. Thus, Jewish students in America and England—countries in which there was a greater openness in Jewish culture to move beyond traditional halakic religious categories—did not have ready access to the works of key sophisticated Jewish philosophical thinkers. As a result, the late nineteenth and early twentieth centuries produced few Jewish scholars who were theologically inclined. Moreover, few academic posts were available at Jewish institutions of advanced learning for serious research on issues of Jewish philosophical and theological thought and culture. Another factor lay in the modern mind-set of most Western Jews of recent generations. For the majority of modern Jews in the West, theology has connoted premodern modes of thought such as dogmatism and religious supernaturalism—notions that modern Jews, emerging from a history of theological polemics and political subjugation within Christian European society, were wont to leave behind. So, whereas "religion" was available for scholarly exploration without intellectual sacrifice, "theology" remained associated with a medieval mind-set. Finally, there was the tradition of Jewish scholarship itself. Historically, Judaism has not emphasized theology as such. Instead of exploring the articulation of theological principles, for centuries rabbinic authorities have been preoccupied with the practice of the Jewish way of life, a preoccupation that had long since become definitive of distinctly Jewish intellectual pursuits.

In the late twentieth century, there have been stirrings of Jewish interest in theology. Some biblical scholars, such as Moshe Goshen-Gottstein and Mattitiahu Tsevat, have explored ways of approaching the Bible from a Jewish theological point of view. One of the leading voices is that of Jon D. Levenson. Currently the Albert A. List Professor of Jewish Studies at Harvard Divinity School, Levenson studied at Harvard under one of the twentieth century's preeminent Semitists, Frank Moore Cross. With a strong background in literature and Jewish religious thought, Levenson has brought his training to bear on the theological assumptions that have historically shaped biblical studies on the part of both Christian and Jewish scholars. Many of his own writings are forays into Jewish biblical theology. In the following essay, "Why Jews Are Not Interested in Biblical Theology," Levenson explains further reasons why Jewish scholars, for all their enthusiasm for biblical studies, have not pursued the theological dimensions of the Bible in the fashion of their Christian counterparts.

For further information on modern Jewish biblical and theological studies:

Brooks, Roger, and John J. Collins, eds. *Hebrew Bible or Old Testament? Studying the Bible in Judaism and Christianity.* Notre Dame: University of Notre Dame Press, 1990.

Goldy, Robert G. *The Emergence of Jewish Theology in America.* Bloomington: Indiana University Press, 1990.

Levenson, Jon D. *Creation and the Persistence of Evil: The Jewish Drama of Divine Omnipotence.* San Francisco: Harper & Row, 1988.

———. *Sinai and Zion: An Entry into the Jewish Bible.* San Francisco: Harper & Row, 1985.

Sperling, S. David. *Students of the Covenant: A History of Jewish Biblical Scholarship in North America.* Atlanta: Scholars Press, 1992.

Tsevat, Mattitiahu. "Theology of the Old Testament—a Jewish View." *Horizons in Biblical Theology* 8 (1986): 33–49.

Why Jews Are Not Interested in Biblical Theology[1]

I

Soon after I began teaching I received a revealing phone call from a colleague in another institution. The caller was teaching "Introduction to the Old Testament," a course for both divinity school and liberal arts students. Among the latter was a Jew upset at what he perceived to be the Christian bias of the bibliography. Eager to be evenhanded, the professor called me to find out what Jewish scholar had written the best "biblical theology." My hesitation in answering was surely sufficient to call into doubt my colleague's confidence in my competence. Finally, I stammered out the names of a few serviceable works concerned with biblical concepts and authored by committed Jews, such as Yehezkel Kaufmann (The Religion of Israel) and Nahum Sarna (Understanding Genesis).[2] The caller thanked me, but I remember thinking as I hung up that he ought to feel disappointed, for what he was hoping to get from me was the title of the Jewish equivalent of Walther Eichrodt's Theology of the Old Testament or Gerhard von Rad's Old Testament Theology.[3] And for reasons that I shall explore in this essay, there is no Jewish equivalent.

I had occasion to recall this little incident several years later, as I sat in a Protestant seminary listening to a distinguished continental biblicist lecture on Old Testament theology. At the end of his talk, he remarked that in a year of research in Israel, he had been unable to find anyone interested in the subject. Finally, he had asked a member of the Bible department at the Hebrew University of Jerusalem about this curious situation, and the latter, a man known for his keen theological interests, replied that he thought no one in Israel, presumably including himself, had any interest in the whole exercise. The lecturer was visibly perplexed as he told this story. Sophisticated Israeli biblicists uninterested in Old Testament theology? It made no sense. In the end, he shrugged his shoulders in a gesture of mingled disbelief and resignation.

The expectation of these Christian scholars was not unreasonable. Whereas for centuries the field of biblical studies was divided along religious and even denominational lines—with little respect and less communication between groups—today the field, at least in North America, boasts a vibrant ecumenicity. Collaboration in biblical work among Jews, Catholics, Protestants, and secularists no longer elicits surprise, except among the laity and the extreme right of each religious grouping. Among professional academics and well-informed clergy, the pluralism of the field is assumed.

---

[1] This is extracted from Jon Levenson, "Why Jews Are Not Interested in Biblical Theology," in *Judaic Perspectives on Ancient Israel* (ed. J. Neusner, B.A. Levine, and E. S. Frerichs; Philadelphia: Fortress, 1987), 281–307. Used with permission.

[2] Yehezkel Kaufmann, *The Religion of Israel* (Chicago: University of Chicago Press, 1960); Nahum M. Sarna, *Understanding Genesis* (New York: Jewish Theological Seminary of America and McGraw-Hill, 1966). —Levenson

[3] Walther Eichrodt, *Theology of the Old Testament*, 2 vols., OTL (Philadelphia: Westminster, 1961); Gerhard von Rad, *Old Testament Theology*, 2 vols. (New York: Harper & Row, 1962). —Levenson

Indeed, it can be readily discerned from the diversity of backgrounds and institutional affiliations among contributors to the two most influential American commentary series, the Anchor Bible (Doubleday) and Hermeneia (Fortress). The old identities have faded and are now often vestigial. On this, my own situation speaks volumes, for, an observant Jew, I teach Hebrew Bible at a liberal Protestant divinity school in a university of Puritan origin, and I am a member of the Catholic Biblical Association and have contributed repeatedly to its journal.

If Jewish participation is plentiful in academic programs, professional societies and journals, excavations, and commentaries, one would expect it to be no less plentiful in studies of "biblical theology" or, at least, in research on its Old Testament side. Instead, we may question whether there is any identifiably Jewish participation in that aspect of biblical studies. To be sure, Jews have contributed studies of the theological themes in various texts of the Hebrew Bible. In his *Preface to Old Testament Theology,* Robert C. Dentan devotes one sentence to these Jewish thinkers, citing Martin Buber, Will Herberg, and Abraham J. Heschel as examples.[4] But whereas Christians have written scores of books and articles with "Old Testament Theology" or the like as their titles, I know of no book with that title or anything similar ("Theology of the Hebrew Bible," "Biblical Theology") written by a Jew. The best approximation is *The Philosophy of the Bible,* by David Neumark, professor of Jewish philosophy at the Hebrew Union College in Cincinnati early in the twentieth century.[5] This book dates from 1918, and even it is more a history of the religion of Israel than a biblical theology. The distinction, as we shall see, is essential.

The meaning of the term "biblical theology" is itself an issue much discussed in the discipline that goes by that name.[6] Dentan notes that the term "might *mean* either a biblical kind of *theology,* or the theological parts of *biblical* studies." Opting for the latter, he insists that "the only definition of biblical theology which does justice to the history of the discipline is that it is *the study of the religious ideas of the Bible in their historical context.*"[7] John Bright sets forth essentially the same dichotomy,

---

[4] Robert C. Dentan, *Preface to Old Testament Theology,* rev. ed. (New York: Seabury, 1963), 81. In his bibliography, Dentan lists the works as follows:

　　Buber, Martin. *The Prophetic Faith.* New York: Macmillan, 1949.
　　Herberg, Will. "Faith as Heilsgeschichte: The Meaning of Redemptive History in
　　　　Human Existence," *The Christian Scholar* 39 (1956): 25–31.
　　Heschel, Abraham J. *The Prophets* (chs. 9–17 on prophetic theology). New York: Harper
　　　　& Row, 1962.
　　————. *Theology of Ancient Judaism.* London and New York: Soncino, 5722/1962 (in
　　　　Hebrew). —Levenson

[5] David Neumark, *The Philosophy of the Bible* (Cincinnati: Ark, 1918). —Levenson

[6] On the discipline in general, see Norman W. Porteous, "Old Testament Theology," in *The Old Testament and Modern Study,* ed. H. H. Rowley (Oxford: Clarendon, 1951), 311–45; Dentan, *Preface;* H. J. Kraus, *Die Biblische Theologie: lhre Geschichte und Problematik* (Neukirchen-Vluyn: Neukirchener Verlag, 1970); Gerhard Hasel, *Old Testament Theology: Basic Issues in the Current Debate,* rev. ed. (Grand Rapids: Eerdmans, 1982); George W. Coats, "Theology of the Hebrew Bible," in *The Hebrew Bible and Its Modern Interpreters,* ed. Douglas A. Knight and Gene M. Tucker (Philadelphia: Fortress; Chico, Calif: Scholars Press, 1985), 239–62. —Levenson

[7] Dentan, *Preface,* 87, 90. —Levenson

although he notes a "third sense . . . , the attempt of certain theologians and preachers to expound the Bible in its unity as authoritative in the church." Bright's own
preference is similar to Dentan's. For him, "biblical theology" is "the theology that is
expressed in the Bible."[8] It is common in these discussions to date the birth of the
discipline to its separation from dogmatics late in the eighteenth century. If biblical
theology has a birthday, it is March 30, 1787, when Johann Philipp Gabler gave his
inaugural address upon assuming the chair in theology at the University of Altdorf.
"Biblical theology," Gabler insisted, "is historical in character and sets forth what the
sacred writers thought about divine matters; dogmatic theology, on the contrary, is
didactic in character, and teaches what a particular theologian philosophically and
rationally decides about divine matters, in accordance with his character, time, age,
place, sect or school, and other similar influences."[9] For Gabler, as for most Protestants, one of the most important of those influences was the Bible. But the distinction
he so lucidly drew between biblical and dogmatic theology ultimately opened the
door for the present pluralism in scholarship. If "biblical theology is historical in character," the affiliation of the biblical theologians is of no account for their work. As we
shall see, this implication is one from which biblical theologians themselves often
recoil. This recoiling is a major reason that this branch of biblical studies is less
pluralistic than the others.

If the distinction from dogmatics is rather easily made, if not easily accepted,
the distinction between biblical theology and the history of the religion of Israel is
more problematic. Dentan contrasts the two thus: "One treats of the story of Israel's
developments in its chronological sequence; the other describes the persistent and
distinctive principles of Old Testament religion in some kind of logical or 'theological' order."[10] In other words, those principles are not examined in a historical vacuum but are assumed to have a stable identity through history, and it is this stable
identity, rather than their growth and minor permutations, that interests Old Testament theologians. They focus not on the "long-cut" but on the "cross-cut" (*Quer-
schnitt* is Eichrodt's term).[11] Bright is of essentially the same opinion, insisting that
"the fact of diversity does not eliminate the possibility of an overarching unity, either
in the biblical faith or any other."[12] If, however, there are "persistent . . . principles"
or "an overarching unity," then it would seem that the historian of Israelite religion
ought to be able to see them as well as can the Old Testament theologian. Bright, I
think, would agree. His historical and his theological work present essentially the
same picture, in which "covenant" and "promise" are the twin centerpieces. They
"run through the whole of the Old Testament and inform all of its parts."[13] If this
were true, it would surely simplify the biblical theologians' task. All they would need

---

[8] John Bright, *The Authority of the Old Testament* (Nashville: Abingdon, 1967), 113–14.
—Levenson
[9] Quoted in Dentan, *Preface*, 22–23. —Levenson
[10] Quoted in Dentan, *Preface*, 92. —Levenson
[11] Quoted in Dentan, *Preface*, 64, 93. —Levenson
[12] Bright, *Authority*, 122. See also 126. —Levenson
[13] Bright, *Authority*, 136, Cf. John Bright, A *History of Israel*, 3d ed. (Philadelphia: Westminster, 1981), 148–62. —Levenson

to do is to describe the religion of Israel as the Old Testament wants it to be, and the result would be both a history of the religion of Israel (with due note of Israel's backsliding) and an Old Testament theology. The fact is, however, that this cross-cut, indeed *any* cross-cut, is really a Procrustean bed that cannot accommodate major segments of the book or, to be more precise, cannot regard as major the segments of the book that it does not accommodate. Covenant and promise dominate the Pentateuch, but they are missing from Proverbs, Qohelet, and the Song of Songs. These books, especially Proverbs, make no attempt to situate themselves within Israel's foundational story; they are unconcerned with the exodus, the revelation at Sinai, and the promise and conquest of the land. Indeed, they demonstrate no awareness of these themes. Bright's claim that in Proverbs "the place of Israel as [YHWH's] people, bound to live under his law, is clearly taken for granted"[14] is specious and circular. One cannot even assume the Israelite origin of all the biblical proverbs.[15] In light of the themes that Bright regards as constitutive of the "overarching unity" of the Old Testament, one is hardly surprised to find that his book on *The Authority of the Old Testament* refers to Amos five times and to Proverbs only twice, and never to a specific verse, even though Amos is less than one-sixth the length of Proverbs. Some themes are more widespread than others, but a widespread theme does not make an "overarching unity." The sad truth is that Old Testament theologians have generally treated the themes that appeal to them as more pervasive in the Old Testament and the religion of Israel than is warranted. Historians of religion without theological commitment would, instead, be inclined to acknowledge the diversity and contradiction of biblical thought frankly. They would feel no need to concoct a spurious "unity."

Dentan insists that the theologian's "concern should be the normative religion of the Old Testament,"[16] but, like Bright, he does not see that this criterion stands at odds with his commitment to the "historical context." The specifically historical context of the authors of Proverbs, for example, may not have included the pentateuchal traditions, and the historical context of the pentateuchal sources may not have included Proverbs. The juxtaposition of these various sorts of literature in the same book is a matter of *literary* context; it becomes a fact of *history* per se only very late in the period of the Second Temple—long after the original historical contexts of the pentateuchal literature and perhaps also the proverb collections had vanished. The construction of a religion out of *all* the materials in the Hebrew Bible violates the historian's commitment to seeing the materials in their historical contexts. The result will correspond to the religion of *no* historical community, except perhaps some parties very late in the period of the Second Temple. The argument that Old Testament theology can maintain both an uncompromisingly historical character and its distinction from the history of Israelite religion is therefore not valid.

---

14 Bright, *Authority,* 136. —Levenson
15 See Glendon E. Bryce, *A Legacy of Wisdom* (Lewisburg, Pa.: Bucknell University Press, 1979). —Levenson
16 Dentan, *Preface,* 108 (the words quoted are the title of a section). —Levenson

If the distinction between the long-cut and the cross-cut is insufficient to differentiate Old Testament theology from the history of Israelite religion, another differentiation must yet be considered. There is a tendency among Christians to insist
that biblical theology requires a measure of faith in its practitioners. "We may assume," writes Dentan, "that the Old Testament theologian of today, at least, will be a
man of faith." "Faith," to quote the title of one of his subsections, "helps make such
insight possible."[17] Gerhard Hasel is less restrained. "What needs to be emphatically
stressed," he writes, "is that there is a transcendent or divine dimension in Biblical
history which the historical critical method is unable to deal with."[18] Similarly,
Moshe Goshen-Gottstein, a Jew, takes special note of the distance involved in the
religio-historians' stance toward their material as against that in the theologians'
stance of "faith, identification, acknowledgment of value and meaningfulness, of taking a personal stand in the present, which draws nourishment from the same spring
from which the teachings *(tôrôt)* of the past flowed."[19] As a means to differentiate
the two disciplines, this idea works far better than the long-cut/cross-cut distinction,
which, as we saw, cannot do justice to the variety and changeability of history. Even if
we do not subscribe to the naive positivism that claims the historian simply tells what
really happened *(wie es eigentlich gewesen ist),* we can still differentiate scholars
who strive after a not fully realizable objectivity from those who openly acknowledge
their transcendent commitments and approach their work in the vivid hope of deep-
ening and advancing them. Here, however, biblical theology purchases its distinction
from the history of religion at the price of its equally essential distinction from dogmatics. For if we shift the focus from the biblical writings to the contemporary theological use of them, even in a nontraditional mode, then we have substantially
reconnected the umbilical cord that Gabler sought to sever two centuries ago. Our
biblical theologian, like his dogmatician, will discuss "divine matters, in accordance
with his character, time, age, place, sect or school, and other similar influences."[20]
Even if one seeks, as Goshen-Gottstein does,[21] to maintain the autonomy of tradition, in his case normative rabbinic law (halakhah), one cannot gainsay that the "personal stand in the present" of any Jew or Christian includes postbiblical elements.
Indeed, if it does not, then the theology in question will be neither Jewish nor Christian but only historical, and we are back to the dilemma discussed in the previous
paragraph, and Goshen-Gottstein's plea for a specifically Jewish biblical theology will
have failed. How can self-consciously *Jewish* biblical theologians take a personal
stand on behalf of a text that they interpret against its rabbinic exegesis? The effect
would be the neo-Karaism against which Goshen-Gottstein cautions.[22] This is not to

---

[17] Dentan, *Preface,* 116. —Levenson
[18] Hasel, *Old Testament Theology,* 173. —Levenson
[19] Moshe H. Goshen-Gottstein, "Jewish Biblical Theology and the Study of Biblical Religion"
(in Hebrew), *Tarbiz* 50 (1980/81): 45; see also 48–49 n. 24. Also noteworthy are his essays "Christianity, Judaism, and Modern Bible Study," Vetus Testamentum Supplement 28 (1975): 69–88, esp.
81–88, and "Tanakh Theology: The Religion of the Old Testament and the Place of Jewish Biblical
Theology," in *Ancient Israelite Religion,* ed. Patrick D. Miller, Jr., et al. (Philadelphia: Fortress, 1987),
617–44. —Levenson
[20] Dentan, *Preface,* 23. —Levenson
[21] Goshen-Gottstein, "Jewish Biblical Theology," 54. —Levenson
[22] Goshen-Gottstein, "Jewish Biblical Theology," 47. —Levenson

say that serious theological study of the Hebrew Bible for a Jew must be restricted to an uncritical repetition of talmudic and medieval rabbinic interpretations. It is to say, however, that the "personal stance" of a faithful contemporary Jew does not allow for the *isolation* of the Jewish Bible (Tanakh) from the larger tradition. Such an isolation is possible on historical grounds, but not on personal, existential grounds. One can, of course, attempt constructive Jewish theology with special attention to the biblical sources—and I believe there is a great need for such studies. But this is closer to what Christian faculties call "dogmatics" or "systematics" than to "biblical theology."

If it be admitted that biblical theology presumes existential commitment and that the commitment will necessarily include other sources of truth (the Talmud, the New Testament, etc.), then it becomes clear that biblical theology is different in kind from the other branches of biblical studies and that, unlike them, it cannot so easily lend itself to ecumenical, pluralistic collaboration. One pursues either Jewish biblical theology or Christian biblical theology, but not both, for the term "biblical" has a different reference for the Jew and the Christian. The first sentence of Dentan's book says it all: " 'Old Testament theology' is one part of a greater discipline called 'biblical theology' and cannot be studied in isolation from the larger subject." This is because "Old Testament theology is a *Christian-theological discipline* and, as such, does not deal with the Old Testament in isolation, but always has some concern for its relation to the New." It is, in fact, "a preparatory exercise for the study of the New Testament."[23] Here, Dentan is typical of the discipline in wishing to have it both ways. Biblical theology must be both *"the study of the religious ideas of the Bible in their historical context"* and *"a Christian-theological discipline."*[24] But Christianity is not the historical context for a single religious idea in the Hebrew Bible, the latest of whose writings predates the earliest Christian material by a full two centuries. The Christian interpretation of non-Christian literature—or, for that matter, the rabbinic interpretation of nonrabbinic literature—may have great strength. It may be defensible, even persuasive. But it cannot be *historical.*[25]

If Old Testament theology is "a preparatory exercise for the study of the New Testament," then an Old Testament theology that did not demonstrate the compatibility of the theologies of the two Testaments would have to be judged a failure. Norman Porteous, after an exhaustive survey of the discipline, concludes that "a theology of the Old Testament, however, will not seek to obscure the fact that Christ did not merely decode the Old Testament but fulfilled it."[26] If this be a criterion for success in the field, then by definition no Jew could ever succeed in it, and the absence of Jewish interest is hardly mysterious. One could, in the spirit of a somewhat obsolescent ecumenism, expect Jews to make the same sort of connection with the

---

[23] Dentan, *Preface*, 15, 94, 98. —Levenson

[24] Dentan, *Preface*, 90, 94. —Levenson

[25] Cf. Friedrich Baumgärtel, "The Hermeneutical Problem of the Old Testament," in *Essays in Old Testament Hermeneutics*, ed. Claus Westermann (Richmond: John Knox, 1963), 135, and A. H. J. Gunneweg, *Understanding the Old Testament*, OTL (Philadelphia: Westminster, 1978), 222. —Levenson

[26] Porteous, "Old Testament Theology," 344. —Levenson

Talmud and Midrash that the Christian makes with the New Testament. Neumark, in fact, tried to do something close to this,[27] and it is still surely the case that the continuity between rabbinic and older forms of Israelite religion is not sufficiently known or appreciated among scholars. Nonetheless, the Jew will feel far less compulsion to make such connections, not least because the Talmud and Midrash do not present themselves as the teleological consummation of the Tanakh but only as the rightful continuation and implementation of biblical teaching. Indeed, since rabbinic Judaism lacks the apocalyptic urgency of apostolic Christianity, the rabbis were not generally disposed to identify events or institutions from their own time as the definitive fulfillment of biblical texts. Their attitude toward the Hebrew Bible and theology in general was more relaxed and more pluriform. As a consequence, the endless discussion among biblical theologians as to the relationship between the Testaments has not found and is unlikely to find a parallel among Jewish scholars.[28]

Levenson goes on to note that historically the rhetoric of Christians engaged in biblical theology has included a (sometimes virulent) depreciation of the Jewish exegetical tradition—an attitude that was not uncommon among Christian theologians of late antiquity and the Middle Ages. Historical-critical methods of Bible study in the hands of Christian scholars tended to produce results that were taken to derogate Judaism in favor of Christianity. So, until only recently, most Jews have been reluctant to practice these methods—and then often applied them to more historicist fields such as philology, textual criticism, or ancient Israelite history rather than to theology. Finally, the fact that biblical theology has been a discipline of Protestantism, with its reticence to read the Bible as it has become embedded in a magisterial tradition (whether Catholic or Jewish), has drawn Jewish scholars to focus on history and to neglect theology in their study of the Bible.

IV

The effort to construct a systematic, harmonious theological statement out of the unsystematic and polydox materials in the Hebrew Bible fits Christianity better than Judaism because systematic theology in general is more prominent and more at home in the church than in the *bet midrash* (study house) and the synagogue. The impulse to systematize among Christians tends to find its outlet in theology. Augustine, Aquinas, Calvin, Tillich, and Rahner, to name only a few, have no really close parallels in Jewry—figures such as Maimonides and Hermann Cohen notwithstanding. Among Jews, the impulse to systematize finds its outlet in law. The Mishnah, the *Mishneh Torah*, the *Shulchan Aruch,* and the *Aruch Ha-Shulchan* have no good counterparts in the church, despite traditions of canon law and moral theology. The views each tradition holds of the other are instructive in this regard. Christians often have the impression of Judaism that its belief system is too amorphous and ill-defined and that its legal system is excessively precise and overdetermined. Jews often have the impression of Christianity that its ethical and liturgical life is dangerously subjective, emotionalistic, and impressionistic and that its theology is too rigid and too abstract.

---

[27] See Neumark, *Philosophy,* xiv. —Levenson
[28] See Hasel, *Old Testament Theology,* 145–67. —Levenson

Joseph Kitagawa, the eminent historian of religion, once put the contrast this way: if you ask Asians to describe their religion, they will tell you about their practices; if you ask Christians, they will tell you about their beliefs. Judaism, concluded Kitagawa, is in this respect more like an Asian religion than like Christianity.[29]

Since the church early on concluded that the particular *practices* of the Hebrew Bible are not incumbent upon Christians, it again follows that the *beliefs* in that book will bear proportionally more weight among Christians than among Jews. Bright's discussion of the laws of the Sabbatical and Jubilee Years in Lev 25 is revealing:

> The chapter can scarcely be called one of the high points of the Old Testament. Indeed, the regulations described therein are obviously so little applicable to the modern situation that the preacher may be pardoned if he told himself that the passage contains no relevant message for his people whatever. . . . So let us say it: The Law, as law, is ancient, irrelevant, and without authority. But what of the theology of the law? . . . It seeks to tell us that the land is God's and that we live on this earth as aliens and sojourners, holding all that we have as it were on loan from him (vs. 23); that God narrowly superintends every business transaction and expects that we conduct our affairs in the fear of him (vss. 17, 36, 43), dealing graciously with the less fortunate brother in the recollection that we have all been recipients of grace (vss. 38, 42). And that is normative ethics! It speaks with an eternal relevance to the Christian. . . . The law we cannot obey; but we are enjoined in all our dealings ever to strive to make the *theology* of the law actual.[30]

In Bright's words one feels poignantly the precarious situation of the Old Testament theologian. A good Paulinist, Bright must steer clear of the heresy of Judaizing. The implication that the laws must be obeyed, whenever possible, cannot be accepted. But across the straits from the Scylla of Judaizing sits the Charybdis of Marcionism, with its bold proclamation that the Jewish Scriptures are irrelevant to the Christian. This, too, must be resisted. Only theology enables safe passage, for by converting law into theology, specific practice into general belief, Bright can grant Paul his doctrine of exemption from Torah without granting Marcion his idea that the Jewish God and the Christ are antithetical. The specifics fade, the laws wither, but Old Testament theology endures forever.

The theology that Bright abstracts from Lev 25 is fully in accord with rabbinic Judaism. The two part company, however, in that, traditionally, Jewish thinkers would not present the theology as a direct *alternative* to the specific legal institutions. Instead, they would have seen these two items as inextricable. Even when historical conditions have rendered a law unfulfillable, rabbinic tradition regards the law as still in effect and worthy of study in all its particularity. For example, in his *Mishneh Torah*, Maimonides codifies talmudic law about the Temple cultus that the Romans rendered inoperative in 70 C.E., early in the rabbinic period and more than a millennium before Maimonides himself. The stubborn rabbinic resistance to losing the

---

[29] In private conversation, October 21, 1983. —Levenson
[30] Bright, *Authority*, 152–53. —Levenson

particular in the general stands in stark contrast to the tendency of most Christian exegesis. In a discussion concerning the adaptation of Judaism to a Gentile audience in Christian tradition, principally by Paul, Erich Auerbach presented the contrast this way:

> The total content of the sacred writings was placed in an exegetic context which often removed the thing told very far from its sensory base, in that the reader or listener was forced to turn his attention away from the sensory occurrence and toward its meaning. . . . [This is] the antagonism which permeates the early, and indeed the whole, Christian view of reality.[31]

Susan Handelman contrasts the Christian inclination toward spiritualization, allegorization, and other forms of abstraction with rabbinic thought as follows:

> One of the most interesting aspects of Rabbinic thought is its development of a highly sophisticated system of interpretation based on uncovering and expanding the primary concrete meaning, and yet drawing a variety of logical inferences from the meaning without the abstracting, idealizing movement of Western thought.[32]

Although one hesitates to tar all of "Western thought" with one stroke of the brush, it must be granted that as a generalization about rabbinic and Christian interpretation of the Hebrew Bible, Handelman's judgment stands. As a result, the search for the one great idea that pervades and unifies the Hebrew Bible is unlikely to interest Jews. Instead, Jewish biblical theology is likely to be, as it always has been, a matter of piecemeal observations appended to the text and subordinate to its particularity. As Gershom Scholem put it, speaking of rabbinic Judaism: "[n]ot system but *commentary* is the legitimate form through which truth is approached.[33] I would amend his remark only so as to limit it to the aggadic dimension of Judaism. In the case of halakhah, Judaism does offer impressive architectonic structures in the form of law codes. But the aggadic and the halakhic dimensions of Judaism are complementary and not antithetical, and when halakhah is the basis for aggadah, the former is not transmuted into the latter by theological alchemy. Rather, the particularities of the law remain alive and in force in and alongside the larger theological and ethical message.

The search for the one idea into which the Hebrew Bible is to be subsumed, for the "center *(Mitte)* of Old Testament theology," as the issue is known in the field, has produced a bewildering array of candidates—for example, covenant (Eichrodt), the holiness of God (Ernst Sellin), God as the lord (Ludwig Köhler), Israel's election as the people of God (Hans Wildberger), the rule of God together with his communion

---

[31] Erich Auerbach, *Mimesis: The Representation of Reality in Western Literature* (Princeton, N.J.: Princeton University Press, 1953), 48–49. —Levenson

[32] Susan A. Handelman, *The Slayers of Moses: The Emergence of Rabbinic Interpretation in Modern Literary Theory* (Albany, N.Y.: State University of New York Press, 1982), 19. —Levenson

[33] Gershom Scholem, "Revelation and Tradition as Religious Categories in Judaism," in *The Messianic Idea in Judaism and Other Essays on Jewish Spirituality* (New York: Schocken, 1971), 289. —Levenson

with humankind (Georg Fohrer),[34] God's acts in history (G. Ernest Wright),[35] communion alone (Th. C. Vriezen),[36] the book of Deuteronomy (Siegfried Herrmann),[37] and the presence of God (Samuel Terrien).[38] It is interesting to note some rather obvious candidates that do not appear in this list and have received little attention in the theologies. One is humankind's duties, a theme that occupies most of the biblical materials, legal, prophetic, and sapiential alike. "What does YHWH require of you?" (Deut 10:12; cf. Mic 6:8) is a theme that cuts across a number of these aspiring centers and covers much of books like Proverbs, as covenant, holiness, rulership, acts of God, and presence, for instance, cannot. I am, for reasons that will become evident, skeptical of the entire pursuit of a center. My point is that with its devaluation of the deed ("works"), the Pauline theology of these Protestant Old Testament scholars has made it unlikely for them to propose a theme like these as the center of Old Testament theology, lest they suggest the Marcionite notion of the antithetical relationship of the Jewish and the Christian Gods. It is instructive to compare their approach with that of John L. McKenzie, a Roman Catholic scholar who explicitly set out to write "the theology of the Old Testament as if the New Testament did not exist.[39] McKenzie put the discussion of "cult" first in his book (whereas Eichrodt, for instance, put "covenant" first) and devoted only twenty-five pages out of 341 to "the message of the prophets" (whereas von Rad, for example, devoted well over a third of his second volume to the same theme). It is difficult to resist the suggestion that the theologians' own personal faith is the determinative factor in their positing a center for the Old Testament. In fact, it is not unusual for the authors to claim that the New Testament, *mirabile dictu,* has the very same center. Given the normative role that biblical theologians, especially the Protestants, tend to ascribe to their discipline, this is not surprising. What is surprising, however, is that the method by which this all-encompassing systemic unity is uncovered is itself seen as compatible with the historian's sensitivity to change, development, contradiction, and difference.

The assumption of the theologians who quest after the center or overarching unity of the Hebrew Bible is that all the books and pericopes therein announce essentially the same message. This has, in fact, a rough parallel in rabbinic thought. "Forty-eight male and seven female prophets prophesied to Israel," reports an anonymous baraita, "and they neither took away from nor added to that which is written in the Torah, with the exception of the reading of the Scroll [of Esther on Purim]" *(b. Meg.* 14a). Here, the assumption is that the first of the three sections of the Tanakh, the Torah (Pentateuch), is prior and normative; the prophets only applied it and did not innovate. It is hard to see how a biblical theology that did not respect the doctrine of the priority and normativity of the Pentateuch could be authentic to the Jewish

---

[34] See Hasel, *Old Testament Theology,* 117–47, esp. 119–21. —Levenson

[35] G. Ernest Wright, *God Who Acts: Biblical Theology as Recital,* Studies in Biblical Theology 8 (London: SCM Press, 1952). —Levenson

[36] Hasel, *Old Testament Theology,* 120–21. —Levenson

[37] Hasel, *Old Testament Theology,* 135–36. —Levenson

[38] Hasel, *Old Testament Theology,* 82–83. —Levenson

[39] John L. McKenzie, *A Theology of the Old Testament* (Garden City, N.Y.: Doubleday, 1974), 334. —Levenson

tradition. The ubiquitous assumption of the biblical theologians that one might learn the biblical message better from a book in another section of the canon and then utilize that book to correct or counterbalance the Torah (e.g., Jeremiah against Leviticus) derives from the modern Christian idea that the unit to be interpreted is the *testament,* an idea foreign to Judaism and in contradiction to the Jewish prioritization of the Torah over the rest of the Tanakh. Like the different conceptions of Scripture held by the two traditions, the different organization of the Tanakh and the Old Testament ensures that a biblical theology common to Jews and Christians is impossible.[40]

In section 1, we saw that this notion that all the literature of the Hebrew Bible, which was composed over a millennium, has one message presents grave historical problems. Needless to say, the idea of the antiquity of the entire Pentateuch does this also. Neither the Jewish nor the Christian assumption is in accord with historical criticism. The message that the Hebrew Bible conveys to any community is necessarily in large measure a function of the tradition in which it is contextualized. In their historical contexts, the numerous passages in the Hebrew Bible represented a multitude of differing and conflicting messages. The continuing lack of consensus as to the center of Old Testament theology offers ironic evidence for the diversity of theologies in that book and the error of attempting to construct a systematic theology directly from it.

I suspect that Judaism is somewhat better situated to deal with the polydoxy of biblical theology than is Christianity. Whereas in the church the sacred text tends to be seen as a *word* (the singular is telling) demanding to be proclaimed magisterially, in Judaism it tends to be seen as a *problem* with many facets, each of which deserves attention and debate. The way midrash collections introduce a new comment is revealing—*dābār 'aḥēr* (another interpretation). The rabbinic Bible *(Miqra'ot Gedolot),* too, surrounds the text with a plurality of commentaries that very often take issue with each other explicitly. And most of the Talmud is a debate, with both majority and minority positions preserved and often unmarked. This is very different from most of the theological literature of Christianity. A tradition whose sacred texts are internally argumentative will have a far higher tolerance for theological polydoxy (within limits) and far less motivation to flatten the polyphony of the sources into a monotony It is not only that Jews have less motivation than Christians to find a unity or center in their Bible: if they did find one, they would have trouble integrating it with their most traditional modes of textual reasoning. What Christians may perceive as a gain, Jews may perceive as a loss.

V

The context in terms of which a unit of literature is to be interpreted is never self-evident. In the case of the Hebrew Bible, the candidates are legion. They include the work of the author who composed the unit, the redacted pericope in

---

[40] See Marvin A. Sweeney, "Tanakh versus Old Testament: Concerning the Foundation for a Jewish Theology of the Bible," in *Problems in Biblical Theology: Essays in Honor of Rolf Knierim* (ed. H. T. C. Sun and K. I. Eades; Grand Rapids: Eerdmans, 1997), 353–72. —Levenson

which it is now embedded, the biblical book in which it appears, the subsection of the Jewish canon that contains this book (Pentateuch, Prophets, or Writings), the entire Hebrew Bible treated as a synchronic reality, the Christian Bible (Old Testament and New Testament), and the exegetical traditions of the church or the rabbis. Each of these locations—and there are more—defines a context; it is disingenuous and shortsighted to accuse proponents of any one of them of "taking the passage out of context." Rather, the success of an interpretation is relative to the declared objectives of the interpreter. The great flaws of the biblical theologians are their lack of self-awareness on the issue of context and their habit, in the main, of acting as though the change of context makes no hermeneutical difference. In point of fact, it makes all the difference in the world.

I can illustrate the difference that context makes by analyzing an elegant little study of Gen 15:6 by von Rad, "Faith Reckoned as Righteousness" (1951). Von Rad prefixed the text as follows:

> He believed YHWH; and he reckoned it to him as righteousness. [Von Rad's question about it is:] . . . [H]ow precisely ought we to understand what we have referred to as the "theological" element here? Is it conceivable that the statement that faith is reckoned as righteousness arose wholly and solely from the reflections of a theologian? What is the derivation of the terms employed in this notable statement?[41]

In answer, von Rad traces the use of the verb ḥašab (to reckon) back to the pronouncement of a priest as he passes "a kind of cultic judgment" on a worshiper: "If any of the flesh of his sacrifice of well-being [zᵉbaḥ haššᵉlāmîm] is eaten on the third day, it shall not be acceptable; it shall not be reckoned [lō' yēḥāšēb] to him. It is an abomination" (Lev 7:18). Similarly, if one slaughters an animal "and does not bring it to the entrance of the Tent of Meeting to present it as an offering to YHWH before YHWH's Tabernacle, bloodguilt shall be reckoned [yēḥāšēb] to him" (Lev 17:4).[42] Since elsewhere we read of the priest's pronouncing an oral judgment announcing the will of God in the matter (e.g., Lev 13:8), it seems likely that in the case of these offerings, the priest also announced whether YHWH "reckoned" the sacrifice to the worshiper, that is, whether it has been accepted or not.[43] Von Rad found a similar declaratory formula in passages like Ezek 18:9, which tells of a man who has done all the right things that "he is righteous; he shall live (ṣaddîq hû' ḥāyōh yiḥyeh)—oracle of the Lord God." Von Rad saw this as "a relic of the liturgical usage" and connected it with the judgment on the fitness of worshipers that one finds in the "temple-gate liturgies," such as Pss 15:2–5; 24:5; and Isa 33:15–16.[44] In light of this cultic background, we see the remarkable transformation that the author of Gen 15:6 has brought about. There we find that

---

[41] Gerhard von Rad, "Faith Reckoned as Righteousness," in *The Problem of the Hexateuch and Other Essays* (New York: McGraw-Hill, 1966), 125. The same ideas appear in Gerhard von Rad, *Genesis: A Commentary*, OTL (Philadelphia: Westminster, 1972), 184–85. —Levenson

[42] Von Rad, "Faith," 126. —Levenson

[43] Von Rad, "Faith," 127. —Levenson

[44] Von Rad, "Faith," 128–29. —Levenson

[t]he process of "reckoning" is now transferred to the sphere of a free and wholly personal relationship between God and Abraham. There is no cultic intermediary, no priest to speak as the mouthpiece of YHWH. . . . In a solemn statement concerning the divine purpose, it is laid down that it is *faith* which sets men on a right footing with God. . . . He says that only faith, which is the wholehearted acceptance of YHWH's promise, brings man into a right relationship—that YHWH "reckons" it to him.[45]

As a consequence, von Rad concluded "that our author lived at a time and place in which ideas and terminology which were formerly tied to the cultus had come to be used more or less unconsciously in such spiritualized contexts."[46]

It is remarkable that von Rad nowhere in this essay refers to the New Testament, for Gen 15:6 was a crucial text in the early church. Paul, combating the insistence of the Jerusalem church that the Mosaic Law obliged Gentile Christians, pointed to Abraham in support of the idea that faith provides an exemption from the commandments:

I ask then: when God gives you the Spirit and works miracles among you, why is this? Is it because you keep the Law, or is it because you have faith in the gospel message? Look at Abraham: he put his faith in God, and that faith was counted to him as righteousness. (Gal 3:5–6)[47]

Later, he made essentially the same point in his letter to the Roman church:

What, then, are we to say about Abraham, our ancestor in the natural line? If Abraham was justified by anything he had done, then he has a ground for pride. But he has no such ground before God; for what does Scripture say? "Abraham put his faith in God, and that faith was counted to him as righteousness." Now if a man does a piece of work, his wages are not "counted" as a favor; they are paid as debt. But if without any work to his credit he simply puts his faith in him who acquits the guilty, then his faith is indeed "counted as righteousness." (Rom 4:1–5)

For Paul, Abraham served as proof that faith (*pistis*) could be detached from deeds and reckoned as self-sufficient. If so, then those who had faith in Christ had nothing to gain by accepting the obligations of the Torah. Von Rad's exegesis of Gen 15:6 supports this line of thought beautifully. Faith spiritualized the cult, nullifying both it and the priesthood in the process. it is now "only faith" that "brings man into a right relationship with God."[48]

It is instructive to compare Paul's handling of Gen 15:6 with that of a Jew of the previous generation, Philo of Alexandria. Philo, too, makes much of Abraham's faith, specifically cites Gen 15:6, and introduces in this connection many ideas unat-

---

[45] Von Rad, "Faith," 129. —Levenson
[46] Von Rad, "Faith," 130. —Levenson
[47] All New Testament translations in this chapter are taken from the *New English Bible* (New York: Oxford University Press, 1970), except that I have capitalized "Law" here because Paul is writing specifically about the Mosaic Torah. —Levenson
[48] Von Rad, "Faith," 129. —Levenson

tested in Genesis.[49] But soon thereafter he notes, "This man carried out the divine law and all the divine commandments,"[50] evidently an allusion to Gen 26:5, which grounds the promise to Isaac in the fact that "Abraham observed my charge, my commandments, my laws, and my instructions." Needless to say, this verse, with its possible implication that Abraham already knew the total body of revelation and scrupulously observed it, is not one cited by Paul. And so, we have two types of interpretations of Gen 15:6, a Pauline type, which takes the verse in isolation and insists on the autonomy of faith, and a Philonic type, in which faith and the observance of commandments are each predicated of Abraham on the basis of texts in Genesis. It is worthy of note that another New Testament document, the epistle of James, takes, in essence, the Philonic position (Jas 2:21–24), citing Gen 15:6 but warning as well that "a man is justified by deeds and not by faith in itself" (v. 24).[51]

One of the great rallying cries of the Protestant Reformers was *sola fide:* humanity is justified (or saved) by grace through faith alone, and not through the church or the sacraments administered by its priests. It was this doctrine that turned Luther against the epistle of James, which was one of four books he printed "separately at the back of his German translation of the New Testament."[52] Paul, in contrast, he much admired, and it is Paul's reading of Gen 15:6 that he explicitly endorsed in his own commentary:

> Accordingly, lest my discussions obscure what the best interpreter says, I shall speak rather briefly here. Read Paul, and read him attentively. Then you will see that from this passage he constructs the foremost article of our faith—the article that is intolerable to the world and to Satan—namely, that faith alone justifies.[53]

Luther goes on to attack "the rabbis of the Jews [who at the instigation of Satan] reveal their folly and the wrath which they harbor against Christ" by interpreting the verse to mean "that Abraham believed the Lord and through that God was just."[54] Here, Luther surely overgeneralizes. Most of the rabbinic commentators interpret the subject of *wayyahšᵉbehā* ("and he reckoned it") as YHWH. But Nachmanides (1195–1270) had argued that it was in fact Abraham who reckoned God as righteous. "A man who had enough faith to slaughter his only beloved son and [to endure] all the other trials—why shouldn't he have faith in good news?" asked Nachmanides. Instead, he argued, the verse shows that Abraham's faith followed

[49] Philo Judaeus, *De Abrahamo,* Les Oeuvres de Philon D'Alexandrie, ed. J. Gorez (Paris: Cerf, 1966), 129 (§262). —Levenson

[50] Philo, *De Abrahamo,* 132 (§275). —Levenson

[51] On the ideas of Abraham in first-century Judaism and Christianity, see Samuel Sandmel, *Philo's Place in Judaism: A Study of Conceptions of Abraham in Jewish Literature,* augmented ed. (New York: KTAV, 1971); and Hans Dieter Betz, *Galatians,* Hermeneia (Philadelphia: Fortress, 1979), 139–40. —Levenson

[52] David H. Kelsey, "Protestant Attitudes Regarding Methods of Biblical Interpretation," in *Scripture in the Jewish and Christian Traditions,* ed. Frederick Greenspahn (Nashville: Abingdon, 1982), 138. —Levenson

[53] *Luther's Works,* vol. 3: *Lectures on Genesis, Chapters 15–20,* ed. Jaroslav Pelikan (St. Louis: Concordia, 1961), 19. —Levenson

[54] *Luther's Works,* 21. —Levenson

from his conviction that God is a God of righteousness. He cited as proof Isa 45:23, "By myself have I sworn—oracle of the Lord—righteousness has gone out of my mouth, and the word will not turn back."[55] Luther's utter contempt for this interpretation originates in his Pauline theology, for, on purely grammatical considerations, either specification of the implied subject is defensible.

This brief sketch of the premodern exegesis of Gen 15:6 enables us to locate von Rad's reading within the Pauline-Lutheran line of interpretation. His assumption that "only faith . . . brings man into a right relationship" implies an exclusion that is not to be found in the Hebrew Bible and certainly not in the J document, the pentateuchal source responsible for this verse as well as for Gen 26:5, which notes the reservoir of merit established by Abraham's observance of law. The facts that cult and priesthood were not spiritualized away in the Hebrew Bible and that righteousness could be imputed not only for faith, but also for observance (e.g., Deut 6:25 and Ps 106:31), are ignored. Von Rad also neglected completely the possibility that it is Abraham who is doing the reckoning and God who is being reckoned righteous. In part, this is owing to the mistaken assumption that he shared with most modern Christian Old Testament scholars that one can be well-equipped for exegesis without knowledge of the medieval Jewish commentaries. In this, Luther, for all his anti-Judaism, was more advanced. Given von Rad's penchant for finding liturgical and cultic origins for things, he should have been attracted to Nachmanides's reasoning. After all, the affirmation of God's righteousness was a common liturgical act in ancient Israel (e.g., Lam 1:18; Pss 119:137; 145:17).[56] What prevented von Rad from even considering the possibility seems to have been an eagerness to endorse the Pauline-Lutheran reading.

The context in which von Rad's interpretation situates Gen 15:6 is one defined first by the verse itself, in isolation from the rest of the Abraham material in the Hebrew Bible and indeed from the Hebrew Bible itself. The understanding of righteousness as derivable from faith alone is a second aspect of context—one that derives from Pauline materials in the New Testament, especially as these materials have been understood in Lutheran tradition and without regard for the Jacobean-Catholic trajectory in Christian tradition. Ultimately, the only context in which von Rad's essay can be considered successful is Reformation theology. He has ignored the historical context of ancient Israel and defied the various literary contexts defined by the J source, by the book of Genesis, by the Pentateuch, by the Hebrew Bible in its entirety, by the Philonic-rabbinic traditions, and by the Jacobean-Catholic dimension of Christian theology. Within the limited context of theological interpretation informed by historical criticism—the context von Rad intended—his essay must be judged unsuccessful. Within another limited context, however—the confessional elucidation of Scripture for purposes of Lutheran reaffirmation—it is an impressive success.

It is precisely the failure of the biblical theologians to recognize the limitation of the context of their enterprise that makes some of them surprised that Jews are not interested in it.

---

[55] Ramban to Gen 15:6. —Levenson
[56] Note also how the lament begins in Jer 12:1. —Levenson

CHAPTER 29

The Illusion of Objective Biblical
Interpretation: Walter Wink (1935–)

After a theological education at Union Theological Seminary that trained him thoroughly in biblical scholarship, Walter Wink joined the faculty there in 1967. This was a time of intense intellectual and cultural upheaval on campuses throughout Europe and the Americas as the younger generation demanded of the established institutions and academic curricula greater relevance for the living realities of the majority of people. In this climate, Wink became increasingly disturbed by the impotence of most biblical scholarship for the spiritual concerns of everyday people. He turned his efforts as a scholar and teacher toward work that situates the relevance of the Bible for contemporary life at the center of the interpretive enterprise.

In 1973 Wink published a little book called *The Bible in Human Transformation*, the opening words of which—"Historical biblical criticism is bankrupt"—have become something of a mantra for those who are persuaded by his thesis. As the following excerpt will make plain, Wink's book set forth in no uncertain terms a frontal assault on the entire historical-critical program that had prevailed in biblical scholarship among the best seminaries and universities in the west for 150 years. Despite the fact that Wink personally held respectable academic credentials and that his book was published by a standard academic press, Wink found himself virtually blacklisted from the guild of biblical scholarship; this included denial of his tenure at Union. He was hired into the continuing-education and research program at Auburn Theological Seminary (a Presbyterian institution housed in the Union buildings), where he has continued to serve as professor of biblical interpretation.

True to the critique leveled in his little book, Wink has focused his teaching and writing on what the New Testament refers to as the "principalities and powers," which he understands to mean the economic, political, and social forces that impinge upon human lives.[1] The resulting books have been so well received that they have won awards.[2] Commensurate with his writing has been Wink's work promoting nonviolent activism in Latin America, South Africa, the Far East, Europe, and North America.

The following excerpt is taken from *The Bible in Human Transformation: Toward a New Paradigm for Biblical Study.* This book was something of a bellwether, drawing

---

[1] Rom 8:38; Eph 3:10; 6:12; Col 1:16; 2:15; Titus 3:1.
[2] Walter Wink, *Naming the Powers* (Philadelphia: Fortress, 1984); *Unmasking the Powers* (Philadelphia: Fortress, 1986); *Engaging the Powers* (Philadelphia: Fortress, 1992).

attention to specific weaknesses in the modern paradigm of biblical interpretation years before other voices would join his. Wink took seriously the social sciences, but not simply to apply them to study of ancient biblical societies. Rather, armed with the insights of sociology, Wink drew attention to the role of ideology in contemporary interpretation of Scripture, pointing out the inevitability of perspectivalism and calling for honest acknowledgment of the class and political interests implicit in so-called objective biblical interpretation. By the 1990s, his cry had been well heeded, as the current generation of biblical scholars recognize their obligation to state the religious and philosophical assumptions that inform their work.

For further information on Walter Wink and his legacy:

Jobling, David. "Deconstruction and the Political Analysis of Biblical Texts." *Ideological Criticism of Biblical Texts.* Atlanta: Scholars Press, 1992.

Jobling, David, and Tina Pippin, eds. "Ideological Criticism of Biblical Texts." *Semeia* 59 (1992): 1–249.

Wink, Walter. "How I Have Been Snagged by the Seat of My Pants While Reading the Bible." *Christian Century* 92 (1975): 816–19.

The Bankruptcy of the Biblical Critical Paradigm[3]

Historical biblical criticism is bankrupt.

I use "bankrupt" in the exact sense of the term. A business which goes bankrupt is not valueless, nor incapable of producing useful products. It still has an inventory of expensive parts, a large capital outlay, a team of trained personnel, a certain reputation, and usually, until the day bankruptcy is declared, a facade which appeared to most to be relatively healthy. The one thing wrong—and the only thing—is that it is no longer able to accomplish its avowed purpose for existence: to make money.

It is in this precise sense that one can speak of the historical critical method generally, and of its application to biblical studies in particular, as bankrupt. Biblical criticism has produced an inventory of thousands of studies on every question which has seemed amenable to its methods, with a host of additional possibilities still before it. It has a method which has proven itself in earlier historical periods to be capable of remarkable achievements. It has in its employ hundreds of competent, trained technicians. Biblical criticism is not bankrupt because it has run out of things to say or new ground to explore. It is bankrupt solely because it is incapable of achieving what most of its practitioners considered its purpose to be: so to interpret the Scriptures that the past becomes alive and illumines our present with new possibilities for personal and social transformation.

How did biblical criticism become insolvent? Here are at least a few of the reasons.

The Method as Practiced Was Incommensurate with the Intention of the Texts

The writers of the New Testament bore witness to events which had led them to faith. They wrote "from faith to faith," to evoke or augment faith in their readers. Ostensibly, historical criticism is not hostile to these intentions, but should serve to make the same decision for faith or unfaith accessible across the gulf of centuries to readers today. In actual practice, however, this seldom happens, and for good reason. For the very essence of scientific and historical inquiry in modern times has been the suspension of evaluative judgments and participational involvement in the "object" of research. Such detached neutrality in matters of faith is not neutrality at all, but already a decision against responding. At the outset, questions of truth and meaning have been excluded, since they can only be answered participatively, in terms of a lived response. Insofar as they are retained at all, "truth" is reduced to facticity, and the text's "meaning" is rendered by a paraphrase.

[3] Reprinted from *The Bible in Human Transformation* by Walter Wink, copyright © 1973 Fortress Press. Used by permission of Augsburg Fortress.

Such "objective neutrality" thus requires a sacrifice of the very questions the Bible seeks to answer. But if our questions do not anticipate a certain type of answer, how can we hope to receive it? If our methodology is not designed to reveal meaning, the possibility that meaning might emerge is blocked in advance, through the manner in which the problem is stated. Having initially turned to the text seeking insights about living, we find ourselves ineluctably drawn by our method further and further from the place where the text might speak.

This detached, value-neutral, a-historical point of view is, of course, an illusion. For all empirical work can be carried out only on the basis of certain metaempirical, ontological, and metaphysical judgments, and the expectations and hypotheses which follow from them. "He who makes no decisions has no questions to raise and is not even able to formulate a tentative hypothesis which enables him to set a problem and to search history for its answer."[4]

Historical criticism did operate, although covertly, on the basis of such metaempirical underpinnings: a faith in reason and progress and an ontology of naïve realism. In the context of belief in progress, historical method became the means to delineate the development of ideas and institutions toward that historical apex *modern times*. It is clear in all this that the "objective standpoint" is none other than the historically conditioned place where *we* happen to be standing, and possesses no neutrality or detachment at all.

We will see later that the historical critical method had a vested interest in undermining the Bible's authority, that it operated as a background ideology for the demystification of religious tradition, that it required functional atheism for its practice, and that its attempted mastery of the object was operationally analogous to the myth of Satan and the legend of Faust. For the time being the point is solely that the fiction of "detachment" made vital relatedness to the content of the text impossible. By detaching the text from the stream of my existence, biblical criticism has hurled it into the abyss of an objectified past. Such a past is an infinite regress. No amount of devoted study can bring it back.

The biblical writers themselves never treated their own past in such a manner. Their past was a continual accosting, a question flung in their paths, a challenge, and a confrontation. But because the scholar has removed himself from view, no shadow from the past can fall across his path. He has insulated himself from the Bible's own concerns. He examines the Bible, but he himself is not examined—except by his colleagues in the guild! This disregard of the voices of the past, this systematic stopping of the ears and restraint of the will do not constitute objectivity but are instead the negation of the manifest intent of the subject matter.

The historical critical method has reduced the Bible to a dead letter. Our obeisance to technique has left the Bible sterile and ourselves empty. The further we

---

[4] Karl Mannheim, *Ideology and Utopia*, trans. Louis Wirth and Edward Shils (New York: Harcourt, Brace & World, 1936), 89. —Wink

have advanced in analysis the more the goal has receded from our sight, so that today many of us might well say with Nietzsche, "Ich habe meine Gründe vergessen"—I have forgotten why I ever began.[5]

The Ideology of Objectivism Drew Historical Criticism into a False Consciousness

Objectivism as used here refers to the academic ideal of detached observation of phenomena without interference by emotions, will, interests, or bias. It can be spoken of as an ideology because it does not correspond to reality and is incapable of realization. The error of objectivism as an ideology lies in its intellectualism, its blindness to the irrational or unconscious, and its separation of theory from practice. Its falsehood lies in the systematic repression of its error.

Objectivism is intellectualistic. Intellectualism, says Mannheim, is "a mode of thought which either does not see the elements in life and in thought which are based on will, interest, emotion, and *Weltanschauung*—or, if it does recognize their existence, treats them as though they were equivalent to the intellect and believes that they may be mastered by and subordinated to reason."[6] Intellectualism is characterized by a complete separation of theory from practice, of intellect from emotion, and finds emotionally determined thinking intolerable. When it encounters a mode of thinking which is necessarily set in an irrational context, as political or religious thought always is, the attempt is made so to construe the phenomena that the evaluative elements will appear separable from a residue of pure theory. Left obscured is the question of whether in fact the emotional is so intertwined with the rational as to involve even the categorical structure itself, thus making the sought-for isolation of the evaluative elements *de facto* impossible.[7]

Here the problem of the academy becomes unavoidable, with its endemic separation of theory from practice, mind from body, reason from emotion, knowledge from experience. Is anything but intellectualism possible when our questions do not arise primarily out of the struggle with concrete problems of life and society, from the blistering exposure to trial and error, from the need for wisdom in the ambiguous mash of events? Can historical criticism, practiced in the academy, ensnared in an objectivist ideology, ever do more than simply refer the data of the text away from an encounter with experience and back to its own uncontrolled premises?

In such a context biblical study is rendered innocuous from the start. Here we are trained to think in a framework which strives to negate every evaluation, every trace of mundane meaning, every proclivity toward a view of the whole. The result is a hermeneutic with whose categories not even the simplest life-process can be

---

[5] Mannheim, *Ideology,* 20. —Wink
[6] Mannheim, *Ideology,* 122. —Wink
[7] Mannheim, *Ideology,* 123. —Wink

thought through. The outcome of biblical studies in the academy is a trained inca-
pacity to deal with the real problems of actual living persons in their daily lives.

Objectivism is not simply in error, however. It is a false consciousness. Error is
unintentional. Falsehood knows but has sought to forget its own face. Objectivism is
a false consciousness because evidence of its error is systematically repressed. It pretends detachment when in fact the scholar is attached to an institution with a high
stake in the socialization of students and the preservation of society, and when he
himself has a high stake in advancement in that institution by publication of his researches. It pretends to be unbiased when in fact the methodology carries with it a
heavy rationalistic weight which by inner necessity tends toward the reduction of irrational, subjective, or emotional data to insignificance or invisibility. It pretends to
search for "assured results," "objective knowledge," when in fact the method presumes radical epistemological doubt, which by definition devours each new spawn
of "assured results" as a guppy swallows her children. It pretends to suspend evaluations, which is simply impossible, since research proceeds on the basis of questions
asked and a ranked priority in their asking. But such judgments presuppose a system
of values and an ontology of meanings which not only give weight to the questions
but make it possible to ask them at all. Even the choice of syntax and vocabulary is a
political act that defines and circumscribes the way "facts" are to be experienced—
indeed, in a sense even creates the facts that can be studied.[8] And finally,
objectivism pretends to be neutral when in fact the scholar, like everyone else, has
racial, sexual, and class interests to which he is largely blind and which are unconsciously reflected in his work. (Why, for example, do German scholars persist in using
the offensive term "Spätjudentum,"[9] as if Judaism ceased to exist with the rise of
Christianity? Why are there so few women and Black biblical scholars in this
country? Why has hermeneutical scholarship so long ignored the rich tradition of
Black preaching?)

On the American scene the problem has been exacerbated by the struggle to
gain standing for departments of religious studies in secular universities previously
closed to all religious instruction. In order to dissociate religious studies from denominational and dogmatic stigmatization, it seemed necessary to assert the scientific
character of the discipline. The descriptive approach became the magic key to academic respectability. This has in actual practice meant objectivism with a vengeance,
and accounts at least in part for the virtual abandonment recently (regardless of theoretical leanings, which were often of the best sort) of the beachhead which Bultmann
had established.

---

[8] R. D. Laing, *The Politics of Experience* (New York: Pantheon, 1967), 62. —Wink
[9] The term is translated "late Judaism." In the nineteenth and twentieth centuries, scholars
conventionally used the term as a reference to the religion of Jews during the latter half of the first
millennium B.C.E. despite the fact that those centuries would better be characterised as the era of
early Judaism. Part of Wink's point is that use of the German term reflects an anti-Jewish bias on the
part of modern Christian scholars, since the Jewish religion of the fifth to first centuries B.C.E. could
only be qualified as "late" relative to the religion of the biblical Israelites—particularly of the
preexilic prophets—which Christian scholars often saw as the roots of Jesus' proclamation.

Objectivity is much to be desired. But objectivity must be separated off from the ideology of objecti*vism* and given new footing. A new type of objectivity is attainable, not through the exclusion of evaluations, but through the critical awareness and proper use of them. Lest this be construed as counsel simply to try harder under the old presuppositions, let us be clear that what is demanded in the face of bankruptcy is not a pep talk to the sales force but new management. If all historical knowledge is relational knowledge, and can only be formulated with reference to the position of the observer, we are faced with the task of developing a radically different model for the role of the interpreter vis-à-vis the text.

Biblical Studies Increasingly Fell Prey to a Form of Technologism Which Regards as Legitimate Only Those Questions Which Its Methods Can Answer

Technique is absolutely essential in any field of inquiry. But technique is essentially value-blind. It depends for its functioning on orders given outside its area of competence. It is all the more crucial then that the technique employed be commensurate with its object, for techniques can only produce those results for which they are created. I have already argued above that the historical method as practiced has not been adequately commensurate with the biblical texts. In this case the carrying over of methods from the natural sciences has led to a situation where we no longer ask what we would like to know and what will be of decisive significance for the next step in personal or social development. Rather, we attempt to deal only with those complexes of facts which are amenable to historical method. We ask only those questions which the method can answer. We internalize the method's questions and permit a self-censorship of the questions intrinsic to our lives. Puffy with pretensions to "pure scholarship," this blinkered approach fails to be scholarly enough, precisely because it refuses to examine so much that is essential to understanding the intention of the text and our interest in reading it.

Preoccupation with technique leads to a self-perpetuating reductionist spiral. Existing technique determines the direction of further inquiry, including the developing of additional techniques, which themselves presuppose the previous techniques, *ad infinitum.* In this process there is no room for an examination of premises, nor is there any capacity to question the appropriateness of the techniques employed for answering the questions which the text might pose.

Technologism need not be disastrous, whether in oil production or in biblical criticism. But it must be subordinated—always, in every field, without exception—to an adequate hermeneutic. Yet, in spite of remarkable strides in hermeneutical thought, biblical technologism reigns unchecked. The horse rides the horseman and the goal is not reached.

Biblical Criticism Became Cut Off From Any Community for Whose Life Its Results Might Be Significant

Historical biblical research, as long as it was situated in an antithetical position to orthodoxy, was the *Wehrmacht* [the Nazi German armed forces] of the liberal church. During this period its relationship to the vital centers of an entire community's life was crucial. Gradually, as success became assured, a shift took place. The community of reference and accountability became, not the liberal church, but the guild of biblical scholars. The guild, however, is not a community but a collective. It is simply a peer group on the model of any other professional guild, subject to the same virtues (preservation of high standards, rewards in terms of prestige to those deemed most worthy, centralization and dissemination of information, etc.) and vices (development of an "expert" ethos, invention of a technical esoteric language, repression of innovation, conformity to peer-group values) which characterize all other professional groups.

This removal of scholarship from a vital community had consequences disastrous for both. For the community it was disastrous because its own self-consciousness as a people under the Word was largely deprived of critical and constructive contributions. For scholarship it was disastrous because the questions asked the texts were seldom ones on which human lives hinged, but those most likely to win a hearing from the guild. Historical criticism sought to free itself from the community in order to pursue its work untrammeled by censorship and interference. With that hard-won freedom it also won isolation from any conceivable significance. For since truth is not absolute, but only approximate and relational, its relevance can only emerge in the particularity of a given community's struggles for integrity and freedom.

Here the crisis in biblical studies links up with the crisis in the churches generally, since they themselves have become problematic as the locus of Christian community. For many liberal Protestant scholars in America, the most urgent question has become that of finding a context in which their interpretations of the Bible might have significance—or, stated more fundamentally, a context which would give that interpretation significance. Here, as at every other point, the crisis in biblical scholarship is seen as an epiphenomenon of a far more comprehensive crisis in the culture itself.

Biblical Criticism Developed in a Historical Context Which Has Now Changed. In the Present Context It Is, as Now Practiced, Obsolete

Far too little attention has been paid to the polemical/apologetical origins of biblical criticism. It was first used as a weapon against existing orthodoxies, and only later was it pressed into more constructive service. One of its first exponents, Richard Simon (d. 1712), a Roman Catholic, used historical criticism to undermine Protestant dependency on the Bible as the sole source of authority.[10] Reimarus [in 1778] used it to assault the historical basis of Christianity itself.[11]

The effect was traumatic. Conservative exegesis had interpreted Scripture in the context of a total theological construction of history. The new analytical approach, on the other hand, broke down every total construction in order to arrive at smaller units which might then be recombined through the category of causality. There can be little quarrel that the historical significance of the Graf-Wellhausen hypothesis (which no one today accepts as then formulated) was its usefulness as a method for destroying the conservative view of biblical origins and inspiration, thereby destroying its entire ideology.

As long as this ideological onslaught was made for the sake of desirable fundamental change, i.e., as long as it was seeking breathing room for the spirit and the right of the intellect to free inquiry, its thrust was utopian in the best sense of the term: it sought to destroy an existent state of reality for the sake of one which it conceived to be better. Today, however, that war is largely over, and biblical critical scholarship has become the established status quo. Now the unconscious ideological elements in its position have become visible. And the unhappy consequence of this unmasking is not just that liberal biblical scholarship also proves to have been ideological, but that it has ceased to be utopian, and no longer moves toward a greater comprehension of truth. It is as if, at the moment of its victory, it had forgotten why it had fought, and settled down on the field of battle to inventory its weapons in hope of discovering some clue as to their further usefulness. Here, as in other revolutions, those who were fit to overthrow were not fit to govern.

The conservative ideology, for its part, was not wholly deceived by the ideology of objectivism, though it was at a loss to know how to overcome it. For it sensed instinctively that the modernist was not nearly so interested in being changed by his reading of the Bible, as in changing the way that the Bible was read in order to conform it to the modern spirit. Conservatism was not, for all that, juxtaposing a "biblical spirit" to the "modern spirit," but was instead trying to forestall the final dissolution of the precritical spirit of orthodox Christendom. One can today more sympathetically appreciate conservative and fundamentalist anxiety at the loss of religious naïveté. But Christianity needed and still needs the acid bath of criticism. In this case scientific criticism performed an iconoclastic function for faith. If we are today moving toward a "postcritical" epoch, it can only be in the literal sense of the term: *after* criticism, not *above* it! The task now is to find a way forward to what Paul Ricoeur calls "a second naïveté," in which faith performs an iconoclastic function in respect to criticism.[12]

---

[10] Richard Simon, *A Critical History of the Old Testament* (London: Walter Davis, 1682).

[11] Hermann Samuel Reimarus, *Fragments from Reimarus; Consisting of Brief Critical Remarks on the Object of Jesus and His Disciples as Seen in the New Testament* (trans. from the German of G. E. Lessing; ed. Charles Voysey; London: Williams & Norgate, 1879; repr., Lexington, Ky.: American Theological Library Association, 1962).

[12] *The Symbolism of Evil*, trans. Emerson Buchanan (New York: Harper & Row, 1967), 347ff.
—Wink

It is in this polemic/apologetic context that the role of "New Testament Introduction" can be understood. "Introduction" was not so much an introduction to the Bible, as to the biblical critical ethos. Students studied the great textbooks—Moffatt, McNeile, Enslin[13]—but seldom read the biblical text. "Introduction" provoked an inferno of debate. People's lives changed as a result of its study. Is it any accident that the victory of biblical criticism coincided with a sharp shift of emphasis away from "Introduction" to that of biblical theology—that is, from assault to reconstruction? I have even heard professors wonder aloud why they ever devoted so much attention to introductory problems. There was also, to be sure, the excitement of discovery, the need to press questions to their limits and to establish a certain consensus. Except for certain outstanding problems (including the periodic reopening of issues believed closed), that work is now a part of the history of the discipline, and was a necessary and vital contribution. All that, however, does nothing to mitigate the fact that the questions asked operated at the level of objectivization rather than self-reflective understanding. Introduction served to distance rather than to mediate the text.

The biblical-theology movement for its part marked a massive defection from the objectivist paradigm. That it was unable completely to free itself from that paradigm is no judgment on its value. In every revolution the thesis lives on in the antithesis for a time. What Brevard Childs chronicles as the crisis of biblical theology[14] is in fact its desperate opportunity to take the next step forward to a total paradigm change. For we have also learned to do objectivistic biblical theology! We can describe Paul's view of grace with as much benign condescension as we adjudge the carbon date of a Qumran fragment. Whatever the excesses of the biblical-theology movement there is only one that counts, and that is its excessive dependence on objectivism.

Bluntly stated, biblical criticism was a certain type of evangelism seeking a certain type of conversion. No depreciation is intended by those terms, loaded as they are. Only those still under the illusion that biblical criticism was ideologically neutral should be offended by their use. Far more fundamentally than revivalism, biblical criticism shook, shattered, and reconstituted generation after generation of students, and became their point of entrée into the "modern world." The failure of historians of missions and evangelism to register the spectacular evangelistic success of biblical criticism is nothing less than phenomenal, and it is but one more indication of the binding power of its objectivist ideology.

To say that biblical criticism has now, like revivalism, become bankrupt, is simply to summarize the entire discussion to this point. It was based on an inadequate method, married to a false objectivism, subjected to uncontrolled technologism, separated from a vital community, and has outlived its usefulness as presently practiced. Whether or not it has any future at all depends on its adaptability to a radically altered situation.

---

[13] James Moffatt, *An Introduction to the Literature of the New Testament* (3d, rev. ed.; New York: Scribner, 1925); Alan H. McNeile, *An Introduction to the Study of the New Testament* (Oxford: Clarendon, 1927); Morton S. Enslin, *The Literature of the Christian Movement* (part 3 of *Christian Beginnings;* New York: Harper & Brothers, 1956).

[14] *Biblical Theology in Crisis* (Philadelphia: Westminster, 1970). —Wink

CHAPTER 30

Rhetorical Interpretation of the Bible's Literature: Phyllis Trible (1932–)

As biblical studies proceeded in the twentieth century, scholars applied a wide range of critical methodologies in order to better answer historical questions about the creation of biblical documents. What sources did the biblical writers use? Source criticism sought to provide answers. How did biblical authors or editors adapt the sources available to them for their specific compositional needs? Scholars applied redaction-critical methods to supply answers. What traditional forms of oral and literary expression did the biblical tradents employ in their worship, teaching, and recollection? Form criticism emerged as a particularly fruitful and enduring critical methodology, for it shed light on more than broad cultural questions. With its focus on the functions for which traditional literary and oral forms or genres were used in specific settings in life, form criticism also helped interpreters understand more fully the social worlds in which biblical traditions developed and to which they spoke.

In 1968 James Muilenburg, an American biblical scholar, delivered to the Society of Biblical Literature an address that helped expand the practice of form criticism beyond simply identifying the typical features of traditional forms and their concomitant social settings.[1] By focusing on the typical features of biblical genres, biblical scholarship ran the risk of overlooking the unique features of specific biblical passages where these genres appeared. Muilenburg drew attention to specific biblical texts showing highly significant adaptations of conventional forms. The purpose for which the biblical writers made use of the conventional forms—a key factor in discerning meaning in the texts—can be found in the subtle changes in literary structure and in the nuances of expression unique to the specific text in question. For example, hymns were a conventional genre in ancient Israelite worship. But the specific ways in which this genre is adapted in Isaiah 40–55 provide important clues to what the prophet was trying to say to his audience—which is not necessarily the same rhetorical purpose served by hymns found in the Psalter. This modified version of form criticism Muilenburg called rhetorical criticism.

Phyllis Trible studied with Muilenburg at Columbia University and Union Theological Seminary in New York, where she earned a Ph.D. From 1980 to 1998 she taught at Union. More recently she was appointed dean at the new Wake Forest School of Divinity in

---

[1] James Muilenburg, "Form Criticism and Beyond," *Journal of Biblical Literature* 88 (1969): 1–18.

Winston-Salem, North Carolina. As a feminist interpreter of Scripture, Trible has pioneered in the application of rhetorical and literary criticism of the Bible to illuminate the
depiction of women in biblical literature and the ways that the Bible speaks to questions of
gender roles. During the nineteenth and twentieth centuries, the democratic impulse in
Western societies to recognize the human rights of women has inconsistently but inexora-
bly included issues of religion and biblical interpretation; Trible's work has contributed
significantly to this cultural debate.

In her practice of rhetorical criticism, Trible concerns herself less with historical
questions about the text and more with literary analysis, focusing on the biblical material
in its present literary form. Her groundbreaking book *God and the Rhetoric of Sexuality,*
part of which is included in the following selection, offers a clear introduction to dimensions of literary artfulness and style and to the sorts of questions that rhetorical analysis
will pose regarding literary design and grammatical and syntactical elements present in
the text. Much of Trible's scholarly work leads the reader through this sort of analysis, as
demonstrated in another influential work, "Depatriarchalizing in Biblical Interpretation."
A section of this article was published as "Eve and Adam,"[2] and a portion of that article is
reproduced on the following pages. Trible argues that although patriarchalism is evident
in biblical texts, careful literary and rhetorical analysis shows that some biblical passages
are actually much less patriarchal than certain feminist interpretations have allowed. For
example, when Gen 1:27 refers to humans as created in the image of God *and* as male and
female, the rhetorical artistry of this passage suggests more of an equality between the gen-
ders than a hierarchy.[3] Her analysis of the Eden story (included in the selection below)
brings her to a similar conclusion. In subsequent publications employing the same methodology, however, Trible draws attention to other biblical texts that advocate or at least express genuinely patriarchal attitudes.[4] Whether treating constructive or oppressive biblical
texts (she specializes in the Old Testament), in most of her writings Trible is concerned to
demonstrate the usefulness of Scripture for contemporary feminist thought.

**For further information on rhetorical criticism and feminist interpretation of the
Bible:**

Bach, Alice, ed. *The Pleasure of Her Text: Feminist Readings of Biblical and Historical Texts.*
    Philadelphia: Trinity Press International, 1990.
Bird, Phyllis. *Missing Persons and Mistaken Identities: Women and Gender in Ancient Israel.*
    Minneapolis, Fortress, 1997.
Exum, Cheryl. *Fragmented Women: Feminist (Sub)versions of Biblical Narratives.* Sheffield,
    England: JSOT Press, 1993.
Newsom, Carol A., and Sharon H. Ringe, eds. *Women's Bible Commentary.* Expanded ed.
    Louisville: Westminster John Knox, 1998.
Trible, Phyllis. *Rhetorical Criticism: Context, Method, and the Book of Jonah.* Philadelphia:
    Fortress, 1994.

---

[2] "Eve and Adam: Genesis 2–3 Reread," *Andover Newton Quarterly* 13 (1973): 251–58.
[3] Trible, *God and the Rhetoric of Sexuality,* 21.
[4] See esp. Phyllis Trible, *Text of Terror: Literary-Feminist Readings of Biblical Narratives* (Philadelphia: Fortress, 1984).

God and the Rhetoric of Sexuality[5]

Clues in a Text

. . .

With increasing emphasis, current discussions of the Bible journey outside its traditional setting in a community of faith to engage the world as their province. The interpreters may or may not be biblical scholars. They may be sympathetic to the text, dispassionate about it, or even hostile to it. They may or may not stand within a religious context. In various ways, with different values and unequal results, these readers understand scripture from the perspective of contemporary issues; or, conversely, they view present interests in light of the Bible.

Trible illustrates with brief references to contemporary biblical interpreters who are motivated by concerns for racial justice, oppression of the poor, political violence, psychoanalytic theory, ecological health, and human sexuality.

Feminism is my concluding illustration of involvement between the world and the Bible. By feminism I do not mean a narrow focus upon women, but rather a critique of culture in light of misogyny. This critique affects the issues of race and class, psychology, ecology, and human sexuality. For some people today the Bible supports female slavery and male dominance in culture, while for others it offers freedom from sexism. Central in this discussion are such passages as the creation accounts in Genesis, certain laws in Leviticus, the Song of Songs, the wisdom literature, various Gospel stories about Jesus and the powerless, and particular admonitions of Paul and his successors. Out of these materials a biblical hermeneutics of feminism is emerging.

All these contemporary interactions between the Bible and the world mirror the inner dynamics of scripture itself. The interpretive clue within the text is also the clue between the text and existence. Hence, the private and the public journeys of the pilgrim named scripture converge to yield the integrity of its life. As the Bible interprets itself to complement or to contradict, to confirm or to challenge, so likewise we construe these traditions for our time, recognizing an affinity between then and now. In other words, hermeneutics encompasses explication, understanding, and application from past to present. Subject to the experiences of the reader, this process is always compelling and never ending. New occasions teach new duties. In pursuing the task here, I am specifically interested in feminism as a critique of culture. . . . [S]uch interpretation requires first the articulation of a methodology, since methodology is one major criterion for evaluating the legitimacy of any interpretation.

---

[5] Reprinted from *God and the Rhetoric of Sexuality* by Phyllis Trible, copyright © 1978 Fortress Press. Used by permission of Augsburg Fortress (www.fortresspress.org).

The Methodological Clue

As the total process of understanding, hermeneutics employs many acceptable methodologies, though a particular interpreter may prefer one over another. My choice is rhetorical criticism,[6] a discipline I place under the general rubric of literary criticism.[7] According to this discipline, the major clue to interpretation is the text itself. Thus, I view the text as a literary creation with an interlocking structure of words and motifs.[8] Proper analysis of form yields proper articulation of meaning.

To study the Bible as literature is to recognize, not prove, that it is in fact literature.[9] I do not argue for its literary status any more than I would argue for the literary character of the *Iliad,* the *Odyssey,* the *Bhagavad Gita,* the *Divine Comedy,* or Shakespearean plays. Instead, I explore the literature to discover its vitality. This artistic pursuit is neither isolated from nor opposed to a religious interest, neither superior nor subordinate. Although aesthetic and religious modes of experience can surely be distinguished "at their more obvious levels," nevertheless, "they discover in their depths unexpected resonances and harmonies out of which a common music may be made."[10] In the totality of interpretation, their visions fuse. Thus, the Bible as literature is the Bible as scripture, regardless of one's attitude toward its authority. And conversely, the Bible as scripture is the Bible as literature, regardless of one's evaluation of its quality.[11]

---

[6] This discussion does not cover the rich history of the terms "rhetoric" and "rhetorical criticism"; see, e.g., Lloyd F. Bitzer and Edwin Black, *The Prospect of Rhetoric* (Englewood Cliffs, N.J.: Prentice-Hall, 1971); Northrop Frye, *Anatomy of Criticism* (Princeton: Princeton University Press, 1957), 243–337; Kenneth Burke, *A Rhetoric of Motives* (Englewood Cliffs, N.J.: Prentice-Hall, 1950), 49–180. I focus on rhetorical criticism as it has been recently proposed for biblical studies by James Muilenburg, "Form Criticism and Beyond," *Journal of Biblical Literature* 88 (1969): 1–18. —Trible

[7] By literary criticism I do not mean source criticism. Unfortunately, the two terms have been confused in biblical scholarship (e.g., Norman Habel, *Literary Criticism of the Old Testament* [Philadelphia; Fortress Press, 1971]). On this confusion, see the review by Edwin M. Good of Habel's book (*Journal of Biblical Literature* 92 [1973]: 287–89); Amos Wilder, *Early Christian Rhetoric: The Language of the Gospel* (Cambridge: Harvard University Press, 1971), xxii; Robert W. Funk, "Foreword," *Semeia 8: Literary Critical Studies of Biblical Texts* (Missoula: Scholars Press, 1977). On literary criticism, see Wilbur S. Scott, *Five Approaches of Literary Criticism* (New York: Collier Books, 1962). —Trible

[8] My use of the word structure bears no relation to structuralism (e.g., cf. Susan Wittig, ed., *Structuralism: An Interdisciplinary Study* [Pittsburgh: Pickwick Press, 1975]). Throughout this study I am concerned with the surface structures of literary compositions and not with the deep structures. —Trible

[9] Cf. Frye, *Anatomy of Criticism,* 315–26. —Trible

[10] Roger Hazelton, "Transcendence and Creativity," The Russell Lecture, Tufts University, October 17, 1972; also idem, *Ascending Flame, Descending Dove* (Philadelphia: Westminster, 1975), 50–59. —Trible

[11] The convergence of the aesthetic and the religious disavows the dualism of literature versus scripture that has appeared in two recent discussions: John A. Miles, Jr., "The Debut of the Bible as a Pagan Classic," *Bulletin of the Council on the Study of Religion* 7 (1976): 1, 3–6; and David Robertson, *The Old Testament and the Literary Critic* (Philadelphia: Fortress, 1977), 1–15, 84–85. Since the word *scripture* itself means writing, it is difficult to set it over against literature. Basically, the word designates the sacred writings of a particular tradition (e.g., the *Iliad,* the Bible, the *Vedas,* the Koran). Secondly, the word identifies authoritative literature for a particular community of faith. Thus, scripture always means religious literature; in specific contexts, this literature is also normative. In pleading for the Bible as literature, rather than as scripture, Miles and Robertson oppose the author-

A literary approach to hermeneutics concentrates primarily on the text rather than on extrinsic factors such as historical background, archaeological data, compositional history, authorial intention, sociological setting, or theological motivation and result. To be sure, these external concerns supplement one's understanding so that the critic never divorces herself or himself from them; yet at the same time stress falls upon interpreting the literature in terms of itself. "The text is like a musical score and the reader like the orchestra conductor who obeys the instructions of the notation."[12] Focus upon an intrinsic reading is, then, one hallmark of rhetorical methodology.[13]

The organic unity of the text is a related emphasis. Form and content are inseparable. On the one hand, the text is not a container from which ideas or substance can be abstracted to live an independent life. On the other hand, the text is not a subject matter from which stylistic and structural wrappings can be removed to exist autonomously. How the text speaks and what it says belong together in the discovery of what it is. To convey content is to employ form; to convey form is to employ content. Though these two phenomena can be distinguished for analytical purposes, their inseparability is the very life of literature.

Exploration of organic unity involves levels of analysis. First, a text can be defined in different ways: e.g., the entire Bible; a major division, such as the Pentateuch or the Pauline corpus; a single book, such as Joshua or James; a part of a book, such as the Holiness Code in Leviticus [Lev 17–26] or the Sermon on the Mount in Matthew; a smaller section, such as Ps 100, the parable of the prodigal son, or even a single riddle, proverb, or doxology; finally, an episode within a story. Basic to all these definitions is the concept of a literary unit, be it large or small. The critic determines this unit by employing the criterion of form and content. Second, a text can be studied from different perspectives. The critic may trace general design and plot movement or offer an exegesis of selected portions. He or she may follow the unfolding of a single motif, a key work, or a particular stylistic device. Again, the interpreter may pursue a close reading of the whole, examining in detail its interconnections. On whatever level analysis takes place, form and content yield the clue essential for interpretation.

A text is both typical and unique, both custom and innovation. Its conventional character is the genre to which it belongs, for every text is a sample of a class or

---

ity, not the phenomenon, of scripture. Conversely, James Barr distinguishes, though not absolutely, between "literary appreciation" and "theological use" of the Bible to find the former inadequate for the latter; see James Barr, *The Bible in the Modern World* (New York: Harper & Row, 1973), 53–74; cf. idem, "Reading the Bible as Literature," *Bulletin of the John Rylands Library* 56 (1973): 10–33. For yet a different view, see Robert Alter, "A Literary Approach to the Bible," *Commentary* 60 (December 1975): 72. —Trible

[12] Paul Ricoeur, *Interpretation Theory* (Fort Worth: Texas Christian University Press, 1976), 75. —Trible

[13] For a classic statement of the intrinsic approach, see René Weliek and Austin Warren, *Theory of Literature* (New York: Harcourt Brace and World, 1956), esp. 139–269; in biblical studies, cf. J. P. Fokkelman, *Narrative Art in Genesis* (Amsterdam: Van Gorcum, Assen, 1975), 1–8. —Trible

family whose members resemble each other. The genre of fairy tales, for example, embraces certain kinds of narratives. Introduced by the phrase "once upon a time," these stories live in fantasy and imagination. Ironically, time is not their essence, since what occurred in the past continues to recur in an imperishable world untouched even by aging. Though brief, these tales are all-inclusive. The natural, human, and supernatural worlds intermingle so easily that miracles are a matter of course. As types rather than individuals, the characters are known through their actions. Stylistically, these stories build on repetition with a precision that leaves no room for ambiguity. Their plots move from danger to redemption, often to conclude with the familiar phrase "and they lived happily ever after." Thus, an entire set of conventions, which includes elements of form and content, classifies innumerable stories as fairy tales. To locate a single text within this genre is to begin interpreting it. In general, to know the literary type to which a text belongs is to possess a clue for reading it.

At the same time, the typical enhances the unique. While all fairy tales exhibit common characteristics, each story has its own individuality. Its life is not interchangeable with any other tale, no matter how similar. Hence, the particular wicked stepmother of "Hansel and Gretel" belongs there and not in "Cinderella." The beauty of Snow White stands apart from that of Sleeping Beauty. Moreover, deliverance by a handsome prince occurs differently in these two stories, and neither of these rescues duplicates the comparable motif in "Cinderella." Every story is unique, as the variants of a single tale illustrate further. The Grimm brothers did not retell "Sleeping Beauty" precisely as they heard it, nor did others who narrated it. The story appears in several versions, each of which is a particular creation. Thus, a single text is "an indissoluable whole, an artistic and creative unity, a unique formulation."[14] To articulate the uniqueness of its form and content is to pursue a clue for interpreting it.

The clue as text, then, involves both the typical and the unique. Within biblical studies, form criticism explores the typical. Along with other emphases, it seeks to identify traditions under such narrative headings as legend, saga, folktale, letter, and exemplary story, and under such poetic designations as oracle, hymn, proverb, lament, and love song. According to this discipline, each genre has its own settings, content, and functions as well as a characteristic structure. The hymn is a song of praise, for instance, that usually consists of a call to praise, a recital of Yahweh's acts or attributes, and a conclusion of praise, blessings, or petitions. On various occasions, this typical structure is fashioned in different ways so that many kinds of hymns result: e.g., victory songs to celebrate success in battle; pilgrim songs to accompany the journey to holy places; and royal psalms to commemorate the enthronement of a king. Altogether, the common elements of the hymn become a key for understanding a single specimen. Thus, form criticism identifies types of literature as they correspond to typical human situations. This emphasis upon genre relates it to literary criticism, which, as we have seen, likewise explores the typical as a major clue for interpreting a single text.

---

[14] Muilenburg, "Form Criticism and Beyond," 9. —Trible

Yet the clue as text is also unique. Within biblical studies, rhetorical criticism focuses on this dimension. Conceived originally as a supplement to form criticism, rhetorical criticism investigates the individual characteristics of a literary unit.[15] While it is true, for example, that all hymns share common elements, a single hymn differs from all the others. The kinds of words used and the ways they are put together make every unit a new creation. In great variety, language plays with imagery, sounds, style, and viewpoints to yield particular distinctions, subtleties, and nuances. Analysis of such literary and stylistic features is the study of form and content as a key to meaning. In general, the practice of rhetorical criticism relates to literary criticism by accenting the unique as a major clue for interpreting a text.

Although it employs learned procedures, principles, and controls, this methodological approach resides in the realm of art. It uses critical tools but is not determined by them. Indeed, it welcomes intuition, guess, and surprise. Moreover, since all methodologies are subject to the guiding interests of individual users, the application of a single one may result in multiple interpretations of a particular passage. Specifically, not all rhetorical studies yield the same results. And while multiple readings are not per se mutually exclusive, not all interpretations are thereby equal. The text, as form and content, limits constructions of itself and does, in fact, stand as a potential witness against all readings. Yet the interpretive task is as compelling as it is inevitable, and rhetorical criticism is one methodology at work in this total process. By using it, I participate in a hermeneutical journey in which the clue is the text. Conversely, a specific text is the clue to my subject matter.

In her book Trible continues with a rhetorical analysis of Gen 1:27 in the context of the creation text of Gen 1:1–2:4a, exploring the interpretive possibilities of humankind as "male and female" made "in the image of God."

Eve and Adam: Genesis 2–3 Reread[16]

The following continues Trible's demonstration of rhetorical criticism. Here she is examining the Eden story.

On the whole, the Women's Liberation Movement is hostile to the Bible, even as it claims that the Bible is hostile to women. The Yahwist account of creation and fall in Genesis 2–3 provides a strong proof text for that claim. Accepting centuries of (male) exegesis, many feminists interpret this story as legitimating male supremacy

---

[15] Muilenburg, "Form Criticism and Beyond," 1–18; cf. David Greenwood, "Rhetorical Criticism and Formgeschichte: Some Methodological Considerations," *Journal of Biblical Literature* 89 (1970): 418–26; Martin Kessler, "A Methodological Setting for Rhetorical Criticism," *Semitics 4* (1974): 22–36. —Trible
[16] Phyllis Trible, "Eve and Adam: Genesis 2–3 Reread," *Andover Newton Quarterly* 13 (1973): 251–58.

and female subordination.[17] They read to reject. My suggestion is that we reread to understand and to appropriate.

Ambiguity characterizes the meaning of 'adham in Genesis 2–3. On the one hand, man is the first creature formed (2:7). The Lord God puts him in the garden "to till it and keep it," a job identified with the male (cf. 3:17–19). On the other hand, 'adham is a generic term for humankind. In commanding 'adham not to eat of the tree of knowledge of good and evil, the Deity is speaking to both the man and the woman (2:16–17). Until the differentiation of female and male (2:21–23), 'adham is basically androgynous: one creature incorporating two sexes.

Concern for sexuality, specifically for the creation of woman, comes last in the story, after the making of the garden, the trees, and the animals. Some commentators allege female subordination based on this order of events.[18] They contrast it with Genesis 1:27 where God creates 'adham as male and female in one act.[19] Thereby they infer that whereas the Priests [in Genesis 1] recognized the equality of the sexes, the Yahwist [in Genesis 2] made woman a second, subordinate, inferior sex.[20] But the last may be first, as both the biblical theologian and the literary critic know. Thus the Yahwist account moves to its climax, not its decline, in the creation of woman.[21] She is not an afterthought; she is the culmination. Genesis 1 itself supports this interpretation, for there male and female are indeed the last and truly the crown of all creatures. The last is also first where beginnings and endings are parallel. In Hebrew literature the central concerns of a unit often appear at the beginning and the end as an *inclusio* device.[22] Genesis 2 evinces this structure. The creation of man first and of

---

[17] See inter alia, Kate Millett, *Sexual Politics* (New York: Doubleday, 1970) 51–54; Eva Figes, *Patriarchal Attitudes* (Greenwich: Fawcett, 1970) 38f.; Mary Daly, "The Courage to See," *The Christian Century* (Sept. 22, 1971) 1110; Sheila D. Collins, "Toward a Feminist Theology," *The Christian Century* (August 2, 1972) 798; Lilly Rivlin, "Lilith: The First Woman," *Ms.* (Dec., 1972) 93, 114. —Trible

[18] Cf. E. Jacob, *Theology of the Old Testament* (New York: Harper & Row, 1958) 172f; S. H. Hooke, "Genesis," *Peake's Commentary on the Bible* (London: Nelson, 1962) 179. —Trible

[19] E.g., Elizabeth Cady Stanton observed that Gen 1:26–28 "dignifies woman as an important factor in the creation, equal in power and glory with man," while Gen 2 "makes her a mere afterthought" (*The Woman's Bible*, Part 1 [New York: European Publishing Company, 1895] 20). See also Elsie Adams and Mary Louise Briscoe, *Against the Wall, Mother . . .* (Beverly Hills: Glencoe, 1971) 4. —Trible

[20] Cf. Eugene H. Maly, "Genesis," *The Jerome Biblical Commentary* (Englewood, N.J.: Prentice Hall, 1968) 12: "But woman's existence, psychologically and in the social order, is dependent on man."—Trible

[21] See John L. McKenzie, "The Literary Characteristics of Gen. 2–3," *Theological Studies* 15 (1954): 559; John A. Bailey, "Initiation and the Primal Woman in Gilgamesh and Genesis 2–3," *Journal of Biblical Literature* (June 1970): 143. Bailey writes emphatically of the remarkable importance and position of the woman in Genesis 2–3, "all the more extraordinary when one realizes that this is the only account of creation of woman as such in ancient Near Eastern literature." He hedges, however, in seeing the themes of helper and naming (Gen 2:18–23) as indicative of a "certain subordination" of woman to man. These reservations are unnecessary; see below. Cf. also Claus Westermann, *Genesis, Biblischer Kommentar* 1/4 (Neukirchen-Fluyn: Neukirchener Verlag, 1970) 312. —Trible

[22] James Muilenburg, "Form Criticism and Beyond," *Journal of Biblical Literature* (March 1969): 9f. Cf. Mitchell Dahood, *Psalms* 1, The Anchor Bible (New York: Doubleday, 1966) passim and esp. 5. —Trible

woman last constitutes a ring composition whereby the two creatures are parallel. In no way does the order disparage woman. Content and context augment this reading.

The context for the advent of woman is a divine judgment, "It is not good that 'adham should be alone; I will make a helper fit for him" (2:18). The phrase needing explication is "helper fit for him." In the Old Testament the word helper ('ezer) has many usages. It can be a proper name for a male.[23] In our story it describes the animals and the woman. In some passages it characterizes Deity. God is the helper of Israel. As helper Yahweh creates and saves.[24] Thus 'ezer is a relational term; it designates a beneficial relationship; and it pertains to God, people, and animals. By itself the word does not specify positions within relationships; more particularly, it does not imply inferiority. Position results from additional content or from context. Accordingly, what kind of relationship does 'ezer entail in Genesis 2:18, 20? Our answer comes in two ways: 1) The word neged, which joins 'ezer, connotes equality: a helper who is a counterpart.[25] 2) The animals are helpers, but they fail to fit 'adham. There is physical, perhaps psychic, rapport between 'adham and the animals, for Yahweh forms (yaṣar) them both out of the ground ('adhamah). Yet their similarity is not equality. 'Adham names them and thereby exercises power over them. No fit helper is among them. And thus the narrative moves to woman. My translation is this: God is the helper superior to man; the animals are helpers inferior to man; woman is the helper equal to man.

Let us pursue the issue by examining the account of the creation of woman (21–22). This episode concludes the story even as the creation of man commences it. As I have said already, the ring composition suggests an interpretation of woman and man as equals. To establish this meaning, structure and content must mesh. They do. In both episodes Yahweh alone creates. For the last creation the Lord God "caused a deep sleep (tardemah) to fall upon the man." Man has no part in making woman; he is out of it. He exercises no control over her existence. He is neither participant nor spectator nor consultant at her birth. Like man, woman owes her life solely to God. For both of them the origin of life is a divine mystery. Another parallel of equality is creation out of raw materials: dust for man and a rib for woman. Yahweh chooses these fragile materials and in both cases processes them before human beings happen. As Yahweh shapes dust and then breathes into it to form man, so Yahweh takes out the rib and then builds it into woman.[26] To call woman "Adam's rib" is to misread the text which states carefully and clearly that the extracted bone required divine labor to become female, a datum scarcely designed to bolster the

---

[23] 1 Chr 4:4; 12:9; Neh 3:19. —Trible

[24] Pss 121:2; 124:8; 146:5; 33:20; 115:9–11; Exod 18:4; Deut 33:7, 26, 29. —Trible

[25] L. Koehler and W. Baumgartner, *Lexicon in Veteris Testamenti Libros* (Leiden: Brill, 1958), 591f. —Trible

[26] The verb *bnh* (to build) suggests considerable labor. It is used of towns, towers, altars, and fortifications, as well as of the primeval woman (Koehler-Baumgartner, 134). In Gen 2:22 it may mean the fashioning of clay around the rib (Ruth Amiran, "Myths of the Creation of Man and the Jericho Statues," *Bulletin of the American Schools of Oriental Research* No. 167 [Oct. 1962] 24f.). —Trible

male ego. Moreover, to claim that the rib means inferiority or subordination is to assign the man qualities over the woman which are not in the narrative itself. Superiority, strength, aggressiveness, dominance, and power do not characterize man in Genesis 2. By contrast he is formed from dirt; his life hangs by a breath which he does not control; and he himself remains silent and passive while the Deity plans and interprets his existence.

The rib means solidarity and equality. *'Adham* recognizes this meaning in a poem:[27]

> This at last is bone of my bones
>   and flesh of my flesh.
> She shall be called *'ishshah* (woman)
>   because she was taken out of *'ish* (man). 2:23

The pun proclaims both the similarity and the differentiation of female and male. Before this episode the Yahwist has used only the generic term *'adham*. No exclusively male reference has appeared. Only with the specific creation of woman (*'ishshah*) occurs the first specific term for man as male (*'ish*). In other words, sexuality is simultaneous for woman and man. The sexes are interrelated and interdependent. Man as male does not precede woman as female but happens concurrently with her. Hence, the first act in Gen 2 is the creation of androgyny (2:7) and the last is the creation of sexuality (2:23).[28] Male embodies female and female embodies male. The two are neither dichotomies nor duplicates. The birth of woman corresponds to the birth of man but does not copy it. Only in responding to the female does the man discover himself as male. No longer a passive creature, *'ish* comes alive in meeting *'ishshah*.

Some read in(to) the poem a naming motif. The man names the woman and thereby has power and authority over her.[29] But again I suggest that we reread. Neither the verb nor the noun "name" is in the poem. We find instead the verb qara', to call: "she shall be called woman." Now in the Yahwist primeval history [the early chapters of Genesis] this verb does not function as a synonym or parallel or substitute for *name*. The typical formula for naming is the verb *to call* plus the explicit object *name*. This formula applies to Deity, people, places, and animals. For example, in Gen 4 we read:

---

[27] See Walter Brueggemann, "Of the Same Flesh and Bone (Gen 2:23a)," *Catholic Biblical Quarterly* (Oct. 1970): 532–42. —Trible

[28] In proposing as primary an androgynous interpretation of *'adham*, I find virtually no support from (male) biblical scholars. But my view stands as documented from the text, and I take refuge among a remnant of ancient (male) rabbis (see George Foot Moore, *Judaism*, I [Cambridge: Harvard University Press, 1927] 453; also Joseph Campbell, *The Hero with a Thousand Faces* [Meridian, World, 1970] 152ff., 279f). —Trible

[29] E.g., Gerhard von Rad, *Genesis* (Philadelphia: Westminster, 1961) 80–82; John H. Marks, "Genesis," *Interpreter's One-Volume Commentary on the Bible* (New York: Abingdon, 1971) 5; John A. Bailey, "Initiation and the Primal Woman," 143. —Trible

> Cain built a city and *called* the *name* of the city after the *name* of his son Enoch (v. 17). And Adam knew his wife again, and she bore a son and *called* his *name* Seth (v. 25). To Seth also a son was born and he *called* upon the *name* of the Lord (v. 26b).

Gen 2:23 has the verb *call* but does not have the object *name*. Its absence signifies the absence of a naming motif in the poem. The presence of both the verb *call* and the noun *name* in the episode of the animals strengthens the point:

> So out of the ground the Lord God formed every beast of the field and every bird of the air and brought them to the man to see what he would *call* them; and whatever the man *called* every living creature, that was its *name*. The man gave names to all cattle, and to the birds of the air and to every beast of the field (2:19–20).

In calling the animals by name, *'adham* establishes supremacy over them and fails to find a fit helper. In calling woman, *'adham* does not name her and does find in her a counterpart. Female and male are equal sexes. Neither has authority over the other.[30]

A further observation secures the argument: *Woman* itself is not a name. It is a common noun; it is not a proper noun. It designates gender; it does not specify person. *'Adham* recognizes sexuality by the words *'ishshah* and *'ish*. This recognition is not an act of naming to assert the power of male over female. Quite the contrary. But the true skeptic is already asking: What about Genesis 3:20 where "the man called his wife's name Eve"? We must wait to consider that question. Meanwhile, the words of the ancient poem as well as their context proclaim sexuality originating in the unity of *'adham*. From this one (androgynous) creature come two (female and male). The two return to their original unity as *'ish* and *'ishshah* become one flesh (2:24):[31] another instance of the ring composition.

Next the differences which spell harmony and equality yield to the differences of disobedience and disaster. The serpent speaks to the woman. Why to the woman and not to the man? The simplest answer is that we do not know. The Yahwist does not tell us any more than he explains why the tree of the knowledge of good and evil was in the garden. But the silence of the text stimulates speculations, many of which only confirm the patriarchal mentality which conceived them. Cassuto identifies serpent and woman, maintaining that the cunning of the serpent is "in reality" the cunning of the woman.[32] He impugns her further by declaring that "for the very reason that a woman's imagination surpasses a man's, it was the woman who was enticed first." Though more gentle in his assessment, von Rad avers that "in the history of Yahweh-religion it has always been the women who have shown an inclination for

---

[30] Cf. Westermann, *Genesis*, 316ff. —Trible

[31] Verse 24 probably mirrors a matriarchal society (so von Rad, *Genesis*, 83). If the myth were designed to support patriarchy, it is difficult to explain how this verse survived without proper alteration. Westermann contends, however, that an emphasis on matriarchy misunderstands the point of the verse, which is the total communion of woman and man (*Genesis*, 317). —Trible

[32] U. Cassuto, *A Commentary on the Book of Genesis*, Part 1 (Jerusalem: The Magnes Press, n.d.) 142f. —Trible

obscure astrological cults" (a claim which he does not document).[33] Consequently, he holds that the woman "confronts the obscure allurements and mysteries that beset our limited life more directly than the man does," and then he calls her a "temptress." Paul Ricoeur says that woman "represents the point of weakness," as the entire story "gives evidence of a very masculine resentment."[34] McKenzie links the "moral weakness" of the woman with her "sexual attraction" and holds that the latter ruined both the woman and the man.[35] But the narrative does not say any of these things. It does not sustain the judgment that woman is weaker or more cunning or more sexual than man. Both have the same Creator, who explicitly uses the word "good" to introduce the creation of woman (2:18). Both are equal in birth. There is complete rapport, physical, psychological, sociological, and theological, between them: bone of bone and flesh of flesh. If there be moral frailty in one, it is moral frailty in two. Further, they are equal in responsibility and in judgment, in shame and in guilt, in redemption and in grace. What the narrative says about the nature of woman it also says about the nature of man.

Why does the serpent speak to the woman and not to the man? Let a female speculate. If the serpent is "more subtle" than its fellow creatures, the woman is more appealing than her husband. Throughout the myth she is the more intelligent one, the more aggressive one, and the one with greater sensibilities.[36] Perhaps the woman elevates the animal world by conversing theologically with the serpent. At any rate, she understands the hermeneutical task. In quoting God she interprets the prohibition ("neither shall you touch it"). The woman is both theologian and translator. She contemplates the tree, taking into account all the possibilities. The tree is good for food; it satisfies the physical drives. It pleases the eyes; it is aesthetically and emotionally desirable. Above all, it is coveted as the source of wisdom *(haskîl)*. Thus the woman is fully aware when she acts, her vision encompassing the gamut of life. She takes the fruit and she eats. The initiative and the decision are hers alone. There is no consultation with her husband. She seeks neither his advice nor his permission. She acts independently. By contrast the man is a silent, passive, and bland recipient: "She also gave some to her husband and he ate." The narrator makes no attempt to depict the husband as reluctant or hesitating. The man does not theologize; he does not contemplate; he does not envision the full possibilities of the occasion. His one act is belly-oriented, and it is an act of quiescence, not of initiative. The man is not dominant; he is not aggressive; he is not a decision-maker. Even though the prohibi-

---

[33] von Rad, *Genesis*, 87–88. —Trible

[34] Ricoeur departs from the traditional interpretation of the woman when he writes, "Ève n'est donc pas le femme en tant que 'deuxième sexe'; toute femme et tout homme sont Adam: tout homme et toute femme sont Ève [Eve is therefore not the woman as a 'second sex'; all women and all men are Adams: all men and all women are Eve]." But the fourth clause of his sentence obscures this complete identity of Adam and Eve: "toute femme peche 'en' Adam, tout homme est seduit 'en' Ève [every woman sins 'in' Adam, every man is seduced 'in' Eve]." By switching from an active to a passive verb, Ricoeur makes only the woman directly responsible for both sinning and seducing. (Paul Ricoeur, *Finitude et Culpabilité*, II. *La Symbolique du Mal*, Aubier, Éditions Montaigne, Paris, 1960; cf. Ricoeur, *The Symbolism of Evil*, Boston: Beacon, 1969, 255). —Trible

[35] McKenzie, "The Literary Characteristics," 570. —Trible

[36] See Bailey, "Initiation," 148. —Trible

tion not to eat of the tree appears before the female was specifically created, she knows that it applies to her. She has interpreted it, and now she struggles with the temptation to disobey. But not the man, to whom the prohibition came directly (2:6). He follows his wife without question or comment, thereby denying his own individuality. If the woman be intelligent, sensitive, and ingenious, the man is passive, brutish, and inept. These character portrayals are truly extraordinary in a culture dominated by men. I stress their contrast not to promote female chauvinism but to undercut patriarchal interpretations alien to the text.

The contrast between woman and man fades after their acts of disobedience. They are one in the new knowledge of their nakedness (3:7). They are one in hearing and in hiding. They flee from the sound of the Lord God in the Garden (3:8). First to the man come questions of responsibility (3:9, 11), but the man fails to be responsible: "The woman whom Thou gavest to be with me, she gave me fruit of the tree, and I ate" (3:12). Here the man does not blame the woman, he does not say that the woman seduced him;[37] he blames the Deity. The verb which he uses for both the Deity and the woman is *ntn* (cf. 3:6). So far as I can determine, this verb neither means nor implies seduction in this context or in the lexicon. Again, if the Yahwist intended to make woman the temptress, he missed a choice opportunity. The woman's response supports the point. "The serpent beguiled me and I ate" (3:13). Only here occurs the strong verb *nsh'*, meaning to deceive, to seduce. God accepts this subject-verb combination when, immediately following the woman's accusation, Yahweh says to the serpent, "Because you have done this, cursed are you above all animals" (3:14).

Though the tempter (the serpent) is cursed,[38] the woman and the man are not. But they are judged, and the judgments are commentaries on the disastrous effects of their shared disobedience. They show how terrible human life has become as it stands between creation and grace. We misread if we assume that these judgments are mandates. They describe; they do not prescribe. They protest; they do not condone. Of special concern are the words telling the woman that her husband shall rule over her (3:16). This statement is not license for male supremacy, but rather it is condemnation of that very pattern.[39] Subjugation and supremacy are perversions of creation. Through obedience the woman has become slave. Her initiative and her freedom vanish. The man is corrupted also, for he has become master, ruling over the one who is his God-given equal. The subordination of female to male signifies their shared sin.[40] This sin vitiates all relationships: between animals and human beings (3:15); mothers and children (3:16); husbands and wives (3:16); man and the

---

[37] See Westermann, *Genesis*, 357.

[38] For a discussion of the serpent, see Ricoeur, *The Symbolism of Evil*, 255–60. —Trible

[39] Cf. Edwin M. Good, *Irony in the Old Testament* (Philadelphia:Westminster, 1965) 84, note 4: "Is it not surprising that, in a culture where the subordination of woman to man was a virtually unquestioned social principle, the etiology of the subordination should be in the context of man's primal sin? Perhaps woman's subordination was not unquestioned in Israel." Cf. also Henricus Renckens, *Israel's Concept of the Beginning* (New York: Herder & Herder, 1964), 217f. —Trible

[40] Contra Westermann, *Genesis*, 357. —Trible

soil (3:17, 18); man and his work (3:19). Whereas in creation man and woman know harmony and equality, in sin they know alienation and discord. Grace makes possible a new beginning.

A further observation about these judgments: They are culturally conditioned. Husband and work (childbearing) define the woman; wife and work (farming) define the man. A literal reading of the story limits both creatures and limits the story. To be faithful translators, we must recognize that women as well as men move beyond these culturally defined roles, even as the intentionality and function of the myth move beyond its original setting. Whatever forms stereotyping takes in our own culture, they are judgments upon our common sin and disobedience. The suffering and oppression we women and men know now are marks of our fall, not of our creation.

At this place of sin and judgment "the man calls his wife's name Eve" (3:20), thereby asserting his rule over her. The naming itself faults the man for corrupting a relationship of mutuality and equality. And so Yahweh evicts the primeval couple from the Garden, yet with signals of grace.[41] Interestingly, the conclusion of the story does not specify the sexes in flight. Instead the narrator resumes use of the generic and androgynous term 'adham with which the story began and thereby completes an overall ring composition (3:22–24).

Visiting the Garden of Eden in the days of the Women's Movement, we need no longer accept the traditional exegesis of Genesis 2–3. Rather than legitimating the patriarchal culture from which it comes, the myth places that culture under judgment. And thus it functions to liberate, not to enslave. This function we can recover and appropriate. The Yahwist narrative tells us who we are (creatures of equality and mutuality); it tells us who we have become (creatures of oppression); and so it opens possibilities for change, for a return to our true liberation under God. In other words, the story calls female and male to repent.

---

[41] von Rad, *Genesis*, 94, 148. —Trible

Nonobjective Validity in Literary Biblical Interpretation: Edgar V. McKnight (1931–)

Apart from occasional fellowships that sent him abroad, Edgar McKnight has spent almost his entire life in the American South. Recently retired from a thirty-six year career as a professor at Furman University in South Carolina—not far from where he was born—McKnight had served in Baptist churches and institutions since his ordination in 1953. Seven years after ordination he earned a Ph.D. in New Testament studies from Southern Baptist Theological Seminary in Louisville, Kentucky. Almost all of his scholarly energies have focused on understanding the documents of the Bible as literature.

Literary study of the Bible is not a recent undertaking.[1] But the assumptions and methods that have been applied to the Bible under the rubric of "literary criticism" have varied over the generations. For the past several centuries, most critical study of biblical texts has been dominated by historical concerns. When literary features of the texts were examined, it was usually in order to help trace the history of the texts' compositional development. For instance, if it appeared that the narratives of the Israelite ancestors in Genesis were derived from earlier written sources, scholars sought to reconstruct the earlier sources and to locate them in the history of Israelite history. So also in the New Testament, the question of the extent and manner of the various gospel writers' use of earlier Jesus traditions has produced several theories about the growth of the gospel traditions. Source criticism and redaction criticism are specific techniques utilized in this sort of literary criticism—with its focus on the production and meaning of the documents within ancient historical horizons.[2]

Developments in general literary criticism (outside biblical studies) in the late nineteenth and early twentieth centuries emerged as a reaction against the dominant historical approaches to literary criticism. The text came to be regarded on its own terms as a text without necessary reference to the world and intentions of the author. Regardless of how a text might have come to be and what influences might have shaped it, once it is written, a

---

[1] For details on the history of literary study of the Bible, see Leland Ryken, "The Bible as Literature: A Brief History," in *A Complete Literary Guide to the Bible* (ed. L. Ryken and T. Longman III; Grand Rapids: Zondervan, 1993), 49–68.

[2] For fuller treatment of these techniques, see Norman Perrin, *What Is Redaction Criticism?* (Philadelphia: Fortress, 1969); William Beardslee, *Literary Criticism of the New Testament* (Philadelphia: Fortress, 1970); and Norman Habel, *Literary Criticism of the Old Testament* (Philadelphia: Fortress, 1971).

text exists independently of its prehistory. It now has an existence of its own, including the potential for meanings never intended by its author or even likely in its originating world. Rather the text now exists in the ideational world created or assumed by the text through the combination of words and forms that make up the text itself. Toward the end of the twentieth century, literary criticism of the Bible took on more the latter sense than a historicist approach.

McKnight emphasizes the role of the text's reader in the phenomenon of meaning, sometimes called the reader-response approach. Not unlike the meaning that works of art evoke in the viewer, the meaning that a literary work evokes is experienced by the reader. In this sense, there is no meaning until the text is read. Authors write texts of all types—narratives, orations, epistles, dreamscapes—with the expectation that readers will be involved in their texts by virtue of reading them. Without participation by the reader, however, meaning is unrealized or yet to be determined. Historical research has demonstrated that the texts of the Bible were produced within specific social and cultural constrictions of convention and expectation. When readers read in later centuries, they did so, and continue to do so, within their own social and religious contexts, which affect the sorts of expectation that will be brought to the text. This mutual interaction between text and reader is what produces meaning.

In this selection from *The Bible and the Reader: An Introduction to Literary Criticism*, McKnight reviews some of the salient factors of a shift from largely historical interpretation of the Bible to literary interpretation. Of particular interest is the question of validity in interpretation, which has long been a central concern in general hermeneutics.[3] In the premodern era, interpretation of the Bible was usually controlled by the expectation that its truth would be assessed via correspondence to religious doctrine; in the modern era, it has been correspondence to historical contingencies. (We might recall, for example, Calvin's conviction that the sole legitimate goal of the commentator "is to lay open the mind of the writer he has set out to explain.") The notion of interpretation created by a reader's interaction with a biblical text irrespective of doctrinal requirements or historical likelihood urgently raises the question of validity. In these pages McKnight addresses that question.

For further information on interpreting the Bible as literature:

Alter, Robert. *The World of Biblical Literature.* New York: Basic Books, 1992.
Powell, Mark Allan. *The Bible and Modern Literary Criticism: A Critical Assessment and Annotated Bibliography.* Westport, Conn.: Greenwood, 1992.

---

[3] Two highly influential late-twentieth-century works on the question of valid interpretation were Eric Hirsch, *Validity in Interpretation* (New Haven: Yale University Press, 1967); and Hans Georg Gadamer, *Truth and Method* (New York: Seabury, 1975).

A Literary-Oriented Biblical Criticism[4]

A literary approach to the Bible has grown logically out of the recent history of biblical criticism. This section shows how literary criticism may be grafted onto the historical approach and how a reader-oriented perspective may allow the Bible to become genuine literature.

A New Situation in Biblical Criticism

The critical method of Bible study which arose in the eighteenth century was concerned with knowledge and understanding that could be authenticated by the presuppositions and methods of the Enlightenment. Rationalism, along with the revolutionary discoveries of geology and Darwinian evolutionary ideas, influenced the development of the historical-critical method. Today, however, the historical confidence or "historicism" that sees the locus of meaning in history is no longer dominant. Moreover, careful attention to the nature of the biblical text has caused scholars to see the necessity of genuine literary criticism to complete the historical task. For example, the narratives telling the story of Israel and the early Christian movement have been treated in succession as historical accounts of the events they depict, as collections of traditions reflecting the history of the communities that originated and transmitted them, and as documents reflecting the period in which they were composed. Contemporary redaction criticism is concerned with studying the theological motivation of an author as this is revealed in the use of traditional material to compose new material and new forms. After a quarter century of massive research using redactional-critical assumptions, Norman Perrin declared that conventional redaction criticism was no longer adequate because "it defines the literary activity of the Evangelist too narrowly." Not only is the full range of literary activity of the author missed, but serious injustice is also done "to the text of the Gospel as a coherent text with its own internal dynamics."[5]

. . .

Reading the Bible as Literature

The reorientation of the critical task whereby the reader-critic is seen as inextricably involved with the text in the creation of meaning gives criticism a new perspective on traditional questions such as "what is literature?" and allows the rapprochement of literary criticism and biblical study. Literature is what we read as literature. Instead of attempting to define the Bible as literature according to descriptive and historical criteria, we read the Bible as literature.

---

[4] Reprinted from *The Bible and the Reader: An Introduction to Literary Criticism* by Edgar McKnight, copyright © 1985 Fortress Press. Used by permission of Augsburg Fortress.
[5] Norman Perrin, "The Interpretation of the Gospel of Mark," *Interpretation* 36 (1976): 120.
—McKnight

What does it mean to read the Bible as literature? Are we to deny that biblical texts grew out of specific historical and theological contexts and were designed to satisfy particular needs in those contexts? Original use is not denied, even though it must be observed that the moment after the text was received by the first readers the limited original use was exhausted. The text began to be read differently almost immediately after its initial reception, even by the first readers. And readers who were not original recipients of the text made sense in their own contexts with their different needs. Our reconceptualizing of biblical texts as literature follows the pattern implicitly followed by readers from the earliest days.

How is it possible to conceptualize as literature those biblical texts that originally had specific historical purposes? The distinction made by Aristotle between literature and history provides a starting point:

> It is not the poet's business to relate actual events, but such things as might or could happen in accordance with probability or necessity. A poet differs from a historian, not because one writes verse and the other prose . . . , but because the historian relates what happened, the poet what might happen. That is why poetry is more akin to philosophy and is a better thing than history; poetry deals with general truths, history with specific events.[6]

Aristotle's distinctions between history and literature may be restated from the reader's perspective and may help the process of translating biblical texts into literature. To read a text as history is to read it as a specific event, as what happened to particular individuals in geographically and temporally limited contexts. To read a text as literature is to read it as a universal truth.

The literary approach not only moves to the more universal so as to be able to be relevant to contemporary readers, it also gives more attention to the linguistic and literary materials used. The historical reduction emphasizes what is said rather than the way it is said; a literary approach places emphasis upon the style and form of what is said.

Biblical critics are so accustomed to the historical reduction that a conscious volitional act may be necessary to change the focus from the historical (or theological) to the literary. Edward Gibbon's *Decline and Fall of the Roman Empire* illustrates helpfully how a work that was originally intended to be history has become literature. As Northrop Frye states:

> In the first place, Gibbon's work survives by its "style," which means that it insensibly moves over from the historical category into the poetic, and becomes a classic of English literature, or at any rate of English cultural history. In proportion as it does so, its material becomes universalized: it becomes an eloquent and witty meditation on human decline and fall, as exemplified by what hap-

---

[6] Aristotle, *The Poetics*, ch. 9 (in *On Poetry and Style*, trans. G. M. A. Grube; Indianapolis and New York: Bobbs-Merrill, 1958). —McKnight

pened in Caesarian Rome. The shift in attention is simultaneously from the particular to the universal and from what Gibbon says to his way of saying it. We read him for his "style" in the sense that the stylizing or conventionalizing aspect of his writing gradually becomes more important than the representational aspect.[7]

Frye is describing what has happened in the history of reception of Gibbon's work, of course. But what has happened in the course of history may also take place in the conscious choice of individual readers. The reader may choose to place biblical writing in a literary frame, emphasizing the style and the universal signification so as to enable him or herself to create world and self both affectively and cognitively through interaction with the text.

History in Literary Study of the Bible

Attention to the original situation of communication does not abolish the work as literature if the total range of meanings and meaning-effects impinging upon the author and reader is considered, if unconscious and implicit meanings are allowed, and if these meanings are not held to apply only in the original situation. The biblical critic, trained as a historian, might find it satisfying and appropriate to continue to use the historical model, giving attention to the original situation of the text but expanding the concept of "meaning of the text" to include the totality of meanings and meaning-effects which impinge upon humankind. As biblical scholars integrate the literary approaches they find satisfying, the original situation may be understood and appreciated more fully. The text will be read as literature in a more comprehensive way. Past and present coalesce, as do thematic content and structure. Continuity may be assumed between the cognitive and affective meaning and meaning-effect; continuity may also be assumed between the original meaning intended by the author, unconscious and implicit meanings of the author, and contemporary meaning-for-the-reader.

Biblical critics are discovering that it is possible to make sense out of literary criticism, to develop literary approaches to biblical texts which, while not completely objective and scientific, are orderly and rational. The literary approaches dissolve the distance between the ancient texts and the modern reader-critic. Such approaches do not depend upon an unacceptable historicism for justification, yet they allow for integration of the rich resources of the historical-critical tradition.

In the bulk of his book, McKnight reviews the major movements in twentieth-century American literary criticism that have contributed to the rise of reader-oriented approaches. These developments provide the basis for his concluding application of contemporary critical theory to the interpretation of the Bible.

---

[7] Northrop Frye, *The Great Code: The Bible and Literature* (San Diego, New York, and London: Harcourt Brace Jovanovich, 1982), 46–47. —McKnight

Interpretation and Validation

Interpretation

The reader's role in the reader-centered concept of literature's function is to enter into a transactive relationship with the text through analysis and synthesis, by means of the codes and rules, conventions and strategies that the reader finds compelling and satisfying. One controlling strategy in the process is interpretation. Interpretation is the translation or recording of aspects of meaning uncovered and experienced by the reader into some sort of language and conceptuality shared by a community of contemporaries. The statements of meaning will be constrained by the community and its critical methods as well as by the text and the reader's capacity and experience in reading and interpretation. The methodological reduction of a text to the various historical perspectives, to existential categories, to contemporary sociological theory, and to other codes, therefore, is legitimate in a reader-centered approach. The interpretive language and conceptuality, however, will not be seen as capable of containing all of the potential meanings or even all of the meanings possible in terms of the given language (history, philosophy, sociology, ethics, theology, psychology, etc.). This is the difference between a positivistic approach and a reader-oriented approach. No one code or system is able to exhaust the potentialities of the text. This awareness relativizes the interpretation resulting from the application of any one code or set of codes.

Those readers and critics who are interested in synthesis of the meanings from various levels, fields, and epochs will emphasize continuity among the different meanings, but this will not result in a completely final synthesis. In the readers' transformation of Paul's Letter to the Galatians into a literary work, for instance, serious attention is given to the linguistic and literary material itself; it is not seen as the dispensable container of an original message. The message, moreover, is generalized. It is no longer directed simply to a first-century congregation in the Roman province of Galatia but to all individuals and groups who face the conflict between external constraint and the vocation of freedom. Attention to the writing as a "letter" and to its rhetorical organization and devices will be coordinated with the "message" to its original readers and to its expanding audience. The world of ideas and values that make such a vision possible will be imaged by perceptive readers; such a world will become the backdrop for evaluating statements of the letter and normative statements that can be made on the basis of the letter. Perhaps the reader will question the nature of some of the statements of the author (attacks upon opponents, for example) in light of the world of values that supports the positive affirmations. The less-positive statements may then be seen not simply as limitations in the historical author but as literary and rhetorical devices.

In spite of the possibility of seeing continuity between meanings of different levels, fields, and epochs, there are discontinuities. Interpretation as a final synthesis eludes us. Because of the impossibility of a final statement of meaning (and because the statement of meaning may be less significant than the process of achieving meaning), the idea of interpretation has been found questionable. Is it not possible to value the partiality of interpretation positively? Is truth or truthfulness in interpretation necessarily ruled out? It is possible, in fact, to reevaluate the relativism of methods and meanings not to say that truth is unattainable but that truth is attainable in all of the various locations and universes of humankind. Truth is discovered and expressed in terms that make sense within a particular universe of meaning. It is not some final transhistorical and transhuman expression of truth, for truth in such a form does not touch us. But meanings that are consistent with the various systems that cohere in a particular universe of meaning are true—or truthful. The universe, of course, includes us, the inhabitants of that universe who use such truth in making sense for ourselves, but it also includes elements over against us that are involved in or making sense of world and self.

Validation

The criteria for validation of reading and interpretation are transformed in a reader-oriented approach. The actual forces that operate to enable and constrain the reading and interpretation are the same for validation: the reader (or readership) *makes* a sense in light of a particular "set," within a particular cultural setting, by means of codes supplied and validated by that culture. The reader is the touchstone for meaning and validation. When a reader says that the text means thus-and-so for her or him, that fact cannot be challenged (assuming the truthfulness of the reader). That is, the reader has come to a satisfying synthesis on the basis of the various textual and extratextual factors that play a part in reading and interpretation. Other readers are not obliged to agree; therefore, the interpreter has to persuade others that the synthesis is in accord with the various factors. Other readers, meanwhile, are able to show that there is a lack of accord or that factors ignored by the interpreter make another synthesis preferable. The validity of interpretation—as it moves from the individual to the community—is intersubjective. An interpretation is valid when a group of readers and interpreters agree that it is valid.

On what basis can such agreement be secured? On the basis of the "fit" between the interpretation and the various textual and extratextual factors. This "fit" is itself not a completely objective criterion. An interpreter or a group of interpreters may favor one factor over another or ignore factors important to other interpreters. Some contemporary reader-oriented interpreters emphasize the significance for the contemporary reader to such an extent that the need for faithfulness to some original purpose and meaning is negligible. The broad role and function of the text as literature takes precedence over the narrow original purpose. Augustine took that position in his approach to biblical interpretation. He distinguished between use and enjoyment. "To use . . . is to employ whatever means are at one's disposal to obtain what one desires." To enjoy a thing is to "rest with satisfaction in it for its own sake." The end of biblical literature, for Augustine, is love of God and neighbor, the "love of an object which is to be enjoyed, and the love of an object which can enjoy that other in fellowship with ourselves." This goal may be achieved even when the meaning drawn from the text is not "the precise meaning which the author . . . intends to express in that place." If a mistake in interpretation tends to build up love, in Augustine's opinion, the interpreter "goes astray in much the same way as a man who by mistake quits the high road, but yet reaches through the fields the same place to which the road leads."[8]

E. D. Hirsch may not be far from that position in his conclusion that validation is not in terms of some narrow original intention of an author, but in terms of the genre, type, or *langue*. When an interpretation is faithful to the *sort* of meaning intended, the interpretation is valid even if it is a meaning not in the mind of the original author. A reader-oriented approach *may* give more attention to the objective criteria for the type or genre noted by earlier interpreters, but the reader may eventually transcend those externally imposed criteria and become equal to the type. Hirsch, beginning from the objective side, says the reader must reproduce in himself the "logic" of the author, the *langue,* in short the "world" of the author, in order to make sense which is valid. Beginning from the other pole, emphasis would be made upon the actualization of the *langue* by the reader, or at least the coalescence of the sort of meaning intended by the author and the sort of meaning intended by the reader.

Conclusion

Readers make sense. Conviction that there is meaning precedes the discovery and creation of meaning. Readers have made sense of the Bible as words and as Word, as human action and divine event, as an object of critical scrutiny and as the subject of human salvation and freedom. The sort of meaning sought has constrained the method used and the meaning found. A thesis of this book has been that reader-meaning has accompanied even the most radically objective historical approach. The reader is the touchstone for the sort of meaning desired, the method, the validity of the result.

This does not mean that "anything goes," for systems of interpretation involve components that must be correlated with each other and with the reader—components that are dynamic in themselves as well as parts of a dynamic system. These components include a world view that constrains the sort of meaning desirable and possible, methods that are capable of discerning those sorts of meaning, and meanings and interpretations that are consistent with the world view and the methods employed and which satisfy the reader.

The method is not static—it is dynamic and capable of accommodating itself to whatever world view directs our living and thinking. It is capable not only of enabling us to achieve meaning today, it is also capable of helping us envision what has really happened in earlier dogmatic, historical-critical, and existential approaches. It is also capable of embracing future world views and helping us develop methods and meanings correlated with those views.

---

[8] Augustine, *On Christian Doctrine,* Book 1, iv, 4–v, 5; xxxv, 39; xxxvi, 40; in *A Select Library of the Nicene and Post-Nicene Fathers of the Christian Church,* vol. 2. (ed. Philip Schaff; New York: Scribner's, 1903). —McKnight

CHAPTER 32

Unmasking Ideologies in Biblical Interpretation: Elisabeth Schüssler Fiorenza (1938–)

After earning her Ph.D. in biblical studies at the University of Münster, German-born Catholic Elisabeth Schüssler Fiorenza taught at a variety of European and American institutions. She has most recently been appointed Krister Stendahl Professor of Scripture and Interpretation at Harvard Divinity School. Schüssler Fiorenza has emerged as a major feminist biblical interpreter, authoring and editing more than twenty-five books on biblical studies, hermeneutics, ecclesiology, and theology. Although the range of her interest in the Bible is wide, we are focusing on aspects of her contribution to interpretation.

One of the characteristics of Schüssler Fiorenza's work is her emphasis on the ethics of interpretation. Scholars in the latter part of the twentieth century have sometimes turned their focus from the hermeneutics of biblical interpretation toward the rhetorics of interpretation. That is, whereas a hermeneutics of interpretation aims to understand the message that a text can speak to readers, a rhetorics of interpretation studies the effect that a text can have upon readers. Such reader-oriented interpretation recognizes that readers are creators of meaning rather than simply discoverers of a determinate meaning that lies dormant in the text. Without exception, all interpreters of Scripture are embedded in social, economic, political, and religious contexts as they carry out their production of meaning. For this reason, no reading of biblical texts can be free of ideological influence. In the light of these factors, Schüssler Fiorenza sees a moral obligation in the situation of the interpreter: interpreters of the Bible are obligated to be aware of the political and social interests that influence their work and that their work influences. The interpretive task, responsibly pursued, is therefore inherently and necessarily critical. It discerns ideological biases that have shaped biblical texts and those that have shaped biblical interpretation—biases that can lead to (and, historically, have led to) the destruction and oppression of human communities. There is, then, an ethical dimension to biblical interpretation.

For Schüssler Fiorenza, however, the interpretive task does not consist simply of describing the rhetorical effects that come from reading the Bible in certain ways. It is also advocative. She advocates in favor of liberation for marginalized groups as the optimum effect to come forth from the work of biblical interpretation. Historically, these groups include women, and as a leading feminist reader of the Bible, Schüssler Fiorenza has helped correct the undervaluation of women in biblical interpretation. But it would be mistaken to categorize Schüssler Fiorenza simply as a feminist biblical scholar. As the following selection makes clear, her concerns for ethical, self-critical interpretation of the Bible have brought her to speak against the unexamined cultural assumptions operative in biblical scholarship that have tended to marginalize *any* "other" racial or social elements of humanity. Hers is a call to a consistently critical practice of biblical interpretation.

For further information on trends in feminist biblical interpretation and the ethics of biblical interpretation:

Patte, Daniel. *Ethics of Biblical Interpretation: A Reevaluation.* Louisville: Westminster John Knox, 1995.

Schottroff, Luise, Silvia Schroer, and Marie-Theres Wacker. *Feminist Interpretation: The Bible in Women's Perspective.* Translated by Martin Rumscheidt and Barbara Rumscheidt. Minneapolis: Fortress, 1998.

Schüssler Fiorenza, Elisabeth. *But She Said: Feminist Practices of Biblical Interpretation.* Boston: Beacon, 1992.

———, ed. *A Feminist Commentary.* Vol. 1 of *Searching the Scriptures.* New York: Crossroad, 1993.

———, ed. *A Feminist Introduction.* Vol. 2 of *Searching the Scriptures.* New York: Crossroad, 1993.

Biblical Interpretation and Critical Commitment[1]

It is told that at a synod in Ephesus, "the robber synod," a sharp dispute arose among the theologians, i.e., about whether or not God had a body. And when the majority of the learned decided that God did not have a body, there was an old Egyptian hermit who left the assembly crying, with the words: "They have taken my God from me and I do not know where I shall go and search for him (sic)." I am in sympathy with the old monk.[2]

Mowinckel told this story in a debate about the church as a "spiritual community." Both the old hermit and the Norwegian professor could not conceive of a conceptualization of religion, the divine, and the church which did not take historical, particular, embodied reality into account. Unlike the hermit and the professor I am concerned here not so much with the concrete embodiment of the divine and of religion but with that of biblical scholarship. Is it possible for biblical scholarship to be value-neutral, objective, detached, and unbiased or should it be? How does the commitment to a particular community, theoretical perspective, and historical struggle impinge on or foster critical inquiry and biblical scholarship? To approach this question it is appropriate to identify my own social location or "embodiment." I speak here today as a woman who traditionally has been excluded from the articulation of theology and its institutions by church law and academic convention. I was invited as a biblical scholar whose academic home is the USA, where the political right utilizes biblical language and authority for sustaining a reactionary and anti-democratic "politics of subordination." And I speak in a German accent as a Christian theologian at the 50th anniversary of the *Kristallnacht* on November 9, 1938, the year I was born.

This particular social location raises important epistemological and hermeneutical questions and concerns. As a woman privileged by education and race, I ask how scholarship in general and biblical scholarship in particular can be changed in such a way that the voices and contributions of the previously excluded "others" can become central to our understanding of the biblical world, religion, and the divine. As member of the US academy I am concerned with how biblical scholarship can transform its "ivory tower mentality" in such a way that it can contribute to the public-political articulation of a religious vision for a more humane future of the world. Finally, as a Christian theologian I must take responsibility for the violence perpetrated by religion in general and Christian theology in particular whenever the divine is "embodied" in exclusive, elite terms of privilege fostering oppression and vilification of the subordinated "others."

---

[1] Elisabeth Schüssler Fiorenza, "Biblical Interpretation and Critical Commitment," *Studia Theologica* 43 (1989): 5–18. Used with permission.
[2] As quoted by Niels Dahl, "Sigmund Mowinckel Historian of Religion," *Scandinavian Journal of the Old Testament* 2 (1988): 17. Dahl derived this quote from an article titled "The Spirit without Body" which appeared 1954 but is not listed in the extensive bibliography of Kvale and Rian, ibid., 95–168. —Schüssler Fiorenza

As a feminist biblical scholar and theologian I do not raise these questions for individualistic and confessional reasons. Rather I have delineated my own rhetorical situation in the interest of changing the discipline that marginalizes such "embodied" scholarly engagement. Therefore, the following three arguments which are engendered by my particular social location will structure this paper. I will argue in the first place that biblical scholarship must recognize its scientist posture of universalist objectivity as masking its "masculine embodiment."[3] Secondly, it must reconceptualize, therefore, its task and self-understanding as engaged rhetoric rooted in a particular-historical situation. Finally, I will indicate how such a reconceptualization of biblical discourse and interpretation in terms of rhetoric can open up the problem of anti-Judaism in the Fourth Gospel for critical reflection and theological evaluation.

The Empiricist Paradigm of Biblical Studies[4]

The positivist value-neutral stance of historical-critical studies was shaped by the struggle of biblical scholarship to free itself from dogmatic authority and ecclesiastical controls. It corresponded with the professionalization of academic life and the rise of the university. Just as history as an academic discipline sought in the nineteenth century to prove itself as an objective science in analogy to the natural sciences, so also did biblical studies. The mandate to eliminate value considerations and normative concepts in the immediate encounter with the text is to assure that the resulting historical accounts would be free of ideology and dogmatic imposition.

This ethos of objective scientism and dispassionate scholarship free of dogmatic controls was shaped in the political context of heresy trials and anti-modernistic sentiment. Therefore biblical scholarship asserts its scientific character by rejecting all overt theological and religious institutional bias while at the same time inhabiting a name and space marked by the traditional biblical canon. To the extent that biblical studies and history-of-religions scholarship continues to mask their hermeneutical character, advocacy position, and rootedness in historical-religious power-struggles, they are not able to cultivate a critical self-reflexivity on how their socio-political location shapes their research practices and self-understandings. Their scientist, value-detached, epistemological "rhetoric of fact" covertly advocates a scholarly political practice that does not assume responsibility for its own engagements and interests.

This scientist scholarly rhetoric of objective detached inquiry insists that biblical critics need to stand somehow outside their own time, have no positive or negative attitude toward the object of their research, and conceptualize biblical time and

---

[3] For the interconnection of the exclusion of women from philosophy and the articulation of "objective" knowledge and "pure" reason see R. May Schott, *Cognition and Eros. A Critique of the Kantian Paradigm* (Boston: Beacon, 1988). —Schüssler Fiorenza

[4] D. LaCapra, *History and Criticism* (Ithaca: Cornell University Press, 1985) elaborates this self-understanding of historiography as "the documentary model of knowledge." —Schüssler Fiorenza

world as totally "Other." Kurt Rudolph, for instance, insists on the scientific character of the history of religions over and against theology normatively understood:

> Historians of religion will, to be sure, have a certain prior knowledge of the object of their research, but to the extent that they have neither a positive nor a negative attitude toward the object of their study, they will be without prejudice. It is in this sense that historians of religion must be objective, that they must be as neutral as possible.[5]

What makes biblical interpretation scientific is radical detachment, emotional, intellectual and political distancing. Disinterested and dispassionate scholarship enables biblical critics to enter the minds and world of historical people and to study history on its own terms, unencumbered by contemporary questions, values and interests.

Although scholars of religion often hold that theological commitments compromise critical rationality and scientific objectivity and confessional theologians in turn show a disdain for the rationalistic criticism of their colleagues, they nevertheless both unite in denying any concrete political-religious commitments and in claiming scientific objectivity and positivist empiricism for biblical studies. Therefore both tend to reject the work of liberation theologians and feminist scholars in religion as ideologically biased and unscientific. Positivist objectivism is blind to the fact that the world of historical data can never be perceived independently from the linguistic conceptualizations of the investigating interpreter. It also denies the relationships of power inscribed in its own discourses.

Such a positivist objectivism is a truncation of the historical impulse of the Enlightenment tradition. The ideal of the Euro-American Enlightenment was critically accomplished knowledge in the interest of human freedom, equality and justice. Its principle of unqualified critical inquiry and assessment does not exempt any given reality, authority, tradition or institution. Knowledge is not a given but a culturally and historically embodied language and therefore always open to probing inquiry and relentless critique.[6] The critical principle of the Enlightenment was institutionalized in the modern university as the rationalist paradigm of knowledge that gives primacy to experienced data and empirical inquiry. Its "logic of facts" relies on abstraction for the sake of rigor, evidence, and precision. Objectivism, literalism, methodolatry and formalism are the hall-marks of the institutionalization of the critical principle in its rationalist form.

The critical principle of the Enlightenment has also engendered three historical correctives of its institutionalized form of objectivist literalism that underline the figurality, complexity, particularity, and corruption of reality. The esthetic or romantic

---

[5] K. Rudolph, *Historical Fundamentals and the Study of Religion* (New York: Macmillan, 1985) 38f. —Schüssler Fiorenza

[6] For this characterization of the Enlightenment and its interventions see E. Farley, *The Fragility of Knowledge. Theological Education in the Church & the University* (Philadelphia: Fortress, 1988). See also the discussion of literature on the Enlightenment and biblical scholarship E. Krentz, *The Historical-Critical Method* (Philadelphia: Fortress, 1975). —Schüssler Fiorenza

corrective stresses intuitive imagination over selective abstraction[7], the religious-cultural corrective insists on tradition as wisdom and heritage, and the political-practical corrective asserts that there is no pure reason as an instrument of knowledge which could lead to a just society. In the beginning was not pure reason but power. The institutions of so-called pure reason—such as the sciences, scholarly organizations, and the university—hide from themselves their own complicity in societal agendas of power. These three corrective paradigms introduce the hermeneutical principle as a second principle of critical inquiry.[8]

To be sure, the argument of these correctives is not with empirical research, analytical scholarship or critical abstraction itself but with an uncritical conception of reason, knowledge and scholarship. The atrophy and anorexia of the critical principle in the modern university has engendered a scientistic ethos of allegedly disinterested impartial research, a proliferation of techniques and specializations and in ever narrower fields of professionalization,—practices that are reinforced by the university's reward system. However, insofar as the institutionalized-empiricist paradigm fails to apply the critical principle of the Enlightenment to its own self-understanding and its institutions of knowledge, it cannot recognize its own dogmatic scientistic character but has to marginalize its correctives as "ideological." Yet by doing so, the modern research-university fails to advance the Enlightenment goal of a just and democratic society.

This is especially underlined by the fourth corrective which—I would suggest—is in the process of being articulated. In interaction with postmodernism and critical theory so-called minority discourses question the Enlightenment's notion of the universal transcendental subject as the disembodied voice of reason. These discourses assert that the political-social and intellectual-ideological creation of the devalued Others goes hand in hand with the creation of the Western Man of Reason[9] who as the rational subject positions himself outside of time and space. By positioning himself as the abstract knower and disembodied speaker of Enlightenment science he claims to produce objective accounts of the world independent of the investigating subject.

Minority discourses such as feminist or Third World theories have shown that the Western "logic of identity" and conceptualization of reason lives from the marginalization, silence, repression, and exploitation of the Others of Western elite men. But in distinction to postmodernism, minority discourses insist that the colonialized Others cannot afford to abandon the notion of the subject and the possibility of de-

---

[7] For this emphasis in Mowinckel's work see M. Ravndal Hauge, "Sigmund Mowinckel and the Psalms—A Query Into His Concerns," *Scandinavian Journal of the Old Testament* 2 (1988): 56–71. —Schüssler Fiorenza

[8] For the presence of these correctives in the discussion of the history-of-religions method see K. Müller, "Die religionsgeschichtliche Methode. Erwägungen zu ihrem Verständnis und zur Praxis ihrer Vollzüge an neutestamentlichen Texten," *Biblische Zeitschrift* 29 (1985): 161–92. —Schüssler Fiorenza

[9] For this expression see the book of G. Lloyd, *The Man of Reason. Male and Female in Western Philosophy* (Minneapolis: University of Minnesota Press, 1984). —Schüssler Fiorenza

fining the world. Rather, the subordinated Others must engage in a political and theoretical process of becoming the subjects of knowledge and history. We who have previously been excluded from theological scholarship have to use what we know about the world and our lives for critiquing the dominant disembodied ethos of scholarship and for fostering appreciation of pluriform difference and particular articulation.[10]

But in order not to become co-opted as the "same," feminist and minority discourses have to consciously undo the rhetorics of unitary otherness. Women are not just the excluded others but the majority of women are the others of the others, doubly invisible and doubly silenced. Whereas elite women and men of subordinated races, classes, and cultures are the others of elite men, women oppressed by racism, classism, religious discrimination and colonialism are the "others of the others." As Jewish feminists[11] have pointed out, as long as feminist theology and biblical interpretation do not explicitly address anti-Semitism as a *feminist* theological issue, it will reproduce the anti-Jewish rhetorics of otherness inscribed in early Christian texts and their subsequent interpretations.

A Rhetorical Paradigm of Biblical Studies

The "inclusion" of the previously excluded "Others" as critical historical and theological subjects particularizes the universalist claims of abstract scientific inquiry as elite men's rhetorical constructions of reality. It requires, I argue, a paradigm-shift in the conceptualization of biblical studies from a scientist to a rhetorical genre, from an objectivist-detached to a participatory ethos of engagement.[12]

Since rhetorical practices display not only a referential moment about something and a moment of self-implicature by a speaker or actor but also a persuasive moment of directedness to involve the other, they elicit not only reason but also emotions, interests, judgments and commitments directed toward common values and visions. Biblical texts and interpretations as cultural-religious practices are rhetorical practices. As an institutional and intellectual discursive practice biblical scholarship is "positioned" within a historical web of power relationships. Intellectual neutrality is not possible in a world of exploitation and oppression. *Bildungswissen*— knowledge for its own sake—functions either as *Herrschaftswissen*—as knowledge for the sake of domination, or as *Befreiungswissen*—as knowledge for the sake of liberation.[13]

---

[10] See, e.g., N. Hartsock, "Rethinking Modernism: Minority vs. Majority Theories," *Cultural Critique* 7 (1987): 187–206. —Schüssler Fiorenza

[11] See especially J. Plaskow, "Blaming the Jews for the Birth of Patriarchy," *Cross Currents* 28 (1978): 306–9 and S. Heschel, "Jüdisch-feministische Theologie und Antijudaismus in christlich-feministischer Theologie," in L. Siegele-Wenschkewitz (ed.), *Verdrängte Vergangenheit, die uns bedrängt* (Munchen: Kaiser, 1988): 54–103. —Schüssler Fiorenza

[12] See C. O. Schrag, *Communicative Praxis and the Space of Subjectivity* (Bloomington: University of Indiana Press, 1986), 179–214. —Schüssler Fiorenza

[13] I have changed here Scheler's use of *Heilswissen* to *Befreiungswissen*. —Schüssler Fiorenza

By rhetorical I do not mean "mere rhetorics" understood as linguistic manipulation but a communicative praxis that links knowledge with action and passion and
discloses that biblical scholarship as a socio-religious rhetorical practice calls for public discussion and ethical judgment. Biblical interpretation understood as communicative praxis unmasks the value-detached scientistic posture of biblical scholarship
as well as the doctrinal certainty of theology narrowly conceived as authoritarian
rhetorics.

Such a rhetorical paradigm would reconstitute biblical studies as religious-
ethical practices of critical inquiry and particular commitments. "The turn to rhetoric" that has engendered critical theory in literary, historical, political and social
studies, I suggest, fashions a theoretical context for such a paradigm-shift in biblical
studies.[14] The sociology of knowledge, critical theory, post-modernism, minority discourses, reader response criticism, and the "new historicism" represent the contemporary revival of the rhetorical tradition.[15]

The analytical and practical tradition of rhetoric utilizes both theories of rhetoric and the rhetoric of theories to display how as historical, cultural, political and religious discursive practices biblical texts and their contemporary interpretations
involve authorial aims and strategies, audience perceptions and constructions. It re-
jects the misconstrual of rhetoric as stylistic ornament, technical skill, cynical deception, or linguistic manipulation, and maintains not only "that rhetoric is epistemic
but also that epistemology and ontology are themselves rhetorical."[16] Biblical scholarship is a communicative practice that involves interests, values, commitments,
and visions.

---

[14] See my article "Rhetorical Situation and Historical Reconstruction in I Corinthians," *New
Testament Studies* 33 (1987): 386–403 and Wilhelm Wuellner, "Where is Rhetorical Criticism Taking
Us?" *Catholic Biblical Quarterly* 49 (1987): 448–63 for further literature. —Schüssler Fiorenza

[15] For bringing together the insights of this paper I have found especially helpful the works of
feminist literary and cultural criticism. See e.g., S. Benhabib & D. Cornell (eds.), *Feminism as Critique* (Minneapolis: Univ. of Minnesota Press, 1987); Gayatri Chakravorty Spivak, *In Other Worlds.
Essays in Cultural Politics* (New York: Methuen, 1987); Teresa de Lauretis (ed.), *Feminist Studies/
Critical Studies* (Bloomington: Univ. of Indiana Press, 1986); E. A. Flynn and P. P. Schweickart (eds.),
Gender and Reading. Essays on Reader, Text, and Context (Baltimore: Johns Hopkins Univ. Press,
1986); G. Greene and C. Kaplan (eds.), *Making a Difference. Feminist Literary Criticism* (New York:
Methuen, 1983); Elizabeth A. Meese, *Crossing the Double Cross. The Practice of Feminist Criticism*
(Chapel Hill: Univ. of North Carolina Press, 1986); J. Newton & D. Rosenfelt (eds.), *Feminist Criti-
cism and Social Change* (New York: Methuen, 1985); M. Pryse & Hortense J. Spillers (eds.), *Conjur-
ing. Black Women, Fiction and Literary Tradition* (Bloomington: Univ. of Indiana Press, 1985); Chris
Weedon, *Feminist Practice and Poststructuralist Theory* (London: Blackwell, 1987). —Schüssler
Fiorenza

[16] Richard Harvey Brown, *Society as Text. Essays on Rhetoric, Reason, and Reality* (Chicago:
University of Chicago Press, 1987), 85. Cf. also e.g., J. Nelson, A. Megills, D. McCloskey (eds.), *The
Rhetoric of the Human Sciences: Language and Argument in Scholarship and Public Affairs* (Madison:
Univ. of Wisconsin Press, 1987); Hayden White, *Tropics of Discourse. Essays in Cultural Criticism*
(Baltimore: Johns Hopkins Univ. Press, 1978); Ricca Edmondsen, *Rhetoric in Sociology* (New York:
Cambridge University Press, 1985); John S. Nelson, "Political Theory as Political Rhetoric," in Id.
(ed.), *What Should Political Theory Be Now?* (Albany: State Univ. of New York Press, 1983), 169–240.
—Schüssler Fiorenza

A rhetorical paradigm-shift situates biblical scholarship in such a way that its public character and political responsibility become an integral part of its literary readings and historical reconstructions of the biblical world. In distinction to formalist literary criticism, a critical theory of rhetoric insists that context is as important as text. What we see, depends on where we stand. One's social location or rhetorical context is decisive of how one sees the world, constructs reality, or interprets biblical texts. Therefore, competing interpretations of texts are not simply either right or wrong.[17] They constitute different ways of reading and constructing historical meaning. Not detached value-neutrality but an explicit interrogation of one's commitments, theoretical perspectives, ethical criteria, interpretative strategies, and socio-political location is appropriate in such a rhetorical paradigm of biblical studies.

The reconceptualization of biblical studies in rhetorical rather than objectivistic terms, I suggest, provides a research-framework not only for integrating historical, archeological, sociological, literary, and theological approaches as perspectival readings of texts but also for raising ethical, religious, and theological questions of contemporary meaning as constitutive to the interpretive process. A rhetorical hermeneutic does not assume that the text is a window to historical reality nor operate with a correspondence theory of truth. It does not understand historical sources as given data and empirical evidence but sees them as perspectival discourses constructing their worlds and symbolic universes.[18] Since alternative symbolic universes engender competing definitions of the world, they cannot be reduced to one and the same meaning.

The rhetorical understanding of discourse as creating a world of pluriform meanings and a pluralism of symbolic universes, raises the question of power. How is meaning constructed, whose interests are served, what kind of worlds are envisioned, what roles, duties, and values are advocated, which socio-political practices are legitimated, or which communities of discourse take responsibility, —such and similar questions become central to scholarly discussion.

Questions raised by feminist scholars in religion, liberation theologians, theologians of the so-called Third World, and by others traditionally absent from the exegetical enterprise would no longer remain peripheral or non-existent in such a self-critical scholarly discourse. Rather their insights and challenges could become central to the scholarly discourse of the discipline.

However, once biblical scholarship begins to explicitly recognize the social interests of the investigating subject, whether defined by race, gender, culture, or class, and once it begins to recognize the need for a sophisticated and pluralistic reading of texts that questions the fixity of meaning constituted by the silencing and exclusion of "the others," then a *double ethics* is called for.

---

[17] Maurice Mandelbaum, *The Anatomy of Historical Knowledge* (Baltimore: Johns Hopkins Univ. Press, 1977), 150. —Schüssler Fiorenza

[18] See the discussion of scientific theory-choice by Linda Alcoff, "Justifying Feminist Social Science," *Hypatia* 2 (1987): 107–27. —Schüssler Fiorenza

An *ethics of historical reading* changes the task of interpretation from establishing historical facts and finding out "what the text meant" to the question of what kind of readings can do justice to the text and can elaborate the rhetorical strategies of the text in its historical contexts. It investigates how the text constructs what it includes or "silences." Such a focus on the ideological scripts of a biblical text and its interpretations does not replace historical text-oriented readings but presupposes them. As literary and historical critical exegesis attends to the text in its historical contexts, so rhetorical criticism seeks to make conscious how the text "works" in its complex historical as well as contemporary cultural, social, religious or theological contexts.[19]

Needless to say that I do not want to be misunderstood as abandoning a careful analysis of biblical sources, as eschewing the reconstruction of their historical-religious contexts or as advocating a return to the pre-critical reading and facile theological imposition of dogmatic frameworks on biblical texts. Rather I am interested in decentering the dominant scientist ethos of biblical scholarship by recentering it in a critical interpretive praxis for liberation. Although such an *ethics of historical reading* is aware of the pluralism of historical- and literary-critical methods as well as the pluralism of interpretations appropriate to the text, it nevertheless insists that the number of interpretations that can legitimately be given to a text are limited. The boundaries set by our sources separate historical reconstruction from historical fiction.

The rhetorical character of biblical interpretations and historical reconstructions requires secondly an *ethics of accountability* that stands responsible for the choice of its theoretical interpretive models and for the ethical-political implications of its interpretations of a different praxis. If scriptural texts and interpretations have been used for legitimating war, nurturing anti-Judaism and misogynism, justifying the institution of slavery, and for promoting colonial dehumanization, then biblical scholarship must not only trace the rhetorical strategies and identity formations inscribed in biblical texts, but also evaluate the discursive construction of their historical worlds and symbolic universes. If the Bible has become a classic of Western culture because of its normativity, then the responsibility of the biblical scholar[20] must include the elucidation of the ethical implications and political functions of the biblical texts themselves and the violence they have legitimated in Western history and culture.[21]

If critical scholarship should not continue to reproduce the "rhetorics of otherness" inscribed in biblical texts, it has to open up its own strategies and contextualizations as well as those of biblical discourses for critical discussion and theological

---

[19] LaCapra, *History and Criticism,* 36–44, elaborates eight ways of how rhetoric bears on historiography.

[20] Krister Stendahl, "The Bible as a Classic and the Bible as Holy Scripture," *Journal of Biblical Literature* 103 (1984): 10. —Schüssler Fiorenza

[21] See also my article, "The Ethics of Biblical Interpretation: Decentering Biblical Scholarship," *Journal of Biblical Literature* 107 (1988): 3–17. —Schüssler Fiorenza

assessment. The last section of this paper seeks to sketch how such a rhetorical approach would interrogate the strategies of biblical interpretations for their operative commitments. I will discuss as a case-study the scholarly interpretation of the anti-Jewish polemics inscribed in the Fourth Gospel.

The Johannine "Politics of Otherness" in Discussion

The anti-Jewish polemics of the Fourth Gospel lends itself for such an exploration of the rhetorical character of biblical scholarship because of several reasons: No one seriously debates the fact of such anti-Jewish language. Exegetes only disagree about its social-literary function and its theological evaluation. Moreover the socio-political location of the debate[22] on whether the language of the Gospel is anti-Jewish or anti-Semitic is apparent and not masked. It is the experience of the Holocaust and the subsequent Jewish-Christian dialogue that has spawned the inquiry as to whether Christian Scriptures in general and the Gospel of John in particular have fostered anti-Jewish prejudice not only in Christian churches but also in Western cultures. Scholars have therefore called for an explicit theological critique[23] and even change of such anti-Jewish discursive practices, although apologetic appropriation of such anti-Jewish texts is still prevalent.

Since the inquiry into Johannine anti-Judaism addresses the "Other" of Christians, it is treated as a "special" topic and therefore marginalized.[24] Many commentaries and monographs on the Fourth Gospel's theology still do not explicitly raise the problem of anti-Judaism. If they do so, they compartmentalize the problem of the Gospel's "language of hate" in an "excursus" but do not systematically develop its impact on the theology, christology, and identity-construction of the writer and audience.

In the last 20 years or so New Testament scholarship has highlighted the sectarianism and anti-Jewish polemics of the Gospel elaborating its social world and symbolic universe. Although the language and "world" of the Fourth Gospel is Jewish, the term "the Jews" is used predominantly as a negative term. It does not include Jesus and his followers as Jews but distances them from the Jews. However, not all Jews have rejected Jesus but many have believed in him. The expression "the Jews"

---

[22] See the review of the discussion by J. G. Gager, *The Origins of Anti-Semitism* (New York: Oxford University Press, 1985). —Schüssler Fiorenza

[23] See, e.g., Eldon J. Epp, "Anti-Semitism and the Popularity of the Fourth Gospel in Christianity," *Central Conference of American Rabbis Journal* 22 (1975): 35–57 who, however, does not seek to change the language of the Gospel but points to its time-bound expression. See, however, the much more extensive hermeneutical and practical suggestions of the Jewish scholar Michael J. Cook, "The Gospel of John and the Jews," *Review and Expositor* 84 (1987): 259–71 for dealing with the problem. —Schüssler Fiorenza

[24] See, e.g., R. Leistner, *Antijudaismus im Johannesevangelium* (Bern: H. Lang, 1974); W. A. Meeks, "Am I a Jew? Johannine Christianity and Judaism" in J. Neusner (ed.), *Christianity, Judaism, & Other Greco-Roman Cults* Vol. I (Leiden: Brill, 1975), 163–68; U.C. von Wahlde, "The Johannine 'Jews': A Critical Survey," *New Testament Studies* 28 (1982): 33–60; J. Ashton, "The Identity and Function of the 'Ioudaioi' in the Fourth Gospel," *Novum Testamentum* 27 (1985): 40–75. —Schüssler Fiorenza

occurs as a positive theological affirmation in the dialogue with the Samaritan woman: "Salvation comes from the Jews" (4:22). However, in the overall context this positive statement reinforce the anti-Jewish polemics of the Gospel and not vice versa. Although salvation originates with the Jews, it is not the Jews but the non-Jews who recognize and accept it.[25] The Gospel's polemics bespeak not just fear of expulsion but aggressive sectarian affirmation.

This anti-Jewish polemic is situated in a cosmological dualism of light and darkness, spirit and flesh, life and death, above and below, "the world" and the believer, God and Satan. One could say that the whole narrative of the Gospel is woven within a framework of dualism. This dualistic framework engenders not only anti-Judaism but also christological absolutism that breeds religious exclusivism and sectarian isolation.

Although it is still debated whether the controversy with gnostic interpreters of the Jesus traditions has engendered the dualistic language and christological myth of the Gospel,[26] the majority of scholars tend to argue that the conflict of the Johannine community with its community of origin and the expulsion of its members from the Synagogue has generated the social-religious alienation of the Johannine community and its anti-Jewish polemic. Relying on the work of J. Louis Martyn and R. E. Brown[27] scholars construct the expulsion from Judaism as the specific historical situation for the vituperative anti-Jewish rhetoric of the Gospel. This traumatic event is retrojected back unto the life and ministry of Jesus. To quote the influential Johannine scholar D. M. Smith:

> Because of the trauma of the rupture, the Johannine community defined and understood itself as the obverse of the synagogue and saw in the latter the enemy par excellence. But the hostility of the Synagogue was matched by the rejection of the world generally, and the community came to regard the Jewish opposition as archetypal of this rejection.[28]

Although Jewish scholars have disputed that such an official synagogue ban has existed at the time of the Gospel's redaction and that the rabbis had the power to enforce it,[29] Christian scholars persist in collapsing the rhetorical situation of the

---

[25] See the reader-response analysis of chapter 4 by Gail R. O'Day, *Revelation in the Fourth Gospel* (Philadelphia: Fortress, 1986), 70, who does however not sufficiently interrogate the anti-Jewish articulation of revelation by the Fourth Gospel. —Schüssler Fiorenza

[26] See for instance H. Koester, "The History-of-Religions School, Gnosis, and the Gospel of John," *Studia Theologica* 40 (1986): 115–36. —Schüssler Fiorenza

[27] L. J. Martyn, *History and Theology in the Fourth Gospel* (2d rev. ed.; Nashville: Abingdon, 1979); R. E. Brown, *The Community of the Beloved Disciple* (New York: Paulist, 1979). —Schüssler Fiorenza

[28] D. Moody Smith, *John. Proclamation Commentaries* (Philadelphia: Fortress, 1976), 70; cf. also 45, 65, 94. —Schüssler Fiorenza

[29] See the balanced judgment of St. S. Katz, "Issues in the Separation of Judaism and Christianity after 70 C.E.: A Reconsideration," *Journal of Biblical Literature* 103 (1984): 45–76. —Schüssler Fiorenza

Gospel with its historical situation.[30] Reviewing the counter-arguments D. Rensberger, e.g., insists

> Nevertheless, whatever the means employed and whatever the role, if any, of rabbinic degrees emanating from Jamnia, it seems incontrovertible from the thrice repeated reference in John 9:22; 12:42; and 16:2 that the Johannine community experienced such an expulsion. . . . We may know less than we would like about the details, but it is surely correct to give this experience a central role in understanding the background of the Fourth Gospel.[31]

This rhetoric "of fact" masks the theological implications resulting from such a scholarly construction of the historical "substory" to the Johannine text. It does not ask why other New Testament writers did not develop such vituperative anti-Jewish language although they know of harassment and expulsion from the synagogue.[32] Such a reconstruction of the Gospel's historical sub-text in terms of its vituperative anti-Jewish rhetorics reinforces Christian anti-Jewish identity formation today, especially if it is connected with a liberation theological posture.[33] It implies that Christians persecuted Jews when they came to power, just as Jews had persecuted Christians when they were in power.

As a reader-response critic Alan Culpepper does not shirk the question as to the function and impact of the Gospel's rhetoric today. He points out that the reading experience of the original reader was quite different from that of the contemporary reader, since the world of the text is quite different from our own. Insofar as modern readers distinguish between empirical and fictional narratives, between history and literature, they assume that they must read the gospels as "literally true."

Culpepper thus shares the concern of modern "progressive" theology when he insists that the real question and issue for contemporary readers is whether John's story can be true if it is not history. In response he argues, if contemporary readers no longer will read the text as a window to the life of Jesus but with openness to the ways it calls "readers to interact with it, with life, and with their own world," they will again be able to read the Gospel as the original audience read it. The rhetorical effect of the Gospel is then profound:

> The incentive the narrative offers for accepting its world as the true understanding of the "real" world is enormous. It places the reader's world under the providence

---

[30] For two distinct but different approaches see W. A. Meeks, "Breaking Away: Three New Testament Pictures of Christianity's Separation from the Jewish Communities," in Neusner/Frerichs (eds.), *"To See Ourselves as Others See Us:" Christians, Jews, "Others" in Late Antiquity* (Atlanta: Scholars Press, 1985), 93–116 and S. Freyne, "Vilifying the Other and Defining the Self: Matthew's and John's Anti-Jewish Polemic in Focus," ibid., 117–44. —Schüssler Fiorenza

[31] D. Rensberger, *Johannine Faith and Liberating Community* (Philadelphia: Westminster, 1988), 26. Therefore he understands the Johannine community as an oppressed community. —Schüssler Fiorenza

[32] See, e.g., Luke 6:22/Matt 5:11 (Q) and Mark 13:9; cf. Gal 1:13ff., 32. —Schüssler Fiorenza

[33] Rensberger does not claim to be a liberation theologian but only to provide "an offering from the realm of critical biblical scholarship of raw material only partially shaped." (*Johannine Faith*, 108). —Schüssler Fiorenza

of God, gives the reader an identity with a past and secure future, and promises the presence of God's Spirit with the believer, forgiveness for sin and an experience of salvation which includes assurance of life beyond the grave. The gospel offers contemporary readers a refuge from all the unreliable narrators of modern life and literature.[34]

Culpepper's summary appropriately underlines how the Fourth Gospel narrative engenders Christian identity formation today, but does not attend to the fact that such Christian identity is articulated in terms of androcentric dualism, christological exclusivism, and anti-Judaism.[35] Moreover, he does not raise the problem as to the political effects of the Gospel's narrative that according to him offers "a refuge from all unreliable narrators" of contemporary society and life.

Assuming that this characterization of "what the narrative offers" is adequate, the whole narrative of the Fourth Gospel and not only elements in it must be interrogated and assessed if we want to unravel its anti-Jewish Christian identity formation rather than repress it as something long past. This identity-formation is shot through with racism. Although in classical and New Testament times "darkness" was not associated with race, and therefore the original readers would not have interpreted the dualistic matrix of the gospel in racist terms, a long history of racist interpretation provides the contextualization for racist readings today. Such racist readings draw out the "anti-Semitic potential" inscribed in the Fourth Gospel.

In conclusion: I have argued that biblical scholarship has the responsibility not only to elaborate the historical-religious meanings of biblical texts but also to critically reflect on the Christian identity formations they produce. It has to do so because the biblical icon has shaped and still shapes not only Christian community but also Western culture. After the Holocaust biblical scholarship can no longer treat the anti-Jewish rhetoric of the Fourth Gospel as an issue of the past divorced from our present that the scholar can approach "without bias and with utmost neutrality." Instead it has to interrogate its own strategies and models of interpretation as to how much they contribute to the proliferation of anti-Jewish prejudice. Just as hegemonic so also feminist and liberation theological biblical scholarship must abandon its apologetic theological gesture, if it should not continue to collaborate in the "rhetorics and politics of otherness" that makes Jewish women the doubly excluded and vilified "others of the others."

Sigmund Mowinckel's work shared the interests of the history-of-religions movement which sought to break out of the confines of canon and ecclesiastical

---

[34] Rensberger, *Johannine Faith*, 235. —Schüssler Fiorenza

[35] In a later article [R. Alan Culpepper, "The Gospel of John and the Jews," *Review and Expositor* 84 (1987): 273–87] he addresses the hermeneutical problem raised by the vilification of "the Jews" in the Fourth Gospel but weakens his proposals by stating: "No one's hands are clean. Dialogue between Jews and Christians requires that we each confess the guilt of our own contributions and those of our respective religious traditions to the sharpening of theological differences into the outrage of anti-Semitism in all its subtle and violent forms." [185]. He thereby draws out the theological implications of a scholarly interpretation that makes "the victims" accountable for their own vilification. —Schüssler Fiorenza

dogma, out of a systematizing theological restatement of biblical texts and the philological confines of source-critical operations (Literarkritik). Instead this approach sought to understand biblical texts as generated by a historical web of religious experiences. Searching for the "Sitz im Leben" [setting in life] of biblical texts it sought to retrace the traditions and transformations in the life of biblical religion intertwined with its socio-political and cultural-religious contexts.

My own argument for a paradigm-shift in the self-understanding of biblical studies, is structurally similar. Just as we have learned from the history-of-religions approach that biblical texts must be understood as embedded in the religious-cultural-political life-world of their authors and communities, so we must cultivate a theoretical self-reflexivity that can explore the experiences and interests which generate and determine biblical interpretation and its rhetorical-historical situation today. For as Eichhorn, the father of the history-of-religions school, more than hundred years ago has recognized: "A historian is only the one who understands the present,"[36] and, I would add, therefore takes responsibility for the past and the future.

---

[36] These 13: "Historiker ist nur, wer die Gegenwart versteht." Cf. H.-J. Kraus, *Geschichte der historisch-kritischen Erforschung des Alten Testaments* (Neukirchen: Verl. Buchhandlung des Erziehungsvereins, 1956), 297. —Schüssler Fiorenza

CHAPTER 33

Biblical Rhetoric and Revelation:
Dale Patrick (1936–)

As other selections in this anthology have attested, the history of biblical interpretation has since antiquity included examination of the Bible's rhetorical dimensions.
In ancient and modern times, attention to rhetorical aspects in biblical texts focused primarily on discovering the point a biblical author was trying to make. The rhetorical situation presupposed behind a rhetorical unit (e.g., a prophetic oracle in the book of
Jeremiah) would be reconstructed through careful observation of the style and structure
of the unit in order to yield an understanding of the text as a response to a rhetorical situation. In recent decades, some scholars have applied the forms and categories of classical
Greco-Roman rhetoric to biblical texts (particularly biblical oratory, such as the Prophets)
whereas others have been more concerned to illuminate the social world assumed by the
texts' rhetoric.[1] Because this sort of interpretation seeks to reconstruct the audience to
whom an ancient speech unit was addressed, it may appear to be limited in its application
to texts that contain an address in the mouth of a speaker such as Moses or Jesus. Since antiquity, however, interpreters have recognized that, like oratory, written discourse aims to
affect or persuade a *reading* audience, such as in Paul's letters or in historical accounts by
the biblical narrators.[2]

In the late twentieth century, rhetorical criticism of the Bible has sometimes been
concerned to simply point out and describe the rhetorical devices that can be found in the
texts. Like Phyllis Trible, Protestant biblical scholar Dale Patrick of Drake University has
for about twenty years sought to move beyond typological description of the rhetorical
conventions found in the Bible, exploring the means by which the Bible functions rhetorically for theological reflection in particular. Patrick's quest concerns the question of the

---

[1] See Yehosua Gitay, "Rhetorical Criticism," in *To Each Its Own Meaning: An Introduction to
Biblical Criticisms and Their Application* (ed. S. L. McKenzie and S. R. Haynes; Louisville: Westminster John Knox, 1993), 135–49; G. A. Kennedy, *New Testament Interpretation through Rhetorical Criticism* (Chapel Hill: University of North Carolina Press, 1984); Vernon K. Robbins, *Jesus the Teacher:
A Socio-rhetorical Interpretation of Mark* (Philadelphia: Fortress, 1984).

[2] See Kathy Eden, *Hermeneutics and the Rhetorical Tradition: Chapters in the Ancient Legacy
and Its Humanist Reception* (New Haven: Yale University Press, 1997). Dale Patrick and Allen Scult,
Rhetoric and Biblical Interpretation (Sheffield, England: Almond Press, 1990), 53–56, make the case
for generic identification of the biblical historical narratives as rhetoric.

biblical texts' religious truth-value.[3] He is motivated in part by a tendency he observes in contemporary biblical interpretation to assume a hermeneutical stance of suspicion, such that the suasive powers exerted in biblical rhetoric are presumed to serve only the justification of the interests of the author and the audience: "The task of this sort of analysis, which often goes by the name of 'ideology critique,' is to uncover the particular power interests being served by a text and the class interests of the audience to which the text pitches its appeal."[4]

Patrick proposes an alternative model of rhetorical analysis: "In its zeal not to be 'taken in' by the text's rhetoric, ideology critique becomes too one-sided—too fixed on the deceptive capacity of rhetoric to give the appearance of truth and therefore blinded to its concurrent capacity to indeed represent the truth. Rhetorical analysis can and should be both an explanation of how a text might have persuaded audiences of its truth and a means by which interpreters can experience that truth for themselves."[5] Not unlike Aquinas seven centuries earlier, Patrick applies insights from contemporary philosophy of language in an exploration of the biblical text as divine revelation, not despite its rhetorical shaping but precisely because of it.

For further information on contemporary rhetorical criticism in biblical interpretation:

Briggs, Richard S. *Words in Action: Speech Act Theory and Biblical Interpretation.* Edinburgh: T&T Clark, 2001.

Gitay, Yehosua. "Rhetorical Criticism." Pages 135–49 in *To Each Its Own Meaning: An Introduction to Biblical Criticisms and Their Application.* Edited by S. L. McKenzie and S. R. Haynes. Louisville: Westminster John Knox, 1993.

Patrick, Dale, and Allen Scult. *Rhetoric and Biblical Interpretation.* Sheffield, England: Almond, 1990.

---

[3] See Dale Patrick, *The Rendering of God in the Old Testament* (Overtures to Biblical Theology 10; Philadelphia: Fortress, 1981); *The Rhetoric of Revelation in the Hebrew Bible* (Overtures to Biblical Theology; Minneapolis: Fortress, 1999); Dale Patrick with Allen Scult, "Rhetoric and Ideology: A Debate within Biblical Scholarship over the Import of Persuasion," in *The Rhetorical Interpretation of Scripture: Essays from the 1996 Malibu Conference* (ed. S. E. Porter and D. L. Stamps; Sheffield, England: Sheffield Academic Press, 1999), 63–83.

[4] Patrick with Scult, "Rhetoric and Ideology," 65.

[5] Patrick with Scult, "Rhetoric and Ideology," 66.

The Rhetoric of Revelation[6]

The concept of revelation was the currency of the realm during the era of the Biblical theology movement, but in the mid-sixties it suddenly depreciated in value and by the seventies was virtually out of circulation.[7] Old Testament theologians lost confidence in it, and there was a scramble for alternative epistemologies. Perhaps the appeal to revelation was special pleading; perhaps the Bible should be forced to make its claims on the same basis as every other purported source of truth and wisdom.

Within the fraternity of theologically inclined Biblical scholars, there was no more trenchant critic of the concept of revelation than James Barr. In the chapter, "The Concepts of History and Revelation," in his *Old and New in Interpretation*,[8] he showed that the Biblical theology movement had distorted the Biblical witness to God by putting too much stress on historical events as the means of revelation. Moreover, the concept of revelation itself was not well fitted to the way God is known in Hebrew Scripture because it suggests that humans were ignorant of the true God until God made himself known, whereas in "the Bible, . . . there is no stage at which God is not known."[9]

This observation is quite cogent. A simple reflection confirms it: The first chapter of Genesis introduces the God who is recognized in Scripture, and at no place in the Pentateuchal narrative do the human personae lose knowledge of this God. He does reveal his name and designs to various figures at important junctures, but there is no suggestion that these revelations re-establish a knowledge that has been interrupted.

> What matters is the question of what more will be added to that which is known; or, whether that which is known has already been falsified by use and interpretation which men have made of it; or, in what ways and under what conditions this knowledge is to be spread abroad to those hitherto outside of the tradition; or, in what way elements within that which is known are now to be replaced or rejuvenated through new relations.[10]

Barr has returned to the question of the knowledge of God in the 1991 Gifford Lectures, this time from the angle of "natural theology."[11] His object in the lectures

---

[6] Our selection is from Dale Patrick's essay "The Rhetoric of Revelation," *Horizons in Biblical Theology* 16 (1994): 20–40. Used with permission.

[7] James Barr paints a much different picture of the last three decades in *Biblical Faith and Natural Theology* (Oxford: Clarendon, 1993), 1–20, 102–37, viz, that revelation has enjoyed unchallenged supremacy in the circles of Biblical scholars and theologians with whom he is familiar. He must move in different circles than I do. Younger American theologians—e.g., Walter Brueggemann, Paul Hanson, Bruce Birch, John Collins, and James Crenshaw—were embracing wisdom and searching for ways to expound Biblical traditions without recourse to any overt claim to privileged knowledge of God. —Patrick

[8] New York: Harper and Row, 1966, 65–102. —Patrick

[9] Barr, *Old and New*, 89. —Patrick

[10] Barr, *Old and New*, 89–90. —Patrick

[11] Published as *Biblical Faith and Natural Theology*. —Patrick

was to show first that a number of Biblical texts clearly do appeal to a universal knowledge of God.[12] Moreover , there are more subtle ways that the authors of the Bible assume and build upon common human experience and the principles of rational discourse.[13]

By arguing that there is an undercurrent of natural theology in Scripture, Barr tacitly accepts its counterpart, "special revelation"—knowledge of God communicated by God, at God's initiative and under his protection, to a restricted body of humans.[14] How Barr would define and treat this privileged knowledge of God is uncertain, for that is not the burden of his argument nor the object of his polemic. Nevertheless, he does implicitly open the door to further discourse on revelation.

Of course, it is not necessary to rely upon Barr for a definition of revelation; there are a broad range of definitions and conceptual schemes to draw from—offered not only by theologians, but philosophers and phenomenologists of religion. One might be tempted to experiment with those to determine which would suit the Biblical evidence most handily. However, it is not in our best interest to range so broadly when what we are searching for is the way the Old Testament depicts the communication of the knowledge of God to the people of God. Our object is not to develop a rationally adequate doctrine of revelation, but to describe the transactions which take place between God and particular humans, transactions which commonly go by the name "revelation."

The term "transaction" is deliberately chosen to focus our attention on the dynamics of communicative events. It derives from the conceptual stock of the "new rhetoric," which understands communication to be an exchange between speaker and audience (text and audience where communication is written) The speaker (or author) initiates and seeks to manage the exchange, to move the audience to think and act in a particular way, but the audience has the power to resist the message, or to construe its relevance in various ways, to fill in the gaps, and so on.[15]

---

[12] Barr, *Biblical Faith*, 21–101. —Patrick

[13] Barr, *Biblical Faith*, 138–73. —Patrick

[14] The Protestant scholastic, B. B. Warfield, *Inspiration and Authority of the Bible* (Philadelphia: Presbyterian and Reformed, 1948), 74, provides a precise demarcation of the relevant terms: "These two species or stages of revelation have been commonly distinguished from one another by the distinctive names of natural and supernatural revelation, of general and special revelation, or natural and soteriological revelation. Each of these modes of discriminating them has its particular fitness and describes a real difference between the two in nature, reach and purpose. The one is communicated through the media of natural phenomena, occurring in the course of nature or of history; the other implies an intervention in the natural course of things and is not merely in source but in mode supernatural. The one is addressed generally to all intelligent creatures, and is therefore accessible to all men; the other is addressed to a special class of sinners, to whom God would make known His salvation. The one has in view to meet and supply the natural need of creatures for knowledge of their God; the other to rescue broken and deformed sinners from their sin and its consequences." —Patrick

[15] The speaker designs the discourse to attain a certain object. The audience can misconstrue or resist the design of the speaker, but language is sufficiently determinate to resist arbitrary construal, acting as a potential critique of audience response. When it is written down, and preserved in community, as the Bible has been, audiences can raise objections to previous interpretations.

The narratives of Hebrew Scripture depict numerous exchanges between Is-rael's God, YHWH, and individuals and groups. Our first task is to describe the rhe-torical dynamics of these exchanges. We shall explore just one example, the classic exchange between YHWH and Moses at the burning bush (Exod 3–4), to test a par-ticular model for describing the transaction in which YHWH communicates knowl-edge of his identity and purpose to his people. It will be argued that what is traditionally designated "special revelation" is communication that requires the re-cipient to "take God's word for it," to speak colloquially: that is, the truth of what is communicated cannot be validated by rational deliberation, communal tradition, or common human experience, but requires trust in and obedience to the speaker.[16] It is expected that this model can be applied generally to divine communications, but it is beyond the scope of this paper to do so.

There is another task that arises from the first: to reflect upon the type of trans-action that takes place between the text and the reader. It is one thing to describe the exchanges between the personae of the narrative world, another to describe the text's communication with the audience. In fact, the word "description" may not be apt for a transaction we ourselves are involved in. At most, we can reflect upon how the text seeks to engage and persuade the audience, and how the interpreter can gain most from the textual communication.

Before we embark on the exposition of the text, the communicative model which I am proposing needs to be sketched.

Performative Utterances

The linguistic philosophers earlier in this century tended to assume that lan-guage intended to describe the world of objects. Scientific knowledge was at first taken as the model of intelligible, meaningful discourse. The philosophers began to realize that the discourse of the vast majority of humans was worthy of respect de-spite its imprecision. However, the model of language still tended to be descriptive. J. L. Austin made a conceptual breakthrough by demonstrating the active force of language, what speakers do when they speak.[17] His work has been taken up by the-oreticians and students of rhetoric, for the study of the actions performed by speak-ing dovetails with the model of communication as a transaction.

Austin distinguishes three aspects of verbal communication—the locutionary, illocutionary and prelocutionary. The locutionary force of a statement is its referen-tial content, what it is about. The illocutionary force is the act of will of the speaker,

---

The text can generate a community of interpreters who continue to discuss and debate the best construal of the text. —Patrick

[16] While these kinds of divine communications are essential components of human dis-course, and in that sense "natural," they involve exchanges which conform in significant ways to both the classical and neo-orthodox definitions of "special revelation." —Patrick

[17] *How to Do Things with Words* (Cambridge: Harvard University Press, 1975); "Performative Utterances" *Philosophical Papers* 3 (New York: Oxford University Press, 1979), 220–39. —Patrick

the "assertion" that he or she makes. The prelocutionary force is the effect of the speaking upon an audience.

All utterances, according to Austin, have these three aspects, but some are constituted by their illocutionary and prelocutionary force; these are called "performatives." In them, the speaker collaborates with the addressee to create in the act of speaking itself the state of affairs described in it.

The simplest example of a performative utterance is giving a name to someone or something.[18] When a person authorized to do so names someone or something, the act causes the person or thing to be so named. The audience must acknowledge this authority, usually by acceptance of the laws and customs of the society to which both belong. In any case, the reality, the name, is constituted by the act, and it would make little sense to ask, is that really her name?

There are many other linguistic acts which are performative in character. Promises, commands and judicial judgments create the state of affairs described in them. When a person makes a promise, the act of speaking binds the speaker to fulfill it; the receiver is expected to trust the speaker and act accordingly. A command binds any addressee under the speaker's authority to act accordingly; the act of communication creates obligation. The verdict of an authorized court of law establishes innocence and guilt within the legal community recognizing the law; the truth of the judgment can be questioned, but when legal appeals are exhausted the verdict becomes a fact within the legal community.

While the types of performative utterance mentioned so far create objective social facts, and depend upon the response of the audience to be put into effect, the expression of a feeling or attitude is self-referential. As the consciousness of one's own feelings and attitudes, when one testifies to them, one's statement has a certain irrefutable character. On the other hand, one has much less control over the response, as many a lover knows. Yet even self-disclosures usually have rhetorical purposes, i.e., they are uttered to elicit a certain response, and the speaker may feel betrayed if the response is wrong; self-disclosure too is transactional.

How We Shall Proceed

Once we become conscious of the way speaking acts upon the speaker and audience, and how the audience completes this action by responding, the dynamics of God's speaking with humans in Biblical literature become much clearer. We discover that these verbal exchanges normally have a performative component. God normally divulges his name, promises, commands, expresses his state of mind, and/or pronounces judgment when he speaks. These utterances cannot be reduced to declaratory statements about God and creatures without doing violence to their

---

[18] I owe the following classification of performatives to Robert Jensen, *Knowledge of Things Hoped For* (New York: Oxford University Press, 1969), 114–18. —Patrick

rhetoric. They are not intended to refer to a state of affairs outside the transaction, so their claim to truth can not be assessed as one would assess an assertion. Rather, they create a social reality between God and the humans he addresses whose truth can only be known in response.

I had recognized that God's verbal revelations were performative in a previous work, but I did not realize the full importance of this fact.[19] In a discussion of the call of Moses, I observed that the voice from the burning bush was making a promise to Israel and commissioning Moses to act as his mediator, both of which are performative in character. I am now convinced that the performative character of God's verbal communications explains the "existential," "self-involving" quality of the knowledge of the Biblical God[20] and confirms, while qualifying, the classical definition of "special revelation."

First we should return to the Biblical text to confirm and refine the identification of the verbal transaction as a network of performative utterances. The refinement entails a working classification of the types of performative utterances within our text and the state of affairs created by them. My exegesis will be narrowly focused on these objectives.

It seems appropriate to return to the text, Exod 3–4, in which I discovered the phenomenon in the first place. The exposition will be of the extant text.[21] This is the text which has informed and still informs the religious communities which recognize the God of Scripture. It is also the text recognized as a "classic" in the culture at large.[22] If one is willing to bracket out the "historical" claims for the text, limiting one's theological reflections to the text's power and imaginative world, the final form is sufficient.[23]

Exposition

The following exposition of the passage isolates the kinds of transaction which takes place in the text. The order is "logical," beginning with the experiential and working toward the central performative communication.

---

[19] *The Rendering of God in the Old Testament* (Overtures to Biblical Theology; Philadelphia: Fortress, 1981), 94–96. —Patrick

[20] As described by philosophical theologians like Ian Ramsey, *Religious Language: An Empirical Placing of Theological Phrases* (New York: Macmillan, 1957) and Donald Evans, *The Logic of Self-Involvement* (London: SCM, 1963). —Patrick

[21] Childs's fullest statement of his canonical approach is found in his *Introduction* to *the Old Testament as Scripture* (Philadelphia Fortress, 1979); the work that has convinced me of its legitimacy is Mark Brett's *Biblical Criticism in Crisis?* (Cambridge: Cambridge University Press, 1991). —Patrick

[22] See Brett, *Biblical Criticism*, 135–46. —Patrick

[23] There are good reasons to believe that Exod 3–4 is a composite text, but in this case the various strands of narrative complement and enrich each other without serious loss of coherence. Moreover, I cannot imagine a source division that would lack performative utterances in any strand. Little would be gained for this rhetorical analysis by distinguishing sources and reconstructing the rhetorical transaction of each, and the reader would be distracted from the real object of the study. —Patrick

Sacred Space

If you were to ask the average person what makes an event revelation, the answer would most likely be an experience of God. Exod 3–4 certainly begins that way. One can identify virtually all of Rudolf Otto's characteristics of the "numinous experience" in this passage.[24] Moses encounters a mysterious presence which inspires fear and awe and the sense of creatureliness, which overpowers his resistance and sends him forth to confront the greatest human power on earth.

Phenomenologically, the account depicts a type of experience found around the world. If one were to take the experience of holiness as itself the essential feature of revelation, there would be no basis for speaking of revelation in the theological sense—privileged knowledge of God. Even though Otto calls the experience "supernatural," antithetical in every way to "natural experience,[25] its universality shows it not to be privileged or "special." Theologians were once wont to call such universal experience "general revelation."

To regard the experience from a rhetorical perspective, the experience "authenticates itself." Moses "knows" its truth in the immediacy of the experience or in the memory of this immediacy. This is the transaction of mysticism. The truth of a mystical experience cannot be demonstrated to others, at least not to their rational deliberation. It can, nevertheless, be evoked because all humans have some intuitive awareness of the sense of the holy.[26]

Within the narrative, the dramatization of the encounter with holiness sets the scene for the exchange that follows. It is a necessary ingredient of the transaction, but not the substance of it. Moses sees a miraculously burning bush, and approaches out of curiosity, only to be warned that he has entered sacred space. By analogy, the account establishes the sacred "space" of the narrative. The narrative of their conversation is itself sacred space, to be approached with awe and humility.

Identification and Naming

If the experience itself were revelation, revelation would not impart a great deal of knowledge. Not a few modern theologians are satisfied with numinous presence: everything else is human interpretation and/or projection.[27] In that case, the truth of revelation is its thatness, not its whatness. The experience itself is sufficient to confirm its reality.

---

[24] See *Idea of the Holy* (New York: Oxford University Press, 1958), 12–40, 75. —Patrick
[25] Otto, *Idea*, 25–30, 35. —Patrick
[26] Perhaps some humans are too secular to share in the experience, and these represent a problem for the claims of immediate religious experience. The advocate must either speak of the "elect"—those with a spiritual mind—or of the suppression of the mystical by secular people. —Patrick
[27] Perhaps Samuel Terrien's *The Elusive Presence: Toward a New Biblical Theology* (Religious Perspectives; San Francisco: Harper & Row, 1978) intends to be taken in this way. —Patrick

The narrative is quick to move on to a particular exchange. Moses is addressed (3:4), then the speaker identifies himself (3:6). Moses and the speaker are set in tradition: "I am the God of your father, the God of Abraham, the God of Isaac, and the God of Jacob." Here Barr's thesis about the knowledge of God is well-substantiated. Moses encounters a God who is already known in tradition. Moses has been given a basis for assessing the truth of this revelation from outside of the experience: conformity to the identity of the God of the fathers. The stories of these ancestors contain promises to them and their offspring, and show how this God demonstrated power and goodwill toward them: any new message must be appropriate to one who had established that identity.

But the identification was insufficient for Moses. "If I come to the people of Israel and say to them, 'The God of your fathers has sent me to you,' and they ask me, 'What is his name?' what shall I say to them?" (3:13) The tradition was probably ambiguous. More than one name may have circulated, indeed more than one deity may have been honored. A person must have a name, it is essential to a centered, cohesive, continuous identity. Moreover, it is privileged access, for address is essential to prayer. If Moses spoke in the name of an anonymous deity, the people would hardly consider him to have had an authentic call.

There ensues the performative act of naming. We would expect a theophanic self-introduction, as we normally have in Biblical accounts of divine communications of this kind (so Exod 6:2). The exchange here retards the narrative to build up expectancy for the revelation of the name. The name is finally divulged (in 3:15), but not until it has aroused our curiosity as to what it means. God begins with a mysterious declaration, 'ehyeh 'asher 'ehyeh, which can be translated in at least four different ways and construed in even more. Perhaps he is suggesting the meaning of the name, perhaps hiding himself in mystery.[28]

Now, giving a name to someone or something is a performative act—an act which establishes the name by which this person or thing will be known; in the case of humans, the name involves access to the person as well. When YHWH divulges his name, it sounds as though he is naming himself for the first time. However, the name has been revealed and used before in the narrative. In the context of the narrative as it stands, YHWH is providing Moses with an answer to the people's question (v. 13). The "God of the ancestors" was not sufficient to establish his credibility.

Nevertheless, YHWH's divulgence of his name has a performative force. After commissioning Moses to use "YHWH" and identifying himself with the God of the ancestors once again—perhaps to avoid any suggestion that he is a new deity—he "institutes" its use: "this is my name forever, and thus I am to be remembered throughout all generations" (v. 15) .This has the force of law, establishing the frame-

---

[28] Among other things, the exchange does hint that the name is found in the structure of language. The verb "to be" reveals and conceals his name/nature. If the history of exegesis is a good indication of its rhetorical force, the utterance elicits the reader's completion. —Patrick

work of all future commerce between God and people. At the same time, it is a gracious act, for it grants accessibility to him in prayer. In that sense, it resembles a stage in a relationship in which one person says to another, "Call me."

Promising and Expressing Feeling

God's revelation of his name comes after the deliverance of a promise. Within the dialog, this act of naming is designed to answer doubts about the veracity of the promise. To trust the promise, the recipient must know who gave it. It is not the name's linguistic meaning, though, that makes the promise more believable, but the fact that he offers with his name accessibility and trust-worthiness.

The promise of deliverance from Egyptian bondage is the heart of the revelation. It is the performative utterance to which everything else is subordinate.[29] The other communications either build up trust in the veracity of the promise or initiate the means of fulfilling it. The promise needs this sort of support because its veracity cannot be confirmed by reason or experience. Moses—and Israel—must trust the speaker's will and power to fulfill what he says he will do. Nothing that is known about the holy One, the God of the fathers, can guarantee that he in fact intends to do this now and is capable of accomplishing it. There is, to quote Kierkegaard, a "leap" to be made from knowledge and experience to faith in the veracity of the promise.

Before YHWH delivers his promise, he expresses his own state of mind: "I have seen the affliction of my people who are in Egypt, and have heard their cry because of their taskmasters; I know their sufferings" (3:7). The wording objectifies God's state of mind by depicting the condition of the people and connecting this with verbs of perception. Obviously this depiction is not meant to inform the audience that God knows what happens on earth; that is expected of a deity. Rather, he is saying, your suffering is on my mind, it dominates my concern. The last of the three parallel clauses, "I know their suffering," underscores the implied emotions, suggesting that God actually enters empathetically into their condition. Rhetorically, YHWH is seeking to persuade Moses that he is so moved by what he sees, hears and knows that he "must" act.

---

[29] The importance of promise in the OT's understanding of revelation was highlighted by the "theologians of hope"; e.g., Jürgen Moltmann, *Theology of Hope*, trans. James W. Leitch (New York and Evanston: Harper and Row, 1965), 42–43, says: "But now the more recent theology of the Old Testament has indeed shown that the words and statements about the 'revealing of God' in the Old Testament are combined throughout with statements about the 'promise of God.' God reveals himself in the form of promise and in the history that is marked by promise. . . . The examination in the field of comparative religion of the special peculiarity of Israelite faith is today bringing out ever more strongly the difference between its 'religion of promise' and the epiphany religions of the revealed gods of the world around Israel." As cogent as this observation is, it is too unitary, too fixed on one of the range of performative transactions that make up Israelite religious tradition. —Patrick

The promise to "come down to deliver them out of the hand of the Egyptians" (3:8) flows logically from the expression of feeling. This is a dramatic logic, of course, for there is no formal logic of deliberation and decision. YHWH does not have to deliver Israel, he is moved to do so. Everything that Israel knows of this God confirms this depiction, but there is much room for doubt. Once the people get out into the desert, for example, they begin to suspect a malicious purpose.[30]

The initial promise goes beyond deliverance to the grant of a homeland (3:8). While that is not the answer to an immediate concern, it does assure the people that their destiny is one of blessing and security. The paradox that the land is already inhabited is presented, but not resolved. For the present, it is sufficient to know that liberation is the beginning of a story with a happy ending.

Commission and Resistance

Verses 9–10 recapitulate the expression of feeling and promise, but this time the promise is couched under a commission of Moses as agent. "Come, I will send you to Pharaoh that you may bring forth my people, the sons of Israel, out of Egypt." Moses is made the subject of the verb which only YHWH in fact can accomplish. The reader must fill in the logical gap by inserting the idea that Moses is an agent of YHWH whose task it is to represent him before both the Pharaoh and the people.

Commissioning is a performative act, an exercise of authority related to the power to command. Again, there is no way to confirm this act by reason or experience. Moses must accept YHWH's authority. Nothing that he has known of the God of the fathers or experienced in this sacred place can make the act of will for him; he must accept the transaction as a reality that includes him.

Moses does not directly deny God's authority, and he is probably pleased that the people he left behind will have a deliverer. But he does resist the commission. Implied in his resistance is the judgment that God does not know what he is doing; if he did, he would choose a more effective agent. On the surface, it is a matter of self-doubt, but behind that is an equivocal recognition of YHWH's authority.

From YHWH's point of view, his promise depends upon Moses' and Israel's response; the compliance of the recipients with the role they are to play is necessary for the fulfillment of the promise. If Moses refuses, the whole thing will have to be called off.

Moses' objections to YHWH's commission give YHWH a chance to show his stuff, as it were. If YHWH has convinced Moses, and the reader, of his will to liberate Israel, there is still the question of capacity. He demonstrates his power in the lan-

---

[30] Exod 14:10–18; 15:24; 16:1–3, etc., dubbed "the murmuring motif," were well expounded some years ago by George Coats, *Rebellion in the Wilderness: The Murmuring Motif in the Wilderness of the Old Testament* (Nashville: Abingdon, 1968). —Patrick

guage of *prediction*. He predicts Moses' return to the mountain accompanied by the liberated people (3:12). He sketches the forthcoming struggle with Pharaoh and how he will win it (3:16–22). He equips Moses with "signs" to perform to convince any doubting Israelites of his power and Moses' access to it (4:1–9). Finally, he promises to make Moses an effective and obedient speaker (4:10–12).

These predictions are not themselves performative, but they are contingent on the promise and commission. One might classify them as assurances that YHWH has planned this all out, and has covered every contingency. Later, in the middle of the struggle with Pharaoh, Moses will recognize that everything is going according to plan; the reader will understand that the whole course of events was under the control of the Deliverer.

After all of Moses' objections are answered, he still is not persuaded. To know is not to do, and without the doing the knowledge—which consists of performative utterances—is empty. Moses can know the truth of the promise and the supporting utterances only if he embarks on the journey. Revelation becomes knowledge of God only when it is received in faith and obedience.

Yet Moses still resists. One more performative act of YHWH is necessary. "The anger of YHWH was kindled against Moses" (4:14). It is the anger, not the provision of Aaron, that turns the tide. Anger intimidates and compels. Moses begins his vocation under compulsion, virtually against his will. The people, who initially accept the news of their visitation with gladness (4:29–31), are soon dragging their feet and grumbling (5:20–21; 6:9; 14:10–12, etc.) and must also be "compelled" to know YHWH.

This is the final proof that revelation cannot be confirmed by reason and experience. According to Kierkegaard, God must not only give knowledge of himself but must also provide the condition for its reception.[31] Here the recipients must be compelled to act upon the promise, and it is the promise that is the knowledge of God.

Between Text and Audience

Thus far we have identified the kind of transaction which takes place between the personae of the story. The case is strong that there is a network of performative transactions between YHWH and Moses, and Moses is commissioned to bear performative utterances of YHWH to the people of Israel Now it is time to consider the transaction between the narrative world and the reader.

We cannot assume that the text engenders a performative transaction with the text's readers. A well-wrought narrative can evoke the suspense of the dramatic moment without setting it as the norm for the audience. Indeed, it would seem that the

---

[31] *Philosophical Fragments*, trans. Howard Hong (Princeton University Press, 1962), 58–67, 85–88. —Patrick

audience is really not in suspense as to the outcome. This means that when one reads the narrative, one does not literally have to make the same leap of faith in YHWH's promise as Moses and Israel does. The promise and its fulfillment have become accomplished "facts" for the audience: we *know* what Moses and his generation had to accept on faith.

To be sure, the ritual re-enactment of the event tries to recreate the original dramatic moment (commanded in Exod 12–13).[32] The narrative itself must do that too, or it will be lifeless. Nevertheless, the audience can only suspend its knowledge of the outcome imaginatively; it knows that its present is not really the narrative's present. The melancholy fact of ritual reenactment is that it is "make-believe." Moreover, the audience lives in the wake of the event, and knows of its consequences and the consequences of those consequences, down to the present. Any identification with the original participants is dialectical; the audience is in the same relationship to the exodus as Moses was to the traditions of the fathers.

There is a narrative strategy for incorporating the knowledge of the reader into the drama. Rather than reproducing the "original" suspense, a successful narrative produces new types of suspense which cannot be resolved by knowledge of the outcome. One way the exodus narrative creates suspense is by portraying Moses and Israel as less than ideals of religious piety. Since the narrator had the freedom to portray them as he willed, the depictions must be deliberate. Moses, as we saw, resists his call until he is virtually compelled to go. This recreates the suspense for the audience; it cannot take the performative utterances as so obviously true that anyone would act upon them. If God's chosen instrument could not respond obediently, it must be difficult indeed. The external suspense has been transformed to a great degree into an introspective one.

The people initially accept the promise joyfully (4:9–31), but the minute the struggle gets tough they begin to waver (5:21; 6:9, etc.). Throughout the plague narratives and departure, they play a rather passive role; they are essentially there as witnesses to YHWH's deed for later generations. However, when they find themselves trapped between the Sea and the pursuing Egyptian host, they begin their "murmuring" (Exod 14:10–15). This continues in the wilderness; indeed, the exodus generation proved so lacking in trust and obedience that they were forced to live out their lives in the wilderness (Num 13–14, etc.). Again, the audience must examine itself about its own staying power.

This narrative strategy is of ritual and theological significance. The introspective suspense recreates the challenge of the performative utterances for the audience. The rhetoric of the narrative seeks to elicit the kind of faith in YHWH's promises and commands that they originally called for. Although they live as benefi-

---

[32] In fact, it is significant that the narrator steps out of the narrative world here to address the reader. This address is performative, requiring the readers to define their identity (through ritual) in relationship to this story. If we were to take this performative as the only implication for the reader, however, the promise would be swallowed up in duty. —Patrick

ciaries of the events re-enacted, their own situation calls for the same faith and obedience that it did in the exodus. The fact that neither Moses nor the people were "models" made the audience realize just how difficult it is to respond properly to YHWH's word. That fact was also a consolation that YHWH could bring about his purposes despite human fallibility.

Despite the efforts of narrators, and the annual celebration of the exodus, the audience was inclined to become complacent and take the exodus for granted. Deuteronomy, Moses' departing address to Israel, is a sustained effort to arouse the people to faith and obedience. The work is permeated with suspense, a new suspense involving the danger of national annihilation because it did not "cling to YHWH with its whole heart," "did not obey his commandments and statutes," did not respond to YHWH's performative utterances in the way that leads to life.

The fusion of the horizons of the narrative and the audience occurs in various ways outside the Pentateuch. Above all, the message of deliverance from exile invited the exodus as an analogue. We find hints of this association in Hosea (e.g., 2:14–15; 11:1–11), Jeremiah (e.g., 23:7–8), and above all the anonymous exilic prophet known as Second Isaiah (Isa 40:3–5; 41:17–20; 42:14–16; 43:16–21; 48:20–21; 49:8–12; 51:9–10; 52:7–8; 55:12–13).[33] The exiles' present is so reminiscent of life in Egypt that they can identify it with the exodus narrative and hear the prophetic message as calling for the same response. Now, however, the future event has eschatological overtones, and generation after generation can wait expectantly without fulfillment.[34]

The canonization of Biblical literature reshapes the relationship of text and audience. When Deuteronomy revived the performative force of the sacred history by placing it in a horizon in which the audience can abrogate the social reality created by YHWH's words and deeds, the audience was still a part of the story continuous with the narrative. Once the canon was closed, the audience inevitably experiences a discontinuity; the reader of canonical literature is no longer living in the sacred time recounted in the Bible. The text is expected to supply a sufficient knowledge of God for the community which maintains its identity by interpreting it; the period of prophecy is over, now it is all interpretation.

The canonical status of Scripture would seem to deconstruct the performative force of accounts like the exodus. The Bible is regarded as the repository of true doctrine and saving facts. The members of the religious community are expected to "believe the Bible;" in other words, to make confessional assertions about what is the

---

[33] Although the theme of the "new exodus" had been recognized by Bible readers from time immemorial, Bernhard Anderson's study, "Exodus Typology in Second Isaiah," in *Israel's Prophetic Heritage* (New York: Harper 1962), 177–95, brought the subject forcefully into the horizon of Biblical theology. —Patrick

[34] Michael Walzer's fascinating book *Exodus and Revolution* (New York: Basic Books, 1985) explores the fusion of horizons in Western culture, showing that it was applied to concrete situations periodically in our history. —Patrick

case. The existential problem, the problem of living according to this doctrine, is separated from the quest for the truth of the Biblical accounts. The Bible is held out as an uncorrupted, timeless truth, a realm of certainty, in an otherwise ambiguous and confusing world.

Thankfully, the history of the synagogue and church has not always been so rigid and dogmatic. While it has been saddled with the doctrine of "plenary inspiration" through much of history, the text was capable of breaking through with performative force again and again. Protestants like to look back to Martin Luther's existential encounter with Scripture. In recent times we have begun to appreciate the radical sects which caught the fever of God's future. And Christians from across the spectrum are enticed by the vividness with which Francis of Assisi could hear the challenge of these sacred words.

God has not left himself without witnesses, but the classical doctrine of Scripture has been a hindrance to the knowledge of the Biblical God. It was a revelation to me, personally, when I was introduced to the critical study of the Bible and discovered that the authors of Scripture, and the characters within their narratives, struggled with the same kinds of questions, and suffered from the same kinds of doubts, as I did. And that God defended them against the dogmatists. Any doctrine of revelation that would be true to the rhetoric of the Bible must avoid encasing Scripture in this debilitating doctrinal framework.

Conclusions

The exchanges between YHWH and Moses at the burning bush fit J. L. Austin's description of performative utterance. They create a "reality," forging a relationship between the parties involving promises, commands, and the sort of personal exchanges that in classical rhetoric went by the name *ethos*. The promise and commission demanded of Moses a risk, a leap of faith that went beyond any knowledge and experience. The experience of holiness and recognition of the God whose identity was passed on in the ancestral tradition provided a basis for judgment, but the veracity of the promise and commission could not be deduced from these. YHWH also built up Moses' trust by offering his name and intimating his state of mind. He instilled confidence by sketching out his plan and demonstrating his power. Yet, after all of this, the "leap" remained and Moses could not take it; YHWH had to force him to act.

This transaction involving divine performative utterances and human response fits the definition of "special revelation" in essential respects. That is, this type of transaction yields a knowledge of God which only God can give, whose truth cannot be known by experience or reason but only by trust and obedience. Not that trust and obedience are necessarily "irrational;" rather, there are aspects of life, kinds of relationships, which are beyond the reach of rational demonstration and experiential confirmation. It may be the "rational" thing to do to trust someone who exhibits trustworthiness. The Kierkegaardian "leap of faith" can be portrayed as irrational, but it is not for that reason unreasonable.[35] On the other hand. the promise of deliverance from Egyptian slavery does fly in the face of power calculations and probabilities, so the act of believing requires a trust which defies the "odds."

It should be noted that the revelation in Exod 3–4 is a part of a larger narrative which could itself be called revelation. The revelation to Moses inaugurated the action, but the social reality created in this exchange could not be sustained without an effective change in the actual conditions of the addressees. A full analysis of special revelation would have to incorporate the events that take place outside the social reality created by performative utterances, but that would expand our study beyond reasonable length. Suffice it to say that the events of the exodus, "God's mighty deeds," could be understood as such, indeed could become a part of an action, only as fulfillment of the performatives;[36] on the other hand, what happens "outside" the social reality created by performatives must confirm and even interpret them to sustain the social reality.

The understanding of revelation as constituted by a performative transaction is probably not the only type of transaction which could legitimately go by the name "revelation," but I propose it as the best way to justify any claim to a privileged knowledge of God.[37] There are theological teachings in Scripture which appeal to wisdom and experience,[38] not just in support of performative utterances but as the court of last resort. Lady Wisdom seems to be an agent of revelation (Prov 8). She does issue a call, which has the quality of a performative utterance, but this call seems to be universal and appeals to common human experience and practical wisdom. It is up to the audience to determine whether to enter the community of the wise, not up to the one who calls.

It may be quite appropriate to speak of the "revelation" of moral and spiritual insight, but that kind of revelation does not cover narratives like Exod 3–4 and does

---

[35] See Kyle Pasewark, *A Theology of Power: Being Beyond Domination* (Minneapolis: Fortress, 1993), 260–70, 313–20, on the irrationality of power and decision. —Patrick

[36] If one could imagine a series of "plagues" without the dramatic context created by the words of YHWH and the Pharaoh, it would not have "led" to anything and the Hebrew slaves would not have been at the border of Egypt without the promises and commands delivered by Moses. —Patrick

[37] The claim to "privileged knowledge of God" certainly does not conform to the cultural values of our era, which purport to grant equality of access to spiritual truth to all religious traditions (except those which claim exclusivity). Perhaps we should abandon the "hard claims" of revelation, and accept a more humble claim—this is our community's experience of the divine. But I cannot imagine how Judaism, Christianity or Islam could live by such a soft claim, for it would abrogate God's commandment to love him with all one's being. All theological language would be translated into "language about" ultimate reality and the human experience of this reality. If the God of the Bible is known in his performative utterances, the claim of God to be both truth and power must be maintained. It cannot be justified by rational argument, though, for the claim made upon us in promises, commandments and judgments can only be known by the appropriate response. God is not an object to be contemplated, but an active persona who has commissioned us to play a role in his purposes. That is our privilege and responsibility. —Patrick

[38] Undoubtedly the wisdom tradition fits into this definition; cf. G. von Rad, *Wisdom in Israel* (Edinburgh and London: Oliver and Boyd, 1962), 53–73, 144–76. —Patrick

not justify the claim to a privileged knowledge of God entailed by the doctrine of election.[39] I am offering the rhetorical model of performative speech to bear this burden.

Finally, in the light of what has been said, the reader should recognize that the performative transactions within the text cannot be converted to declaratory statements about reality. To be sure, there is room for praise, but praise should not resolve or relax the performative claims made by the text on the reader. Classical Christian doctrine sought a body of objective doctrine in revelation, truths which do not depend in any way on the human response to them. The model I am proposing requires a transaction between text and audience; the revelatory texts of the Bible cannot be said to be "true" except as they enter into exchanges which elicit faith in and obedience to the God rendered in its stories, laws, prophecies, psalms and other texts. It is in the act of interpretation and appropriation that these texts engender either truth or falsehood.

---

[39] Cf. my entry under "Election, Old Testament" in *Anchor Bible Dictionary,* vol. 2; D. N. Freedman, et al., eds. (New York: Doubleday, 1992), 434–41. —Patrick

CHAPTER 34

The Multiple Voices of Postmodern Biblical Interpretation: Fernando F. Segovia (1948–)

A s he pursued theological education toward Roman Catholic ordination, Cuban-born Fernando F. Segovia was schooled in the prevailing methods of historical-critical study of the Bible. Further study at the University of Notre Dame refined his skill in these disciplines. But as he has narrated in several of his own publications, the "de-culturalization" that such education presupposes and expects of its practitioners did not fully take hold in his case. That is, Segovia became increasingly aware of the shortcomings in the proficient Bible critic idealized by Western historical criticism. This would be the reader who assumes that "textual meaning and historical development were retrievable, to the extent made possible by the sources, through the proper exercise of the right methodological tools" by means of a thorough divestiture "of all presuppositions and preconceptions, mostly framed in theological terms but also extending in principle to all matters sociological or ideological."[1] Late-twentieth-century developments in literary criticism as applied to biblical literature have convinced Segovia and many other biblical scholars that meaning does not reside autonomously in the biblical text, waiting to be discovered like a vein of ore and brought to the surface through skilled manipulation of extractive tools. The emergence of cultural criticism has further persuaded them that, because of the inherently culturally contextualized construction of all knowledge, no biblical interpreter operates free of ideology. Any reading of any text takes place by virtue of some predisposed interpretive interest—some combination of cultural factors stretching from the text and its world to the reader and the reader's world—that will influence the meaning that is thereby created. "[A]ll interpretation is contextual and ideological."[2]

In Segovia's view, then, biblical interpretation is a thoroughly cultural phenomenon from start to finish. The cultural factors operative as actual (as opposed to theoretical or ideal) readers of the Bible construct any hermeneutical dimension of the text and its meaning must be critically identified and brought into dialogue with other cultural factors that would result in different constructions. Segovia outlines an essentially dialogical mode of biblical interpretation: mutually engaging multiple perspectives are brought to bear regarding what the text is and what the text says and what the text means. Culturally

---

[1] Fernando F. Segovia, "My Personal Voice: The Making of a Postcolonial Critic," in *The Personal Voice in Biblical Interpretation* (ed. I. R. Kitzberger; London: Routledge, 1999), 26–37.

[2] Segovia, "My Personal Voice," 31.

dialogical biblical interpretation, of necessity, calls for greater recognition of previously suppressed voices from venues beyond the halls of the Western academy. It can no longer be assumed, for the sake of maintaining "scientific objectivity," that the vibrant traditions of biblical interpretation through generations of nonwhite and non-Western faith communities do not produce legitimate, worthwhile knowledge or interpretive results. On the contrary, these communities of interpretation have often had broad cultural impact greater than the academic guild itself can claim. Yet in the modern era, they have been denied legitimacy by the guild of professional biblical interpretation. In the postmodern vision cast by thinkers such as Segovia, all perspectives brought to bear on the text are worthy of consideration but at the same time must also be subject to the same critical scrutiny. The prospect is potentially daunting, as vast new horizons of cultural expression beyond the narrow range of academic publications must be taken into consideration—sermons, films, songs, and communal devotional exercises, to name just a few. The scholarly conversation we have known as biblical interpretation is bound to grow with the reverberation of many, many voices.

"Cultural studies" is the label sometimes given to the academic examination of the myriad factors (including institutional, sociological, political, religious, and ideological) that play into the construction, representation, and validation of human identity and values. In a number of essays published in the 1990s, Segovia explored the theoretical possibilities of cultural studies as an overarching model for biblical interpretation. The following selection is taken from one of his most programmatic reflections on the future of biblical interpretation within a framework of ideological criticism, "Cultural Studies and Contemporary Biblical Criticism: Ideological Criticism as Mode of Discourse."

For further information on postmodernism and biblical interpretation:

Adam, A. K. M. *What Is Postmodern Biblical Criticism?* Guides to Biblical Scholarship. Minneapolis: Fortress, 1995.
———, ed. *Postmodern Interpretations of the Bible: A Reader.* St. Louis: Chalice, 2001.
Inglis, Fred. *Cultural Studies.* Oxford: Blackwell, 1993.
Loomba, Ania, ed. *Colonialism/Postcolonialism.* New York: Routledge, 1998.
Sugirtharajah, R. S. *The Bible and the Third World: Precolonial, Colonial, and Postcolonial Encounters.* Cambridge: Cambridge University Press, 2001.
———, ed. *Voices from the Margin: Interpreting the Bible in the Third World.* New ed. Maryknoll: Orbis, 1995.

Cultural Studies and Contemporary Biblical Criticism: Ideological Criticism as Mode of Discourse[3]

Segovia's essay on the future of biblical interpretation begins with a review of the three-stage development of biblical criticism in the twentieth century.

The three stages in question proceed as follows. To begin with, a thoroughly entrenched and dominant historical criticism (the first stage)—which had been firmly in place since, in effect, approximately the middle of the nineteenth century—is rather swiftly displaced, beginning in the mid- 1970s, by two different and largely unrelated movements: literary criticism and cultural criticism, each of which rapidly gains strength and sophistication through the 1980s and into the 1990s (the second stage). Subsequently, a number of developments within each of these two paradigms in the late 1980s gradually begin to point the way toward another such paradigm or umbrella model of interpretation, cultural studies or ideological criticism (the third stage), with a specific focus on both texts and readers of texts—real, flesh-and-blood readers.

On the one hand, literary criticism is eventually forced to wrestle with the fundamental issue of real readers on two counts: first, insofar as it gradually moves from an analysis of the formal features or elements of texts (narrative criticism) to an analysis of readers (intratextual readers, that is) and the reading process in the construction of meaning (reader-response criticism); second, insofar as it increasingly entertains the notion of multiple interpretations, whether based primarily on the text (via the polysemy of language) or on the reader (via the filling in of textual gaps). On the other hand, cultural criticism is also brought to confront this crucial issue of real readers on two counts as well: first, in the light of the persistent emphasis of neo-Marxist interpretations on readers and readings as socioeconomic and ideological products; second, in the light of the turn toward readers and readings as socio-cultural products in anthropological approaches.

This gradual turn toward the reader on the part of both literary criticism and cultural criticism eventually brings biblical criticism face-to-face with the question of real, flesh-and-blood readers, and, in so doing, shifts it into a very different model of interpretation with its own mode of discourse and theoretical spectrum. The end result, once again, is the existence of four competing paradigms within the discipline at one and the same time: not at all a new consensus, therefore, replacing the earlier one of historical criticism, but rather a situation of radical plurality (or perhaps a consensus about no consensus).

---

[3] This essay first appeared in F. F. Segovia, "Cultural Studies and Contemporary Biblical Criticism: Ideological Criticism as Mode of Discourse," in *Social Location and Biblical Interpretation in Global Perspective* (vol. 2 of *Reading from this Place*). Most of Segovia's extensive footnotes have been excised for easier reading. Reprinted by permission from *Reading from this Place*, Volume 2 edited by Fernando Segovia and Mary Ann Tolbert, copyright © 1995 Augsburg Fortress (www.fortresspress.org).

At the same time, besides such methodological and theoretical developments in the discipline, the proposed plot [tracing the story of biblical criticism in the twentieth century] involves a crucial demographic and sociocultural development as well. Following a pattern at work not only across the entire disciplinary spectrum but also within theological studies itself, biblical criticism, which had remained since its inception largely, if not exclusively, the preserve of Western males—Western male clerics, to be more precise—begins to witness an influx of outsiders, individuals now making their voices heard for the first time: Western women; non-Western theologians and critics; and racial and ethnic minorities from non-Western civilizations in the West.

Such individuals, to be sure, received their training almost exclusively in the academic institutions of the West, where historical criticism reigned supreme and where they were duly introduced to the fundamentals of the method at the hands of Western male scholars in their role as *Doktorvätern,* master researchers and teachers as well as founders of or links in all-important pedigree lines. As such, these outsiders were very much subject to the powerful centripetal and homogenizing forces of this training, with its emphasis on the classic ideals of the Enlightenment: all knowledge as science; the scientific method as applicable to all areas of inquiry; nature or facts as neutral and knowable; research as a search for truth involving value-free observation and recovery of the facts; the researcher as a champion of reason who surveys the facts with disinterested eyes. A further, fundamental—though much more implicit—dimension of this socialization, quite in keeping with the cult of modernity emerging from the Enlightenment, should be noted as well: the conviction that such training not only represented progress over against traditional interpretations of the Bible (the triumph of light over darkness and reason over tradition) but also reflected the superiority of the West over against other cultures and civilizations (the hermeneutics of over/against and the white man's burden). In other words, historical criticism was perceived and promoted not only as the proper way to read and interpret the biblical texts but also as the ultimate sign of progress in the discipline, the offer of the (Christian) West to the rest of the (Christian) world and the means by which the backward and ignorant could become modern and educated.

Despite this overwhelming academic socialization, many of these individuals slowly began to question the program and agenda of such biblical criticism, especially the construct of the scientific, objective, and impartial researcher—the universal and informed reader—operative in one form or another not only in historical criticism but also in the other two emerging paradigms; these individuals then also began to raise the radical question of perspective and contextualization in biblical criticism. This growing insistence on the situated and interested nature of all reading and interpretation would bring additional, pointed, and unrelenting pressure on biblical criticism to come to terms with the question of flesh-and-blood readers, further pushing the discipline as a result into a quite different model of interpretation, with its own mode of discourse and interpretive spectrum.

Thus, the long-standing project of the Enlightenment, as embodied in historical criticism and its emerging rivals, was ultimately being called into question, as
were a number of attendant principles and notions: the character of biblical studies
as *science* and the use of the *scientific* method; the nature of *history;* the possibility
of *value-free* observation; the role of the *rational, disinterested* researcher; the notion of *progress*. In the process, historical criticism along with the new competing
paradigms began to be analyzed (like the Enlightenment itself) in terms of perspective and contextualization, agenda and social location, inextricably tied as these
were to the gender and origins of its practitioners—Western male clerics. In other
words, the thoroughly Western and gendered character of the discipline lying just
behind the scientific facade of the universal and informed reader began to be exposed and critiqued. In effect, reading and interpretation were no longer seen as
value-free and disinterested but rather as thoroughly enmeshed in the public arena
and thus as irretrievably *political* in character and ramifications, from the point of
view of both the narrower meaning of this term (the realm of politics within the
sphere of the sociocultural) and its broader meaning (the realm of power within the
sphere of the ideological).

From within and without, therefore, on the basis of internal disciplinary developments as well as external sociocultural developments, biblical criticism was being
pushed to take into account not only the texts of ancient Judaism and early Christianity but also the readers and interpreters of such texts—the twofold focus I have advanced as central to the emerging paradigm of cultural studies.[4] Such a plot [in
biblical criticism's story] I have described in terms of liberation and decolonization.
This I do on two counts: first, with respect to models and strategies, insofar as a
tightly controlling paradigm is displaced by enormous diversity in the theoretical and
methodological realm; second, with respect to reader-constructs, insofar as the construct of the scientific and detached ideal reader as well as the faceless and nameless
constructs of intratextual readers are displaced by enormous diversity in the
sociocultural realm. As a result, the Western and gendered nature of the discipline,
operating under the mask of objectivity and impartiality, is unveiled, and the issue of
perspective and contextualization is brought to bear as much on the texts as on the
real readers and interpreters of the texts. Such a denouement, I would readily confess, represents for me, inscribed as I have been and continue to be in a variety of colonial realities and discourses, a most welcome and attractive situation of liberation
and decolonization, whereby other voices can now speak in their own tongues and
no center controls the discourse. If the result be a situation of anomie, and I believe
that it is, I find that neither regrettable nor deplorable but rather something to be
welcomed and embraced.

---

[4] I should explain that by "biblical criticism" I mean not only criticism of the canonical
texts, whether of Judaism or Christianity, but also criticism of all other texts surviving from ancient Judaism or early Christianity. I use the term "biblical criticism" throughout merely as
a shorthand for such comprehensive studies and for lack of a better inclusive and concise term.
—Segovia

Cultural Studies: The Text as Construction

For this still-emerging paradigm of cultural studies, then, real readers lie behind all models of interpretation and all reading strategies, all recreations of meaning from texts and all reconstructions of history; further, all such models, strategies, recreations, and reconstructions are seen as constructs on the part of flesh-and-blood readers; and all such readers are themselves regarded as variously positioned and engaged in their own respective social locations. Thus, different real readers use different strategies and models in different ways, at different times, and with different results (different readings and interpretations) in the light of their different and highly complex social locations. Consequently, for cultural studies a critical analysis of real readers and their readings (their representations of the ancient texts and the ancient world) becomes as important and necessary as a critical analysis of the ancient texts themselves (the remains of the ancient world), since these two critical foci are seen as ultimately interdependent and interrelated. In other words, all recreations of meaning and all reconstructions of history are in the end regarded as constructs or re-presentations: re-creations and re-constructions.

As such, cultural studies has recourse to a broad variety of theoretical frameworks and modes of discourse, ranging from the more traditional historical and theological discussion of historical criticism, to the more recent dialogue partners of literary criticism and cultural criticism, to the field of cultural studies as such. Cultural studies within biblical criticism thus seeks to integrate, in different ways, the historical, formalist, and sociocultural questions and concerns of the other paradigms on a different key, a hermeneutical key, with the situated and interested reader and interpreter always at its core. As a result, a new mode of discourse, bearing its own analytical wherewithal and corresponding nomenclature, comes into play—a mode of discourse best characterized as *ideological*, given its central focus on contextualization and perspective, social location and agenda, and hence on the political character of all composition and texts as well as reading and interpretation. Such a mode of discourse is by no means monolingual but rather quite varied, profoundly polyglot, given the complex nature of social locations and agendas. In the end, a different model of interpretation begins to take shape, calling yet again for a very different type of reading and application on the part of its subscribers.

With this background in mind, I now proceed to an overview—again, I would stress, preliminary and tentative, given the absence of precious hindsight—of the basic principles I see as guiding and informing this umbrella model in biblical criticism. In so doing, I follow my earlier analysis of the other paradigms with respect to the categories of comparison employed: location of meaning; reading strategy; theoretical foundations; the role of the reader; theological presuppositions; and pedagogical implications.

1. *Location of Meaning.* The cultural studies model approaches the text as a construct, insofar as meaning is taken to reside not in the author of the text or the world behind the text (as postulated by both historical criticism and cultural criti-

cism) or in the text as such (as postulated by literary criticism of the text-dominant variety) but in the encounter or interchange between text and reader. For the model, moreover, the reader in this interaction is seen primarily in terms of real readers rather than intermediate and formalistic reader-constructs (as in literary criticism of the reader-dominant sort), although the latter are not at all ruled out in the process of reading and interpretation.[5] Meaning emerges, therefore, as the result of an encounter between a socially and historically conditioned text and a socially and historically conditioned reader.

From this perspective, the text—no matter how approached, whether as medium or means, or by whom, whether oneself or others—is always looked upon not as an autonomous and unchanging object, as something "out there" with a stable meaning that precedes and guides/controls interpretation, but rather as a "text," as something that is always read and interpreted by real readers.[6] The text, therefore, may be approached and analyzed from a variety of angles.

First, it may be viewed as a medium, as a message between a sender and a receiver, an author and a reader. The focus would then lie on the text, with a corresponding emphasis on its artistic and/or strategic character and an examination of its formal aesthetic and/or persuasive features—the text as a literary and rhetorical creation. Second, it may be approached as a means, as evidence from and for the time of composition. The focus would then rest on the world behind the text (the world presupposed by, reflected in, and addressed by the text), with a corresponding emphasis on contextualization and perspective and an examination of its historical, sociocultural, and political dimensions—the text as a historical, cultural, and ideological creation. Third, it may be understood as a construct, as the result of interaction or negotiation between the text and its reader(s). The focus would then lie on the text as actually read and interpreted, with a corresponding emphasis on its various readings, whether historical or contemporary, and an examination of the

---

[5] Two points are in order. First, such reader-constructs (see the section below entitled "The Role of the Reader") would be explicitly identified as such, justified in terms of reading strategies, and acknowledged as constructions on the part of real readers, variously positioned and engaged in their respective social locations. Consequently, the readings produced through the use of such intermediate and formalistic reader-constructs, regardless of the goals and purposes adduced for their employment, are not seen as more neutral and objective productions but rather as thoroughly contextualized and ideological productions. Second, real readers themselves would ultimately have to be seen as analyzed in terms of constructs as well. —Segovia

[6] Such a position need not deny altogether the existence of authorial intention (whether realized or intended), literary or rhetorical elements and features, and sociohistorical context or sociocultural scripts and codes. Self-reflection has taught me in no uncertain ways that, when writing or speaking or acting, I very often do so with certain goals and purposes in mind, which I then proceed to formulate in certain ways in the light of the context at hand and under the influence of a variety of sociocultural scripts and codes. At the same time, experience has taught me that there are usually many other goals and purposes at work—many other subtexts behind the texts—of which I am not aware at the time of acting, speaking, or writing. Experience has further taught me that any perception or rendering of such intentions, elements, context and script of myself and the various "texts" I put forth—and hence of texts as well—always constitutes a reading and interpretation, contextualized and perspectival, that in the end reveal as much about myself and my "texts" (or about texts) as about my readers and interpreters. —Segovia

contextualization and perspective of such readings—the text as a creation on the part of readers and interpreters.

In the end, however, whether the text is approached directly or indirectly, cultural studies remains keenly aware throughout of the fact that any reading and interpretation—any account of the text, whether in terms of its historical and theological, literary and rhetorical, sociocultural and ideological dimensions, by oneself or by others, in the present or in the past—constitutes a construction or re-presentation on the part of real readers: a *re-creation* of its meaning and *re-construction* of its context on the part of readers who read and interpret from within specific social locations and with specific interests in mind. For cultural studies, therefore, this character of the text as "text" ultimately makes a joint analysis of texts and readings of texts indispensable and imperative. There is never a text out there but many "texts."

2. *Reading Strategy.* In principle, in terms of theory, cultural studies would be as interested in layered as in holistic readings of the text. In other words, both the largely vertical reading of historical criticism, that reading that is based on *aporias* and textual ruptures, and the largely horizontal reading of both literary and cultural criticism, that reading that is based on the unity and coherence of the text, are seen in terms of reading strategies and underlying theoretical models on the part of real readers. As such, the presuppositions and ramifications of such strategies and models become a primary focus of attention: Why is it that some readers see disunity in the text to the extent that a reading of it as it presently stands is deemed impossible, proceed to identify the seams and ruptures in question, and engage in an excavative sort of criticism whereby literary layers are sifted out and chronologically arranged for a proper reading of the text? Why do other readers find unity and coherence in the text as it stands, downplay or rule out altogether the presence of ruptures and seams, and opt for a horizontal type of criticism with an emphasis on literary anatomy and flow or social script and codes?

In practice, therefore, in its own approach to texts, cultural studies would neither rule out the presence of textual ruptures nor find it necessary to argue for unity and coherence. Indeed, it could very well argue, along the lines of deconstruction, that there are *aporias* in the text but that such *aporias* point not to conflicting literary layers but rather to a fundamental lack of unity or coherence in the text. Any decision would be made ad hoc, as the occasion were deemed to require. In the end, however, regardless of the particular decision reached and applied with respect to the text in question, the result would be regarded as a "text," a reading and interpretation on the part of real readers, involving and thus calling for an analysis of contextualization and perspective: situated and interested flesh-and-blood readers arguing for disunity and incoherence as evidence for underlying literary strata, unity and coherence, or disunity and incoherence as evidence for ideological contradictions and implosion.

3. *Theoretical Foundations.* With cultural studies the spirit of positivism and empiricism—so prevalent in historical, literary, and cultural criticism—draws to a close. To begin with, the meaning of the text is no longer regarded as objective and

univocal, nor is the critical approach employed in the analysis of the text presented as scientific in the sense of yielding, when rigorously formulated and applied, an accurate retrieval and recreation of such meaning. Similarly, the path of history behind the text also ceases to be regarded as univocal and objective and thus open to scientific retrieval and reconstruction. For cultural studies the text has no meaning and history has no path without a reader or interpreter—without a creation of such a meaning and a construction of such a path from within a contextualized perspective; likewise, there is no critical approach without a critic—without a construction of methods and models out of a contextualized perspective.

Given its location of meaning in the interchange between text and reader (real reader, that is) and its view of the text not as something out there, both preceding and guiding/controlling interpretation, but as "text," as something that is always read and interpreted, cultural studies accepts a plurality of interpretations not only as a given but also as a point of departure for an analysis of texts and history. As such, it approaches the question of validity in interpretation as a problematic, since even the very criteria used for judgment and evaluation are seen not in essentialist terms, as universally valid and applicable at all times and in all places, across all models and social locations, but as themselves constructions on the part of real readers and hence as emerging from and formulated within specific social locations and agendas. For cultural studies, therefore, the concept of multiple interpretations is, in the end, much less circumscribed and much more open-ended than in literary criticism.

Consequently, cultural studies focuses on the variety of readings and interpretations of texts. As such, scholarship tends to be seen less as evolutionary and progressive, with serious aberrations and deviations along the way, and more as multidirectional and multilingual, reflecting different reading strategies and models at work on the part of real readers, whose contexts and interests call for critical analysis as well. It should be pointed out in this regard that the critical situation envisioned is not necessarily one where "everything goes," since readers and interpreters are always positioned and interested and thus always engaged in evaluation and construction: both texts and "texts" are constantly analyzed and engaged, with acceptance or rejection, full or partial, as ever-present and even shifting possibilities. At the same time, that sense of sharp competition, of demolition and exposé, that has been at the heart of the discipline for so long (reflecting no doubt its primary context in both the male world and the capitalism of the West) yields as well to a realization that no final recreation of meaning or reconstruction of history is possible—beyond all perspective and contextualization; that all recreations and reconstructions are productions—creations and constructions—on the part of real readers; that such readers are differently situated and engaged; and that all constructs call for critical analysis and engagement in a spirit of critical dialogue.

4. *The Role of the Reader.* It is the role assigned to the reader that, without doubt, most sharply differentiates cultural studies from the other competing paradigms in contemporary biblical criticism. For cultural studies the reader does not and cannot ever remain faceless: the reader is a real reader whose voice does not and cannot remain in the background, even if so wished and attempted, but is actively

and inevitably involved in the production of meaning, of "texts" and history; who does not and cannot make any claims to objectivity and universality, but is profoundly aware of the social location and agendas of all readers and readings, including his or her own; and who does not and cannot argue for sophisticated training, of whatever sort, and the creation of corresponding ideal readers as essential for a correct and proper understanding of a text, but is keenly aware of the nature of all readings as "texts," whether high or low, academic or popular, trained or untrained.[7] Such a foregrounding of the reader's face and voice has immediate consequences for the critical task.

First, cultural studies calls for critical analysis of reading strategies. On the one hand, strategies are to be identified, with a broad variety of options regarding reader-constructs available: internal readers or readers "inscribed" in the text, such as narratees, implied readers, or implicit readers; external readers of a historical sort, such as original, intended readers and ancient, Mediterranean readers; external readers of a suprahistorical sort, such as first-time, naive readers and sophisticated, ideal readers; external readers of a contemporary sort, whether considered as individuals or as social beings; any combination thereof. On the other hand, since all strategies are regarded as constructs, their use is also to be justified: What goals and purposes are served thereby? What are the presuppositions and ramifications of the approach adopted? Why are different strategies invoked at different times?

Second, cultural studies also calls for critical analysis of real readers—of those who lie behind, opt for, construct, and apply such strategies. Real readers are seen as neither neutral nor impartial but as inextricably positioned and engaged within their own different and complex social locations. For cultural studies, therefore, the contextualization and perspective of readers are seen as impinging, in one way or another, upon their readings and interpretations, thus calling for critical analysis of such social locations and agendas in terms of the various constitutive factors of human identity: sexuality and gender; socioeconomic class; race and ethnicity; sociopolitical status and affiliation; socioeducational background and level; intellectual moorings; socioreligious background and affiliation; ideological stance; and so forth. For cultural studies all these dimensions of human existence must be studied not only with regard to texts, their representation in texts, but also with regard to readers of texts and their readings, their representation in "texts."

---

[7] The argument is not, lest I be misunderstood on this score, that education and scholarship are unnecessary and superfluous. Indeed, I for one see both scholarship and education as vital for liberation and decolonization. It is no accident that a primary tool of the colonizer is either to deny formal education altogether to the colonized (What would it benefit them?) or to undertake it in such a way as to deny the social location and interests of the colonized (Let us make them in our image and likeness!). The argument rather is that education and scholarship—a high socioeducational level—represent no privileged access to the meaning of a text or the path of history, but are simply another constitutive factor of human identity affecting all reading and interpretation, and in this sense are no different from any other such factor. It should be clear how such a position is inscribed in both modernism and postmodernism: in the former, insofar as education and scholarship are regarded as most valuable and liberating; in the latter, insofar as they are also seen in terms of social context and ideology. —Segovia

Finally, cultural studies calls for critical analysis of all readers and readings, whether located in the academy or not, highly informed or not. In effect, the traditional distinction between high and low is collapsed thereby: the readings of, say, base Christian communities *(comunidades de base)* or marginalized social groups, such as millenarian groups, are regarded as being as worthy of analysis and critique as the readings emerging from prominent scholars following the latest intellectual movements. As such, the position of the critic ultimately emerges as much less powerful and authoritative, at least in principle. On the one hand, the critic ceases to be a necessary intermediary between texts and readers, since the critic also has to acknowledge a particular reading strategy or set of reading strategies based on certain theoretical frameworks as well as certain social contexts and interests. In other words, the critic is no less positioned and interested than any other reader. On the other hand, the critic, given the highly privileged socioeducational training received, is *presumably*—although experience often indicates otherwise—in a better position to articulate not only his or her reading strategy but also those of others. While the former position tends to diminish the highly powerful and authoritative role of the critic, the latter tends to perpetuate it. All in all, however, the open admission of contextualization and perspective does serve, in the end, to relativize and hence subvert the highly privileged education and position of the critic. In this regard, to be sure, a fundamental question regarding the role of the critic in society and the church comes immediately to the fore, a question that lies, however, beyond the scope of the present essay.

5. *Theological Presuppositions.* The model of cultural studies is no less theological than any of the other models, but it does call for radical openness in this regard as well. Besides the factors of sexuality and gender (the male nature of the discipline) and sociopolitical status and affiliation (the Western character of the discipline), a third factor has been highly influential as well in biblical criticism: socioreligious background and affiliation. In fact, the socioreligious matrix or ambit of the critic—his or her institutional, religious, and theological moorings—has been more explicit or evident than any other factor as regards the recreation of meaning from texts, the reconstruction of history behind texts, and the use of critical methodologies in relation to texts. Even when a critic pretended to the highest levels of objectivity and impartiality, his or her socioreligious identity proved unconcealable and undeniable in reading and interpretation, with the representation of ancient texts and communities bearing the unmistakable stamp of the world of that critic.

For cultural studies the socioreligious factor—the question of belief systems, their discourses and practices, and their relationship to ideological worldview and stance—is not and cannot be denied or put aside but rather must be brought out into the open and critically analyzed, not only in texts but also in the reading of texts. In other words, all recreations of meaning from texts, all reconstructions of history behind texts, and all critical models and methods used to approach texts are seen as profoundly religious, whether by way of affirmation or negation, reflecting once again the contextuality and perspective of critics and readers.

On the one hand, therefore, cultural studies is interested in the deeply socioreligious character of texts: both the theological positions, conflicts, and developments present in texts and a comparative analysis of these in the light of other socioreligious traditions are seen as worth pursuing from a critical point of view, as an important dimension of the text's meaning and history. At the same time, on the other hand, cultural studies is also interested in the socioreligious matrix of real readers and hence in the relationship of interpretation to theology, howsoever conceived or articulated: as an exercise in the history of religions, divorced from the wider theological enterprise and yielding facts or data for the theologians to deal with in their respective contexts; as an exercise leading to a greater understanding of the text in its original setting—whether conceived along historical, literary, or cultural lines—and thus ultimately to a more informed hermeneutical appropriation of the text as the "Word of God" in the contemporary religious community; or as an exercise on the side of the oppressed and with liberation in mind, sifting from the text what is liberating and putting aside what is oppressive.

For cultural studies, therefore, all readers and critics are theologians, implicitly or explicitly, by way of negation or affirmation, and all approaches to the text are theological in one respect or another. It is, then, this socioreligious dimension of reading and interpretation that needs to be surfaced and examined, in terms both of belief systems and of their ramifications for ideological worldviews and stances. For cultural studies there is simply no escape from the socioreligious dimension. Moreover, given its fundamental conception of texts as constructs or "texts," there is not and cannot be a meaning for all readers at all times and in all cultures. No meaning can dictate and govern the overall boundaries and parameters of Christian life; in effect, such boundaries and parameters are radically problematized thereby.

6. *Pedagogical Implications.* The educational implications of cultural studies are radically different from those of the other three paradigms. A number of factors call for a complete rethinking and reformulation of biblical pedagogy, its discourse and practice, within theological education: the broad variety of interpretive models; the conception of all readings as constructions on the part of real readers; the emphasis on social location and perspective with regard to real readers; the view of the critic as being as contextualized and perspectival as any other reader of the text. Certain consequences of such a revisioning are immediately clear.

First, there can no longer be a demand for a common methodological approach and theoretical apparatus on the part of all readers, regardless of theological moorings or sociocultural contexts, in order to become informed critics. Diversity in methods and models has rendered such a call not only unworkable in practice but also and above all groundless in theory. Indeed, one could very well argue that what is now necessary to become an informed reader or critic is metatheory, a grasp of theory and its history, not only within the discipline itself but also across the disciplinary spectrum. Second, informed readings can no longer be perceived as hermeneutically privileged and hence inherently superior to uninformed or "popular" readings, since both modes of reading involve, in their own respective ways, contextualization and perspective on the part of real readers. In this regard the call for readers to become informed, to become critics, has to be reconceptualized as well. Finally, readers can no longer be called upon to put aside their "faces" and voices in order to become informed, but rather must be called upon to become self-conscious and self-critical regarding these in the process of reading and interpretation, that is, learn how to read not only texts but also themselves and their readings.

In the end, the long-established model of learned impartation and passive reception, carried on within a seemingly ahistorical and asocial vacuum, must yield to a model of self-conscious, highly critical, and global dialogue involving constant and ever-shifting impartation and reception. In so doing, the pedagogical model would follow closely upon the interpretive model, becoming in the process highly decentered (or multicentered) and multilingual.

Concluding Comments

Such, then, are the basic principles that inform and guide the paradigm of cultural studies. Following this overview of the model, I should like to conclude, as I did in the case of the other three paradigms, with some remarks on the consequences of this new paradigm for theory and methodology as well as culture and experience in the task of biblical criticism. In so doing, I make use once again of the fundamental themes of liberation and decolonization invoked and deployed in my plotting of [story of] the discipline—its past, its present, and its future.

First, from a methodological and theoretical point of view, cultural studies represents a further and profound liberating step in biblical criticism, insofar as it allows for a diversity of reading strategies and theoretical models, while calling for critical awareness and engagement regarding the grounding, application, and ramifications of all such models and strategies. Cultural studies does not argue for any one strategy or framework as the sole and proper entry into the text to the exclusion of all others, for a totalizing narrative as it were; it contemplates instead a creative use of historical, literary, and cultural perspectives and concerns. In so doing, cultural studies finds itself in conversation with a wide variety of disciplines and critical frameworks. It does regard, however, all strategies and models as constructs on the part of real readers and thus calls on all readers to be quite up-front regarding their reading strategies and theoretical frameworks as well as their social locations and agendas.

Second, from a historical and cultural point of view, cultural studies represents an even more profound and liberating step in biblical criticism, insofar as it moves well beyond diversity in the methodological and theoretical realm into diversity in the sociocultural realm. Cultural studies is interested in analyzing not only the social location and agendas of texts but also the social location and agendas of flesh-and-blood readers and "texts," their readings of texts. Since all reading strategies and "texts" are regarded as constructs on the part of real readers, the task of criticism is seen as encompassing both an analysis of culture and experience vis-à-vis texts and an analysis of culture and experience vis-à-vis their readers, in the fullness of their diversity. For cultural studies, therefore, all *exegesis* is ultimately *eisegesis:* interpretation and hermeneutics go hand in hand.

Through such a joint analysis of texts and "texts," readers and their readings, cultural studies moves well beyond the implicit and dominant Western moorings and concerns of the discipline to embrace the concerns and moorings of readers throughout the rest of the world, to let everyone speak in their own tongues and from their own place. With cultural studies, therefore, the process of liberation and decolonization in biblical criticism takes a crucial step. What happens when the inculturation of the critic as gendered and Western ceases? What happens, in effect, is what can be presently witnessed in the discipline and what takes place whenever any process of liberation and decolonization begins to prove successful: a situation of simultaneous celebration, wailing, and conflict. First, the outsiders rejoice over their newfound identity and history on the periphery. Second, the insiders wail over the decline of standards and "scholarship" represented by the center. Third, there is conflict: on the one hand, sharp and inevitable criticism of the center, of its discourse and practice (the what-have-you-done-to-us syndrome), by the outsiders; on the other hand, ready dismissal of the periphery, of its discourse and practice (the after-all-we-have-done-for-you syndrome), by the center.

At the same time, beyond the celebration, lamentation, and conflict, new and fundamental problems arise. To mention but a few: If no master narrative is to be posited or desired, how does one deal with the continued abuse of the oppressed by the oppressor, the weak by the strong, the subaltern by the dominant? If the ideal of the master teacher is to be put aside, how does one carry on the task of biblical pedagogy and theological education? If the critic is neither objective nor disinterested, what then becomes the role of the critic in society and religion? If biblical criticism is not to be regarded as scientific, nontheological, and nonreligious at heart, what then should be its relationship vis-à-vis the other classical theological disciplines and the so-called fields of religious studies? Anomie, to be sure, does have its price. A consideration of such issues must, however, wait for another occasion.

A final comment is in order. I have argued that cultural studies calls for and demands dialogue, critical dialogue. I would also argue, however, that there should be no romantic illusions whatsoever about such dialogue. Were one to plot the discourse and practice of dialogue along an interpretive spectrum, the following three positions would readily come to mind: toward one end, the totalitarian position, whether of the left or the right, of no dialogue whatsoever, with dialogue seen as profoundly subversive; in the center, the liberal-humanist position of genteel dialogue—perhaps the most common position in both professional and graduate theological programs—in which the political questions of power and ideology are distinctly frowned upon and actively skirted as disruptive and politicizing, as undoing or not building "community"; toward the other end, the democratic and liberative position of critical dialogue, according to which all voices have a right to speak up, loud and clear, and no subject remains untouched, including that of power and ideology. I see cultural studies as fully ensconced within this latter end of the spectrum and thus as both a progeny of conflict and a progenitor of conflict: such dialogue is born out of conflict and engenders conflict. Such, I would add, is also the inevitable result and mode of a postcolonial world and a postcolonial biblical criticism.

TIMELINES

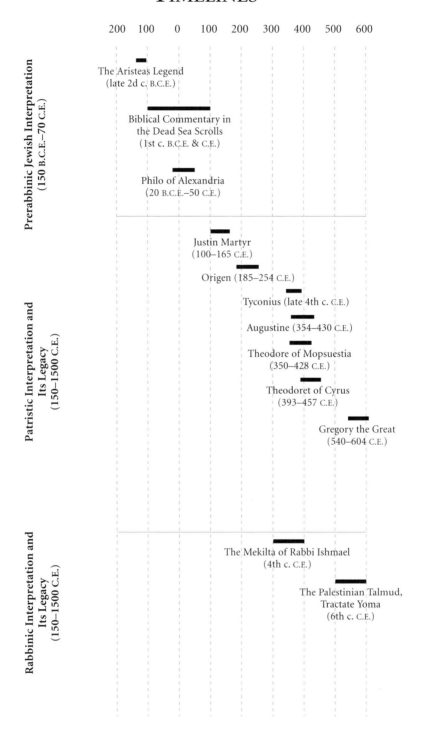

| | 200 | 100 | 0 | 100 | 200 | 300 | 400 | 500 | 600 |

Prerabbinic Jewish Interpretation (150 B.C.E.–70 C.E.)

The Aristeas Legend
(late 2d c. B.C.E.)

Biblical Commentary in
the Dead Sea Scrolls
(1st c. B.C.E. & C.E.)

Philo of Alexandria
(20 B.C.E.–50 C.E.)

Patristic Interpretation and Its Legacy (150–1500 C.E.)

Justin Martyr
(100–165 C.E.)

Origen (185–254 C.E.)

Tyconius (late 4th c. C.E.)

Augustine (354–430 C.E.)

Theodore of Mopsuestia
(350–428 C.E.)

Theodoret of Cyrus
(393–457 C.E.)

Gregory the Great
(540–604 C.E.)

Rabbinic Interpretation and Its Legacy (150–1500 C.E.)

The Mekilta of Rabbi Ishmael
(4th c. C.E.)

The Palestinian Talmud,
Tractate Yoma
(6th c. C.E.)

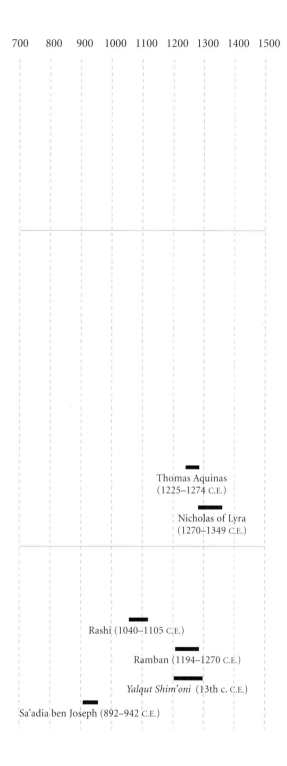

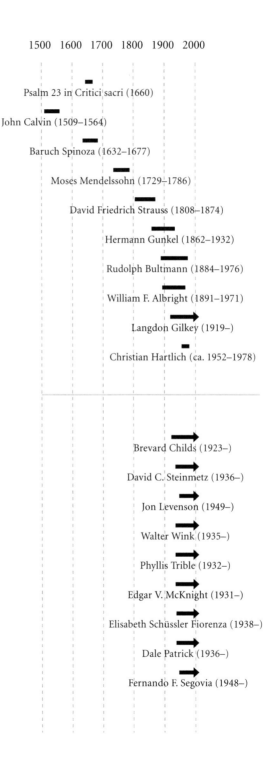

Author Index

Scripture Index

3:6   162, 406
3:7–10   407–8
3:12   409
3:13   138n, 406
3:13–14   223
3:15   215, 406
3:16–22   409
3:18   162
4:1–9   409
4:9–31   410
4:10–12   409
4:14   409
4:14ff.   247
4:22   163
4:29–31   409
5:20–21   409
5:21   410
6:2   406
6:3   215
6:9   409–10
7–12   279, 282
9:3   154–5
10:5   157
12   123
12–13   410
12:14   314
12:26   246
12:26ff.   314
13:14   246
13:20–22   279, 282
13:21   145
14:10–12   409
14:10–18   408n
14:19–31   279
14:21–30   282
15   268
15:8   157
15:17–18   15, 268
15:24   408n
16:1–3   408n
16:4   144
16:13   144
17:1   154–55
17:14   16
17:15   142
18:4   369n
19–24:11   279, 282
20:2   142
20:5   44
20:8–11   121
20:9   126
20:10   123, 125
20:13   123n
21:1   114n
21:14   163
22:1   124

23:17   163
24:10, 154
25–31   45, 138n
25:23   xix
25:40   48n
29:45   161
31   123, 126n, 129, 133
31:12–17   121–22, 127n, 138n
31:13   124n, 132, 134, 137
31:14   124, 134
31:15   125
31:16   124, 125
31:17   134
31:18   138n
33:19   186
34:5   162
34:6   317
34:23   163
34:29–35   235
35   123
35:2–3   121n
35:10–39:43   45
40:38   144n

Leviticus
5:1   203
7:18   347
11:1–8   6
11:13–19   5
11:29   7
13:8   347
16:29   132
17–26   365
17:4   347
19:17–18   203
19:30   139
21:9   163
23   129
23:4   127
23:28   130
23:28–30   130, 131
24:10–11   133
25   343
25:8–55   90n
25:17   343
25:23   343
25:36   343
25:38   343
25:42–43   343
26:10   25
27:32   181

Numbers
4:27   156
6:25   155

10:35   162
11:8   143
11:13   144
11:18   155
11:22–23   144
11:31   157
13–14   410
14:1   24
15:31   115
15:38   6
16:32   157
21:18   xiii
22   167, 222
22–24   268
24:15–19   233

Deuteronomy
2:7   143
4:16   154
4:20   153
4:24   153, 200
6   101
6:4–5   101
6:7–9   6
6:25   350
7:18–19   6
8:3   23
8:4   143–44
10:21   6
11:12   155
14:1   163
16:16   163
18:15   227
22:6   179
23:3   15
24:8   130
25:4   47n, 67
25:17–19   280
25:19   16
28:48   127
29:20   179
31:9ff.   314
31:21   212
31:24–26   212
32   212
32:4   128
32:5   163
32:9   162
32:22   44
33   268
33:1–29   212
33:2   101
33:7   369n
33:26   369n
33:29   369n
34:5   211